Hi, Meredith,

You look like a Peace Corps potential. Consider becoming a Volunteer in your later life. Why not. It would be a win-win for you & Uncle Sam!

Best!

John Gery LaPlante

# 27 Months
## in the

## Peace Corps

### My Story, Unvarnished.

## *John Guy LaPlante*

I went in at 77. It was tough but good.
Not every Volunteer serves the full hitch.
I did. I tell you all you should know.

*'If Peace Corps interests you
for any reason, this is a* must-read*!'*

Woody (WR) Boynton, Volunteer 1966 / See P. iv

**145 pictures! Advice! And Tips, Tips, Tips!**
*Thinking of joining? Bravo! Be proud! But read this first.*

All rights reserved. No part of this book shall be reproduced or transmitted in any form or by any means, electronic, mechanical, magnetic, photographic including photocopying, recording or by any information storage and retrieval system, without prior written permission of the publisher. No patent liability is assumed with respect to the use of the information contained herein. Although every precaution has been taken in the preparation of this book, the publisher and author assume no responsibility for errors or omissions. Neither is any liability assumed for damages resulting from the use of the information contained herein.

Copyright © 2011 by John Guy LaPlante

Peace Corps/Voluntering/Travel/Adventure

ISBN 0-7414-6676-7

Printed in the United States of America

Published September 2011

INFINITY PUBLISHING
1094 New DeHaven Street, Suite 100
West Conshohocken, PA 19428-2713
Toll-free (877) BUY BOOK
Local Phone (610) 941-9999
Fax (610) 941-9959
Info@buybooksontheweb.com
www.buybooksontheweb.com

*"Ask not what your country can do for you. Rather, ask what you can do for your country!"*

**John F. Kennedy**
Inaugural Address, 1966

*'If you're not making your life an adventure, you're short-changing yourself.'*
John Guy LaPlante

*'Travel is fatal to prejudice.'*
Mark Twain

# *'If Peace Corps interests you, this is a <u>must-read!</u>'*
## ~ *Woody (WR) Boynton*, Volunteer

**His comments in full:**

"I was a Peace Corps Volunteer. I got assigned to Micronesia in 1966 when the Peace Corps went there. Things have changed a lot.

"One thing is still the same. A Peace Corps tour is not easy. It takes mental toughness to survive and flourish. You get sent to a far-off place to do worthwhile work. You've probably never heard of the place. You'd never go there for a vacation.

"You may still go to a primitive place. Or you may go to a more advanced place, but tough in a different way, such as John's Ukraine. The culture shock, the challenges, the problems, the anxiety are much the same. It isn't easy!

"But there are big rewards and satisfactions, too, wherever you get sent. You'll be proud. And you'll come home stronger and better equipped.

"John deals with this. He tells about the good, the bad, and the ugly of his tour. A lot of good, in his case, but a bit of ugly, too. His stories will make it alive for you.

"A tour is not for everybody. John's book is the best picture of a full tour (some Volunteers don't finish). It's a fine read for anyone interested in Peace Corps—this is its 50th anniversary, and it has accomplished a whole lot.

"And his book is a *must-read* if you have any thought of signing up. You'll find out if Peace Corps *is* for you.

"Read it on the beach in July. Or by a warm fire on a cold night. Or when flying somewhere. Anywhere, anytime. For good info, and pleasure, too. Especially before you commit!

"He's loaded it with tips and advice. And photos."

~ *Woody (WR) Boynton* / Volunteer, 1966.

---

## Credits for Photos and Front Cover

I took most of the photos. Some came from friends and associates. Thank you! In some cases, I don't remember exactly who. Sorry! The two JFK photos in Chapter 2 are courtesy of Peace Corps / Washington.

*Photos on the Front Cover:* The photo montage is intended to suggest the variety of the things I did and of the folks I met along my path.

*Cover Design:* A pleasure to work with Melissa Craig.

On this 50th anniversary of Peace Corps
# I Dedicate This Book
To the many Volunteers who have done good for our country and so many other countries. And to you readers who may decide to join Peace Corps and continue this noble and patriotic work.

**Bravo!**

~ ~ ~

SPECIAL THANKS to milady Annabelle (a *good sport!*) and my dear sister Lucie and my loving children Arthur, Monique, and Mark and their families, and their mother, Pauline.

AND TO MANY OTHERS, including the special friends who did not forget me while overseas and helped me through that. I am pleased to name you, which I do alphabetically: Dale Winchell, Ivan Otterness, John Stratton, Len Poulin, Olwen Logan, Peter and Angela Galera, Sheila Connelly, Sulekh Jain, Ton and Susan Coppejans, Woody Boynton, and Wu Bin.

MY THANKS also to the four of you who vouched for me with the recommendations that Peace Corps required: Andrew Katsanis, Artie Lynnworth, Donald (Skip) Routh, and Timothy Haut. You also remembered me through those long months.

There have been others.
I would like to name you all but fear a grievous omission.
And warm thanks to special new friends in Ukraine
...Iryna and Victoria and Tatiana at the library; my Russian tutors Luda and Sasha; Olena and Lina at the language school; my fellow teachers Marina and Louba; my expat friends Rich and Renato and Alain; my two special students Anton and Valery; the regulars in my English and French Clubs; my friend Wayne Purves; my students; and numerous Volunteers and Kyiv Headquarters staffers!

If I've missed anyone, it's been unintentional.

~ ~ ~

# Chapters

**1 / Why this book?** ................................................................ 1
*Simple. To tell you what Peace Corps is like. It's tough—but good. Maybe you will join...*

**2 / The Corps' surprising start** ........................................... 5
*1960: President Kennedy's Call inspired many. Including me. But I get to respond very late.*

**3 / How I got this weird idea** ............................................ 15
*Strange how it popped up! At a concert, of all places. And it just wouldn't go away.*

**4 / I am nominated!** ........................................................... 23
*I'm nearly in. But there are "if's" ahead. Now it's time to break the news to everyone!*

**5 / The Staging. Exciting!** ................................................. 35
*Bad luck getting to Philadelphia for it. But Peace Corps gives us a rousing start.*

**6 / Yes, we're in Ukraine!** ................................................. 44
*Our Peace Corps bosses welcome us.... and warn us. Training starts. This is for real.*

**7 / My first 'family'** ........................................................... 52
*I move in. They're so nice to me as I suffer through these three months of "boot camp."*

**8 / Russian! So hard!** ......................................................... 73
*For 12 weeks we sit, concentrate, memorize. I'm getting up at 3 to study. Fear I will flunk!*

**10 / Where will I be posted?** ........................................... 100
*Suspense. Then surprise: right here! I'm upset when I hear that. Then delighted.*

**11 / I take the oath** ........................................................... 114
*What a memorable ceremony. Then, we rush to our posts. For me, it's back to Chernihiv!*

**12 / My job at school** ....................................................... 122
*I teach but only in a sense. The job shifts and changes. I'm happy. And unhappy.*

**13 / Things at school sour**.................................................134
*Dean Olena and I are not hitting it off. Things are not good. I blow my stack!*

**14 / My second 'family'** ...............................................153
*I move in with Ira and her son, Slava. It works out fine for a while. But then...*

**15 / I follow orders**......................................................172
*Peace Corps tells me to get set up with the police and the bank. Not that easy.*

**16 / I'm given a second job!**........................................179
*I'm to start an English club. Well, I start a French club, too. Also a project more dramatic.*

**17 / I have a fantasy!** ..................................................199
*It's to digitalize this great big library! It must get with it. Or for sure it will die.*

**18 / A chance meeting**.................................................218
*My new American pal gets to play a big role in my English Club. And my life.*

**19 / One more fantasy!** ...............................................225
*What a crazy public transit system here! I see a way to make it better. I get started.*

**20 / A Rotary Club here!**.............................................243
*I am a Rotarian. This city needs a Rotary Club. I'm eager to start one. Finally, a big surprise!*

**21 / I move to Family 3!**..............................................247
*For good reasons! My friends Iryna and Sasha help me to move. Ira takes it hard.*

**22 / My computer life!** ................................................259
*I needed a computer here from Day 1! Finally I get set up. How good it is.*

**23 / The mail! Oh, my!** ...............................................268
*The problems started soon and caused me big headaches—especially at IRS time!*

24 / **My expat friends** .......................................................................280
    *I meet all four of them by accident. How they have made my life better!*

25 / **'Expect the unexpected!'** ..........................................................298
    *It's good advice. Mishaps befall me. Quirky things come up. I get hurt.*

26 / **Getting thru the holidays** .........................................................311
    *They're happy...but sad, too. It's true for Volunteers everywhere. It's hard for me, too.*

27 / **I meet the PC doctors** ..............................................................326
    *I get to see them for this thing and that. And then, two emergencies come up!*

28 / **A troubling op-ed** ....................................................................343
    *A former Volunteer criticizes Peace Corps. I respond. Our top director has his say.*

29 / **Off I go to Shanghai** ...............................................................353
    *My friend Wu is getting married there. Annabelle flies from L.A. and joins me.*

30 / **Annabelle visits me** .................................................................367
    *It's time! She flies to Ukraine, meets my friends, and gets to see my life close up. Just as I hoped.*

31 / **I get involved in SNAC** ..........................................................392
    *SNAC is our Seniors Club. It's not long before I get involved deeper and deeper.*

32 / **My life with Tanya** ..................................................................410
    *She gives me a good home away from home. A wonderful gal. But oh, what frustrations!*

33 / **My life with the bosses** ...........................................................431
    *I get to deal with the brass. I develop a big problem and some irritations*

34 / **I came here to write** ................................................................444
    *I start early. Compose articles...feel I'm being censored! Begin my book.*

**35 / I get to travel a lot** .................................................................... **455**
   *Peace Corps offers tempting opportunities. I pack up and go. Even to other countries.*

**36 / And back home, what?** ........................................................... **478**
   *27 months of separation can generate stresses. And some things can go sour.*

**37 / My successes & failures** ........................................................ **485**
   *I put my best into all this. I work hard. Some things go well. Some could go better.*

**38 / Preparing to go home** ............................................................ **496**
   *It's a process to join Peace Corps, another to get out. But at the finale, there's fun, too.*

**39 / Life after Peace Corps** .......................................................... **511**
   *Peace Corps can be such a life-enlarging experience—how good to have tried it.*

**40 / So, what do I think now?** ...................................................... **516**
   *It's natural that I've formed strong opinions. I like Peace Corps. But it needs changes.*

**41 / Tips & Advice for you** ........................................................... **529**
   *I learned so much during my service. I want to be helpful, so I'm passing it on.*

**42 / Thinking in the night** ............................................................ **537**
   *What would JFK think now? How will Obama carry on? What's coming up?*

**43 / Now what about YOU?** ........................................................ **542**
   *Are you interested in becoming a Volunteer? Yes? No? Maybe?*

~ ~ ~

# Ukraine

*The capital, Kyiv, is in the North on the Dnipro River. Chernihiv, where I spent all my service, is on the smaller Desna River.*

## A Snapshot per the U.S. State Department

**Where:** In Eastern Europe. Largest in Europe. Nearly the size of Texas. Russia is larger but extends into Central Asia.
**Geography:** Vast agricultural plain, mountains in the Southwest, Black Sea and Sea of Azov in the South.
**Natural resources:** fertile soil, coal, iron, mineral deposits, timber.
**Economy:** Free Market. Agriculture and manufacturing primary.
**Climate:** Mostly Continental Temperate, Sub-Tropical in the South.
**Population:** 43.6 million, down from 50 million in 1991.
**Languages:** Ukrainian (official), Russian, and others.
**Religions:** Ukrainian Orthodoxy, Orthodox Greek Catholicism, others.
**Life expectancy:** males, 65: females, 76.
**Income:** Per capita annual: (est. 2007) $1,746.
**History:** Independence from the Soviet Union on August 24, 1991. Peace Corps has been there since nearly then.
**Administration:** Parliamentary - Presidential.
**Suffrage:** universal at 18.
**Literacy:** 99%.
**Education:** 70% have secondary or higher. About 150 colleges and universities; numerous institutes.
**For more:** www.state.gov/r/pa/ei/bgn/3211.h

# My fault! *Mea culpa!*

This book has been self-published. Like my previous two. For the same good reasons. At my age, I don't have the time to fool around and deal with this conventional commercial publisher or that one and perhaps go on to collect a folder full of dreadful rejection slips.

And if I found a publisher, I didn't want to give up control. To somebody who would compose the title and design the cover and make all the decisions, from choosing the photos right down to the type faces. Who might order me to re-write something or chop out many words or put something in. Who would decide the publishing date. On and on!

This may surprise you but all such commercial books are a team effort, though only the author is mentioned. There's an editor, designer, marketing expert, copy editor, to name just the barest minimum!

I did 97% of it—nearly every single thing prior to the printing technicalities. The big exception is some photos provided to me. There's a downside to this. I am wholly responsible. If there's a mistake it's my fault.

~ ~ ~

## *Your Attention, Please!*

Let me be clear.

In the pages ahead I have written what I truly believe is an honest and fair story of my 27 months in Peace Corps in Ukraine. A full hitch.

You'll find that I speak of Peace Corps in high terms. I am pleased to do so. It is only fair. I found Peace Corps an impressive organization. I like it. I am proud to have been a Volunteer. I encourage others to be Volunteers. On special occasions I make it a point to put on my Peace Corps pin.

But I do made recommendations and some criticisms. I make known my true thoughts only because I want to make Peace Corps even better, for our Volunteers, for our country, and for its own self-esteem. And I want you, my readers, to better understand what will await you if you sign up.

# 1 / Why this book?

*Simple. To tell you what Peace Corps is like. It's tough—but good. Maybe you will join...*

I was 77 when I applied to Peace Corps, 78 when I went in, and nearly 81 when I came out. Yes, not a youngster. But very young at heart.

One day while I was a Volunteer in Ukraine—that's where I was sent for my whole 27 months—I was in a meeting at Peace Corps headquarters in Kyiv with Diana Schmidt, our Ukraine director. Excited

She told me that she had just received an e-mail from Washington. I was now the oldest Volunteer not only in Ukraine, which I knew, but in the world. There were nearly 8,000 of us serving in 74 countries.

I asked about my predecessor, of course.

"Oh, he was 84," she said. "He just went home. An emergency. He was flown out by Medi-Vac. He won't be going back."

Oh? It sounded very ominous to me.

"Congratulations!" she said.

"Thank you, Diana. But it's nothing I earned. Totally accidental. I'd rather be the youngest...21, say!"

She laughed and so did I. But I was telling her the truth.

Then she asked me a question. "Washington has asked me to ask you, would you give permission to be interviewed by the press?" She had a document in her hand.

"Certainly. I'd be very happy to do that."

She handed me the document. It would allow Peace Corps to use me for publicity purposes any way it wanted to. I signed it.

"As a matter of fact, Diana, I hope Peace Corps will get going on this. I like Peace Corps. I believe in it. I am proud to be a Volunteer. I think additional Volunteers would be wonderful. Particularly older Volunteers. I hope this publicity will help that."

I am telling you all this because it explains succinctly why I am writing this book. Peace Corps' success story needs to be told anew. And I want you to know Peace Corps was a good thing for me. And believe it may be good for you. Whether you're 21 or a retiree.

But first, one point. Know what? While in Ukraine I was interviewed by local TV stations and newspapers because of my elderly status. They heard about me through locals. I was positive and upbeat with those media—that was how I felt. But not once was I interviewed by anyone contacted by Peace Corps—and Peace Corps Washington has a full PR staff! Even after I returned home. Its mission is to promote Peace Corps. That says something not good about Peace Corps' follow-up. I came to feel there were things quite weak, even amiss, with the Peace Corps Washington administration.

But now, why did I join? I am sure you are curious. It's a question I am asked often.

I joined for a grab bag of reasons. It's true of most Volunteers, I believe. In my case, I like to travel. I like to see and do new things. I like to meet new people. I need a smidgeon of adventure in my life. I never served in the armed forces; I felt that finally I could do something for my country.

I liked the idea that late in life I could also do something just for the good of it rather than for money. I like to write and report, and quickly I saw this as a golden opportunity for articles and a new book. I like to teach, and teaching turned out to be my main job. And maybe deep down I was trying to deny I was an old man. So, mine was a very big grab bag, don't you think?.

Do any of these thoughts strike a chord in you?

**N**ow, do you know that it was a shock when I found out I was going to be sent to Ukraine? Yes, a great shock. I expected to be sent to a French-speaking country. I speak French. Ukraine is not one. Also shocking because Ukraine has cold winters. Ice and snow! After growing up and living all my working years in New England, I had made it a point to escape to easier climes every winter for the last 15 years. Also a shock because of other reasons. But I'll explain all this in due time.

There's a saying that when you join Peace Corps, you agree to go anywhere and do whatever. True, but I expected there would be more common sense in assigning me. Only months later did I learn that Peace Corps had used common sense, but differently. Again, more later. Be patient!

Now a few words about Ukraine. I'll be telling you a lot about it throughout the book. Here I want to give you some essential starting information about it.

Notice I say just "Ukraine." Not "The Ukraine." Most people say "The Ukraine." I used to say it that way. That is a remnant of Soviet times. As one Ukrainian teacher said to me, "You do not say 'The Texas,' or 'The Massachusetts.' Now that we are independent, we prefer just 'Ukraine.'"

So be it.

Volunteers first went to Ukraine in 1992. Ukraine had dropped out of the Soviet Union and become independent just the previous year. That's when it abandoned communism and a rigged economy in favor of democracy and market capitalism. It didn't take the new republic's leaders long to ask Washington for Volunteers.

This, by the way, is the standard policy. It's not Peace Corps that asks a country if we can serve in it. It's that country that asks us.

Well, our Volunteers could help Ukraine in a number of ways. By teaching English in a country getting ever closer to America, and it has happened that it is now English—American English—that has become the dominant international language around the globe.

And could help in other important ways also. In community and business development. In youth development, and in a variety of public health initiatives, from clean-water development to containing HIV/AIDS. All Volunteers, regardless of their main job, are trained to emphasize the urgency of the HIV/AIDS crisis in Ukraine, and to explain in the simplest terms how to avoid the disease by insisting on practicing safe sex. And to bring up the subject at every reasonable opportunity.

Our Volunteers are still at it in Ukraine nearly 20 years later. As I write this, 340 Volunteers are serving in some 240 communities there. Some 2,000 have served in the country. It remains Peace Corps' largest program.

Nevertheless, I got to like Ukraine very much despite its troubled economy and deeply-veined corruption, and the Ukrainians also, well, 99.9 percent of them. And I liked the job...in fact, it turned out to be several simultaneous jobs, though there were days when still I felt under-employed. This last statement may surprise you. Again, the details later.

Very few things are perfect, and my 27 months of service were not perfect, but I gave up hoping for perfection of any kind when I was about 13. However, I am not lying or exaggerating when I tell you my 27 months were very good. Some of my colleagues didn't feel this way. Many quit and went home. It was a shock when I saw this happening.

I had a great time in Peace Corps but a couple of bad times, too. I feel that I did some good, although at times I wished I could do more. I had some disappointments. I had some wonderfully memorable experiences, and some that re-enforced my belief that perfection is rare indeed. I met a lot of fine people, including students, some that I hope I will see again and that I will cherish till my last breath. And I was happy most of the time, despite some rough living conditions and bouts of missing home and my loved ones.

To repeat, I am writing this book because I like to write. I have a good story to tell. I have worked hard to write it honestly, truly, and totally, and, I want to say, charitably. I hope that some of you, regardless of your background, your gender, your age, or your motivation, will be encouraged to follow my example and will become Volunteers.

Right away I noticed some things worth mentioning to you. I was surprised to find that more women than men serve, but I also saw that this was not a problem in any way. I saw that some people have good reason to get away for a couple of years. Peace Corps is a fine outlet, and this could be a good thing for them and Peace Corps.

I also saw minority people serving, although in numbers probably less than their percentages in our national demographics. I made it a point to speak to them and I found that they considered Peace Corps a worthwhile endeavor, though they got more scrutiny from Ukrainians. And I really saw that older Americans could be valuable Volunteers, all as I became convinced Peace Corps should modify its training for them.

And if Peace Corps does not fit into your plans, nevertheless I hope all of you will get to know Peace Corps better and will esteem it as never before. It's an excellent outfit that really tries to do good work and spend its money effectively. It does try to make good friends for us around the world, in places where we do need more friends. And it succeeds.

Peace Corps' 50$^{th}$ anniversary is coming up soon—September 22-25, 2011—half a century to the day of Congress' passing of the Peace Corps bill. It will be a grand affair in Washington, D.C., with celebrations in major cities as well in Peace Corps countries around the world—countries past and present. There will be huge publicity and coverage, all well-deserved.

I hope to be I in Washington for that celebration. And to cheer with all my fellow men and women who took the oath—yes, to cheer and say a silent prayer of thanksgiving and hope as Peace Corps commences its second half century.

Few things in this world are perfect. Peace Corps is not perfect. It has had problems and has problems now. I write about some that I noticed. But I completed my hitch with admiration and enthusiasm for it.

Peace Corps' history has been a proud one. We Volunteers have achieved much in far and strange lands. Small things individually but great things hand in hand. I am proud to wear my Peace Corps pin on the Fourth of July and other special days.

Now back home in the U.S.A., I am doing whatever I can to promote Peace Corps and celebrate its good work.

I hope you will think about joining Peace Corps. Why not? And please suggest the idea to anyone you might consider receptive.

~ ~ ~

# 2 / The Corps' surprising start

*1960: President Kennedy's Call inspired many. Including me. But I get to respond very late.*

**H**ow time flies by. Half a century ago, what a radical and, some thought, crazy idea when they heard Senator John F. Kennedy of Massachusetts, hard-campaigning presidential candidate, propose what became the Peace Corps. He didn't even have a name for it.

It was late on Oct. 14, 1960. He was running hard to beat President Richard Nixon at the polls in three weeks. He had been on the go all day and was hours late for a quickie evening speech to students at the University of Michigan in Ann Arbor. Most too young to vote, mind you.

It was a dark and cold night. He thought they probably all had gone home. He was utterly astonished—a crowd were anxiously waiting outside the Student Union. Thousands of them, it seemed. When they heard he had kept his promise and had pulled in, they started chanting his name. Incredible. He was amazed by the rousing welcome.

He felt inspired. He chucked the speech he had used in many places. He came up with something new. He had never spoken about this before. New even to his staff. Later some wondered how he came up with the idea.

Looking at the crowd, pausing a moment, suddenly he said, "How many of you who are going to be doctors are willing to spend your days in Ghana? Technicians or engineers, how many of you are willing to work in the Foreign Service and spend your lives traveling around the world?

"On your willingness to do that, not merely to serve one year or two years in the service, but on your willingness to contribute part of your life to this country, I think will depend the answer whether a free society can compete."

It was reported he spoke for just a few minutes. But passionately. All he had was an embryonic idea. No details. But he captivated his young audience. It was all new to them—an exhortation! And they felt it. JFK noticed. At his hotel that night, he felt he had hit a home run.

What he was hinting at was so different. And exciting. Little did he realize that he was giving birth to a program that was to become one of the most important of his presidency. One that would add a new dimension to how we saw our role around the world. One that in time would help people in more than half the countries of the world, all in need of a boost. One that would win a secure place in the hearts of generations of Americans and win high rankings in public opinion polls time and again.

Yes, he went to bed that night thrilled. But little aware of the significance of his speech. Some news stories failed to mention what he had proposed. But enthusiasm flamed, all sparked by students. He was amazed by the response that developed far and wide.

JFK's speech got young Americans thinking about taking time off, shelving their personal ambitions, flying off as high-spirited groups to distant poor countries, and getting to work at mundane jobs often too ridiculous to consider as a career.

Mundane but potentially so rewarding because of the core notions of idealism and patriotism and altruism.

All to make life better for the ordinary people in those undeveloped countries in what was really a noble way. All while making new friends for our country. And surprise—maybe while changing their own lives for the better.

Droves of students began signing a petition. Then they rushed it to other universities. Thousands more signed. There was wide eagerness.

In the next few days this huge endorsement energized him. His idea continued to swell. He talked more about it. He developed it, adding details, changing them, weighing counter ideas. And morphed it.

The Foreign Service angle never took root; no, it would not become a part of the State Department. Some thought it might tie in with the C.I.A. as a new way to do intelligence work, spying! Quickly discarded.

About the only things clear were that it was intended to attract young people and send them overseas for a limited period of time to do good. The name Peace Corps still did not exist. Nor the word Volunteer.

On Nov. 8 he won the election. He became President. His new idea was high in his priorities. In his presidential address he brought it up again. That's when he said, "And so, my fellow Americans, ask not what your country can do for you. Ask what you can do for your country!"

Those words sparked the imaginations of young people beyond number. Not everybody was excited. JFK was a Democrat, as we know. Pres. Ike Eisenhower, who had preceded him in the White House, knocked the idea as "a juvenile experiment." He was a Republican. Maybe that's why he spoke that way. Plenty of others also nixed it. Scoffed.

JFK acted. He didn't wait for Congress to pick up his idea, deliberate it, maybe hash it to death. Less than six seeks after being sworn in, by executive order on March 1, 1961, he founded the Peace Corps— astonishing when you think about it. It's a name that had come up only later.

Congress gave its authorization Sept. 22. It was the first time that such a big new program got launched strictly on the swell of public opinion.

"Ask not what your country can do for you. Rather, ask what you can do for your country!"

Yes, those words of his have become embedded in our nation's memory. I am sure you know them. Maybe like me you were stirred by them.

The results were immediate and dramatic. Queries piled in. The name of final choice was the Peace Corps. Those chosen were called Volunteers, with a big V. It became a proud title that quickly entered our vocabulary.

**I** have always thought of it as the Peace Corps. That's how I always read about it. Once I joined, I found those in it called it Peace Corps—no, "the." I found that hard to get used to but eventually managed. Truth is, I have found just about everybody on the outside calls it "the Peace Corps."

Thus was Peace Corps launched. Some say it was the best idea President Kennedy came up with during his brief presidency. Interestingly, historians have pointed out that a similar idea had been proposed earlier.

JFK gives Sargent Shriver the pen he used to sign Peace Corps into law.

In 1952, Sen. Brian McMahon (D. Connecticut) proposed the creation of "an army of young Americans to serve as missionaries of democracy." And in 1957, Sen. Hubert Humphrey (D. Minnesota) introduced a bill supporting essentially the same thing. It's thought this is how JFK got the idea.

Anyway, thousands of people applied, and on Aug. 28, 1961, the first group of Volunteers, 51 of them, departed for Ghana, which had requested Volunteers, thanks to the efforts of Sargent Shriver, the brand-new director. He was beating the bushes to get the new agency going.

The pioneer Volunteers were an enthusiastic group, motivated by thoughts of adventure, travel, service, patriotism, and altruism, the mix varying with each person probably. Such a mix motivates applicants today. They were ready to roll up their sleeves and get started. They were very young and unseasoned, as you'd expect. Their average age was early 20's.

Their exuberance was contagious, and they set up an excitement in the countries they shipped out to. Some people there were cynical. Laughed. How much could such kids accomplish? Well, nearly 50 years have passed and the answer is still the same, "A lot!"

All these years Peace Corps' goals have remained steady. There are three. To go work in less-developed countries as worthy representatives of our country. To make life better there for ordinary people by undertaking simple but practical and achievable projects. And when they returned home, to give fellow Americans a better understanding of these foreign lands and people and of Peace Corps' work there.

*The President and Shriver see the first Volunteers off—Ghana has the honor. Shriver worked day and night to get Peace Corps up and running fast.*

There was sound thinking behind it all. What a good way to generate good PR for our country in so many places where our reputation could stand buffing. What a good way to lend a helping hand in poor and desperate countries at the ground roots level where folks could really see improvements happening and things getting better. What a good way to make friends abroad.

And what a good way to season our idealistic Volunteers for further challenges when they came back, and possibly in the public domain.

And to accomplish all this at relatively little cost. After all, isn't it much cheaper to send Volunteers abroad in work shirts and jeans with just books and blackboards and simple tools than in army uniforms with rifles?

**N**ow, about the founding director, R. Sargent Shriver. He was JFK's brother-in-law, married to his sister Eunice. He had political ambitions of his own, but he set them aside to campaign for Jack's presidential bid—as everybody in the family was mandated to do, per the orders of the do-as-I-order patriarch, Joseph P. Kennedy.

## 2 / The Corps' Surprising Start

JFK had tossed the raw Peace Corps idea in his lap It was up to him to develop it. Every angle of it. He set a dynamic pace. One thing he did was search for a director for it. Gave JFK a list of solid names. JFK looked at it, put it aside, and pointed his finger at Sarge, as he was called. Sarge was it!

Truth is, Sarge was an unknown quantity. It turned out JFK was lucky to have such a smart and energetic implementer. The President had a terrific idea but it's Sargent Shriver who made it the great success.

Appointed three days after Peace Corps was created, Sarge gave it his all. There were so many ideas to be considered. So many aspects to be thought out. A big one was finding countries to accept Volunteers. He traveled overseas, button-holed leaders. Ghana, the first country to agree, gave a reluctant yes.

In time Peace Corps was glad to accept requests for Volunteers from interested countries. Shriver had to coax, bargain, and wheedle. Nowadays, there is a waiting list of countries.

He was a masterful leader. Within six years he had Volunteers serving in 55 countries, more than 14,500 of them. He turned out to be a man of enormous talent and drive, so successful and admired that charges of nepotism never got serious attention.

Those were heady times for Peace Corps. The press coverage was enormous. It was a rare American who did not get to know about Peace Corps. An aura of success and goodness developed, and it continues to this day.

Oh, there were older Volunteers but they were few. It's the young people who responded in big numbers and were actively recruited. They were the ones who, it was thought, would find the challenge exciting. Peace Corps was a young person's game. Older folks were signed on because they turned up at the door.

One of the older ones in the early days did get heavy publicity. For one thing, Lillian Carter was much older—in her 60's—and stood out by her age. The press loves subjects who stand out. She also stood out because she was the mother of Jimmy Carter, who was becoming famous in Georgia politics and would go on to be elected President. She was serving in India as a nurse in the late Sixties.

Journalists got to like her because of her frank comments and no-nonsense ways. By all accounts, she was an impressive Volunteer, doing the job seriously and engendering respect and appreciation. She was worth her weight in gold in good publicity in Peace Corps' formative years. She motivated many others to serve.

Truly I thought of Lillian Carter when I reported for my first interview at the Los Angeles recruitment office.

The years and the decades rolled by. Before long it became certain that Peace Corps was not just a passing fancy. It was here to stay. Oh, there were occasional questions about its effectiveness and once in a rare while a bad headline when a Volunteer acted badly. Steadily the program grew.

Volunteers were dispatched to more countries. They undertook a broader variety of tasks. The returning Volunteers took their places in society and started their career climbs. Their Peace Corps service became an impressive and even prestigious add-on to their résumés. Leadership is a natural part of every Volunteer's day, and this experience overseas served them well in civilian life.

Many went on to careers of accomplishment and prominence. Their Peace Corps service was often mentioned when they made the news. Peace Corps likes to drop names. There is a long list of Returned Peace Corps Volunteers—RPCVs"as they're called—who became leaders in government and business and academia and journalism.

The press coverage has continued routinely favorable. Study after study has reported the good feelings that the program generated and continues to generate in the host countries and among folks back home.

By and large, Americans have considered Peace Corps an excellent program, with the funds budgeted for it well spent.

From the beginning, Peace Corps was determined to send over a cross-section of recruits representative of our demographics. Sure, they were primarily young but an effort was made to attract them from all races and nationalities and religions.

We wanted the host countries to see us as we really are—a multi-racial and multi-cultural nation made possible by citizens flocking to our shores from countries all over the world, all in search of a better life.

As the years passed, its diversity continued to be a hallmark. And it became manifest in its leadership. It's the President who appoints the national directors as well as its other top officials.

This diversity has been dramatic from the top down. There have been 20 national directors. Four have been women; three black, including one of the women (Carolyn R. Paton) and the present director, Aaron Williams; one Asian-American (Elaine Chao); and one Hispanic-American (Gaddi H. Vasquez).

The longest to serve were Loret Miller Ruppe (highly regarded), who served eight years; Sargent Shriver, six years; and Mark D. Gearan and Gaddi H. Vasquez, both four years. Many served for less than that.

Ronald A. Tschetter was the director when I entered. I got to meet him when he visited us in Kyiv. It was a memorable encounter, as you'll get to read in Chapter 28. He was succeeded late in my service (after temporary service by assistant director Jody Olsen) by Aaron Williams, appointed by President Obama.

The program did have ups and downs over the decades. Enrollments fell sharply, then rose again. The last three years, with numbers hovering near the 8,000 mark, have been the highest in the last 30 years.

President George W. Bush called for Peace Corps to be doubled as part of the War on Terrorism but that did not happen. Barack Obama recommended the same thing several times in campaign speeches.

Sen. Christopher Dodd (D, Connecticut) filed a bill to greatly expand Peace Corps and to reform it. More about this in Chapter 39.

The list of countries being served changed from year to year. The total list approaches 140—there are some 200 countries in the world and the number changes, as we know. Currently Volunteers are serving in 74.

It was very recently, during the administration of Tschetter, that the idea of actively recruiting Volunteers 50 and older– Fifty-Plus is the buzz word—took solid root. It was his signature idea. Yes, why not seek older folks?

Here is the rationale. Older men and women have the work and life experience that younger ones lack. They have important skills. They have maturity, even some wisdom, perhaps. And undoubtedly the same patriotism and altruism that motivate younger ones.

Many are retirees who have time on their hands and have an interest in keeping busy at something worthwhile. Probably also a greater appreciation of other cultures.

Many feel a pent-up desire to finally travel and do something exciting. More and more are joining. Doesn't it make sense that they'd be good role models for the younger ones?

It can be argued that older Volunteers command more respect and attention. After all, some cultures regard elders with particular esteem and admiration. And it would do no harm for more placid retirees back home to notice that some men and women among them still had enough steam and gumption to get up and going, and to become inspired to remain active.

**N**otice that I said men and women. It was unexpected, I think, that the Peace Corps would attract more women. After all, isn't it men who are expected to rally to calls of adventure? To turn up for hard work in difficult living conditions? Well, a different pattern developed early. More women enroll than men. We'll leave it to the psychologists to explain that.

In the beginning, the training was skimpy and the assignments quite basic. You went overseas and taught and helped. Maybe in a classroom.

Maybe on farms or plantations Maybe in a medical setting. Maybe among village leaders.

Ever since the beginning, the notion of Volunteering has been the core principle. You are giving of yourself. You are not doing this to make a career or even to earn a livelihood. You are doing this to help others. It is taken for granted that you will be willing to sacrifice and accept some hardships.

You will find everything quite Spartan. You may live in a hut or an apartment or a house, but nothing fancy. You will live the way the locals live. In fact, you will be cautioned against displays of ease or luxury. This would be counter to what you are striving to demonstrate. There will be frowns if you use your own money to make your life better.

You certainly will not ride around in your own automobile. Prohibited! You won't even be allowed to drive one. Sure, you may be issued a bicycle or a motorcycle, but chances are that wherever available, you will ride the buses and trams like nearly everyone else.

But quickly some got to see that Peace Corps in some ways can be a good deal in its own right. How come? Sure, Volunteers do not get paid for their labor but of course they have to be supported. Who of any age can go far off for more than two years without financial help?

Of course they are flown to their country and back by Uncle Sam.

Volunteers get a stipend instead of a paycheck. Peace Corps calls it an allowance. It's enough to support a Volunteer in a lifestyle similar to that of a local person doing that kind of work, with a little extra thrown in for travel and recreation and fun.

It varies from country to country, and even at times within a country —so much in an expensive city, less in a small town or village. But Volunteers serve in very few expensive cities. Peace Corps feels it gets more bang for its bucks by placing Volunteers in smaller places.

There's more good stuff. Volunteers get two days of vacation per month (24 days per year), but they can't take any of them during the three months of training or the last three months of service.

During their service, Uncle Sam takes on their medical and dental care. Peace Corps sets up medical care for them even in the smallest country—a nurse practitioner or physician's assistant or even full-time MDs. If something serious comes up, Volunteers will get expert care, even if it's back in the U.S.A. While they're in Peace Corps, they can suspend their private medical and dental insurance knowing they can pick it up again without penalty when they get back. It is mandated by law.

They will participate full-time in three months of training in the host country—practical training that may have real dollar value.

They will learn a language (or attempt to, as in my case), and Peace Corps has become expert at teaching languages. It may not have great value to learn Swahili or Tagalog, but who knows? Life is strange. They are lucky to land in a country where they have to learn Russian or Mandarin (China's major language), both spoken by millions of people. Knowledge of these can have substantial value on their post-Peace Corps résumé.

If during their service a family emergency develops, Peace Corps will send them home for two weeks at its expense. Of course, it will be the one to define what "family emergency" means beyond the death of a parent or sibling. During vacations they can travel as they like, in their host country or beyond it, but at their expense. They can even fly home for a visit.

I must mention that bad things can happen over there. Peace Corps has recorded murders and rapes and assaults and robberies and accidents. I was bowled over by a drunk. I had a potentially serious accident getting off a bus. Homesickness and culture shock and harsh weather and tough living conditions and disappointment and boredom can drive some Volunteers to quit. I was surprised by how many go home, though for other reasons, too.

This said, it's to be remembered that such bad things might happen to a Volunteer who spent the same time in the U.S.

There's a dollar bonanza at the end. Not huge, but helpful. They will go home with money in their pocket. During each of their 24 months of service (after their three months of training), Peace Corps will set aside $225. This will add up to $5,400. This is transition money for them, paid in two installments.

Peace Corps will pay for their flight home, either by handing them a ticket or giving them cash in lieu of a ticket (Volunteer's choice). Additionally, they may use this transition money to support them on a journey of many weeks or even months before reaching home. Or to get married or pay a debt or begin graduate school or start a business or buy a car or support themselves until they get a job. For whatever. They can use it as they like.

There's more. They can enroll in some graduate programs which give credit for Peace Corps service, or which will entitle them to financial help. They can apply for some competitive federal jobs with extra points awarded to them for their PC service.

And they can get active in the National Peace Corps Association, which is a private group independent of Peace Corps. It is based in Washington. There are chapters around the country. It's a nice way to socialize, network, build a career, promote Peace Corps, and have fun.

And of course, Peace Corps service does look good on a job application. Countless Volunteers will attest to that. Many people consider Peace Corps service prestigious.

As mentioned, this year, 2011, Peace Corps will observe its 50th anniversary. We'll see a fanfare of publicity. Many commemorative events. It will climax with a great turn-out and celebration in Washington.

Over the years, books and journals and articles and newspaper reports and TV shows and DVDs and now blogs have poured out about the Peace Corps experience. Peace Corps service has become enshrined in our culture.

It's assured the media will focus their spotlight on the anniversary. We'll all hear about it aplenty. Certainly there will be fresh books and TV specials telling its story, appraising it, glorifying it, perhaps criticizing it. Undoubtedly there will be a re-dedication of it, a new call to service.

It is my belief that Peace Corps will sail on securely. If anything, it will be expanded. I'm betting on it. President Obama spoke of doubling it by the 50th anniversary. He missed that by a thousand miles but a significant budget increase did make it to his desk for signing.

Peace Corps' history is one of twists and turns and compromises and new visions. Certainly Peace Corps will be modified to meet changing circumstances wherever it serves.

As in its beginning, Peace Corps really does do good. I've witnessed that. Enthusiasts say it really makes friends for us and is cost-effective. I know I made friends for us, but I saw a way or two it could be more cost-effective. Detractors knock it for this and that. I'm on the enthusiasts' side.

I believe that overall it has added sparkle to our Stars and Stripes. Even in the not-long-past years when our foreign policy in great parts of the world cost us friends and esteem by the bucketful.

Yes, this 50th anniversary will be a big celebration. John F. Kennedy would be astonished to see what he launched on that evening in Michigan in 1960, He had no idea he was making history.

I believe that Peace Corps will reach its 100th! I'm sure it will still be finding many places in the world in need of its help. Maybe we'll have 100,000 Volunteers serving!

~ ~ ~

# 3 / How I got this weird idea

*Strange how it popped up! At a concert, of all places. And it just wouldn't go away.*

By and large, Peace Corps is considered a youngster's game. I am no youngster. My idea of joining sparked in the fall of 2006. I was 77. I was happily busy at this and that. Me a Peace Corps Volunteer? Preposterous. But the idea became tantalizing.

Milady Annabelle and I were in Connecticut, my home state since I retired. We were enjoying another fine concert at the Coast Guard Academy in New London.

I live only a 30-minute drive from the academy. It has a beautiful campus overlooking the Thames River. And it has a terrific band. It performs all over the U.S.A. and even abroad. And it gives marvelous concerts in its auditorium at the academy.

Its concerts are often standing-room only. They attract many senior citizens. These fans are as rabid about the Coast Guard Band as Bostonians are about the Boston Red Sox.

Well, the band starts every concert with The Star Spangled Banner and the audience joins in, of course. Then it goes on with the Armed Forces Medley.

When the Army anthem starts, all the former soldiers in the audience stand until it ends. Then the Navy anthem starts and all the former sailors stand and then sit. And so on for the Marine and Air Force anthems. And the Coast Guard band's own "Semper Paratus," of course. It's a wonderful and stirring start to the concerts.

I never stand. A simple reason. I never served. It just worked out that way. But how I wish I, too, could stand during these concerts. At this concert I looked around and saw all the proud men and women who had worn a uniform for the defense of our country. I was too old now to even think of serving. I felt a great regret.

Then a magical thought came up. *Maybe I could serve in the Peace Corps!* Remember, I was one of those who had heard President Kennedy's clarion call back in 1961. His words had lodged in me in a subconscious way. I was so excited when we drove home. But I didn't mention a word to Annabelle. Such a crazy idea!

Oh, something had happened two days earlier. A friend had confided in me about his daughter. She was 10 years out of college and not doing well in a career of any kind. Had moved back home and was floundering. He was very worried.

"Get her to join the Peace Corps," I suggested off-handedly. "She may discover herself. And when she gets out, she'll have something decent to put on her résumé."

In fact, that evening I researched it for him online. I thought joining the Peace Corps would be easy. But only one applicant in three gets accepted. I also read that Peace Corps was recruiting older people. I didn't give it any special attention. I must tell you that my friend did go on and mention Peace Corps to his daughter, but she was not interested.

But now I found myself thinking, *Why not me?*

Once again I accessed the big Peace Corps website and began reading in earnest. This is when I got to appreciate Peace Corps' interest in older recruits. It makes sense. After years of work, we have a lot of experience to offer. As retirees we have time on our hands. And with the clock running down for us, we're more conscious of doing something important and significant, and primarily for the good of it. And giving back to our country.

I kept thinking about Peace Corps. But there were big difficulties. One in particular. Milady Annabelle.

For 12 years I had been blessed to be in a fine relationship with her. Wouldn't entering Peace Corps squash this relationship? That would be a huge loss for me. And her, I felt sure. I let the idea rest. And rest. But it persisted. The idea would not be denied.

I pondered a few more days. Then I made my big decision. I would try to get into Peace Corps. Maybe they would look askance at a near-octogenarian. But maybe they'd consider my idea crazy. Well, I'd see.

Then a happy discovery. I found out Peace Corps encourages family and friends to visit Volunteers at their overseas post. It's good for everybody, including Peace Corps. So, immediately I decided that if Peace Corps took me, Annabelle would come for a visit. I'd make that happen.

By this time we were back in southern California, at Annabelle's condo in Newport Beach. We had been shuttling back and forth this way like ping pong balls, Connecticut in the summer and southern California in the winter.

Neither of us likes snow or ice. As a New Englander I had endured a lot of it and wanted no more. Annabelle, a native southern Californian, had experienced it a few times during travels but was fond of swimming outdoors year around.

We were enjoying good times and a good life. I was in retirement mode but still actively working, though I didn't consider it work. I was finishing and preparing to publish another book, I was writing frequent feature stories and a column (with remarkable freedom about the subjects I chose) for our local newspaper in Connecticut. I had finished a string of public talks to various clubs and organizations about my world travels and I had a few more scheduled for when I returned there.

I loved southern California but life had become much more quiet. And life had changed for us. I had given up riding my bicycle four or five years earlier, and so had she, and we had been active riders. I had enjoyed canoeing and rowing and sailing small boats, and she had also, but now my three boats weren't getting used much—I had a Grumman sailing canoe, plus a wooden canoe that I had built three years earlier, and a sailing pram that I had spent many hours rebuilding.

We also had been active ping pong players and that was calming down. I continued writing my column from 3,000 miles away, but now the days were a cycle of breakfast, reading two daily newspapers, going for a walk for an hour, having lunch, puttering at this and that, taking a nap. Then going to one of our local libraries followed by a stop for coffee and then marketing and shopping, preparing and eating dinner, and then an evening of reading and television and reading again—always a bit of reading in bed before turning off the light. We liked a game of Scrabble and chess now and then.

Oh, there were pleasant breaks. We ate out. We liked to take rides, I particularly, and often we'd combine a ride to a nice place with a walk, and quite frequently a picnic. We had friends over for dinner, or we went to friends for dinner. We'd attend concerts and talks. On Sundays we'd often have dinner out, then go to a concert or to a park to walk, or to a shopping mall to walk and shop. Sometimes we'd go off for a weekend.

And when in California, I would always visit my daughter Monique and son-in-law David for a week or so farther up the coast, in Morro Bay. We'd visit Annabelle's two brothers, Hugh and Paul and their spouses, also up the coast in the San Francisco Bay area.

I was always busier back in Connecticut than in California. I was active in our Deep River Rotary Club and was chair for a couple of active projects. One was to develop a wasted piece of land overlooking a pond in our village center into a little green park with a pretty gazebo.

Another was to organize an annual patriotic Independence Day Observance with a ceremony on the morning of the Fourth. It included a fife and drum corps, public readings from the Constitution, the Bill of Rights, and the Ten Amendments, and addresses by dignitaries, followed by fun and fellowship. These responsibilities took some time and energy, but I enjoyed them.

That was our life. It was a fine retirement and one that many people would have been content with. But I felt restlessness. Even emptiness. For the first time in many years, I did not have a formidable purpose. I had always had projects to do, a whole variety. From building a house to starting a sideline business of buying and managing income real estate, or buying and converting it into condos, or of course running my main business. This was providing public relations and graphic arts services, primarily to non-profits. I had started it and nurtured it for 16 years. Now I felt idle and un-challenged, and I didn't like it.

A small article caught my attention in the Los Angeles Times. It was about Peace Corps' new emphasis on recruiting older people.

As I read it, I recalled the thought that I had had back at that concert at the Coast Guard Academy: *I wish that I could stand up with these folks who had really served their country!*

And an exciting notion came to my mind: *Is it still possible to serve? For me? At this stage?*

The idea had surfaced but it remained just that, a mere possibility. But one day I again went to www.peacecorps.gov, Peace Corps' website.

There was a lot there and I gave it a lot of time. Yes, Peace Corps was looking for older folks—Fifty Plus, it called them. I was far beyond that, in fact, far ahead of the age 65 which is our big official retirement time. Another few days went by.

The year ended, and in a few more days, without having said anything to anybody, I sent an e-mail to Peace Corps' Los Angeles Recruitment Office. In the subject line, I typed: "Can you use me?" I wrote some words about my interest and a résumé.

I got a reply from Allan Paloutzian, the head recruiter. He said, "Yes, we probably can!" Not his exact words, but close.

I made a brief visit alone to scout the office and pick up a few brochures. And I was lucky; I got to meet Mr. Paloutzian. We sat in his office and I found myself speaking with a warm and engaging man. He told me about his experience as a Volunteer in Africa and later his career as a banker in Scandinavia.

It's when he retired that he heard of the possibility of becoming a recruiter. His time as a Volunteer had been a transforming one, and now in his later years, he liked the idea of serving Peace Corps in a new way, all while doing something interesting.

I got good vibes about Peace Corps from him and then a couple of staffers I met. On the ride home I resolved to apply for admission. I knew it might take a while. I didn't want to lose a day. I started the process.

And the time had come to commit myself publicly. First, I had to tell Annabelle and my family!

Finally, steeling myself, I brought it up with her. I knew that she had thought about Peace Corps for herself at one time. So many of us have. She herself was the kind who might do it now but a knee problem ruled that out. She would be a terrific Volunteer.

"My!" she said. She just stared at me.

Of course, she was shocked. But she didn't blow her stack. She asked questions. She was puzzled, naturally. She wondered whether I was motivated because I was unhappy about us. A natural question. Ours was not a perfect relationship. Is there one? But it was very good and I was content. If anything, she had more reason to be discontented than I.

I laid out my reasons. I was retired, true, but only in a sense. I kept working, but at things that interested me, on my own, for my own pleasure. I enjoyed work.

As usual, I needed a challenge. An adventure. Maybe this was my way of repressing the idea that I was becoming an old man fast.

And a new idea excited me. All my adult life I have been a writer. Peace Corps would give me a lot to write about!

Few big decisions in life are ever crystal-clear. It's a matter of looking hard to see which way the scale tips. So it was now.

Finally she said something special. "John, you would be a terrific Volunteer!" How that made me happy! It nearly brought tears to my eyes. She was so understanding.

Mr. Paloutzian had told me that some of his staffers gave talks about their own experiences in Peace Corps. He gave me a schedule of such talks. One was coming up at a nearby Barnes and Noble bookstore. I invited Annabelle. A surprise: she said Yes. Very nice.

About 40 attended, the great majority very young, and about half and half men and women. Annabelle and I were about 50 years older than anybody else. Our presenter was about 30, and he spoke in a relaxed and interesting way.

He had a job to do, to recruit new Volunteers, but his pitch was low key. He spoke of the many advantages that Peace Corps offers, and he let those facts be his argument. He showed a DVD about Volunteers at their varied jobs. Interesting but I didn't care to grow crops or work in a medical clinic. He fielded questions and I paid attention to the answers. I enjoyed it all. He had brochures and hand-outs and I snatched some.

On the way home, Annabelle and I chatted about it. I said, "Well, it was a nice morning's entertainment." And she said, "Peace Corps is considered a very good program." That was it.

Another such talk came up a week or two later, in a different bookstore, and I went alone. Again it was interesting. I heard nothing to dissuade or discourage me.

I decided to take the next step, a bold one—to set up a formal interview at the Los Angeles office and apply to join. And I invited Annabelle to come along. A sensible idea, I thought. I wanted her to be in on everything. And she would become very savvy about Peace Corps. Again she said Yes. I gave her a kiss!

Allan Paloutzian welcomed us warmly. He introduced us to a young woman who would be my recruiter of record. She was Melanie Thurber, also a former Volunteer, in Africa also, I believe. She was pleasant but all business. She would do all the work today and would be my guide through the several weeks that would come next in the process.

Unfortunately, Annabelle could not be present with me for this part with Melanie. She made herself comfortable in the waiting area and began riffling through Peace Corps literature.

Melanie took me to her office and began asking serious questions, which I expected, of course. How I got the idea of this, career experience I had, why I was interested. More. She covered a lot of ground. She was satisfied for the moment. Then she handed me a form.

She said, "This gives Uncle Sam permission to look you over any way he wants to. Please sign it here." She pointed where and I signed..

Then she took a photo of me and showed it to me. Not the best mug shot I had ever had. Next she finger-printed me. I did not recall going through this before. She told me that we were through for now and what I would have to do next. I'd have to write some statements, supply records, get recommendations, do other things. There was a list. Finally, this visit was over. It had taken more than two hours.

On the way out I chatted with Mr. Paloutzian again.

"Congratulations!" he said. "You are taking a big step! I hope it works out well for you."

So, the process had been started, but there was no guarantee about its outcome. "It will take time," he said. "In fact, maybe even a year."

I got the feeling that it would take that long not only because of Peace Corps' various procedures, but to make sure that I was firm in my resolve to become a Volunteer. Peace Corps surely wanted to be certain this wasn't just a flash-in-the-pan idea.

The next big step would be what Peace Corps calls the Nomination, which would come by mail. That's when it would accept me as a serious candidate. This would conclude its preliminary steps. Again, nothing was guaranteed. Something might come up to disqualify me. Perhaps some finding in my physical exams that I would have to go through. If all went well, finally I would receive what was called the Invitation to Serve. I could accept or decline it. Nothing would happen overnight.

On the ride home, I filled in Annabelle. She had little to say. But no complaints. No sarcasm. The days passed in their usual quiet way. Annabelle and I continued to do everything as usual.

I broke the news to my three children. They were all adults, of course, all married and settled in their professions. Yes, it was a surprise for them, but not so surprising, everything considered. They have grown used to my "adventures." They began taking interest. Particularly my son, Mark, who began calling for updates. I heard a comment or two that I would make a great Volunteer. I liked that, of course. I felt encouraged.

I continued to research Peace Corps. I came to a conclusion all my own. I began to think that some people look at Peace Corps as something like the French Foreign Legion!

We are familiar with this famed outfit from books and movies. Legionnaires come from foreign countries and sign up to serve France as mercenaries for five years. Maybe it's seven. Some have good reason to go far away for a while! Maybe some view Peace Corps as a chance to duck out—maybe for good reason but maybe a bad one..

And something strange began to happen. I became aware of all the pleasant moments in my everyday life with Annabelle. Our visits to the library. Our Sunday rides. Our games of Scrabble. Our luncheons at Annabelle's favorite Chinese restaurant. Our walks. Our visits to favorite stores. On and on.

I would find myself thinking, *"Annabelle and I won't be able to do this. We won't be able to do that. For 27 months! That's a long time."*

I would ask myself, *"How will I feel when all these wonderful things are no longer possible? Will I be able to take that?"*

I began anxiously checking the mail every day. I knew when Harvey, our mail carrier, would arrive, and I would be on the look-out.

Annabelle was aware of all this going on in me. How could she not be? But she never brought up the subject. I wondered what her feelings were. Her deep-down feelings. No clue.

Many days went by. It seemed to be taking so long.

One day I called Melanie at Peace Corps. She told me, "I know how you feel, John. But be patient. We always have a lot of applications in process, and we have to do them all step by step, all one by one."

I was becoming fascinated by Peace Corps. One day, I arose with a new thought. I knew I would write articles if I got appointed. Now my new thought was, *"I will write a book about it! Explain the whole experience! It will be a wonderful project!"*

Peace Corps had changed in many ways since its early days. It was now focusing more than ever on recruiting older men and women. I enjoy writing articles and books. There would be much to write about. Important factual stuff. And my personal experiences going through it. The good stuff. The bad stuff if some developed. A book made sense.

I was sure many people would be interested. My book would help them if they entered Peace Corps. Now I really felt excited. I wished I had a book like it right now. It would help me.

But whoa! Nothing was certain yet. I still had to be nominated! I continued to watch for Harvey every day.

~ ~ ~

***Did you know*** .... that it's comforting when you head to your assignment overseas to be guaranteed that you will return home at the end of it with cash in your pocket.

Peace Corps will give you transition money. For us in Ukraine, it amounted to $240 per month for every month of service. This money was held in reserve. A full hitch was 27 months. But Peace Corps did not cover the three months of Training.

This will be given to you in two sums. One will be when you prepare to depart for home. The other will be some weeks later when you are in the U.S.A. I think Peace Corps learned that it was unwise to hand it over all at once. Maybe at times not much of it was left when the Volunteer did reach home.

You will appreciate this kitty as you buy your first groceries and search for an apartment or a job or buy a car or start in graduate school or get engaged or whatever.

If inflation continues (who believe it will not?), it will probably be more when you serve.

# 4 / I am nominated!

*I'm nearly in. But there are "if's" ahead.*
*Now it's time to break the news to everyone!*

**O**pening my mailbox, I scanned my letters and spotted the envelope from Peace Corps. Wow! Was this my good news? I tore it open.
 Yes, it was. The words jumped up: "You are nominated to Peace Corps!" What good news. Hallelujah! What this meant was that I would be accepted as a Trainee if I passed the checks and tests coming up.
 I read on. I would be a university English-language teacher. My 27 months of service would stretch from Dec. 21, 2007 to Dec. 21, 2009. And the big news: I would be posted somewhere in eastern Europe.
 Yes, eastern Europe! That was not good news. It was a shock! I expected to go to a country where French was important. For a simple reason—I speak French. Eastern Europe did not fit that bill!
 It went on to emphasize I would find other opportunities for service. That sounded interesting.
 It was signed by Melanie Thurber, my recruiter. This was good news and bad news.
 Good news because I had reached another big step in getting into Peace Corps. Bad news because I didn't like where I'd be sent.
 Then right away a doubt. Did I really want to do this? Separate myself from Annabelle and my children and their families and my friends? Leave home for more than two years? Go off to a strange land and eat strange food and put up with strange ways? Struggle to learn a new language? When I was just short of age 80?
 It's with chaotic feelings that I scooped up my mail and headed to tell Annabelle. I had hoped and prayed for this news. Now I wondered. And worried. For one thing, my destination was a great concern. For another, I feared Annabelle's reaction when I told her I was now a nominee. This was now for real. This would not be easy.
 She had been a good sport so far. Yes, she had learned early in our dozen years that I need stimulus…a challenge of some kind.
 But did it have to be something as momentous as this? Something necessitating such a huge displacement for such a long time at an age when two years represents a big chunk of whatever time we had left? A displacement that would affect her severely also?

She was playing the piano. She played every morning.

"I have something to show you," I said. Seldom did I interrupt her at the keyboard. Instantly she knew this was important. I gave her the letter. I did not mention my concern about eastern Europe.

She read it, then handed it back.

"Congratulations," she said. She said it flatly, the way you say something when you're expected to say it, even if you may not mean it. "Looks as if you're serious about this."

"Yes. But this is far from being decided. There are big steps ahead. It will be weeks before they make their final decision."

"Oh, they'll accept you." She began playing again.

The conversation ended right there. Much had been said. But even more had been left unsaid.

I sat and watched her play. I had the letter in my hands, but my excitement had died. I stared at her. I was sure she knew I was sitting there and looking at her. She played on. Finally she paused and began looking for another piece to play. Things were not good.

Before she could start again, I said, "How about a game of Scrabble this evening?" We both love the game. Playing a game was always fun. And it was always a nice way to smooth things over.

"I'm not in the mood." A long pause. She opened the new music and put her fingers on the keys. "Oh, all right. We'll play a game. After dinner." And she began playing.

After dinner, we set up the game. It had been a long day. Slowly her mood lifted. I relaxed. But we went to bed without speaking any more about the big, big subject in our minds.

We didn't bring it up the next morning. It came up again only when I got another communication from Peace Corps and had to tell her about it. We each had a great weight on our spirits.

I had realized from the start that this decision of mine would greatly change things for her as well as for me. But a remarkable thing happened. In the months ahead she never argued against my decision, never berated me, never bemoaned the sacrifices she would have to make.

Now the immediate thing I had to do was to resolve my feelings about being sent to eastern Europe.

When I applied to Peace Corps, I was confident that if accepted, I would be assigned to a country where French is spoken. Maybe Haiti. Maybe Morocco or elsewhere in Africa. Maybe southeast Asia or Vietnam. Why? Not only do I speak French easily. I read it. I write it.

French was my first language. My parents were French-speaking immigrants from Québec. I was the first born, entering this world in

Pawtucket, R.I., and thereby staking my claim to citizenship in the greatest country in the world.

I learned French on the laps of my mother and father. I learned English later, on the street and in school. And for 16 years—all through college—I went to bilingual schools, with the instruction in English and French. Sounds unusual, but yes, it all happened here in the U.S.A. Subsequently over the years I visited Québec often and also visited France eight or ten times.

In fact, just two years before all this, Annabelle and I had done a house swap with a doctor and his wife in Poitiers, France. We walked into their circle of friends and relatives in Poitiers and they walked into ours in Deep River—it was total cultural and language immersion for us and them. I spoke French with all of them. It's easy to lose a language through lack of use. I always kept up my French. So now why would I not expect to go to a country where French would be useful?

I had another big concern. Eastern Europe is cold and snowy. For nearly 20 years I have escaped the snow and cold of New England by going to warm places like the southern United States, Mexico, and particularly southern California. I started escaping New England in the winter after I slipped on an icy sidewalk and bonked my head. Lucky I didn't suffer a concussion. Could I handle tough winters again? Not sure.

So, imagine my surprise—eastern Europe! Somebody at Peace Corps must have misunderstood. Immediately I called Washington.

"Here's the situation," I was told. "We ask host countries what kinds of Volunteers they need and we get their lists. Then we look at the Volunteers we have. Then we do the best job we can matching the two.

"Other factors come into play, such as the Volunteers' talents and experience, their age, yes, their preferences. There's a whole list. Impossible to do it perfectly. You have to be flexible!"

It reminded me of that saying about Peace Corps. "You sign up to go wherever and do whatever, even with hardship!" Okay. I'd be flexible!

I checked the list of countries in eastern Europe that Volunteers serve in. There were six. I was hoping for Romania. I considered it interesting and attractive. And most important, Romanian is a Romance language, based on Latin. This meant it uses our abc's. Not a different alphabet, which is what the other countries used. This was encouraging.

More time went by. I got impatient. I called Peace Corps again. "Can't you tell me where I'm going?" I asked. "I'm on pins and needles."

"Sorry," I was told. "We'll tell you in the letter we send you. We call it the Invitation."

"Can't you just whisper it?"

A big laugh. "Just be patient. We've got rules because rules are needed. Have a nice day." And that was it.

But on another day I called again and said to the clerk, "What country? Can't you please tell me?" She was irritated and spoke sharply. "No!" In my shoes, she would have felt just as I did.

Finally came the invitation. I was invited to go to Ukraine! I was surprised because it was not on the list of Eastern Europe countries I had seen! I would be a university teacher in Ukraine! And I was told I would have to learn Ukrainian. Yes, what a shock. Ukrainian uses the Cyrillic alphabet! So different! I got a headache thinking about this.

I had never considered Ukraine a possibility. I still called it "the Ukraine." That's the way I always heard or read about it. But it was a new democracy now, struggling hard, with its own hard-won identity. A new country.

It was explained to me this way: we don't say "the Texas," do we, or "the California"? This was now rightly and proudly simply "Ukraine"!

*What a shock! I'm going to Ukraine! Ice and snow! Russian! Well, okay.*

**R**ight away I rushed to my Encyclopedia Americana and looked up Ukraine. I picked up Volume "U" and began flipping through. On the way to "Ukraine" I got to "Uganda." I had thought I might be sent to Africa, remember? I took a few minutes to read about Uganda. There were pictures. I saw how poor and undeveloped Uganda was. I saw ramshackle housing and primitive streets.

Then I got to Ukraine in the book. I saw how magnificent Kyiv, the capital, looked. Yes, magnificent. I saw beautiful Orthodox churches with golden domes. Tree-lined avenues with impressive buildings. Modern trams and buses. Well-dressed people. I thought, "I'm glad it's going to be Ukraine and not Uganda!"

Then I went online to Google and typed "Ukrainian universities." I'd be heading to one! I found several. I looked at impressive buildings. Very promising.

I did more research. Ukrainians speak Ukrainian. It is the only official language. But Ukraine is right next door to Russia. Many Ukrainians are ethnic Russians and speak Russian as their first language rather than Ukrainian. Some are campaigning to make Russian the second official language. Sound familiar? Like the people in our country who are advocating that Spanish be made an official language?

The disturbing news was that both Ukrainian and Russian use that strange Cyrillic alphabet. It has more letters. Some look like ours but have different sounds. Some look very odd. It appeared dreadful.

A lot that I was reading was scary. But flexible I would be! I had 10 days to decide Yes or No. Promptly I said Yes. I would give the assignment everything I had. And I'd do my best to adjust and fit in.

I wasted no time in getting started. I went to Amazon.com and searched for helpful books. Right away I ordered Lonely Planet's "Ukraine." Also Culture Start's "Ukraine—A Quick Guide to Customs and Etiquette." Also Teach Yourself's "Teach Yourself Ukrainian," with two 60-minute audio CD's. I began studying the minute they arrived.

I quickly realized that much more lay ahead before I might get in. But I had no idea it would be such a demanding and trying experience.

I had been told that the process would require that I be cleared four ways. Personally. Medically. Dentally. Legally. I had only a vague idea what all that meant.

**But** some of this had already been done. The Peace Corps had determined that I met all the basic criteria. They had studied my résumé and my application form. You need a master's degree in education to teach English as a Second Language at the university level but they said I qualified with my master's in journalism. Besides, I had done some teaching at that level.

They had required a detailed medical history. Financial and credit information. Statements why I wanted to join and about this and that. In my case, a statement about my relationship with Annabelle.

They had required three letters of recommendation covering my personal and professional background. There was a form these three persons would have to complete, with every question to be answered. I had supplied not three persons—four! They had to mail their letters directly to Peace Corps, not via me. And each had to sign his name across the joint where the flap is glued to the envelope. Security!

All four had kindly supplied me with copies of their evaluations, and I had seen they had gone overboard for me.

And Peace Corps had my transcripts from Assumption College, Brown University, and Boston University.

These had been late in coming, and that had made me anxious. I joked about it. I told friends, "I went to those schools so long ago that the registrars are still down in the cellar poking in the archives with their flashlights for my record. All that was more than half a century ago."

One transcript after another got mailed to Peace Corps with a copy to me. I had a general recollection of how well I had succeeded at those schools. But looking at each course I had taken brought back many memories. I had passed every course everywhere, many with distinction, but a couple had been difficult.

I had to be legally cleared also. Some of this had happened in my first interview. The finger-printing, for instance. I assumed that my prints had been checked and cleared. Never have I been in serious trouble with the law. Once when I was very young I had ignored a parking ticket and had been hauled into court and fined, but that was trivial.

As you remember, at my interview with Melanie Thurber I had checked off that Uncle Sam could scrutinize my past in any way he deemed necessary. That was not a worry. I had no skeletons in my closet.

But I didn't know whether this legal checking was over. Was the FBI or the CIA or some other government agency scurrying around talking to my friends and acquaintances and neighbors? Or was this whole business nominal, being done just for the record and not for any red flag that might have popped up? I did not know. And I never found out.

Medically and dentally cleared also. This was a different matter. This, I felt, might be a simple requirement for somebody 23 years old, say. Such a person would not be burdened with medical problems.

But I had many decades to look back on, and although I was in good health and felt strong and peppy, I had had some illnesses and some surgeries. I was surprised at the detail that Peace Corps wanted and the vigor with which they pursued the answers.

In fact, supplying Peace Corps with evidence that I was okay in every way became a problem.

I filled out every form with painstaking accuracy. The forms wanted specifics, not generalities. Came a form that asked about operations. One question asked if I had had surgery to any artery. I answered yes. It had been a trivial procedure. But if surgery is the cutting into the body with a scalpel by a surgeon, then I had had this particular surgery.

Here's what it was about. Some 20 years ago I had come down with a strange illness. Well, very strange to me. It's called Temporal Arteritis. Note: not arthritis; arteritis! There's a big difference.

Temporal arteritis generally affects older people, and women more often than men. It involves the temporal arteries, which run up the side of the head. Temporal arteritis has several symptoms and one is major headaches, but I never got headaches. Still don't.

The big danger of T.A. is that it can lead to sudden blindness in one or both eyes. I had had some scares. One day my right eye began to close down as if somebody had pulled a curtain over it. It went nearly black. In seconds the curtain had risen. My vision was perfect again. It happened again. Then again. My oh my! Would the next time leave me blind?

After tests, the possibilities pointed to temporal arteritis. There was one definitive test left: a microscope examination of a tiny piece of the artery. This required a biopsy. This was a simple procedure done late in the afternoon by a surgeon, his last little job of the day. An injection of anesthesia and a nick or two with a scalpel. That's all. In 15 minutes that minute surgery was done. The lab report said I had T.A.

In one sense, this was good news. T.A. can be treated well with corticosteroids. Prednisone is a leading one! Take it as prescribed and the disease would run its course. You can get T.A. only once. So they say.

That's what happened. I took varying doses of Prednisone, some very large. I would get better, then things would get worse, then get better. Finally I was told the T.A. had been licked. Wonderful! It had taken a couple of years. Finally I got off the Prednisone.

But suddenly I had cataracts in both eyes. They had advanced so quickly that it was guaranteed I would fail my next driver's-license eye examination. This was scary because I was a consultant and I scurried around in my car to see my clients. Losing my license would threaten my livelihood. The cataracts, I was told, were a side effect of the Prednisone. How nice. I had cataract surgery. The results were marvelous and still are.

**B**ut now two things were red flags on that Peace Corps medical form. The T.A. surgery. And the Prednisone. Prednisone is misused by some folks. Peace Corps demanded more information.

I contacted my rheumatologist of 20 years back in Massachusetts. A kind and understanding lady. She had steered me safely through those frightful months. She lost no time. She managed to locate my old records and assured me I had no reason for concern. She wrote a letter to Washington and that finally settled the matter. Well, nearly.

But within the past few months I had suffered something else quite nasty. All new to me. A terrible itchiness on my palms. I had seen a dermatologist. She had prescribed a medication and it had worked. Now Peace Corps demanded that I have a dermatologist take a second look. I went back to her and she reassured Peace Corps I would be all right.

I had also gone through extensive dental-implant surgery. In fact, the work had been completed in California a few weeks earlier. This also had to be checked out. Now I was home in Connecticut. It involved a detailed new dental examination and set of full-mouth X-rays. All this was done and sent to Washington and it paid the bill. Well, a tiny part of it. Peace Corps allowed $60. My dentist charged me $525.

My cataract surgery also made Peace Corps nervous. They demanded an examination by an eye doctor. An optometrist found everything satisfactory. He also gave me a prescription for new eyeglasses. Peace Corps demands that each Volunteer who wears glasses report for duty with two pairs, and I wanted them to be right up to date. I paid for this also.

But because of my age, Peace Corps put me through some extra precautionary steps. As I have said, I was in excellent health. I saw a physician regularly, as regularly as I did a dentist. I was lucky to have good doctors. One in California because I live there part of the year, and one in Connecticut because that is my home base.

I was in California then and went to see my esteemed doctor there. I told him what I was up to. "The Peace Corps?" he said with surprise. What kind of guy would want to do that at such an elderly age? He questioned me and I assume my explanation was satisfactory.

That reaction of his was common. My being a Volunteer always evoked surprise, whenever and wherever I mentioned it.

He looked over Peace Corps' medical questionnaire. He's a practical man. "Well, it's your regular time to be checked over," he said. "Why don't we check everything to see whether you might have a problem satisfying their requirements."

We did that. Oh, I did have a problem or two. A few pounds too heavy. And my diabetes test had edged up a few points. Diabetes is rampant in my family. I do not have the disease but I must be extremely cautious. I was still on the safe side—I controlled the problem with proper diet and exercise; no medication was required. So I looked forward to Peace Corps' medical studies with some confidence.

But now Peace Corps insisted that I see a cardiologist. Just for the record! I had never been to a cardiologist. I went to one recommended by a friend. This doctor examined Peace Corps' paper work. "Interesting," she said. "This is the first time I go through one of these."

What a process! First, a stress test. A first for me. Of course, I was apprehensive. I stepped on the treadmill, the machine started, the speed got stepped up, and I did my best to keep going. The lab technician smiled. "Terrific!" he said.

I've always made exercise part of my daily routine. When I pull into a large parking lot, I always park far back, to get in more walking. I shun elevators and use the stairs. It's a habit. We all know how hard it is to break a habit. That's why it's important to build good habits.

In California Annabelle's condo is on the fourth floor of her building. I always take the stairs up and down. She takes the elevator. We split up this way even when we're going out together, or returning home together. Yes, it seems strange. She definitely thought so when we first met. She now accepts it. Maybe this is why I did so well on my treadmill test.

The cardiologist also made me wear a Holter monitor for 24 hours. I wore it when I walked around, ate, took a shower, went to the toilet, walked up the stairs, down the stairs, carried up the groceries, did everything. My results were excellent.

I also had to have an echocardiogram and a full electrocardiogram. Both satisfactory.

All this wasn't easy to get done. Each test required a different appointment at a different hospital or doctor's office. Each test created the anxiety of waiting for the results. All ran up bills. Peace Corps was willing to spring for some of this, but pitifully little—I mentioned the $60 for the dentist. Only $20 for the optometrist! Unrealistic! And so on.

Fortunately, it was decided that because of my age some of these tests were justified anyway, and Medicare and my private insurer agreed. But I had decided to go ahead with all of this before that became known. It tested my determination. I was willing to do whatever it took.

Later I found that some people go to great lengths to satisfy Peace Corps Medical. One woman told me she spent $3,000 for hearing aids. One man told me that he spent many hundreds for dentistry.

I was excited when the books about Ukraine that I had bought arrived. I got them within a week and I started right in on them.

**B**ut Peace Corps wasn't losing any time, either. I thought the training would start only when I reported for service, which I was told would be in another four weeks or so. Hah!

Quickly they sent me a Ukrainian-language set of their own and told me to start studying right now! So, I had their books and those I had just bought. I got to it, although I had a zillion other things to do in order to go overseas for 27 months.

And Peace Corps kept sending me things. Brochures, folders, handouts. Forms to fill out. Booklets to read. Incredible how much stuff.

I spent hours on the Cyrillic alphabet, trying to memorize each character. I would give myself little tests. Slowly, slowly I got better. But I hated every minute. Why hadn't they found a country for me where I could speak French! Then another stunning surprise. Came a new message. "You won't be studying Ukrainian. You'll be studying Russian!"

What! I couldn't believe it. But again I made up my mind: "I will be flexible!" I started studying Russian.

Throughout all this, I kept Annabelle informed. She was my priority. She took it all in stride. I found it remarkable. One day I heard her speaking to an old college friend on the phone. I heard her say, "Oh, they'll take John. He was made for the Peace Corps!" Her words made me so happy!

My personal To Do list seemed endless. I owned real estate, in fact two condos, one a rental. I had to make sure these got cared for. How would I maintain these from 4,500 miles away? This required planning. I decided to rent out my own condo also rather than leave it unoccupied. I had to put many things into storage. I began advertising for a tenant.

I was not a millionaire but I had a varied financial portfolio and it required supervision. I had to copy many documents and records that I would need overseas, including IRS records. I'd still have to file federal and state returns. I had to automate some financial payments, including tax obligations. I had to suspend all my utilities—my electrical and telephone and computer and TV service.

I had to arrange for the storage of my car. I had to find a good realtor. I made changes in insurance policies. I wrote a new will. I had to make arrangements at my post office. I notified various businesses and many friends. On and on. The list was intimidating.

I had been writing a newspaper column. I had to discuss this with my editor. I arranged to write articles from overseas. This would require Peace Corps approval. I would take that up in due time.

Came the date I should report to Peace Corps' Staging in Philadelphia. September 28! I discovered Peace Corps has its own travel agency. It would give me a plane ticket. I said a train would be more convenient and probably cheaper. They agreed and sent me an Amtrak ticket.

Oh, they also said they would issue me a passport. But I already had one. "Ours will be limited to your Peace Corps service," they told me. "Use ours all through Peace Corps." I did that but I took my own along as well.

Staging is when recruits gather and prepare for departure overseas. I prepared a timetable for the many things I had to do. I am an organized person. Something terrible happened. Somehow I miscalculated. I ran out of time. I spent the last 48 hours without a single hour of sleep! True.

On the evening before my departure, I was frantic. I put in an S.O.S. to my friend Dale Winchell. He rushed over to help me. He was stunned by what he saw. So much more to be done. He called his wife Amy and she rushed over. She worked with us until midnight...apologized...had to go to work the next morning. Dale slogged on with me for nearly two hours more—to 2 a.m.—and then excused himself and departed. He, too, had to get up early. I worked on through the night.

My friend Rev. Timothy Haut, pastor of the Deep River Congregational Church and a fellow Rotarian in our Deep River club, had told me he'd pick me up at 7 a.m. to drive me to the train. He arrived on time.

He was startled to see me still packing things. He pitched in. It was a frenzy! Finally, finally I took a three-minute shower, changed, and the two of us lugged my two mammoth suitcases down to his car. Peace Corps emphasized only two! My two were the biggest I could find.

On the way out I grabbed a wastebasket I had packed some important papers in—it was the only thing available—and carried that along.

It was 8:10 a.m. The train would pull in at 8:32. We had six miles to go. Tim looked at his watch, did not say a word, stepped on the gas. We zoomed ahead. In 5 or 6 minutes, he looked at his watch again.

He glanced at me. "John, it's hopeless. We'll never make it."

"You don't think so?"

"Impossible." Silence. Then, "I'll tell you what. Let's relax. Let's stop and have a nice breakfast. We can have a good talk. Then I'll put you on the next train. I think it comes in around 11:15."

My mind was racing. How awful! I'd be showing up for the Staging hours late! How terrible! But...but...there was no other choice.

"You're right, Tim. Breakfast sounds good. I'm so sorry about this. This is the first time something like this happens to me. I feel awful."

"No problem, John. The next time we see one another, we'll laugh about it."

I doubted it but said nothing. Tim had slowed down now and we rolled on, saying little. We approached the station. We had to pass it to get to the restaurant Tim had in mind.

"Tim," I said. "Why don't we stop at the station? I'll run in to check the time of the next train."

"Good idea." And he turned into the parking lot. It was 8:49 a.m. We had missed my train by 17 minutes.

**S**traight ahead I spotted a stopped passenger train. And headed in the right direction! "Tim! Tim! Look! Maybe that's my train!"

"Maybe it is!" He put his foot to the pedal...drove right up to the train...stopped just 15 feet short! People were getting onto the train. I jumped out and yelled up to them. "Is that the Philadelphia train?" Nobody paid attention. I yelled a second time.

A businessman looked down at me. "Yes, it is!"

I dashed back to Tim. He had opened the trunk and was taking out my suitcases. He had heard!

"Tim, let's go! Let's go!"

I grabbed a suitcase. He grabbed a suitcase. I grabbed the wastebasket with my mail.

Somehow I got up onto the platform and ran for an open car on the train, dragging along that enormous suitcase. A conductor was standing in the door. I handed my case up to him. Tim was right behind me, huffing. I took his suitcase, handed it up. I jumped onto the train.

"Thank you, Tim!" I yelled down to him. "Thank you! We made it! You must have been praying all the way!"

He laughed. "Good luck, John! All the best! Write often!" He headed to his car. Then looked back. He was smiling. "Good luck! Take care!"

The conductor motioned me forward. "Good thing our train was late, my friend!" he said. "You made it by a whisker."

He led me to a seat, stacked my suitcases in a corner, checked my ticket. I dropped into the seat, pushed my head back, closed my eyes, tried to calm down. "Thank God!" I thought. "Thank God!"

I felt the train start. We made up the lost time and got to Philadelphia on schedule. Before pulling in, I asked the conductor about a taxi.

"I'll have a Red Cap waiting for you. He'll get you a taxi."

I took all my mail and papers out of the wastebasket and managed to stuff them into a suitcase. What to do with the wastebasket? It was a beauty. It had been a housewarming gift. No way could I take it along. What a shame. I left it at the door of the train as I stepped out.

I made it to the Staging on time. Wow! I thought of the story Tim would be telling our Rotarian friends. I could foresee the joking. And I thought of the challenge ahead. Would I be up to it?

~ ~ ~

***Did you know***…that there are some 200 countries in the world and that no other has a Volunteer civilian service like Peace Corps?

I have heard of one or two other countries which have a service, but much smaller, more limited, and more short-term.

Imagine what good works could be accomplished around the world if all major countries shared this vision of ours.

Imagine what good works could be accomplished around the world if all major countries shared this vision of ours.

Let's hope that other countries will be inspired by our Peace Corps.

# 5 / The Staging. Exciting!

*Bad luck getting to Philadelphia for it.*
*But Peace Corps gives us a rousing start.*

The Staging would be easy, I thought. I'd have time to again visit Benjamin Franklin's great Philadelphia Public Library. Enjoy the Philadelphia Fine Arts Museum. Maybe celebrate on the last night with a concert at the famous Curtis Music Institute. Hah! I barely got to take a walk around the block.

The Staging—it's a word we don't hear often. Its military meaning is to get ready for a big campaign. That's how Peace Corps looks at its efforts overseas—a great big campaign to achieve its mission. We were here to prepare for it in double time.

It was impressive from the first minute. Super-organized. We had meetings, classes, seminars, discussions—yes, all these things—all through the three days. To make everything even more effective, we were divided into two sub-groups, each with our own "faculty."

This made it easier for our teachers to get to know us. "Cheer leaders" is a better description. Gave them a better chance to look at each of us right in the eye and keep us alert and fired up and determined.

We were all put up at the Holiday Inn in the Historic District, and that's not only where we slept, but ate, met, studied, discussed, pondered, socialized, and bonded. Bonding was a big part of the deal. The Historic District? We were right there, but don't ask me anything about it. Never got to explore it.

Right away I found out how serious and motivated Peace Corps is. I was enormously impressed. I even had a good time. I had expected one lecture after another. No, no. Lots of variety. I kept thinking, *This is how they must teach in universities nowadays. I hope so.*

Our bonding started in the first 10 minutes. Eighty-six of us were reporting for service from all over the country. We were called Group 33. That's how many groups have gone to Ukraine since it became its own country in 1991. Two a year. There were still some PCVs in Groups 31 and 32 on duty there.

PCVs are Peace Corps Volunteers. PCV is the first new word I learned! Then I learned another, RPCV. It stands for Returned Peace Corps Volunteer—"alumnus." I think all our cheer leaders—excuse me, instructors—were RPCVs. We'd become RPCVs at the end of our 27 months. But we newcomers weren't PCVs yet. We were Trainees. That was emphasized. We'd become Volunteers only when we took the oath at the end of our training.

By the way, the normal hitch is 27 months in all—the three months of training and then the 24 months of service. I say "normal" because you can quit and go home earlier without penalty and without shame, well, on the record books. It is said the typical attrition throughout Peace Corps over 27 months is 30 percent. That got my attention. I didn't want to become part of that percentage.

As I looked everybody over, I was struck by several facts. Three-quarters of us were women! Three quarters were under age 30! We seniors were just a handful! How multi-cultural we were! Truly we represented the diversity of our country.

We were White, Black, Latino, Asian. I didn't see anyone noticeably Native American but I was sure some of us had at least some of that blood. I did get to meet one during my service and I believe there were one or two others. It will be a pleasure to tell you about him later.

Peace Corps is known as a young person's game and that was still true despite the recent intense effort to bring in older persons. We were still only 7 or 8 percent—the goal was 15. Most of the guys and gals around me were in their early 20's, it seemed. What also struck me was the many women. I was astonished. Nationally some 60 percent of PCVs were women. I never realized that. Why does Peace Corps appeal more to women? I'm still trying to find out.

Only eight of us were seniors, meaning age 55 and over (that's AARP's definition of "senior," it seems; not Uncle Sam's). Such a tiny group. And I at 78 was the oldest by far. At times I felt like the odd man out though nobody did anything to make me feel that. I did attract stares.

I was struck by the many decades between me and most of the others. I admit I did wonder, *What the heck am I doing here?* I am sure a lot of the younger people were asking the same question about me.

Right now there was a lot of hand-shaking and "glad to meet you!" going on. We were all gathered in a large lounge, some relaxing at tables, others standing and chatting. Peace Corps had given us name tags to make the bonding easier.

Among the first that I met were Mary and John Evans. In their 60's. This was their second hitch—they had served earlier in the South Pacific. I considered this remarkable and very encouraging. They were going over as teachers also. In fact, all of us would be teaching.

"You'll love the Peace Corps, John," he told me. "It's great. That's why we re-upped!" First time I heard that expression. I got to meet a couple of others who were re-upping.
Mary smiled. "We've looked forward to meeting you," she said. "We thought we'd be the oldest. But no. That's you!" And that's how I found out I held that title!

What had happened is that in the last week, Peace Corps had e-mailed us a master list of all of us. It included our e-mail addresses. So, many had dashed off e-mails to many others. I had read each and every one, of course.

What an impressive group. It was clear they were people of some accomplishment. All had academic degrees, I found out. Many had graduate degrees. Many had worked at exciting and important things. Quite a few had traveled abroad, even studied abroad. And by definition as Peace Corps Trainees I knew they were competent, motivated, energetic people. The Peace Corps selection process assures that.

To all these writers I had sent the same reply. "Dear Friends, I am looking forward to meeting you and working with you. I won't be hard to miss. I could be the *dedushka* of you all!" *Dedushka* means "granddaddy" in Russian. See, I knew that now! Maybe in Ukrainian, too. I got kidded about that.

Some knew some things about me. I have an e-mail "signature" that gets tacked onto all messages that I send out. It's simple. It mentions where I live. And it gives the titles of two travel books that I have written and where they can be ordered.

Soon I was astonished. Some people had spotted this and had looked me up on Google. Even my books on buybooksontheweb.com and on amazon.com. What a surprise. Several had ordered my books and told me nice words about them.

Quickly the program geared up. It ran on for the afternoon and the next two days. Peace Corps had been doing stagings like this for a long time. They had it down pat. I quickly got to understand this was a super-serious undertaking. It was slick and effective. They didn't want to lose a minute and they wanted us ready and raring to go.

All our instructors seemed thoroughly seasoned. Mostly women but the men held their own. What an enthusiastic, high-energy team! They were so practiced. They did this for group after group of Trainees.

What they strove to do was intensify our pride and get our *esprit de corps* firmly rooted, familiarize us with Peace Corps traditions and ways, strengthen our bonding, give us all the essential know-how we needed, and make us realistic about what was waiting for us in Ukraine.

What followed was a fast-paced schedule of welcome, orientation, briefings, and earnest training. It was serious—I say it again for emphasis. And it was fun. I want to emphasize that also. I learned a lot. I got to feel good about my buddies. And about Peace Corps. I was becoming more and more impressed about this outfit.

One program followed another, each 90 minutes long. Our leaders made it look easy. They did it all in an entertaining way. Delightful.

Many topics were covered. The history of the Peace Corps. The selection process. The money and perks we would receive, and the paperwork and forms we had to fill out. What was expected of us as Volunteers. How we would travel abroad, and how we would be welcomed and processed there and what would happen next.

The constant theme was that we were an elite group, though I don't remember that word "elite! being used. We had been selected with care. I had read that only 1 in 7 applicants make it in—incredible! Elsewhere I read that it was 1 in 3. I believe the latter is the correct figure. Anyway, we got to understand that for each of us here, several others were back home, disappointed.

Emphasized was that being a Volunteer is a no-nonsense commitment. Toss away any notions of lolling on a beach under palm trees for 27 months. Chuck any hope of doing light duty, or nominal duty, and then returning home to lap up the respect and prestige that come with having been a Volunteer.

The Peace Corps had spent many years building its reputation as a can-do, will-do outfit. That reputation now rested on us. We were here because we had been judged capable. Peace Corps would prepare us thoroughly with three months of training in Ukraine before sending us to our assignments. The training would be intense. And the assignments would be meaningful.

We were familiar with the Peace Corps' publicity. One of its favorite lines was, "It's the toughest job you'll ever have!" *It's all exaggerated,* I thought. I for one had had some tough jobs. I doubted this would be tougher than some I'd gotten through. But I got the feeling Peace Corps meant it.

I had expected a series of lectures. That had been my experience all through college and graduate school. A teacher would stand in front and talk to us until time ran out. Oh, he (not many women profs back then) might put a few questions to us, or read something, or crack a joke. But lecturing was the established style. Here I was astonished by the richness of techniques and how well done it all was.

I mentioned we were now two sub-groups. Yes, and that was effective. But one disadvantage of course was that we stuck with our own group. I for one did not get to meet those in the other group. I regretted it later. I went the whole 27 months without getting to know more than one or two in the other group.

At times we would be broken into still smaller groups of six or eight. We were given a topic to discuss, always a fragment of a broader topic. Afterward, one of us would be designated to stand and give a report to the other groups. And we would hear reports from the other groups. I thought that worked well. Of course, some groups did a better job than others. We all noticed who did best. We did cover a lot of ground. The hours flew by.

Other sessions involved games. We learned all while having fun. Others used a question and answer format. Throughout, we were encouraged to be active and even pro-active. Participate! Jump in! That was the idea. Later I saw this technique being used in our training in Ukraine.

Strange the way I kept running into two other Trainees. A gal and a guy. How lucky I was. She was in her 30's, I believe. Eunice Bonaparte, a black gal from New York City. So energetic and friendly. She had taught in public school. Had done other things, too. We happened to sit at the same table for work sessions. I liked the way she spoke so forthrightly. And she was fun. I took a big liking to her.

Another was Matthew Rodringo from New Jersey, who seemed in his mid 20's. He listened carefully and when he spoke, he made a point. I got a feeling of earnestness and solidity. We did not sit at the same table. What happened is that wherever we were, I found him often at my side. It became clear he was looking out for me!

I was certain both would be fine Volunteers. I hoped all three of us would be assigned close together. But just the opposite happened.

I got to meet numerous others and had good chats. I could see Peace Corps had selected with care. I liked them. I wish I could name more of them. They deserve that.

We were sleeping two to a room. My roommate was Keith Gough, in his early 20's, a public school teacher from the Midwest. He had trained to be a teacher, and he had had some solid classroom experience, and he took pride and pleasure in being a teacher. I felt he was in teaching to stay.

I am sure he did not expect to be bunking with a septuagenarian. We got along fine. He was interesting. He spoke of his fiancée. He was engaged! That surprised me. He was so young and going away for so long. But that gave the two of us something in common: Annabelle and I were not engaged but we were in a committed relationship also.

Late into the night he worked on his laptop in bed. We had Wi-Fi! I had never experienced Wi-Fi. Amazing. But it was everyday stuff for all our younger people.

On the second night as we were in our beds and chatting, Keith kept working on his laptop. And as we talked, he looked me up on Google! I was astonished. I found it incredible how easy and rewarding this high-tech way of life was becoming.

Later I saw that most of my colleagues seemed to have a laptop. They would work on them every minute they could. I felt like a digital klutz.

I had a computer also, but not a laptop. Mine was a Mac Mini, a small and just-out Apple processor about the size of a cigar box (if you remember what that is; cigars are not that popular any more). Along with it I had a full-size flat monitor and a keyboard and track-ball mouse plus small accessories. Not things that you could set up at a moment's notice, but that I looked forward to setting up wherever I wound up.

In our brief free time, we had the chance to go outside for a quick walk. But no possibility of real sight-seeing in the City of Brotherly Love. This was not a vacation. I did not even get to Independence Square, which was nearby. The best I managed was a noon-time walk for a couple of blocks in one direction one day, and in the opposite direction the next day.

On one quick walk I spotted a pedicure shop. I looked in. An Asian man worked at the front desk as pretty young Asian women in blue tunics and white slacks worked on customers. Modern. Elaborate flip-back chairs. Very clean. Both my feet had painful calluses on the soles. I was familiar with podiatrists, but I had never had a professional pedicure. I walked in and showed him my calluses. "Yes! We help you!" he said.

"But how long will it take?"

"Just half hour!"

Did I have the time? I decided to take the chance. He led me to a petite gal with a gorgeous smile. First, a hot soak for my feet. Then a vigorous massage and toweling. A nail clipping. A lotion. Most important, the painstaking trimming of my calluses. Then a cream with more massaging. She was terrific. What a delight. But it took 40 minutes, and I had to rush. But my footsteps back were wonderfully pain free.

**F**inally, Staging ended. Time well spent. We were now a close group. On departure morning, the instructions were precise. Every piece of luggage downstairs by 9! I was early this time! Our three chartered buses would be waiting for us.

Astonishing how much luggage we had. We had been told only two suitcases but I spotted plenty of other things. Bulging backpacks. Countless laptops. I even saw two guitars.

This was for real now. There was seriousness to it. We were going off for a long time. I'd be in my 80's when I got back! Many of my colleagues were traveling out of the U.S.A. for the first time.

There was a lot for us to wonder about. And worry about. This wasn't a joy ride. Peace Corps had high expectations. We had been told this time and again. This was a mission. I am sure there was uneasiness. Undoubtedly some second thoughts. I admit I felt some.

But there was laughter and joking and bantering. It was all so exciting. Finally we got the word and clambered aboard.

Members of the Staging staff were out front, watching us go, waving to us, giving us a thumbs up. They knew us now. Theirs was no longer just an academic interest. They cared. We could tell. And away we rode. We were a jolly bunch now.

In 90 minutes we were at the airport. We were scheduled to fly to Frankfurt, Germany, on a United Airlines flight. Approximately eight hours. There to transfer to a Lufthansa flight for the two-hour ride to Kyiv. We had heard a lot about Kyiv, the capital of Ukraine. Beautiful, everybody said. We were excited.

We had to stand and slowly move forward in various lines, of course. That's the way it is at airports nowadays, even for important, official U.S.A. officials like us—just joking! Again it was surprising how often I found Matt at my side. He kept trying to wrest one of my big suitcases from me. Sometimes he succeeded. What a good fellow.

As we approached Customs and Immigration, somebody yelled, "This is our last chance, guys! If you want to change your mind, do it right now!" I saw no takers.

United and Lufthansa were billed as "partners." Interesting. United is American. Lufthansa is German. Well, it turned out to be Lufthansa all the way, and on an Airbus. I wondered how American taxpayers would feel about us, all on official American government business, being transported on a foreign carrier and a foreign-made plane. It was explained to me later that United and Lufthansa are "code sharers," and this seemed to make it okay.

I had flown Lufthansa some 15 years earlier, on a trip to India. That was on an Airbus also. That was unforgettable for a remarkable reason. The aircraft had a video camera in its nose. The captain turned it on for our take-off and landing. We watched it all on TV sets in our cabin. How exciting. "Wait till you see it!" I told everybody. "Marvelous!"

Well, if this plane had the camera, the captain never turned it on. I was so disappointed. Others who had heard me were also.

I had flown across the Atlantic a number of times. I found this flight strangely tedious. Couldn't wait to get off. Finally we got to Frankfurt. An astounding airport. So big and modern. So many planes landing and taking off. So many shops and services. But we had just enough time to go to the men's room. Well, that's how it felt to me.

Our second flight was good. We were getting excited. We were about to arrive. But I kept thinking: I will be here for more than two years! I had never been away on foreign soil so long. How would it go? So many things could happen, good and not so good. Back home, also. It was a concern. Surely my buddies were thinking the same things.

For me this had been nearly a full year of hoping and anticipating and preparing and worrying. Now was the great moment. I was about to step onto Ukraine soil. The future was becoming the present. Would it turn out to be the grand adventure that I hoped? Or might I be disappointed? Time would tell. This is such a trite exception. But so true.

Perfect! We were flying into Kyiv in broad daylight, and we slid through a hole in the clouds, and there below was the great expanse of Ukraine. I couldn't see Kyiv. What I saw was fertile table land stretching as far as could be seen. Just as my guidebook described it.

The whole of it looked beautifully cultivated, with big rectangles of fields strikingly outlined with trees. Hundreds of trees. It was obvious that every each had been planted with care. What an impressive sight.

Ukraine has often been called the bread basket of Europe. It is famous for all the cereals it raises, wheat and rye and buckwheat and oats and others also. It also grows fruits and vegetables by the tons. I had heard about the bountiful harvests. But manufacturing is big also.

Now I got a glimpse of our airport, Borispil International. Quite small, well, by American standards. It's the country's main airport. I expected bigger. After all, more than 40 million people live in Ukraine. But very neat, as modern airports tend to be. I spotted just a few jets on the ground—not the great line-ups that are usual at major airports around the world. Everything looked quiet. Strangely so.

We made a smooth landing and of course we all cheered. Our pilots must have been startled. We were here! Our Airbus stopped short of the terminal, in fact, out on the field. We transferred to a huge bus. We were piled in shoulder to shoulder. It drove us right to the door. Customs and Immigration were a breeze, and soon we were all fetching our luggage.

The bags began sliding down a chute, spun around on the carousel, and we grabbed our own. Soon all my buddies had taken off with their stuff, but I was still standing there, waiting. And waiting. I had my big suitcase but my smaller one still had to appear. Finally I was there all alone. The carousel had been turned off. I was missing one suitcase.

Where was it? Maybe back in Frankfurt, where we had changed flights? That had happened to me before. How awful that would be.

I found an attendant and he began a search. I fidgeted. Everything in that bag was essential. In 10 minutes he located it. It was way over in left field, so to speak. How it got there, no idea.

I managed to catch up with the others in the terminal. They were assembled in a loose group and looking at a cadre of smiling officials who faced them. This was the Peace Corps' reception committee—all come from Headquarters in Kyiv to greet us and smooth us through.

There were eight of them, maybe more, all the top people. What a line-up. One thing struck me. How well-dressed they were compared to us. I looked around. What a sloppy, motley group we were! Oh, well.
It they thought so, too, they didn't show it. What a warm welcome they gave us! It made me feel so good.

~ ~ ~

***Did you know*** ... that Volunteers may welcome relatives and friends from the United States to come and visit them at their post?

In my case, milady Annabelle came twice, once at mid service and then just before my hitch ended. It was wonderful for her and me because she got to see what I was doing, what my life was like, and what Peace Corps is all about.

It was a morale builder and good public relations for Peace Corps. I believe this is how Peace Corps looks at it.

# 6 / Yes, we're in Ukraine!

*Our Peace Corps bosses welcome us....
and warn us. Training starts. This is for real.*

There at the airport, our top boss, slim, sixty-ish Diana Schmidt, took a step toward us. She was surrounded by top administrators. She looked us over and smiled. "Welcome to Ukraine!" she said. "Are you tired?"

A lot of laughter. Some of us yelled Yes! Some No! She laughed also, knowingly. We felt she understood.

Her title was Ukraine Country Director. But all of us knew she had started out in Peace Corps as a Volunteer. That had impressed us. We had heard she had been a college professor, then a marketing expert of some kind. She and her husband Hugo had joined as older Volunteers—what are now called 55-Plus Volunteers. He was a dentist. I got to meet him later.

She congratulated us. Told us she was confident we were up to the challenge. Told us that in a few minutes we would head to an orientation program in a suburb of Kyiv for three days. She smiled again and said, "So, sorry, there won't be time for any sight-seeing right now." Some laughter. But I heard groans, too. I groaned.

The intent there, she said, would be to give us some practical preparation and background for the Training we were about to begin. Peace Corps always spelled it with a capital T—it was a big deal. Actually they called it PST. It stood for Pre-Service Training.

At this orientation we'd get to deal with various experts on her staff and meet the Peace Corps doctors. They would review our medical records and give us shots. And we'd sit through talks and seminars. Then we'd go off to our training sites. There were three of them in different communities. Questions and suspense, of course.

We all knew by now that every Peace Corps group abroad is led by a country director and run by a distinct administrative staff. Here in Ukraine, 75 people worked in the Kyiv headquarters full-time. Only the top two were Americans. The others were Ukrainians. Oh, I must tell you Ukraine had the most Volunteers in the world, so I assume the largest headquarters staff.

She introduced some assistants. Each said a few words. Their messages were essentially the same. "We are pleased to see you. We are confident you will do good work. We stand ready to assist you in whatever way we can. Your individual contributions to the people of Ukraine will be important ones, and they will be appreciated." Then she wished us luck at our posts. "You can reach any of us whenever you have to," she said. "Count on us!"

With this over, it became informal, in fact friendly. We got a chance to mix and meet. Two of her people came to me and said hello. It was obvious that they recognized me as the old man in the group. I wondered whether I was the oldest ever to have come to Ukraine. Maybe.

Obviously our arrival was a big deal for them as well as for us. It took many weeks to plan and ready everything for the two groups that arrived every year. This was the culmination of a long process for both the Headquarters staff and us.

Then it was time to board the buses with all our luggage and set out. Our exit road was lined with beautiful matched trees, full grown now, their trunks painted white chest high. I thought, *"They're standing at attention for us!"* A crazy idea, yes, but I liked it.

It was a perfect fall day. Blue sky, golden sunshine, beautiful autumn colors in the foliage.

I was excited about seeing Kyiv. We were all excited. It was not to be. We got just the smallest view. A large city—three million! Quite modern. Lots of traffic. We got a glimpse of the Dniepr River (sometimes spelled Dnipro), which cuts through the city—the fourth biggest river in Europe. Quite broad—as broad as my Connecticut River back home.

We were all excited to notice some gorgeous gold-domed churches on a hilltop. Orthodox churches—Ukraine is officially Orthodox. I heard many "Oh's!" of appreciation. Volunteers scrambled to take snapshots through the windows. Yes, many beautiful things in Kyiv, I knew.

Then, on the fly, I spotted a McDonald's. Our American fast-food giant was here! Somebody yelled, "Hurray!"

The bottom line: though we got just a glimpse, Kyiv was a more impressive city than I expected. I think we all felt this way. It re-enforced my feeling we weren't in a really backward country. This was not Uganda!

In half an hour we pulled onto landscaped grounds. Someone yelled out the name. It was a Ukrainian name and I didn't get it. A post-graduate school, someone said. No classes right now. The place would be all ours. Someone mentioned it was the Post-Graduate Institute for Diplomacy. That impressed me.

It was four or five stories high in a plain, modern architecture. It set back off the road on a big yard in a neighborhood. A curious building. It seemed like three or four buildings touching one another side by side, with each one set back from the next. Inside, I found it hard to find my way from one to another.

We were told this was a nice neighborhood where high-level Soviets used to have summer homes (dachas). In fact, that Dyebek had been a sanatorium—a vacation hotel—for good Communists. They were rewarded for work well done by coming here for a couple of weeks and re-energizing.

I was surprised to see nothing luxurious about it. It was spartan and quite worn. It wouldn't qualify even as one of our budget motels.

It was cold inside. We all noticed. Chilly! We were here for three days and I wore two sweaters all day long and even my woolen hat. Yes, in all our meetings. Some of the staff kept their coats on. Peace Corps distributed supplemental electric heaters (the small, portable oil-filled models that we can buy for less than $100 or so) for use in our bedrooms.

I was lucky and was able to snag an extra blanket. Was this the way it would be all winter in Ukraine? I worried. But I was impressed that Peace Corps supplied these heaters to us. That was auspicious.

It turned out that our Staging in Philadelphia had been Part 1. This orientation was Part 2. As in Philadelphia, we would attend a tight schedule of talks and discussions.

I was assigned to sleep in Room 319. Again, we were booked two to a room. My roommate had already arrived. An intense, wiry fellow in his early 20's, and Asian though his name Derek didn't seem so. He had claimed a bed in a corner and was unpacking his suitcase.

He extended his hand. "Where are you from, sir?" Very friendly.

We chatted for a minute or two. I went to my bed and started organizing my things. But we talked as we worked. Interesting fellow. Surprising how much foreign travel he had managed.

**W**e went our separate ways during our stay but had several nice talks in our room. I was surprised by how he had gotten around. At his age my world had been a small corner of New England. Again I was reminded of what remarkable people Peace Corps attracts.

Another thing struck me. I had found that Volunteers in Ukraine worked in several fields. Education was the biggest field. All of us would be teachers. Some in secondary schools, some in universities. I got to believe education was Peace Corps' dominant program around the word.

Others here worked in public health, including heavily in the HIV/AIDS sector. Some in community development, which could cover many kinds of jobs. And some in youth development.

HIV/AIDS was so rampant that all of us were expected to do whatever we could in this sector—to talk about prevention, especially condoms. Community development seemed quite varied. It seemed to focus on working for NGOs (non-governmental organizations). This was an appellation new to me. Apparently it meant what we call non-profits.

One important item on the calendar here was our medical interview. I knew that each Peace Corps country had at least one medical worker or two. One physician in a country with a bigger Peace Corps deployment, maybe a physician's assistant or a nurse practitioner in one with a smaller group. There were four full-time doctors here! Yes, all Ukrainians. Each of us was scheduled for a 15-minute appointment.

The doctors were ready for us. They had our medical histories, they knew about us individually, and they were prepared to give us whatever final inoculations might be necessary to keep us from catching nasty diseases. It was hard for me to keep track of all the shots I had been getting. They spoke good English.

I looked forward to my 15 minutes and went eagerly. I got to meet two of the doctors. First, Dr. Oleksander Gonta, about 40, I thought, and then Dr. Valery Gontarenko, maybe in his mid 50's, the senior physician.

They were all business—with so many of us they had to be—but the tone was definitely friendly. We reviewed small matters. No problems. I walked out feeling good about Peace Corps Medical. This feeling got emphasized over my whole service. In time I met all four and got to like them.

We got into the swing of things fast. Many meetings. Busy!

As in Philadelphia, this was highly organized. Much planning had been done. As expected, most of the speakers were staff people. They were giving us good information and we were attentive. All this was important. But it didn't have the fun and excitement of Philadelphia.

The many speakers we encountered besides Diana Schmidt and Juan Carlos Campos, the affable assistant director, during our stay were all native Ukrainians. These native Ukrainians made us aware that we indeed could learn to speak Ukrainian or Russian, whichever we were assigned to study.

After all, they all spoke to us in English, in fact American English, and very good English it was. They had all learned it as a second language. They were terrific proof it could be done. I found this heartening. I would try hard.

One thing I definitely enjoyed. Veteran Volunteers were brought in to talk to us about their experiences in the field. I listened earnestly. I wanted to pick up every tip I could and I wanted to get a feeling for what being a Volunteer was really like. I think we all enjoyed that.

One message was emphatic: the 12 weeks coming up would be difficult. But then everything would become easier and more enjoyable. Those words turned out to be prophetic.

Our first speaker again was Diana Schmidt. We learned more about her. She had a master's, an M.B.A. and a Ph.D. in industrial psychology, somebody said, whatever that is. She had then started out in college teaching, then had gone on into marketing, I heard.

Again she was pleasant and welcoming, but very serious. She reminded us of the jobs we were here to do. She emphasized that we were representatives of our country and many eyes would focus on us wherever we worked, in large community or small. Those eyes would focus on us even when not at work. It would be imperative to behave ourselves.

She told us that there was a daily plane to the United States at 10 a.m. and certain behaviors would get us a seat on that plane. I had read what they were.. Here are a few.

~ Embarrassing our country.
~ Breaking a serious law.
~ Having sex with a minor.
~ Being a public drunk.
~ Doing a terrible job, of course.
~ Making money off our experience while in the country.

And there were others.

She told us that PST would be tough. "Very tough. The good news is that it will come to an end in just 12 weeks!" That got chuckles.

She told us that we would probably experience a roller-coaster of emotions. Highs and lows. We would be confronting so many differences. A different country. A different climate for many of us. A different culture. A different language. Different food. Different money. Different this and that. And we'd lack many things we took for granted. Too many to enumerate.

"You will be living with families you have not chosen and have not yet met. You will have so many new things to learn and so fast. How to get around your city. How to make yourselves understood. How to use the different kinds of public transit. How to use the phones. On and on.

"You may think all this is crazy and impossible. You may get depressed. You may think of quitting and going home. Do not make a hasty decision. You may regret it.

"Give it what I call the 10-day test. If you develop bad feelings and they linger for 10 days, then consider resigning. But make sure you talk it over with us. We are here to help you. We are committed to helping you in every way possible. Do not quit impulsively."

I was to seriously consider this advice in the difficult weeks ahead.

We heard other interesting speakers. Iryna Krupska, the training manager, went into interesting detail about our 12 weeks coming up. She, too, said it would not be easy. It would keep us busy. "But I am sure you will find it very interesting. Imagine, for one thing you will be learning a new language! So exciting!"

She was the first of the staff Ukrainians to speak to us at length and I was amazed by her easy and fluent English. And how energetic she was. I liked her. But that was how I came to feel about all the Ukrainians

There would be two parts to the training, language learning and technical training.

We would be divided into two language groups. One would study Ukrainian, the other Russian, this because, as I've explained, some areas were heavily, even dominantly populated by Russian-speaking Ukrainians, and for the ones assigned to those areas Russian would be essential. Of course, I knew I would be in the Russian group.

Someone pointed out that for anyone interested in learning a language for career purposes, Russian was the better choice.

We found out Russian was spoken by 400 million people, Ukrainian by 45 million. I found this interesting. It was a big consideration for our young people but unimportant for me.

I was curious about the technical training. What could it be? It turned out mostly to be our training as teachers of English as a Second Language, which is a specialty unto itself. And it included special attention to how the Ukrainian Ministry of Education looks at education, what it insists on, and what it will not tolerate.

Another speaker was Juan Carlos Campos. About 40, I thought. He made a good impression also. He spoke easily. He had been a Volunteer also.

He spoke reassuringly. "I know you may feel some tension, even apprehension. But you are here because Peace Corps felt you will be successful. I am confident you will do fine."

*Ukraine is big! All of us kept thinking and talking about where we might be sent.*

I found out he spoke Spanish. I liked that because I speak French. We had that in common—fellow Americans who spoke another language easily.

And I found out that he, too, was a Rotarian. I brought that up with him afterward. He told me he belonged to a Rotary Club in Kyiv and gave me a man's name and address.

I made up my mind to contact this man once I settled in. I hoped somehow to participate in Rotary/

Farewell! New friends see Trainees off. In two days they'll take the oath and head off to their posts.

A forceful speaker was Serhiv Pashynsky, safety and security coordinator. I heard he had been a colonel in the Soviet army. Erect, direct, plain-spoken, he would have been well cast as such in a movie.

He discussed possible safety risks—assaults, accidents, stupid actions—and outlined specific procedures. He discussed the all-important "Pink Card" given to each of us. "Important to carry it all the time!" It would identify us to police if ever we got stopped for any reason as American Volunteers permitted to be in Ukraine. Another card listed Peace Corps officials with their contact information. "Carry that, too!"

He said Headquarters was staffed around the clock seven days a week. "For any serious problem, call immediately!"

The highlight for me—probably all of us—came on our second morning. We had been told Ambassador William Taylor might show up. Ambassadors are busy people. I was skeptical. Well, he came. He spoke. And he conquered. It's the best way for me to put it.

He addressed us for close to an hour, then answered questions and kept answering them until nobody asked another. He spoke easily and candidly and encouragingly. He stressed the importance of Peace Corps and us Volunteers—which was not un-expected, of course.

But he said two things that struck me. "You will see more real, everyday Ukrainians than I ever will, and you'll get as good a perspective on what this country is like and what its problems are as I will probably."

Another was, "I get around a bit. Whenever possible, I like to stop by and chat with the local Volunteers. Don't be surprised if I come by."

Later I was told he did do this. When he said goodbye to us, I hoped that all our ambassadors made as good an impression for our country.

Later I read that he was a graduate of West Point, had served in the Army and then had joined the State Department and worked up. So, he was not a political appointee.

Throughout, we were kept busy with talks and meetings and administrative matters. Of course, we continued to meet our fellow Volunteers and friendships began. There were numerous opportunities. At meals we could choose to sit at any table. In meetings there were opportunities to chat and meet new people. All natural and desirable.

It was amazing all the materials we were given. Handbooks, folders, photocopy hand-outs. They piled up! Something I noticed was that the staff dressed better than we did. All of us, men and women, were attired neatly enough. But "casual" was our key word. These professionals, men and women, were dressed up like executives in a high-class business enterprise.

We had been told we should give much attention to our attire: "It is the first impression!" The staff took it seriously and set a good example.

Very soon we would find out where we'd be assigned for Training. And later, where we would be assigned for our two years in the country. Nobody was assigned to Kyiv. The capital was considered too expensive.

Very few went to the larger cities. Nearly all of us would go to smaller cities or to towns or even villages. These questions were much on my mind. I'm sure we were all wondering. I didn't know what others wanted. But I wanted to go to a fair-sized city for both Training and work.

Then we found out. For Training, I and about 30 others would go to a city of about 300,000 people. Well regarded. It was called Chernihiv and it was located in the north central part of the country. It was two hours by road north of Kyiv. A busload of us would be going. I was excited. Apprehensive, too.

~ ~ ~

***Did you know*** ... that a surprise upon returning home to the United States can be reverse culture shock? True. The difficulties of re-adjusting after more than two years in what may have been a strikingly different country overseas can be troubling.

Peace Corps is aware of this, warns of it, and prepares departing Volunteers to recognize and weather it.

# 7 / My first 'family'

*I move in. They're so nice to me as I suffer through these three months of "boot camp."*

I knew—we all knew—our three months of Training would be tough. How tough they were! We all groaned and complained. So tough I considered dropping out. But one thing made it bearable—my 12 weeks with Natasha and her two sons. They were my first host family in Ukraine. I got to live with three families over my 27 months.

Peace Corps selected our first family and insisted we live with it for the whole three months of Training, one recruit per family. I struck extra-good luck.

The idea was to make things easier for us. It relieved us of having to search for an apartment when we could hardly say more than *"da"* and *"nyet"* (yes and no). We Trainees simply did not have the time to shop for food, cook, keep house, and so on—all as we strove to fit into the strange new culture and get around in our new temporary city.

And of course, boarding with a family made it easier to concentrate on learning the language, pick up on the culture, and plunge into the everyday life of the people.

At the close of our orientation in Dyebeck, some 30 of us—a third of our Group 33, boarded a bus with all our stuff and started north for Training tin mid-size Chernihiv a couple of hours away. It had 300,000, thus mid-size in Ukraine. In many of our states it would have been considered big.

Our bus made its way along a divided four-lane highway. It was one of the best in the country but just fair by American standards. It got dark fast and the night was black. We were covering flat country—the famous Ukrainian agricultural steppe.

After an hour we poked into a small town with modest houses. I didn't make out any downtown area. We were here to leave off a handful of Trainees. That's all we knew. Nothing else was explained to us.

They would spend the next three months here with their LCF and their TCF—Peace Corps nicknames for Language Cultural Facilitator (teacher) and Technical Cultural Facilitator. The driver finally stopped on a dark street. I could make out a vague building on the left.

Their LCF, brought in from somewhere else for 12 weeks, would live and hold classes in an apartment rented by Peace Corps in this building. Her Trainees would live with families nearby. LCF stood for Language Cultural Facilitator—our full-time instructor teaching us our foreign language throughout Training.

None of us had any idea what was going on. Apparently someone came out and greeted the Trainees assigned here. They picked up their suitcases and backpacks and followed in the dark toward the building. I didn't hear any goodbyes from them.

But others got off the bus as well. This was their opportunity to go to the toilet. I had the same need and scrambled behind them.

It was black inside the building. We groped our way in. Finally someone found a switch and turned on the hall lights.

We followed one another up the stairs right to the top, to the fourth floor, I think it was.

My first home. I lived here with Natasha and her two sons. I was happy. Private housåes are rare—most folks live in huge apartment blocks.

Someone unlocked the door to the apartment and we crowded in. We were in the kitchen. It was our first time in a Ukrainian apartment. Plain and humble indeed.

I didn't spot anyone who seemed to be a teacher or an official. Nobody seemed in charge. We queued to use the tiny toilet. No way could it have been made smaller. It was hard to turn around in it.

The Trainees staying here checked the various rooms. This was going to be their base for the whole 12 weeks. The rest of us made our way back down and out to the bus. Few words had been exchanged. So strange, I thought. We rode on in the dark. Such a small town! I was so glad I hadn't been left off there with them.

We arrived in Chernihiv an hour later and how dramatic by contrast. We came in on a long road. A black night. Now and then a house with a light on. Straight ahead high on a rare hill was a stunning sight: a big, magnificent three-dome Orthodox church. Aglow! Spotlights illuminated its pure-white façade and gold domes. Stunningly beautiful against the black night. "Wow! Gosh! Look!" Those were the comments all through the bus. We kept staring at it as we rolled on. I felt better about Chernihiv.

Now we entered the city. Street lights! A beautiful park appeared, then big beautiful buildings, then a vast cobbled square. Bright with lights. Stately buildings—edifices is a better word—on all sides. It was late; few people out. On the right I saw what looked like a classic Greek temple, very large. A drama theater, we found out later. Chernihiv was fantastic!

The bus stopped right in front of the temple. Some cars were parked here in a cluster. A crowd was waiting. Fifty or so people surged toward us. Our host families!

I saw five or six people heading right for me. They

*A bit of togetherness after dinner: Natasha, ailing Nikita with kitten, and Kyrill. I kept to myself a lot but felt at home. A good time.*

were MY family! They must have been told I was the only old man and had spotted me. They surrounded me.

They were smiling and telling me things I did not understand. Insisting on taking my suitcases. All so friendly. What a big family. So helpful.

I kept saying, "Hello! Hello! Thank you!" In English. I knew those words from my primitive Russian but they just didn't pop up. Awkward.

**T**hey had a big sedan. I knew such cars were rare here. They managed to fit in all my luggage. They sat me in the back and then all squeezed in. The motor started. I didn't have time to say a single goodbye to any of my buddies. Gosh. I saw that other cars were also loading up. We drove for 15 minutes. They were saying things to me in Russian but I didn't understand a thing. We stopped.

We seemed to be out in the country. I could not make out any houses. But one was there, back a distance in the dark. We clambered out and walked through a high gate, then up a path to the door. Someone fumbled for a key, opened it, and snapped on a light.

With pats on the back and lots of merriment I was led inside. My luggage was carried in. I was in a small house. I saw that right away. This would be my home all through Training plus one month afterward—all arranged by Peace Corps. But my family seemed wonderful.

I was introduced to everyone. Only two spoke a bit of English. I heard their names but could not absorb them. Quickly several began to leave. Just one woman and two boys left.

Then I figured it out. Those leaving were friends who had taken my family to meet me. My family did not own a car. They had prevailed on these kind folks for a favor. These three were my family!

Natasha, my "host mother" in Peace Corps parlance, was tall and pretty with such a nice smile. About 40. Her sons were Kyrill, 18, and Nikita, 12. Kyrill—with a big smile—was studying electrical engineering at the local Polytechnic University. It turned out he spoke good English and liked to talk; how lucky for me. Nikita was shy. Said nothing. But he smiled a lot, too. I liked that.

There was no man of the house, it seemed. Natasha took me by the arm and showed me around. The boys came along, eager to catch my words. Soon she shooed them off. I understood. School in the morning.

Quite old this house. Just one floor. Everything clean and neat. Small kitchen. Tiny kitchen table with stools for four. No real chairs. Then a modest dining room with a shiny wooden table and chairs.

Natasha would see me off every day. Then she'd change and go off to her own job.

The living room had just a couch on one side and a TV on the other side. And off it, a bedroom. Natasha was all smiles as she led me in. It was small and long and narrow She pointed to everything in it and then to me and spoke. In Russian.

She knew no English. She pointed to me again and to the bed. Now I understood. This would be my bedroom! She beamed. I could see how proud she was of the room.

It had a single window at the end. It had nice curtains and potted plants on the sill. The bed was squeezed in at the other end. It was a double bed, so plenty of room for my tossing and turning. It had a reading light above it. That pleased me.

There was a bureau and a wardrobe, I noticed, and a desk with a straight-back chair. That pleased me also. There was a rug. That was it. No two pieces of furniture matched, but all were sound and good. The room didn't have a single extra foot of space but it had all the necessities. Very clean. Very neat. I was impressed. I could be okay here.

Later I found out this had been her bedroom. She had moved out for me. She took me to another bedroom.

Kyrill was sitting at a desk in a corner. "My room," he said. "I spend many hours here." He spoke in English. Quiet fluently. I smiled and gave him a thumbs up. He smiled. He understood.

I was surprised to see a full computer set-up. He had a narrow bed and it was neatly made. All his clothes were neatly hung. His books—he had many—were lined up. He was a neat fellow. Or he had a neat mother.

Then to another bedroom. It was tiny and crowded with stuff. Her young Nikita was sprawled on a small couch. She pointed to him. I got it. This was his bedroom. She pointed to a narrow bed and then to herself. She slept on that bed.

I guessed Nikita slept on that couch he was relaxing on. There were piles of clothes and things. But everything was just so. I could see she was making sacrifices for me.

*Privately owned "marshrutkas" were new. More expensive than trolleys and buses but faster. But crowded and dangerous, I found out.*

The big surprise was the bathroom. It waas an old room but in the process of being modernized. Everything in it was obviously new. I noticed the attractive new counter with gleaming sink and the gleaming toilet.

She pointed to two buttons on the toilet and tried them. One gave a short flush and the other a long one. She was so proud. It was better than mine at home.

But what was startling was the gleaming fiberglass shower unit in a corner. It had two curving doors forming a quarter circle. Beautiful. They rolled open and shut on tracks.

It had eight water nozzles! They were spotted strategically—one in the ceiling and the others on the circular walls. She turned on the water to show me. You could get the water to shoot from just one nozzle, or two, or all eight. Remarkable! This was a first for me. Again she was so proud. She pointed to a label—"Made in China."

Oh, the room also contained an automatic washing machine, small by our standards, made in Italy I noticed. Again gleaming new. But no clothes dryer. She pointed outside. She dried the clothes on cords in the backyard.

She led me back into the kitchen. She had the table set for coffee and tea and insisted that all four of us sit. We had to crowd. As I said, small stools! They made sense in this small space. Comfortable for them but not me. I leaned my back against the wall. Better.

Everything here was old. A small refrigerator, its paint worn off behind the handle. A four-burner gas stove. Plenty of mileage on it. The sink was white cast iron and it had chips. The faucet was an oldie.

The counter was crowded with stacked pots and pans. Jars of cucumbers and preserves lined the back. There was a big pan of potatoes on the floor. But I saw order and neatness.

There were open shelves on the wall and they were crowded with everything needed by a growing family. Everything organized.

Kyrill was by my side. "We will do here what we did in the toilet room," he said. "When we get more dollars!" And he laughed. I got the idea that my living with them would provide some of those dollars.

*Natasha, Kyrill, and Nikita at the dinner table. Food aplenty. I sat at the other corner. Stools. No room for chairs.*

On one wall I recognized an instantaneous electric water heater. Most of us Americans are not familiar with such heater.

I had seen many such units around the world. Turn on the faucet and instantly the water is heated as you draw it. Turn the faucet off and the heating coil turns off.

It supplied hot water for the kitchen and the bathroom. No big tank of water to keep hot all day, or to spring a leak. Much more economical. Took much less room. Yet surprisingly effective.

I nodded and smiled. I wanted them to see my appreciation.

"I'd like to have one just like yours back home in the United States!" I said. Kyrill beamed. Again he translated and did a good job of it. Natasha beamed, too.

The four of us sat at the table. Natasha poured me tea and offered cookies. They were home-made. She pressed me and I ate three. Very good. Later I got to see that she made just about everything. Excellent cook.

It was late. It had been a long day. Physically and emotionally.She pointed to the clock and led me back to my room. Good. *"Dobrie noche!"* she said pleasantly. That was Russian and I knew what it meant! "Good night!" I said *"Dobrie noche!"* to her. She grinned. A pretty woman.

It took me just a few minutes in the fantastic new bathroom. I slipped into bed. Just a thin mattress on plywood. Oh, well. This was Ukraine. Not everything could be good and modern. I'd get used to it.

I got to learn that owning a private house like this was unusual. She had inherited it from her parents. Most people live in big apartment blocks. The city was full of them. I called them Soviet blocks, and I'll explain further on. She had lived in one before. I could see she was putting a lot of herself into this house.

Where was her husband—the boys' father? For certain he did not live here.

The language classes were starting at 8:30 the next day. Natasha knocked on my door at 6, as I had asked her to. I had had a good night's sleep. She did that for me five days a week. She skipped it on Saturdays and Sundays so they could sleep later. I had more training on Saturdays. She left it to me to get up.

*7:45 a.m. It's cold out! Hot coffee from a kiosk was perfect on my way to class at Tamila's.*

She had a huge breakfast set out: *blini* (pancakes) and sausage and cheese and cookies. No fresh fruits, but a tasty fruit drink she called *compote*, and some stewed apples. Kyrill and Nikita joined us. "Mama cook all these good things," Kyrill told me proudly.

She came in and said "Good morning!" Yes, in English. How nice.

I had worried about getting to my classes on time. I had only a written address. This would be my first day there, of course. I was anxious. No need to worry, Kyrill assured me. "Mama will go with you today."

At breakfast it was usually just Natasha and me. It became my practice to take my brand-new two-way English-Russian dictionary to the table for every meal. She had one of her own, worn with age.

I would look up a word in the English section and show her its Russian translation. She would look up a word in the Russian section of hers and show me its English translation. Very slow, but it worked.

Sometimes we would sit in silence through much of the meal, just the two of us, but it was a comfortable silence. I came to feel close to her, and she to me. I sensed that all the time.

With Kyrill with us at other meals, no problem. It was remarkable what good English he spoke. I loved his frequent smiles. Nikita was a nice boy, but so quiet. Strange. Was something amiss? I suspected so.

On our first Saturday, after I got back from class, Natasha and the boys took me outside. They put a spade in my hands and led me to the backyard. Most of it was a garden. This was October, so dormant now. Natasha carried a sapling—apple, Kyrill said.

I was shown where to dig a hole. They made sure I dug it just right. Not something I do often. Kyrill placed the little tree in it. His Mom spread its roots carefully and mounded it with her hands. Nikita poured a can of water over it. We stood back and studied the little tree, Not a word was said.

Then Natasha spoke. Kyrill translated. "John, we will always remember that you planted this tree. With this tree we will never forget you."

Natasha's house was on Gagarina Street. It was named for Yuri Gagarin, the Soviet cosmonaut who in 1961 was the first to enter outer space and orbit the earth. Great hero. Natasha's house was near the far end.

Home from the forest with mushrooms. A harvest to keep us for the year!

Nearby were two bus stops, one on each side. The buses from the city stopped on our side. It would take me three minutes to walk home. Those to the city stopped on the other side. A five-minute walk.

There were several possibilities. In either direction we could use buses No. 101 and 41, which cost 70 *kopecks*. Or trolleybus No. 5, which cost 60 *kopecks*. Or several *"marshrutkas,"* the 16-passenger minibuses. They cost 100 *kopecks*. They had more comfortable seats and were faster. All very cheap, well, for me an American: 100 equaled 1 *hryvnia* and 5 *hryvnia* was $1. So the most expensive ride was 20 cents. That was then. But galloping inflation! The fares shot up often. I quickly got to see that.

On this first morning Natasha led me to the stop across the street. It was a sunny but cool day. Beautiful out. We waited under a tin roof. Several people were waiting.

The leaves were turning into reds and yellows. It reminded me of my Connecticut. But I didn't feel homesick. Yet.

Gracious of Natasha to accompany on this first day but I was sure it had been mandated by Peace Corps. Just as we Trainees had been briefed on how to live with our host family, all the host mothers had been trained on how to deal with us.

Incidentally, "host mother" was a Peace Corps expression, at least in Ukraine. It's what we called the woman who was paid to let us live with her and her family in her house or apartment. She also might cook for us. Even do our laundry along with the family's laundry—whatever was negotiated. And be our coach every step of the way.

"Host mother" bothered me from the moment I heard it. Apt maybe for the younger Trainees. I thought it ridiculous to call a woman 40 years younger my "host mother." But I couldn't up with the perfect word. The closest I ever got was "landlady." And that fell short.

During my service, I got to have three host mothers. All three were excellent, as you'll see. I was unusual. It was my impression Volunteers went on to set up apartments of their own.

Now, back to Natasha accompanying me that first morning. Gagarina was a major street but I saw just an occasional car or truck pass. Private vehicles were rare. A few older folks pedaled bicycles. Public transportation was it for most people. Minutes passed as we waited.

I got to appreciate this tin roof in harsh weather. Always lots of litter all around. No trash can. People just dropped things. I made up my mind that when I started teaching, I would tell my students they should not litter!

It was Bus 41 that came along first. I mean, before a trolleybus or *marshrutka*. Quite squat by our standards. There were already a dozen aboard. There was a rush to get on. Natasha and I managed to get seats.

A woman with a blue and yellow smock—the Ukrainian colors—was the *conductora*. She collected fares and gave out tickets.

Natasha paid for me and explained the ticket was important. No ticket, a big fine! However, in the next many months, I never met an inspector and never saw someone get fined.

It was 20 minutes to downtown. The bus stopped at every quarter mile. People piled in. All the seats got taken. Then people jammed the aisle, shoulder to shoulder. Awful. At the next stop, two got off but five shoved and got on. At the next stop, still more forced themselves on. No room left.

The Institute bus stop—that would be my stop, Natasha said. Half the people got off there. We got off. She pointed to the cigarette kiosk with the name Tiou-Toon. The roof was purple, and there were two soda machines next to it. "Remember all this," she told me in Russian, pointing around. But there were many Tiou-Toon kiosks and it could be confusing!

She led the way to the end of the block and we took a right. This was a business neighborhood with shops and stalls all along. We walked seven or eight minutes to a big apartment block, then around to the rear of it.

It was five stories high. The front door was locked but had a combination lock: five buttons above five buttons, 1 to 10. Push three buttons and it would unlock. I liked it. No fumbling for a key. She told me the three-number combination. "Don't forget it!" she said.

This was my first time inside a Soviet block. It turned out to be typical. The hallway was dark. Hard to see our way. Easy to stumble and fall. I learned to leave the front door open and study the inside with the incoming daylight, then walk in. We walked up eight flights of stairs, two per floor. A long climb. I was nearly out of breath. There, a button to ring. I heard somebody unbolting the door.

"*Dobrie utra,*" a smiling woman said—Russian for "Good morning!" "*Dobrie utra,*" Natasha replied. I said "*Dobrie utra!*" I'd get the hang of it.

This was Tamila, our friendly but insistent LCF for the next three months. LCF stood for Language Cultural Facilitator. On Saturdays we would go to our TCF—Technical Cultural Facilitator. LCF and TCF—strange words! They became second nature to me.

Tamila was in her early 40s, I judged. Warm and cordial but all business. She drew me in and said goodbye to Natasha, who gave me a wave and smile and left. Tamila showed me where to put my jacket and hat and shoes.

No shoes in the apartment! And led me to the living room. Two young women there.

I recognized them. My colleagues Clare and Amy. They were on a couch. It faced a broad wall covered with hand-lettered placards. Some written in red. Some in blue or green. So many! All Russian stuff Tamila would teach us.

"Welcome, John!" Clare said to me. "Hello, John," Amy said. Their smiles made me feel good. Two more were still due. We'd be five in all—a typical cluster. We remained together right to Swearing In.

Tamila told me to sit in a stuffed chair on the right of the couch. That seat became mine for all the hard days coming up—until Tamila decided I needed special help and ordered me into the kitchen to study alone.

The two others arrived. Mandy and Evonne. Evonne was in her 50's, I believe. Clare and Amy and Mandy were just recently out of university. So, we were one man and four women—I the very senior person—then Evonne, maybe 30 years younger, then the three young gals. We became good friends. I am pleased to tell you that.

Tamila got started. She smiled, "Welcome, my dear students! You will make me happy if you will arrive on time every morning!"

She did not waste a minute. She was going to turn us into Russian speakers! This became a drama in itself, and I will reserve it for the next chapter. All I'll tell you now is that five days a week we would have class from 8 to 12 in the living room with a 15-minute break at 10. Then 20 minutes for lunch and then class till 2. I found it intense and grueling. I got to worry a lot.

That afternoon after class I walked around the neighborhood, just to explore and exercise. I could not linger. I had a heap of homework to do once I got home. It would get dark at 4 and I had to get home on my own.

I was terribly anxious. I found the right bus stop across the street from where I had gotten off. Many buses came along and finally No. 41. Again it was jammed. I pushed myself aboard just as the others did. I had hand-printed a card with the name of the stop near Natasha's. I showed the card to the *conductora* and when we got close she alerted me. Hallelujah! What a nice lady. I felt proud of myself.

Now I found out that my host mother, Natasha, was a free-lance interior painter. In fact, she did plastering also. She had a little business.

She went off every day by bus or trolleybus to a house or an apartment with her bagful of tools and did her work.

Then came home to start a second shift as a mother and homemaker and lady do-it-all. She was always upbeat and cheerful. And she could do it all! I got to admire her greatly.

She always prepared a full dinner, varied and generous. She never skimped. She made many of the dishes from scratch. She always offered me more. One problem was that I was increasingly vegetarian, and I eschewed many of her entrées. She offered and offered, and I would say, "No, thank you, Natasha." It was hard for her to accept that.

We quickly established a routine. As I said, usually the two of us ate breakfast alone. The boys ate later. We'd exchange the same simple greetings in the morning, I in Russian and she in English, and make a comment about the weather. That would be it. We became good friends despite our few words.

I would gather the dirty dishes and carry them to the sink. One day I started to wash them. She put a quick stop to that.

One morning she made up a little bag of cookies for me. "For your friends at tea time," she said. She did that for me every morning.

She was a beautiful woman and when she dressed for a party, she was a knock-out. But it was obvious to anyone who noticed her hands that she did very hard work.

Her own house was beautifully painted inside and out. She said she and Kyrill had painted it all.

One day she explained to me how she would have to stand high up on a scaffold sometimes and sand and sand and then paint. I asked if she wore a kerchief over her nose and mouth. She said no.

The sanding that she did worried me. There was a big outdoor bazaar near Tamila's apartment. It had hundreds of stalls. Everything imaginable was sold there. I enjoyed strolling around it.

One day at the big central outdoor market I went shopping for something special. It took me a long time but I found it: a professional painter's respirator mask. I bought it and a supply of filters. That evening I gave it to her. She gasped. Then beamed. She was so happy. I'll never forget it.

But in the evening all five of us would eat dinner together. Again I was grateful to have articulate Kyrill at the table. His English was such a big asset for us. He made communication possible for me and his Mom.

He liked every dish that she served, and every subject that I brought up, and dinner was always a pleasure for me. For him as well, I felt.

Afterward it was TV time and they would invite me to sit with them. But I have never been much of a TV person. Anyway, I had much to do.

All their programs were in Russian and I should have gotten into the habit of watching. But I didn't care for the shows and always felt rushed because of my study load every evening.

I would exit my room only to go to the bathroom. I would cross the living room to do that and the three would be on the couch, watching TV.

They were always pleasant and cheerful, and so was I. They had their life, and I had mine.

Kyrill would help me whenever I asked. He'd give me directions. Help me to set up my desk. Once he repaired my desk lamp for me.

One problem was that I couldn't use my computer because the monitor that went with it was broken. I asked him where I could get it repaired. He had no idea. But he made no attempt to find out. I was greatly disappointed.

On my second morning I walked to the bus stop totally on my own. I started 15 minutes early, just in case. This time I became one of the standees on the bus. We were so many that I could not see outside. I kept trying to see. I was so apprehensive. I kept struggling to spot the Tiou-Toon. Finally I saw it and got off.

The wrong Tiou-Toon! The wrong stop! Where was I?

I had Tamila's address on another card, fortunately. In Russian! Only by flashing it to passersby did I manage to get to her place. I had to walk a long way and I got to class 25 minutes late. She was understanding.

But the same thing happened again the next day! Tamila shook her head. No smile this time.

My problems did not end. One evening when returning home, I overshot Natasha's stop in the dark and had to ride to the very end. My thinking was simple: I'd remain on the bus and get off at my stop when it went back. At the end of the line I was the only passenger still aboard.

The driver and the *conductora* remained parked for 20 minutes and shared a picnic supper and tea from a Thermos. They kept glancing my way. I could tell they were talking about me. I am sure they wondered, "What is that guy doing?" At one point she came and offered me a cookie. I accepted it. Very nice. It pleased her that I took one.

I finally got home. Natasha was alone. I did not have the words to tell her about my bad experience, as much as I wanted to.

I told Kyrill later, and he told her. She glanced at me and shook her head sadly. First my Tiou-Toon experience, and now this one!

I had other bad experiences. On one bus going to class, I was the last to get off at my stop. I was at the rear door. I stepped onto the bottom step of the bus with my right foot and extended my left foot to step onto the ground. Just then the driver closed the door. It pinned my right foot against the jamb! I couldn't move my foot. I fell forward. Luckily a woman was ready to board. I fell against her, but didn't knock her over, thank God.

Good thing she was right there. I would have fallen onto the ground and smashed my face. I might have snapped my ankle.

Every morning I tried to get ready with time to spare. I had to make sure I had all my right books and reports. All the right clothes. As it got colder, I had to layer up. Had to remember to take an umbrella just in case, or my precious Stabilicers. These were Canadian-made, an overshoe—a skeleton really—of tough rubber that slipped over my boots. Its soles had steel cleats that gripped into the ice—life savers! They were a gift of my friend Len back home. I thought of him often throughout my many icy months over my two winters. I used them time and again. People envied me.

In the park, we came upon newlyweds! I told Natasha and Kyrill that our couples mark the big day much the same way.

Sometimes I forgot something and had to go back to my room. This meant I had to take off my shoes or boots (no shoes in the house!), pick up what I needed, and then put my footwear back on. What a nuisance.

Natasha would see me to the front door. How nice. Sometimes she would turn up my jacket collar to make sure I stayed good and warm.

One morning she saw me rushing. She threw up her hands and stared at me. *"Ya ne ponimaiou!"* she said. *"Pachemu?"*

By now I knew enough to understand. She was saying: "I don't understand! Why are you going through all this? You, such an old man!" She did not say those last five words, but I knew she had them in mind.

No way could I explain. In fact, sometimes I asked myself the same question. Why? Yes, why?

Two or three times she did my laundry and I let her. She would fold my clothes and leave them in a neat pile on my bed. But she had too much to do and I insisted on washing my own clothes.

More than once I put a $10 bill in her hand. She always protested, but I prevailed. That was significant money in Ukraine.

After a month, our teacher Tamila organized a dinner for us five students and our host mothers. What a nice idea. We met at a very pleasant rustic restaurant. It was a log cabin! It perched by the pretty Desna River, which coursed through the city.

We all sat around a very long table. Good food. Good wine. Our host mothers sang beautiful old songs for us. Great conviviality. A wonderful get-together. Tamila told us that our host mothers were springing for it!

I felt badly for Nikita at home. Just about to turn 13. A nice boy. He did not go to school. He had a mysterious illness although he looked very healthy.

He would dress and then spend the day in the house. He would loll on the couch and watch TV, or sometimes play on the computer in his brother's room. It was understood that he should not exercise. No exercise!

He would remain alone until his mom returned in late afternoon. Once a week a public school tutor would come instruct him for two hours.

Chernobyl was often on my mind. That community was less than an hour's ride away. Who had ever heard of Chernobyl? Then awful melt-down at its nuclear plant on April 26, 1986!

So many people killed. So many afflicted with terrible cancers and illnesses including young children born long after the catastrophe. I kept wondering, *Was Chernobyl the cause of Nikita's plight?* I never found out, but I suspect yes. Chernobyl had spewed radiation for hundreds of miles, but most westerly, away from Ukraine.

It was only later that I found out that our city, Chernihiv, had a hospital just for people suffering from health problems caused by Chernobyl. There were so many of these people.

Much later I found out how Boston's CCPUSA (Chernobyl Children's Fund U.S.A.) was helping victims who needed services unavailable in Ukraine. It was a wonderful charity operated by the Boston Area medical community (doctors, medical schools, hospitals, labs, nurses, therapists, pharmacies) to help children affected.

CCPUSA was bringing dozens of children and young people to Boston for treatment and/or surgery every year. All free of charge. I wish I had known about CCPUSA when I was living at Natasha's. I would have tried to get Nikita into it.

Every two or three weeks a man, about 50, would stop by and visit. Most often in time for dinner. He was greeted warmly by Natasha and the boys and Natasha made sure he ate well.

I was introduced to him. Although we could not speak, unfortunately, we did become quite cordial. We'd smile at one another and sit side by side and it would be pleasant..

Then I found out that he was Natasha's former husband … indeed maybe present husband…and the boys' father. He would chat a little, watch TV with the family for an hour or two and then say goodbye. What a strange relationship. There seemed to be no knowing when he would stop in and have dinner with us.

I was told that he was a *vrach*, a medical doctor. He lived in a flat downtown. I think Natasha and the boys lived with him until she took over her parents' house.

Kyrill told me he was the head of a three-person team that would respond by ambulance to psychiatric emergencies. Much like firefighters rushing to a blaze.

Sometimes it would be a drunk lying on a street. There were many of these. Sometimes something far more serious.

On our walk I got to see many fine statues. This is Shevchenko, the great writer.

**W**hen Natasha or one of the boys got a cold or something, he would stop by and give them a medicine—a home-brew or home–mix of some kind. Kyrill had great faith in his dad. "Very good doctor," he would say. I never got to see any of these cases of his with Natasha or the two boys. I would have liked to see their outcomes.

I had wonderful experiences with Natasha and her family. One fine autumn Sunday, she and Kyrill and I took a bus downtown. Nikita stayed home, as always.

They led me on a walk through the city's park. Beautiful. So impressive. It was a block wide and ran right through the heart of the city. Nearly two miles long!

Here and there, avenues cut across it. It had pleasant paths, hundreds of great chestnut trees, benches in shady spots. It offered peace and quiet, a rare thing in many cities. The leaves were bright yellow. A carpet of them was forming.

The park ran on to a hill called the Val. It's the spot where the city was founded 1,300 years ago. Chernihiv is an ancient city, one of the oldest in Ukraine. The hill looks down on the pretty Desna. Up on the Val's bluff, ancient cannon aim down. It's by river that enemies would come.

We walked the whole length. Saw all the large statues—great figures in their history, including Soviet heroes. We stopped at this one and that one. I'd take pictures of Natasha and Kyrill here and there. Lots of fun.

The most notable was Lenin, the history-making enforcer of Karl Marx's Communist teachings. He had the biggest statue of all. Enormous—maybe 20 times life size. The big surprise was that his statue was still standing. After Independence, many cities took down their statues of him.

In fact, the main avenue nearby was now World Avenue. "It used to be Lenin Avenue," Kyrill told me. "But some old people still call it Lenin."

We had a fine day. I learned a lot.

Natasha was always wonderful about inviting me to participate in birthday parties and other family celebrations. It emphasized some important things I have discovered over the years. One, people all over the world are much the same. Two, families are much the same everywhere. Three, people everywhere have the same problems and pleasures. The differences are those that relate to income—how much or how little.

**I** got to see meaningful glimpses of their family life.

For instance, now and then in the kitchen Natasha would ask Kyrill to fetch something. In Russian, so I wasn't sure what. I was startled the first time. He opened a trap door in the floor. There was a room down there!

He clambered down some crude steps. It was a cold storage. Shelves lined the room. They were stocked with big jars of preserves— fruits and vegetables and other goodies. They had been put up by Natasha at the end of the past harvest season for the long winter. Dark. Hard to see. But he managed to pick out a jar of pickles and one of mushrooms.

Of course, Natasha had to do the big job of replenishing these good things every year. No problem, or so she made it seem.

Her backyard—where I had planted the apple sapling—was an amazing garden. She took pleasure in working there whenever she could. Sometimes just for 20 minutes, sometimes for two hours.

She saved every scrap of left-over food from the dinner table, plus all the outer cabbage leaves, all the peelings from carrots and potatoes and turnips and beets, all the impossible pieces of meat, all the scrapings from the dinner plates. All went into a bucket by the sink.

When it filled, she'd carry it to the backyard and add it to her big compost pile. That compost pile was precious! She'd turn it over herself with a pitchfork. Sometimes I had an urge to tell her to ask Kyrill to go out and do it. That compost would be the natural fertilizer for next year's crop.

I became so interested when they began planning a Saturday to a forest some kilometers outside the city. They were going on a mushroom search. Even little Nikita. I felt hurt when I wasn't invited. When they got back and told me about it, I was pleased they hadn't asked me. Would have been awfully hard. They went every year.

They assembled storage bags and some grubbing tools and a big picnic basket full of bread and cold cuts and cheese and apples and cookies. They arose at dawn and took the early train to the village near the forest, then headed into the woods.

They spent the day harvesting mushrooms, all kinds. There are many varieties and some are poisonous. No problem, Kyrill assured me. His mom had learned from her mother. His mom was an expert.

They had to explore and feel for the mushrooms with their bare hands below the rotting leaves—under the bushes—in moist, shady spots. It was dirty work. Hard work. Lots of bending and squatting.

"Last year a snake nearly bite me," Kyrill said.

They would make a grand day of it again. And they did. They returned exhausted but joyous. In the kitchen they pushed the table aside. Spread a plastic sheet on the floor. Dumped bags and bags of mushrooms on it. Big ones, little ones, so many different kinds. All muddy and dirty, with leaves and grass on them. A mountain of mushrooms. I rushed and got my camera!

They spent the next day sorting them. A huge job. Dirty. They tossed out a few. Not good. Maybe dangerous. They bagged all the others and Kyrill opened the trap door and lugged them down.

As the days went by, he would bring some up as needed and Natasha would clean and slice them and put them up in big jars. There would be enough for the whole year. Next year they'd go back to the forest for another fun day. Yes, great fun for them.

Winter was a season that took much work to prepare for. It would be awful to run out of food before the next harvest. A family had to be prudent. Had to make clever plans. Had to work hard. Every member had to do his share. Even the youngest and even the oldest if capable.

Another time they planned a weekend bus trip to a distant village for a very different reason. It was famous for its outdoor market. "Big,

big, big," Kyrill told me "Cheap prices!" It offered the best shopping in Ukraine. Natasha prepared a list of things she wanted to buy. Things for the house, clothing for herself and her sons, gifts for this one and that one.

Again she packed her big picnic basket. They planned to board the bus at 8 in the evening, try to sleep a bit through the night as it rolled along, and get off at the village at dawn. Everybody on the bus would be going for the same reason. Natasha and her sons would find a place to wash and eat breakfast, then spend the day scouting the hundreds of stalls for the best deals and hopefully buy every single thing on her list.

The next evening, I was excited as I waited for them to come home. They got back after midnight. They staggered in with enormous bags of stuff. I couldn't believe it. Again, exhausted. But grinning, Had stories to tell. Hard for me to understand it all, but I could see how happy they were.

They opened their big bags. What riches. So many things. Kyrill tried on for me a beautiful formal overcoat. He was about to graduate as an electrical engineer, and he'd be proud to wear this coat to job interviews. New shoes and trousers for Nikita. A stunning Sunday jacket for Natasha herself. She looked gorgeous in it. Finally they had neat piles of things set up all over the dining room and even on the carpet. Best of all, the joy of all the money they had saved!

Fellow PCV's. My cluster mates (l. to r.) Evonne, Sarah, Mandy, Amy, and Clare.

I kept saying "Oh!" and "Ah!" I wasn't faking. They could feel my enthusiasm. It made them feel good. And seeing that made me feel good.

Natasha handed me a package. Two pairs of dress socks—a present for me! Excellent quality. How thoughtful!

As the end of Training approached, I learned I was going to be posted right there in Chernihiv. (Much more about this in the next chapter.) I would be free to have an apartment of my own or to find other living arrangements. I gave these options a lot of thought.

In our last week together, I wanted to do something nice for them. In fact, our teacher Tamila hinted strongly we should give a gift. I really wanted to—I thought the world of my little Ukrainian family. What could I do? I spotted Natasha's ancient kettle. She was always vigilant to turn off the gas the minute she saw steam emerge from the kettle's spout. She did not want to waste a penny's worth.

I got an idea and went shopping at the big bazaar. I looked at many kettles and bought a beauty. Had a thick bottom which would hold the heat. Would last for many years. Would look terrific on the stove. And when it started steaming, it would let out a piercing whistle. Natasha could turn off the gas immediately! She'd love that. This was the feature that clinched it.

I had it wrapped in gift paper and gave it to Natasha at our last Sunday dinner together. You should have seen her joy!

And surprise. She had a present for me. A big, fluffy pink bath towel, a bow around it. She smiled. "You will remember us when you use it!"

Then, remember that marvelous dinner when our host families treated us Trainees at the log-cabin restaurant? Well, now it was our turn. Good food. Much laughter. Many toasts. Singing. They loved it. We loved it.

Finally I made my big decision. Instead of moving into an apartment of my own after I took the oath as a Volunteer, I would stay on with Natasha and the boys.

After all, I was going to be working right there in Chernihiv. It would be a good deal for me, and a good deal for them.

I kept hoping that she or Kyrill would mention that my last day was approaching. I hoped Natasha would ask, "John, what are your plans now?" Then I could speak up and talk about staying with them. Not a word from them. The last day came and still they said nothing. I wondered, *Why are they letting our relationship lapse? Why are they letting me walk away? Didn't the money for my room and board mean a lot to them?*

I knew they planned a complete re-make of the kitchen. My money would help a lot for that. Or were they tired of having me in the house? Had I offended them in some way? Maybe Natasha was tired of sleeping on that small bed in that tiny room with Nikita, their clothes in piles on the floor?

I never found out. We never discussed it. They maintained their high spirits and good humor till the last minute on the last morning. So did I.

But when I sensed their lack of interest, I had started looking for another place. I had to! Through *Coursi*, the language school I was starting to teach at, I had found another family. They lived in a flat in a big Soviet block. Not a house like Natasha's. It was a suitable apartment.

And they seemed a nice family, including a university-age son also, Slava. Like Kyrill, he spoke good English. What an asset for me.

I had arranged with Slava to pick me up in a taxi on my final day. Unless I called him (maybe Natasha would invite me to stay!). Slava arrived right on time. I had all my stuff ready. He helped pack it into the taxi.

Natasha and Kyrill and Nikita were all standing there, watching every minute. They looked on as the two of us made numerous trips to the taxi. Finally it was time to say goodbye.

I kissed Natasha on both cheeks and she returned my kisses. I hugged Kyrill and Nikita. We said sweet words and wished one another good luck.

Then I got into the back seat with Slava and we drove off. On the way to his flat, I had a new thought: *maybe they had been waiting for me to open the subject*! How awful if that was so. I knew that whatever happened, I would never forget them.

I hoped that Natasha would have a long and very good life. I was sure Kyrill would be successful as an engineer. I worried about Nikita.I felt no Trainee could have had a better first family.

Well, my final decision was a good one. Yes, our living with other Ukrainians gave me a better understanding of the country and its people. A most valuable experience for me.

~ ~ ~

**Did you know**... that in every country where Peace Corps operates, there is a full-time staff supporting and directing the Volunteers?

Typically this staff is directed by two or three Americans and everyone else is a local. This includes teachers, bookkeepers, medical personnel, secretaries, chauffeurs and guards. Besides their specific specialties, they bring knowledge of the country and the culture.

This can be a surprise to Volunteers when they arrive. So many locals! Including some who will be their bosses. But I found these people competent, helpful, and welcoming. It was a pleasure to get to know them.

# 8 / Russian! So hard!

*For 12 weeks we sit, concentrate, memorize.*
*I'm getting up at 3 to study. Fear I will flunk!*

Learn Russian! I was reminded firmly and frequently that this was our Number 1 job in Chernihiv during our Training. Others of us were straining to learn Ukrainian, but for my group it was Russian, Russian, Russian. Russian became our life for three months.

Please notice the capital T in "Training." Training is Peace Corps' intellectual equivalent of the Marine Corps' physical Boot Camp. We devoted hours beyond number to it, in class and on our own. For me Training began as a challenge but quickly morphed into a nightmare.

Russian is a world-class language. Some 400 million speak it. It is an elegant language, I'm told...the language of some of the world's greatest writers....Tolstoy and Pushkin in literature, Karl Marx in political philosophy, Pavlov and Mendeleev in science, and so many others.

But it is not Ukraine's legal language. Only Ukrainian holds that sanctity although only a much smaller number of people speak it. Russian is important because so many Ukrainians are ethnic Russians. The easy way to explain this is that they were born in Ukraine and live there but they learned Russian on their mom's lap and Ukrainian on the side.

The story behind this is interesting. During Ukraine's 70 or so years in the U.S.S.R., Russian had been emphasized constantly and insisted upon. Ukrainian was not only downplayed and discouraged, but depicted as an inferior and lower-class language. It was learning Russian and speaking Russian that got you ahead in the system.

After Independence in 1991, Ukrainian was established as the sole national language. The legal language of the land! This law was a natural reaction to the oppression that Ukrainians had suffered at the hands of the Russians. This mandate has angered many ethnic Russian speakers in the country, who are some 20 percent of the population. There is strong lobbying to make Russian the second national language.

Well, we were broken down into clusters of five. It turned out I was the only male in my group. I stood out for another reason also. My age. I could have been the father of the next oldest, and the grandfather of all the others, and with years to spare.

The following was the task set before us. We were to master the strange Cyrillic alphabet, grasp the grammar in all its notorious complexities, and build up a vocabulary of at least a thousand words, some horribly unpronounceable. Well, in my opinion.

Peace Corps insisted it could be done. Peace Corps has been teaching a hundred or more languages over its nearly 50 years, and it has developed a top reputation for teaching languages fast and well.

We would have Russian language classes five days a week, from 8:30 to nearly 2, then go home to put in hours of study on our Russian. Each of us would also get one hour of private tutoring on Friday afternoons.

And we were expected to soak up vocabulary every minute possible. Not only from our textbooks but during our shopping, at the café, on the street.

So on the bus or trolleybus coming and going, I would peer out the window and try to read the store signs and understand them.

Sometimes the crush of passengers standing in the aisle made it impossible. In a restaurant I would study the words on the menu. At the grocery store I would study the words on a can of peas or a box of soap or a bottle of wine.

We were also expected to watch TV with our host family. TV was considered an important learning tool. In the evening the two boys, Kyrill and Nikita, would turn on "The Simpsons." Yes, "The Simpsons" in distant Ukraine, with Russian dubbed in. After that, they would click to other programs, often remarkably similar to American TV fare. Often this would turn me off. I preferred the quiet of my room. A big mistake, I found out.

Peace Corps teaches language by immersion and believe me, we were dunked in deep. It emphasizes "facilitating" rather than teaching. A silly distinction to me. I always thought of Tamila as my teacher, not my facilitator...a very nice and very good teacher.

She was a pleasant, energetic, and very earnest Ukrainian in her late 30s, I judged. Russian was her native language. She was from another city, assigned in Chernihiv for our training. She had been an LCF several years and was seasoned.

She had learned English as a second language, and mostly as an adult, I believe—it's so much harder when you start as an adult. So she had gone through all the difficulties and pains that were now our daily burden. She had done a remarkable job. Still, now and then her pronunciation was off and her vocabulary lacking and her fluency limited. But all in all, she was amazing. An inspiration to us.

Her living room was our classroom, and we took our mid-morning coffee break in the small kitchen, squeezing around the table. And sometimes our lunch, just before leaving for the day. My cluster mates were interesting. I must mention that all of us had master's degrees. At least a master's was a must to begin training as a university-level teacher. Here's more about them.

The next oldest to me was Evonne, 50 or so, who had served a Peace Corps stint some years earlier in Malawi in southern Africa, and in fact had taught in China for many months in a private English-teaching program. She was happy to be back in Peace Corps. I think that she considered it a good job. She was enthusiastic about learning. She was determined to match our three much younger classmates.

Lunch time at Tamila's. We were all different. Our big bond was "getting through this."

They were Mandy, Amy, and, all in their early 20's. I believe that Clare looked at Russian as I did. The two of us were studying it because Peace Corps demanded it, period.

After college, she had gone to London to study and get a master's degree in international relations, and had succeeded. I think that she had entered Peace Corps for the adventure of it.

She was a fervent Catholic and found it essential to start the day by attending Mass—she kept hoping she would find a closer church. And she had a serious boyfriend back home.

She had Skype on her laptop—the magical free long-distance phone program—and whenever she could she would Skype him and chat.

She was my closest friend. She kept an eye out for me. She is the one that I would ask for clarification about something. One day I lost an important hand-out. Clare lent me hers. I returned it after making a photocopy.

Mandy and Amy were different from us. They were eager to learn Russian. They were "ignited." They saw Russian as a terrific career asset.

Mandy had two master's degrees, one in library science. She loved libraries and told me being a librarian was her dream job. She had worked as one, and now her big hope after Peace Corps was to get a professional job in the library of the American embassy in Moscow.

Amy aspired to a career in the State Department. She saw her future in Uncle Sam's Foreign Service. She had spent some months working and studying in Ghana in a private program. She mentioned to me that good Russian would be a definite plus during the difficult State Department application process.

She and I would often find ourselves on the same bus in early morning. She would have her backpack and her laptop. She was loaded down. But Not once did I see her daunted. Or even a bit discouraged. At times a person would give up his seat for me all because I was old. I would urge Amy to put her stuff on my lap. She would do so reluctantly. She was tough.

*Tamila went all out to teach us. Here she's explaining some verb endings. She gave me special help and always did it so generously.*

Day after day Tamila's living room was our classroom. She had a long couch positioned against one of the two long walls, with an upholstered chair on each side. The five of us would sit in a line there. Tamila, of course, would stand in front of us to teach us.

The wall behind her was something to behold. There were dozens of placards taped to it. She had drawn each one with big, bright color markers. The photo above gives you only a small idea.

**T**amila had the technique down pat. Perhaps it was a standard thing to do everywhere that Peace Corps teaches languages. She had a handful of Magic Markers in a dozen colors. She had reams of paper, some as large as 2 by 4 feet. With her markers in hand, she would spend whole afternoons, I believe, creating these things. Maybe she brought many of them from a previous Peace Corps teaching assignment. That would make sense. If she ever lost them, a huge loss!

One might be a list of words describing foods. Another might show the declension of verbs in the First Conjugation. Another might list all the Possessive Pronouns, and another all the Possessive Adjectives.

Another would show how adjectives change their endings according to whether modifying a masculine, feminine, or neuter word.

As the weeks went on, Tamila made more and more of them and put them up. They soon blanketed one wall. Then she went on to the other walls. I was so happy when she ran out of space.

Peace Corps seemed to give her a fresh supply of markers and paper every couple of weeks We'd joke that soon she would start taping her creations to the ceiling.

On some days she would show us a new one, and the only way she could squeeze it in was by putting it over another temporarily. After a while it became difficult to decide where to look to locate what you were looking for. I found it frustrating. We all did.

One day Dr. Oleksander Gonta came from Kyiv to give us medical advice. He set up for us in Tamila's living room. Of course, he noticed all the placards. How could he not? His eyes scanned one wall, then another, then another. He stood back and looked at all four walls. He shook his head. He seemed dazed. He muttered, "How do you know where to find something?" Our exact problem!

At times she would show us a new game she had devised. This would change the pace and could be very effective. At first a simple game, then more intricate. One might involve a winding path that she had drawn. Along it were instructions carefully numbered.

Each of us would have a small paper with our name on it. We'd take turns with a pair of dice. Let's say I rolled a 3. I'd follow instruction at No. 3: "Put the word *yabloko* (apple) into the genitive plural." Not easy. A triumph if I got it right. If wrong, I'd get penalized.

Then it would be Mandy's turn. Then Evonne's, and so on. Whoever finished first won. It was often fun. We learned!

Tamila charged ahead from the first minute. She insisted on brutal memorization. She believed that if we repeated something often enough, it would stick! That might work for my four classmates, but not for me. Not any more.

They could hear a word once or twice and yes, the word would stick. With me, it was in one ear and out the other. One evening I would labor to memorize a list of a dozen words and then feel satisfied and proud. The next morning I'd remember only half of them. That evening, only a quarter.

Then I'd strive to memorize a new list. And as I did, the previous words would fade into oblivion. It was awful.

To make a word stick, what I had to do was create an association for it. Here's an example. Try as I might, I couldn't remember that the pretty river that slips through town was the Desna River. Desna! Desna!

Desna! I just couldn't get it pounded in. Then I thought of Disney...like Walt *Disney...like Disneyland. Desna...Disney*! That became the association I needed! Now Desna sticks!

So I found myself continually searching, searching, searching for associations. The more, the better.

Another good trick was to try to recognize cognates. I didn't know what they are. They are words that have the same linguistic root. I found many cognates. One example is "Etage." In Russian it means 'floor." It's easy for me to remember because it means the same thing in French.

In fact, the Russians borrowed it from French. They borrowed a lot of words from French. I admit I had fun identifying cognates.

Peace Corps went all out in giving us whatever was needed. It was remarkable how many books and booklets and hand-outs were given to us, and we were expected to bring to class everything that might be required. With our daily sessions nearly six hours long, Tamila could ask us to open a surprising number of these. So we were all loaded down with books when we arrived at her apartment.

*Peace Corps gave us so many books to study. I just had to spread them out for a photo. That's Kitty in the right corner.*

Toss in a couple of notebooks plus a lunch and an extra sweater because the heat might not be on and you had a hefty load. In my case, a big shoulder bag full. But by now it was getting easier to get up all those stairs. I was getting more exercise than ever, and it was good for me.β

I was so impressed by the quantity of all these books and booklets and hand-outs given to us. One Saturday at home, I took them all out and arranged them on the floor.

Surprising how many square feet they took. Then I snapped a picture of them. What a souvenir this would make in years to come. Later I saw I had overlooked three books, including a big one.

I mentioned that Peace Corps believed in language instruction by total immersion. The trick was to start using Russian right away. The first line we'd learn might be, "My name is John." Yes, in Russian.

That would be followed by many other everyday expressions, "I am American," or, "I am from the state of Connecticut." We would repeat them over and over. Gradually new words and expressions would be added. If we didn't know the meaning, we were encouraged to guess it. Often we guessed right. That was a valuable tip and I used it.

Every time that I cursed the Russian, I had to remember that all these Ukrainians on the staff had had to suffer through the same miseries to learn English. They had been successful. If they could do it, why couldn't I? I tried and tried.

Tamila also used a lot of flash cards. They were another standard Peace Corps technique. I made sets of flash card of my own. For the days of the week. For the cardinal numbers 1 through 10, then 11 through 20, then 21 through 100, and even 1,000. For the months of the year. For the big question words: who, what, when, where, why, and so on.

I carried the flash cards in a pocket and worked them while waiting for a bus. I would master one set, but get it only part right on the next day. But I learned little by little. But not enough. I had a problem all my own. A bit of deafness. Until now, I never considered it serious. I always managed. Sometimes all I had to do was place myself in front of the person speaking. If I faced the person, no problem.

Dr. Oleksander came and spent a day giving us advice on staying healthy in body and mind. An excellent job.

In this classroom, it was difficult for me to do. As I said, all of us sat in a long row, side by side. I was the last on Tamila's far right. If Tamila spoke to someone way on the left, I missed some words. And so my problem was compounding.

Whenever my friends spoke to her—to answer a question or make a comment—I often missed it. I would ask her to repeat, and she would do that, but too softly.

I thought that she—all of them—would become aware of my problem and speak louder, or even swap seats, but it didn't happen.

In the second week I developed a dental problem and had to go to Kyiv for a day. I tried to catch up the next day, but did not manage to. I got more behind.

I must say that my classmates were impressive. They learned by leaps and bounds. Every day I would learn a little, but they would learn more. They got much better than I did. And as they did, Tamila focused more on them, all quite naturally.

**T**amila gave each of us one hour of private tutoring every week. She would work on our weaknesses, our deficiencies. Mine were endless. Sometimes she asked me something simple, which she rightfully expected me to know. "John, what state do you come from?" Or, "John, what kind of work did you do back home?" She wanted more than a one-word answer.

I would think and fumble and come up with a wrong answer. Frustrating and embarrassing for me. Terribly discouraging for her, I was sure, although she managed to conceal it. I must say that she did her best for me. Nothing would have made her happier than my succeeding.

But sometimes she would grope for a word in English and we'd supply it, just as she would supply one for us. She was learning, too.

Our mornings were filled with frustrations…well, mine were…and I suspect hers were also. My constant frustration was, "Why can't I learn this stuff better?" And hers undoubtedly was, "What, oh what can I do to make John get it?"

One day when I knew I was taxing her patience, I said to her, "Tamila, I know that I am your Purgatory!" I meant it. I was giving her a hell of a hard time, though not deliberately. In fact, I would have done anything to lighten her burden.

*I was always checking the value of the dollar at exchange shops. Nice to see it go up. We liked that trend.*

"Purgatory? I am very sorry, John. I do not know that word."

The next day she said. "John, I looked up that word. No, no, no. You are not my Purgatory. It is my job to teach you!

How could I not love her? I held her in highest regard for her enthusiastic and unrelenting efforts to do a fine job. She began each morning with a smile and ended it with a smile.

On our mid-morning break we would sit together around the kitchen table and she would join us. We'd have just 15 minutes. Never 16 although I am sure she would have enjoyed sitting and chatting with us longer. I kept mentioning one thing to Tamila: I was interested in what I called Survival Russian—just basic words and phrases that would get me through the day. Not all this heavy-duty grammar.

I mentioned that after class I planned to go to the outdoor bazaar just a few minutes away. I needed another necktie. She said, "Are you sure you can do it all right? Can I help you?"
"Thank you, Tamila. But no, no. I'll do fine."
She looked doubtful.
In the vast market I walked to the section with all the clothing stalls. I couldn't find any neckties. I walked up to a shopkeeper and mimed putting on a necktie.

I made believe rolling up my shirt collar, draping a tie around my neck, pulling down the wide end lower than the narrow end, then making the knot. She understood immediately and pointed me to another area.

I walked there but could not find a tie. I put on my little act for another shopkeeper. He got it and pointed to another stall. And there I found a nice selection of ties and bought one.

I wore my new tie to class the next morning. Tamila noticed it but said nothing. I could not resist. "Survival Russian!" I said to her, and then explained how I had succeeded. She laughed.

**B**y now I had learned something else. Most people on the streets spoke neither Russian nor Ukrainian. They spoke a bastard mix called Surgeit. And of course it included lots of slang—just like our English. This made me skeptical of how useful all this textbook study of pure Russian would be.

I learned something else. I mentioned to you that I had been studying the words on all kinds of items in the big grocery store I went to. Then it dawned on me: all those words were in the legal Ukrainian, not Russian! But there was a saving grace. Some of the words were the same in Russian.

To be fair, I must say that Tamila wanted to make our learning practical. One day she cut our class short and took us all on a walk to the bazaar. Then she let us loose. Our task was to buy a list of foods for a meal we would cook together. Could we manage that?

Absolutely. In an hour we were back in her apartment with everything needed. It was easy. Most of the items were on display. All we had to do was point to them.

On another day she took us onto the streets again. This time she challenged us to find our way to a certain shop, just by asking people for directions. What I did was write the shop's name on a slip of paper. In Russian. I intended to show it to passersby. She nixed that fast. She wanted us to ask in Russian. Well, we managed and found the shop.

Frankly, I never expected to have such difficulty learning the school-book Russian.

I had had a lot of experience in studying languages. My first language was French, as I've explained. Then English. Then Latin—for six years! Then Greek—one year.

Sounds strange, I know, but I had unusual schooling. Then some 20 years ago when I started going to Mexico, I studied Spanish and picked up some of it.

But Russian was more difficult. And I wasn't getting younger. It seemed that my memory had tanked up. No more room. It was that simple. My frustration grew. I began worrying. How would I get through all this?

Late one night at home at Natasha's, I had quite an experience. An epiphany! I am a morning person. I like to get up early. And I like to go to bed early, at 9 or 10. This became my habit at Natasha's.

But all I was thinking about now was Russian. I was uptight about it. I began getting up at 3 a.m. I would sit at my desk for two hours and study grammar and vocabulary. Then at 5 I would go to bed for an hour. At 6 Natasha would knock on my door. Up I'd jump and launch into a new day.

On Friday evening at the end of our first week with Tamila, I finished dinner with Natasha and Kyrill and Nikita and stretched out on my bed for an hour. Then I'd get up and study. Well, that's what I intended. I woke up the next morning! My body knew better. I needed sleep.

But I continued my middle-of-the night routine for three weeks.

I couldn't get the new words to sink in! At 4 a.m. one night my frustration got the best of me. I closed my Russian workbook and threw it aside. I despaired. I picked up my pad. I began scribbling.

I wrote: *"I am the worst Russian-language student Peace Corps has ever had. I will never read Tolstoy in the original. I will be lucky to be able to read the headlines in the newspaper.* "

Then I had another thought. *"But I am the best 78-year-old Russian-language student Peace Corps has ever had. I will not quit and go home. I will not go home until Peace Corps sends me home!"*

I was its first 78-year-old Russian-student, I was quite sure.

Then I turned off the light and went to bed to squeeze in as much sleep as I could before Natasha came to wake me. I felt better right away.

Peace Corps saw my problem. They adjusted my hours, letting me study more on my own. They let me find a private tutor of my own and show up for one-half of each session at Tamila's. None of that really worked. What it did was put me farther behind the others and made me feel all the more alone. But I can't fault Peace Corps.

I gladly acknowledge that Peace Corps is expert at teaching foreign languages. They teach dozens of languages around the world. They've had half a century of experience. I marveled at the progress of my young companions, well, some of them. The problem was me, not Peace Corps. There is an age for everything. I had long passed the age for this.

But my worrying did not end. I was so overwhelmed and doing so poorly that I began thinking the unthinkable. Maybe I should quit. Maybe I should go home. Others were quitting. Why shouldn't I?

In our group of 86, there were eight of us who were seniors. Four had already quit and gone home. I was the oldest in this group of eight. In fact, I was about 17 years older than the next oldest.

If some of these younger ones couldn't take it, why should I feel that I had to suffer through this? But maybe the language difficulty was not their big problem, though I thought it might be.

I also thought of my four friends back home who had written recommendations to Peace Corps about me. And all the friends who had turned out for my Going Off to Peace Corps Party back in Deep River. How would I be able to face them?

But as a young man I had learned that quitting is not a good solution to a difficulty. And I remembered something else. How back in Kyiv on our second day in Ukraine Diana Schmidt had addressed us. She had covered many topics. One was discouragement.

"The training is tough," she said. "Do not quit impulsively. Give it the 10-day test! Yes, please!"

A nice thing was that my bad feelings would brighten the minute I left class and walked through the bazaar nearby, with all its color and action.

And I would get comfort in what older Volunteers—those already working at their posts—kept saying to us. "There is life after Training! Yes, there is!" That cheered me on.

Then we got a substitute LCF for two weeks, Pasha, a likable young man. That was a pleasant change, but I don't mean this as a reflection against Tamila. Heck, no. I admired Tamila. Peace Corps wanted us to hear "another voice." Good thinking. In fact, Tamila had gone off to teach Pasha's class for two weeks.

Pasha was 24 maybe, very tall, and as earnest and patient as he was tall. He told us that he was a public school teacher. His father and mother were teachers. "Teaching is our family vocation." We all knew how poorly teaching paid. I was impressed by his sense of vocation.

He was always encouraging. One day I mentioned I knew I was a terrible student. He stared at me, then shook his head sternly, in contradiction! "No, no, no, John!" he said. Nice of him, but I knew differently.

**P**asha also wanted to make our learning practical. Before long we'd be going off to our permanent sites as sworn-in Volunteers. We'd travel by train. He took us to the big Chernihiv Railroad Station. For two hours it became a laboratory of sorts.

He told us, "Soon you will be assigned to your posts. You will be going by train. You must know basic things."

He showed us how to understand the big train boards showing Arrivals and Departures. There were many ticket windows. Some for express trains. Some for locals. He explained these things.

Luda was my first private tutor. Such a sweet gal. I look so glum! I must have just finished a very tough Russian lesson!

He took us out to the track platform and made us look at a stopped train. How the coaches were numbered, from which end of the train, and the different kinds of cars…sitting cars, sleeping cars…and the different levels of service.

Back in the station, he sent us off to find the toilets, the money exchange, the luggage-storage service, the emergency medical room, on and on. All excellent stuff. A great session.

It was about then that Tamila asked to speak to me. She suggested that I spend only 90 minutes with our group every morning, then leave and study on my own. She told me, "You will do better that way, I think." Then she changed it a bit. She told me that after our tea break, I should remain in the kitchen and study on my own at my own pace.

The classes had become a misery for me. I took her idea one step further. I told her that I would get a private tutor of my own, at my expense. She was pleased. And so was I.

I did find a tutor. Here is how. I had started going to the Korolonko Library every afternoon, the city's public library. I got into little conversations with Nadia, the young librarian in the Foreign Language Department. She spoke English so well and was so pleasant that I asked if she would tutor me.

"I am sorry, John." She smiled and patted her tummy. "I am going to be a mother." She sounded so happy. "I will have no time.

"But I have a friend. I'll talk to her. Her name is Luda."

Luda called me. She liked the idea. She was 22 years old, very attractive. More importantly she spoke good English.

She had graduated with a major in English with Nadia at the local Pedagogical University and was now in a master's program. She was also studying German seriously, she said.

"I have a job also," she said. She was a clerk in a business office. She could tutor me for 60 or 90 minutes a couple of evenings a week.

We started, and it was helpful. I liked her. But it didn't last long. Surprise! She said, "I have been accepted by Aerosvit Airlines."

She was excited. She would train as a flight attendant at Borispil Airport outside Kyiv. Aerosvit was the big national carrier.

It flew to the major cities in Ukraine and other European countries and to the U.S.A. and even to China.

She was glowing. "I will be able to improve my English! I will be able to see famous places." I understood. I congratulated her and resolved to find a new tutor.

One day Diana Schmidt came to visit. We were reaching the end of Training. She wanted to chat with each of us. I was sure that back at Headquarters somebody was figuring where each of us should be assigned. I felt maybe she wanted to pick up clues about where we might serve best.

My turn came. She was pleasant. She asked, "How are you doing?"

"Not very well." I explained my problems. I was sure she knew how I was doing. I decided to level with her. I looked at her squarely. "Tell me, Diana. Are you thinking of sending me home?"

"Not yet!" she said. I was struck by how straight-forward she was. It had to be admired. It sounded very ominous to me. Quickly she added, "We are impressed by how hard you are trying. We'll wait and see."

I didn't sleep well that night.

I had another big worry. A scary prospect was coming up for all of us. It was our Language Proficiency Exam. Two language experts would come from Kyiv and invite each of us into a room for a private 20-minute conversation in Russian. They'd tape the conversation for later study. And as evidence if necessary.

All of us talked about it. We were all jittery. But one Trainee after another would tell me, "John, nobody ever gets sent home for a bad performance."

Oh, no? Well, I might become the first.

Came the big morning. I had done my best to prepare. I was uptight. I was one of the first to be called in. Surprise, only one examiner, not two, as we had been led to believe.

She was sweet. As kind and gentle as she could be. She made it easy. But it was a disaster. An embarrassment. A humbling experience. But my conscience did not bother me. I had been doing my best. That was my only consolation.

I was upset by one thought: *I was so bad at this language learning that Peace Corps might decide to no longer accept Volunteers my age!*

Well, Training finally ended. Many of my young friends did very well. They were proud, rightly so. I was so relieved it was over. And what I had heard so often seemed proven. Nobody flunked out for poor language-learning performance. If anybody deserved to go home for that, it was I.

I knew I would be accepted as a Volunteer. But another surprise. Two or three weeks before the Swearing In, I was told I would teach not at a university, but at a school called *Coursi*. What a shock. But I'll tell you about that in another chapter.

Oh, this is a good time to tell you about a terrific tip I got. Finally I could tell instantly if something was written in Russian or Ukrainian. I got the tip from a fellow Volunteer.

She told me, "Look closely at the words, John. If you spot a letter 'i', that's Ukrainian. Not Russian. Russian doesn/t have an 'i']."

Why didn't one of our teachers mention that during Training?

~ ~ ~

***Did you know***... that in this 50th Anniversary Year of Peace Corps' founding, celebrations and commemorations are being held all over the world. Yes, in many countries where Peace Corps served in the past and is serving now. Also in Washington, D.C., which is Peace Corps' home base. And in many states and many cities—besides their national association (the private, not government National Peace Corps Association), former Volunteers have numerous state and local associations. And at some universities where significant numbers of students have decided to become Volunteers, such as the University of California in Los Angeles (UCLA).

The big national celebration, long planned, carefully orchestrated, and heavily publicized, will be staged in Washington in September, Wednesday to Sunday, the 21st to the 25th, with thousands attending from near and far. Those days will be busy with memorial ceremonies, get-togethers, celebrations, much speech-making, and plenty of fun and festivity.

This is a fine celebration of past accomplishments, of course. But I'm sure it is planned as a springboard to a bigger and brighter future. The plan for Peace Corps is to get bigger. All this publicity should give that effort a huge jumpstart.

# 9 / Saturdays...more study!

*Now we're tackling 'Technical Training.'*
*Practical stuff! But a tough new teacher!*

Technical Training—we kept hearing about that. Back in Dyebeck we were told we'd attend Russian classes Monday through Friday all through Training. And Technical Training every Saturday. "What's that?" we wondered. It turned out to be a grind of a different kind.

I just told you about Tamila, our LCF. Now we got a TCF—a Technical Cross-Cultural Facilitator. Natalia was in her early 30's, I guessed. A beautiful woman. Dressed like a fashion model.

She spoke English extraordinarily well—rare for someone who learned it as a second language. She knew her stuff. She had a Ph.D. in education, we were told, or maybe it was literature. And she was a professor at a centuries-old university back in Lviv, over in the west close to Poland. And she was tough—too tough.

I got to dislike her. Then something good happened, and I had to change my opinion. I wound up liking her a lot.

Technical Training turned out to be a different deal. It was one day a week as opposed to five, but that was the classroom part. But it stretched through the week, too. A big part was learning how to teach Ukrainian-style. And this took two forms. We had to go observe Ukrainian teachers doing their thing in actual classrooms. And we had to teach classes, as well, and under an expert Ukrainian teacher called our Counterpart.

We'd do this at two universities in the city. One was the Pedagogical University, which trained teachers and prepared students who were majoring in things like literature, history, philosophy.

The other was the Polytechnic University, which prepared students to be engineers, computer whizzes, and science-focused graduates. I went and observed at both, but did my practice teaching at Tech U, as I called it. All that got decided for me—for all of us—by Headquarters, of course. And all this got fitted in after our Russian classes. So, in late afternoon and on into the evening. Not much time to loaf.

There was another difference. There were only five of us in language class. But there were a dozen of us in the technical sessions. We would meet in the apartment that Peace Corps rented for Natalia. It was smaller than Tamila's, and her living room seemed only half as big. We were jammed in there. Some of us had to sit on the floor. Natalia would keep us three hours, sometimes longer. Nobody was unhappy when the class ended.

Natalia's role was to train us to teach in Ukraine. Well, isn't teaching just teaching wherever your classroom happens to be? No.

Cultural differences must be taken into account. And Ukraine had ideas and regulations of its own. We had to become familiar with them. And Peace Corps had additional things that it wanted us to pick up.

Specifically, her job was to prepare us to be good Volunteers and good teachers. She strove to teach us Peace Corps policies and expectations. To instruct us in Ukrainian teaching methods and educational philosophies.

And to prepare us for the day not far off when we'd go off alone for 24 months to teach here or there across the country. In a university—that would be my assignment. Or in a secondary school—a high school to us.

Like Tamila, she was here in Chernihiv only for 12 weeks, so in her own way she was roughing it also. We could see this in their apartments. Living out of a suitcase, so to speak, and making do with skimpy pots and pans and kitchen things. But both ladies were neat and tidy to a T, and good sports about it, I must tell you.

Natalia's teaching style was similar to Tamila's in one way. She too would prepare posters and pin-up sheets. This was an essential part of her style. But there was far less brute memorization here, of course. Our challenge was to understand.

Her creations were detailed and elaborate. And she would teach by pointing to an item, speaking about it, then moving down to the next. They'd make me think of an iceberg. The biggest part—the part under water—must have taken her hours to prepare.

I told you she was tough. And how! One of her favorite lines was, "You are expected to do this!" Another was, "This is your responsibility!" She said these things over and over. It got to rankle. It was no way to make friends and influence people. An undercurrent of resentment developed.

This part of the class would take her 30 minutes or so. Then she'd fire broad questions. "What do you think of this?" Or, "Is there a better way to accomplish this?" Or, "How would you react in a case like this?"

As I said, we went to her apartment every Saturday. And on every Saturday one of us would have to make a presentation on a topic she assigned. And afterward, our fellow students would quiz us. All of us became quickly aware that it was important to participate actively—ask questions, make comments.

Yes, she tossed the ball to us a lot. And that was good. She could see how well we understood, and hopefully what we said contributed to the topic. But I also got the feeling it was simplifying her job a lot.

Also she had to make sure all of us got practical teaching experience. She was the one who assigned us to the two universities, for observation or to teach. We were supposed to teach twice a week. Our schedules couldn't take that, so our practice teaching got reduced to once a week.

For this stand-up-front performance, we had to prepare a detailed teaching plan in the prescribed Ukrainian style.

Each of us was assigned to a teacher at the university, and he or she was called our Counterpart. We conferred with our Counterpart on what we would teach and how.

I'll never forget my first ride on the trolley to Tech U. It was in a strange part of town. We had to find the right departure point, and exit point. It involved a ride on a bus, then a transfer to a trolley. I was uptight about it. I am sure all of us were. One problem is that the rides were always crowded and we had to stand at least part way. Hard often to see outside.

And the language difficulty was so enormous. I was afraid I might get off at the wrong stop—even with the right stop spelled out on a card that I could show somebody on the bus or trolley. This had happened to me. Or miscalculate how long it would take to walk this portion, or that one.

Well, I got to Tech U. Four floors. A sprawling building. It was recess time, and the university halls were jammed with kids. I had a job just finding my way to the right department way back on the second floor.

**M**y counterpart was Alexander Kot—English teacher of what I would call Business English. A handsome man. Natty dresser. Low-pressure.

He was a veteran teacher—more than 30 years' experience—and right away I saw that he took his role with me with a big grain of salt. He always sat through my entire class—would stand over on one side of the room, actually, and keep his eyes on his charges. His big contribution would be to keep the students attentive.

"Make notes of what Mr. John is explaining to you!" he would bark. Or, "What Mr. John just said is important. Remember it!"

He gave me plenty of freedom. He was always pleasant and often funny. I got to love chatting with him afterward. I would gladly have taken him on as a close friend.

It turned out he spoke French— his French was even better than his English, which was good. He liked to chat with me in French after my sessions, just for the practice, I think.

But I never got any feedback from him about how I was doing, good or bad. I would have welcomed that. I got to believe that he was simply going through motions.

His chairperson had assigned him to do this, and he was doing it. Period. Maybe he felt that if Peace Corps had selected us to do this work, that was good enough for him.

During our teaching sessions, at times Natalia would sit in also. Even a visiting Peace Corps expert from Kyiv might come in. They would sit in the back, observe us and the students' reactions (or lack of them), and scribble notes. This was unnerving.

After our class, they would check their notes and "de-brief" us, with brutal frankness. Always advice to give. They'd write long comments in our Practicum Journal. What fun.

The Practicum Journal was a blank Peace Corps workbook each of us was given at our first Tech Session. We had to fill it in week by week for all 12 weeks.

*We got off to a bad start with Natalia. Then we got her to begin smiling. A great transformation! Better for her, and for us. Good!.*

We would detail the classes we taught, our lesson plans, and our own assessments of what we had learned and still had to learn.

We turned it in to Natalia every Saturday. She wrote in comments—at length, doing a lot of work—then returned it to us.

I got off to a bad start. I lost my Practicum Journal. Accidents happen. There was no extra blank copy. What I finally managed to do was borrow my friend Clare's and photocopy it.

Clare had already filled some pages in it—I couldn't copy those. So I made extra copies of the pages still blank to get the number of blank pages that I needed. Then I stapled all the pages together. It worked, but it was an untidy thing. Really was. I was sure I lost points with meticulous Natalia.

She had a tough job, no doubt. We would hand-write in our Practicum Journal with a pen. As good as her English was, Natalia knew it as a second language. So she had to struggle not only with some of our colloquialisms and even slang, but with our handwriting, which was far different than her native Cyrillic. She complained about it. "Try to write carefully," she would say. "Please!"

I understood. She certainly had a big problem, especially with me. Sometimes I had a problem understanding my own scribblings! I was sympathetic. I would have hated her job.

Besides all this, we were urged to go observe the Ukrainian teachers at workF in their classrooms in our "spare time" after our Russian class. And we would write reports about all this in our Practicum Journal.

As you see, we were working and studying six days a week. In my case, what really happened is that Training took over my life. I was in Training or thinking about it 98 percent of the time. True for most of my friends as well, I believe.

*It's wet and gray and late and I'm happily going home after one of my practice classes at Tech U.*

I forgot to mention one thing I enjoyed. After class every day, I liked to stop by the Dba Gucia Restaurant downtown. The name means Two Geese. Just a short walk away. It was a cafeteria with a liquor license. Cozy and quite nice. It was our hang-out. All I wanted was a cup of tea..

Often my friends would be there, sitting at tables in two's and three's, laptops open, studying and working away. But I didn't have a laptop.

Oh, everybody was always nice to me, but I never felt I fitted in. It was my *dedushka* thinking again—my grandfatherliness. My age.

This team studying was a great assist for them. I was on my own. They had an advantage.

When alone, I would head for the bazaar. There was always a lot going on. I liked the walking.

I got to learn so much about the people and their ways. And I got to use bits and pieces of my Russian, of course.

Now back to Natalia. She also tutored us one hour a week privately and I got to know her better that way. At this time, a different personality! What a happy discovery.

She could be warm and engaging. How pleasant. So different than in the classroom, where she was so stiff and formal. I was positive that she would be more effective in class if she loosened up and smiled once in a while and maybe even joked or showed a bit of sympathy instead of her frequent "This is your responsibility!"

One time we were sitting together, just the two of us, and I saw my opportunity. I said to her, "We all see what a great facilitator you are, Natalia. What a great teacher. Would you mind if I made a suggestion or two?"

"Of course not, John."

I mentioned that in American higher generation, by and large there is more informality between professors and students although professional distance and respect are maintained. True especially in advanced classes and in small groups. Well, that had been my experience.

I mentioned to her the enthusiasm and pride that infused all us Trainees.

We all had our own reasons to join Peace Corps, I believed, but feelings of patriotism and altruism were part of them.

I told her that as Volunteers we would be offering our services free to the people of Ukraine, with no expectation of payment for specific services. And that we all received the same living allowance, regardless of our age, experience, or background.

*To relax, I'd stroll the huge bazaar nearby. Clear my mind! Loved to see the people, the variety, and all the activity.*

She knew some of this, but not all. And I mentioned the difficulties and hardships we were going through far from home in a strange land and a different culture. It wasn't just a sob story. I wasn't sure she appreciated all this.

Then I got to my point. I said, "Know what, Natalia? We would like it so much if you relaxed more in class. Laughed and joked a little. Let your hair down." She didn't understand this, but I explained and she smiled. And kept listening.

Emboldened, I even suggested that she stop saying "This is your responsibility!" and "You are expected to do this!" I said a word or two about our being mature people and having met high standards to get into Peace Corps."
She was gracious about it. She thanked me, and sincerely, I thought. I noticed that in class she began acting differently. She was loosening up. We all noticed it. To me it was a mark of her professional attitude about trying to do better. And it showed her good will toward us. I admired her.

**O**h, I told you that in our Russian class we got a substitute LCF for a while, the young man Pasha. Here in Tech Training we got a substitute TCF. Oksana Yurchuk came into our life.
Apparently someone noticed Natalia had an enormous load and Oksana stepped in to lend a hand. She became my tutor for that one hour a week. And she took over as my supervisor in my practice teaching.
We got to know one another and hit it off. She was warm, pleasant, and low-key but serious. And sympathetic! She was in her late 30's, I thought, and had a husband and daughter back in Kyiv.
In our weekly sessions in her temporary apartment, she would review the entries in my Practicum Journal, ask questions, and make comments. Like Natalia and Tamila and Pasha, she was a pro. I appreciated her interest and suggestions. Helpful.
Shortly later, she played a larger role. She is the one who helped me get set up with my second host family. That was not long after I took the oath as a Volunteer. More about this in a chapter coming up. Interesting!
Oh, I got help from another person. Olya was another LCF teaching another cluster of Trainees in Chernihiv. I met her. Was sympathetic about my Russian difficulties. Offered to tutor me, and free. I saw her three times. What was best were her re-assurances, "John, do not worry!"
I have told you Training was difficult. So much work, such high expectations of us. We were all affected. I got to see three big emotional upsets in just a short time. They were unpleasant to behold for all of us, sad to tell you. We never expected such.

*When sunny May arrived, what a relief. Little markets sprang up on corners, and folks shed the hardships of winter.*

One morning in Russian class, one of the gals broke down. Began crying uncontrollably. Ran out of the room to the kitchen.

What was wrong? I jumped up, left the class and went and sat with her at the kitchen table. She was still sobbing, her head buried in her arms.

"I am doing so, so badly," she blurted. Well, I didn't think so, and told her so. I held her hand and tried to console her.

Finally she roused herself and wiped her eyes. Together we returned to the living room. Tamila was carrying on with the class, or trying to. Did not want to show she was upset. We took our seats and paid attention.

The same thing happened to another gal on another day. An emotional collapse. An explosion of tears. For the same reason.

Certainly Tamila was not being cruel or unkind. She had a warm heart. Was well-intentioned. If anything, she wanted to make things as easy as possible for us, but she had her job to do and was doing her best at it. I am sure she was distressed by these upsets. I'll bet that she met with these students individually later and tried to be helpful.

It was a fast pace. The intellectual challenge was huge. There were all the associated shocks of living in Ukraine and trying to adjust to so many changes.

I saw another breakdown at Tech U. Terrible. At the end of our practice teaching, each of us had to put on a demonstration class before a group of live university students. It was the usual 80-minute class, and it was important to perform well.

In other words, we had to show our stuff. There would be our TCF and one or two other official Peace Corps observers at the back of the room plus fellow Volunteers. All would be watching the Trainee's performance with eagle eyes and taking notes and trying to find things about the performance to talk about during the usual "de-brief."

This Trainee was a gal about 23. I'll call her Beverly. She did a fine job, I thought. She was lucky, too. She was teaching a class of only eight students. Much easier than 18, say.

Ahead of time, she had filed a detailed lesson plan explaining every phase of her class, with so many minutes allocated to this and so many to that. And she had to give a copy of her plan to every observer—eight observers in this case. I was one of them.

During her class she did what I thought she was supposed to do: engage every student, mix lecturing with inter-active dialog, and so on.

As she proceeded, she had to make adjustments. Spend more minutes on this, fewer minutes on that. It's very natural. It's expected. That's what good teachers do. They adapt to the circumstances.

Meanwhile, the eight of us in the back row watched and scribbled. I had counted and had noticed there were as many of us observers as there were kids in the room! Well, too my eye, the students were kids.

As usual, a couple of the students took the lead in putting up a hand and asking questions or answering questions. Others said little. Beverly tried to engage them and stimulate them. Finally the class ended. Well done, I thought. The students dashed out.

Then came the mandatory de-brief. All of us observers were supposed to make helpful comments. We took our turns with our notes in hand. Our intention was to make her a better teacher. The de-brief was supposed to last 45 minutes. That's a lot of criticism.

We had hardly started when Beverly began sobbing and fled the room. We looked at one another. We were distraught.

This was a bad experience for all of us. We tried to chat. Finally she walked back in. Her eyes were red and she was clutching a handkerchief. "I am so sorry," she said. She said a few more words of apology. But for what? She hadn't done anything wrong! I really thought that.

Who wouldn't have been intimidated by all us observers? In fact, the kids themselves had been intimidated by us. I was sure that that our big group had changed the climate in the room, and for the worse. Our presence surely had affected the kids and created an artificial atmosphere.

My turn came to put on a demo class, of course. I was teaching a class of business students. About 18 of them, 16 of them girls, average age 20. Why such a lop-sided division? I asked Professor Kot.

"Because they are more interested in English than the boys are," he told me. It's he who had suggested my topic. It was "The Typical Big American Corporation."

Well, some universities in America spend whole semesters discussing that subject. I had 80 minutes. But I already knew something about the subject. Then quickly I had gone to www.wikipedia.com to prepare even more.

One Sunday at the big square I ran into Tamila, Natalia, and Olya. Olya was an LCF who tutored me a bit. We chatted—but not about classes. And look at Natalia smiling now!

I made up a Vocabulary List for the class—even wrote all the definitions myself, trying to make them as simple as possible. Prepared graphics. Spent a lot of time on my lesson plan. Made all the copies for my observers. My TCF Oksana was one of them. So was Professor Kot. I felt ready.

**M**y class went well. I have a firm belief: learning something should be fun. I always manage to make students chuckle now and then.

In the back I counted five official observers—I was lucky that I had so few. I began my class. But now I had two audiences in mind, my students and my observers.

I kept studying my students for their reactions, and I did the same for my observers. It's only natural. And of course I strove to please both. So, not a typical classroom by far.

And I could see that my students were reacting differently. They had the observers sitting in the rear on their minds also. What a distraction.

I finished my class. Pretty good, I thought. I felt my students had learned something. I felt it had been time well spent for them. They left. I walked to the back of the room and took a seat facing my observers.

Came the de-brief. They studied their notes, took turns making comments. Oksana had the most to say, and Alexander Kot the least. They were all kind. There was one big criticism: I had talked too much, and that had prevented my students from participating more.

"Thank you," I said to one and all. "Much appreciated." If I had to do the class again, I would not change much. The topic had been a very technical subject. If I had opened the class to wide discussion, I never would have been able to cover even the modest outline I had written in my lesson plan.

Oh, I must tell you about a previous class, also under Professor Kot's supervision. The topic assigned to me was, "American-Style Advertising." Again I was familiar. I had prepared. I had put together a Vocabulary List and copied it for each of my students.

Again, I had made the definitions simple. Still I felt some students would not understand. Some knew very little English. So I said to them, "If you do not understand some of these words, look them up in your two-way dictionary when you get home." Meaning their Russian-English/ English-Russian Dictionary."

 One like mine. I used it every day. Pretty basic advice. In fact, I had printed this at the bottom of the Vocabulary List.

I was shocked to learn most of these kids did not have a two-way dictionary. The university did not supply dictionaries and the students could not afford one. How can you possibly study a foreign language without a two-way dictionary?

I must tell you that at one time Alexander—that's what I called him when we were alone—had worked as a translator for a French company working at Chernobyl after the great melt-down. He loved American culture...was familiar with many of our writers and composers and singers. When his cell phone rang, what it gave out was some vertydelightful Frank Sinatra!

**I** took a liking to Alexander immediately. He was an older man, and that was a factor. His love of French was also a factor. One of his passions was stamp collecting—he was a serious philatelist, and to me that spoke volumes about him. He considered his precious stamps windows to the whole wild world.

I told you that he was a natty dresser. "That's a beautiful cardigan you are wearing," I said to him one day. "Second hand," he said.

I thought he was joking. Not so. I had noticed second-hand shops all over the city. That's what their signs said, "Second Hand," in English. Second-hand was big business all through Ukraine. I visited a few shops. Most of the clothes that I saw came from the United States and Western Europe—affluent countries.

His remark was another reminder of how little teachers were paid, even in universities.

I got to see him at the university at a later occasion, long after Training. In fact, I stopped by just to visit him. He was happy. He had just received his first monthly pension payment. "Now I can ride on the trolley buses free!" he told me, smiling.

So, was he retiring? "No, not yet." His pension was too meager. And he had just made a down payment on an apartment for his daughter.

Technical Training kept us busy in other ways. One of our projects was to create a community map. Yes, a map of Chernihiv. Each cluster of five Trainees was to work together on its own map. So Evonne, Mandy, Clare, Amy, and I got started on ours with a big blank piece of paper.

On long, balmy summer evenings I loved to sit outside and people-watch at our one and only McDonald's. With no thinking about work!

We were to create our map from scratch, drawing major avenues and streets, rivers, lakes, and so on.

And then we were to note anything and everything that we came across that we considered important ... schools, churches, bazaars, hospitals, railroad and bus stations, parks., neighborhoods.

*Prof. Kot and I having fun at the blackboard. He supervised me during my training at Tech U.*

A nice idea, but who had the time to do this? Each of us had been given a detailed map of the city. A fine map in full color published commercially in Kyiv, for sale in book stores. A beauty. Why go to all this effort when it was already done for us? It would have been smarter to give us a test on our understanding of this map.

Also, each cluster had to do a community project as well. What should that be? Anything that would help the community! I suggested a Peace Corps Night at the Pedagogical University where we were involved.

Students and faculty saw us roaming through its halls. Were curious about us. Were told we were Peace Corps Volunteers but knew nothing about Peace Corps. A Peace Corps Night would fascinate many.

Everybody would be welcome. We'd show an interesting video about Peace Corps, answer questions, talk about what our 300 Volunteers did in Ukraine, introduce ourselves, hand out literature, and serve nice refreshments and soft drinks. It would be a true public service. And it would be good publicity for Peace Corps. It would be easy to do. It got nixed.

So finally we decided we'd produce a Friday evening show. Our guests would be fifth-year English students—in other words, the most advanced. We called it "The first American-style Open Microphone Coffee House." That took a lot of explaining, but we got it done.

We would be the talent. We'd serve refreshments. It would benefit the needy...an orphanage, say. There would be a small admission fee—a toy for an orphan. This idea got a lot of excitement. Each of us got special assignments in preparation for it.

One for me was to design a poster advertising it. Another for me was to find an orphanage to which we could turn over the proceeds of this modest effort.

In the show itself, I had to be part of the talent. What could I do? I can't sing. Can't dance. Can't do somersaults. My friends decided for me.

My friends concocted a funny little skit involving the five of us singing and acting. Each of us would have a title role. The skit called for a mouse. A tiny, endearing mouse. The mouse would stick its head up at one point and act cute, then at another point, then at another.

I wanted to be a good sport and said, "Yes. Of course I'll be the mouse." No chance to rehearse. We did it cold. We got a lot of applause. I was hailed as a most cute and lovable mouse. Everybody had a good time. I had a swell time.

**O**h, about the orphanage. How to locate an orphanage? No Yellow Pages in Chernihiv. I gave it a lot of thought. So simple, it turned out. I went to the library and asked a librarian. She made phone calls and chose an orphanage. It took all of 20 minutes. No wonder I love librarians.

Two days later, Mandy and Amy took a bus to the orphanage and presented our bagful of toys. They reported to us that it was a nice place and the director had been appreciative.

The two facets of our Training—Russian Language and Technical Training—ended at the same time. What a relief. Both had helped us a lot, some of us more than others, as usual. Peace Corps had been earnest about it all and had put a lot of thought and energy into it. Our facilitators had put everything they had into it. No doubt about that.

All of us (well, I think all) recognized that everybody involved had to be applauded for their enthusiasm and good intentions and sincere efforts. But what's perfect, right? I for one had minor complaints. No major ones. I was grateful to Peace Corps for being so generous about my Russian. Had not sent me home!

I was ready to take the oath as a Volunteer. I would do so with pride. And I would do my utmost to be a good Volunteer.

~ ~ ~

***Did you know*...** that Peace Corps has a rule perhaps unique in our federal government? The rule is that all its executives are limited to five years of service. It's called "Five and out!"

It dates back to the very start. The rationale was that it would continually infuse Peace Corps with fresh blood. Enthusiasm can peter out after a few years. Some consider it a bad rule. Makes it hard to develop expertise. The fifth year often is spent in looking for a new job.

# 10 / Where will I be posted?

*Suspense. Then surprise: right here! I'm upset when I hear that. Then delighted.*

Yes, I'd be working in the very city where I had just finished training! I admit that at first I was disappointed. All my fellow Trainees were headed for towns and small cities across the country. So exciting. Then I thought, *I'll bet Peace Corps is keeping me here as a concession to my age.* That bothered me. I didn't want any favors.

But then: *How lucky I am to be staying right here! I know my way around.* I know lots of people. I'm familiar with the places where I'll be working. This is a very nice city—and just the right size. It's wonderful!

When word about my assignment got out, I found out that some Volunteers assigned to isolated villages envied me. They had to rough it with cold running water and backyard privies!

After all, consider some key facts about Chernihiv. Population: 300,000. That's a lot bigger than Hartford, the capital of my Connecticut, and that's one of the largest cities in New England. Yet surprisingly Ukrainians consider Chernihiv a small city,

Chernihiv was an attractive city. The beautiful Desna River flowed right through it. Well laid out. Beautiful avenues. Parks. Trees on nearly every street. Big enough to give me everything I wanted, small enough to get around.

Not one, but four large outdoor bazaars. Even a modern shopping center downtown and some big American-style specialty stores—for computers and electronics, household supplies, clothes and shoes, other things. Bookstores. Restaurants of many kinds, movie theatres, a fine symphony orchestra where already I was a regular. So important to me, the wonderful Korolonko Public Library.

Four universities and numerous institutes. Banks, hospitals, services of many kinds. A handsome railroad station with connections to all points of the country and even beyond. Ditto, a big inter-city bus station. And nearby, dozens of picturesque villages.

And it was only two hours north of Kyiv by highway. It would be easy to get to Headquarters whenever I had to, and I could look forward to getting to the beautiful capital and its attractions now and then.

Consider—some Volunteers were assigned to the far corners of Ukraine. Some 24 hours away by train, even 40. How fortunate I was by comparison.

There was one big concern. Chernihiv was too close for comfort to Chernobyl, just 90 minutes or so away to the northwest. I've already told you about Chernobyl and its catastrophic nuclear accident. When friends in the U.S.A. heard that I was training in Chernobyl, they were concerned and told me so. Why? For people all over the world, Chernobyl has become the most famous place in Ukraine—far more than even Kyiv. "Famous" is the wrong word. "Notorious" is better. Chernobyl was a small city that had a big nuclear power operation—one of many in Ukraine. At that time it was a Soviet republic.

One of its reactors suffered a terrifying melt-down. Catastrophic loss of life. Thousands. Many hundreds of square miles of the vast area were made uninhabitable. Its wildlife blighted with radiation. And its fields and forests and streams ruined for all practical use...agriculture, fishing, habitation, tourism, everything. Chernobyl became a ghost town.

And the tragedy was not over. Scientists say that for centuries the area will be contaminated with radiation. Generations of people and wildlife will be affected.

Of course, when I heard I would be training so close, I did plenty of worrying. I admit that, too. After all, right after the accident, the news media had broadcast awful Chernobyl's dangers all over the world

*"I'm not going anywhere near Chernobyl!"* I said to myself. But Peace Corps had assured us that Chernobyl posed no danger. I took Peace Corps at its word.

Many scientists had studied the situation and proclaimed there was no problem. For one thing, the wind had blown the radiation in the opposite direction from Chernihiv. Many tests had shown Chernihiv safe. I took Peace Corps' word.

During all my time in Ukraine I never visited Chernobyl. I could have. But I had seen many photos of the ruined reactor building and the stark desolation. I had read about it and kept seeing it in the news. One of my students gave me a book about it, with graphic pictures. That was enough. Some Kyiv tourist agencies ran trips to Chernobyl. I had zero interest

But it was much on my mind during my first weeks in Chernihiv. When I began riding public transit in the city, I noticed people with growths on their faces, small and big. "*Chernobyl!*" I said to myself. I believe I was correct. Even more so when I learned Chernihiv had a hospital just to care for people suffering from radiation. Including many infants.

The more I learned about Chernihiv, the more I appreciated it. It was famous for its long history. It had a monastery a thousand years old! It was settled even before that. It became the second most important city in Ukraine but it had been eclipsed by three or four others. Still it was known far and wide.

The early settlers located there because it had a bluff overlooking the Desna River. The bluff provided great protection—enemies would come by the river. The natives built fortifications, of course. Today that strategic point up there is a beautiful park but ancient cannons still point down toward the river.

The Desna had commercial importance, well, until highways were built. Not totally true; it still had importance. Folks loved the beautiful river and flocked to its sandy beaches and cool waters in the summer. It attracted tourists. And fishermen, even now when they knew the fish were contaminated by Chernobyl.

Amazing how many men in the cold months chopped holes in its ice and sat there dangling line and hook. What surprised me even more, how many folks love a dip in the frigid waters.

Once my fellow Trainees got spread out on assignment all over the country, I'd get an e-mail back now and then that would say, "John, how lucky you are to be in Chernihiv!" Very true. I got to realize that. Not unusual for them to return for a visit. To see their host family, of course. But also because Chernihiv was such a nice city.

There was not the hassle and expense of living in the country's half a dozen large cities. Nor the heavy traffic and congestion. For one thing, cars were expensive. Few families had one, but more and more were achieving that dream. I never saw a traffic jam.

People walked here and there as an everyday thing or took public transit. That's the way I got around. I might take a taxi in a heavy rain. Walking turned out to be very good for me.

A prime reason it was so attractive and modern is that it was re-built after the massive destruction by the Germans in World War II. So much got destroyed that massive re-building was necessary. The re-building had to be rushed because of the thousands desperate for housing.

Still, the careful planning was obvious Where the broad avenues should be located. How the railroad should be laid out. Where the apartment complexes should be built. How stores were sited to serve the people in the big blocks. Where factories should be located, and schools and hospitals also.

The infrastructure was good. All the houses and apartment blocks had electricity, indoor running water (though we Volunteers were ordered to drink only bottled water or boiled), flush toilets, and central heat and hot water supplied by the city. Telephones were common, and thousands had cell phones. Amazing.

It was a civilized place. I was impressed, believe me, when I learned that Chernihiv, like the rest of Ukraine, had one of the highest literacy rates in the world, as high as ours in the U.S.A., with many books published every year, newspapers, magazines, cable TV with many channels.

The main library, called the Korolonko, boasted more than a million volumes, and it had neighborhood branches. I started going to the Korolonko for relaxation—I had no idea that I'd be working there.

Chernihiv had book stores and movie theatres and two drama theatre and a concert hall. A history museum, an art museum, and a military museum. I got to know all of them. A big soccer stadium with a team known all over the country. Restaurants aplenty. Even a McDonald's, and popular it was.

And the churches! So many of them. I emphasize them because they were so important in the post-Soviet life. For decades folks had been forced—yes, forced—to profess atheism but many never lost their Christianity. The great majority were Orthodox churches—there were three distinct branches—but there were others also. I knew of a Roman Catholic church and a synagogue.

When I got assigned to Ukraine, I thought there might be as many as a dozen universities in the country. How wrong I was. There were some 1,000 schools of higher education. Chernihiv itself had some eight universities and institutes. Institutes were specialized schools for law, economics and management, health care, music, sports and physical education. And there were vocational schools for the various trades.

Many of my students were quick to tell me all about their schools—all public schools. They were proud of them and I came to see why.

Numerous hospitals, of course, including specialized ones for maternity and coronary and child care—I mentioned the one for people with problems stemming from nuclear radiation.

Little by little I became familiar with the city's remarkable history and that of Ukraine. For centuries it was called "the Ukraine," meaning an area or district, albeit a huge one. Early in the last century, it was annexed into the developing U.S.S.R. and in fact became one of its key republics.

It was prized for its enormous agricultural output on vast farmlands that stretched beyond the horizon, and also its great industrial might, especially in the large cities in the east.

After independence in 1991, it became "Ukraine." A democracy under itself, and a free-enterprise one. A dramatic start to what so many hoped would be a bold and proud new chapter in the evolution of Eastern Eruope.

It seemed to have so much of what was needed for outstanding success. My city, Chernihiv, for instance, was a good example.

Chernihiv had important factories that gave it a high rank in the Soviet republics. It produced goods for all of them. Manufacturing remained an important activity and seemed poised for growth.

"Oh, Chernihiv is a small city!" I would hear that often from Ukrainians. It amazed me. Small with 300,000 people? Why did they feel that way?

I found out. They were talking of physical size rather than population. It's all because of the huge apartment buildings I've mentioned. I called them "Soviet blocks." They could accommodate hundreds of people in few acres. Chernihiv was dotted with such blocks. There were individual homes—I lived in one, as you know. But it was awesome to see the numerous big blocks.

Our American cities sprawl because once outside the center, we find so many people living in single-family houses with garages and lawns. They take up a lot of room.

I found these Soviet blocks in every city in the country. During my tour through seven countries on my vacation in my last summer, I saw them wherever I went. They exist all over what used to be the U.S.S.R.,,I believe.

I got to live in two blocks on opposite sides of city. They were typical and quite similar. See one and you've seen them all. Let me tell you about the second one. I lived in it for a year and a half.

There were six blocks in our development. Some had 5 floors, and some 9. Some developments had blocks of 14 floors. I never understood those odd numbers. Well, I thought 9 and 14 odd. Why not 10 and 15? Never found out.

They were all built of re-enforced concrete. They seemed to have been assembled from pre-formed panels. The same plan seemed universal in all the cities I traveled to. The buildings were plain boxes. Their flat roofs emphasized this.

Those with five floors were walk-ups. Those with 9 or 14 floors had tiny elevators that could carry just three or four people. Furniture was designed for the most part to fit in the elevators. If not, it had to be carried up and down the stairs. Many times I saw someone carrying a bicycle up or down. Or a baby carriage.

Zero attention was paid to beauty or attractiveness in putting up those buildings. "Economy" and "utilitarian" were the key words. Not a single kopeck was spent on ornamentation. The front door, for instance, was just a sheet of steel. It reminded me of a back door in an American factory or warehouse. The stairs were grim concrete. Dark and dingy very often.

I thought the buildings ugly and still felt that way when I left. The apartments were tiny by our standards, but comfortable. A basic one consisted of a living room, a single bedroom, a tiny kitchen, and a hallway. The hallway had a bathroom—with a tub and a sink—and a toilet room, so small that it was hard to turn around in it. To wash your hands, you had to go to the bathroom next door. That's where the sink was, also a bathtub with a shower.

Each apartment had a balcony with sliding windows. Not intended for sitting in the sun and the fresh air, mind you. This is where you hung your laundry to dry. This is where you stored produce. Or your bicycle and baby carriage and all your extra stuff.

A big apartment would have two bedrooms. I saw one once with three bedrooms. It was a rarity. When I thought about it, I realized that this smallness was one reason why most families had only one or two children. Very difficult to accommodate more, especially once the children started school. And most university students lived at home, going to the local university the way our American kids go to high school.

Interesting the way young married couples invariably started married life by living with the bride's family, but sometimes the bridegroom's. That continued after the first child, sometimes longer. Apartments were very expensive to buy and rent.

A universal practice was to use the living room as a bedroom also. Couches and sofas were designed to convert into beds.

The water was supplied to all of them from a central source, by the city and also the hot water that supplied big cast-iron radiators. The hot water was turned on for everybody on the same day in the fall throughout the city, and turned off on the same day in the spring.

Before and after those dates, it might get quite cold. This was why Peace Corps supplied Volunteers with small, plug-in electric heaters (we had to pay our host families for the extra electricity).

Originally all the buildings and all the apartments were owned by the city (Communism!). Now more and more apartments were owned by the families in them. They paid for water, electricity, and heat. This was the case at the two apartments I got to live in.

The owners paid these bills at the post office. When I first went to the post office, it was to mail something, naturally. Always long lines of people, which surprised me. But not all there to buy stamps or pick up mail. How strange. I quickly found out they were paying for other services rendered. These utility services, for one thing. There were branch post offices all over the city for convenience.

I said a lot of attention was paid to urban planning. Consider the second development of blocks that I lived in. It had eight buildings. All were set differently on the site with an eye to both economy and efficiency. All were cookie-cutter buildings. All were set off from the next with large lawns. It was a priority to plant trees. Always trees. I loved that. And there was a large central lawn.

This common area would always include a playground. There would be a sand box and swings and a seesaw. What always caught my eye was the way the playground was set apart.

Somebody somewhere got the idea of planting old tires standing up in the ground about one-fifth deep, one next to the other, as a boundary. Each tire would be painted red or blue or green or purple, some in multicolors. Quite clever, and attractive once I got used to them. Whoever got this brainstorm got to see the idea picked up all over the country.

There would be an area for pick-up soccer. Kids could roller-skate or bike on the black-topped paths connecting the buildings. Over time people would short-cut across the lawns, and these would become established paths. Oh, they weren't really lawns. The grass would just grow and grow. Once in a while a man would appear with a weed-whacker and get to work.

There would be an area of clothes lines for anyone to use. You had to carry your laundry downstairs and upstairs, of course. There would always be a rug-beater stand. This would be two steel poles with a horizontal bar between them at the top. You would lug down a big carpet, say, spread it over the bar, and whack away at it with your steel beater. Its working end was a big steel pretzel, so to speak.

This was considered women's work, but now and then I would see a husband going at it. The two families I lived with in the blocks had vacuum cleaners, which was unusual.

On nice days, mothers and grandmothers would come outside to supervise the children and get fresh air. They would sit in pleasant groups in the sun and chat. I was always glad to see that.

And there would always be a table with a little roof for protection from the sun and the rain, and a couple of trees close by. This was usually reserved for men. They would sit and play cards and dominoes, but usually chess. Very popular. Often many kibitzers.

Each building had a tiny garden in the front for bushes and flowering plants. And each had a bench by the front door. Men and women would sit there and socialize, often with a cigarette and a bottle of beer in hand. Sometimes even in the winter, which always surprised me. I found out many people loved winter. Not I, though I admired their attitude.

And there would always be a parking area. But in my development—with maybe more than 200 apartments—the parking lot would be large enough for only a dozen cars. More and more cars now. Some cars would park on the lawns. There will be more and more cars, of course. It will be interesting to see how these will be squeezed in.

There were nice traditions. On a Saturday in the fall, sometimes two Saturdays, neighbors would come out and rake up the litter (always big piles of it) and carry it away. And on a Saturday in the spring, they would come out to rake the sand in the children's sandboxes, re-paint the tires around the play areas and the fences in the front of their buildings, and neaten everything up. This was a left-over of "community days" in Soviet times. A wonderful idea, I thought. I observed it several times. But just a few would turn out and nearly always mostly women.

New blocks were much more attractive. Some were handsome, even beautiful. But the basic idea was still to pack in as many people as possible.

During my 27 months, I became familiar with the sections of the city that were part of my life—the neighborhoods where I lived and where I taught and the downtown. But there were many sections that I never got to. No reason to go to them.

Besides, not that easy on public transportation. I have owned an auto all my adult life, and I've always appreciated it. Living in Chernihiv emphasized how wonderful owning one is. To my surprise, it also taught me I could get by happily without.

I got to like Chernihiv. I felt it was just right for me. I felt comfortable. I lacked very little. I enjoyed its beauty. When I visited other cities, invariably I returned impressed by things and features that I had seen, but always glad to be back in Chernihiv. I began to think of it as "my" city!

Even in my short time I saw interesting changes—numerous new buildings going up, for one thing. Quite attractive. Then came the national financial crisis (concurrent with ours in the U.S.A., and that was not accidental), and I saw nearly all these construction jobs stop dead.

I saw many people laid off with little notice, if any. Meager back-up resources. The crisis was still intense when I left for home. Very sad. I would love to hear of a vigorous upturn.

Now some words about the people. I got to see them close up, of course. I have learned that most people in the world are much alike. Are interested in the same things and have the same priorities. Family. Health. Safety and security. Good jobs and income. Education. Advancement. A good social life and recreation.

And the same concerns. Earning enough to make possible some extras. Giving their children the best start possible. Having interesting and secure employment with future opportunities. Being able to live without fear of being conscripted into an army. Having time for leisure and vacations. Saving for a good retirement. The differences are in the details.

Now I caution you: the statements that I make below are generalities. There are exceptions, as in every society.

Ukrainians are intelligent and resourceful. Hard times have taught them how. They know how to work hard.

The family is tight-knit and fundamentally important, despite widespread divorce. Paradoxical, it seemed to me.

The women work harder than the men. They work as employees at jobs and then return home to begin Shift 2 as homemakers. Both men and women retire in due time (earlier than we do) but women never really retire. As grandmothers they take on a new role: to care for their grandchildren while their mother continues her dual role as a salary earner and housewife.

Couples get married very young, and have children very young, and increasingly have fewer children, just one or two. Birth control is easier than ever—condoms and pills are available everywhere—and, from what I have heard, abortions are common.

We have a high divorce rate in the U.S.A. but I believe it is higher in Ukraine. It is surprising how many families have no father in the house, no husband. It was true of all three families that I lived with.

In Soviet days, Communism gave people a bigger safety net. Everybody had a job and nobody worried about unemployment (though sometimes locked into terrible jobs with no chance of anything better.) Everybody had a place to live and keep warm in the winter. Everybody got a pension. There was free education, right up through university for those judged capable of it, and free medical care. But the quality of these social services could be disappointing.

However, there were few freedoms. You were afraid to express your real opinions. You had to follow and preach the party line to get ahead. You had limited choices in elections—sometimes a single slate of candidates. Everything you read or heard on radio or saw on TV was carefully controlled. You were taught that there is no God and your churches were locked or turned into museums. You waited in line for just about everything—to buy food, to pay bills, to see a doctor, to get a larger apartment. And the choices often were nil or extremely limited. You wore the same tired clothes day after day. Sometimes you could never leave your city.

This fledgling democracy of Ukraine, born in 1991, has had tough sledding. It's been difficult to give up the old ways and feel comfortable in a new environment of fierce competition and free enterprise.

I saw that many people associated government leaders with corruption and particularly bribe-taking. "You elect somebody and in a year or two you find out they are rich!" Many people were afraid of the future.

"You go to the university and study hard and then you have to work as a *marshrutka* driver to get by!"

Some people still thought Communism was the better system and pined for the good old days. "Everybody had a job. Maybe it was a lousy job but it was a steady job."

In many societies there seem to be a few more females than males. In Ukraine the split was bigger, because of men killed at war, I was told. I noticed intense competition for a man. I saw this in the dramatically different ways that young women and men dressed.

The young women—so very many were so beautiful—dressed so fashionably and so skimpily. I was amazed how they flaunted their femininity. Their "sexiness" is a better word.

On summer days they would strut the downtown streets in their meticulous hairdos and makeup, their high heels, their mini skirts or skin-tight shorts, their bare bellybuttons, their proud barely-covered breasts, their jewelry, and their fashionable boots and enormous designer handbags.

And their cell phones! Cell phones were a must, although I was told that some young people didn't have the money to keep them charged. I wondered how they could afford all this stuff.

The young men were the opposite. They went around in what I considered the national young guy's drab uniform: black or dark dungarees, un-ironed T-shirt, sneakers or scuffed shoes. Too often with a cigarette in hand and even a beer.

With so many desirable and desperate young women available, Ukraine has developed a huge marriage-agency industry. Men all over the world go online to peer at and hopefully meet Ukrainian dream girls.

Some fly over expressly to meet one. Some of my expat friends went to Ukraine for this reason and succeeded in finding one. It was easy.

Ukraine has developed a big sex trade. It is fueled by two realities: one is that it is hard for young women to get jobs that will give them a decent week's pay. The other is that they have dreams of their own—to find a good man who will support them well, and who may even take them to one of the glamorous and always touted countries—the U.S.A., Canada, Australia and New Zealand, or the better countries of western Europe, even Poland right next door. I heard of numerous folks emigrating to Poland.

I would read about these aspects weekly in the Kyiv Post. It was a bold and forthright newspaper. All in English. Every issue would headline articles about problems in the society. Widespread corruption at every level. The financial crisis. Political in-fighting. Unemployment. Alcoholism and drug abuse. The sex business.

I would be amazed by the newspaper's daring and bravery. It would name names and cite bribes and give details of scandals. What impressed me was that its articles seemed backed up by solid research and reportage. They were true exposés.

No surprise that journalists have had a hard time. The free world knows about one Ukrainian journalist who was highly critical of high officials. He was found decapitated. His murderers were suspected but were never brought to trial while I was there. Numerous journalists have disappeared. I would be afraid to be a writer on the Post!

Here is one glimpse at the sex business. A friend who operated a retail business told me a story. I'll call him Rudolph. A woman customer of his, quite respectable, asked him one day whether he would be an agent for her.

It turned out she was a madam and wanted him to find customers for her girls. She told him prostitution was a legitimate business like any other. Her girls were offering a desirable and important service. Nothing wrong with it. Her gals did it not because they were naughty. They were good women. They needed the money, some for their families.

He turned her down. But he told me, "I understand her point of view. I know that the need for money is what leads many women into that work. Well, most of them."

But Ukraine has paid an astronomical price for this rampant sexual looseness. It has one of the highest HIV/AIDS rates outside Africa. My city of Chernihiv had one of the highest rates in the country. So I was told.

One day a young woman of high accomplishment that I knew well told me that she had just had a physical exam. It had included a routine

HIV test. No problem, she thought. Then a nurse had phoned her to come in to discuss the results. "I was in shock," she told me. "So scared." She went with the greatest apprehension. A false alarm, it turned out. Whew! Her story surprised me because I thought she was sexually innocent. It opened my eyes to how widespread her behavior must be.

This was one of our constant focuses in Peace Corps—to inform people about HIV/AIDS, to caution them, tell them how to prevent it and what to do about it if they came down with it. I was an English teacher, and I rarely lost an opportunity to bring it up. I felt that students were bored hearing about it. Yet so many people got the disease because of their indifference and negligence.

I was lucky in an important way. By the nature of my work as a teacher, I met and worked and associated with good people. They were the students and young career people that I taught at school and attracted to the two clubs I started (more about this later). And the people who were my fellow teachers. And the librarians and clerks at the Korolonko. And the families that I lived with and their friends that I got to know. And the Ukrainians who worked for Peace Corps.

I got to see many things and gather many impressions in my daily comings and goings.

A grave problem was alcoholism. Alcohol was part of the culture. No big dinner—in some homes, no dinner—was eaten without vodka. Other hard booze and wine were popular. Everybody drank beer, some people for breakfast or lunch. In the summer, beautiful tents in bright red and blue went up on every spare lot.

They were beer tents, erected just to sell beer and snacks. Men and teen-age boys gathered to drink and smoke, play cards and dominoes, and pass the time. And drink. I noticed women but they were rare. It was legal to drink beer on the streets openly—no bag required as it is in some of our communities in the U.S.A. I saw boys drinking quart-size bottles of beer after school.

In my supermarket, the booze section was as big as or bigger than any other, whether meat, produce, bakery, or sweets. It was surprising how cheap vodka was, well, to my American eyes. Just $3 or so for a liter bottle. It seemed an essential part of many a dinner. Men would hold up a glass of it, offer a toast (always a toast!), then take pride in gulping it in one big swallow. I got to see three or four men finish a liter in one meal.

Beer was considered a soft drink, so to speak. Anyone could drink it, even teen-agers, and openly. You could buy it from vending machines, like Coke. And their bottles seemed bigger than ours.

I got to see stumbling drunks on the streets, some unconscious on the pavement. Yes, numerous times.

Consider this daily sight. My language school was right next to the Polytechnic University, which had a large plaza out front with benches. The students gathered there after school to chat. Even in winter. Very nice. But it seemed mandatory to have a beer in hand. It's was pack psychology. Young women joined in.

I got to see that some people didn't drink just to enjoy a drink. They drank to get drunk. One day I noticed a young man sprawled face up on the lawn next to a foot path that I took every day. In mid-day, mind you. About 20. His arms were flung straight out sideways. What to do?

I bent and shook his hand. No response. I thought he was dead. I did. Then I noticed he was breathing, but barely. I could smell the alcohol.

Nobody else around. No idea who to call. Anyway, my Russian was too poor to explain to anybody. Reluctantly I got up and walked on. I hoped the next person coming along would be able to help him.

Vodka seemed the national beverage. I would watch people drinking it. To me it seemed a nasty drink. They would fill a big shot glass and down it in one swallow. That was expected. Some would shudder—fellow drinkers would laugh. The drinkers would follow the vodka with a gulp of orange juice or cola and a bite of bread. If you were a macho man, you would prove it by drinking the whole bottle of vodka. Or fall over trying to.

Corruption was another problem. It was another recurring topic in the Kyiv Post. Corruption was a fact of life on every level, from high elected officials right down to traffic cops. I was told reliably that nobody could conduct a business without considering bribes a routine operating cost. That's just the way it was.

I saw another problem. Rampant gambling. Casinos dotted the city. Four months before I left, the government ordered a shut-down. Yes, it closed every casino in the country. What a public outcry! It put thousands out of work and incensed many gamblers. When I left, the ban was still on.

Another was littering. I found it nearly as bad as in Mexico, where on several trips I found the littering shocking. I found it awful in Ukraine. Have an empty cigarette pack? Empty bottle? Just toss it. The city of Chernihiv made an effort to clean up. I saw squads of workers—always women—sweeping the main streets.

But in other areas, the littering was ignored. Benches in the beautiful park downtown were always surrounded with bottles and cigarette packs and butts. And hundreds of beer bottle caps. Disgusting.

I found another thing offensive. Bubble gum! I would see globs everywhere, on the sidewalks and in many buildings. In the two apartment blocks that I lived in, every step all the way up was dotted with dried globs.

Mind you, I found Ukrainians who found these behaviors as appalling as I did. And who did their best to correct them. And yes, we have these same problems in the U.S. But less so.

How do you change such a culture? Well, we had widespread littering much like Ukraine's years ago. I remember that. I give credit to Lady Bird Johnson, wife of President Lyndon Johnson. Back in the 70's, while in the White House, she started a big campaign. "Keep America beautiful! Let's not litter. Let's clean up! It's our country."

I used to litter. I listened. I stopped. Many listened. It turned the situation around. It has been dramatic. Our country is much cleaner now. Ukraine needs a Lady Bird Johnson.

One peculiarity was how cool and detached people were to strangers. On the streets, nobody would make eye contact. That's normal on a busy street. But two strangers—two men, say—approaching one another all alone on a long sidewalk would pass with zero recognition. A fixed visage with eyes aside was normal.

I can't pass that way. Yet once two strangers got introduced, smiles and hellos and handshakes. Wonderful graciousness. Instant friendship.

I brought this up with friends, including Ukrainians. I'd get the same explanation. Over the centuries Ukrainians have suffered through so much warring and exploitation and brutality that they must be wary. Caution has become inbred. Could be so.

I must say that once I broke through, I found Ukrainians to be warm, solicitous, and even generous. I could give you many names and instances. You'll read about some in the chapters coming up.

I came home to the U.S. with many new friends in Ukraine. I felt so lucky to have them as my friends. I want to say to them: "Dear friends, I know I may have offended you by my remarks. Sorry. I'm a journalist. The truth as I see it has to be the truth when I write about it. But you may find this illuminating and helpful.

"If you come to the U.S., you will find some things to complain about, too. We're not Paradise. My complaints are dwarfed by the admirable things I saw in your country."

The thing to remember is that Ukraine is a new country and a new democracy. And just a teen-ager at it. It's struggling to improve. What intelligent citizen would not want a better country and better ways? Our working there as Volunteers was one effort to make things better. I tried to do my bit.

~ ~ ~

# 11 / I take the oath

*What a memorable ceremony. Then, we rush to our posts. For me, it's back to Chernihiv!*

Finally December 19th arrived—our long-awaited Swearing-In Day in Kyiv! The end of Training and the beginning of our Service! We'd take our oath as Volunteers and immediately head to our assignments for our 24 months in Ukraine. Imagine our excitement!

The day before, we were bused to Dyebeck near Kyiv—where we had attended orientation right after arriving from the U.S.A. We had everything we owned with us. Suitcases, backpacks, computers, guitars, Ukraine tour books, the works. Three inches of snow on the ground there, and we trudged through it up the long walk to the front door.

This time we were here at Dyebeck to be prepped for the big ceremony. There would be more talks and discussions.

My young cluster mate Amy was behind me, bent over under her huge backpack. I grabbed one end of it with her and helped her up to the front door. "Thank you, John!" she said. "You shouldn't be doing this." I admit I was breathing a bit hard.

All the important officials from Headquarters were there. One after another told us to look good for Swearing In. They handed out half a dozen steam irons and said, "Do a good job!"

So many gals were in line ahead of me for one that I had to go back to my room empty-handed. Somehow I managed to look half decent.

Again Dyebeck was cold! Again Peace Corps had supplemental heaters for us. Very thoughtful. And I managed to snag an extra blanket. Was this the way it would be all winter in Ukraine? I worried about it.

December 19 morning turned out terribly gray—no fresh snow, thank goodness—but our spirits were anything but. We were in high spirits. Yes, excited, and very proud.

We were a jolly bunch—and a well-groomed one, too—when we clambered onto our chartered buses and rode into the capital. More than one Peace Corps official gave us a double look. Their smiles told us they approved. I gawked all the way—an impressive city, Kyiv.

We were let off at an elegant building with classic columns and a big dome—Teachers' House, our invitation called it. It was the old Parliament, someone said. We admired the lobby and entered an ornate chamber—lots of gold paint and filigree. It had tiered seats. We'd all have a perfect view right in front of the stage! The audience seated behind us, too.

Of course, we were looking one another over. We had never seen one another all dressed up. The gals were beautiful. And we guys looked spiffy.

We were quite a crowd and more were arriving, dignitaries and guests. One thing I liked is that the chamber was just the right size. There wouldn't be many empty seats. I noticed a distinguished man nearby. Just a few years younger than yours truly. A pin on his lapel caught my eye.

"Hello, sir," I said and extended my hand. He took it. I introduced myself. He was Hugo Schmidt, the husband of our Diana. A retired dentist. As a Volunteer with her, he had the assignment of teaching native dentists how to improve their practice, or so I heard. I did not know whether he still had a Peace Corps role of any kind.

"**W**hat is that beautiful pin?" I said, pointing to his lapel.

"Why, that's the Peace Corps pin." He lifted his lapel to give me a better look.

I had never seen the pin. Impressive! Right away I recognized the circular Peace Corps logo proud in its red, white, and blue.

I saw two tiny flags criss-crossed over the logo, which represents the globe, I believe.

One was our Stars and Stripes. The other was the blue and yellow Ukrainian flag—blue for sky and yellow for golden fields. The two flags

We had high spirits at Dyebeck—Swearing In the next day! I hated the snow—have shoveled too much of it. But Evonne (left) and Amy enjoyed it.

crossed that way symbolized the partnership of our two countries, of course. In a small way, I felt I had a role in this developing partnership.

"Beautiful," I said. "Will we get one as part of this ceremony?"

He shook his head. "No, you'll have to buy one if you want one!"

That surprised me. I was disappointed. "Well, I want one." I felt that receiving that pin should be part of this ceremony, and I told him so.

"I agree," he said, "but today it isn't." He told me how to get one eventually. A few more pleasant words and I headed for my seat.

Then I spotted Olena, beaming so happily and beautiful in a stylish get-up. I had met her a few days earlier and she would become a big part of my life every week from Monday to Friday. I soon found that I would never ever see her un-stylish. She had gotten here on her own, to be with me.

I haven't told you about her. It's a pleasure for me now. Olena Pavlovska was the dean at *Coursi*, the language school in Chernihiv that I would teach at. She was here for the best of reasons. She would be my official Ukrainian Counterpart—notice the capital C. Every Volunteer had one. The Counterparts were selected for us by Peace Corps.

She would be my mentor and "spiritual advisor" and friend, I hoped. Counterparts were men and women at whatever institution we were assigned to.

They were selected to smooth our way and cheer us on and help us throughout our service. I knew by now that Olena was a dynamic, exuberant lady. In my case, she was also my boss, and it wasn't long before I found she had a mind of her own, believe me.

Peace Corps had invited all our Counterparts to attend. And here she was, a gorgeous long-stemmed rose in her hand and eager to present it to me and give me a hug. All the lady sponsors held one, compliments of Peace Corps. She looked lovely. She always did, I found out.

**N**ow we took our places of honor down in the front seats. We faced a big stage. Olena sat at my side. It is surprising how many people were attending. I speculated who they were. Maybe government officials, American and Ukrainian. Maybe people from the business community. But I recognized some key staffers from Headquarters who had worked with us and a couple of our doctors. The hall filled. This was really a big deal.

Several people took their places on the stage. Somebody flicked the lights and everybody quieted. We stood for our National Anthem. It had special significance today. We were not military. We were not government officials. We were just average Americans, ordinary in many ways.

But we were all present here because we had made the decision to serve our flag and help the people in this struggling country. I don't mean to get maudlin, but we had answered the call of President John F. Kennedy "to do something for our country."

Then we sat and the program got under way. Several people spoke. I was all ears, but as usual I missed some words. Some at the microphone had heavy accents. Every one of them spoke earnestly.

I paid special attention when our Country Director Diana stood. She was just Diana to all of us now—it was part of her style.

She offered us congratulations and good luck, of course, but also good advice. For me it had a ring of special value because she had been a Volunteer herself. She really knew the score. In fact, at a glance I thought she was the only one up on the stage who had been a Volunteer. But then I noticed Juan Carlos Campos, our second-in-command. He had been a Volunteer also, so I had been mistaken.

I looked forward again to hearing our Ambassador to Ukraine, William B. Taylor, Jr. As you know, he had made a big and good impression on me back in Dyebeck on our first day.

I was impressed by Teachers House. It gave our Swearing In the right tone. Very appropriate.

He had not been a Volunteer but had graduated as a cadet at West Point and then had worked his way up in the Army and then had switched from arms to diplomacy. A significant change. I wished I knew how that had come about. I knew from Dyebeck that he was a gifted speaker.

**H**is topic was much the same: it was noble of us to have made this big decision to serve our country:

We had trained hard and well and the time had arrived for us to go forth in the finest spirit of Peace Corps. We would have important work. It would be a challenge. Would we meet it?

We would perhaps find it difficult to find our way, but we had been chosen because we had the background and the potential. We were following in a proud tradition.

Each of us would be an ambassador in our own right. We should set a shining example—all eyes would be on us.

The Ukrainian Minister of Education was next. Sorry, I didn't catch his name. He was gray-haired and spoke dramatically. He spoke in Ukrainian and a beautiful woman translated as he went along. I understood nothing from his mouth, of course. Her fluency wowed me.

He offered us his country's thanks for our upcoming service, which he said would be service in a new country struggling with great needs but bent on democracy and progress. He thanked our country for this generous support at the important grass-roots level.

I knew now Ukraine had thousands of public schools, plus hundreds of institutions of higher learning. I mused that he must have his hands full.

Finally, the big moment. We were about to take our oath. In two minutes we would become Volunteers for two years. We were asked to stand, and our Counterparts were asked to stand at our side. Olena and I glanced at one another. She saw how happy I was. Again I saw that she was beaming.

Up on the stage a woman was reading our names from a list. One after the other—more than 80 of us. And each of us acknowledged our name by nodding. Everybody was listening in silence.

But when my name got mentioned, applause. Terrific applause. Because of my age as the oldest, I was sure, though it was not mentioned. I was stunned. There could be no other reason. I guess people could tell just by looking at me. This was not a good thought.

I had looked all around and I had realized I was undoubtedly the oldest in this whole auditorium. All this applause had made me blush wildly. No need for this attention.

Then, still standing, we were asked to raise our right hand. Ambassador Taylor led us in the oath, and we repeated, phrase by phrase. Let me tell you what I, and all my colleagues, swore to do:

"I, John Guy LaPlante, do solemnly swear that I will support and defend the Constitution of the United States of America against all enemies, foreign and domestic, and that I will bear true faith and allegiance to the same....

"That I take this obligation freely, without any mental reservation or purpose of evasion, and that I will well and faithfully discharge my duties in the Peace Corps of the United States of America, serving Ukraine to the best of my abilities and demonstrating the respect and consideration due its people. So help me God."

I had pondered the oath. I understood what it meant. And I took it seriously.

In mere seconds we passed from being Trainees to Volunteers! We were in! We had made it! I was jubilant. Remember, I had had nightmares I would not make it. I looked around.We were all jubilant.

But I had one unhappy twinge. One thing was missing. We were not military, did not have uniforms. We were not government officials—we wouldn't even be able to get into our American embassy nearby easily.

I felt Peace Corps should have presented us something symbolic but tangible and memorable as part of this Swearing In. To make us feel proud. And remind us and show everybody we were Volunteers.

A Peace Corps pin! One like Dr. Schmidt's. And having it pinned on with ceremony should have been a part of this ceremony. Peace Cops should have sent photos of us being pinned to our hometown newspapers. It would have been terrific PR.

Incidentally, I did buy one as soon as I could. In fact, three. I wanted one for each of my jackets. I did not wear a pin every day. Only on special occasions. But I wore it with pride. When I met a new group of students. Or at important sessions of my English Club. And always when I was interviewed by a journalist.

This happened a number of times by print and TV journalists. If they had a camera with them, I'd always point to my pin for any picture-taking.

The price of a pin, it turned out, was trivial—just $4. Peace Corps said it had no budget for them. Ridiculous when you consider the multi millions of dollars Uncle Sam was pouring into Peace Corps every year.

I considered this idea so important and relevant that I decided that I would bring it up on the right occasion. The day did come.

After the Swearing In, a gala reception. We congratulated one another, of course. High Fives all around! Wished one another well—we would be splitting up. Within minutes!

We were surrounded by hundreds of people—officials of both countries, Headquarters staff, Ukrainian friends from our Training, who knows who else. All crowding around, all eager to reach the endless line of tables with goodies and drinks of many kinds.

I knew very few of them. True for all us Volunteers. But all this fervor and excitement and attention felt so good. This really was a unique day.

*I was proud finally to get my Peace Corps pin. But I was upset. I had to buy it!*

The long tables were covered with a vast buffet. So many plates of fancy foods. But most amazing was the assortment of chocolates. So many boxes of gorgeous chocolates were open and spread out for us. Dozens of them, all open. Incredible. Only one conclusion.   Somebody high up in our Headquarters surely was a chocoholic.

I realized the Peace Corps purchasing manager must be a chocoholic. I was beginning to see what a huge sweet tooth Ukraine has. And a thought—the cost of all these chocolates could easily have paid for pins for all of us, with plenty of chocolates still left over for us.

As I said, this day was important for one more reason. Each of us would be heading to our individual assignment—one in a city or town where most likely we'd be working alone. Yes, with no other Volunteer around.

This had been a huge surprise. And to me a disappointment. I did not want to be alone! How nice to have a couple of Volunteers to get to see

To travel to our assignments, some of us would be facing enormous train rides. Some 19 hours long, even 24. Some with transfers to another train. Certainly overnight for many. But I was going back to Chernihiv, just two hours away. How lucky I was. I knew many envied me enormously.

Some of us had to leave within minutes to catch their trains. In fact, some had had to skip the buffet! They had to make their way to the mammoth and thronged railroad station by bus or trolley or Metro with all their suitcases and stuff. Not easy. Scary. And find the right train among the many pulling in every few minutes. Missing a train would be awful.

A sadness welled up in me. We were parting! It might be weeks or months before we saw one another again. Maybe not at all until the end of our service. A sad thought.

True, I knew only a scant few of my buddies by name, but still we were fellow Volunteers in Group 33! We had become bonded. We were glued together by this esprit de corps in Peace Corps.

Now, another surprise. What a good one. Suddenly Olena and I had it made. A Peace Corps chauffeur was driving back empty to Headquarters and had noticed the two of us. He told us to hop in—he'd leave us off at a convenient Metro stop.

How nice. We didn't have to find our way in the tangle of buses and trolleys and *marshrutkas*. He also invited a young Volunteer nearby. I'll call her Arlene. This was good luck for her, too. She was assigned to a town far to the east. An enormous train ride. Alone! She had loads of luggage.

The three of us crowded into the back seat. Arlene between us. But! Arlene began weeping. I was startled. So was Olena. What was the matter? Arlene dabbed her eyes. "Oh, Oh! I don't have enough money!" More tears.

"What!" I took her hand.

"I'm so worried. What Peace Corps gave me will not be enough to get settled." More sobbing.

What to do? I took out a $20 bill and put it in her hand. Yes, an American $20. That was a lot more in Ukraine than in the U.S.A.

"Oh, John!" she blurted and looked at me in amazement. She fingered the $20 bill. Was silent a minute. "No, John," she said. "I am sorry, but no. Thank you very much. I cannot accept this." She shoved it back. I was nonplused. But she had her mind made up. She dried her eyes.

The driver left the three of us off at the Metro station. What a good guy. Arlene strapped on her big backpack. She had stopped weeping. Hefted her other things. Looked resolute. "Goodbye, John," she said. "Good luck to you!" And headed toward the swinging door.

"Good luck, Arlene! I'm sure you'll do fine." I managed to say it just before she disappeared in the shoving crowd. Olena echoed me.

Olena and I were less rushed. We picked up our few things—all I had was an overnight bag—and entered the Metro. We would be taking a different train than Arlene. It was jammed as always. But two young people gave up their seats for us. It was a long ride, as usual. We got to board a *marshrutka*. Again, crowded. In two hours we would be back in Chernihiv.

Olena and I talked a little. We were tired. By now I knew that a *marshrutka* ride was never pleasant. We both sank into our own thoughts. I had a new one.

This was December 20. Tomorrow would be the first day of winter. It had already been dark outside for more than an hour and it was barely 4 p.m. I dreaded what I was sure would be a cold, tough winter. I had come to hate winters in New England. No way could I escape this one. Chernihiv was farther north than my Connecticut!

And I was disappointed about not having been assigned to a university. Was worried about my difficulty with the Russian language. Wondered how things would work out with my new host family. Had concerns about doing a good job with the young people who would become my students.

Were these worried thoughts bad omens? Time would tell. Yes, I had a lot on my mind. But I was determined to do my best. At everything that came my way. And with everybody.

One thing was sure. Peace Corps had done its utmost to train us in every way. Now it was time for us to get started and show our stuff. Would I be up to it? The answer would reveal itself before long..

~ ~ ~

# 12 / My job at school

*I teach but only in a sense. The job shifts and changes. I'm happy. And unhappy.*

No, I was not at some university teaching as I had hoped to be when I arrived so enthusiastically in Ukraine. I was still in Chernihiv where I had trained and I was teaching at an evening language school, mind you. What a surprise. I had misgivings aplenty. For one thing, an evening school! I wouldn't get home till 10 p.m.!

But before long I came to appreciate my good fortune. *Coursi*—the school's nickname—was a serious, high-minded school with a good curriculum and faculty. And, I quickly got to see I had a good deal at *Coursi* and in Chernihiv.

Peace Corps indeed did its job and got me a teaching assignment in a Ukrainian university for my two years of service. I never learned its name or location. But it turned me down for being too old, which was 78 going on 79. True, 80 is quite old in Ukraine—men here have a shorter life span than we American men. And yes, I was the oldest by far of the nearly 300 of us in Ukraine.

To me, that rejection was blatant age discrimination. That is illegal back home. But it wasn't Peace Corps discriminating against me. It was that university. Such discrimination apparently was okay in Ukraine.

I was crestfallen. I had planned on going off on a teaching adventure like all my friends. I felt bitter.

But I had to admit that if I were the dean of a university, I would have my doubts if I happened to review the résumé of a teaching applicant who was nearly 80. However, if Peace Corps had told me that candidate was worthy and capable, I would have given such a recommendation great weight. I certainly would have invited the old-timer to come in for an interview. I would have looked at him and listened to him and then passed judgment. That university did not do any of this. Shame on it!

But I admire Peace Corps for what they did next. They beat the bushes to find me a suitable and fulfilling job. And succeeded. They told me that I would be a teacher at a Ukrainian Government language school, and it would be university-level teaching.

I would be teaching English, of course. And also French, it turned out. Talk about a surprise! I'll explain about the French in a minute.

As word got out, my friends sent comforting words back. I would get an e-mail saying, "John, you are so lucky to be teaching in a school where foreign languages are everything!"
Or, "John, I got to visit *Coursi*. It's a wonderful school."
Or, "John, Chernihiv is the perfect-size city. It's got everything anybody would want. And it's beautiful."
I began to feel better. I did like Chernihiv. I was impressed by *Coursi*. And I got to like my work there. The work was interesting. I felt truly welcome and appreciated. Well, till things deteriorated.

I must tell you I got off to a slow start at the school. It was the Christmas and New Year season, and I kept getting messages that Olena, the dean, was tied up. She had been my Counterpart at the Swearing In, standing at my side as I took the oath. A charming lady. I loved her right away.

But as the days went by she kept putting me off. I was eager to get started. "In a week or two," she assured me. I hadn't even gotten to see the place! You can imagine my curiosity.

The school's full name was awkward, at least in English: The First Kyiv State Courses of Foreign Languages. No wonder everybody called it just *Coursi* (Courses). Enormously easier.

Yes, it was a government school, but it was never explained to me how. In fact, I soon saw that it was totally self-supporting. Every *kopeck* to keep it running came from student tuitions.

It was based in Kyiv and its Chernihiv branch was one of 14 in the country. Ours taught five languages: English, German, French, Spanish, and Italian and in that order of popularity. English was the biggie with some 250 students, and Italian the smallest, with just 8 or 10. I would teach English and, strangely, French.

Yes, the French assignment was a big surprise. And puzzling. Why would Peace Corps want me to teach French? Well, somebody had noticed that I speak, read, and write French. In fact, that it was my birth language. Apparently they felt that teaching it was another way I could be of service. So, why not? I could be a good ambassador doing that also. Anyway, the prospect delighted me.

Actually, I believe that it was Olena's doing. She had probably noticed the French on my résumé and thought, "How interesting! Let's make use of John in the French program also."

I couldn't wait to visit the school but I had to bide my time. It was Oksana at Headquarters (one of my TCFs during Training) who had been coordinating this with Dean Olena. Oksana came to Chernihiv and took me to *Coursi* for my first visit.

It didn't look like a school. What we went to was a modern hotel on the edge of the city. It had 8 or 9 floors and it set back a hundred yards from the street. Plain but neat and attractive. We entered the lobby. On the right was the registration desk. On the left was a small café...a few stools at a counter. And beyond it, also on the left, was a large dining room.

"The school is on the second floor," Oksana said. There was a small elevator but we took the stairs.

We walked down a broad corridor. Attractive carpeting. Many cheerful paintings. A large auditorium on the left, very modern. An open space on the right caught my eye. It had large windows. Plenty of sunshine. Gorgeous potted plants on the attractive carpet.

We walked nearly to the end of the corridor and entered a pleasant office. I thought it was that of Dean Olena. An attractive young woman was busy at a desk.

Quickly she stood and smiled and came forward. "Welcome!" she said in English. It was obvious she knew who we were.

But she was not Dean Olena. She was Lina, Olena's right-hand assistant. Very pleasant.

She led us down the corridor to the next office. Dean Olena was at a big desk. She was busy on the computer. "Welcome, Oksana!"

*Students leaving after classes. The school was in this hotel. All classes were in the evening. This was summer time. I got used to the hours.*

she said with a big smile. "Welcome, Mister John!" also with a big smile.

It truly was a warm welcome. We sat at a table and Lina served us tea and cookies and sat with us. Cozy. The conversation was light and easy. I liked these two. In just seconds I felt right at home.

"How do you like Ukraine now?" Olena said. "It is a rare opportunity for us to have you on our staff. We never had a journalist and writer before. How exciting that will be for our students!"

I beamed. "I know already that I will enjoy *Coursi* very much!"

Oksana had alerted me that I should bring a gift. "A box of chocolates will be fine," she said. "It is our tradition."

I gave Olena and Lina my present. They smiled with delight. They unwrapped and opened it and placed it on the table between us. We all took a piece. What a propitious start.

And they had a present for me: a beautiful bottle of cognac. I enjoy a glass of wine now and then but that's about it. I didn't mention that. "Such a beautiful bottle!" I said. "This is my first bottle of cognac ever." True. They were pleased.

I had brought my travel books to show them. Olena took one and Lina the other—they insisted that I call them by their first names—and thumbed through them, pausing over the many pictures.

"Our students will learn so much from you," Olena said. "We ourselves enjoy listening to you!" Lina said. "Your English is interesting for us. We were afraid it might be difficult for us. But no problem!"

I felt the same about them. I was already impressed by Olena's English and now was impressed by Lina's. I knew that both had learned English as a second language, and in fact, had undoubtedly started with British English, gradually easing into American. Not easy. I had to tip my hat to them.

I thought that surely we'd discuss the specifics of my work. That did not happen. "The next time," Olena said cheerfully. Leaving, I said to Oksana, "What a good start. It couldn't be happier." She nodded and smiled.

Finally some days later Olena explained my assignment. I would not teach! What? Peace Corps had sent me here to teach!

She explained. "You will not teach grammar and punctuation. You will teach in a different way. You have something unique to offer our students. You are a native American speaker. They have never met one!

"It will be wonderful for them to hear you. To listen to you. Your vocabulary. Your pronunciation. Your slang. They will be inspired."

**I** had to smile. The truth was that I spoke English with President John F. Kennedy's famous accent. We were both from the Boston area. Everybody knows about the Boston accent. It occurred to me Olena and Lina had no idea of the many accents in the U.S.A. Suppose instead of me they had a Volunteer from Louisiana, or Texas, or Montana! A good experience!

However, I understood her thinking. This way many students—not just two or three classes—would be exposed to my English. I cheerfully agreed to give talks. But what about?

"Well, you have traveled a lot. You have traveled all around the world! Many countries. Talk about that!"

And that's what I began to do, not to the beginning students, but the intermediate and advanced ones who could follow me better. I was a hit. It was easy for me to see that. Their eyes were fixed on me.

The teachers eagerly put me on their schedules. I spoke to class after class. I felt I was giving my students everything Olena wanted and something more. They were learning that they too could travel to far places. That travel was important in a person's development for many reasons. I could see that I was having an impact. I felt good about it.

But, oh! I must tell you that my very first class had some fireworks. Olena wanted me to start off with a bang. She arranged that three teachers would join their classes together in a single session. About 40 students in all. It would be my début. I walked in beaming. Introduced myself by writing my name on the blackboard and pronouncing it. Made a joke.

Talked about my background. Explained Peace Corps. Told them what I would strive to accomplish with them. The three teachers were all seated in the rear. They listened eagerly, as did all the students. Except one.

He was about 22 or 23. Kept talking to a neighbor, a pretty gal. She resented it. He continued. I got the feeling he was ignoring me. Deliberately. What to do? I stopped speaking. Seconds passed. More seconds. Everybody was wondering. Finally he turned away from the gal and looked at me. I was glaring at him.

"Please pay attention, young man!" I barked at him. "You are here to learn. Not to waste your money. Not to distract other students. I will not tolerate your behavior. If you continue, I will ask you to leave the room."

Silence. I stared at him. Stared him down. I resumed the class. He paid attention. It ended well. If I had ignored his bad behavior, that would have been a terrible message for the other students.

I wondered what the three teachers at the rear thought of all this. Only one brought it up later. "You were firm!" she said. "Very, very good." I brought it up to Olena and Lina and realized they had heard about it. They said little. I felt they didn't wholly approve. Strange.

I spoke in the advanced French class also. It had just a handful of students. It was a far smaller commitment for me than my English one. Most of my work by far was in the English classes. But what a wonderful diversion. I felt I was helping the students. It was helping me to keep my French alive and fluent. For me it was a bonus. I looked forward to every session.

There was only one French teacher, Louba, in her 50's. I got to love her, and her students. She made me feel right at home.

She was ethnic-Russian. She had learned French as a second language and loved it and the French culture. She had visited France once and it seemed to have charged up her enthusiasm forever. I thought she was terrific. She invited me back whenever she could and I always said Yes.

I smiled to think that her students were hearing me speak French with a Québec accent—the accent of my forebears. But I assured them I had been easily understood in the French-speaking world. French Canada, of course. France. Switzerland. Lebanon. Morocco. Vietnam.

We always think that it's the other person who has an accent. Everybody has an accent. You do, too.

In both the English and the French classes, I made it a point to do more than speak. I encouraged the students to ask me questio comments. In other words, to talk! But it was rare that they would. I pleaded. I cajoled. They were embarrassed. Felt inadequate. I understood.

I felt the same way about my Russian. But I tried and tried to get them to speak. I admit I got frustrated though I tried never to let them see that.

I stressed one thing often. "You must continue to use your new language skills once you graduate. Once you begin your careers. You must never stop improving them."

I would say, "If you don't continue to move forward, you will move backward. Your new language will get rusty. It is hard to learn a new language but easy to lose it. How awful that would be!

"Continue to study on your own. Find someone to speak with. And read, read, read. In fact, read aloud to yourself!

"Hearing the words—not only seeing them—will be very helpful. You will remember them better.

"Not only books and newspapers. There are English words and expressions all around you. So many things that you buy come with English on them. TV sets. Detergents. Beauty products. Home appliances. DVD movies! Read! Watch American DVDs. Listen to

*My favorite photo of Olena, my dean at the language school. Busy. Big smile. Beautiful.*

songs. The harder you study today, the more successful you will be tomorrow. It's up to you."

I quickly learned a lot about *Coursi*. It had some 300 students and a faculty of 20. The students were of two kinds. Young adults already launched in careers and professions, and university students studying the language on the side. The classes were in the evening, from 6 to 9, after the day's normal work.

All the teachers except for Olena and Lina were part-timers. They taught in the public schools and then at *Coursi* after hours. Some had been carrying this double load for years.

Olena and Lina were administrators but they also taught classes.

Olena was in her late 40's, I estimated. A buxom, quick-to-smile lady whose title was deputy director in charge of this branch in Chernihiv. I never understood the "deputy" part.

She ran the whole shebang with an iron hand. I am the one who told her that in the U.S.A. her title would be "dean." I would call her Dean Olena. It amused her but she got to like it.

She opened the branch and was its first and only teacher for a while. She had plenty to do running the school—everything from advertising and recruiting to hiring and planning courses and supervising and worrying. She did a lot of worrying—bore the suspense of recruiting enough students every semester, for one thing.

Still she found time to continue teaching. She had regular classes and private students, including high-profile managers in banking and business and industry plus business owners.

She chuckled when I told her she was the first woman I ever met from Siberia.

But I had met a commercial fisherman from Siberia in Hawaii,

Lina, the "methodologist" and Olena's aide. I worked closely with her. We got along fine.

strangely enough. "Boris was a good guy," I told her. "You look pretty good, too." She smiled.

I told her the little I knew about Siberia. How in Soviet times I would read in newspapers how people in the various republics of the U.S.S.R., often political dissidents, would be "exiled to Siberia." Yes, that was the expression. It made Siberia sound like the closest thing to hell on earth. Siberia sounded like such a cold and dismal and terrible place.

"Yes, it is remote," she told me. "And it is very cold in winter. But the people are so warm-hearted!"

Well, if all Siberians were like Olena, they were cheerful and positive people, quick to laugh and help and charge ahead. I got to see all this in her. But tough and thick-headed at moments. I got to experience this also—it became a big problem. I'll get to that.

As for Lina, I found out that her big role was as the school's "methodologist." That was her title. It was a new word for me. What is a methodologist? She told me. She oversaw the quality of the courses and the instruction. She was the direct supervisor of all the teachers. She made sure they were up to the job, carried out the curriculum rigidly, and kept the quality up. And she taught classes also.

I got to see the library, only one room but thickly lined with books and adequate when you considered the specialized nature of the school. Also the photo-copying room.

This was a busy place and a key one. Textbooks were not affordable for the students, so teachers would photocopy pages from their own textbooks and distribute them at every class. I got to doing the same thing.

Maria ran both the library and the photo-copying room. She knew even less English than I knew Russian but when she saw me coming, she'd begin a rapid-fire sally totally impossible for me to grasp but it would give her kicks. I'd fire back in English. We had fun.

Both Olena and Lina had attractive offices, fully equipped with computers and printers. The school had numerous tape recorders that teachers could use to play audio tapes. And lots of CDs and DVDs.

The class groups were small, so the small classrooms were perfect. And the large auditorium was ideal for large group meetings—it was also hired out to business and professional groups for special assemblies. The whole place shined. Everything was neat and organized. Paintings on the walls. An abundance of potted plants. It was a proud operation. Olena deserved the credit.

She herself always showed great pride in her person. She was a heavy person. I admired how she came to work every day so impeccably and fashionably dressed. Sometimes I wondered how she developed such a glamorous and extensive wardrobe. It was another of her talents.

I went to work at *Coursi* with enthusiasm. I gave it a lot of myself. It was assigned to me as my major effort and it remained that all through my service. I didn't want to shortchange the students in any way.

But gradually I took on other challenges in the city as well. Because *Coursi* was an evening program, I had spare time during the day, Peace Corps urged Volunteers to develop secondary initiatives.

My attitude was that I was in Ukraine to be helpful in any good way that I could. This was why I had become a Volunteer. These extra projects taught me more about the people and the country. And I enjoyed keeping busy. I'll tell you more about these projects in an upcoming chapter.

I found *Coursi* a friendly place. I got to see that the teachers liked their students. Sure, the teachers might complain. They worked long hours. It could be tedious and even boring. I saw they were devoted.

It was scandalous how poorly teachers were paid, even at university level. None of them went into it for the money. They did it because they liked teaching and enjoyed getting to know their students. Of course, like teachers in the U.S.A. they enjoyed the many weeks of vacation.

Olena and Lina were both generous to me. One thing they did for me was remarkably wonderful. They found out that I went to the Korolenko Library and the Post Office a lot to use their computers—both to write and to access the Internet.

*I admired the students. Smart. Ambitious. Nice. They were with me to learn English. "Speak more!" I would urge them. "Speak more!"*

"Use ours whenever they are free, John," they told me. "Any time."

And I did, and on a daily business. *Coursi* was closed on weekends. But I'd go to school for a few hours on Saturday and sometimes even Sunday to use a computer. I'd get a key from the receptionist on the first floor and let myself into Lina's office. What a blessing!

One day I happened to mention how I missed toasts at breakfast. I had not had a toast since I arrived in Ukraine. On my birthday, Olena presented an electric toaster to me!

I got to know the school well. I got to see that a three-hour class at the end of a long day was hard for everybody, teachers and students. At first I got upset when students would come in late, which was not uncommon. Nobody had a car. They had to walk or take the buses and trolleybuses and *marshrutkas*.

If somebody came in late, we did not frown. We understood. I learned that fast. And it was a good thing I did.

Yes, all classes were held from 6 to 9. This was because two-thirds of the students were adults in their early career year—engineers, doctors, teachers, bankers, entrepreneurs.

They could come to school only after their day's work. The others were university students who couldn't squeeze a language into their program, or who thought *Coursi* did a better job.

The students had to pay for their courses (the public universities were free), and this was hard for them, especially when the big recession hit.

All the other teachers were women. I was the only man. All had learned English—or the French or German or Spanish or Italian that they taught—as a second language. I soon saw they were doing a good job of it. I admired them.

I found out something else. Teaching a foreign language is as tough as teaching mathematics or philosophy. Oh, I had never taught these but had studied them, so I knew.

English has an earned reputation of being a tricky language. It's full of quirks and pitfalls, although we native Americans may not think so. That hard reputation is deserved.

*A one-ring traveling circus came to town and I just had to go. I was the oldest little kid there.*

There was much more involved than just grammar and vocabulary, though these could be enormously challenging. There were other difficulties. Correct spelling—so many exceptions to memorize. Proper pronunciation—again many exceptions. So many idioms. Such incredible slang. It takes a lifetime to master all this, and still we fall short.

I spotted a problem right away, and of a different kind. So many students saw the U.S.A. as heaven on earth. So many dreamed of moving to the U.S.A. They kept asking me how they could get in. I felt the responsibility of giving the students a realistic perspective.

The U.S.A. was a very nice country, yes. One of the best in the world, and that is why so popular. But like Ukrainians, we had plenty of problems. Economic problems. Poverty. Discrimination. Class alienation.

Substance abuse. Illegal immigration. They should know this. I made it a point to tell them.

I found out that *Coursi* was not quite heaven either. For me personally, I mean. And it was Olena mostly who made me feel that way. Here's how that started. A few weeks after I began, Olena mentioned that the school could really use an IWB set-up. "It would be a wonderful teaching aid," she said.

An IWB? I had no idea what she was talking about. It stands for Interactive Whiteboard. That didn't help me much. It turned out that the IWB is the computer world's snazzy version of an old-fashioned blackboard.

We used to write on a blackboard with white chalk, remember? An IWB uses a whiteboard so that images from a projector can show up nice and sharp on it—think white movie screen. The projector is operated by a computer. And because you are using a computer, you can do all kinds of marvelous things.

You can "write" on the whiteboard, as you would with chalk, and in many colors. Can show photos and graphs and movies on it, in fact, any kind of graphic, and in gorgeous color. Can simultaneously play music or narrate a script. Can print out anything that's on it with a couple of clicks.

Olena was excited by all the possibilities. All our teachers would love the IWB, she told me. And what terrific PR it would be for us to publicize that we had this whiz-bang technology for our language students.

A blackboard is cheap. An IWB is expensive. A good set-up costs thousands of dollars. No way could *Coursi* afford an IWB. But boy oh boy! She knew that Peace Corps had funds available. She knew about Peace Corps' SPA (Small Project Assistance) grants.

"Do you think we'd have a chance," she asked me.

"I'll check," I told her. I did check and yes, SPA had funds. But not for the purchase of equipment. Only for programs. I reported this bit of news back to her. Her smile disappeared.

"Maybe that's not a big problem," I said. "Isn't the reason that we want an IWB so that we can do a better job of teaching?"

And I elaborated. "Aren't we going to have to develop a strong, substantial program to teach our teachers how to use an IWB and get the most of it? Aren't we going to want to develop a good program to also teach language teachers in our public schools how to use an IWB?

"After all, it's the technology of the future. Every school will get its own IWB some day. Wouldn't it be a fine public service for us to prepare them for that day? Isn't something like that expected of us as the most important—in fact, the leading—language school in the area?" To all these questions she nodded yes, yes, yes. She was excited. I was excited. We were off and running.

Together we cooked up a "program." It would involve a curriculum, a syllabus, seminars, a schedule, a whole package of good-sounding essentials. We hoped it would be a winning strategy.

If we were lucky and won an SPA grant, we'd have to solicit bids. To get an idea of the money involved, we shopped for an IWB set-up. More than $7,000! But the highest request SPA would consider was $6,000.

In fact, the average grant was only about half that. And 20 percent of that would have to come from private funds, but these could be our own funds—meaning *Coursi*'s funds. We could put in that much. So the net amount we finally asked for was $4,800.

I wrote it all up. We reviewed our proposal and sharpened and polished it. I sent it off to Peace Corps to give them a preliminary look. They reminded us that they would not fund equipment. That's how our proposal still looked to them. So I beefed up the program aspects.

SPA kept saying it was interested in "capacity-building" projects. In plain English, that meant helping a lot of people to do a better job as much as possible. I expounded on the capacity-building dimension of our program. Sent it off again. Back came more comments. Their tone was less than sympathetic.

We did more tinkering, then forwarded the final official request. We had put so much effort into this. We got turned down! And I thought she blamed me. That was a black day.

Olena was disappointed, to say the least. Upset! For one thing, *Coursi* would have been the first in all 14 branches of the school to get an IWB. Slowly our relationship soured.

And that deserves explanation. It's coming up.

~ ~ ~

***Did you know*** ... that about 7 percent of all the Volunteers are now over the age of 50? And that Peace Corps is trying hard to increase this percentage. Director Tschetter launched the Fifty Plus program. The goal was set at 15 percent, but it's elusive. Presently the average age is said to be 25. So any older recruit can expect to be surrounded by younger Volunteers. It's important to be young at heart!

# 13 / Things at school sour

*Dean Olena and I are not hitting it off.*
*Things are not good. I blow my stack!*

Something about my work was irritating Dean Olena. One day she startled me. "You are not a teacher," she said. "All you do is talk. You are an entertainer!" She said it in a bad way. A contemptuous way. And in front of her assistant, Lina. Whew! I needed an aspirin.

I fretted about her remark. It was inexplicable. After all, I was doing in the classroom exactly what she had told me to do. Giving talks, talks, talks to my students about helpful and interesting things.

She made a remark like that another time. Again she criticized me in front of other teachers. I was being maligned. My reputation was at risk.

I knew better about myself. I knew I was a good teacher. I felt it in every class. I could tell that I was engaging the students. Holding their attention. Getting them to understand.

Invariably the regular teacher would sit in as I talked. I could tell if she was just daydreaming or actively listening…and invariably she was. The teachers always complimented me, and sincerely, I thought. Plus, I was a journalist. I was experienced at sensing when someone was lying.

True, I had never been a full-time teacher. I had never taken courses in pedagogy. But I had done considerable teaching over the years. And I had spent many years as a student, and students are the first to know who is a good teacher, and why.

And of course, during Training I had gotten through the practice-teaching at the Technological University nearly next door to *Coursi*. I was bothered but I held my tongue. Kept my temper. And I had been positive about one thing a long time. Education is more effective if it is fun. I tried to teach my students solid stuff. But I tried hard to make it entertaining. And was succeeding.

In truth, I had gotten to question Dean Olena's own effectiveness in the classroom. I had come to see she was no expert. In the beginning, she often asked me to assist her in her advanced classes. I saw that she was earnest and tried hard to teach well. But in some ways she wasn't doing the job, sad to say. Disappointing.

She loved to involve her students in little games. She would divide them into groups of four and tell them, "Match this with that!" Or, "Discuss this and then tell me about it."

It sounded good. But I could see it was ineffective. Why? Because in each group of students, usually only one would do the work. Maybe two. The others would just go along. It filled up the class time but it was a waste.

What to think? I concluded Olena was making it easy for herself. She didn't have to perform every minute.

One day when she criticized me again in front of a third person, I blew my top. Very rare for me. I contradicted her. "Not true!" I said. "Come and sit in my classes! Come see for yourself! I am effective!" She never did.

She attacked me again a few days later. Her behavior was intolerable. I tossed and turned all that night. The next morning I wrote her a stern letter. I said I was a good teacher and many would vouch for that. I told her I resented her demeaning me in front of my colleagues.

I told her that if she persisted, I would report her to the Peace Corps Country Director in Kyiv and provide a substantiating account. I put the letter aside for a couple of hours—didn't want to act in haste. Reviewed it. Changed a word or two. Put it on her desk while she was away.

She never mentioned it to me. But obviously she had read it. She did not speak to me for days, even when we were with other teachers and she spoke to all of them. She would turn her back on me. The teachers noticed. I continued to greet her cheerfully. "Good morning, Olena." Or, "Have a nice weekend, Olena."

One day my boss, Iryna Shevchenko, asked me how things were going. Should I tell her? Should I not? I told her. In detail. As factually as I could. It was painful. She decided to investigate and made an appointment to visit the dean.

I attended that meeting. I was uptight. Suppose this got serious! Might this escalate? Could Peace Corps even dismiss me over this?

Olena was remarkably sweet. She made light of it. "John is not a trained teacher," she told Iryna. "He does not do things our way. He does not write lesson plans. He has a mind of his own! But we like him." And she smiled.

Iryna looked at me sharply. "John, you were taught how to write lesson plans in Training! You must write them according to the prescribed government regulations!"

I protested. I did indeed plan my classes. Carefully. I admitted that I wrote my plans differently. Not with the prescribed Ukrainian rigidity. I started by stating what I hoped to achieve. I detailed a beginning, a middle, and an end. Chose exercises. I built in flexibility to take into account what might come up in the class itself.

This was common sense. Things happen! And teachers must seize what I called "teachable moments" and make the most of them. The goal was to achieve a good result. Getting the students to understand. And—important—keeping them interested.

Iryna decided she would sit in on one of my classes. Dean Olena liked that idea. We set a date. But an evening class, of course. Three hours long!

Iryna drove out all the way from Kyiv to attend. I explained in class that we would have a visitor.

*A few of my fellow teachers at tea. They worked hard. I liked them all. Louba, the teacher who invited me to her French class often, is the tall one. It was a good time for her students, her, and me.*

Iryna entered and sat and watched and listened. I felt some pressure, of course. But I taught in my regular style. Nothing different.

Half through at the coffee break, Iryna said, "I am satisfied, John. You are doing all right." She smiled. "You even inject humor in the class!" And went home.

Whatever she reported to Olena seemed to be acceptable. I appreciated Iryna's common-sense approach. And I conceded. I did turn in rigid plans, as foolish as I thought they were.

And slowly, slowly Olena's attitude mellowed and her behavior improved. It was surprisingly good in the final weeks of my service, thank God. Neither of us ever spoke of the bad days. I was always aware of them. I suspect she was also.

One of her priorities, and mine, was to keep me productive. But our priorities differed in an important way. My priority was to help my students. Her priority was for me to help *Coursi*, meaning, to bring in money by luring more students. That's why, for instance, she arranged for me to be interviewed by a journalist.

She would charge students who attended my own classes when those got under way. I came to have two private students and she hoped I would have more. They had to pay. I had mixed feelings about this. Remember, my services to *Coursi* were totally free. I got no salary from *Coursi*.

It was a Peace Corps principle that the institutions where we worked not make money off us. But I understood Olena's problem; tuitions were the lifeblood of her school—I did not mind if she charged for my services.

Sometimes I wondered whether my students thought I made money off them. Now and then I would slip in that Volunteers never get a penny for whatever work they do, or how much work they do.

She got a new idea: I should offer a course called Creative Writing. She thought that would have appeal. I liked her idea. It was up my alley. After all, I had earned my living in good part by writing.

But how many students would be interested? In the United States, creative writing courses had become popular, in my opinion largely because the title was so catchy and clever. I inquired: had Ukrainians ever heard the expression? No.

Most people, I have found, don't know what creative writing means. Does it mean a poem....a short story or novel...a song....what? Yes, all those are creative writing. But to me, so is a good business letter. Or an effective marketing plan. Or an attention-getting news release. Or a letter of application—especially for students applying for their first big job. That could be the most important creative writing they ever attempted.

To me, creative writing is any piece of writing that is important and that requires you to use all your wits to achieve the desired result. That you do your very best to create.

Such writing is creative in the same sense that cooking well is creative, or sewing well is, or painting well is, or dressing well, or doing any challenging task well.

Yes, I welcomed such a course. I would do it as a workshop. I would teach the principles and would guide. And my students would write and write. And I would correct and critique. You become a good carpenter by measuring and sawing and hammering time and again. And you become a good writer the same way. You must write, write, write.

One thing I preached again and again. Every serious piece of writing must be written at least twice. Write it. Let it cool; do something else to change your ideas. Look at it again. You'll see ways to make it better. Always go through this process.

To promote my workshop, I went from class to class. I'd tell students how *Coursi's* new course would help them throughout their career and in fact their life.

I stressed that the principles of good writing are the same in all languages—so, what they would learn from me in my English creative writing class would be transferable to their Russian or Ukrainian writing.

I expected a full class. Hah! I got only two students, Kristina, 16, a precocious secondary school student, and Diana, early 20's, a clerk in a government office, also very smart.

We met for three hours every Wednesday evening for 16 weeks, and I got them to do as much writing as I could. Active writing is basic!

*Coursi* was realistic and practical about some things, such as not frowning when someone arrived late. I explained this to you earlier. Fine. No problem. We were understanding. But of course, they would miss part of the instruction, and that wasn't good.

*Coursi* was considerate in another way. I would assign home tasks, always a writing project. Kristina always did it, and I always made corrections and added comments.

But Diana would disappoint me. She would show up now and then with the assignment not done. "I am so busy at work!" she would tell me with a charming smile. I didn't like it but I would not get outwardly upset.

Of course, if she didn't turn it in, I would have less homework to correct, which made my life easier. But loafing was not my goal. How would she learn if she did not do her homework? *Coursi's* reasoning was, "It's wonderful if they do their home tasks. That's an important part of learning. But don't growl if they do not!"

How come such a lax attitude? I soon caught on. *Coursi* did not want to lose a student. Every student was precious. The thinking was, "Do everything you can to keep a student, even if it means not pressing for missing homework." This was never said to me but I got the point.

What was remarkable is that little Kristina did her homework week after week and was getting somewhere. Diana, five years older, was ignoring it too often—and was stalled.

**T**hen Olena decided to change Creative Writing to English Business Writing. It was my idea. I thought that would be more descriptive and have more practical sizzle. We offered it for the new semester. Again, only two students, both gals.

Tatiana was 25 or so. An "economist." The word had a different meaning in Ukraine. It meant someone who had majored in business. She was a head accountant in a bank. Natalia was about 20, finishing her third year as a mechanical engineering major. They were excellent and worked hard. I felt my efforts worthwhile. Very nice gals. I enjoyed teaching them.

One day Natalia, the engineer, mentioned that she was building a machine at the university. Natalia with the perfectly painted fingernails! Natalia in the fashionable dresses! Natalia working with wrenches and an oil can! Unbelievable. I brought it up.

"No, no, John, " she said, and laughed. "I am building it on paper. On a drawing board!"

So, I was learning things, too.

I also had two private students—Anton and Valery, private meaning that my classes with them were always one on one, and my instruction always focused on their specific needs. The classes would be for an hour and a half but sometimes we'd go on for two hours. Both students turned out to be a pleasure.

Anton was 14. He became my student shortly after I started at *Coursi* and continued all the way through. Nearly two years. He was younger by far than any other student at *Coursi*. How come?

The first thing Olena told me was that he was the grandson of a famous mathematician, deceased. His daughter, Anton's mom, was the chair of the mathematics department at one of our Chernihiv universities.

Quickly I got to see that Anton's mother was a close friend of Olena. She had her own car and always drove Anton to class—that in itself was an extraordinary thing in Ukraine. While I gave Anton his class, sometimes she would sit with Olena in her office and they would have tea and chat. Then she would drive him home.

When his mom couldn't drive him, he would come with his grandmother by *marshrutka*. She was his mom's mother.

She would sit and wait in another room. He never came alone. That, too, was unusual for a 14-year-old. It was common for kids to use public transit and do so alone.

She and I couldn't converse because of our language difficulties, yet we became close. She was sweet, smiled a lot. One thing astonished me. She would pass the time by working difficult math problems—just for the fun of it.—surely the genes of her mathematician father.

Anton and I met on Friday afternoons. A terrific boy. We'd sit side by side at a table and talk. He already knew a lot of English and was eager to learn more. And came prepared for every lesson.

He was interested in a whole range of subjects, and I would latch onto one and use it as teaching bait. Who invented the computer mouse. Esperanto. China's manufacturing advantage. The amazing Barack Obama. Architecture (Anton's dad was an architect and his dream was to become an architect). The controversial Dr. Kevorkian. The significance of the Equator. On and on. Anton loved it. I loved it.

At the end of our class, I'd pick an interesting aspect of that day's topic and have him research it and write a paper. In the process, I taught him how to use Google and Wikipedia, the Russian versions (yes, in Ukraine!) as well as conventional encyclopedias.

He'd arrive at the next class with his paper written. He'd do it every time—this in addition to his regular school work. I would correct his paper in front of him. We'd discuss it. I got to like him a lot. He was my student for nearly my whole time at *Coursi*. Truth is, I was a grandfather five times but sometimes I'd muse I'd love to have Anton as another of my grandchildren. And I could see that he liked me. His mom saw it. Olena saw it. Lina saw it. They would kid me about it.

After some months I got another private student. He was very different. His name was Valery. He was 39. A mathematician.

He had read an article about me in a Russian newspaper. He came to *Coursi* specifically to meet me. He made an appointment with Olena and asked whether he could have private lessons from me. He wanted to improve his English. Was determined about it.

He was a shy man, but gentle and very engaging. Enormously likable. He already spoke excellent English. How could I possibly help him with his English? He also spoke German easily. Remarkable, I thought.

What he wanted was earnest conversations on many topics. I found that appealing. And that's what we did, once a week. All I did was to steer the conversation…keep it moving…make suggestions and corrections. I looked forward to our sessions.

Valery worked in Chernobyl, the site of the nuclear power plant that suffered the terrible nuclear melt-down. Now just a ghost town.

He was employed by a firm of consultants studying the disaster. He liked the work. It sounded dangerous to me because of possible continuing radiation but he didn't think so. He said his office was a distance from the catastrophic reactor. I thought he was still far too close.

He lived in Chernihiv with his parents and his brother. It was my impression that he had never married. He would take the train and work in Chernobyl for five days, returning for the weekends

We hit it off. I learned many things about him that intrigued me. He had worked and done graduate work in Germany for several years and that's why he spoke German easily. His language skills were so impressive.

He had gotten a job in the Emirates for a while and had enjoyed that. His current work focused on preparing reports of various kinds and made use of his math and analytical skills.

I learned that he was an ABD. It was a term that he had never heard and I explained it. An ABD, I told him, is a person who has studied for a doctor of philosophy degree (a Ph.D.) and has completed all but the dissertation. No dissertation, no Ph.D.

Usually this is a great disappointment because the Ph.D. is a must for a career job as a university teacher. I picked up the expression from my son, Mark, who is a Ph.D. university teacher.

Valery told me that he had done his graduate work at the most prestigious polytechnic university in Moscow. It was not clear why he never completed the degree. I got the feeling it was something to do with the professor who had mentored him.

I felt that maybe I could help him by encouraging him to complete the degree. Why not? Possible. Sometimes what somebody needs is just a strong push. Encouragement. And emotional support. We discussed ways and possibilities. The usual stumbling block was his explanation that "I have found it very difficult to find the right professor to sponsor me." We never got beyond that.

One thing he was fervent about was emigrating to a better country. He had explored getting a visa to the United States but too difficult.

He had an aunt who lived in Ottawa and he was busy researching how to get a visa to Canada. He spoke to me about it often. He was intent.

"She has invited me to live with her when I arrive. That would be wonderful." We talked about Canada a lot. I was quite familiar. The weather. The cost of living. Opportunities and salaries. Other topics.

*The courses were not free. The students had to pay Coursi. I was free. Volunteers cannot accept a single 'kopeck.' My reward was in helping them as best I could.*

Often he brought a gift. Usually a book from his big collection or a map. "Thank you, Valery," I would say to him. "But no need. I feel embarrassed accepting this."

Some of my students would tell me that it was not unheard of for a university student to bribe a teacher for a better grade or a recommendation.

This was not the case for Valery and me. Ours was a loose and informal arrangement. Besides, no grades!

All he would ever be able to claim was that I had tutored him in English conversation for a few months. He was being generous because he was appreciative and liked me.

Our exchanging gifts started when I began giving him my back issues of the Kyiv Post. I've told you about it—the good, brave English weekly that gave the lowdown about much going on in Ukraine.

I also gave him back copies of the International Newsweek magazine. Peace Corps supplied it to all Volunteers. Well, until it cut it to save money. I gave him these because I saw he was an avid reader and they would build up his English skills.

One day he gave me a paperback in English that I found very interesting. It was written by a man in Ireland who lived on a tiny island, had built a small marine research station there, and was conducting various studies.

"He is a very impressive man," Valery told me. "I wrote to him and asked him whether he would accept me as an assistant."

Gosh, that surprised me. Of course I said, "What happened?"

"He thanked me for my interest but he declined. Told me life on the island would be too difficult for me. He sent me his book as a present."

*My student Valery. His wanted to converse in English. That's what we did—we talked. He was donating these books to a public library.*

That's the way Valery really talked! He spoke better English than most Americans. My opinion.

One day he arrived with a satchel full of books. No, they were not for me. He told me, "After class I am going to our branch library near here. I will give these to the librarian. They are books I no longer need. She is always very grateful."

I saw him come with a satchel full like that several times. Always for the branch library.

Then one day bad news. He had been laid off at Chernobyl! He didn't explain why. Maybe research grants had been slashed. Maybe his project had been completed. I felt sorry for him. I offered to write a letter of recommendation for him. He thanked me. But never asked for it.

The weeks passed. He kept applying for jobs. He was interested now in a government job because of the security. He went to interviews. He waited to hear from this official, then that one. He never got an acceptance.

He was lucky to be living with his family. It was my impression he spent his time on the Internet prospecting job leads. I never understood why the consistent bad news.

The semester ended and he did not return. A money problem, I thought. He was paying *Coursi* for my services. I would contact him and invite him to our English Club meetings at the library. He came two or three times, but not consistently.

Shortly before I left to go home to the U.S.A., I received an e-mail from him. He wanted to know what I thought of his taking a job on a commercial fishing boat in Alaska!

He had spotted an ad seeking workers. He was a slight man, at home in an office or library but not doing the grueling work that job required, and I told him so. He gave up the idea.

Just recently I received an e-mail from him, yes, here in the U.S.A. After these many months, he is employed in a government agency. I am so pleased. I write more about Valery in another chapter.

In one of Olena's classes I got to know a 15-year-old girl named Nastia. Very bright. Sunny personality. Earnest student. I suggested to Olena that Nastia would be a good FLEX candidate. She agreed and suggested that I coach the girl. I said yes.

What's FLEX? It's an American State Department program. It stands for Future Leaders Exchange Program. It operates in a number of countries. But it is not an exchange; it operates only one way—to the U.S.A.

Every year FLEX was sending more than 200 boys and girls to the U.S.A. for an academic year, 10 months. They went to different cities and towns. They lived with a host family and participated in its life.

Attended the local high school, engaged in as many of its activities as possible—athletics and clubs and field trips and so on—learned about life in their community and what America is really like.

Going to America was a life-changing experience for these kids—a dream come true. Many dreamed of going.

When they returned home, they spoke American English quite well, were invariably delighted with their experience, spread good words about it all around, made friends for our country, and got a terrific start in becoming leaders.

Marina—what a teacher! I taught in her class often. A pleasure..

We were doing something wonderful for these kids, and promoting our country in their country.

The competition to become a FLEXer was enormous, of course. Only the better kids were encouraged to apply. They got into FLEX by passing three progressive exams and surviving several interviews. The exams were held all over the country.

It was costing FLEX $12,000 for each boy and girl going to America. It covered everything, from round-trip air right down to everyday pocket money. I think it included a stipend for the host families. That year, 220 were going, I believe.

Multiply those two numbers and you'll be amazed by how much Uncle Sam was paying out—and just for one year's FLEXers from Ukraine. It operated in numerous countries.

It could be difficult to sell the idea of FLEX to a child's parents—a 10-month separation could be painful for them. And scary. Maybe when the children returned, they might be very different, with very different values, and be very dissatisfied with life in Ukraine—and might talk of emigrating to the U.S.A. some day. Not happy news for some parents.

Olena sold the idea of applying for FLEX to Nastia and her mother, and Nastia was overjoyed to try. Olena asked me to help Nastia any way I could in preparing for the exams. I was eager to help her.

But what could I do for her in just three weeks? How much new English, or how much of any other subject, could I teach her in that short time?

Anton and I deep in a lesson. He was only 14. We worked together two years.

I got an idea. The exams emphasized writing essays. What I did was draw up a list of possible essay topics. "How do you think a year in America will change you?" "Why do you want to be a FLEX scholar?" "What do you think might be your biggest problems in America?" And so on.

Nastia and I sat together and discussed the questions and worked to come up with good answers. I didn't tell her the answers. That would not be right. I guided her to them.

Thousands participated. Some students got dropped after the first exam, some after the second. Nastia made it through all three. Through the interviews also. She did beautifully. Olena and I were so happy. So hopeful. Then Nastia had to wait four months for FLEX's decision. Four months! Can you imagine her anxiety? I was anxious myself.

During that time, I turned 80, and *Coursi* gave me a party—just Olena and Lina and my fellow teachers. Imagine my surprise to see Nastia come walking in. And she had a box of chocolates for me. So nice.

But my first words to her were, "How did you do?"

She gulped. "I flunked!"

She used that American word!

I could see she had expected me to ask. What a brave girl to come and face me. It took spunk.

"What?" I was shocked. What could I say? I embraced her. Looked her straight in the eyes.

"You did not flunk! You were a great success. It was just bad luck. All you finalists were super students. You were qualified. It's just that FLEX did not have enough openings for all of you. You were all excellent. What to do?

"Finally they just picked the number of names they needed out of a hat. That must be what happened. You were a terrific candidate. No way did you fail. You will be a great success in life."

I meant every word. I could see how she was devastated by her bad news though she tried to veil it. I hoped my words set her perspective right. And consoled her.

In one of my writing classes, I had met another 14-year-old, Galina. Also bright. Very outgoing. She was very different—she was Vietnamese. Her father and mother had emigrated to Ukraine for a better life. They ran a stall selling jeans in the bazaar. She was the only Asian student I ever saw in Chernihiv. She had heard about me at my English Club. She signed up for my writing class.

She, too, was going to try for FLEX. One day she asked if I would coach her. That took a lot of moxie and I admired that. I am not sure she knew Nastia, who was also hoping for a FLEX. I agreed and we got to work. I proceeded with her the way I had with Nastia—by training her for the essays. She, too, made it through the strenuous process. She waited and waited for the results also. I waited anxiously with her.

She burst in late at class one day. She was so excited. "I made it! I made it! I am going to America!"

Wow! We all congratulated her, of course. I hugged her. "Wonderful, Galina! You will have a great year. You will be a terrific FLEXer!"

Life is so mysterious. Nastia, no. Galina, yes. Some things are so hard to explain. More about Galina farther on.

As the months went by, I tried to help *Coursi* in any way possible. *Coursi* was a fine school, operating under difficult conditions, the huge economic recession for one thing.

One day in a section of the city new to me, I came upon another language school! It was in a storefront. A commercial operation. I had never heard of it. English was its main offering. I went in. I wanted to learn everything I could about it. Several young people with books in hand were lounging in the office.

It had two or three small classrooms and I could hear teaching going on. Many students were participating. I approached a young woman who was the clerk.

I told her I was a Peace Corps Volunteer. She knew about Peace Corps. Told her I had been trained to be an English teacher and that's why I was fascinated to have come upon her school. Never mentioned that I was teaching at *Coursi*, her school's big competitor for sure.

She was pleasant and gave me a brochure. Told me her school was one of three branches operated by the same company. I thanked her, said goodbye, and left.

My only purpose was to inform Olena of everything I had learned. My information might be helpful. She thanked me but told me she knew all about the school. "We have a much better program," she said. But I couldn't help wondering why so many had chosen to study there.

*Coursi* advertised for students. I saw its ads in several newspapers. Small ads. Nothing exciting. There was also one *marshrutka* that was a rolling ad for the school as it covered its route.

"We teach five languages!" it proclaimed on its flanks, and listed them. "Learn a second language and get a better job!" Well, words like that.

More and more young people were using computers. I felt a website was an essential marketing tool. *Coursi* did not have one. I offered to create one. Olena told me that Maxim was already at work on one.

I knew Maxim. About 30. A talented IT specialist who handled *Coursi's* computer problems. Quite friendly. I went to him several times about problems with my own computer at home, and he fixed them easily. I was sure he was a master at the technical aspects of websites. But I doubted he knew much about marketing. I had done a lot of marketing for non-profits back home.

So, I partnered with Maxim. I took photos of a dozen teachers and students in school situations for the website. I wrote all the copy. It would be important for the website to be accessible in Ukrainian, Russian, and English. My English text would be translated into the other languages. He would do all the technical stuff. We planned to get the website up and running by August 1 at the latest, in time for the next semester.

Eventually I got to see the finished website. I spotted some of my pictures, but not much else. What a disappointment.

For the next semester, I made my offer again. I would sharpen the website as a recruitment tool. I waited. And waited. Olena did not take me up on it. Imagine my frustration.

Then I suggested an English Conversation class and Olena agreed. Students were reluctant to talk in English. Talking in English would be what this course was all about. No writing. I got five students, all in their early 20's. Three men and two women. Four young professionals and one Tech U. student. Obviously far-seeing and ambitious people.

I prepared a list of topics. They added more. I asked each to choose one. He or she would prepare it thoroughly and lead a discussion, one for each class each Friday evening, then another cycle. The others were duty-bound to ask questions, make comments, contribute! I would keep it lively and make suggestions and corrections. A success.

I made another suggestion. Riding the *marshrutka* to school, I noticed attractive small billboards along a main street of the city. Quite effective, I thought. Must be affordable.

Fifteen years earlier I had designed a huge billboard in a key location for a hospital client of mine in Worcester, Massachusetts. I knew something about effective billboards. I recommended these small billboards to Olena and offered to create an ad for them. "No money!" she said. That was the end of that.

One day I had another idea. Wild, I admit. I typed out a memo: "Olena, *Coursi* should begin teaching Chinese. Do not laugh! I am serious." And I stated the reasons in detail.

I was there when she read it. She began to laugh! I had to urge her to please read my reasons. All convincing, I believed.

China was becoming pre-eminently important on the world stage. I had been to China. I had seen and felt the might and energy of Beijing and Shanghai and another city or two. China was Ukraine's most important foreign supplier. I believed that this might be China's century—just as the last century had been ours in the U.S.A.

I had a good local example for her of China's growing importance in Ukraine. Aerosvit, the national Ukrainian airline, was now flying regularly to Shanghai and Beijing. That demonstrated how close the two countries were becoming. And surely the flights would increase with Ukraine's expanding economy.

Some students surely would be attracted to studying Chinese. I mentioned Andrei, the younger son of my then current host mother, Tatiana. He had just gotten a master's in physics from the leading university in Kyiv, and he had been studying Chinese for a year.

On the side. Out of personal conviction. Not at a language school; no school taught Chinese, it seemed. He had gone out and found himself a Chinese student who would tutor him. Andrei could see its importance.

I said to her, "Someday some school in Chernihiv will be teaching Chinese. We are the leading language school in this whole area. We should be first, not last! Think of the enormous, powerful publicity that being the first to teach Chinese would get us."

She objected. "Where would we find a credentialed teacher? How would we pay for this?" I made suggestions.

·And I continued, "We're teaching Italian. We're teaching Spanish. But we have very few students although those are important languages. Isn't Chinese much more important than Italian and Spanish when you see China's huge role in Ukraine?" She closed the door on the whole idea.

**S**ummer came. *Coursi* emptied for two months. Teachers went off on vacations. I did, too. I spent a month on the road. I describe all that in a chapter coming up. Classes resumed in September.

It was nice to catch up with my teacher friends just returned from trips—Egypt was the favorite because exotic and low cost. It was a pleasure to say hello to returning students. I looked forward to my new classes and new students.

But for me this fourth semester—my last one—became a disaster.

I got off to a very slow start. I had no teaching classes, only speaking classes. No Creative Writing, no Business English Writing classes. Olena seemed to do little to promote them. My assignment again was to go talk to various classes.

About what? "Well, you did a lot of traveling on your vacation. Talk about that." Just a continuation of what I had been doing.

And that is what I did. But I didn't want to merely entertain my students and give them the pleasure of my New England accent. I wanted to really teach, and I did. Not necessarily English. I would talk about how to find a job, how to choose a career, how to become more interested in politics. My students paid attention.

I considered this last topic—politics—most important. After all, this was their country. They should become interested. Become immersed. I would say, "Ukraine is going to need new leaders in 10 years, 20 years, 30 years. Why couldn't you be one?"

They thought I was out of my mind, of course. Everybody knew politicians were corrupt. But there must be some good ones, I argued. I would tell them, "You could be a good one!"

There was a complication. It was a complication for Olena. The semester for me would be short—my Peace Corps service would be ending two months before the end of the semester!

Furthermore, all Volunteers had to attend a Close of Service Conference (C.O.S.). It was held in a small resort hotel in the Carpathian Mountains in western Ukraine, close to the Polish border. With the long train rides back and forth, it took up most of a work week.

It was interesting and I'll tell you more about it shortly. So, I was away from *Coursi* all that time.

Soon after returning from that, the swine flu epidemic hit the country. Grossly exaggerated, I believed. But Ukraine closed all schools for three weeks, including *Coursi*.

And then, just as they re-opened, I came down with a plain, old-fashioned cold. My first illness in my more than two years in Ukraine. I lost another week. Then I broke a molar. I had to go to Kyiv for several days for a root canal operation and reconstruction and capping of the tooth.

As you know, it was a long process to get into Peace Corps, and now it was a long one to get out. Besides the C.O.S. retreat, all of us in my group had to undergo a comprehensive exit physical exam, culminating with a mandatory HIV/AIDS test. More about all this later also. The running around and the paper work took several days. Of course, all this posed a big scheduling headache for Olena.

Meanwhile, another group of Trainees had arrived in Chernihiv and they were practice-teaching here and there in the city. *Coursi* had two that it could use. I was no longer so important.

"Everything is fine, John," Olena would tell me when I called. "Just take care of your health."

One thing that distressed me was that I was out of contact with my students. There were a number of them that I liked very much.

And one thing that I hoped to do was to speak to all the students at *Coursi* in a final school-wide assembly. I wanted very much to say certain things. That I admired them. Believed that they would have a good future if they continued to work hard. Believed that their country would improve—after all, it was less than 20 years old. And so on.

Time ran out. I never got to see my students again except for two or three who came to my clubs at the Korolenko Library,

There was a small farewell party for me at *Coursi*, hastily squeezed in, and I appreciated that. Just for my fellow teachers. Not my students. It was on a Saturday at noon. This meant that all the teachers who came had to come in on their day off.

I have explained that all of them worked full-time at day jobs, mostly as teachers, and then taught at *Coursi* in the evening. Think of how demanding for women who were also wives and mothers and in some cases the sole support of their family. Ten of them came, including my favorites.

The culture in Ukraine calls for the person being feted to host the party. It is true for birthdays, and true for an occasion like this. I was game. Olena and Lina suggested a list of things for me to provide.

Annabelle was in Ukraine—she had come from California to be with me in my final days. The two of us stopped at a market and picked up everything. But at school, I found some things lacking. I went back and bought more items.

The conference table in Olena's office was perfect. All the teachers helped. There were bottles of wine and fruit juices. Red caviar—I was told they liked it better than black. And bread.

I did not realize that the way they liked their caviar was neatly arranged on a slice of bread slathered with butter—I rushed off to buy the butter. Cheese. Gourmet olives. Pickled mushrooms. Apples and oranges and grapes and bananas. Cookies. Chocolates. Ukrainians love chocolates.

The centerpiece was a gorgeous box of Whitman's Sampler Chocolates. An extra-big box with a double layer of them, sent to me by my daughter-in-law Marita and saved for this specific occasion. It was opened wide for all to see. They had never seen Whitman's famous box.

Everybody was eager to try the Whitman's. Fingers reached in to grasp two, three, four chocolates. They were nearly all gone when I thought of pointing out the famous chart that tells you exactly what every chocolate is, and why the box is called a "sampler."

Later I got the feeling that it was the Whitman's that they talked about when they got home.

Olena sat directly across from me at the table, and Lina farther on the left. Olena was sweet and smiling. I had insisted—really insisted—that there be no gifts, but she quickly handed me one—a traditional Ukrainian folk tablecloth with matching napkins. And other teachers had gifts for me. Such kind people.

As is the custom, I was asked to give the first toast. This was just two days after Thanksgiving (a holiday unknown in Ukraine but which everybody at the table was familiar with). I raised my glass of wine and said that for me this was a true Thanksgiving. That was my theme. I was thankful to *Coursi*. I was thankful to all of them. I was thankful to my students. They could tell that I was sincere.

Olena raised her glass. "Thank you, John, for coming to our school and working so hard to help our students. You have accomplished much. You have been a good Volunteer. A good ambassador for your country. We wish you a happy journey home and good health!"

Lina caught my eye. "I will give the next toast," she whispered to me. But she never did. Not sure how come.

We were a strangely quiet room. Maybe it was Annabelle's presence. Maybe because everything had to be said in English. Maybe because of Olena's presence. But I knew I had very warm friends sitting at the table with me. They would lean toward me and say something endearing.

One was Marina, always bubbling with gusto. Another was Louba, the French teacher. She knew no English. I excused myself to the others at the table and turned to her and said words of appreciation to her in French.

Olena's dour side soon showed, sorry to say. One of the things Annabelle had brought from the United States at my request was a Scrabble set—a gift from me for the teachers and the students at *Coursi*. I had it on the table. They had never heard of Scrabble. I was sure it would interest them.

I explained that after our party I would have four teachers sit and try the game as I explained it, with the others observing. "No time," Olena snapped. "We can read the directions later." I was disappointed.

One after another they departed. They were sweet. I could see one or two were close to tears. "I will keep in touch," I promised. But who knows?

Finally only Olena and Lina remained, plus another teacher. Annabelle presented gifts to Olena and Lina...beautiful necklaces bought especially at her favorite store in Newport Beach back home. Chosen with the two of them in mind. They seemed pleased. I was embarrassed I had nothing for the lone teacher. Alas!

We were all tired. I got the idea of taking a taxi home. Olena quickly ordered one for us. She lived in our neighborhood so I insisted she join us, and she did. I invited Lina also, but she said no. She planned to visit her parents in another neighborhood.

Olena, Annabelle, and I had a pleasant ride together. Annabelle and I got out first. Olena would be riding on. She got out to say goodbye. Warm hugs. Genuinely warm hugs.

She smiled. "I will never, never forget you, John," she said.

"And I will never forget you, Olena. The best of everything always!" She got back into the taxi.

I cringe at the thought of her reaction when she reads this chapter. But the truth has to be the truth.

Many close relationships become a love-hate relationship, of course. Ours was such a relationship for some weeks during our many months. Mostly a loving one for sure. I'm so happy we parted with best wishes and genuine affection.

I'll always admire her for the school that she created out of nothing and kept going. Remember how she stood at my side at Swearing In. Be grateful for the many kindnesses she showed me.

If I offended her, it was never intentional, and never done maliciously. I have read that it is liberating to forgive. I forgive her. Time will soften my memories of the anxieties she gave me. I'll never forget the good memories.

~ ~ ~

*Did you know* ... that the Peace Corps' foreign-language teaching program is one of the most extensive in the world? At this time Peace Corps operates in 74 countries, and this means that it teaches scores of languages.

Some countries have more than one official language. My Ukraine, for instance. Peace Corps teaches Ukrainian and Russian there. A few countries use English officially, and that makes it easier.

I have known Volunteers who found this a major reason to sign on—the chance to learn another language. Rarely do they have a choice. They study the language that they are assigned to study.

Some languages have global significance. Others, of course, have much less.

# 14 / My second 'family'

*I move in with Ira and her son, Slava.
It works out fine for a while. But then...*

It started this way. When I first met Dean Olena at *Coursi*, I told her I would be moving out from my host mother Natasha's. Two days later she told me, "I know a lady who has a very nice flat. She is a wonderful person. She makes good food. Is clean. You would be very comfortable there."

That recommendation from Olena carried a lot of weight. Even more when she told me that she and this lady—Ira—had been friends for many years.

"Ira is an entrepreneur!" Olena added.

Believe me, that was a high compliment in this newly capitalist country. Especially when said about a woman. *Maybe Ira runs a factory,* I thought.

It all sounded good. But Peace Corps would want a say in this. And so I got Oksana, the TCF that I knew well by now, to call this Ira and make an appointment for the two of us to visit. The visit would really be an inspection, of course.

We took a taxi. This was a surprise. Our Peace Corps officials always seemed to be driven around by professional chauffeurs in huge Toyota wagons. That impressed me every time. None available, she told me. I assumed we'd go by trolleybus. She said taxi. I liked that idea. So much easier. In fact, this would be my first ride in a taxi in Ukraine.

Small ordinary sedan. Man driver (nearly always). She gave him the address, and he drove us—in fact, he speeded—right to the development of big apartment blocks and right to the door of the right block. This guy really knew the city. She paid. No tip. That was an insight. "Same price for one or four—even five passengers!" she told me.

Good info, and incredible, though I found it to be true. And no tipping. But I'm sure this will develop, given the new capitalist spirit.

The blocks all looked alike—huge, squat, generic, functional buildings, totally devoid of ornamentation. In fact, ugly. Oksana gave me some pointers. "These buildings usually come in three sizes—five floors, nine floors, and fourteen floors. Don't ask me why. This is just the way it is. Those of five floors don't have an elevator. You have to use the stairs. The taller buildings have elevators and stairs. I know it sounds odd."

This building had nine floors. We went to the front door—just a plain piece of sheet metal. It was dark inside and I followed Oksana in cautiously, groping my way up six or seven steps to a landing.

This place didn't have the charm and convenience of Natasha's nice little house, believe me. What was I getting into?

We located the elevator, surprisingly tiny. Graffiti covered its walls. Wads of dirty bubble gum dotted the floor. Oksana pushed a button and we started up with a jerk. We got off at the fifth. We faced three doors. She found the correct door and pushed a buzzer. I noticed the door had a peep hole. The person inside could look out and check who was at the door.

A woman opened the door. "*Stradzvuite!*" she said. "Welcome!"

This was Ira. She was smiling. Iryna was her formal name. A little dumpling,, about 40. Behind her was a young man, her son, Slava. He was smiling also. He was 19, in his second year at the nearby Pedagogical University, majoring in physics and computer science. Oksana had told me there was a daughter, Olya, but she did not live here.

They led us into the living room. One big window with lace curtains. Modern upholstered furniture, quite new. A shiny coffee table. A big TV set. All quite attractive. It made me feel better.

We sat on the couch and they sat on chairs opposite us. The room was bright and pleasant. There were cookies and a pot of tea on the low table in front of us. Certainly they had prepared for us. Ira smiled a lot. That pleased me.

Oksana introduced me and they nodded. Slava spoke. "We know about you," and he gestured toward Oksana. "We are happy to have you here today." I was impressed by his English. His mother said something to him. "She asks if you would like some tea?"

Apparently she didn't have his ability. Natasha couldn't speak English either but still we made out.

"Yes, thank you," Ira served Oksana and then me and insisted I take a cookie. More small talk. Two more minutes and I got down to business. I mentioned what was important to me. I took a shower every morning. Had strong vegetarian leanings, ate very little flesh but liked vegetables and fruits. Did not smoke. Had a glass of wine or beer on occasions. Then I asked about washing machine, their daily routine, things like that.

Slava tried to translate for his mom, but it was slow going. Oksana took over. She'd tell me what Ira said. I was eager. In a few minutes Ira insisted on giving us a tour. From the first, Oksana had made me understand this was a superior flat because it had two bedrooms. Most had only one. A good thing she explained this. Back home in the U.S., I would have considered this a modest and ordinary apartment. Later I got to see other flats. Oksana had been right.

Ira led us to the end of the narrow hall and opened a door. The toilet. Just a closet just large enough for the toilet itself. Nothing else. So tiny. Difficult to use. Its right wall was open to the studs, exposing a water pipe—a plumber had had to break through to make a repair, I assumed. The wall had not been repaired. Not good.

Next to it was the bathroom. Plain but clean. It had a bathtub with a shower and next to it a hand sink. Squeezed in was a compact washing machine. Smaller than anything I had ever seen back home.. There was a neat pile of towels on it. Next to it a hamper with clothes in it. Natasha had had only a shower. This bathtub had appeal.

Ira took us into a bedroom. She said something to Oksana, and Oksana said, "This would be your room."

It looked crowded. But everything was neat. At the back it had a door and a window. The door had a window, too, which helped a lot. Out there was a covered balcony. It was glassed in with big windows. Clotheslines were strung from one side to the other. Blouses and trousers were drying on them It was jammed with odds and ends. Also a bicycle. Slava's, I assumed.

It turned out that every flat had a balcony like this. An important feature. You did not sit out there for pleasure. Nobody ever did that. This is where you kept your potatoes and cabbages and onions through the long winter. Stored stuff. Dried your clothes.

Back in the bedroom, I noticed the bed. So small. Just a cot. It reminded me of my boarding school days. Back home in Connecticut I had a nice big double bed. Could I get along with this tiny thing?

"Where does your Mom sleep?" I asked Slava. He pointed to the couch we had sat on in the living room. It converted to a bed. I learned that such couches were standard. The living room became another bedroom.

Ira led us into the kitchen. Tiny. Compact. Everything needed seemed to be here. The table was in a corner—large enough for four, five if you squeezed in. But no chairs. A padded L-shaped bench was built in. Two stools on the other sides. Like at Natasha's. Everything neat.

Ira led us back to the living room. Slava had gone off to his room. It must have been the one with the closed door I had noticed.

More tea. Ira excused herself for a minute. Oksana and I talked hurriedly. "Will the apartment be all right?" she asked. "Yes, I think so. It is clean. They look like nice people. A good location, you say. It will be okay."

This was several steps below what I was used to back home in Connecticut. Not as nice at Natasha's little house. But I knew things would be rougher wherever Peace Corps sent me. This would be adequate. More important—how well would the three of us get along?

And so, when Ira returned—Slava was with her now—I said I liked her home and would be pleased if she became my "host mother." I smiled as I said it. "Host mother" was quite a stretch. I was nearly twice her age! Oksana translated for me.

Oksana mentioned the price....1,000 *hryvnia* for room and board....and I accepted it. And that sealed the deal. I would move in a week, on the Saturday. I gave Ira a deposit. That sum would be the biggest chunk in my monthly Peace Corps allowance. It's about what I had been told was normal.

I asked Slava if he could help me to move in with all my stuff. "Yes!" No hesitation. That pleased me. We made a plan. He would come in a taxi at 10 a.m. that day.

Later, outside, Oksana said, "You will be happy here, John. They are good people." I appreciated that. I thanked her. Again I appreciated Peace Corps' assistance. A good outfit, Peace Corps.

Later I wondered about Slava's bedroom. In time I got to see it. Yes, that closed door was his. I understood why Ira hadn't opened it. The bed was unmade. Blankets were in a heap. Clothes on the floor. Also books and newspapers and this and that. He had a small desk jammed with a computer and stuff. An exercise machine was squeezed into a corner. Lots of posters on the walls, helter-skelter. I wasn't surprised. He was a teen-ager. My room looked like that back then.

**B**ack at Natasha's, I made my arrangements. On Saturday morning I had everything packed and ready. In Chapter 8, I told you about my leave-taking from her and her two sons. Brief but heartfelt. Peace Corps could not have placed me with a better family. I hoped they enjoyed me, too.

Slava showed up exactly at 10 in the taxi. Again tiny. He helped me pack everything in it. I had a lot by now. It was a trick. I paid for the taxi. Less than $3. Slava apologized for the big expense. For him a dollar was a significant sum. We drove off.

Natasha and her sons were standing close by. I gave them a wave and a smile, and they responded. The big question in my mind: *why hadn't they invited me to stay on?*

Slava's mom was waiting for us. A hearty welcome. She wanted to help carry in my things. How nice, but I said no. Slava was a big help. She went and made lunch. Tasty. Substantial enough. I was off to a good start. I began putting my things away. I crossed my fingers for good luck.

I got to know the family well. And I got to like them. Yes, good folks.

It turned out Ira was strong-willed—truly a matriarch. She was the head and heart of the family. The total support for herself and Slava, if not for her daughter. All I knew was her name was Olya. Ira was admirable in many ways. Again, no man in the house. I never heard of the husband / father.

Ira was a dynamo. A tireless worker. Slava told me she drove taxi for many years, "20 hours a day." Napping at the wheel between passengers, he said. I believed him.

He called her an entrepreneur, just as Olena had. That title was a big honor in what until not long had been a Communist society which proclaimed capitalism evil. I was eager to hear about her big enterprise.

Well, she was a sales agent for Oriflame, which is a European sort of Mary Kaye, if you're familiar with that—selling cosmetics and household products to customers who in turn become agents selling to other customers.

Oriflame was a huge Swedish outfit, operating all over Europe and parts of South and Central America. She had been selling for Oriflame three years. Now she had 300 customer-agents. It was a major achievement. But I didn't think she'd be called an entrepreneur back in the U.S.

She was up at 7 on most days, made breakfast and served me, did chores, did some cooking for dinner, and was out the door to her office at 10 a.m. She returned at 8:30 p.m. and sometimes later, made dinner, washed the dishes, watched half an hour of TV, and then to bed. Yes, on that couch!

Never, never a complaint from her. Every day was a good day, even when it wasn't. She loved Oriflame and was highly successful. Two weeks after I moved in, she came home with a shiny new watch, an award from Oriflame.

A month later Oriflame gave her a laptop computer for high performance. Slava was giving her daily lessons how to use it.

She had just attended a sales seminar in Kyiv and came back excited—she had spoken to a couple who indeed had become millionaires through Oriflame.

She told me she hoped to own a car in two years. A used one, most likely. Very few people owned a car. Gas was the equivalent of $5 a gallon and the average family income was $350 a month. I believed she would buy that car.

"I will be a millionaire!" she told me. I believed her.

She tried to get Slava and Olya interested in the business. Slava worked at it on his vacations, but half-heartedly. Olya had other plans and they seemed realistic. I'll tell you about her shortly.

With both host families I had been lucky in a special way. Natasha's children and Ira's children spoke English! Both women could speak a few words. This made it easier for me to communicate. I spoke a few words of Russian—just a few. But Ira and I made ourselves understood. When something important had to be said, we did it through her children. But this was an impediment. Without them I would have learned Russian better.

My room was adequate. Quite comfortable except for that cot. A lot of natural light. A couch. It opened to make a bed except that the mechanism didn't work. A small gateleg table with two leaves. I was amazed how big when opened. It became my desk.

I had a wardrobe, too. I needed every square foot I could scrounge for all my stuff. The wardrobe had many heavy boxes piled high on top of it. Candles. Ira had left them up there when she cleared the room for me. Slava had a tiny business selling candles, and this was his stock. I had my eye on that space. Eventually I got him to move them out and in fact helped him. I never saw him sell a single candle. And I piled my stuff up there.

One thing I didn't like. The family would enter my room to get to the balcony, sometimes when I was out. But they kept it to a minimum.

The Robinson Crusoe in me led to a lot of improvements. I read "Robinson Crusoe" when I was eight or nine—could not understand all the words—but was forever changed, and for the better.

I like to create and improvise and come up with "10-cent solutions." I made improvements, big and small. I changed the couch into a dresser of sorts with a couple of long boards and some boxes. Then I made myself a filing cabinet. I converted an old sewing machine cabinet into another table. Other improvements, too.

To gain more space, I had to shift things around, and Ira and Slava went along. I needed a better arrangement for my Apple computer set-up. The only solution was to buy a table for it. Slava told me about *Bena*, which in Cyrillic is pronounced "Vienna," like the Austrian city. It was a small copycat of one of our Home Depots or Lowe's. Impressive.

There I found a satisfactory table. But it came as a kit. It was only about $39, which was a lot in Chernihiv, but that included the 20 percent sales tax that applied to everything, including food. Yes, 20 percent on everything!

But how to get it home? Slava offered to help me. I took him to *Bena* by trolleybus. The rear of all trolleybuses had some seats removed. This allowed more standees to crowd in. It also gave space for people

bringing on a baby carriage or TV set. We'd take my table home this way.
I expected to pick up a cardboard box with all the pieces packed in. No. This was a demo table and the last of this model in the store. So all set up. A crew had taken it apart for us, piled all the pieces neatly together, and wrapped them. Slava lifted the bundle. He was strong but this was too heavy. What to do? I got the crew to take the bundle apart and make two bundles. One for him and one for me. We could manage these.

As we walked out, I spotted a taxi. It left off a passenger. I told Slava to rush over and ask how much to take us home. He did. "Eleven *hryvnia!*" he said. "Much too expensive!"

That amounted to $2.20. I would have jumped in. Slava thought it was exorbitant so I went along with him. I was mindful of what Peace Corps kept telling us. "Do not act like rich Americans! Please do not create that impression."

"Which way to the trolleybus stop?" I said to him. He pointed across the street. "Let's go," I said, and we started toward it. Even separated, the bundles were heavy.

Then Slava let out a yell. A small, old sedan had just pulled in. He recognized the driver, who was alone. "Andrei, my neighbor!" he told me, and rushed to where it had stopped. He persuaded Andrei to give us a ride home. But first, we had to wait for Andrei to finish his errand in the store, which would take only 5 minutes but took 35. Then Andrei packed our bundles into the trunk, barely getting them in, and we squeezed in, Slava in the front. It was only a 10-minute ride back.

I was ready with some cash in my hand. After we stopped and took out our bundles, I put the money into Andrei's hand. "For *pivo*," I said. "Beer!"

"No, no!"

I pressed it upon him. Again he refused it. I changed my pitch. "Then for chocolate for your children!" I said.

"No, no!"

He won. Later I learned he was Ira's boss in Oriflame. That explained things. Slava and I assembled the table. It took only 20 minutes. It was the finishing touch to what became a pleasant and functional room—except for my cot. It was a pleasure to set up my computer equipment on it. I spent hours at the computer every day.

One thing annoyed me besides my cot. It was the gateleg table that I used as my desk. I had to sit at the middle on one side—it was the most practical position. But my knees knocked up against the side of the table, which was a rectangle of plywood about 18 inches wide.

I got a brainstorm. I decided to cut away a curved vertical slice on each side of this panel. It would leave about eight inches of plywood. It would still be plenty strong. This way I could straddle this narrow panel with my knees and be closer to my work.

I brought it up with Slava. He brought it up with his mom. They stood at my side as I explained. I penciled two light lines on the plywood panel. I explained how I would saw off these twin sections. "Slava, see what an improvement that would be!" I said.

They had a discussion. They frowned. Slava looked at me. He looked doubtful. "You will not be with us many more months, John. Is it necessary to do this?"

"Slava, I spend many hours at this desk every day. Look!" I showed him how I had to hold my knees sideways. "I will do a good job. And if you do not like my work, I will buy you a new table."

They looked at one another. Finally they agreed.

I had no tools. I thought of buying an electric jigsaw but too expensive and I would never use it again. I returned to *Bena* and after careful checking bought two hand tools—a coping saw and a sheetrock saw. I needed the two. And two grades of sandpaper. These simple tools would do.

On Saturday I cleared everything off the table, put sheets of newspaper on the carpet, and put the table on its side. And got to work with my

*Our Sunday dinners were wonderful. That's Viktor pouring for Olya. I liked them.*

saws. I worked very carefully. It was hard, tedious sawing. I took breaks. I finished one cut and started the next. Finally I cut off the second piece. Then sanded and sanded, all by hand. Finally I finished.

Ira and Slava had heard me sawing, I was sure, but had not ventured in. I was sure they were worried. All done, I invited them in, showed them my work. I sat at the desk and showed them how I could now tuck my knees under the table. Before, I had to sit diagonally. So awkward. They saw my pride.

Slava said, "Very, very good, John." Ira smiled and patted my shoulder. What a happy day it turned out to be. I took photos as a souvenir.

Another thing irritated me. When I came home, I always had trouble unlocking the apartment door. It was hard to stick my key into the lock and turn it. I told Slava, "A few drops of oil would make a big difference."

He nodded but never bothered. I told him again. Nothing happened. I was annoyed every time I unlocked the door. One day I returned. Viktor was replacing the lock—I'll tell you about Viktor in a minute. Slava was watching but did not explain. Too embarrassed. Viktor explained to me. "Slava broke the key in the lock!" I was so happy I could have grinned. But I managed to muffle it. I had warned Slava! A drop of oil can perform a miracle. He would never forget this!

I went all out to be nice. She made it a point to serve a varied menu. One Sunday she made a delicious pudding. She asked me if I liked it. I gave her a loud *da*! (yes). "Please make it every Sunday!" I said it as a joke. Well, she made it every Sunday.

At breakfast, she'd make something fresh. A stack of *blinis* (pancakes), or an omelet. But she also put on the table all the left-overs from the evening before. A left-over fish. Or half a pizza, Ukrainian pizza—not real pizza to me. Or some *salo*, a great delicacy. It's raw pig fat, sometimes seasoned. No appeal for me. Sorry. Or *borsch*, the famous beet soup. I liked that.

We each got a spoon and a fork but no knife. Only one knife was placed on the table. It was a big knife to slice the bread (machine-sliced bread seemed unpopular) or to cut a piece of *salo* or cheese. We passed the knife to one another.

If you had a chicken cutlet on your plate, what you'd do was stab it with your fork and lift it to your mouth and bite off a piece. Then you'd put it down and take a bite of potatoes or something else. Then you'd stab and lift the cutlet again. This was completely proper.

Dinner plates were much smaller—like our saucers. Maybe this was a carry-over from the hungry times many families experienced. Maybe this was why most people were thin. Very little obesity.

Plenty to eat. No problem. But all through winter, it was potatoes, cabbage, beets, carrots, onions. Potatoes and cabbage were mainstays. Potatoes were served mashed or fried. I never got to eat a baked potato. Cabbage was served at every meal, usually uncooked as a slaw. Sometimes with grated carrot or onion. With vegetable oil and salt and pepper and a bit of parsley. Tasty. Or drenched with mayonnaise. I liked it both ways.

I never got celery or lettuce of any kind. In the winter, tomatoes and other fresh vegetables and many fruits were prohibitively expensive. At Ira's I never saw a banana served, or a pear, or a plum. I got to eat these because I bought them as a snack for school.

I had arrived in Ukraine with a jar of Skippy peanut butter but it was long gone. Juan-Carlos Campos, the assistant Peace Corps director in Kyiv, had assured me that Ukrainian peanut butter was available and quite good. I searched for it but no luck.

I had one problem with the food. As I said, Ira got home at 8:30 or 9. Then she made dinner. Fried many things—they would drip with oil. I went to bed at 10 or 11. Immediately I had to take an ant-acid tablet. Not good.

I decided to talk to Ira and Slava about a new food set-up. Then he would talk to his mom about it. I would eat breakfast as usual. I would eat lunch on my own—they were never around. But have only *chai* (tea) and a snack when I got home after my classes at night, with him and her if available. So, no more dinners.

"How much would this save me?" I asked him. Quite a bit, I expected. He checked with his mother. She trimmed my monthly tab just a few *hryvnia*. I did not dispute it. The new system worked fine.

Oh, a very sad happening. Slava had a serious girlfriend. I met her only once. Attractive. Seemed a nice girl. Never got to chat with her. They would enter his bedroom and close the door. One evening I arrived home at 9:30 and found Ira silent and abrupt. Unusual. Slava was not around. Unusual. I wondered, *What the heck is going on?*

The next morning I found out his girlfriend had died.

"Cancer," his sister Olya told me. "There was no hope. Everybody knew."

Slava closeted himself in his room for three days. He emerged only for the funeral. I did not get to participate. Ours became a very sad home. Slowly things got better.

*Ira went all out at every holiday. She worked hard in her business of selling cosmetics, but her family came first.*

During Training, I was up and hopping at 6 a.m. Now I was a working Volunteer.

My classes were in the evening. It would be 7:45 a.m. and I'd be just getting up. At first I felt guilty. But I was not due at school till 11.

It was the first time I would sleep so late. Maybe due to the tough pace of my first three months. Maybe because it was winter. At 7:30 a.m. the sky was just brightening.

**M**aybe I was in an emotional slump now that all my buddies were gone and I was alone. Still, I was always up before Ira and Slava.

I showered and did my morning limbering exercises, a habit of 30 years. Stretching, squatting, bending. Many sets. I never missed a morning.

Then Ira and I ate breakfast together. Slava stayed in bed. She insisted on serving me, then sat across from me. Few words would pass between us. My Russian and her English were so poor. We'd pass my English /Russian dictionary back and forth.

I would look up a word in the English section. "Snowy," for instance. I'd mark it with a dot, then pass the book to her.

She would read and nod. Then she'd look up a Russian word and dot it. I would read its English translation. So it went. Amazing how many dots my dictionary was collecting.

You would think that I was picking up a lot of new words. No. For me, it was in one ear and out the other. Every word needed constant repetition. Yes, constant repetition.

And best of all, what I called an "association." It was so discouraging. But I could see her progress! How I envied the young Volunteers. My consolation was that I was quick like them once!

Sometimes for me our silences were awkward and uncomfortable. Here we were, face to face! Unable to have a decent conversation. I'm sure Ira felt the same way. But we managed.

I never saw her not cheerful. Ask her how her day was and her answer was always the same. "Very good day!" She meant it.

**W**hat a worker she was. Up early, made her bed and tidied her room. Made breakfast for us, kept me company, cooked the main dish she would serve in the evening. Washed the dishes and tidied the kitchen. Then dressed for work. Gave Slava instructions if up.

At 10 a.m. sharp, she popped her head in my room. "Have a good day!" she would say brightly. She had her high heels on and her lipstick and her nice coat and fancy hat, and her briefcase in hand. Quite a transformation. She was off to her office. She'd return at 8:30 or 9 p.m.

She insisted that I lock the door behind her. She put great emphasis on keeping the door locked, even when all three of us were inside. Made me wonder what might have happened in the past.

Slava rarely joined us—slept as late as he could, sometimes until noon on no-school mornings. No wonder. Sometimes I'd get up at 3 a.m.

to go to the toilet and I'd see the light under his door. A night owl. He'd get up only after his mom reminded him two or three times, and just in time to rush out and catch a *marshrutka* to school.

On Sunday, when he did have breakfast with us, he'd be very pleasant. He'd talk about wind power or tidal power as good alternate sources of energy, which he happened to read about during the night, or some other technical subject that had caught his eye. I enjoyed chatting with him.

His English surprised me time and again. We always spoke in English, never Russian. In one sense his interest in English was a problem. If it had been poor, I would have practiced my Russian more. Using English was the easy way out for me, sad to say.

There was a further problem. Necessarily his mom got left out of our conversations. Time and again I would say to him, "Slava, tell her what we're talking about! She is curious." He would tell her just a couple of words. She felt frustrated. It made me angry.

One day he told me his favorite sport was competitive rifle target-shooting—shooting at tiny tossed targets at a range. Quite a surprise. He told me that he was a champion-level shooter at the national university level across the nation. He had medals to prove it. He explained how precise and demanding the sport was, and what split-second reaction it took.

He owned a beautiful 10-speed derailleur bike. He told me how proud he was when his mom bought it for him. It was the most beautiful bike in the neighborhood. All his friends were envious. He kept it on the balcony. But he never used it.

I talked with him a lot about bikes and biking because I had been an active rider for many years. In fact, right into my 60's.

Never a competitive rider. I loved to ride for the fun of it. And the exercise.

Mine was a 10-speed model, also. Like his. I would tell him about my biking adventures, and my travels with one. It was always on its rack on the front of my VW Microbus during my rambling travels around the United States and through Mexico.

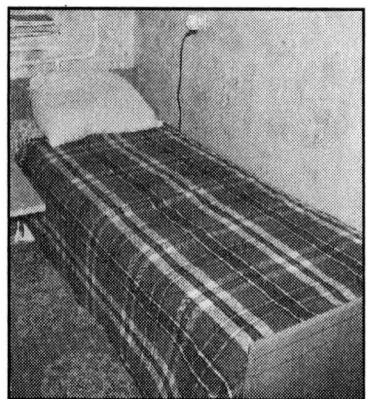

*Too narrow. Never got used to it. Little I could do about it. For now.*

I would park and go off pedaling on jaunts in cities and towns—wherever I happened to be. He enjoyed my stories.

**F**inally spring came and I prodded him and he cleaned and oiled his bike and decided to take a ride. He had to take it downstairs in that tiny elevator, of course. Not easy. He was gone for a couple of hours. When he returned, he thanked me for my encouragement. But it was the only time I saw him use it.

I stressed how our Chernihiv region was perfect for bike-riding. No mountains, only a few easy hills. I told him how at many universities in the U.S. and in many other countries, it was common for students to bike to school.

I talked about the money he would save, the exercise he would get, the wonderful fresh air, the freedom to roam here and there.

"Somebody will steal it," was his usual reply.

I talked about good locks and how to use one. About bike-parking lots at universities and other public places. "But there are no such lots in our country!" I told him that if enough students demanded these improvements, they would get them. He listened but my words had zero impact.

**I**ra served a full breakfast. She might make something fresh, an omelet or some tiny pizzas, but she would also cover the table with all of last night's left-overs. Maybe a plate of salo, the raw pig fat Ukrainians love.

Or the remains of a fish (cold). Or mashed potatoes (re-heated), a *salat*, the last pieces of a cake, or a plateful of miscellaneous cookies.

Plus bread, always two kinds, white and rye, and cheese and butter. And whatever else that she might might see deep back in the fridge—maybe her homemade stewed tomatoes, or a jar of pickles.

A *salat* was a salad. A totally Russian salad. Not the lettuce and fresh tomatoes and cucumber salad that I was accustomed to. It consisted of finely shredded *kapushta*–cabbage. She would include shredded beets, or onions, or carrots. I ate her *salat* every morning. Good for me!

My "office" with my kit table assembled. Every inch of my room was taken up. I was happy.

Oh, there were other veggies available, such as tomatoes or eggplant, but so expensive that she bought them only at the height of the harvest when prices dropped.

In early spring when the radishes came in, she'd serve a bowl of them. In fact, often. I'd dip them into salt. She'd also add slices to her *salat*. When the cucumbers arrived, she'd offer a plate of length-wise slices, always with the skin on. All my life I had eaten cucumbers peeled.

She had never heard of a salt shaker. She served salt in a tiny dish. Want to salt your cucumber? Take a pinch and spread it. Surprising how hard it was to spread it evenly this way. Ah, ethnic cultures are so interesting.

Surprise! One day she asked me what I would like for breakfast. "Cold cereal," I said. "Muesli would be good. With cold milk."

That night she showed up with muesli—oats and corn flakes with raisins and chopped apricots and prunes and a few nuts. And milk, which had been a rare treat. She served the muesli for the next three days, until it was gone.

Then she replenished the supply. But this time she bought the cereals and the dried fruit and everything else separately and mixed them herself. Good idea. Frugality was a national trait. I am frugal myself.

But she had so much fruit in it that it tied up my bowels. I protested and she let me mix the proportions. I cut down on the fruit, which helped not only me but her budget. She took a liking to muesli and ate it often.

One thing I missed were toasts. I like one or two at breakfast. I went for five months without eating a toast! What a happy day when Dean Olena gave me that toaster at school.

Ira and Slava watched me set it up. They stood by curiously when I dropped in the first two slices. They popped up perfectly. I buttered them and gave them to them.

Slava took an immediate liking. Ira took longer. But soon they were eating toasts every day. Even bought sliced bread—a first for them. See what a powerful influence a Volunteer could have in spreading American culture! Just joking. But seriously, it was surprising the impact Volunteers could have in various ways.

She liked to serve pizza, but her version. She'd cut a slice of bread, plop a slice of tasteless cheese on it, and put this in the microwave. "Pizza!" she'd smile. Soggy. Awful. A small piece would be enough for me.

Ira and I had a little routine. Before breakfast one of us would check the thermometer in the window. She would say *dva plus* or *chetire minus*. That meant "two above zero" or "four below."

Celsius scale, by the way, not Fahrenheit. We'd look out to see if there was a wind. The wind made the temperature a lot colder, of course.

Then she'd refill our tea cups and we'd do 15 minutes of vocabulary together. We were both struggling to expand our lists of words. It was a serious business. Again we sat across from one another.

I had bought myself a dual Russian / English word and phrase book at a newsstand—an inexpensive paperback. It listed everyday practical words and expressions in categories. Excellent. I carried it with me all the time. I'd study it while waiting for a bus. I got more out of it than the big volumes Peace Corps had provided.

One day I bought one for her. A small gift. "Oh, thank you, John!" Her words were so sincere! From that day on we'd work at the table each with our own copy in hand.

We'd both turn to a certain page and I would read off English words and she would try to repeat them and memorize them.

Then she would read off Russian words and I'd do the same. We'd list our new words on a pad we each kept. Truth was, she was learning more English than I was Russian.

I must tell you about our Sunday dinners. They were truly family dinners. They included daughter Olya and Viktor, the man she lived with.

Now about Olya. Very smart. She was 20, a year older than Slava. She was majoring in psychology at the same university. My room used to be hers. I'm sure my narrow bed was fine for her.

For a year she had been living with Viktor, who was 41, I believe. He owned his own business. He sold veterinary medicines wholesale. He had recently bought a new Ford SUV, very expensive in Ukraine. He was the only Ukrainian I knew who owned a car.

*I put my table on its side, drew the two cut-outs, and started sawing. It was an improvement I got to appreciate every day.*

Olya was a knock-out. Beautiful with the classic Slavic attributes: tall, fair-complexioned, skinny-slim, beautiful long tresses. Always elegantly coifed and manicured and dressed.

Her English was as good as Slava's, which means attention-getting. And she was a brilliant student. Her grades were so good that the university waived her tuition. Slava had to pay, which was strange to me because he was smart also.

Schools throughout the country sent their best students to compete in national "Olympiads" in physics, literature, English, psychology, and so on. The previous year she had come in thirtieth in psychology in the country, and this year fourth!

She came nearly every Sunday for the family dinner, occasionally with Viktor, who seemed a nice guy. Ira told me she liked him. I was aware that in many countries, people think it's wiser for a younger woman to link up with an older man...more worldly and experienced and well off, hopefully. The five of us were a big crowd in the tiny kitchen. Viktor was a big man, so he always sat at the head of the table.

**I** would shake my head when I'd think about her with Viktor. I liked him. He was friendly and personable. And I had to admire his success. But I didn't like his thinking in taking up with Olya.

There she was, so young, beautiful, a dean's list student, perhaps naïve in the ways of the world. And there he was in his 40's, divorced and a father, I had learned, and a seasoned businessman. I thought it was terrible but kept that to myself. But Ira and Slava seemed to accept the situation, even approve it.

Olya seemed most happy. It was amazing what beautiful outfits she sported and what nice accessories she had. I doubted that other girls at the university had the equal. I wondered how it would work out in time.

Ira went all out for the dinners. She served not one, but three or four meat and fish dishes, plus two or three *salats*, plus everything else needed. The food took up every inch on the table. Alcohol was essential. Ira brought out a left-over bottle of wine and served a big bottle of beer sometimes. Viktor always bought something high-powered...vodka, the country's beloved iconic booze—or perhaps cognac. I always brought a bottle of wine and a box of chocolates.

Sweets were also essential. What a sweet tooth Ukrainians had! Ira always provided a big store-bought cake, elaborately decorated with thick, multi-colored frostings. It was the only time that she bought a cake. I always enjoyed the dinners, although I had only the vaguest idea ...sometimes no idea... of what they were saying. Viktor loved to talk and was good at it. We always focused on him.

He drank a lot of alcohol, and whenever he poured himself another shot, he poured a little bit of it into our glasses.

Toasts were essential and frequent, and there had to be something in every uplifted glass! Nothing elaborate, though.

Just "To Family!" Or "To Love!" Alwsays "To Prosperity!" Then Viktor would drain his glass in one gulp!
A dinner could last 90 minutes or even longer. I never saw an unpleasant moment. They were big beautiful events. Every family should have such dinners. But with limited alcohol, please.

Sunday dinner. Ira and Slava always asked me to join them and I always said *a quick yes.*

**F**or extra big dinners, meaning for more than the five of us, the table was moved into the living room next door. Such as for Ira's mother's 65th birthday. A beautiful lady, quick to pitch in and help. Ira went all out! She was the guest of honor at our dinner.

Also present was Ira's younger sister, who came with her 14-year-old daughter as well as her twin daughters, only 14 months old. They were so cute. The attention we gave them! Again, never a mention of a husband.

For that dinner, the only two real chairs were brought in—one of them from my desk. And all the stools were carried in.

Ira labored from 7 a.m. right to the dinner at 6 p.m., finally sitting and dining with us. Everybody had a good time, including me. It always made me feel good to be invited.

It was amazing to me that after all these big dinners, Viktor looked in decent shape to drive home. I would be afraid to ride with him.

I had a habit. After dessert, I excused myself and returned to my room. I left them to their privacy. I'm sure they enjoyed having a break from me.

Slava's birthday was soon. What could I give that would be different?

I invited him to our McDonald's Restaurant downtown. It was the only McDonald's in this whole section of Ukraine. It was considered expensive. You went there only for special occasions. A big date. Maybe just once out of curiosity. He glowed when I told him, and we went by *marshrutka* on the next Saturday. "Order anything you want," I told him.

He went all out. A Big Mac. The biggest order of fries. Chicken Fingers. The biggest Coke. A sundae, then an apple pie. Ate it all. More Coke.

I liked the McDonald's and would go now and then, but only for a coffee or one of the tiny ice cream cones. Sometimes I would splurge with fries. That's all that I had with Slava—fries, a cone, and a coffee. We had one of our good chats. I told him about founder Ed Krock and Hamburger University and other McDonald's lore. They loved it all.

Then I saw dark clouds on our relationship. More and more, Ira began complaining about inflation. I got to feel that she was making her remarks pointedly. I was aware of the double-digit inflation, of course. I shopped for things myself. My friends and students talked about it.

At night I would see old men and women roaming the streets and scrounging for empty returnable beer bottles. But the good news was that Ira was prospering with Oriflame and proud of it, and rightly so.

But the only way that I was a factor in this inflation was the food that I ate and the bit of electricity I used. I ate small portions and never took seconds; that happened to be my style. And I never ate meat or fish...in other words, her most expensive items.

I had only one light in my room and I turned on my computer only for a couple of hours. That was it. Bottom line: all their other household expenses would have gone up just as much even without me.

That 1,000 *hryvnia* a month which I was paying her was the average monthly income for many families. It was the price set by Peace Corps, and Peace Corps paid it my first month at Ira's. This included my room and my laundry and my electricity and my breakfast and evening dinner every day. My monthly payment to them was a huge plus in their budget!

One noon at table Slava brought it up. "We must ask you for more money, John," he told me." And Ira spoke up. "Yes, John," she said. "Inflation! Inflation!" And she threw up her hands in frustration.

"How much more would you like?" He mentioned a 33% increase. I was taken aback. In fact, I was shocked. "Let me think about it, Slava."

I let a week go by, then another. And another. He did not bring it up but I knew the matter was high in his mind. And in his mother's.

I was delaying because I had an important matter of my own that I was considering. I had invited milady Annabelle to come from California and visit, and she had agreed. In fact, I had mentioned this to Slava and Ira. Summer was approaching—the best season.

I wondered whether somehow things could be re-arranged in my room to make it possible for her to move in. Not possible, I had decided. I had considered getting a flat of my own and had looked at a nice one.

But I preferred having someone like Ira and Slava to come home to at night. How good they had been that frigid winter evening when I got knocked over by a drunk—a frightful experience that I will tell you about in Chapter 23. And I greatly appreciated not being burdened with all the shopping and cooking and housecleaning.

So I decided find another another "host mother." I found a woman who would charge exactly the same. She was well recommended. I could walk to downtown! It had many other advantages. Even a big bed!.

I made arrangements to move to the new place on the first of the month. Two weeks to go. Should I mention it to Slava and Ira now? It seemed the right thing to do. Should I not? I decided that if I did, there would be enormous tension between us during the interlude.

I mentioned it to Slava just the day before I moved out. I had to steel myself. Yes, it was a shock to him. "Annabelle is coming," I said. "This room of mine is too, too small!"

He was dumbfounded. I had to explain again. He just walked away.

It made me feel I had made the right decision by delaying my announcement. Two weeks with this over our heads would have been difficult. I had just about everything packed and ready. And I had friends ready to come and help me.

It was an emotional parting. "You are good people," I told them. "I like you very much. I have had happy days with you. I won't forget you." It was all true. And they were very nice to me when I said goodbye. Ira was dabbing her eyes with a tissue. I felt very emotional myself.

~ ~ ~

*Did you know* ... that Peace Corps takes the safety and security of its Volunteers most seriously? In Ukraine, we had a full-time security director—a former Soviet colonel, or so the rumor went. He did an impressive job.

From what I saw there, I know that Peace Corps takes great precautions in every country and gives detailed training.

There are dangers that go with being a Volunteer, and we were warned of them. How to act, how not to behave and where not to go, how to get emergency help, and how to get all that started.

There are accidents and assaults and robberies and hate crimes and there have been numerous murders and rapes over the years.

But of course these can happen at home in the United States, too.

# 15 / I follow orders

*Peace Corps tells me to get set up with the police and the bank. Not that easy.*

*I'd better get with it*, I thought. I had moved in with my second family and had started teaching at *Coursi*. But I had not followed through on two Peace Corps demands!

"Go introduce yourself to the police as soon as you can," Peace Corps had told us. "And to the bank! Important!"

Okay!

They wanted the police to know that I was a new Volunteer in town and where I was living. And for me to know how to contact the police if need be—emergencies do come up.

And to the bank so they could pay me my monthly allowance. I needed it to live. I had to open an account in the local branch of the national ProCredit Bank. Peace Corps would deposit my money in my account. And I could draw it from a teller or an ATM as needed. I was running low of *hryvnia*.

But where was the police station? The bank? And how would I explain things there? Would they use Ukrainian, the official language? Or would it be Russian, which was what most people spoke here? I was positive about one thing. I would need assistance!

It was easy to get the address of the police station. Not easy for the ProCredit branch in Chernihiv. Finally I found a brochure which listed all its branches. Some cities had many branches. Chernihiv had only one, near Red Square, the most beautiful square in town. I wrote down its address.

I asked Dean Olena about assistance. "No problem, John," she said. "Speak to Lina. She will help you."

Lina was the methodologist at *Coursi*. Always ready to lend a hand. She had good news—the police station and the bank were in the same neighborhood. "I shall accompany you!" she said. Her English was amazing.

"*Harrasho!*" I said. That's Russian. It means "Great!" That made her smile. It pleased her that I was using a bit of Russian.

We started out together late one morning. *This will be easy,* I thought. We took a trolleybus to close to the Police Station and had to walk only a few yards. It was a grim, nondescript building. Lots of activity inside. We were told to wait in the hall and we sat on a bench there. Twenty minutes later an official came out and invited us into her office. She examined the forms I had filled out. Wrong office! The right office was upstairs. Up we went. That office was busy. "Wait in the hall, please," a clerk told us. Finally we were called in.

A large room with a high ceiling—a corner room, which made it even more impressive. A man in uniform sat at a big desk. He had gold stars on his shoulder pads. Fifty-ish. Tall and muscular. He was on the phone, talking loudly. Barking! In Russian or Ukrainian, certainly not English. He went on for a long time. Whoever was at the other end didn't have a chance.

**F**inally he slapped down the phone and looked at us. His attitude changed 180 degrees. He smiled. He shook hands with us. "Please sit down," he said, indicating two chairs in front of his desk. I still couldn't tell whether he was using Ukrainian or Russian. I'd have to ask Lina later.

She did the talking. He listened politely, glanced at me, asked her a question or two, and looked at me again and smiled a bit, shaking his head. He examined the papers Lina gave him. Looked at me again. Obviously he was puzzled. I thought I knew why. He saw on the papers that I was a Volunteer. But Volunteers were young people. He asked Lina more questions. I could tell she was re-assuring him.

He examined the papers again, then signed them. He kept some papers, returned two to Lina. He looked at me again and began talking to me earnestly. I had no idea what he was saying.

Lina translated. He was welcoming me to Chernihiv. And he was telling me to beware of thieves. Every city in the world has thieves. Not to keep my wallet in my back pocket. Not to open my wallet in public. To make sure I had back-up copies at home of all important documents. To carry only essential cards and documents and to leave all the others at home. He was emphatic. Very. He meant business.

Then he rose and extended his hand and I took it. Said nice words. Not sure what but I thought I got the drift. "Enjoy our city! We appreciate your being a Volunteer here. We appreciate what you Volunteers do. Good luck! Do not hesitate to call us if you need us."

Now I could make out he was speaking Russian. In fact, it was the street version called *surgeit*, a mixture of both. He spoke all these words in the mildest tones and most cordially. Hard to believe this was the tough man we had walked in on. And he shook my hand.

"*Spacibo!*" I said. "*Ochen spacibo!*" – "Thank you very much!" He smiled and gave me a pat on the shoulder.

Outside, Lina said he was not just an officer. He was the police chief!

Now on to the bank. Oops! This had taken us a long time. Lina apologized—she had to get back to *Coursi*. The bank was nearby. It was at 11 Shevchenko Street. She told me how to get to it. "They will speak English," she said. "No problem."

She turned left and I went right. It was just a few minutes' walk to the bank. No ProCredit Bank. Yes, I was on Shevchenko Street. I walked along looking for Number 11. Many buildings did not have a number. At what I thought was Number 11 was a TAC Bank! I couldn't figure this out.

It was 1:10 p.m. The bank was closed. Lunch break. Would re-open at 2. What to do? Come back on another day? No, better to finish this now.

I took a walk and spotted an interesting café and went in. Upscale place. The nicest café I had seen so far. I was delighted. Big assortment of fantastic pastries. Cappuccino coffee! Ordered a cup. The pastries were too fattening. I ordered a gorgeous fruit cup. Putting in my order was not a problem. All I had to do was point to what I wanted. Delicious.

But still 30 minutes to go before the bank re-opened. I strolled through the neighborhood and got back to the bank at 2:03. It was open.

I showed my documents to a clerk. She did not understand and I could not explain. A lot of good all that language study was doing me! She called another clerk. Same problem. Lina had said they would speak English! Hah!

An older man at a far desk came over and looked at my papers. He told me his name was Yuri. "I speak English." He smiled. "But just a little bit!"

"But am I in the right bank? This is a TAC bank. I am supposed to go to the ProCredit Bank."

"You are right. This is a TAC Bank. But we are a…partner bank…. I think 'partner' is the right word? How can I help you?"

I got him to understand I wanted to complete the paperwork and withdraw money. "Yes," he said. "Come to my desk, please."

He asked for my passport. *No problem*, I thought. I did not have my passport but I had a photocopy. The passport was precious. I left it at home. The photocopy always worked fine. He could see my photo on it. He double-checked by glancing at me. Yes, I was the man of that photo.

But then he frowned. "Sorry, Mister," he said. "This not good. Real passport necessary."

But it was at home! I didn't want to go back for it and go through this hassle again. I offered him my Peace Corps "Pink Card," which we had been told to carry at all times for instances like this. He looked at it. He shook his head vigorously and gave it back to me. "No!" he said. "Very sorry!"

What to do? How irritating. I had an inspiration. On the Pink Card I showed him the name and phone number of our security expert at headquarters in Kyiv, Sergey Sukhov. I made him understand to please call Mr. Sukhov. He did! What a decent guy. Sergey had impressed me. A very forceful and authoritative man. I waited with confidence.

They had an amiable conversation. Everything would be fine, I was sure. He put down the phone and spoke to me. He believed I was who I said I was, but without a passport, no initial withdrawal!

"Please return with your passport," he told me. "We have rules! They are for your protection and the bank's."

I understood. But damn!

**I** returned the following day. He spotted me and approached smiling and gave me his hand. I showed him my passport. "Excellent," he said. "Everything okay now." Yes, he said "okay"—he knew a bit of our slang! He put on his overcoat and led me to the ATM machine outside. No buttons in English! They were in Ukrainian, he said.

He punched the keys for me. I tried to memorize his sequence for my next visit. I managed to withdraw 1,000 *hryvnia*. Sounds like a lot. It was $200—what I needed to keep going for one month..

I noticed the bank was paying 12.4% on savings accounts. A huge return! I wondered, *shouldn't I open a savings account?* I had a stash of dollars under my mattress in my room that I had brought with me from home just in case. Well, I'd think about that.

We said goodbye. He told me to stop in and see him personally. "Please call me Yuri!" he said amiably. "Have a good day. Good fortune!" I knew he meant good luck but I didn't correct him.

On the way home I kept thinking about the 12.4% interest. Very appealing. But the high inflation would erode most of that. Still, it was better than the 0% interest on the account I had just opened!

I was tempted. Then I found out Peace Corps did not allow a savings account. Something about not earning money off our Peace Corps service while in service! Silly, I thought. But I wouldn't start an argument about it.

**W**hy have I given you all this detail? To show you that many ordinary things for us in the U.S. were very complicated in this new world of mine. They could become very time-consuming and irritating. This is the way it was in going to the Post Office...or taking a bus...or ordering a meal in a restaurant...or finding the right shop to buy something.

I know what you're thinking about finding the right shop: "John! Just look in the Yellow Pages!"

Good idea, thank you. But there was no Yellow Pages phone book here that I knew of. Not even a White Pages book. This was Ukraine.

Back at *Coursi*, I thanked Lina and gave her my sad report.

She nodded sympathetically. "I know, John," she said. "I know. I am sorry. Sometimes things are not easy in our country. It goes back to the way things were in Soviet days. Things were very, very complicated! Long lines for so many things! Even bread!"

So with this hard start, how did things go in my two years?

I took the police chief's advice very seriously about being prudent and careful. I never had a problem. I never had anything stolen. I never had to summon the police for anything. Yet I must tell you that I heard of several instances that Volunteers got into trouble...got robbed...were mugged. Usually it happened late at night, involved alcohol, and occurred when the Volunteer was unaccompanied. I did have a run-in with a drunk one night. Very bad. I'll get to that before long.

The chief's advice was advice that Peace Corps gave us time and again. Peace Corps warned us about specific behaviors that could precipitate trouble. It was important to heed that advice.

**N**ow about the bank. I used it only once a month, and that was to take out the cash I needed. Nearly always I did it from the ATM machine outside next to the front door. I always did it from this specific branch, never from any other, even on travels through the country.

The next time I needed money I went right to the ATM. I slipped in my card and got the machine working. But despite my repeated efforts, could not punch the right keys in the right sequence. As I said, they were all labeled in Ukrainian. I went inside and looked for Yuri. "Come in and see me at any time," he had said. Well, he was not around.

I found another manager, a young man. He took me to a teller's window. "No, no!" I said. "I want to learn how to use the ATM."

He cheerfully put on his hat and overcoat and came out to help me. He slipped my card in. Looked the other way while I punched in my password combination. Asked me how much I wanted to take out. I had to specify the amount in *hryvnia*, not dollars. He tapped the right keys, and out clicked the money. Nice crisp bills. He insisted that I count them. The total was correct.

The machine had also spit out a receipt. It was in Ukrainian. Later I studied it and finally managed to understand everything it said.

"Have a good day," he said, and turned to go back into the bank.

"Please," I said. "One minute!" I asked him to go through the proper sequence on the keyboard in slow motion. "I must learn," I said. He did and I jotted down the sequence on a card and put it in my wallet.

I used that card every time I used the machine. In time, I memorized the moves, of course. I did see Yuri a couple of times. "You should put English words on the keys," I told him. "Some Volunteers in other cities have told me they have English on the machines they use."

"Yes, I know," he said. "It is true. But we must be patient."

"It is important for tourists." I said. "If you have English on your machine, you could tell hotels and restaurants. They would tell their customers. It would be good business for you."

He nodded and smiled.

Some six months later I noticed the machine had been modified. You could choose Ukrainian or English! I clicked English and clicked also for a receipt. It was in English. How nice. No way could I say, however, that that was because of me. Yuri no longer worked at the branch, by the way.

**A** few months before I completed my service I was surprised to see that the branch had changed its name. It was now called Svedbank. What was going on? But I had no problems conducting my transactions.

And then in my very last days in Chernihiv I went to the bank to close my account and pocket whatever balance I had. I made sure this time to have my passport with me. It would all be very simple, I was sure. Not so.

Not possible to close the account. The manager—a new man—tried to explain to me. He spoke even less English than I did Russian (which had some similarity to the official Ukrainian). And less than Yuri. I did not understand him. His accent threw me off.

Finally he put in a call to Kyiv. He was calling the main office. Then he handed the phone to me. A woman at the other end told me in halting English that the only way to close my account was by going to the bank in Kyiv! She gave me an address. I was dumbfounded and asked her to repeat. She insisted that I had to go to Kyiv! What a nuisance.

I did that on my next trip to Headquarters. Milady Annabelle had arrived from California and she accompanied me. It took us more than two hours in Kyiv to go by Metro to the right neighborhood, walk and walk to find the right address, then wait in line and finally complete the transaction. What I cashed out was the equivalent of $182. Not exactly a fortune.

A good thing that I never took a chance and opened that 12.4% savings account at the bank. In my last months a financial crisis gripped the country. Some banks refused to honor withdrawal requests! If they did, they insisted on a notice of a specific number of days. Some banks closed…collapsed! No FDIC in Ukraine!

More than once I found myself saying, "God bless America!" What was surprising was that I was bearing up under all this.

~ ~ ~

*Did you know* ... that a problem that affects nearly every Trainee is culture shock? "Shock" is the right word. It can be intense—a challenge and a half. I found it difficult, and I have traveled in numerous countries. But never for a prolonged period

Culture shock is the result of confronting the so many differences that await you at your post. Differences in the weather, the food, the money, the way of life, on and on.

Plus the challenges of learning a new language and the other stuff essential to do the job and fit into the society.

The cure is the same as for seasickness: time! But it is a reason that drives some PCVs to quit.

# 16 / I'm given a second job!

*I'm to start an English club. Well, I start a
French club, too. Also a project more dramatic.*

I am always on the prowl for a new library. I discovered the Korolenko Library on my fourth day in Chernihiv—just one week after arriving. I never thought I would enjoy it so much, or—what was extraordinary—have an official role there or—again extraordinary—start a big project to keep it alive and well.

I love libraries. I put them very high on any list of important institutions. I try to get to the public library whenever I visit a new community. I found my way to the Korolenko 30 minutes after I found there was a big library in the city.

It was easy to locate it. Right on Prospect Mira, one of the two main avenues. Hard to miss with its massive stone tower and fine arched entrance. A big, striking edifice, built of stone and mortar for the ages. Three floors with tall window, which meant high ceilings.

It was built 130 years before as a bank for peasants. Sounds intriguing, doesn't it? Such a big building for a bank. I never found a clear explanation of how it functioned. It had something to do with making land available to peasants—a very radical and reformist idea.

Over time the building served many purposes. Headquarters of the Communist party in this section of the country. Then Nazi Gestapo headquarters during World War 11. Then a Soviet headquarters after the war. Then a museum. Finally the library moved in about 40 years ago when it needed more room. Nearly a million books now!

That's when it was named for the writer Vladimir Galaktionovich Korolenko (1853-1921). To me it became just the Korolenko. I read up about him. I marveled that it bore the name of such a good and courageous man.

I walked in through ponderous wooden doors 10 feet high, up marble steps worn down by countless footsteps, to the main floor. I saw posters and notices tacked up, as in libraries everywhere, but I understood nothing—everything was in Ukrainian. Or maybe Russian. Not sure.

I walked around. Woman staffers were stationed at strategic desks here and there. I saw some "readers"—that's what they were called, but not many. University students. A few older people. Things were quiet.

I walked along a corridor as far as I could, and then reversed to the other end of the building, hoping to peek into rooms. Not easy. Big doors, closed. I could take a peek when somebody came out. Each seemed a department by itself. I could see a central desk in each with a clerk or two, some tables and chairs. Shelves loaded with books. A pleasant reading and study area.

On the second floor I stumbled into the very large and impressive main room. Beautiful. Thirty or forty tables to read and write at. An exhibit of paintings on the walls—40 or 50 of them. Golden light streamed in through the windows.

Straight ahead, on the wall at the far back, was an enormous portrait of a striking man. A strong man, 65 or so, with an amazing head of white hair and an amazing white beard. In a fine suit. Compelling. It was his eyes, I decided. So fierce.

I quickly inquired: Vladimir Galaktionovich Korolenko himself!

**K**orolenko was a Ukrainian writer. Mostly short stories. Just one novel. But also a courageous journalist.

He was revolutionary even as a teen-ager—got kicked out of two schools for his progressive ideas. He opposed the czar. Hated the very idea of czarism.

Was deported to Siberia for five years, one of the most notorious places in the world at that time.

Released, he crafted one story after another, focusing on peasants and other little people. Wrote warmly about them. They were a hit. He took off for the U.S.A.—Chicago!—got to work and wrote a

Wow! The Korolonko. So grand! I had no idea that soon it would my second home.

powerful story about a Ukrainian struggling to make it as an immigrant in the U.S. It was an enormously popular and inspirational piece.

He wanted big change and campaigned for it. Turned his pen to journalism in his last two decades and continued to criticize. He was delighted to see the czar toppled in the Bolshevik revolution. Soon, however, he was disappointed.

He took a great dislike to the new Communism. Spoke out for minorities. Was sympathetic to the Jews. Returned to Ukraine and died in his homeland four years later. The more I got to know about him, the more I admired him. The whole country admired him. Numerous libraries and institutions carried his name. Even a city.

This was a major library. It was the head library for the whole province (*oblast*), and there were 26 in the country. It directed operations for a number of other libraries in Chernihiv and other cities and libraries in the province.

I spotted a men's room and walked in. Squat toilets! Ceramic. Very clean. But yes, squats!

I came to a big door with a sign that I could understand: Foreign Language Department. English is a foreign language, of course! This was one department I had to see. I was interested in books in English. I opened the door slowly. A young woman sat at a desk behind a counter. She smiled. "*Stradzvuite*," I said to her. "Hello!" She understood!

"Welcome," she said. In English! It made me realize my pronunciation was not good. She was working at a computer behind an L-shaped counter.

"I am John," I said, keeping it simple. "I am American. I am a Volunteer in what we call Peace Corps."

She was maybe 22 or 23. So friendly. Attractive. I liked her smile. We chatted. I told her I was a Trainee and a few words about myself.

"But you are not young!" she said. Apparently she thought all Volunteers were young. I said a few words about that. I was the only visitor in the room. She seemed willing to chat.

She pointed to a wall of shelves. Beautiful shelves. Looked new. They were loaded with books. Good-looking books. Brand-new-looking books. Impressive.

"They are American books," she said. "Yes, all from your country. They are our Window on America books," she said.

I didn't know what she was talking about. She walked me to them. Several hundred books—fiction, non-fiction, dictionaries, three sets of encyclopedia, and other reference books in various fields. She pointed to shelves of CDs and DVDs. Music and movies.

All were a gift sent by our Embassy in Kyiv. What a gift! She handed me a pamphlet that explained Window on America. It was written in English and Ukrainian.

It was called Window on America because all the books and disks gave a good view of our country. People could learn about us. All kinds of things about us. Big bucks! For sure. Nadia mentioned all the beautiful shelving was part of the gift from us. Later I heard that all this in this room had amounted to $40,000. And that our Embassy had made a similar gift to every major library in every province.

I really took to this Foreign Book Department. So bright and attractive. Paintings and engravings on the other long wall. Big cactus plants on the sills of the tall windows. I noticed five or six small reading tables. Each had two chairs. Cozy.

I spotted two computers. A big flat-screen TV in a corner. A large whiteboard with color markers. A big photocopier. In another corner, another computer. All this came from Uncle Sam! Oh, except the computer in a corner. It was a gift of the European Union. The EU had also donated a collection of books and disks behind her desk. But much smaller than the Window on America collection.

"Very nice," I said. I was surprised by how much we and other countries were helping out. In time, I was astonished by the amazing largesse of our country to the people of Ukraine. It was considered a good way to make friends in this developing country which still had strong links to Russia right next door.

Looking back toward the entrance door, I spotted a big bank of catalog drawers next to it. The kind we had in every library until 10 years ago or so. Thousands of index cards in them, I was sure. But where were all the books for all these cards? I asked Nadia.

**W**e were standing by another door. She pointed inside. It was jammed with tall steel bookcases. Loaded with books squeezed in tight. Row after row of books. Thousands and thousands of books in. Such narrow aisles.

"They are the books of our Foreign Language Department. We have books in 41 languages!" I noticed her pride. "English books are the most popular."

"May I go in and take a look?"

"No. I am sorry. It is against our rules."

"So how do you choose the books you want?"

She pointed to the card catalog. She explained that you'd search through it. Jot down the information about each book that interested you on a slip of paper. Hand her your slips. She'd enter this Stack Room, look for them, and bring them out to you.

Right away I saw the limitations. Say you were interested in "Elephants." You might find 20 cards about elephants. You might pick out two that sounded best, jot down the info, give her the slips. She'd disappear, then return with only one book.

"The other is out on loan," she'd explain. The other 18 books might be there on the shelves. If you were allowed to enter, you could examine all 20 of them, or the 3 or 4 that looked best. It would save you a lot of time. It would save her a lot of time. And it would be a lot more fun. Back in the U.S., all these drawers and cards were long gone. Now we used computers instead.

I looked longingly at the computers. I asked her, "Is it all right for me to use one? I would like to see if I have e-mails."

"Yes, of course. You do not have a library card yet but you are a Peace Corps Volunteer! I shall permit you." She pointed to the nearer computer. "Today we have Internet. Some days we are not lucky."

I sat down and worked for 40 minutes. Until now I had gone to the Post Office to use a computer. There sometimes I had to wait for my turn. I had to pay. This was such a nice set-up. And free. I said a silent thank you to Uncle Sam. Well, his taxpayers really. I was one of them. You probably are, too.

I came back the next day for an hour after language class. And the next day. Soon I was a regular. Very soon I met Victoria. She was the head of the department. About 50. A beautiful woman. Also spoke good English.

And Tatiana, the other clerk, about the same age as Victoria. Also beautiful. She didn't speak English as well. But she knew a bit of French. She liked to say *"Bonjour"* to me, and *"ça va?"* Lots of fun. I got to know them well. They always welcomed me with big smiles. I had a good time every time I entered. In fact, they became my dear friends.

**I** soon realized that the centerpiece of the room was the Window on America collection.

The books were a mix of fiction and reference materials, all quite recent, about 1,000 in all. All published within the last five years, it seemed. All displayed in the handsome bookcases. Also two sets of encyclopedias, a variety of dictionaries, almanacs, reference books covering many fields.

Lots of books about history and immigrants to our shores and American colleges and universities.

The Window on America collection included a series of beautiful books called "The Library of America." Big, handsome books, all of them with matching black jackets. More than 150 in the series. The volumes were the works of our greatest writers. Mark Twain, Eugene

O'Neill, Saul Bellow, Willa Cather, Washington Irving, Herman Melville, and so many more. What a magnificent gift.

The librarians prized all these books so highly that they would not let any of them be taken out.

I can understand that policy for the reference materials, a volume of the Encyclopedia Britannica, let's say, or The New York Times Almanac. Readers would use those for only minutes. But Mark Twain's "Huckleberry Finn"? How can anyone read a book like that without taking it home? Impossible.

*I'm giving my big talk at the library. A gorgeous room! I want to get people excited about joining my new club.*

Not one book had ever been checked out. Ridiculous, I thought. The whole point was to make these books circulate.

The library applied the same restrictive policy to CDs and DVDs in the collection. An American librarian would be stunned by this, I'm sure. The Korolenko reasoning, of course, is that it prized these books, did not want to risk losing them. It did not have money to replace them if something went wrong.

One day I was told that two Peace Corps Trainees had checked out some of these books…and never returned them. I was appalled. It made all of us Volunteers look bad. "How awful!" I told my new friends. "If ever I catch them, I'll cut their hands off!" That made them feel better.

Then I suggested an idea. "Why not consider doing this?" I said to Victoria. "'If somebody wants to borrow 'Huckleberry Finn,' say. Yes! Simply remove its beautiful jacket and save it.

"When the book returns, put the jacket back on. Then put the book back on the shelf. It will look just as beautiful! As if never been opened!"

She adopted the idea.

One day Nadia said to me, "You are going to be working here!"

"No, no." I said. "I am going to be a university teacher."

"Your name is LaPlante, yes? Well two ladies from Peace Corps came here. They talked to our director upstairs, Mr. Grishchenko. You will be working here!"

Gosh! Could it really be true? I had my doubts.

One day Oksana, my old TCF, told me I was being assigned a second job. She told me, "It is at the Korolenko Library!"

Yes, she said it with an exclamation point! Somehow she knew that I was going to the Korolenko just about every afternoon. Except on Fridays. The Korolenko was closed on Fridays. Nadia had been right. All Volunteers—not only I—were supposed to find themselves a secondary job. My primary job would be at *Coursi*, the language school.

So what would my job be at the library? Well, it would be to start an English Club. It's a common project for Volunteers. Peace Corps likes the idea of English Clubs. So many people are interested in English, American English especially.

*Flowers for Victoria. Women's Day—a big holiday indeed. Doesn't she look pleased?*

Our country is the most important in the world, and our brand of English is the most important in the world. So many people dream of living in the U.S.A. Even more, of emigrating our blessed land.

The idea is to encourage people…usually university students, but other people also…to come and join the club and attend meetings and get to learn about the Window on America program. And become appreciative of our country and way of life and values.

An English Club is a good way for them to meet a Peace Corps Volunteer who, Peace Corps hopes, will be a nice, friendly person, one who will create a favorable impression of our country. The natural setting in the library was its Foreign Book Department.

I got started right away. I suggested it to Victoria, the department boss. She liked it. Nadia was already enthusiastic. And Tatiana went along.

Victoria suggested it should meet once a month. I laughed. I said, "No, Victoria. Every Sunday!" She frowned and said, "I do not think we can get enough members to come every Sunday."

Well, we'd see. How to give the club a good start? With a good shot of publicity, I decided. I suggested a public talk open to anybody and everybody. On a Sunday afternoon, when more people could come. Free.

I would talk about my trip around the world—alone—for my $75^{th}$ birthday. I believed most people in Chernihiv had never been to Kyiv, two hours away. Who wouldn't be interested in hearing what it's like to travel around the world?

There would be no translator to explain, and the talk was publicized this way. This would assure that those who came understood at least a bit of English. After my talk, we would announce our new club, explain it, and urge people to join it. Free. No charge. Lots of fun.

*At times I'd sit at the side. A member would do the speaking. Good experience! I'd coach.*

All three liked the idea and made many phone calls to get it launched right. It worked out fine. Before the event, I got interviewed on TV and for print, and that helped.

We booked the library's main reading room for the talk, its biggest room. I was anxious, of course.

Would it be a hit or a flop? I had no experience with such things in Ukraine. The three gals were uncertain. The library had never done this before. A talk by an American in English? It could be argued both ways. Only time would tell.

The day and the hour came and people began to arrive. I watched nervously from a wing. Slowly the room filled. Only a few seats were left at starting time. I was delighted.

I spoke loud and slow. Paid special attention to my enunciation. I got my audience's attention.

Their eyes were fixed on me. Of course I spoke about the most dramatic events of my trip. I managed to spark some laughs. I was delighted to see a TV crew covering me. Wonderful. I saw a woman journalist busily taking notes. I was eager for publicity. I wanted lots of members. I spoke for an hour. Bottom line: it was a hit

Then I launched into a pitch about our new English Club. A perfect opportunity to improve their English. To make friends. To learn good stuff. Finally I was done. Applause!

A woman rushed up and gave me a lovely bouquet. Some people came forward to chat. Victoria, Tatiana, and Iryna surrounded me. They were glowing. How good.

For our English Club first meeting the following Sunday, we had standing room only. A balanced mix of men and women.

We held it in the Foreign Language Department's reading room. It was hard to crowd everybody in.

I counted 33. Mostly young people. Our topic for the day was, "Would you like to be a Peace Corps Volunteer?" Impossible, of course, because Peace Corps is for Americans only. But it gave me the opportunity to explain what Peace Corps is all about.

*My expat friend Rich explains Scrabble. They loved it. I donated the set to the library.*

At one point I asked, "Would you join if your country had such a Peace Corps?" Hands went up. That pleased me.

Right away I developed a standard procedure. I would introduce myself as a Volunteer and say a few words about myself. I'd insist they call me John. Just John. Victoria thought that it was a bad idea—elders command high respect in Ukraine. She said I should at least use my patronymic. My patronmic? She explained.

Men and women must honor their father by adding the patronmic. My father's name was Arthur. I should say I was John Arturovich LaPlante. Polite people would call me John Arturovich. I tried it a couple of time. People chuckled. I became simply John.

*All those books in back were American books—a gift from our country. They were greatly prized.*

Next I would ask every person to self-introduce. Give his or her name, what university or profession, a hobby or special interests. That would break the ice. I hoped it would lead to friendships..

Then I would announce the topic for the meeting. It might be "Higher education in the U.S.A. and Ukraine." Or "How the bicycle changed many things in the U.S.A." Or "Vegetarianism. Could you live without eating meat or fish?"

Time and again I would urge people to speak. To make a comment. Ask a question. After all, they were here to improve their English. They had to practice. I would get few takers. Same situation as at *Coursi*. They were embarrassed. I understood. I was embarrassed about my Russian.

I would wind up doing most of the speaking. Then I began bringing in guest speakers. One day it was a young Ukrainian who had settled in the U.S., had done very well, and was home to visit his parents. He had learned English by watching TV. He impressed us all.

Another time it was Jim and Robyn, a married couple who were Volunteers. They spoke about spending six months back-packing through Central America. Wonderful. They were excellent. They were from Alaska. I got them to return and do a program about living in Alaska! Wonderful.

Our meetings lasted an hour and a half, but often they went longer.

Just as the club was getting started, Nadia told me she would be leaving. "I am going to have a baby," she told me happily. How wonderful. But sad for me. I loved to chat with her.

She was replaced by Iryna. About 35. Also a beautiful woman. Ukraine is a land of beautiful women. She had been on maternity leave and was resuming her job. Working mothers were allowed three years off to raise a new baby. It was a law—a hold-over from Soviet days.

She spoke English well—she had graduated from the Pedagogical University as a teacher of English. We became close friends. She took a great interest and assisted me in many ways. Not only in the club, but other projects as they developed. I took an interest in her and her family. She became so involved that I began calling her my "partner." She deserved the title.

We did meet every Sunday! Victoria was delighted. The club made her department look good. I believe it was considered tops in the whole library. After every meeting, Victoria would send a report to the Embassy. At every meeting she would snap photos and include them.

About a year after we started, I learned that Victoria was invited by our Embassy to go to the U.S. on a junket with a group of librarians from around the country. All expenses paid. They went for 10 days. First to Washington, D.C.

They visited the Library of Congress and other libraries in the city. Library officials came and gave talks to them. And they went sightseeing, of course. So exciting. They were busy every minute.

Then they were sent to different cities. One here and one there. Victoria went to Pittsburgh. She was the house guest of a librarian there. She visited the main library, then a branch library, even a library in a prison.

She saw how our digitalized libraries operate. How readers can walk right into the stacks and look at any and all books. How librarians give wonderful service. So important for any library.

She came back thrilled and excited. She was gushing with good things to say. She gave an impressive talk to her colleagues at a special assembly. I was sure the junket would have a good domino effect.

Everybody in the library would get to know how fine American libraries serve their readers and solidify their public support in their community. Our Embassy deserved compliments for its brainstorm.

I couldn't help thinking that one reason she received this golden invitation was the success of our club in the Embassy's eyes.

One day one of our members approached me. "John, why don't you start a French Club also?"

"A French Club?" I was astonished. I wondered, *What will Peace Corps think of that?*

"Yes. We have some people who are studying French. They would enjoy a French Club. Just like the English Club!"

Well, it happened. We would meet every Sunday at 1:15 and carry on for 80 minutes. The same format as the English Club. Le Club Français was tiny. It attracted 4 members, sometimes 6 or 7. They enjoyed it and so did I.

For me it kept my French alive. Peace Corps thought the idea was fine. That pleased me.

Right afterward would come our English Club. Both right there in the Foreign Book Department. Nearly all the members would stay on to attend the English Club also!

*One of our members leads a discussion. In English! This was the whole point.*

I maintained the two clubs all through my service, right to the end.

The Korolenko became my second home. I loved the place. It needed substantial repairs. The great building was showing its age.

One day workmen arrived and started to erect staging in one of the broad corridors. It was the beginning of an extensive program of patching, sanding, and painting.

They tackled the ceilings, the walls, the floors. New windows were installed in several key areas. The hard work went on for weeks and progressed from one section to another.

And what a surprise. Much of the work was being done by women. They were the ones doing this hard and dusty and painstaking work—moving furniture, patching and sanding and painting high up on staging.

It made me think of my first host mother, Natasha. This was the kind of work that she did, but as a free-lancer. Not easy.

The women worked as hard and as well as any men could. Amazing how beautiful the library was becoming. Finally both main floors were finished. What a transformation!

Throughout, it was difficult for the staff and the readers. Inevitably some services got disrupted, but we carried on. In the end, it was enormously worthwhile. I was fascinated from the first day to the last.

The workers got to know me and would greet me with a smile. I checked the progress whenever I came, which was six days a week. The library was closed on Tuesdays—the staff spent the day catching up at this and that.

In just three months I came up with my Digitalization Project. That's what I called it. Some of my best ideas have popped up while in bed at night. So it was with this one.

From the beginning I felt it was essential for the library to improve its services. It was so difficult and tedious for readers to choose and check out books. And in several ways, I felt the library was in danger.

The solution was to digitalize—to use another word, to digitalize. To emulate our American libraries and libraries throughout modern Europe and in other advanced countries around the world. So many have put the power of the computer to work to make their libraries more efficient and better.

I decided to make it happen. An enormous undertaking, but critical to the Korolenko's future, in my opinion. I was going to be here only two years. Possible? I was excited. I set to work.

Digitalization became quite a project. It engrossed me. I devote all of the next chapter to it.

# 16 / I'm given a second job!

As the seasons went on, one month of my service at the library morphed into another. I became "part of the family" there. I got to notice tension in our department. Between Victoria, who was the boss, and Tatiana and Iryna, her assistants. Three lovely ladies. What a shame.

All were long-time employees. All three were dedicated to the library. This obviously was their life. It was clear that all three would work in the library until they retired. Many more years! The tension became hostility.

Ira (left) is hamming it up. Lilitt is on the right. Behind is Victoria, department head.

I got caught in the middle. Victoria would unburden herself to me. She would complain about the others.

Iryna would unburden herself to me. Tatiana would have done the same but her English was limited.

I was friends with all three, but with Iryna especially. She was interested in my projects and became a sort of Gal Friday.

She was essential in my Public Transit project, which became a big deal. I'll tell you about it further along.

Anyway, this tension dragged on. It got worse. All three made appointments individually to go upstairs and complain to Peter, the director. Word of the feuding spread through the library. Much gossip, plenty of tittering.

Peter tried to reconcile the three. It didn't work. He cut their annual bonuses! The feuding continued. Peter recommended that Tatiana and Iryna transfer to different departments. They refused.

With my librarian friends Tatiana (left) and Iryna. I got to see them often.

They said they'd talk to their labor union. I didn/t know such existed.

Finally Peter refused to see them for any reason. He told them sternly, "Come and visit me when you have made peace. Not a day before!"

I felt their jobs were in threat. But apparently they felt protected by their union.

I tried to be the peacemaker. Futile. I liked all three of them. But I was in a bind. I was closest to Iryna. How would this sad tale end?

As I explained, she played a big role in my English Club. Plus, she was always ready to help me with anything. Her husband, Sasha, was now one of my friends. I felt this feud was hurting her professionally and socially.

*That's the New York Sunday Times. They had never seen such a thick paper. What I emphasized was its high quality.*

**I** would take her aside. She would complain about her boss, Victoria. But it was hard for me to judge who was right, or to what degree.

They had worked together for many years. Little aggravations had become magnified—too much to tolerate.

I would say to Iryna, "Now all three of you hate to come to work. All your colleagues in the library talk about you. All three of you are living on aspirins.

All three of you have become pests to Peter. He is punishing all three of you. It will get worse if you don't change your attitude and make peace. You are ruining your future.

"Swallow your pride. Let bygones be bygones. Become friends again. You will be better off. You will be happier. Now please go tell Tatiana what I have said to you." I tried to say a few words to Tatiana also. We liked one another. But the language difficulty made it hard.

Then I would go to Victoria. I liked her a lot. Knew she was a fine person. Admired her many qualities. At times we would have tea together. I would say the same to her. But she would complain about Iryna and Tatiana.

They were trapped in a dead-lock. All three did get to realize they had much to lose and not much to gain. Slowly things did become better. Bit by tiny bit. The feud was still simmering when I left to fly home. But since then, Tatiana transferred to another department. Victoria and Iryna are getting along. Peace is restored, I am happy to tell you.

Half way through my second year, I made an interesting and, it turned out, an important new friend. At a Philharmonia concert one evening, I heard a man directly behind me speaking English. American English. I thought, This must be a Trainee I have not met. At intermission I looked at him. A good-looking man, white-haired, about 65, in casual clothes, but impeccable. I introduced myself. "I'm from Connecticut. I'm a Peace Corps Volunteer here."

*My French Club was smaller. We had a good time and got to be close—friends, actually.*

"My name is Wayne Purves. From California. I live here. I was a Volunteer years back."

"Gosh, I live in California in the winter!"

We had a lot in common. We made an appointment to meet at a downtown restaurant one afternoon at 4. I arrived early. He never came. What is this, I wondered.

My telephone rang. Wayne: "John, I forgot! I am so sorry. Believe me, this is not my style!"

He invited me to dinner at his home. "Take *Marshrutka* 27," he said. "I live in a development of new homes." He gave me specific directions I went the next day and found it easily.

I had no idea that such fine homes existed in this city. Yes, all quite new. His was a two-story brick building with a red roof. It rose high above an impressive eight-foot-high brick wall. He had told me the combination to unlock the solid steel gate.

I opened it. I noticed the attached garage. A BMW sedan was parked in the driveway. I noticed the house was about 98 percent finished. The landscaping remained to be finished, for one thing. What a beautiful property!

He greeted me at the door. Immediately he gave me a tour. Greeted me with a big smile. The first floor was sparsely furnished but everything was top quality. Large rooms with large windows. A spectacular spiral staircase up to the second floor. Kitchen cabinets from Germany, plumbing fixtures from Germany.

He took me to a sunroom at the back. Beautiful. I noticed its ceiling still had to be finished. We looked out on the backyard. Large, with an extensive garden. Many things growing, flowers and vegetables and fruits and berries.

"I enjoy gardening," he said. "But Larisa comes and does most of the work. She's a teacher. But like all Ukrainian women, she is a fine gardener."

He knew I was vegetarian and was ready for me with a big Greek salad and garlic toasts right out of the oven. He added a roasted chicken breast to his plate. He chose two beautiful wine glasses from a selection of several sizes.

On a club walk. The main square. Our guide is explaining. That's a theatre in back.

"Dry red wine all right?"

"Yes, Wonderful!" I stopped him after he had poured just an inch or so. He poured himself a generous measure.

"To friendship!" he said. And raised his glass.

It turned out to be a toast amply fulfilled. We met many times.

He was the best thing that happened to me in my final six months. And I got him to play a big role in my English Club. How nice to have another older American here. I felt Peace Corps was wrong in assigning Volunteers alone.

I dined with him often. Sometimes just the two of us. Several times as one in a party of 8 or even 12—once even larger. I talked him into attending my upcoming Sunday English Club. I introduced him as a former "Volunteer." That interested everybody, of course, and he explained.

One Sunday after our meeting, he led half a dozen of our members, men and women, across the park to play volleyball in the gym of the high school there. They went and played every Sunday after our session.

For the Fourth of July he invited a big group to his house for an American cook-out. The weather threatened so it was a cook-in. Members still talk about how wonderful it was. On another day, he organized a summer picnic by the river.

In the summer, when I went touring on vacation for a month, I got him to substitute for me. I hated the idea of suspending our meetings for a month. He did a fine job. Everybody loved him. And I talked him into taking over after I returned to the States. I felt lucky to have him as a friend.

Christmas was approaching. He was preparing to fly home to California for the holidays. And while he was gone, I would be completing my service and returning home to the U.S.

I have much to tell you about him, but I reserve it for a chapter about to come up, "A Chance Meeting."

*Our largest turn-out! We had new Trainees in town and some joined us. We ran out of chairs— a perfect excuse to go outside and enjoy the sunshine.*

Truly the meetings of my two clubs every Sunday afternoon became the highlight of my week. They were a lot of fun. The members were all smart, ambitious, hard-working people who wanted a better life
and were willing to work toward it. They realized the importance of English in their developing country.

I felt that I was doing something very good and very important. To me, this is what Peace Corps service was supposed to be about.

I got to know some well. Lilitt, the beautiful Armenian girl who always attended both clubs.

And Denys, the ambitious young engineer who had worked in a resort restaurant in America for a summer and who spoke both English and French so well. Sveta, who became such an excellent English speaker. Gorgeous Yulia, with such strong leadership skills. Quiet but determined Sasha. He never missed a meeting. He had a university degree in history and was a father of a young girl but couldn't find a better job than as a security guard. He had a remarkable religious streak and became a Mormon (there were Mormon missionaries in the city.)

*My friend Ken Mattingly and Russian tutor Sasha with me on a stroll.*

Tall and quiet and efficient Sergei who did so much to get the volleyball games going after our club meetings. I was sure he would be a success.

So many others. Little Iryna, so brilliant. I convinced her to go on for her doctorate. Effervescent Yulia—our second Yulia—so thoughtful and generous. Beautiful Natasha, who was already working on a Ph.D. in Kyiv—I had helped her with a special project. All inspiring young people.

Viktor, our oldest member in his 50's, a brave dissident who had fled from his native Russia and spent every minute scheming how to topple "the terrible, corrupt leadership in Russia today."

They were what gave me such a strong faith in Ukraine. They were the future of the country. I did not hesitate to keep reminding them of this. "Take a big interest in your country. In its public affairs, " I would tell them. "You can become a leader. You really can. Why not you?"

I will never forget the final meeting of our English Club. There were 25 or 30 members—we ran out of chairs in the Foreign Language Department. Some had to stand at the back. And milady Annabelle was at my side. She had flown in from California to share my last days.

Also present were Victoria and Iryna of the Korolenko staff. It was their day off, too. But Iryna came every Sunday, sometimes with her two sons and husband, Sasha. He was an engineer who felt he could make more money operating a tool kiosk at the central bazaar.

The highlight came when Lilitt and Sasha stood and started a question game, "What do you really know about John?" They asked questions about me, and members were asked to supply the answers. My home state in the U.S. How many children I have. Grandchildren. How many books I have written. Why I joined Peace Corps. The nationality of my parents. How many Volunteers in the world. How much we got paid. On and on. Surprising how many facts they came up with. Lots of fun.

16 / *I'm given a second job!* / 197

*Our last meeting before I left for the U.S. A wonderful party. Lots of fun. Milady Annabelle is next to me. How lucky I was to make so many friends.*

I was given presents though I had insisted that there be no presents. One was a colorful peasant tunic. They insisted I try it on. And it fit! (Earlier in the week my landlady Tanya had asked to take one of my shirts. I thought she wanted to replace a button. It was to check its size!)

They gave Annabelle a fetching princess' headpiece...a colorful crown with long streamers running down its back. It looked good on her.

Sveta came up to me and whispered her thanks. Little Iryna approached and said nice words to me. Tanya squeezed my hand and made me promise I'd tell her when my book got published. On and on.

Natasha came forward and gave me a tiny book of poetry. It was inscribed to "John. Writer. Traveler. Teacher. Inspirer!" I was bowled over by her kindness.

One present I'll treasure was a thick photo album. Thoughtful Yulia had decorated its cover with tiny beads. It showed two hands meeting in friendship—an American hand and a Ukrainian hand! How symbolic.

The album was a labor of love. It was chock-full of individual photos of members. And each member had written a comment about me. Some funny but most touching. The album was her idea.

In preparing us to return home, Peace Corps told us that Volunteers often experience cross culture shock when they return to the U.S. Well, if that happens to me, I'll feel better by leafing through this album with its many photos and comments. Fine food for the soul.

Then we had our farewell party. Juices, cookies, candies, fruit, so many other good things. Then the picture-taking. Just about everybody had come with a digital camera. I posed with this one, then that one, nearly everybody in the club. An unforgettable experience.

Then, it was over. Annabelle and I walked home through the cold night. But I felt so warm deep down. I had come here a total stranger. And now I was going home with so many new friendships in my heart—

so many good memories tucked into my emotional bank. I truly felt appreciated and loved. And I felt that they knew I loved them. And knew I had done my best to help them, each and every one.

It was the best pay-off of all in my total Peace Corps experience

~ ~ ~

***Did you know***…that there's a new book out that is must reading for everybody who is interested enough in Peace Corps to be reading this book of mine. It appeared just as I was readying my book for printing.

It's Stanley Meisler's "When the World Calls: the Inside History of the Peace Corps and Its First Fifty Years."

It's the only overall history of Peace Corps written in years that I know of. Meisler is a journalist of wide experience with books about the United Nations and Kofi Annan to his credit. He worked in Peace Corps in its early days as an evaluator of some of its overseas programs. It was his job to go look, judge, and report back. He was an insider.

He's very savvy. A digger. It seems a balanced book—he mentions some stalls and embarrassments. A colorful writer. One warning: I believe he started the project tilting toward Peace Corps. He's an admirer of it. (As I am.) What institution is perfect?

I'm glad he mentioned his wife works for USAID. Numerous people in USAID jumped to it after service in Peace Corps. Still do.

Amazing to me how much he crammed into the book's 227 pages of text. An additional 30 pages of notes detail the depth of his research, travel, and interviewing. And a 19-page index provides a great assist.

He gave me a better grasp of the agency's development, evolution, crises, and principal players. Plus many valuable insights and juicy tidbits. I do dispute a thing or two. A fascinating read. I couldn't put it down. I wish he had given it another 200 pages. Highly recommended.

The Peace Corps gave us Trainees a ton of things to read. They should include this book. It would fill a big void in its curriculum.

# 17 / I have a fantasy!

*It's to digitalize this great big library!*
*It must get with it. Or for sure it will die.*

So exciting the day I got started at the Korolenko. It took me longer than I expected to figure out how it went about its job. Definite differences. When I did find out, I realized that by the standards of modern libraries in the U.S. and around the world, it was horribly behind the times. Not surprising, given the huge challenges that beset Ukraine.

But with computers and the Internet, going to the library was not as important as it used to be. Even in Ukraine! A lot more people were getting computers and connecting to the Internet. The way to continue to attract "readers" was to digitalize. Or computerize, to use another word.

Every general library in the world is a collection of departments, of course. This was so at the Korolenko.

The bigger the library, the more departments. The usual departments are Literature, Science, Fine Arts, Periodicals and Newspapers, Philosophy, Religion, History, Languages, Computer Science, Natural History, Business and Economics, Government, Geography, Music, Law, Health Care. On and on.

In these departments you could find books and media dealing with every aspect of our world. This is why libraries are so important. So essential.

The Korolenko was rich in these intellectual resources. But there was a big difference. Each of its major departments was a mini library. Each had its own staff. Its own card catalog. Its own reading room with tables and chairs where patrons could sit and read and research and write. And its own stack room with bookcases groaning with its books.

I know that you're thinking this doesn't sound very different. But it was different because each department seemed to operate by itself.

Maybe your business was at just one of these departments. You would go through the Korolenko's ponderous front door, go up marble steps, sign in and get a pass from a librarian at the top, and then go directly to the mini library of your choice.

You would go to its card catalog, thumb through its many cards to select the book or books you wanted, jot down the information for each book on a separate slip of paper, and hand these to a librarian. Let's suppose you wanted two books from this department.

She would go to the stack room with your two slips. You would have to wait in the reading room. You were not allowed in that room. She would be searching for your two books in there for all the time it took. She would return with one book and hand it to you. She would say, "I am sorry. The other book is not available." This meant that the missing one was out on loan, or maybe lost—somebody had borrowed it and never returned it.

But maybe there were other books in the stack room on the subject that interested you. She did not bring them out because you had not requested them. A considerate librarian on a light day might bring one out and suggest it to you, but she was not obliged to.

You would sign out the book and take it with you. Maybe you had business also in another department—another mini library, to use my term. You needed another book. You would walk there and go through the same process. Check the catalog, write out a slip and give it to a librarian. Then wait and hope for the best.

You might even need a book in another mini library. You went to it and did the same thing. When you were finished, you would return to the main desk where you had checked in, go through formalities there, then head home with your books.

If a busy day—Saturday, for instance—you might have to stand in line at the first desk, then at the desk in the mini-library or libraries, then at the original desk again. It could take much time. Could be enormously irritating and frustrating.

That was one way. There was another way. You could enter the library, check in at the top of the marble stairs with the librarian, then go up two more flights of stairs to its Grand Catalog Room. Well, that's what I called it. It was grand indeed.

It was lined on three sides with catalog drawers. There were hundreds of them. They were stacked up as high as it was comfortable to use them.

They contained millions of index cards. This was the Korolenko's brain. Its memory. The cards in the mini libraries were duplicates of the cards in this Grand Catalog Room.

This was where you would probably start if you wanted books from more than one mini library. Easier here. Let's say you were interested in elephants. You could go to the appropriate drawer. You might find 32 cards, each one describing a book about elephants.

You would begin examining the cards. Some might be new, beautifully typed, for books recently purchased. Some might be handwritten for books acquired years ago. You would choose the book(s) you wanted and write out slip(s). All that would take many minutes.

But you were also interested in Beethoven. You had to write a paper about him. You proceeded to the right catalog drawer. Oops, sorry. Somebody else was using it. Well, you waited, and eventually you found 21 cards about him. You selected the two best, then copied the info on two slips. Many more minutes.

You might want to find a good novel to relax with on Saturday evening. A popular detective story. You would go get the right catalog drawer and search for the book.

But it might be out. To play safe, you'd choose another detective novel and copy down the info. More minutes.

Now with these slips in hand, you would find your way to the Natural History Department and go through the routine there. Then on to the Music Department.

Then on to the Popular Fiction Department. It could take you the whole Saturday morning. And you might go home unhappy because you did not find all the books you wanted.

Now imagine a different scenario: you were allowed to go into all the stack rooms. How wonderful. If you did not find a book that you had a slip for, you could search for an alternate. The alternate might even be better! You'd save a lot of time. And would go home happier.

Now imagine still another scenario: instead of going to a card catalog, you could go to a computer. And search on it for the books you wanted. Much easier and faster.

Also you could find out immediately how many copies of each book were available. If only one, whether it was in the library or out on loan. If out, you could instantly reserve it, knowing you would be notified by e-mail when it got returned. And so on. You could do this also from your own computer at home—no need to take a bus or a *marshrutka*—or both—to get to the library to do this checking.

This is how it is done in our American libraries today. You can do it from home.

If this were a busy day...Saturday, or Sunday afternoon...again there might be numerous readers seeking books. You might have to wait in line. Finally you'd exit the department, your books in hand.

But you weren't finished. On the way out, you'd have to stop at the main desk near the front desk, and turn in your pass. Only then would you be finished.

I saw long lines many times. I suffered for these poor folks. A visit to the library could consume hours. Think about it...having to ride public transport downtown, walking to the library, going through this nightmare of a process, and then repeating the same steps in reverse to get home. Awful. No wonder some readers came to the library very reluctantly. Then you'd have to return the books. That involved another process.

How all this made me appreciate our libraries back home in the U.S.! All of them, even the smallest, now use the power of the computer to make everything so much easier. I am sure you know this. And our libraries have an enormous difference: we can walk into the stacks to look over books and pick them out for ourselves! I never realized what a huge blessing this was until I got to see the Korolenko.

To take the books home, we'd simply carry our books to the take-out desk. All we'd do is identify our self with our magnetized library card and pass our books through a scanner. Many of our libraries have such automated service. It not, we'd let a clerk do it for us. And that would be it! Home we'd go. To return the books, we'd bring them into the library, but after hours we could just drop them into a book box by the door. How could it be any easier?

And wonder of wonders. At my library in Connecticut, I can use my computer at home to scan its collection of books. In fact, can search for a particular book in public libraries throughout the state. If my library doesn't have a book I want and I see it at another library, I can get my library to order it for me. Free.

In fact, I can enter any other public library in Connecticut, even in a town or city a hundred miles away, one where I am a complete stranger. Can browse its stacks, select a book or books, and borrow them instantly, just by using my card! No questions asked. When I am finished with them, I can return them to my own library, and it will take charge of returning them to the original library.

I mentioned this to students in my English Club. They shook their heads in wonder. It was unimaginably wonderful to them.

In fact, if you're an invalid or house-bound in any way, your friendly library will probably deliver books to you and retrieve them when you request new books. A free service!

I'm familiar with all this because I have loved libraries ever since my dear *Maman*, an immigrant from Québec who became passionate about her adopted country, took me by the hand and led me into our Slater Memorial Library in Pawtucket, R.I., and got me my first library card. I was 11 or 12. I loved to read—I was such a curious kid.

I thought that that building with the marble steps and the big dome was the finest place in town. Over the years, I have seen the services expand, and dramatically so with the advent of the Computer Age.

I have visited libraries beyond number. And used more than I can count. I make it a point to visit the library in any interesting community. I have been to libraries, big and small, all over the U.S. Also in Paris and London and Prague and Lisbon and Québec City and Montreal and Guadalajara and Hong Kong and Singapore and Shanghai and Nairobi. Yes, in numerous countries.

There are only two libraries where I have ever been denied admittance. One was in Hanoi in Vietnam—I was stopped at the gate. The other was at the new and great British Royal Library in London because I did not have a card. I did have a disappointment at the new and grand *Bibliothèque Nationale* in Paris—I had to pay to enter. That goes counter to our library principles. We believe our libraries should be free—perhaps it's the poorest among us who need them the most.

Long ago I learned that libraries are the most welcoming institutions anywhere. I believe that in any community the library is the second most important institution of all, right after the grocery store. We do have to eat, of course. At libraries we get to enjoy a different sustenance.

No wonder I got the idea that the Korolenko should digitalize. I realized that very early. I became convinced after Victoria took me on a tour and I got to see how cumbersome using it could be.

Then I had an illuminating experience. I was doing my practice-teaching at the Technological University. One day Prof. Aleksander Kot asked me to give a class on "The Modern American Corporation." Some American universities devote a whole semester to that topic. How to do this in an 80-minute class?

I went online to www.google.com and then www.wikipedia.com. In an hour or so I had the information I needed. I organized it and gave my class. Ten years earlier I would have had to go to my library and spend hours. No search engines then.

And I found out more and more Ukrainians were using search engines now. No need to bother going to the Korolenko! I realized something immediately: if the Korolenko did not shape up, it faced a dismal feature. More and more people would stay away. They would do their research the way I had just done mine—online! Its staff would get trimmed and trimmed. Eventually it would be a silent warehouse with thousands of unused books.

**D**igitalization was the solution! Automation! The Korolenko should get with it! This became my sermon and I preached it to Victoria, then to Iryna, then Tatiana. They listened politely. They quietly agreed with me. But I suspected they were only being nice.

It dawned on me that yes, they realized that computers could save a lot of time and work…but the computers might put them right out of their jobs! They loved their jobs. This was a genuine fear.

But I was convinced I was right. If the library failed to digitalize, it would attract fewer and fewer readers. The staffers would lose their jobs because they'd no longer be needed. But if it did digitalize, it would become more attractive. Would pull in more users.

The more I thought about this, the more I realized that digitalization was a priority project. More significant even than my teaching assignment. Computerization would benefit countless people.

I had to address this fear of job loss. Of course, I mentioned to them that with so much work to do to digitalize, it would be a long time before any staffer got a dismissal notice.

And with enlightened leadership, the staff reduction would take place only through attrition. Staffers would not get dismissed. Some older employees might appreciate a "buy-out." As natural attrition took place—retirements, resignations, deaths—these positions would remain unfilled until the library achieved the right percentage of staffers. Humanitarian policies could make the impact of all this easier and kinder.

I also stressed the significance of the project. This might be the first library to digitalize in the whole country. It could be the pacesetter for the many other libraries. They would follow suit. Digitalization would be the salvation of all of them.

Nothing was guaranteed, of course. So many technological breakthroughs were changing people's reading habits, and of course this would impact libraries. For instance, the development of www.amazon.com's history-making digital book reader, the Kindle. And of Sony's. And Barnes & Noble's. And then, Apple's stunning Ipad. And others. And most importantly, the free availability of books, magazines, and newspapers online, although publishers were beginning to see the essentiality of having to charge for them.

And all this that was happening in the U.S. was happening in advanced countries around the world. It would happen in Ukraine eventually. Without a doubt.

Then Victoria and I got to attend a practical and most timely Peace Corps In-Service in Kyiv. In a nutshell, about how to plan any big project and carry it through. It was limited to 25 Volunteers and 25 Counterparts.

A Peace Corps tenet is "Train, train, train!" Our "Friday e-Digest" from Headquarters would regularly announce seminars and mini-courses and "camps" and Russian- and Ukrainian-language "refreshers." I gave every such offer my attention.

I jumped at this one and rushed to bring it to Victoria's attention. She saw its aptness and was excited in joining me—if we got chosen. We got in!

Why were we interested? Our library Digitalization Project! Ours was a big project indeed. We could use any and all practical advice and tips we could on how to organize it and carry it to completion.

The title of the program was "Project Creation, Design, and Management." It was being held at the Post-Graduate Institute in Kyiv that we Trainees had gone do for our orientation upon arriving from the U.S. Attending were Volunteers and their Counterparts planning or active in a big project of any kind. So many kinds, it turned out.

My big question was, how can anyone teach you how to carry out any—yes, any—big project to fruition? In the abstract, I mean? Without knowing its nature or purpose, its special features and special challenges? It seemed preposterous. Well, I found out. We had good teachers, all from the Headquarters staff. And they had much to teach us.

Directing the in-service was Iryna Krupska. I knew Iryna well. She was the training manager for all of us. She had been part of our life since our first day at this same institute.

In fact, she was one of the two who had come to Chernihiv to announce that I had been rejected by that awful unknown university because of my advanced age and, sob, would remain posted in Chernihiv.

As usual, she did a good job. Early in our first session she asked us to set our own ground rules for all our sessions. One Volunteer suggested "Arrive on time!" I made the second suggestion, "Stay awake!" Laughter! But she put it on the list she was scribbling on a big whiteboard. Other suggestions followed. Interesting.

We learned that all projects have common traits and common problems. Have a generic nature, so to speak.

First, an Idea of something that needs to be done…a Vision! Next, its Elaboration. Then a Goal, or Goals, quite specific. Then its Objective, or Objectives, in detail. Then required Tasks. Then an Action Plan. And a Timeline. And a Budget. And a list of Resources and Deficits. Then Monitoring and Evaluation. With Modifications as needed (speaking of the real world!). Quite a list, but quite logical and remarkably comprehensive—an effective master plan!

**FU** bunked in a modest twin-bedded room with Mike, 30. Victoria roomed with a woman from the Ukrainian-speaking western-side of the country. We ate in a pleasant dining room. We soon found this was serious business. We did have opportunity to make friends and spend social time together.

Mike had signed up for Peace Corps with his wife. He left a federal government job in Washington, D.C. Not sure what she had been doing. The two were serving in a small city in the eastern part of Ukraine, which is the industrial and mining and Russian-speaking section. She was not attending this program. Like me, they were new to Peace Corps and were just settling into their assignments. He called her every evening. I was glad to see that.

He was proud of his wife's Russian-speaking ability. She had had a serious interest in Russian language and culture and had taken courses over the years. "Far better than my ability," he said. "We were lucky when we found out where we were being assigned to eastern Ukraine."

We had long talks at night. One of his concerns was his youthful age and his married status which he felt set him apart from other Volunteers. I had a similar problem, except mine was my high age.

Another, he said, was the difficulty of getting launched in his work. I told him that my limited experience told me that many of us had to carve out and shape our own specific jobs.

I said, "I think your counterpart organization is just as concerned as you are. You are wondering what you are going to do. They are wondering what to assign you to do that will be helpful to both of you." Volunteers really have to use imagination and initiative to find significant work and become effective. It's my true belief.

All of us, Volunteers and Counterparts, spent an hour in class together early every day and another in late afternoon. In between, Victoria went to classes taught in Russian and I in English. We met for meals but made it a point to sit at different tables, eager to see old friends (I didn't see any) and make new ones (I did do that).

During class we listened, asked questions, took notes. Victoria filled a whole notebook—I was so impressed. I learned some things, though I had to fight an urge to nod off every afternoon around 4. Funny because of the original "ground rule" I suggested, which was to stay awake! I noticed others had the same difficulty.

We left for home happy to have attended. I'm sure I didn't get as much out of it as some of the younger people. Frankly, over the years I had handled a wide variety of challenges in managing big projects and had learned a thing or two. Still I was delighted to have participated.

I wrote up a report which I sent to my boss at Headquarters. Victoria wrote up a report to give to Peter, our library director. I never found out his reaction to it.

Now I was all the more fired up to make digitalization happen.

But back at the Korolenko, I noticed something else that disturbed me. It had a culture all its own. A culture not completely good. For instance, the staff would delight in a quiet day, meaning a day when few readers came in. The librarians could carry on with their regular work of maintaining records, writing reports, dusting the books, but also enjoying longer tea breaks in their alcove in the stack room. Readers could be a big bother.

I'm sure the staffers would deny this, but I got this feeling many times. I felt this attitude was bad. Every reader should be Number One!

**F**inally one day Victoria agreed to take me up to Peter, the eminent director, and to broach my ideas about digitalization to him. She always spoke of him as "Our Chief." She said she had briefed him but he had not been receptive. My being present would add weight to her presentation.

Peter knew me. He had attended my talk in the big reading room, and he had come forward to shake hands afterward. He would smile and always utter a pleasantry when we'd pass in the hall and I'd respond. Neither of us knew exactly what the other said. He knew even less English than I knew Russian. Conversation was impossible.

A nice man certainly, warm and welcoming. In his 60's, meaning already an official pensioner, receiving a monthly stipend but one too small to live on. I was told he loved to garden and maintain bees. He would sell jars of honey to friends. He was hanging on in his job because he had to. That's the impression I got from Victoria.

His secretary ushered us in. He was cordial, as expected. He pushed the papers on his desk aside to give us his full attention. His secretary brought us coffee. Victoria began speaking. At length. And he replied to her, and quite fully. Then she would turn to me and sum up his reply in a mere half a dozen words. I fumed. How could I understand? I felt so frustrated.

I would make a point with some detail and she would translate it to him, but in just a few words. Sometimes she spoke much longer and I'd have no idea what she was saying. Maybe she was adding to what I said, or subtracting from it. And vice versa when she told me what he was saying. This was not a conversation! Very unsatisfactory. Finally the session ended.

Peter rose, clasped my hand, gave me a great big smile, and said, "*Da svedania!*" I understood that. "Have a good day!"

Afterward Victoria explained everything in just a few sentences. She said, "Our chief believes in digitalization. He has read about it. He fully agrees with you. But this is not the right time. The library does not have the money. And he has his hands full with all these repairs."

Maybe he was right about the money. He certainly was busy with the repairs. It was a massive job. Workmen had been laboring for months. Very difficult for staff and readers during that time. Still, I felt that the library—that Peter—should get with it. What could I do to help?

**I** got an idea about how to raise the money needed. At that time Peace Corps was using space for its headquarters in Kyiv in the USAID building. The U.S. Agency for International Development is a State

Department agency that operates in many countries. It gives out money for many kinds of programs helpful to a host country.

On my next trip to Headquarters, I finished my business at Peace Corps. Then I simply took a detour in the building and walked to the top floor. This was advertised as off limits. Getting entry would have been impossible from the street without an appointment. But easy from within.

I located the director's office and strode in. A woman at a desk looked up. "May I help you?"

"I am a Volunteer. I am hoping that I can have a few minutes with your Director." And I explained my pet project and how the Korolenko needed money. I could see that she was interested. And approving!

"Hello!" a man said behind me. And that is how I met Peter Argo, the director of USAID in Ukraine. He had heard me from his big office in a corner. He invited me in and pointed to a couch. He told me that he had been a Volunteer. How wonderful.

I told him what I had just told his secretary, but in detail. He, too, was interested. Very interested. He asked, "How much will it cost?"

"I'm not sure. Maybe $5,000. Maybe $10,000. If you feel the project is feasible, I will go back to my library director and tell him that. He will be excited, of course. Then I am sure we could launch a study and determine exactly how much is required."

He nodded. "I think it's great. I am impressed that you have given this so much thought and are so enthusiastic. But it's not a project for us. We deal with projects in the six figures. And that's a rock-bottom minimum. Most are much bigger."

I was disappointed. We chatted some more. Then he said, "My tour is over. I am leaving for home in three days. If you want to, you can talk some more about it with my successor. I'll brief her. But I am sure she will tell you what I did." And he gave me her name, Sarah Wines.

I went home glum. Later I got another idea. A better idea. I sent her an e-mail mentioning my conversation with Peter Argo. I said, "I know now this project is too small for you. But every library in Ukraine faces the same challenge of how to digitalize.

"What I now suggest is a grand project. Involving all the big libraries in Ukraine! They all need to digitalize! That would bring it up into the big dollar figures that you deal with. Think of how it would benefit Ukraine big time!" That was the essence of my e-mail. It wound up much more detailed.

Time went by. No reply. I re-sent my message. No reply. Finally I got irritated. I sent an e-mail about all this to Diana Schmidt. As our director, she was an officer of the Embassy. I was sure she knew Sarah Wines.

I got an e-mail from Ms. Wines the very next day. Diana had alerted her. She was all apologies. "I receive hundreds of e-mails. I am so sorry!"

My first thought was, she should get an additional secretary! How could she ignore e-mails? Including an e-mail from a fellow American who happened to be in Ukraine, in fact, a Volunteer in Ukraine?

Anyway, she explained that all U.S.AID projects must be approved by Washington, and in fact nearly all are initiated by Washington. In her I definitely did not sense the approval and enthusiasm that I had felt in Peter Argo. But I didn't quit. I was resolved to pursue it.

I carried on with all my various tasks at *Coursi* and elsewhere. But I harped on this project.

One day Victoria broke good news. "Peter has found some money. He is buying a software program. It is for libraries to do what you want. It is called Irbis 64, a very good program. It is Russian."

I was thrilled. The Korolenko would digitalize! How good. But I worried. It was important for any such software to make it possible for all libraries to inter-connect and to work from the same core database. Could Irbis 64 do this? For instance, could Irbis 64 tie in with the Library of Congress and its vast data base?

"Yes," I was told. "Absolutely."

"Good!"

I wondered how much Irbis 64 had cost. I never got a definite answer. But I was told through the grape vine that its price tag was $10,000, but the Korolenko had paid only $4,000. It was said it was an earlier version. Well, this was the all-important start. I was excited.

In a few weeks an Irbis library consultant arrived. He spent a week at the library. He gave a talk to the staff. Then he met with small groups for hands-on teaching of the software. I was not invited to any of the meetings. No problem. I would not have understood a thing, of course.

But I did finally meet him when he visited our department. "I am Leif," he told me. About 45, pleasantly rumpled, very earnest. He smiled when we shook hands. "Good!" he said to me. "Very, very good!" In English. I felt it was the best he could do in English. I wasn't sure what he meant. I got a hunch that maybe he had heard of my role in promoting this project and was complimenting me.

I had many questions to ask him but impossible because of the language impediment, even with the help of Victoria and Iryna.

I was sure, for instance, that once we got started, whatever we accomplished would be beneficial for all the libraries that followed us. They could import our digitalized data and use it as a contribution to their own data base, and what a head start that would be for them.

I sent e-mails to good friends in the U.S. who were librarians. I asked for advice. I sent one to Ann Paietta, the director of the Deep River Public Library in my own town. I sent one to Michelle van Epp, a librarian at the Acton Public Library in Old Saybrook, next door to Deep River.

They both replied promptly. Both were enthusiastic. Both gave me advice from their own experience. Both referred me to professional websites for librarians. I peeked at them and learned things. But my time was limited. What I wanted most was an outline of how the work should proceed, step by step, in the most efficient and economical manner. I did get such an outline and studied it.

The work got started in our department. That pleased me enormously. But it crawled along. How I was impatient! I felt it wise not to complain.

Many of the volumes in Window in America had barcodes. They were a great head start, I reasoned. But we did not have a scanner to read these barcodes! And no money for one!

Iryna, working at her computer, would pick up such a book and scrutinize its barcode. The barcode had a long string of tiny numbers above it. Then, so carefully, she would type the numbers into her desk computer. Irbis 64 had been installed on it. Must not err! It took time. But finally a book could be said to be "digitalized."

What we needed was a big PR impetus, I felt. It was important for the public at large to know of this momentous beginning. I sat down and wrote a news release. I had written many news releases over the years. This one would be sent to area newspapers and television stations and radio stations and anyone with influence. Important for them to understand. Its headline said, "The Korolenko Goes Digital. It will become better than ever."

I told the whole story in my release. Made it as interesting as I could, I, the old feature writer. I even included quotations originating from Peter's mouth. Yes, I fabricated them. I never heard him say these things. But there was method to this madness of mine.

My intention was that Iryna would translate my release into Russian for Peter to read and to approve, of course. It could not be sent out without his approval. He would read my quotations merely as suggestions of what he might say. He could re-write any or all of them and even delete them. My idea was that he would be stimulated to express his own thoughts in his own words.

We took a picture of the first book being digitalized this way. A beautiful volume named "*Ukraina*" – "Ukraine." So appropriate, we all thought. The photo showed Iryna at her computer, the book in hand as she typed in the many tiny numbers of the barcode. Behind her, watching this dramatic moment, were Victoria, Tatiana, our consultant Leif, and myself.

Well, my release never got upstairs to Peter, so far as I know.

Then a terrible economic crisis had come upon the land. Right in the wake of our own crisis...our big recession...in the U.S. Maybe as a result of our crisis! Ukrainian banks failed. Thousands got laid off. Many people who kept their jobs took big pay cuts. This was a poor time to start a program even as exciting as this one.

I had an expatriate American friend, Alain. He ran a small café. Alain became important to me and I talk about him at length in my later chapter, "My Expat Friends."

He had just bought a scanner for use in his café. He showed it to me. A simple, hand-held model, like a pistol. Point it at a barcode, click it, and instantly it would read the barcode. Alain told me there are six basic types of barcodes, and this scanner could read all of them.

He told me he could buy me one at a good discount right here in Ukraine. He quoted me a price. Affordable!

I told him to buy one for me. I would present it to the library as my gift. It would give my friends there such a morale boost.

Then I had another thought. "May I borrow this overnight, Alain? I'd like to take it to the library and show it to my friends."

"Of course!"

I took it to the library the next day. Yes, they were excited. This was the missing piece of technology. With this, so much labor would be saved. They had never seen one. Even more excited when I told them one like this would be my gift to the library. I walked to the Window on America collection, picked out a book, made believe scanning its barcode with my "pistol." Then did it with another book, then another.

They saw how fast I could do it. They had been scanning books manually, as I've explained, by typing in all the little numbers that were lined up above every barcode, at a rate of 100 books a month. It would take decades at that pace! They could do hundreds a day with this little marvel.

Then they had questions. Could it really do the job? I said yes. I showed them the literature in its box. Showed them the different kinds of barcodes it would recognize.

Victoria immediately took the scanner up to Peter. She came back disheartened. "He said we would not need this for another five years!"

I couldn't believe it. It was incomprehensible. What had happened to his enthusiasm? Dejectedly I took the scanner back to Alain. "Thank you," I said. "But the library will not be ready for this for a long, long while."

I for one would be going home in December—in just a few months! I'd never get to see the project get up to speed! But I kept preaching. When I began planning my summer vacation, I decided

*A big moment - the library's first book gets digitalized!! Only a million more to go!*

that all while having fun in my travels in Ukraine, I would visit libraries on the way to get a broader picture. Victoria, the department head, suggested libraries along my travels.

I visited three where to my astonishment, I saw digitalization projects under way! I had thought my library in Chernihiv would be the first! Not so. One in Poltava in a library of about the same size, one in a bigger library in Kharkiv, which is the country's second largest city, and a third in the opposite corner of the country, in ancient Lviv, close to Poland.

This was a big library—more than 10 million volumes in several buildings. All recognized the importance of digitalization. All were hampered by limited funds and limited staff. But all had made a start!

Oh, in one I came upon a librarian who was scanning a famous English book about the history of musical notation. A book of several hundred pages. It was taking her days!

I said to her, "This book may be available online free."

She did not understand. I explained that some important books out of copyright were being digitalized as a monumental public service by Google and others. "Let's see," I said, and I sat at her keyboard and accessed such a service and typed in the title of her book. And I found it online!

"See! The job is all done for you. From now on, please check this way before you start any such book!"

Imagine her amazement!

I brought all these glad tidings back to the Korolenko. But the pace did not pick up.

Then came a remarkable meeting at the library. One day Victoria told me that a delegation was coming to visit from our Embassy in Kyiv. It would be led by the director of its Window on America program. She would come with two assistants plus some librarians from nearby Georgia—native Georgians.

Our embassy in Georgia was starting the same Window on America program there. It wanted to have them see how a successful Ukrainian library was promoting the program. A nice compliment to the Korolenko! I was asked to give a talk to them on our Window on America program.

I was pleased to do it. It was entirely about WoA. I said not a word about digitalization. We had a fine morning. Peter attended. Of course, I spoke in English and a fluent visiting librarian translated for her fellow Georgians. Then Peter, to my surprise, invited all of us to lunch at a nice nearby restaurant. It was a fine gesture to show his appreciation for our Embassy's continuing support.

At lunch I happened to sit across from Valentyna Pashkova. She had given me one of her Embassy business cards: she was Chief of Information Services. In other words, its librarian. I was so excited. This was my opportunity to bring up digitalization, and I did. She handed me a second card. She was the president of the Ukrainian Library Association! I was astonished. In fact, she was its founder. How fortuitous. She was gung ho about digitalization.

I began asking question after question and she answered them. We were running out of time. I asked if I could meet her at the Embassy for further talk. Yes!

We met there two weeks later. She was a charming lady in her mid-50s, I would say. Her father and mother had been librarians. She had become a librarian in Soviet times. There were even more libraries then, she told me. Even the smallest village had one. "They were ideological incubators," she said. "That's where they began preaching the party line to us."

She handed me a recent fact sheet. The country had more than 40,000 libraries of all kinds, including 18,000 public ones. Astounding! The public ones had some 279 million books. There were more than 16 million users, more than a third of the population. It all sounded so impressive.

There were dismal aspects. In all those libraries, there were only 5,346 computers. Most libraries had no computer. Only 1,754 computers were accessible by the public, and only 567 were connected to the Internet.

Then came her big news. The Bill and Melinda Gates Foundation had very recently announced a $26 million grant for computer and Internet support to Ukraine libraries. The news nearly knocked me off my chair. Unbelievable…fantastic!

It was called the *Bibliomist* program. It would work in partnership with the Ukrainian Library Association, the Ukrainian government, U.S.AID, and a non-profit group called IREX, which would manage the whole shebang.

Quite complicated, but over four years the biggest libraries, 1,000 of them, would get computers, all with Internet connections! Aides of librarians would be trained in their use. Great numbers of card-holders would get to learn and enjoy this new technology in up-and-running Internet Centers within these libraries. All these computers would be free to the public. And through technical training, the libraries would get an enormous assist in preparing to serve their users better.

Valentyna, like Victoria at the Korolenko, had been sent to the U.S. to see how our libraries were functioning in this new computer age.

She said to me, "This magnificent grant is not about getting libraries to digitalize their collections. It's more than that. It's about bringing our people into the wonders of the Internet age through our libraries. It's to give us a big push forward in expanding our knowledge and intellectual sophistication.

"But how can it not simultaneously propel us toward the wholesale modernization of our libraries…a step so important to all of us?"

These were not her exact words but they certainly come close. I came home excited. There was a good chance after all that the Korolenko would not decline into just a big warehouse of musty books.

Later Valentyna asked me to write an article for the Journal of the Ukrainian Library Association. She had founded the journal and was its editor. She asked me to give my impressions of how the Korolonko functioned and how digitalization would help it…and indeed assure its future. I wrote it and sent it to her.

Then, just one week before exiting Peace Corps, I gave a special talk to the professional staff of the Korolenko. It intended more than a talk.

I jumped at the chance. In fact, I asked for it. I had something important to say to all of them.

*I visited Valentyna at the Embassy. We learned that a few libraries in Ukraine were indeed digitalizing.*

It was the last Tuesday of November. The library was closed to the public on the last Tuesday of every month. The staff attended in-service training sessions. All would would be present. Good.

We met in the big reading room on the second floor. Such an impressive room with paintings displayed all around and the great portrait of stern Vladimir Korolenko on the front wall.

We were about 60 in all—a huge turn-out. Everybody on the professional staff was present. Victoria introduced me and then milady Annabelle—she had arrived to be with me for my final days in Ukraine (more about this in a chapter coming up). Peter, looking distinguished in his best suit, said nice words about me and surprised Annabelle with a bouquet of white carnations and a beautiful Ukrainian-style tablecloth.

I was certain his words were fine words though Impossible for me to understand him. I say this because he was speaking in Russian and I had to depend on Victoria to put them into English.

I spoke in English, of course. All the staffers

*Going to lunch after my briefing to the librarians from Georgia. Peter is at the far right. Victoria is behind me at my left. The lady at my left is Valentyna Pashkova from our Embassy. Also head of the Ukraine Library Assn.*

would have considered my Russian laughable, and rightly so. Victoria had to put my English into Russian nearly sentence by sentence. It sounds clumsy but it went quite well. It boiled down to this:

"As you are aware, my dear friends, I know your library well—I have come to it hundreds of times. Sadly, it is declining. You know this. Fewer people are using it And it's dying because it has not been able to keep up with the times. It's too hard for people to use it. You know all the reasons why, I am sure. So, if it is to thrive, the library must change. Must digitalize. It has finally agreed to do it. And that is wonderful news. Well, I think so, although some of you do not.

"The work is starting, but at a snail's pace. Many of you resent it and are opposed to it. You are scared of losing your jobs because of digitalization. But it doesn't have to be that way!"

And I explained how. "Your jobs could be guaranteed. A smaller staff would be required, but that would be achieved through normal attrition. Not dismissals. Do not be afraid! The Korolonko will have a new life. Without digitalization, it is my opinion it will not!"

I told them I was leaving for the U.S. soon. But would return for a visit. "I will be back in 10 years...in 2019!" I said it with a straight face. They all laughed. They all knew my age, of course—2019 was impossible! Their laugh was just what I expected, and had hoped for.

I said, "I have a dream." If that reminds you of Martin Luther King, that's not just coincidental. "This is what I want to see when I return.

"One, the library fully digitalized. Meaning every user with a digital ID...a plastic card. And every book, document, music disk, and DVD with a barcode. The enormous card catalog with 3 million items long gone. There will be computers for readers to use in the main hall and in every department! And the library will function like a major modern American library!

"And one more thing. I hope to see a huge change. The readers will be able to enter the stacks and look at and handle books themselves! Right now they can't do that, as you know. They have to give one of you librarians a slip for each book they want. You go into the stacks to fetch the books. That will all change.

"It has to change. It's too easy for readers nowadays to read books and do research without using the library. Just by using their computers at home or at work or at school to access the Internet. And more and more are acquiring computers."

I was treading on thin ice as I talked about all this. I knew it. I kept glancing at Peter. His looked deadly serious. Solemn. I couldn't tell whether he was favorable or unfavorable. But finally he was backing digitalization. Surely he had to agree with what I was saying. I forged ahead. Somebody had to say these things. I was leaving in just a few days. I had little to lose.

Of course I mentioned the whopping $26 million gift coming from the Bill and Melinda Gates Foundation. All this money to be used for computers and Internet for Ukraine. Can you imagine that? I wasn't sure the staffers knew about it.

"This is for real," I told them. "The contract has been signed. The money will be spent over four years. Each of your 'oblasts'(provinces) will receive money. The total expenditure will average nearly $1 million for each library. Isn't this wonderful news for all the libraries? And for our Korolenko?

"It will be spent on computers, computer training for staff and the public (it must be free of charge!), and modernizing the libraries...which means digitalization, of course. It's a big, big deal. So my 10-year dream is based on rock-solid reality!"

When I finally got through, applause. Peter came forward and shook my hand warmly. That was more than I expected.

And he turned to the audience and said, "We shouldn't let John go home. He must stay here and become the new director!"

Lots of laughter. A nice joke. It was all very friendly. I felt relieved. And happy.

As I walked out with Annabelle, there arose a swell of applause. I must mention that. I'd be a bad reporter if I didn't.

For me, the Gates' magnificent gift was completely fortuitous. No way could I take credit for that. But how nice that Bill Gates and this humble Volunteer seemed to have the same thinking for Ukraine—digitalization was essential. So I was on a euphoria of high hopes when I began packing to leave the country. The fates had been smiling down upon me!

I am now back in the United States, of course. I do hope that when I go back to Ukraine—it will be long before 2019, God willing—my dream for the Korolenko will have come true. Users will have a digital ID card.

They'll search for books by computer, not index cards. Will be able to reserve books from home. CDs and movies and audiotapes, too—everything! Will be able to roam the stacks and look at any and all books they want to. Will be able to check out their own books and other items—again because of the computer.

And no staffer will have been let go because this huge labor-saving project took place! And the Korolenko will be serving more people than ever, and making their life better.

I had no idea that I would get involved in such a far-reaching project when I flew to Ukraine, or took the oath to serve the Ukrainians I fell in with to the best of my ability. Peace Corps service truly is an adventure.

~ ~ ~

*Did you know* ... that you will receive the same pay as every other Volunteer in your country or region? This is regardless of your age, your job, your field of work, and your experience or lack thereof.

This is why Peace Corps calls it an allowance rather than a salary.

This allowance is designed to carry you through comfortably and provide pocket money for travel and other niceties. It definitely will not support a lavish lifestyle. Peace Corps would frown on that.

But I did know of some Volunteers who dipped into their own cash at times.

# 18 / A chance meeting

*My new American pal gets to play a big role in my English Club. And my life.*

**H**alf way through my second year, I made an interesting and important friend. At a Philharmonia concert one evening, I heard a man behind me speaking English— American English, not British. I thought, *"This must be a Peace Corps Trainee that I have not met."*

At intermission I turned and looked at him. He was with a woman. A good-looking man, white-haired, about 65, in casual but smart clothes. I introduced myself. "I'm an American.. I 'm a Peace Corps Volunteer here."

He said to me, "My name is Wayne Purves. From California. I live here. You're a Volunteer! Well, I was a Volunteer also. In Armenia. But that was 10 years ago."

I didn't catch the woman's name. A Ukrainian teacher, he said.

I was fascinated by him. Later I called him and we agreed to meet at the *Dba Gucia* restaurant. I arrived early. He never came! What's this? I was so disappointed. I had looked forward to another American friend.

He called the next day. "John, I forgot! I am so sorry. Believe me, this is not my style!"

We did meet this time. We met many times. Wayne was one of the best things to happen to me in Peace Corps.

He invited me to dinner at his home. "Take *Marshrutka 27*," he said. "I live in a development of new homes." He gave me directions.

It was on the edge of the city. It had been vegetable-gardening land. There were still gardens. But I saw many new houses. Big. Two floors. Many rooms. Attached garages. Large yards. Protective front walls. I had no idea such fine houses existed in the city.

I found Wayne's easily. It fit right in with the others—a big, handsome, two-story house with a red roof. An eight-foot wall ran all along the front. A heavy steel gate led to the attached garage. I walked to a smaller gate. It had a punch-the-numbers lock. He had told me the combination. Talk about being trusting! I let myself in. The landscaping work was still unfinished.

He greeted me at the door. "Welcome, John! Come in!" I started to take off my shoes—it was the national custom. "No need!" He swept me inside. My first impression: the house was still not completely furnished. My second: he had spent a lot of money here. The beautiful floor. The spacious and elegant kitchen—cabinets and fixtures from Germany. Large windows of the best quality. A stunning spiral staircase led up to the second floor.

"Beautiful, Wayne," I kept saying. "It's all so impressive. You are going to be set up here for a long time!"

"I live here only part of the year. I go home to Sacramento regularly."

In the garage I noticed a shiny BMW sedan. Later he told me that he had shipped it from California. "It came here through the Panama Canal," he said. "But it's not worth as much as you think. It's a few years old."

He took me to the back of the house and showed me a sunroom. The ceiling still had to be finished. Big windows with expansive views. I looked out on the backyard. Large, with a big garden. Many things growing, flowers and vegetables and fruits and berries. "You are quite a gardener!"

Wayne with some of our club members. He took over after me.

"'No, no. Larisa comes and does it all. All Ukrainian women are good at growing things. But I do like gardens."

He told me Larisa was a school teacher. She was the wife of Nick, who lived nearby. Nick was a retired Ukrainian Air Force pilot—a colonel. "Nick is a capable guy. Has been my building superintendent, so to speak. He chose the craftsmen and supervised everything."

**H**e knew I was vegetarian and was ready for me with a large Greek salad and garlic toasts right out of the oven. For himself he had made a roasted chicken breast. He chose two wine glasses.

"Dry red wine all right?"

"Wonderful!" He poured for us and raised his glass. "To friendship!" he said. "I'm glad you are here."

It turned out to be a toast amply fulfilled. I spent many happy hours with him. Our talks often touched upon important things. I always enjoyed my time with him.

He talked about his Peace Corps days in Armenia, of course. "It was a good experience. I worked in a village. Wine country. I worked to

The Chernihiv Philharmonia, founded by Conductor Sukaj. I loved it and tried to attend every concert. Young Chil Lee was conducting this concert.

He, too, had been an older Volunteer, though not a real oldie like me. So we had that in common also. But his group in Armenia had been much smaller than ours in Ukraine. I felt that their group morale was better than ours. To me our being fellow Volunteers, the two of us, was a big bond.

He liked to give parties and I was always a happy participant. But I always enjoyed our private get-togethers more. I dined with him often, nearly always at his house mostly but sometimes downtown.

One day I said, "Wayne, you were a Volunteer. You must come and talk at my English Club about that." I was always on the look-out for good speakers. He agreed. He came and did a great job.

Here is his story in fuller detail. I had never heard the name Purves. "It's Scottish," he told me. He was a Californian. After university he had gone to work for AT&T and had become an executive. Telephone electronics was his specialty. He didn't call himself an engineer but I saw that he ran some big projects for the company. After AT&T's break-up, he had gone to work for Pacific Bell, I think it was. He handled challenging projects there also.

It was a hugely competitive time for that industry. One day he was offered a buy-out. "I hadn't planned on retiring early. But it was irresistible. I accepted it."

He bought a large RV and toured the country solo—it reminded me of my travels in my tiny VW Microbus. Then he moved up to an even bigger RV—one as large as they come. More road adventures.

"I had some cyclists preparing to bicycle across the U.S. I accompanied them in my RV. I'd park for the night up ahead of them and they'd rendezvous with me and stay with me. We did that all the way across the country. A good time!"

He lived the RV life for several years, favoring the West Coast.

He had divorced but was on good terms with his ex. He had a son and daughter and both were doing well. And a younger sister. He was close to her. He had been coming to Ukraine for about five years. I would have bet that like so many other foreign men, he came to meet a woman. No. He had met a Ukrainian couple in the U.S. They became friends. They invited him to visit in Ukraine.

He took them up on it and got to Chernihiv—he always called it the Russian "Chernigov"—and liked what he saw. For one thing, he saw how so many things would be a bargain for an American, such as a house.

He bought his big lot, hired an architect, designed the house with him, and got it built. "I am sure it will be a good investment," he told me.

He spent about half the year in Ukraine, returning to Sacramento for the Christmas holidays and then the spring income-tax time.

He became a regular at the English Club and took a leading role. Made friends. Was an innovator. Created a volleyball club. One Sunday after our meeting he led a group of our members, men and women, young and not so young, across the park to the high school.

He had arranged to use the gym. They played volleyball and had a grand time. He'd play as hard as the others, and he was the oldest. It became part of the club routine.

I did not participate, as you can understand. And I hated the idea of being the only one standing on the side lines.

For the Fourth of July he invited a big group of us—all members of the club were invited—to his house for an American cook-out. The weather threatened so it became a cook-in. Fabulous. Hot dogs. Corn on the cob. Fine salad. Watermelon. Ice cream aplenty. Soft drinks and wine and beer and even more potent. All on the house!

Some folks admired his garden. He handed them plastic bags and said, "You go pick whatever you want!

Our party at Wayne's on the Fourth of July. A first for our members. They talked about it for a long time.

Tomatoes. And corn. And lots of zucchini!" Some eagerly took him up on it and ran to the garden. They were a happy group.

We had gotten to his house by *marshrutka*. Too many of us for just one. We broke up and used three. The next day I asked Iryna at the library how they got home. "We all walked. Together!" she said. "It was fun!"

I was sure it was. Certainly it was a very long walk. Also a way to save car fare. The economic recession was harsh.

He loved to host dinner parties for five or six. And he loved to cook—and to wash the dishes. I balked at this. I would jump in and help despite his protests.

If it got very late and someone had a wee bit to sip, he would back out his BMW and pack us in and drive us home.. Always cheerfully. I was aware how expensive gasoline was.

Wayne with conductor Mikael Sukaj and Valya, one of our English Club members, after a concert at the Philharmonia.

Then for a beautiful summer Sunday not long later, he organized a picnic by the river. Swimming. Sunbathing. Snacking. Lounging. Another great success. It would not be forgotten soon.

I had accumulated a month's vacation time and I planned to go off and travel all that time. I hated the idea of the club lapsing while I was gone. An idea!

I said to him, "Wayne, how about substituting for me? You'll do a great job!" He hesitated but then agreed. He lived up to my expectation. I heard happy reports when I got back.

Like me, and like my friend Renato (who became his friend also), Wayne loved the Philharmonia concerts—remember, the two of us had met at one of the concerts. We attended every concert. It was Renato who had introduced me to Mikael Sukaj, the conductor. And I introduced Wayne. Often we'd chat with Mikael during intermission.

One day I got an idea. I said to Wayne, "Why don't we invite Mikael to dinner? Wouldn't that be fun?"

"Yes. A great idea! But where?"

"Your house!"

It happened. And a fine dinner it was—and Wayne did all the cooking. Mikael attended with his wife. Renato was at the table, of course. So were Nick and Larisa and another Ukrainian couple. Language difficulties were a problem but Larisa was a good translator.

Mikael was an enthusiastic participant and talked plenty. Just as we had hoped.

He had guest-conducted in numerous European cities and, in fact, had been to Las Vegas and California. I believe he had performed in both places. He had CDs of great pieces that he had conducted with his baton—100 of them—as a gift for each of us. A wonderful evening. His CD was among my prized souvenirs when I came home to the U.S.

Wayne outdid himself as a host. Many toasts. Afterward, Renato and I felt it only fair that we be allowed to contribute to the expense. And did so.

At one performance of the Philharmonia, a guest conductor took the podium, Young Chil Lee. South Korean. Deliberate and demanding and forceful. About 40, I estimated. Was on a tour through Eastern Europe. I managed to chat with him and his manager—a beautiful Korean woman—during the intermission. I was amazed—both spoke good English. It turned out he had studied at the Juilliard School of Music in New York. He told me he would return to Chernihiv and conduct again some weeks later.

Again I approached Wayne. "Let's have a dinner for him when he comes back!"

Wayne hosted it again. Young Chil Lee—I never found out what part was his family name and what part his given name—was delighted and at ease. It was another gala dinner. Mikael Sukaj and his wife were among the guests. Yes, my Peace Corps service in Chernihiv had interesting moments.

Wayne was readying for his Christmas trip home to Sacramento. I knew he would be traveling light but carrying two big suitcases. "I've got a list of things to buy at Costco and bring back!" he told me.

Inspiration struck! I was preparing to exit Peace Corps. "Wayne," I said to him in a brave moment, "could you take some things home for me—I am over-loaded! When you get home, you could mail them to me in Deep River. What a blessing that would be!"

Instantly he said yes. I prepared two large packages for him. I told him, "I have no idea of the postage. Let me know and I'll pay you."

"No problem!" And he took them with him. How about that?

I had dinner with him at his home on the eve of his flight. Larisa was with us. She would look after his place during his two months away. She left right after dinner to go home. Wayne and I lingered at the table.

I would be going home in just a month, and for good, my service finished. So this was our last time together. We talked lightly about all the things we had done together. So many. Now we were quiet for a minute. I was deep in thought. He, too, it seemed.

Then Wayne looked squarely at me and said, "John, my meeting you turned out to be a transcending experience."

"What?"

"Yes. It was. It has changed my life for the better. I had just about finished my house. Had a lot of time on my hands. You changed all that! And interesting new things began to happen."

Well, time to say goodbye. A frigid night. I bundled up. Wayne offered to walk me to the bus stop a quarter of a mile away. He did this often. He bundled up. But a clear night. The stars stood out. We talked little.

At the bus stop we were alone. I said to him, "That concert at the Philharmonia when I we met that first time was a big event for me, too."

He smiled, shook my hand, and turned and walked off into the night. I stood alone in the cold. I turned my collar up and watched for my *marshrutka*. I kept hoping it would be right along. I thought again of his words to me, "a transcending experience." Then I saw the *marshrutka's* lights getting bigger in the dark. Well, a transcending experience for me, too.

~ ~ ~

*Did you know* ,,,, that Peace Corps strives to be truly representative of our American people. Meaning that it has Volunteers of all races and major background demographics.

Not only religions and, ethnic origins, but educational backgrounds in the fields of expertise that Peace Corps provides in the various countries where it serves. But the in-country representation may not match our actual national percentages.

# 19 / One more fantasy!

*What a crazy public transit system here!*
*I see a way to make it better. I get started.*

Isn't it strange how ideas spring up in our mind? What's amazing is that this new idea of mine was about the city's public transit system. It came to me while I was thinking of something totally different: how to find a way to raise money to help the Korolenko Library's big digitalization project.

I found the public transit system a mess to understand. A daily puzzle. Oh, the city had plenty of buses and trolleybuses and *marshrutkas* and taxis even. They were all essential to its daily life because few people owned cars. The problem was figuring out where each type went and which was best to use. You had to be born in the city to master the system.

You would spot Trolleybus No. 8 arriving. Then Bus No. 8. Then *Marshrutka* No. 8. Wouldn't you assume they all traveled the same route? Maybe yes, maybe no. And how would you know which to take to get to the main hospital? Or the Polytechnic University? Or the northeast bazaar?

Maybe for a single journey it would be best to take a combination of buses, trolleybuses, and *marshrutkas*. What would be the best combination? There were many stops in the downtown area. Which stop should you wait at?

At times all of them would pull up at the same stop. But sometimes they'd pull up at different stops, so that if you waited there, you didn't have the choice of taking one kind or another. It was all so baffling.

I would be traveling alone nearly all the time. I would be waiting for a certain bus or a certain trolleybus or a certain *marshrutka* and others would come by. Often I would think, *Maybe one of those would work fine.* But I had no way of knowing without asking somebody. And my Russian was too poor to do this. What frustration! Especially on a cold or rainy day.

In the United States all bus and trolley and subway systems publish route maps and departure schedules for each route and each stop. It's expected. It's taken for granted. In big cities like New York and Los

Angeles and Chicago, and even in smaller cities like Providence and Hartford.

I would ask my host mother or a professor at the university, or one of my fellow teachers at school. I carried a card in my wallet listing the various possibilities for my routine trips. And I became more savvy.

In my early days I made mistakes aplenty. More than once I found myself on a bus or *marshrutka* going to the wrong place—had to hop off and find my way back and start again. Got to school late more than once.

And if on the right vehicle, how would I know where to get off? True, each vehicle had a small map posted on board, but often inaccessible because so many standees in the way. And too small to really see. And it was all in Ukrainian.

Sure, I could ask the person sitting next to me. I would show them the name of my destination written on a card. Sometimes that would work. But rarely easy. I would think, *There must be some central place where all this is explained.* There was not.

So how did the locals figure these things out? They started when they were tiny tots, learning from their mothers and fathers as they used the system with them.

Most people had certain travel routines. They'd go to and from work the same way every day, to their favorite bazaar the same way, to church the same way every Sunday, to visit a certain friend, and so on.

If they had to visit a new friend in an unusual part of the city, they would get directions from that friend. If they heard of a new store opening somewhere, they would ask a neighbor, or the woman who operated the newsstand at the corner.

In time, I got to use every type of vehicle the system offered, including taxis. In the beginning, I would take Trolleybus 5 to get downtown, then change to Trolleybus 1 to get to my classes at *Coursi*. Then I discovered I could save time by taking the same Trolleybus 5 to downtown but then *Marshrutka* 27 to my classes.

Then I discovered that if I left from a different stop I could take *Marshrutka* 31 all the way to my classes, but I would have a longer walk before starting the ride and at the end of the ride. It was a challenging learning experience for me.

**W**hat made it more complicated was that *marshrutkas* ran far more frequently than the buses, and the buses more frequently than the trolleybuses. But for me as a senior the trolleybus would be free. But I would have to pay on the buses and the *marshrutkas*. But the *marshrutkas* would cost 50% more than the buses. The mental juggle was a daily thing, but it got easier.

My big question was, Is there some way to make this complex triple-layered system of trolleybus, buses, and *marshrutkas* easily understandable to everybody? Is there anything I can do about it?

That's when I got my brainstorm. I would publish an annual handbook! It would cover all three types. It would provide schedules for each type. And a map for each type. Plus I would include essential information about the taxis. The handbook would be loaded with advertisements. It would be a money-maker. The Korolenko Library would run it! The profits would fund its digitalization project!

The handbook would have to come out at least annually because its information would be in continual flux. Annual updates would be essential What a great help such a handbook would be for the people! I would call the first one "The 2010 Chernihiv Public Transit Handbook."

Designing it would not be a big problem. For years I had been designing printed things. Ads. Pamphlets. Brochures. Booklets. Newspapers. Even a billboard or two. I felt comfortable with this part of the project.

The thorny part was the maps. Sure, I could publish one map for the buses, another for the trolleybuses, and another for the *marshrutkas*. That would work but it would be clumsy.

For a ride involving a bus and a trolleybus, say, you'd have to study two maps. If you included a *marshrutka*, three maps! Wouldn't it be possible to design a master map that would include all three types? Wouldn't that be wonderful?

Then came my second thought. This annual handbook could raise a lot of $$$ for the library!

Now let me tell you a bit about each type.

The trackless trolleybuses were the successors to the original horse cars, which were the first public transit system in the city. The trolleybuses were what served the city when Ukraine became independent.

But when I arrived in Chernihiv, the trolleybuses ran the smallest number of routes and were the fewest in number. They were operated by the city, they had the lowest fares, and they offered discounts to students. and they were free for pensioners.

So they were the vehicle of choice for old people, and most of the passengers by far were old people. I got to like them, and not only because as a senior I didn't pay. They were fun, well, when not jam-packed.

Because of a lack of money, most of the trolleybuses were old and worn and scruffy. They had not been washed in years, and you would think that some should have been junked years ago.

I saw a couple that broke down on their route and had to be towed away. But they gave a nice smooth, quiet ride. They lumbered along, heaving and swaying. Sometimes I was reminded of my sailing days on Narragansett Bay, and I liked that.

Definitely they were the slowest and you had to wait the longest for one. One or two buses or *marshrutkas* going to the same place might stop by while you waited for a trolleybus. From where I lived, they took twice as long as *marshrutkas* to get downtown.

Six months before my time in Ukraine was up, a brand-new one was put into service—butter yellow with bright blue trim, and state of the art. Magnificent. It would just glide along, amazingly silent. What a pleasure to ride it. Everyone gawked the first few times it went by. And it was manufactured right there in Ukraine, a matter of great pride for everybody.

A trolleybus had a driver, usually a man but sometimes a woman, plus a conductor who was usually a woman but could be a man. The conductor collected the money and provided information.

In peak hours they were a sardine can. Every seat got taken and often there were as many standees as there were seated riders. But this was true of buses and *marshrutkas* also. It was surprising there were not more accidents of standees being knocked down when the vehicles braked or lurched.

They offered a special advantage. In a society where private automobiles are rare, how do you get a big purchase home? A new television set? Or three or four boards eight feet long? Or get your baby in its baby carriage on board?

Well, the rear of the trolleybus was clear of seats. You got on with your bulky stuff through the rear door, and stood back there with your stuff, resting in on the floor if easier. Then exited through that door.

It was impossible to carry such stuff on a bus or a *marshrutka*. You could do it in a taxi, but that was expensive, and the taxis were generally small. Impossible with a baby carriage, say.

**O**h, one thing. When new in Chernihiv, I always paid on the trolleybus, just as I did on a bus or *marshrutka*. But when I paid, I noticed people would stare at me. It was the custom for the *conductora* to walk up and down the aisle to collect fares. It was hard. She had to hold her balance and squeeze between the standees. If I did not offer to pay, she would skip by me with nary a look.

That's when I realized that seniors rode free. I stopped paying. Not once was I ever asked for my fare. At first I felt guilty. But then I thought, *Heck, think of all the things I do free for the people of Chernihiv as a Volunteer.* That worked nicely.

The buses were the second to arrive on the scene. They were privately owned and operated and in fact by several individuals and companies. They carried fewer passengers than the trolleybuses but they covered more routes, extended farther out in the city and even into the suburbs, and were far more numerous.

They had a driver and a conductor, usually a man and a woman. No discounts. The only ones who didn't pay were those who carried a government pass (several categories) but these people were a minority.

Next came the *marshrutkas*. They were the newcomers, coming on the scene after Independence.

Relatively few just a few years back, but now the most numerous of all. Hundreds of them. Owned and operated by different people. They traveled the most routes, were the fastest on the road, and offered the most frequent service.

They were the first choice of people with better jobs and a better income and those who needed to get somewhere as quickly as possible—job or university, say.

A *marshrutka* was a van with an extra-high roof. Typically a *marshrutka* would accommodate a dozen sitting plus eight or ten standing in the aisle. Older people did not ride the *marshrutkas* because too expensive. Invariably I was the only old person on a *marshrutka*. University and school children could save money with a pass.

Being a standee was unpleasant. You had to hold on for dear life. You could not see outside—I was always anxious about where I was on the route. And dangerous. The driver was always a man, often a young man. He didn't give a hoot about the passengers.

He drove as if handling a sports car. Sharp turns! Hard braking! Lots of bouncing! If he slammed on the brakes, the more standees, the better... you were all in so tight that you held one another up! There was no room to fall down. I never heard anyone protest to a driver about his driving. Everyone was so meek. It was amazing that I was never in one that got into an accident. I heard about accidents.

At peak time, once in a while someone would rise and offer me his seat when I got on. At first I would decline. I was embarrassed. But that passed. Many times I stood for a long time while teen-agers remained sitting and looking the other way from me.

The driver also collected the fares. I might pay when I got on. But maybe he was too busy, or in a rush to get started. I would take my seat in the fifth row, say. Then hand my fare to the person in front of me, who would pass it on. If I had change coming to me, it would be passed back from passenger to passenger. It worked beautifully.

The fares varied according to type of vehicle. The trolley buses were cheapest. There was continuing inflation. When *marshrutka* prices went up, more people rode the buses and the trolleybuses or walked (it was surprising how many walked), but then they gravitated back. In my 27 months I saw the fares triple.

This became painful for many when the financial crisis struck. People began using shoe leather even more.

Then of course, there were taxis. As everywhere, they were used when public transit just wouldn't work out, for whatever reason. Also by people who could afford them on a regular basis.

I used them, but only because I had to. I would be very late in getting to class, say. Or it was raining hard. Or it was late in the day—they operated all day; public transit shut down during the night.

They had one peculiarity. Three or four people going together in the same general direction would pay the same fare as a single person, even if the taxi had to go out of its way to leave them off at different spots. Didn't seem smart, but that's the way it was.

Classes at *Coursi* ended at 9 p.m. Quite often three or four teachers would share a taxi. I did that. That beat a 10-minute walk to a transit stop, waiting there, then riding, and then walking home. Especially on a winter night. The final fare broke down to just a few *hryvnia* more than a *marshrutka* ride. I'm talking pennies more, now.

The taxi drivers spent so much time waiting and lounging. Reading newspapers, chatting with colleagues. When they got a fare, they would speed! It was amazing. And dangerous. The idea seemed to be to set a new speed record.

One stormy, rainy night, four of us shared a taxi after class. I sat in the front, Olena (my dean) and Lina (her assistant) and Marina (a teacher) sat in the rear. Our driver was speeding, of course. The windshield wipers couldn't keep up. Big pools of water on the road and he splashed through recklessly. I had buckled up immediately. The driver forged ahead. I was scared.

"Are you buckled up?" I yelled to them in the back. I was sure they were not. "This is dangerous! Buckle up!"

Marina laughed at me. "This is not America, John. This is Ukraine! We don't do that!"

They did not buckle up. I was astounded. And Marina had spent months in the U.S. as a visiting teacher on a grant! She knew better.

So that was the complex and baffling system in Chernihiv. Every city had the same mix of trolleybuses, buses, and *marshrutkas*, I knew. How could all this be made more efficient and more convenient for the riders? With my handbook! It could do the trick in Chernihiv. And could be adopted by every city in the country.

Now let me tell you how my handbook would provide essential money for the library. My handbook would have two sections. The first would offer detailed and accurate information. How many vehicles of each kind. Their average age. Who owned and operated them.

Were there compulsory vehicle inspections? Was there insurance for riders? Who drove them. What did you have to do to become a rider. How many hours a day did a driver work. What authority ran the system. Set the fares. Sets the schedule. Who decided on new routes. How route numbers were assigned. On and on.

The second section would have a map showing every route for every type of vehicle. Would show all the transit stops. Would show all the transfer stops...where riders could change to another vehicle of the same type or a different type.

You could study the map and find out exactly how to get from one transit stop to another anywhere in the city, and decide the best combination for you ... whether a trolleybus followed by another trolleybus, or a bus followed by a *marshrutka,* and so on.

And schedules would be posted, with pick-up times at all the major stops, with

Public transit is all-important in a country with few cars. We had a mix of buses and marshrutkas (above) and trolleybuses. A map was needed!

special schedules for Sundays and holidays. It was obvious to me how useful this would be. No such book existed. I decided to start the project.

The handbook would be supported by advertising. Every family would want one and would use it. Advertisers would love to be in it, I was sure. Clearly the handbook would be a money maker. Why? Because many people would buy it, of course.

But the cover price should be kept as low as possible in order to maximize the handbook's circulation.

The real income would derive from the advertising in the handbook. The handbook would be an excellent medium for all kinds of businesses and services.

Think Yellow Pages! That would be the inspiration for my handbook.

And here was the beauty of the scheme. All profits would go to the Korolenko Library! The profits would pay for its digitalization work and maybe other things, too. Finally the library would have a source of income apart from its meager funding by the government, and the paltry fines that readers paid for late books. A source of income year in and year out.

The handbook would be the Korolenko's project! It would own it. Would create a special small department to run it.

The rights to sell the advertising might be franchised out to the highest bidder, for four years. say. After all, it takes special expertise to sell ads and design them and make sure they get printed right. I thought that franchising this out would be the best solution.

All bidders would have to be thoroughly experienced advertising companies. By the way, franchising was very novel in Ukraine—a truly capitalist concept!

Promptly I got the project started. I talked it up with my friends the librarians in the Foreign Book Department.

I spent days digging up all the information needed, then wrote a draft of the whole information section.

I tried to imagine every detail that was required, typing "xxx" wherever a number of some kind was required. A date, say. Or the number of *marshrutka* routes. Or how many trolleybuses there were. On and on. I labored to make the handbook comprehensive in every way.

I planned that later, during meetings with different officials, I would demand the right answers for every "xxx" and type them in.

I designed the handbook, laid out the various sections, wrote all the headlines, made every-thing as accurate and exact as I could. To illustrate it, I took photos of buses and trolleybus and *marshrutkas* and of people waiting and getting on and off.

*A rare sight —a young man with a car. Denys, here with his fiancée, was in my French Club. He saved for his Russian Lada working in New York.*

Then my friend Iryna at the Korolenko translated the whole thing into Ukrainian. It's the only official lan-guage, as you know. Many people in Chernihiv spoke Russian, but all could at least read Ukrainian.

I must tell you that Iryna became my partner in this project. She took a great interest, was always quick to help me, and was my go-between. I would not have been able to move ahead without her. As you know, Iryna was her formal name, and Ira her informal one. In other places in these pages I have called her Ira. In this chapter she is Iryna all the way.

Well, my idea was the handbook would have two versions. The one in Ukrainian for the local people. And one in English for tourists. The city was intensely interested in attracting more tourists. An English version would be helpful because it is the main international language. Even many people from non-English countries spoke English a bit.

If many Germans or Spanish-speaking tourists started coming, editions in German or Spanish could be published, of course.

Then Iryna made an appointment for me with the City Commissioner of Public Transportation. The two of us went to his office. His name was Vladimir and he dealt with this whole complex transit business.

I had a prototype of my handbook with me. He received us cordially, listened, and looked at my sample.

"Very nice," he said. "But everybody already knows how to use the buses and trolleybuses and *marshrutkas*."

He turned to the front pages with all the background information. "And much of this at the front is not necessary." He grimaced dismissively and flipped it back to me. He was speaking in Russian, of course. Iryna was doing the translating.

I felt he was absolutely wrong. From my own experience I knew people were sometimes at a loss about what kind of vehicle to take, or what route number. And I felt that people had a right to know all this basic information.

*Advertising lady Olga (left) had designed a clever map. I wanted to buy it. Here Iryna is negotiating with her.*

This was their city. They paid the taxes. And the fares. I made a further point.

"The city is interested in developing tourism. That's an excellent idea. Chernihiv could be a great tourist city. Americans would come here. The handbook should be published in English as well. It would be a great aid to them. English is the most important language in the world."

And I said more. "Americans could stay here for a month for what two or three days in Paris or London would cost them!

"And just imagine! The booklet could be loaded with ads targeted to tourists: ads of restaurants, hotels, cafés, nightclubs, theaters, on and on. Think of the money!"

I could not convince him. Baffling. He did get an assistant to plug in the missing bits of information indicated by all my "xxx's." That was progress. But later when I reviewed the work, I could see there were obvious exaggerations and even untruths. True.

Meanwhile, I worked on the map. The map was all-important. The task of including routes of all buses, trolleybuses, and *marshrutkas* was a complex challenge, more so because I insisted on making the map as simple as possible. Simplicity was key. I developed rough ideas, selected the best, created a concept, and showed it to some savvy people.

One was a new Peace Corps Trainee. A very sharp gal, Barbara. A computer whiz. She had good ideas of her own. She told me she was up to the project, was willing to tackle it in her limited spare time, and went to work. I felt so encouraged.

She refined her scheme to the point that she had a map that covered two of the three types of vehicles. It was shaping up and she was ready to tackle the final challenge. But then she was sworn in as a Volunteer and sent off to a distant village close to Russia. Suddenly she was up to her chin in her new responsibilities. She no longer had time for our map. Sob!

I carried on. Iryna and I visited Vladimir, the commissioner, several times. Very cordial. Always laughter. But the bottom line was always the same: I was getting nowhere. I would leave his office frowning.

But one day he surprised me by showing me a new map. It was what I was dreaming of! Exactly what I wanted. I was so excited. He told me it was created by a local advertising woman, Olga.

"May I use this wonderful map?" I said to him.

"No! It is not mine to give you!"

But he did let me photograph it after I assured him that I would not use it without permission. I wanted to study it.

In one sense, Vladimir's refusing me impressed me. He was recognizing the importance of intellectual property! Intellectual property rights weren't well developed in Ukraine. There seemed to be no concept of such rights. "Borrowing" copyrighted and trade-marked materials was thought perfectly all right.

I had had an eye-opening experience about this. One day I was talking to one my students. He had a master's in computer science and was working as a lead programmer. He had Microsoft Word on his laptop. This may sound unusual to you, but remember, this was Ukraine, and I assumed all the programs on his machine were Russian programs. "Where did you buy Microsoft Word?" I asked him.

He laughed. "It was free!"

"Free? How could it be free?"

"I lifted it." He said it whout embarrassment. "Everybody lifts programs. Easy to do."

"I can't believe it."

He seemed astonished. He said, "Ukraine would collapse without such free programs. All kinds of programs are available on certain big file-sharing websites.

"You just download them! For instance, from eMule.com. Or from BitTorrent.com. People on these websites share all their programs."

I had never heard of these websites. I investigated and as far as I could tell, I found he was accurate in everything he had told me. Imagine that! I thought it awful! Made me think I'm an innocent in the woods.

But bad things were happening. A huge financial crisis clouded the country, precipitated by our own, it seemed. Americans suffered greatly, I know. It was difficult to make comparisons, but I believe Ukrainians were suffering more.

They did not have our safety net. In Ukraine you could be dismissed on the spot—without even a day's notice. And unemployment compensation existed in name only.

Those suddenly dumped had none of the established resources that most Americans have to support themselves for a while and hopefully find another job. Much harder here.

I saw construction crews walk away from buildings partly built. Once- popular businesses shut down. More empty stores appeared. Newspapers got thinner. Goods on store shelves got scanty...more and more cheaper goods started to be offered for sale. Banks were shutting down. Some banks froze accounts; you could not withdraw your own money! Scary.

*Always many people downtown. Their choices: walking or riding public transit. But what type?*

I realized that my idea of a printed handbook was unsupportable. There would be no ads. No ads meant no financial support for the Korolenko, of course. What to do?

I switched. I decided to publish a website instead of a printed booklet. Websites are cheap. A website could offer advertising but its ad rates would be cheaper. No paper. No ink. No expense in distributing the booklet. But a website would have a serious limitation.

It would be limited to people who knew how to use a computer...who owned one or had access to one. This would be a small percentage of the community, and a much smaller segment. Computer use would grow, of course, and maybe with better times the idea of a printed booklet—one mass-distributed—could be revived.

At least, this would be a start. It would establish the concept. One big plus: information on a website could be updated much more quickly and more often than in a printed booklet.

The months rolled on. As my Close of Service date got approached, I concentrated on completing my projects. I focused on this one. I considered it such a good idea. If I did not get it created, my idea might die.

Iryna and I would talk about it often. She had invested a lot in it herself, in hours of work and enthusiasm. She had translated everything into Ukrainian. Quite a task. And she was emotionally involved. She knew that her name would be on the website as a co-producer.

She would be a key person in its continuation after my departure. She believed in our project! And she saw how much it meant to me. She wanted success!

One day she made an appointment for us with another official in the mayor's office. His name was Vladimir also! He was the tourism promoter.

We misunderstood and went to the wrong building. She called him. He said, "Stay right there. I'll pick you up in my car." He did. A good start!

But then, disappointment. Much conversation but little action. He talked and talked. We met with him three times. I got irritated. I said to him, "It's all words. No action!" And I folded my

*Barbara, a Trainee who was a computer whiz, started designing the map. But then got assigned to a far-off village.*

papers and put them in my bag. And we walked out.

I was frustrated in the extreme. One day I said to Iryna, "Let's go see this Olga. The lady who made the terrific map for herself! Please see if you can make an appointment."

We went to her office a week later. Her ad agency. Our appointment was for 10 a.m. Iryna told me, "She is giving us 30 minutes." It was on the first floor of a Soviet block like the one I lived in. In fact, like Iryna's block.

Olga was a thin, intense gal. About 45. Dressed in jeans and sandals. Nothing glamorous about her.

She noticed us but paid no attention. She was all business. She was leaning over the shoulder of a young man at a computer. He had created an ad and she was critiquing it. Meekly he agreed to every change she suggested. I knew who the boss here was.

I was looking around. It was a busy office. Piles of publications. Pamphlets pinned on the wallet, ads, posters...all samples of her work obviously.

We had arrived a few minutes early. At exactly 10, she turned to us. I introduced myself, introduced Iryna, and explained our project from A to Z. I spoke in English, of course. I thought she was getting the gist of it, but Iryna translated as we went along. Olga said little, merely nodding now and then. For me, this was just a guessing game. Again I felt so frustrated.

I came to the big topic: her remarkable map! I told her I had seen it, in fact had photographed it. I mentioned it was exactly what I had in mind. "I promise you I will not steal it," I said with a little laugh.

"Good!" she said, looking me straight in the eye. "You had better not!"

I explained I had no profit motive. I was a Volunteer going home in just a few months.

"I am doing this project because it will be a good step forward for the city. Chernihiv needs this. May we use your map on our website?"

She did not answer directly. "This is how I earn my living. This is what supports this office."

"Maybe we can work out an arrangement of some kind?"

"I must think about it. Call me in about two weeks. But excuse me. I must get back to my work." I looked at my watch. It was exactly 2:30. Quite a gal, this Olga.

Two weeks soon became four weeks, became two months. Then Olga agreed to see us. Iryna put down the phone and said to me. "She is giving us just 30 minutes. A busy lady!"

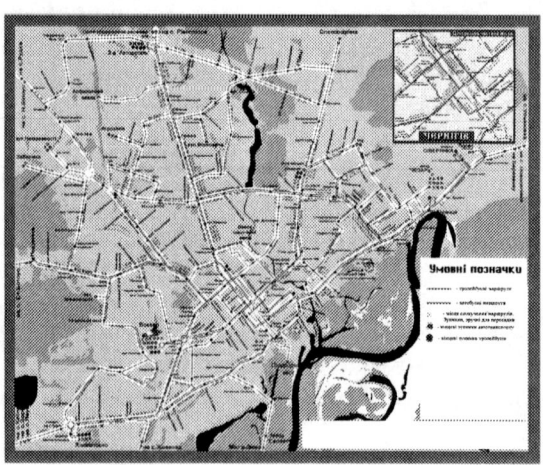

This is the Transit Map as now seen on the city website, but in full color. What a challenge to get it done. The inset at top right shows the downtown area.

When we arrived for our 3 p.m. session, she was busy again. She invited us to approach her desk at 10 past. I wasted no time. I was emphatic. "I am returning to America soon," I said. "I am eager to complete this."

Again I stressed how this would make life better for everybody. As I spoke, I reached into my pocket, pulled out a crisp American bill that I had ready for this moment, and placed it on the corner of her desk. It was a $100 bill. My own money. She never looked at it but I knew she was aware.

"I want to buy the rights to your map. We must settle this now. How much will you take?"

She answered instantly. "One thousand dollars."

I chuckled. "I am just a Peace Corps Volunteer. I do not receive a salary, as you know. The price you ask is impossible."

She forgot all about her 30-minute limit. We went on for more than an hour. She opened her map on her computer and explained it. I appreciated the cleverness of it. I understood all the work she had put in.

I repeated, "This is how much money I can spend."

She took the $100 bill! "I will give you a receipt," she said, and wrote it out. In Russian, of course.

I know that $100 sounds trivial to you. Not so trivial in Ukraine. It was a month's pay for a lot of people.

On our next visit to Vladimir, I told him about my paying Olga for her map, and her agreeing to turn it over to me.
He looked at me with eyes wide. "Really?" he said.
"Yes. Really!"
A week later Iryna called me. She said, "Vladimir called. He said to go get your deposit back from Olga. He has contacted another artist.
"This artist will complete the map we need. It will be ready in four days. It will cost exactly the same. Give him the $100 you paid her."

**W**ow! Well, I got the money back. Olga was not happy And I gave it to Vladimir. His intentions were good, I think, but the realization dragged on.

The four days became eight weeks...ten weeks. I brought it up with Iryna time and again. Dutifully she would make a call to him. Then she would report back. "He says it is a difficult project. Takes time."

Or, "Vladimir says he always keeps his word. Be patient."

*Kyiv had some beautiful new buses (made In Ukraine!). What a sensation when our city got one. Just one. No money for more.*

One day she called me. Very excited. "Vladimir has e-mailed me the map. It is not finished. But we will get the idea."

We bent over her computer. His map looked good. But there were only two route lines, a red one and a blue one. For trolleybuses and buses. There should have been three. The third would be for *marshrutkas*.

Iryna told me, "The trolleybuses are separate because they are operated by the city. But the buses and *marshrutkas* are the same category. Both types are operated by entrepreneurs. That's why only two colors."

"No! The buses and *marshrutkas* have to be shown separately. For one thing, the buses charge 1.5 *hryvnia*. The *marshrutkas* 2 *hryvnia*. Users must be given the choice of which type to use."

Iryna tried to persuade Vladimir. On and on it went. Steadily the map improved. More detail. Then Iryna reported a new message. "Vladimir says they have done enough!"

Not so. The sad truth was a reader still could not tell clearly what trolleybus, buses, and *marshrutkas* should be selected to get most efficiently from one place to another in the city.

She had a new message from him for me. "Who is going to pay for all this work? You are about to go home to America!"

We visited him again. I said to him, "It is the city's responsibility to improve and maintain this map. The city licenses all the transit operators.

"Isn't it the city that pays for the street lights? That operates and maintains the traffic signals? That paints the crosswalks on the streets? That plows the snow in the winter so the public can ride the system and get to work?"

My voice was rising. "Giving the public the information that they need for the trolleybuses, and theF buses, and *marshrutkas* is also the city's responsibility. This is what modern cities everywhere do!"

He threw up his hands. "We can do only so much!"

Forty-eight hours before I departed for the U.S. I had one more meeting with Vladimir. As always, Iryna went with me to his office. Truly she was my sidekick. She was enthusiastic about all this.

*During this, I got to know Iryna and her husband Sasha well. After our project shaped up, we celebrated.*

**A**gain it was the usual: half serious communication, half jovial banter. We were four. Iryna and I sat at a table with Vladimir and a young woman, Anna. She was the graphic designer. This map was her work. It was our first meeting with her.

As usual, I spoke in English and they in Russian and Iryna did her best translating. Vladimir would speak for two minutes, sometimes passionately. And she would translate it all in a mere 15 words! Surely I was missing a lot. The process was barely adequate. In fact, frustrating.

Remember, the map would show three different types of transit: by bus, trolleybus, and *marshrutka*. Each carried a different fare. Furthermore, the trolleybus offered discounts for old and young and veterans and university students.

My key question, which I repeated several times, was, "How can someone use this map to get from Point A to Point B most effectively? Depending on his or her own priorities. How to use it best way to save money? Or to make the trip fastest? Or most conveniently? There are many possible answers. How can this be solved?"

Again I emphasized that the map's website should have two versions of the map, one in the official Ukrainian and the other in English.

And I insisted that the map also indicate important places—parks, universities, hospitals, bazaars, and so on.

Vladimir's bottom line to all this was: "This is a work in progress! This is the beginning map. It will improve steadily. We agree with everything you say, John. But this is the best we can do right now."

And he added: "I guarantee you! It will be up and running on the website next week! It will be a fact. No longer just a dream."

He laughed. "And we will put your name on it as the Peace Corps creator! You are a pioneer here! And Iryna's name as your partner."

I added, "It must also carry Anna's. She is its designer!"

"Of course. Absolutely!"

Then he said. "I am a Russian. I am proud of our Russian soul," and he placed his hand over his heart. He was very serious. "I promised you I would complete this map. And I have kept my promise, though it took longer than I thought. "

I nodded to Iryna. All this time she had been holding the money that I had given her to pay for this project. She counted it out and gave it to Vladimir. He took it and handed it to Anna.

She smiled and said, "Thank you!"

I thought that was very nice of him. We shook hands all around, then Iryna and I left.

On the street, she said, "Anna was Vladimir's daughter."

"Oh?"

"Yes. At one point she called him Papa."

"Why didn't he tell us that?"

"I have no idea."

I did. I suspected that he saw the opportunity to funnel my $100 to his daughter. I understood. As a father, I suppose I would have done the same thing for my daughter.

Iryna lived nearby. She invited me to her flat. Her husband Sasha had just arrived from work. He was a mechanical engineer but could earn more by selling electric tools in a stall he rented at the central bazaar. A smart guy. I liked him.

She served us tea and cake. He took out his guitar and played. Very nice. But Iryna had our map on her mind. She had discussed it with Sasha. They had studied it together. Now the three of us looked at it together at the kitchen table. Sasha spotted some mistakes: Bus stops that were wrongly located! He pointed to another mistake. And another. Iryna promised she would bring them to Vladimir's attention.

It was raining out. Sasha walked me to the nearest stop. Wanted to make sure I got on the right trolleybus. A good guy. We shook hands.

"Gold luck, John," he said. "You have been a good, good Volunteer!"

"Good luck to you also, Sasha. You are a good man. It is a pleasure to know you."

My trolleybus came. On my ride home, I realized that I had just had my very last dealing with the map! It had originated as a much grander idea. But it was alive. Very modestly alive. But as we kept saying, it was a start.

When I flew home to the U.S., I knew I would keep abreast of this project. Iryna sent me an update now and then. It was barely moving along. How discouraging. Then she sent me an e-mail that made me whoop with joy. "John, the map is on the website! And it will be used on other websites also!" She gave me a link to check, www.map.cn.ua.

I did. The map was supposed to be big. It was small. It was supposed to be in color—different colors would make it simple to distinguish the trolleybus, bus, and *marshrutka* routes. It was in black and white. I wondered, *What the heck is going on! I am on the eve of sending this book off to be published!*

Then I received another e-mail from Iryna. The map was now in color, and it could be enlarged with a click to enlarge it and see details! She said it would be available on four major websites serving the city! I believe her.

~ ~ ~

***Did you know*** ... that you will be disappointed serving in Peace Corps if you go in thinking that you will have privileges at our embassy and consulates (if these exist) in the country you go to.

Americans with jobs in such State Department posts overseas have very attractive privileges and perks, and it's easy to envy them and expect the same. No!

Most Volunteers never get to one of our embassies or consulates, and in some cases, even to see one.

# 20 / A Rotary Club here!

*I am a Rotarian. This city needs a Rotary Club. I'm eager to start one. Finally, a big surprise!*

This is a good time to mention another project of mine in Chernihiv. It was to start a Rotary Club. It was one that I never managed to pull off, sad to tell you. But an interesting angle did develop.

Back in Connecticut, I had been an active member of the Deep River Rotary Club. I had become a Rotarian after choosing Deep River as a fine town to retire in. But I had gotten the idea of joining decades earlier.

When I was a graduate student in journalism at Boston University, I served a short internship on the Amherst, Mass., Record-Journal. A small weekly a hundred miles away, but a good one. I was recommended by one of my professors. That was long before the concept of internships got developed for professional training outside medicine.

The editor gave me small assignments and I loved it all. One was to write a feature about a well-known hunter who had written his own cookbook on how to cook game that he brought home. Porcupine was one recipe, and wild duck was another.

One day my boss brought me to the Amherst Rotary Club. He was a member. I had only vague notions of the club. The club's weekly meeting was held at the Lord Jeffrey Inn, the finest restaurant in town.

I remember the white tablecloths, the men in their crisp business suits strolling in and hailing one another and sitting down to dine (that was long before Rotary went coed). The enthusiastic president at the lectern. The banter and good fellowship. The fine lunch. And then the guest speaker of the day, and then the question and answer period afterward. My job was to write a story for the paper.

I left the meeting greatly impressed. I thought, Maybe someday I will be able to be a Rotarian. Back at the office I wrote up the man's talk—I have no recollection of his topic.

But over the years I was always too busy and away too often to join. When I retired in Deep River, one July day I made myself a sandwich and rode my bike to the nearby Connecticut River. I planned to sit by the water and enjoy my little lunch.

There was a beautiful gazebo in a small park down there. I noticed 15 or so men and women in the gazebo. They were seated in a circle. An energetic bearded man was standing and speaking to them. I recognized him—Rev. Timothy Haut, minister of the First Congregational Church. My friend! He had been one of my best teachers when I was director of the Elderhostel program at the Episcopal Center in the next town.

He spotted me. "John!" he called. "Come over here and say hello!"

I walked my bike over. He introduced me to the group. I saw they were eating picnic lunches. "This is a meeting of our Rotary Club," Tim said. "We have our meetings here on nice Tuesdays in the summer. John, why don't you join Rotary?"

"What?"

"Yes. It's a great little club. You'll make new friends. Be able to pitch in on some good projects."

"Yes, Tim! I will join if you will have me!"

It happened that fast. All because of that indelibly beautiful memory of that Rotary meeting many decades earlier. And because of Tim.

I loved the club and was active all the time I was in town. I had the chance to develop a couple of projects and carry them to completion. Just before I left for Peace Corps, Tim presided at a farewell party for me. The club honored me by naming me a Harris Fellow.

When I left for Ukraine, I brought along some small Rotary pennants. I planned to present them to any Rotary Club I might be lucky enough to find in Ukraine. After all, Rotary is an international organization. It could happen.

At Peace Corps Headquarters in Kyiv one day, I was chatting with Juan Carlos Campos. He was the second in command. A smiling, outgoing, former Volunteer himself. He told me he was a Rotarian and attended the meetings of the International Rotary Club in Kyiv.

It was made up of Rotarians from other countries who were working in the capital. They conducted their meetings in English. I loved the possibility. But no way could I join—Kyiv was just too distant from Chernihiv. But I wondered, Why not a club in Chernihiv? The city is big enough.

Juan Carlos had given me a contact in the Kyiv club. I sent several e-mails. I asked whether there might be a club somewhere closer to Chernihiv. Never a reply. I mentioned this to Juan-Carlos when I saw him again some months later. "I had to drop out," he said. "Too busy."

Quite late in my second year in Peace Corps, I mentioned all this in an e-mail to a friend in Connecticut, John Donnelly. He was a fervent Rotarian who had moved up in the club regionally and was savvy.

John quickly replied. He put me in touch with a Rotarian in Finland. He said, "Jorma Lampen is a great Rotarian. He was once Rotary's

District Governor in the whole U.S.S.R. That was when Ukraine was part of that. Contact him. He will be able to help you, I am sure."

I followed through and before long I got an e-mail from him.

He wrote, "There are at present 40 Rotary clubs in Ukraine, one also in Chernihiv. This club meets on Thursdays at 13,00 o'clock in Clara Zetkin Street 5. President of this club is Boris Gabelev, and secretary is Natalya Makarenko." And he gave me their email addresses."

He encouraged me and gave me practical advice. An existing club in Chernihiv! I was flabbergasted.

Victoria, my librarian friend at the Korolenko, knew Natasha Makarenko. "A remarkable lady," Victoria told me. "An entrepreneur. Active in many things! I will approach her for you."

*Then I got lucky. I found a Ukrainian Rotarian, Natasha Makarenko! We hit it off.*

All this happened only about 12 weeks before I was scheduled to exit Peace Corps and return home. Victoria made phone calls.

Natasha was busy in her business of selling cosmetics and pharmaceuticals, as I understood it. Through Victoria she invited me to attend a meeting of the Chernihiv Club. I was delighted.

One late morning I went. Victoria and my Italian expat friend Renato accompanied me on the *marshrutka*. I had been selling them on the idea that Rotary might be wonderful for them. The meeting was being held in her office. It happened to be in her nice old home on a quiet street with shade trees. There were five men and women at a round table when we arrived.

"Welcome," Natasha said, smiling and drawing us in. "This is our modest Chernihiv Rotary Club." And she said it in French. Her English was sketchy but her French quite good. Victoria had told her that I spoke French.

We sat at the table with them. We met the other members, including Boris Gabelev, the president, a quiet but genial plumbing contractor. Natasha told us about the club. Victoria translated into Russian for me and Renato, then translated back to her friends for us.

"Yes, we are very small," Natasha said. "In fact, we are struggling. It is not easy to spread the word about Rotary in our city. The idea of an international service club is a strange concept here. But we are trying. And we have been working on a very big community project."

She told us that the club had developed a relationship with partner clubs in Florida somehow. These clubs had raised thousands of dollars for the Chernihiv Club. The club had used the money to completely rehabilitate a nearby orphanage for boys.

"An enormous job," she said. "The boys had pit toilets. Now they have real flush toilets! A new roof! Many improvements! All because of Boris here." She turned and smiled at her friend. "He made it all happen. He did some of the work himself."

It turned out to be a fine meeting. We were all friends when we said goodbye—they had to get back to their jobs. We all shook hands and talked about future meetings. That's the way Rotary is.

On the way out, I invited Natasha to attend my French Club at the library. "It is small but nice people. We speak French! It will be good practice for you. Please do come."

She did come two weeks later. "I have been so busy," she said. "And in a few days I am leaving for India. A vacation—a dream come true! I will be gone for a month."

We made the best of our meeting. She joined our conversation easily. Afterward, I talked her into attending our English Club which would be starting in 20 minutes. "Many more members in that club," I told her with a smile. "And you can practice your English!" And she accepted. That, too, turned out well.

She went off to India. When she returned, I had Victoria call her for me. "Please ask Natasha to come to our French Club Sunday."

She came again. Arrived with a big smile and photos of her travels around India. She charmed our little group. At one moment I gave her one of my Deep River Rotary Club pennants. I had forgotten to bring it to our first meeting. She understood this traditional ceremonial gesture.

"Thank you, John," she said. "I will place it in an honored space on our wall. You are our first American Rotarian to visit our club!" And then she grinned. "Now I have a surprise for you."

And she gave me a pennant of her Chernihiv Club! I was taken aback. Never expected it. "Thank you, Natasha. What a wonderful gesture! I will show it to my friends in Deep River and tell them all about you."

We parted with considerable affection. "I am so sorry that we did not meet 18 months ago," I told her. "A year ago. We could have worked together!"

"Well, now we are friends! Better late than never."

So true.

~ ~ ~

# 21 / I move to Family 3!

*For good reasons! My friends Iryna and Sasha help me to move. Ira takes it hard.*

Last night was my night to pay Iryna back for a huge favor. She helped me to move out of my old place into my new one. A huge job. I never would have managed it without her. How to show my thanks?

Iryna was the librarian at the Korolonko who kept helping me. She and her hubby Sasha and their two boys had just gone all out for me. I got an idea of something nice for them. It wasn't really a big deal. But they loved it. Will remember it a long time, I believe.

Here's what happened. Overnight I moved out of Ira's apartment and into Tatiana's on another side of the city. I had ruled out getting an apartment of my own. I worked out an arrangement with Tatiana for room and board similar to the one I had at Ira and Slava's.

Ira and Slava were fine people. Very nice to me. I liked them and they liked me. I had lived with them nearly six months. Never a bad word between us. Not even a bad look.

I had a pressing reason to move. Milady Annabelle was coming from California to visit me for a month. I wanted a nicer, more comfortable place for her. But also I was tired of trying to get a night's sleep on my narrow bed—just a cot! Also I had come to Ukraine hoping to absorb as much of the local culture as possible. Ira and Slava had been my second family. Living with a third family would give me a third window to look out on Ukrainian culture, so to speak.

Yes, I looked at apartments for myself. A lot of Volunteers rent furnished apartments. But I nixed that. I did not want to spend time shopping for groceries and cooking and doing all the housekeeping involved and paying the monthly bills for electricity and heat and water and gas. Plus I liked the security of living with a family. I had had a couple of scrapes and it was nice to come home to somebody.

Suddenly, good luck. Rebecca, a fellow Volunteer, heard I was out searching and recommended a woman named Tatiana—Tanya informally. Tanya had been landlady to Rebecca and her husband David here in Chernihiv during Training. They left Tanya's when they got assigned to another city.

Rebecca told me, "Tanya is a good person. She keeps her place sparkling clean. And she will serve you good food. She will really, really try to please you."

Sounded good. At the library I mentioned this to my friend, Iryna. You know about her now. She spoke excellent English. She could be the essential translator in my dealings with Tanya. Iryna didn't hesitate a second. "Of course I'll help you," she assured me.

I gave her Tanya's phone number and she made the call. She told me, "Tanya will come here tomorrow at 4 to meet you. She sounds very nice."

Tanya arrived at 4 on the dot. Attractive blonde, about 50, well made up and dressed, a single mother also, with two grown sons. Smiled a lot. Knew a smattering of English—a bit more than I did Russian—and answered my questions quickly and with a remarkable scarcity of words. Iryna sat at my side and translated everything, to me and to her. Wonderful.

I had a long list to take up with her.

First, I was increasingly vegetarian. Could she emphasize veggies and fruit instead of meat and fish? Ira had fried everything. I didn't like that. Could Tanya steam some veggies, maybe even roast some? Bake some?

Next, how warm was her flat in the winter? How often would she change my sheets? What buses and trams and *marshrutkas* went from her place to downtown? Did any go across town to *Coursi*, where I taught?

At what time did she go to work? At what time did she get home? My teaching schedule got me home around 9:30 every night. Could I have tea and a snack then? And on to more questions.

**H**er answers were quick and favorable. Except for my commute to school. That would require two rides each way. Now I did just one ride. And that would triple my riding time. And would be more difficult in the ice and snow of January and February, I was sure.

Next, how much would I pay? At Ira and Slava's I was paying 1,000 *hryvnia* a month. That was about $200. Peace Corps gave us about $280 a month, and that was for everything, including transportation to work and clothes and entertainment and even our vacation spending. But Ira kept moaning about inflation, inflation, inflation—prices going up, up, up—so I knew a raise was imminent. That was another reason that made me think of moving.

Tanya told me she would charge 1,000—exactly the same amount. And would not raise it unless inflation became sky-high. That made me very happy.

Tanya made a good impression on me. But I wished she had expanded her answers a bit. Every answer was just a word or two. But she smiled a lot and I liked that. I felt encouraged. We made an appointment to visit her apartment—"we" meaning Iryna and myself. I was so lucky to have Iryna helping me. She was such a generous person.

The next day after Iryna got through at the library, the two of us took Trolleybus 5 to Tanya's place. It took less than 10 minutes. That was a plus. She lived in a neighborhood that was all new to me. But middle-class and pleasant.

On the way, I asked Iryna what Tanya did for a living. "She works at the macaroni factory. Maybe she operates a machine. I will find out."

The macaroni factory? Interesting. I couldn't wait to find out all about it. I had never visited one.

"This is our stop," Iryna said. We walked about 10 minutes and entered Tanya's development of Soviet blocks—the big, boxy buildings you are now familiar with.

This development had eight or ten big blocks. We walked by a nice children's playground. Kids were playing in a sand pile. The playground was lined with used truck tires. They were propped straight up in the sand. Somebody had painted each one red or yellow or blue or green. Had done a good job.

It was a clever way of putting old tires to a new use. I had seen the same thing in many developments. The kids were having a grand time crawling through them and hopping over them.

We strode on. I noticed litter and empty beer bottles along the walk. But that was common.

Old men were playing chess on a table under a shade tree. Three or four others were looking on. Two dogs were chasing one another. Four old ladies were chatting on a bench. A toddler was trying to chase a cat.

**W**e reached Tanya's block. It was older than the one I was living in but in better condition. In the front was a nice garden of flowers and trees and shrubs.

It was a five-floor block. This meant there would be no elevator. Buildings with more than five floors must have an elevator. At Ira's, I was living on the fifth floor of a nine-floor block, which meant that I could ride up and down. Here Tanya lived on the third. We walked up. It will be good for me, I thought. I can rationalize just about anything.

Iryna rang the bell and we could hear Tanya coming. Then we heard a lock unlock. Then a second lock! Then a third lock! Three locks! Yes, security was a big concern in Ukraine. I am not sure why. Everything always seemed peaceful.

Tanya waved us in. First impression: a very small apartment. Tiny kitchen—like the galley of the sailboat I went sailing on in the Bahamas 20 years ago. Second impression: very neat and clean and nice. But would it be kept this way after I moved in?

The living room was strikingly attractive. Gleaming walnut bookcases along one wall. In fact, two walls. Hundreds of books, all perfectly arranged. A handsome divan with big matching chairs. A TV set, of course. A painting or two, vases and bowls and baskets, family pictures, souvenirs of vacation trips. A definite step up from my present place.

Cleverly tucked in one corner—a kind of alcove—was a desk with a full computer set-up. In fact, it looked more like a home office.

The room looked out on a balcony. Small, yes, but even so, a balcony, like Ira's. And used to store things and dry clothes, like Ira's.

I took a second look at the kitchen. Yes, compact. Smaller than Ira's. Lined up along one wall were a tiny clothes washing machine, a tiny four-burner gas stove, a tiny counter, and a tiny sink. Cupboards above. On the opposite wall were a small fridge with top freezer, and a tiny dining table with not chairs, but small stools, and just two. No room for chairs. Everything was a tight squeeze.

A big window looked out on a lawn. No, not mowed. I hadn't seen a lawnmower since I arrived in Ukraine. They just let the grass grow. That's what Nature intends, or so Ukrainians think. I had gotten used to it.

The toilet room was tiny, of course. Just room for the toilet, but at least you could turn in this one—impossible at Ira's.

The bathroom was next door. Tiny, too. The claw-foot tub and the sink were arranged in a right angle. One faucet: swing it over the tub for water there, then swing it over the sink for water there. I tried the faucet. Yes, cold water, and yes, hot water. It was important to be sure. And yes, there was a shower hose. Everything neat and clean.

Tanya had the usual dozen lipsticks and a score of bottles of creams and lotions and shampoos tucked here and there. So many that I wondered where I'd find room for my toothbrush and razor.

Next, the one bedroom. My room! Small, yes, but nice. Not a foot of lost space. The wallpaper was pleasant and fresh-looking. At the far end, two large windows, ceiling-high. Lacy curtains without a wrinkle. Green carpeting. No spots on it. A double bed! Yes! No more narrow cot!

On closer look, I saw that it was a divan opened up. The inevitable divan! But she had a smaller divan also. That was a plus. And a desk with drawers! A long bank of bookcases along one wall! All very satisfactory. I was impressed.

**I** took a good look at the bed. Stretched out on it! Tanya and Iryna smiled when I plopped down. I had to test it! I would spend a third of every day on this bed. Firm. I like a firm mattress. I could definitely feel the three sections that made up the mattress. But not bad. I could get used to it.

Tanya and Iryna were watching me, of course. Judging my reaction to all this, I was sure. I made it a point to remain deadpan.

When I got up, I winked to Iryna. She smiled and nodded. I knew she agreed with me. This was a nice place.

Then I spotted something else that pleased me: there was enough room along one wall for the computer table that I had bought for my room at Ira's. That table was all-important to me. And my computer would be right across from the smaller divan. It would be possible to sit there and watch a DVD on my computer!

Oh, a built-in closet also. Some bedrooms in some blocks did not have built-in closets. This one was small, but I could manage.

It was obvious Tanya was an excellent housekeeper. Assuming, of course, that she hadn't worked day and night cleaning and arranging everything to impress me. It was obvious also that she liked nice things. She was a lot like milady Annabelle.

Back in the living room, I glanced again at the hundreds of books on the shelves. The home office. The many travel souvenirs. This Tanya at the macaroni factory did more than operate a machine. I was sure of that.

I inquired about her children. Two sons, the older one age 26, here in the city with wife and child in their own place, and a younger son at a university in Kyiv. "University in Kyiv" was code for "expensive school." No mention of a husband, or a man in her life.

I had one question more. At what time did Tanya leave for work in the morning? She said 8 a.m. That would work out fine. It meant that five days a week we'd see one another probably only late in the evening, after I got through my evening class at *Coursi*. Excellent!

As I've explained, back at Ira's my room was really a tiny apartment within her apartment. I kept to my room. Kept the door closed. Saw her and Slava only at meals and at noon I usually ate alone because they were out. It was a friendly relationship, yes, but basically a business relationship. This is the way I would want it here. Another arm's-length relationship. I liked my privacy and enjoyed my own company.

There would be one big difference. In my present place, Slava was the go-between me and his mom. He would always speak to me in English (he was eager to learn English) and I would always speak to him in English. He would translate to her and then from her to me. No go-between here! But this would be better for me. I would have to get better at Russian!

When could I move in? Suddenly this became a problem—in three days Tanya was going to Russia on vacation for 10 days! She said I would have to move in before she departed!
But I had another week coming to me at Ira's and I did not want to lose it. Besides, I could use that final week to get ready. Impossible, Tanya said. We went back and forth and finally I gave in. I would arrive with all my stuff on the morning of the day that she'd take the train to St. Petersburg at 4 p.m. Meaning I'd move here on the day after tomorrow! Wow!
I took out my money and gave her a deposit of 250 *hryvnia*. I'd give her the other 750 then. And I assured her I would always pay in advance. She wouldn't have to nag me for the rent.
She smiled. And she made a little joke, which I did not understand but Iryna did and chuckled. She did not explain. Tanya was happy. I was happy. This seemed a win-win situation for the two of us.
I glanced at Iryna. She was happy, too. I moved closer and gave her a hug. Felt I had to. Such a wonderful helper. This would have been impossible without her.
We said goodbye to Tanya and rode the trolleybus back downtown. On the way I became aware of something: Tanya would be sleeping on the divan in her living room, just like Ira! Gosh! I mentioned this to Iryna. She just nodded. She had realized this. It was the usual thing in Ukraine.
Then she said, "Tanya told me what her work is at the macaroni factory. She is a manager. Has to buy and keep records of many things." So my suspicion had been correct. Not a machine operator.
We got off by the library. She was late in getting home to her husband Sasha and two sons. I took her hand and said to her, "You were terrific! I must do something nice for you."
"No, no, John. It was a pleasure. Come to the library tomorrow and we'll talk about what we must do next." She smiled and strode off.
Now I had to go home and tell Iryna and Slava. This would not be easy. I'm sure they were expecting me to be their tenant until I completed my service in another 17 months at 1,000 *hryvnia* per month! Yes, this definitely would not be good news for them. I decided to wait as long as possible. Announcing it early would make our remaining time together only difficult and embarrassing.
I started planning right away. I had to notify Peace Corps, then Dean Olena at my school, then other people. I began figuring how to pack. Astonishing all the stuff I had. So ironic. I had been telling myself I

had to keep things simple. After all, I wasn't going to spend the rest of my life here! But I kept accumulating things!

The next morning, at the end of breakfast, I broke the news to Slava.
"What?" he said. He was startled. "I didn't understand all."
I spoke more slowly. I explained about Annabelle coming, but he knew about this. I told him about the big bed in the new place and my small bed here. Then I said, "I will be moving out tomorrow morning very early!"
His eyes widened but he said not a word. He turned to face his mom. She had noticed something was up. Had stopped peeling her potatoes and was looking at him. He spoke. She stiffened. She asked him a couple of questions.
He said to me, "Is this just for the time that Annabelle will be here?"
"No. I will stay in the new place. Please understand that I like you and your mother very much. In one way this will be good for you. Your mom will be able to have my whole room all for herself."
I did not mention any complaints. They were few and minor. "You and your mother are very good people. I have been lucky to live here with you."
"I see," he said simply. He explained to his mother. Not another word was said. She went back to her potatoes. He made himself another toast. In my toaster, by the way. Neither one of them had ever eaten a toast until I brought in the toaster and set it up—actually it was a gift from Dean Olena. I would be taking it with me.
Quickly I put my dirty dishes in the sink and rinsed them, as I always did, said thank you in Russian, as I always did, and returned to my room, as I always did.
First, I called Iryna at home. It was too early for the library. Quickly she said, "I will help you move. Sasha will also. He has a friend with a van. He will take all your things for you."
"Thank you, thank you! I will go see you at the library this afternoon."
Then I got to work. Began packing earnestly. I worked till I left for the library at 2. I was tired. But excited. It seemed this would work out very well.
There Iryna had a surprise for me. She handed me a *babushka* bag filled with neatly folded *babushka* bags—"grandma" bags. A dozen of them! All grandmas used these bags, often loaded with stuff. They were big, squarish things made of lightweight but strong plastic fabric. They folded compactly. Everybody used such bags, not only grandmas. I had

two or three. We should have them in the United States! I planned to take mine home with me.

"Use them all," she said. "Better to carry many small bags than a few big, heavy ones. We'll be there to help you tomorrow morning at 7:30. Sasha opens his shop at 8. Tomorrow his assistant will open up."

Sasha was a university-trained mechanical engineer. He worked as an engineer for a while, then felt he wanted his own business. He opened a stall in the *rinok*—the big outdoor bazaar. He sold electric tools. Not easy because he stood and worked outdoors all year round. It was a tiny business but he seemed to be doing all right.

Thanking Iryna, I returned home and worked till midnight getting ready. Then I set the alarm on my cell phone for 5 a.m. I had never owned a cell phone but Peace Corps insisted that we have one. This was only the second or third time that I used its alarm. Would it go off? At the right time? I slept fitfully. It did. I hopped up and got to it.

Iryna and Sasha arrived 15 minutes early, at 7:15. Iryna told me, "His friend Andrei will arrive with his truck at 8:15."

They had brought their two sons with them! Nikita, 14, and Damien, 12. Two strong boys. The four had taken the trolleybus here. Like most folks, they didn't own a car. I wondered at what time they had gotten up to make it all the way here this early!

But already I had all my possessions moved from my room, I had carried them out of the apartment and piled them in the hall by the elevator. I had filled all Iryna's babushka bags plus many cartons and bags of my own. And my two huge suitcases, of course.

Peace Corps also issued us a chemical fire extinguisher and a combination smoke and gas detector. We were obliged to return these at the end of our service. I had already carried these smaller things to the elevator. And yes, my precious toaster!

Everything, that is, except my computer table and my big electric heater, this issued by Peace Corps to all Volunteers. These were still in my room.

In all these trips back and forth, I had to walk by the living room. Ira was still asleep in there. I walked on my tip toes but she must have noticed. She emerged only when she heard my friends arrive. That's when Slava emerged also. I made introductions all around and I was pleased that everything was pleasant.

Iryna and Sasha and their sons went right to work, packed the tiny elevator time and again, and got everything downstairs and out the front door. The truck arrived on time. Sasha introduced me to Andrei. Andrei helped us to put everything aboard. Sasha kept telling me to take it easy. Not to work so hard. But I was eager and felt up to it.

I had my camera handy. At the end, I got everybody into a picture, meaning even Iryna and Slava. I clowned a little. I wanted them to smile. Everybody did smile. I clicked the camera.
I looked at Ira. She was dabbing her eyes. The language barrier had made it nearly impossible for us to talk but we had gotten along with never a spat and I knew she liked me and she knew I liked her. She gave a little wave and tried to smile.
I said to her, "Is it all right if I come back for a Sunday dinner?"
"*Da! Da!*" Ira said, brightening. "Yes! Yes!" Slava smiled, too.
"I will come with Annabelle!" I said. Then I looked at Slava. "You, Slava! I have one thing to say to you. Do not become an Oriflame salesman. Become a physicist. Or a computer scientist. The money will take care of itself. You can do it!"
He nodded politely.

Now I double-checked that I was not forgetting anything. And in 20 minutes we were at Tanya's. She wasn't home! Where was she? What was wrong? Then she arrived, smiling, a heavy babushka bag in hand. She looked at her watch. It was 8:30. She had said she would meet us at 8:30!
She had been to the market. She had bananas and tomatoes and cheese. "These are for you while I am in St. Petersburg," she said. "And I have made you a pot of borsch. And here is a jar of *smetana* to go with it." *Smetana* is the Russians' all-important sour cream.
Now everything on the truck had to be carried up to her floor. No elevator, remember. Well, we got it all up. I had suggested putting everything out on the balcony. Then I could bring things in and sort them out and put them away. But my eager helpers piled everything in my room helter-skelter. What a mess.
I took out my wallet to pay Andrei. "No," Sasha said. "I will pay him later." Andrei nodded and seemed agreeable. I shook his hand and said, "*Spaciba bolshoi,* Andrei!" "Thank you very much." He drove off.
A few minutes later Iryna and Sasha and Nikita and Darien said goodbye. I gushed with thanks. They trudged off to the trolleybus stop. No room in Andrei's truck for them. What a big favor they had done me!
The next day at the library Iryna told me Andrei was asking for 30 *hryvnia*. "That's because he was on his way to his own work so there was not a big gasoline expense." Gas here was close to $5 a gallon.
I put 300 *hryvnia* into her hand.
"No, no, John! I said 30. Not 300!"
"Yes, I know. But I want you to keep the change!"
That 300 amounted to about $60. It sounds like not much, but Sasha had told me that on the previous day his assistant had earned 17

*hryvnia*—he got paid a straight 10 percent commission. "But I gave him an extra three." In other words, about $4 in all.

Iryna was very firm. She said, "No, no, John. We did this because you are our friend. Not for money." She pushed the money back. "You yourself are a Volunteer!"

"All right. But you must let me do one thing. Tomorrow night, let's all of us go eat at McDonald's. All five of us."

Her eyes sparkled. "Very, very nice! That will be fun."

I told you about the McDonald's earlier. The only one in the city. It was right on one of the most important corners. It was a very big, very nice McDonald's even by American standards. For average Ukrainians McDonald's food was expensive. You went to McDonald's out of curiosity or for a big date.

She had been there only once. "I bought a hamburger. It was good."

"It is time for you to try a cheeseburger!" I said, smiling. She smiled, too.

We met there the next evening right at 6 p.m. I had no classes. A beautiful evening, warm and clear. I said, "Please let me do the ordering! You just stand by and watch."

I bought four sandwiches. A Big Mac. A McChicken. A McFish. And a McSomethingelse—it was a new sandwich; I couldn't make out what kind. I made up that word for laughs. And four orders of fries. And two big drinks and two teas, which were the drinks they wanted. And for myself, just a basic cheeseburger and a tea. I was watching my weight.

We went outside to the patio to eat. Nikita and Damien carried out the two loaded trays. We sat at a table under one of the big bright parasols. Very pleasant. The breeze was wonderful. We could see the little kids playing on the McPlayground.

I knew that my friends were wondering who was going to get what sandwich. I had a surprise. I took out my pocket knife. They watched me. What was I up to? I unwrapped one sandwich—it was the McFish—and cut it into quarters, telling each to take one piece.

I made up a little story. "In America, whoever does the cutting like this must wait and take the final piece for himself."

They nodded knowingly and smiled.

I did this with the other three sandwiches. By the time I finished quartering the fourth one, they had eaten their first piece.

"Very good," Sasha said. Iryna said, "Yes, very tasty!" The two boys were already on their second pieces.

I was pleased. "This way you will get to taste four of McDonald's most famous sandwiches. The same ones sold at 13,000 McDonald's in the United States."

Maybe I had the number wrong. Maybe it's 18,000.

I told them a couple of McDonald stories. How in Hong Kong at one intersection I had spotted a McDonald's nearby on all four streets! And how in Mexico some families insist their son or daughter work at a McDonald's for a summer! If the kids are lucky enough to be accepted—the application process is tough. Only the top kids in school get in. Why do they insist on a job at McDonald's?

I explained to my friends. "They will see how America's most successful fast-food company does everything. Insists on high standards. On quality control. How everybody must become part of a crew—wear a uniform!—and jump and help another crew member who needs help. If a sandwich sits under a hot lamp for more than 10 minutes (I think it's 10), throw it away! How the toilets must get checked every 90 minutes.

"How the computer keeps track of everything, not only the routine figures about daily—even hourly—sales and supplies on hand and supplies needed, such as buns and frozen hamburgers and ketchup and toilet paper, but how successful—or what a flop—the new McSomethingelse is!

"It's a valuable education for any smart, eager young person, regardless of what he goes on to do in life."

I explained it all in the simplest words I could. Iryna and Sasha were all ears. Nikita and Damien, too.

I enjoyed my cheeseburger. That was all I needed. I did snitch a few fries from them.

Afterward I handed Nikita money to go back with Damien to the counter for five *rishoks*—McDonald's ice cream cones. They went off and I asked Iryna what the word *rishok* means.

"One of those twisty things on some big, big animals we read about! You know, above their eyes!" Then the right word came to her. "A unicorn!"

*Rishok*! Unicorn! The little cone was well named.

Soon the boys were back with the cones and my change.

"I like this!" Nikita exclaimed as he licked. Damien agreed. They were their first *rishoks*. Iryna said, "This is the best, best ice cream in all Chernihiv!"

I took snapshots of them. They were delighted to pose. I could see all of them were having a grand time. And I could see how Iryna and Sasha were enjoying their boys. But then she whispered a disturbing story to me.

"One night last week Nikita had a bike accident and bruised his cheek and lacerated an arm. He had hit a pothole in the dark and tumbled. Eventually he went home and his Mom took care of his wounds. But her sister had seen the accident and told her, "Nikita was drunk! The 14-year-old had been drinking beer!"

It was his first experience with too much beer. He got a stern talking-to! Iryna leaned close and said, "It is so hard to raise children!"

"Yes, it is." I had noticed the bandage on Nikita's arm and could see the red on his cheek. But he looked fine now. I got up and took a picture of all four. Then Sasha insisted on a picture with me and them, and Nikita took that one. We spent another half hour together. Then time to split up.

I had paid McDonald's 122 *hryvnia*. Roughly $25. Sasha had noticed and said, "John, you are spending so much money. Too, too much!"

I knew that 122 *hryvnia* was more than he made in a day. Maybe more than both he and Iryna made. This was not the good old U.S.A.

I was sorry Iryna had refused my 300 *hryvnia*. Even that would have been a bargain for me, although a fair chunk of my monthly take-home. But how can you put a price on anything done out of friendship?

I watched them stride off. They were chatting. They were happy.

I was sure that my McDonald's "sampler" would be remembered a long time.

I planned to give her my snapshots at the library tomorrow.

I had loved my first night in my big new bed. I felt I was off to a good new start.

~ ~ ~

**Did you know** ... that quickly you will pick up Peace Corps lingo? For the first three months you will be not a Volunteer but a Trainee. Then you will become a PCV—a Peace Corps Volunteer.

When you return home, you will be an RPCV—a returned PCV. And you'll get to know various other expressions also. It will make you feel like an insider!

# 22 / My computer life!

*I needed a computer here from Day 1!*
*Finally I get set up. How good it is.*

From the minute I thought of entering Peace Corps, I hoped and hoped that a computer would be available in whatever corner of the world I got sent to. One connected to the Internet. How could I survive otherwise?

I was delighted when I found out I could take mine with me. But an Internet connection? Not at all sure. But so vital to me.

I had to keep in contact with my family and friends. I planned to send newspaper articles back. And I planned to write a book about my experiences. Of course, many Volunteers found a way to get such things done in pre-computer days. They used postage stamps. Where there's a will, there's a way! Right? But I had become spoiled by my computer. And time was of the essence.

Sure. I had managed all this in my own pre-computer days. I remember 50 years ago traveling around the U.S.A. and writing newspaper stories on my tiny Olivetti Lettera 32 portable typewriter (very basic but wonderful). And mailing them home, along with a roll of exposed film for the darkroom techs to develop.

But I was now a computer enthusiast. I depended on the computer every day. Realized that many Peace Corps countries still had not become digital. Or barely. How unlucky to get sent to one of them! Still I would go.

Truth is, the Internet had become all-important to me. Strange considering how late in life I discovered it. I first began using it about 20 years ago. Very unsurely and timidly. That's when my newspaper suggested that its life, and mine, would become easier if I began e-mailing my work to it rather than driving it over.

I took to this fabulous technology because of practical reasons. It saved me time. It saved me trips. It saved me paper. It saved me stamps. And it was instantaneous!

Then I discovered the great big new wide world out there that I could access online. The Internet! Unbelievable. I became hooked.

It was then that I got the idea of celebrating my 75th birthday with a trip around the world. Immediately I decided that I would write reports about it as I traipsed from country to country. I realized that the only way

I could do this practically was through e-mail. If I used slow-mail, I'd get home long before some of my articles arrived!

I completed that huge trip. Along the way I used e-mail shops nearly every day. Not easy but I coped. I sent back enough reports to fill a book. In fact, they led to a book, "Around the World at 75. Alone, Dammit!"

You will understand better if I hark way, way back to Summer, 1960. My wife Pauline and I took a six-week camping trip around the country. Yes, literally around the country, in a long ellipse all the way from Massachusetts to Oregon and then down through California and back. With my home-made tent-trailer in tow.

A tent-trailer was a remarkable innovation at the time, but in fact it's what made our trip possible. And with our two little tots, Arthur and Monique, playing and napping on a foam-covered platform I had built over the back seat of our new Falcon station wagon.

I mention this because I had the same plan way back then as I did circling the globe—to write articles about our adventure as we went along. The technology was different then. I had a string of interviews arranged all along our trip—more than 11,000 miles. I would find our way to the movie actor or airport manager or young married couple or other interviewees I had lined up—all of whom at my newspaper's insistence necessarily had to have a Massachusetts connection.

Pauline would watch our kids in the car while I went and did my interview. I'd also snap photos. That night, at our campground wherever, I would take out my little Olivetti typewriter and write my feature story. I would include my roll of Kodak Tri-X film and mail everything back to my paper. I did that numerous times.

Contrast that with my experience using the Internet during my solo 36,750-mile trip around the globe over nearly five months in 2003. I planned it as my 75$^{th}$ birthday present to myself.

At a hostel in Nairobi, Kenya, I met a remarkable young Chinese digital engineer named Wu Bin. He was on vacation alone. We became friends. Once I finished my book, he took it upon himself to have it translated into Chinese (Mandarin) and published in China. He invited me to Shanghai for its publication. Very exciting.

Annabelle couldn't go with me, so I took my dear sister Lucie along. Wonderful events in Shanghai. The two of us traveled on to other Asian destinations. She had to return home for a big engagement but I went on.

All that, too, was an adventure…and led to many more e-mail reports for a newspaper back home. It also led to my book, "Around Asia in 80 Days. Oops, 83 Days!" All this was created on computers rented by the hour here and there at Internet shops.

With that finished, back home I continued writing newspaper articles and a frequent column.

As I've told you, I had a number of reasons to volunteer in Peace Corps. Writing...and reporting...are driving forces in my life. Peace Corps is a dramatic subject and is fascinating to many, whether they are thinking of joining or just want to satisfy their curiosity about it. Anybody who knows me would expect to read a lot of words about it.

So, I would need a computer wherever I got assigned. I was familiar with laptops. I had been tempted to buy one for my global trip. But I got good advice: don't! Lugging a laptop is a bad idea. A laptop weighs a lot and is awkward. It's possible to lose it. It can break down. It is too often irresistible to thieves. It requires a telephone connection—unavailable in many places. Plus a big bagful of electrical adapters. It is useless much of the time. It can lead to airline overcharges.

Much of this still applied in going to a Peace Corps country, I believed. I did not buy a laptop. I took along the computer I already had. I had resumed my normal life with Annabelle—some months in California, some months in Connecticut. That's when I read ecstatic reviews about Apple's brand-new Mac Mini. I placed an order sight unseen. It turned out to be ideal.

It was a tiny, full-featured, powerful processor. Just the size of a cigar box if you remember what that is. It was a Mac, which meant superb quality. And it came loaded with fabulous programs. But I was used to Microsoft Word, which is a PC program, not an Apple one. But through my generous friend, Ivan Otterness, I acquired Microsoft Word for Mac. How wonderful!

To go with the Mac Mini I needed a monitor, a keyboard, and a mouse, of course. No problem. I picked up a flat-screen monitor. My son Mark gave me a fine Mac keyboard. I bought a Logitech "golfball" mouse. Well, that's what I call it. The mouse stays put—you don't have to nudge it all over the place. It has a golfball in a tight-fitting cup on top. With my index finger I roll the ball in its cup, this way and that. I love it.

But this was not an outfit that I could take on trips. Too cumbersome. On trips I'd still use Internet shops. But I'd pack my Mac Mini and components and use them when I got to Annabelle's, then at home.

This was the outfit I decided to take to Ukraine for 27 months. I placed everything in a suitcase and padded every item with underwear and pajamas and sweaters. All set! But in Ukraine I opened my suitcase tin Ukraine to find my monitor in two pieces. The screen had parted from the base! They were connected by an umbilical cord of frail wires. Some airline baggage attendant had given my suitcase a hard toss! Everything else was fine. Still, that put me out of business for more than three months. Training was too hectic for me to even think about getting the monitor repaired...if at all possible.

In Chernihiv for Training, I located an Internet shop within walking distance. I'd stroll over for an hour after Russian classes, stand in line, and rent a computer by the minute.

It was operated by the Ukrainian Postal Service. It had about 40 computers, quite good. The service was cheap—I could pound away for 90 minutes for less than a dollar.

But sometimes I'd have to wait in line 5 minutes, 10 minutes, 15 minutes for a computer. Irritating! The keyboards were lined up elbow to elbow. No room for a pad or notes.

But some machines were set up solo in tiny cubicles along a wall. More space! I preferred these. I wondered why the two different set-ups. One out in the open, another in the tiny cubicles. A few times I glanced at a monitor n one or another of these as I walked by. Always occupied by a man, it seemed. One glance explained it all. Pornography! It seems to have universal appeal.

One of my regular after-school stops was the Dva Gucia Restaurant nearby. We called it the Two Goose. That's what the name means. Upscale and pleasantly relaxing. It featured a food buffet. Enormously important for me—no need to struggle with a Ukrainian menu. Just point to this dish or that one.

But sometimes all we'd do is order a cup of tea or coffee and hang out with our friends. Plus it had Wi-Fi. Trainees would come in with their laptops, buy just a beverage, and spend two hours online or word-processing. How fabulous.

I thought that maybe I should have a laptop. Then my good sense prevailed. My friends had to lug their laptops back and forth every day, plus their satchel of books or backpack. Always the big risk of theft. Often one of my friends in the café would be at the keyboard—and a friend would come and sit at the same table. All work would stop. Using the Internet shop a block away made more sense to me.

**I** must tell you that throughout my service I also did a lot of writing the old-fashioned way. By using a pen or pencil! Shortly after arriving, I began writing a daily journal. Essential! My book would need facts! I could not trust my memory. Brute memory plays bad tricks. I decided to put everything down on paper every day.

I had a fresh 200-page notebook, full size. I numbered all the pages in advance. Every evening I'd scribble and scribble. Record the day's significant events. The new persons I met. What had happened, good and bad. Amusing things. Bad moments. My impressions. My emotions—these were very important. A word about the weather—in fact, many words at times...rain, snow, ice. By the time I flew home, I was well into my fifth notebook. Nearly 1,000 crammed pages! I was astonished. Sometimes this nightly writing was difficult. I would be exhausted. I'd force myself. One evening at 6, I took a short nap—and woke up at 5 a.m.! I hadn't written my entry! I sat right down and wrote it. That was the only time I did not write my journal entry the same day. I would keep up my journal even when I traveled. My scribblings became so valuable when I wrote reports home, and for "Peace Corps Journals (more about this later), and for this book.

A lucky day it was, as you know now, when I discovered the Korolenko Biblioteka—its Foreign Language Department—and its two Internet-connected computers. The Korolenko became a stop for me every day except Tuesday. It was closed on Tuesdays. But the Internet might work one day, might be off the next. Unexplainable.

And only two computers. I might be working happily for an hour and then a couple of people would stroll in and want to use one. I'd have to give it up. Not a happy moment.

What then? If I still had a lot to do, I'd walk to Poshta—that's the word for the Post Office—and take the chance of having to stand and wait for a computer. And that's how I kept in touch with everybody and sent off a lot of newspaper reports.

So I felt I was in Heaven when I started at *Coursi*, the language school. Dean Olena was wonderfully gracious. "Use our computers, John. Mine when it's free. Or Lina's." And she meant it. I would use hers when she was out. Lina had two in her office next door, hers and Iryna's. She was the bookkeeper. She went home at 4, and I would time it to arrive at 4:05. How good it was. At other times, Lina would let me use her computer if she could. She was so generous.

At 6, I'd have to do what I was there to do, which was to teach. That required preparation, but I could do that at home. But there were difficult moments. All the computer menus were in Russian. Not easy. But for word-processing, I memorized the Russian words for Cut, Copy, Format, Insert, and so on. But at times I'd have to call on Lina for help. True at the Korolenko also. The three gals on staff were always wonderful.

*Coursi* was closed on Saturdays. But Olena had given me free access. A clerk in the lobby would unlock her door for me, or Lina's. Sometimes I'd spend all Saturday afternoon working up there alone, undisturbed. I really had it made.

It's when I moved in with my second family—Iryna and her son Slava, if you remember—that my computer life became much better. My new bedroom was so much bigger than at Natasha's. Immediately I thought of making my Mac Mini operational.

No problem with that. The problem was my broken flat-screen monitor. In two pieces! Chernihiv was a big, modern city. I tried some of the electronic stores. Many monitors for sale. It would be easy to buy one. But I had my own. Could it be repaired?

Then Luda, my first Russian tutor, and very soon my good friend, told me about a computer *remont*...repair shop. In fact, she walked me over to it on her lunch hour. I carried along my broken monitor in a big babushka bag.

Luda led me inside. Several technicians were at work on computers. The place was a mess of disassembled machines and tools and parts. The kind of place I love. I was impressed. And prepared for bad news.

Luda did all the explaining, of course. Two technicians looked over my hapless monitor, turning over this part, then that one, and studying the wires. Then they explained something to her.

*The sign says Ukraine Telephone. It was a big Internet shop. I came nearly every day. On the way out, I'd buy an apple at that stand.*

"It's a small problem," she said. "You can wait while they do the work." She excused herself...had to get back to work. In an hour, I was handed my repaired monitor The screen was solidly attached to its base. They explained the two had been designed to be taken apart for easier packing! The charge was only 18 Hryvnia. About $3.50. Imagine my smile.

I quickly installed everything in my room at Iryna's. I told you how I had converted a folding table into a desk. And how I went out and bought a table specifically for my computer set-up.

These were marvelous improvements. Now I could do my entire computer word-processing here in my room at home. Wonderful beyond words.

Right away I began actual work on my new book. Life was good. Doing this work at odd moments was a refresher from the tedium of studying and my hours of teaching, which were usually enjoyable. But still.

But the Internet was out of reach at home. Not possible. I still depended on *Coursi* and Poshta to go online.

Then I moved in with my third family—Tanya's. You haven't read about that phase of my life yet, but it's coming up. I got all set up in my room in her flat. Even brought along the computer table I had bought for Iryna's. Immediately I saw that Tanya had a computer set-up—and used it every evening...and went online! At times she let me use it. But why couldn't I get mine connected?

One weekend her student son Andrei came home from his university in Kyiv. Andrei spoke good English and was computer savvy.

He told me, "Yes, John, you can connect here in your room. No problem. I will talk to Mama. She will arrange it."

Tanya called the company and in a week a technician showed up. Within 30 minutes he had run wires and connected them to my Mac Mini. Then he sat at it to get it connected. He tried for 30 minutes. For an hour. He tried this and that. Nothing worked. He called his office and spoke to somebody. He sat down and tried again.

"Big problem," he said. "No understand." He had to give up but said he would return. It was a week before he showed up. He smiled. "I think I can fix." He tried. And tried. Finally he threw up his hands. He tapped the computer. "This is Mac," he said. "I think this is problem." And he said goodbye.

You can understand my huge disappointment. I continued to write my reports on my Mac Mini. But to e-mail one, I would download my report onto my flash card, go to *Coursi*, load it onto a computer there, and then e-mail it out. It worked. But what a nuisance.

That's when I met Maxim, about 30. A graduate in computer science from the Technological University. He was the IT specialist at *Coursi*. *Coursi* was a tenant in the building, and he did all the computer trouble-shooting for everybody in the building.

He had studied English at the university. It was rusty. But he enjoyed having me stop by because in talking with me, he refreshed his language. I persuaded him to come look at my Mac Mini and new set-up. We took a marshrutka together late one evening to my flat.

He looked at the machine, checked all the cables and connections, tried this and that, found some numbers somewhere in the recesses of the machine and jotted them down. "I go online and do research maybe tomorrow. Or when I have time. I try to help you."

I got him to return a week later. He opened a notepad and from it typed some numbers on my keyboard. He performed magic! Suddenly I was online!

I was so happy. "What did you do?" I said excitedly.

"I had to write code. Yes, lines of code. Everything okay now."

It changed my life. I gave up using Poshta and spent less time at *Coursi* and at the Korolenko.

Then another breakthrough: I learned about Skype and downloaded it. It's the revolutionary digital telephone service. But more problems. One was that I could not pre-pay Skype the way I was supposed to—in fact, the way every user is supposed to. Phone calls on Skype are free if you call another Skype user, but there's a fee if you call a landline—a most reasonable fee, in my opinion, but still a fee.

When you make such calls, Skype draws down these charges from your pre-paid deposit. The suggested deposit was 10 Euros, to be paid with a credit card. When the deposit runs way down, Skype automatically boosts it to 10 Euros, and the process continues. Neat.

I tried and tried to give Skype my 10 Euros. Nothing worked. I e-mailed my friend Artie Lynnworth back in Florida. He loves Skype and knows it inside out. He advised me.

The problem persisted. My friend Sheila Connelly in Boston came to my rescue. She is a whiz—runs her own IT consultancy. She sent me an e-mail, "You're all set now, John!" And so I was.

But a start-up problem. You need a microphone and earphones. Easily available in Chernihiv for a PC but not for a Mac. That got resolved when I received a set from my son Mark in Athens, Georgia. But that took a couple of weeks.

I was eager to thank both Sheila and Mark and I flipped a coin. I called Sheila first. "Sheila, this is John in Ukraine!" I said after connecting

"John!" she said. "Wow!"

My sentiment exactly. We had a nice talk. And yes, because we were both using Skype online, there was no charge. My 10 Euros remained untouched. How amazing. And there seemed to be no limit to how long we could talk. And the connection was so strong and steady! It was another of those high-tech marvels that I can describe only as a "miracle"!

Next I called Mark in Georgia. Same enthusiastic reaction. We were both amazed. He had his web camera on, so I could see him smiling and speaking and scratching his cheek. That was another "miracle."

And I got a big bonus: Mark brought Annalivia, his daughter—my new granddaughter, to the phone. He held her in his arms. Only a few months old. She wasn't talking yet. But I did get to hear gurgles and murmurs and even a bit of crying. I had seen photos of her, but this was my first time live! She was squirming and screaming, but still. And then Stacie, Mark's wife, came on. How good that was. All unforgettable!

By the way, I did not have a web cam. Maybe you are not familiar with that. It's a tiny video camera on your monitor that points at you as you sit at the keyboard. If the person at the other end of the line has a similar camera on, you can see one another as you talk. Sounds wonderful. I refused one. Didn't want people to see me the way I am at the computer.

I admit that in the ecstasy of my Skype honeymoon, I went nuts using it. But that slowed down as the newness wore off. For one thing, there was often the problem of a 7- to 10-hour time difference (Atlantic coast and Pacific coast). We tried making calls by appointment but that was hard. We went back to the pleasant routine of exchanging e-mails.

Oh, in all my calls, it was surprising how often the same questions came up. "What is the time there right now?" And "What is your weather right now?" I, too, asked such questions. And always the same comment, "You sound so clear! Like right next door!"

With Skype, no longer did I have to trudge to the Post Office, stand in line to use a pay telephone, hand over a deposit, go to an assigned booth, and dial the call. I was always delighted when my call got through. Sometimes I would get an answering machine. That would be only half satisfactory. Sometimes a busy signal. Sometimes nothing at all.

Then at the end, I'd have to go back to the clerk to collect what was left of my deposit. Surprising how pricey those calls could be. Of course, for a call that didn't get through, I'd have to go back for another try.

Now I could also receive calls. In my own room!

For the first time I was able to chat with Volunteer friends here and there. What a morale booster that became.

It was a while before I learned of another Skype plus. At times I had to make 800 calls to the U.S.A. To speak to an official at my bank, say. Again I had to go to the Post Office. It charged for outgoing 800 calls just like ordinary calls. But 800 calls were also free on wonderful Skype!

Yes, in my second year, these computer improvements vastly enriched my life. Often I marveled at being so blessed with these technical wonders. I was so fortunate. Think of Volunteers in backward parts of Ukraine! In other undeveloped countries!

More than once I wondered whether I could have made it as a Volunteer in pre-computer times. No way! But who knows? In Ukraine it definitely transformed my life for the better.

~ ~ ~

# 23 / The mail! Oh, my!

*The problems started soon and caused me big headaches—especially at IRS time!*

My mail problems! They started early and went on and on. They boiled down to one complaint: I wasn't receiving some mail that I was positive was being sent to me! Important mail!

    I must explain. I never had a problem with keeping in touch with my family and friends—I did all this mostly by Internet, but also postal mail at times. . And every letter that I mailed to the U.S.A. got delivered, I am pleased to say. And as I just explained, in my last six months I had Skype, which was wonderful

    And I never had a problem receiving parcels from the United States. They took a long time but they got through. Peace Corps warned us they might be a target for thieves. But all arrived safely, although one or two got banged up.

    For this service, Peace Corps recommended a Ukrainian company called Meest. It specialized in delivering packages from the U.S.A. to Ukraine. I did receive a couple sent through Meest. No problems. But in time I found that USPS—our U.S. Postal Service—was more convenient and did an excellent job.

    In fact, I never had a problem receiving letters mailed directly from an address in the U.S.A. to me in Chernihiv. I found all this impressive. So what am I complaining about? I am complaining about all mail that was mailed to me at one of my two addresses in the U.S.A. My primary one in Deep River, Connecticut, and secondary one in Newport Beach, California. And then forwarded to me by USPS—specifically, by my Deep River Post Office. I am talking about _forwarded mail_. This was a major problem for months.

    For many months, most of that never made it to Ukraine. Anxiety, frustration, and trouble! I couldn't keep current on what was going on, especially in my financial affairs. I had major problems filing my U.S. and Connecticut income tax returns in my first year, and lesser but still difficult ones in my second year.

    Sounds crazy, I know, but one reason that I looked forward to going home was that I'd file my next returns from home instead of Ukraine! I'd be spared all these headaches finally!

During our three months of Training, mail from the U.S.A. was to be sent to us care of Peace Corps Headquarters in Kyiv. Peace Corps had given us two addresses in Kyiv (not sure why), and I had given both to my Post Office in Deep River. It could choose whichever it preferred. Then Peace Corps would get it to us.

Any mail that arrived in Kyiv would be sent to us as part of the regular biweekly mailings from Headquarters—routine official announcements. Along with the Kyiv Post, a weekly which was the country's leading English-language newspaper. As well as the international edition of Newsweek—but it was eventually discontinued to save money.

I did not receive a single letter during those three months of Training. I arrived Oct. 1 and received my first letter on Jan. 22. An eternity! Why was this extraordinary? Because back home, it was a rare day that I did not receive some first-class mail.

**B**efore leaving for Peace Corps, of course I had filed a change of address at my Deep River Post Office. In fact, I had handed it to Chris, my mail carrier, who was a friend. Super-efficient. I was sure he would do his best to provide fine service for me abroad. "Just the first-class mail, Chris. Not the junk mail." I wanted to make it simple and easy for him. Later I wondered whether he was authorized to decide what was junk and not junk.

Filing address changes was second nature to me. I did this every fall when I moved to southern California for the winter, and every spring when I moved back to Deep River. And all the forwarding went nicely.

After Training, Peace Corps would no longer accept mail for us. So as soon as I got settled in Chernihiv, I sent out my new address in Ukraine. It was PCV John Guy LaPlante, 105-a, Shevchenko street, 205, Chernihiv, Ukraine 14027.

That happened to be the address of my language school. "PCV" stands for Peace Corps Volunteer. Peace Corps told us that tacking that on would give our mail more respect.

Using *Coursi* as my permanent address turned out to be a smart move. During my service I lived with three different families. Imagine if I had had to keep sending out alerts of these changes!

During Training I quickly got antsy about not receiving mail. I was positive I was receiving mail back home. Why was it not getting to me in Ukraine? What was wrong?

I would call Headquarters in Kyiv and ask, "Do I have mail?"

"No. Nothing." I became really concerned after the first six weeks. Something was amiss. I called my postmaster in Deep River, Barry

Donahue. Not easy to make the call—I had to go to the big central post office and had to keep the time differential in mind.

Barry was—is—a friend. When he was brought in as postmaster, I happened to be the chairman of our weekly speakers' program at the Deep River Rotary Club. I invited him to speak to us about our town's postal operation. He did a fine job and made new friends in the process.

Now I got him on the phone and he was pleasant and assured me everything was being forwarded!

When I expressed doubt, he said, "John, I have checked. Nothing is being returned to us here!"

So where was it winding up? Who had it?

I called Peace Corps about it. Then I e-mailed Peace Corps. And I spoke about it when I went to Headquarters. I went right to three people who might have a role. They investigated, making calls to the Kyiv Post Office.

No answers. No explanations. My problem had become a mystery. Talk about frustration!

A thought came to me. Maybe it cost extra postage to forward a letter overseas! I hadn't thought of asking my postmaster about that. Maybe it had not occurred to him that it might.

I didn't want to bother him. So I e-mailed Skip Routh, a friend in Deep River, and asked him to check this for me the next time he went to the post office. He e-mailed me, "No, John, extra postage is not required for forwarded mail. However, it does cost more to send a letter directly abroad." Which we both knew, of course.

**S**kip is a clever fellow. He set up a simple test. He wrote me a letter, put on the right postage (90 cents), and mailed it. It arrived! It was my first letter from the United States in four months! It proved that the mail could get through.

As I think about it now, a better test would have been to mail it to my home in Deep River. Then would it have been forwarded to Ukraine?

Then I thought of another possibility. Maybe the Ukraine Post Office required extra payment at its end? I called Peace Corps about that. I was told somebody would inquire. Never an answer. I think they were getting tired of my queries.

By now I was receiving other mail, both through the U.S.Postal Service and independent deliverers. Christmas cards and packages, for instance. But all that mail was being sent directly, with no forwarding by an intermediate required.

Then a break-through! In one week, I received three letters forwarded from Deep River. Now a new thought. Why so many in such a short time? Was it that my Deep River Post Office was being more careful? Whatever the reason, I was happy.

The big question remained. Where was all that lost mail? It was important to me. I was sure some was Christmas mail from friends who had not switched over to e-mail, and I had a number of such friends. And some was business and financial mail, including mail very important for IRS reasons. That mystery was never solved.

Now let me tell you about my income tax problems. They were the direct result of my mail problems.

I arrived in Ukraine on Oct. 1, 2007. New Year's Day came and I faced the same problem as you, preparing and filing my returns. It's an enormous headache for all of us, don't you agree?

The first requirement is having all our financial data. Much of it, of course, is supplied on statements sent to us as required by law by financial institutions and businesses and organizations with which we are connected.

I knew how many statements to expect every year. Well, I got just a paltry few. I didn't know who should be blamed, the U.S. Postal Service or the Ukraine Postal Service.

Like many Americans I have an assortment of financial accounts. I needed more statements! I sent letters and e-mails and made phone calls to the U.S.A. to get the missing ones. I never got replies from some. Astounding. What to do?

*Maxim was a whiz with computers. He bailed me out more than once.*

There was only one solution. I would have to re-construct the missing numbers from my checkbook and credit-card records. But I did not have these records for the last months of 2007, and by now you understand why. So I had to guess-timate a lot of numbers. Fortunately I had brought copies of my 2006 federal and state returns, and they gave me some clues.

Missing even was my 2007 Social Security statement. I sent an e-mail to Social Security, and then wrote a letter to its office in Middletown, Connecticut, even tried to place a phone call. No luck. Not a reply. I e-mailed and called others on my list. Few results.

For Social Security receipts, I tallied the deposits in my checkbook. Easy, even for the missing months. It was a fixed sum times 12. But still we were supposed to attach the official statement.

But in other cases such as for dividends and capital gains (or losses), much more difficult. What a headache. I worked at it. It took weeks.

And in a fluke, I had more income than expected and I now had additional tax to pay, although I had made advance quarterly tax payments, as required.

The deadline was April 15, of course. But as a Volunteer serving abroad, I was entitled to an automatic three-month extension and I took it. In my bad luck, I was lucky, however. I had a friend back home who had assisted me with this painful annual ritual. I wish I could mention his name. He is entitled to loud thanks, but I know this would embarrass him.

He assisted me by e-mail. I would query him: "What should I do?" He would shoot a reply back. Numerous e-mails went back and forth. What a good guy. Finally I got the awful job done. Please remember, I had a lot else going on. I was busy from morning till night.

I signed my names to both returns. I signed guess-timated checks to the IRS and Connecticut. Then I sat down and wrote a detailed letter explaining my problems to both.

I stressed that I was a senior-citizen Peace Corps Volunteer serving in poor Ukraine, praying that this would evoke special sympathy from an official who I hoped would be a kind soul of Ukrainian descent!

These were important letters. I didn't dare drop them into the local mailbox two blocks away. I didn't want to take a chance. I made a special trip downtown and slipped them into the big box in front of the main post office. And I crossed my fingers.

My sixth sense told me that I would hear back from IRS and I would not like what I heard.

Many weeks passed, and then I got the long-feared letter from IRS. What tortures of research would they put me through now? I decided I would take it home and then read it. Then I told myself, Open it now! Find out the bad news immediately! Get it over with.

**I** ripped it open. They accepted my return as prepared! Hallelujah! But they fined me $141.16 for being late. That included $6.14 of interest.

Obviously they had not read my paragraph about being entitled as a Volunteer to a three-month extension. Should I write and complain? I decided to drop the matter—to just write it off as a lucky citizen of the best country in the world. I paid the fine and interest.

I never heard from the Connecticut tax office. Maybe I hit a very sympathetic tax reviewer there.

All that was for my 2007 returns. But I was still in Ukraine in 2009, so I would have to go through the same pain for my 2008 returns. But I was determined to make it easier. Early in the New Year I sent alerts to the various banks and businesses and institutions I was depending upon.

I wrote, "Do not send your statements and reports to my Deep River address. Please send them directly to me here in Ukraine. If you cannot do that because that would cost extra money (you cheapskates!), send them to my daughter Monique in California." I gave her address. And I authorized them to do that.

I had coordinated with Monique, of course. She would gather the statements patiently until the end of February (surely all of them would have their statements out by then), and then would mail all of them to me in one big envelope.

That worked quite well.

She also called Barry Donahue, my postmaster, and gently refreshed his memory about my difficulties of the past year. She asked that if any mail did arrive in Deep River despite the alerts I had sent out, that he hold it and a friend there would pick it up and she named him.

And that friend would arrive with a signed authorization from me permitting him and also his dear wife to retrieve my mail, just in case he was tied up. They too would wait late in the season. No need to make repeated trips!

Monique sent me an e-mail. "Dad, Mr. Donahue was very friendly. Very helpful. He asked all about you." That made me feel good. I resolved to stop by and thank him personally when I got home.

A good thing that I had arranged that. Some mail did indeed arrive in Deep River. My friend—he prefers not to be mentioned—picked it all up, sorted out the "junk," and sent the good things on to me. They arrived safely.

Monique had also managed to speak to a live person at the Middletown office of Social Security—a very kind lady, as it turned out. She was first-class. She said she'd make sure that I'd receive my statement although that was supposed to be done automatically by machine.

**B**ut not everything went smoothly, unfortunately. There were irritations and delays. But this time the process was gratifyingly better and I signed and e-mailed my returns punctually. This time with the glowing satisfaction that this would be the last time that I did this as an American in a far-off and different land.

Speaking of taxes, I must tell you one aspect that went superbly well. And at first I thought it would be a periodic nuisance. I am speaking of my real estate taxes and water and sewer payments and automobile taxes in Deep River. They had to be paid twice a year, by a deadline, of course. I would write and mail checks each time.

Now I was heading abroad for 27 months. What a chore it would be to do this from 4,500 miles away—from across the Atlantic Ocean and half way across the European continent. By slow-mail. And without forgetting to do it on time.

I spoke to my bank, which paid some of my routine bills automatically for me. I was told, "Sorry, we cannot pay taxes!"

There was another way, of course. I could pre-pay an estimated total amount for the whole 27 months. That would require a big chunk of money, and the Town would not pay me a penny of interest on it. It also would be a bookkeeping nuisance for our Deep River tax collector, Arthur Thompson.

Then came my idea. Ridiculously simple. But I needed the sympathetic understanding and approval of Mr. Thompson. Living in a small town has great advantages. He listened. He was sympathetic. He understood my idea in 10 seconds flat. And he approved it!

Here's how my scheme worked.

I gave him a series of checks written to cover 27 months with every important detail on them except one: the amount for each check.

Here's an example of one: Pay to: "Town of Deep River. Date: July 15, 2008. Memo: Tax for Unit 228, Piano Works Condominium."

And I signed each check. The only item left blank was the amount of the check because unknown—taxes usually go up, don't they? I also owned a second condo there, so I signed a series of checks for it. I did the same thing for my Nissan Maxima. And the water and sewer bills.

Mr. Thompson placed them all in an envelope with my name on it, tucked it away, and wrote an explanatory note in my account. When the time for payment came, he would pull out the pre-dated checks and write in the proper amounts, whatever they were, and deposit them. That was all there was to it. So simple.

Sooner or later, I would receive my bank statement and notice the canceled checks and their amounts. As my Peace Corps service progressed, I began getting these statements online.

What a good man Art Thompson was. A month ahead, he would send me an e-mail telling me the amounts due. And he would ask, "John, would it be a problem to deposit these checks?" He didn't want me to face a bounced-check penalty! It might happen. But there was never a problem.

This is the right moment to tell you about other post office and banking problems. This time my postal problems were with my post office in Chernihiv, my city in Ukraine. It became such a nuisance to mail and pick up parcels!

I ran up against it the first time when I mailed some thank-you items to my friend, Peter, in Connecticut. An extraordinary can-do fellow of many skills who had been a career Navy man, serving on submarines.

In a bookstore in Chernihiv, I had come upon a remarkable book about Soviet submarines—the very subs he had trained to fight and destroy if necessary. In all his years at sea, he never got to see one up close, I suspect.

The book was in Russian, of course. He would not understand. But there were photos of many subs in different classes, and some looked remarkably strange and different and huge, even to my amateurish eye. Each type was identified and the launching date of the first sub in that series stated. And there were tables of statistics.

He wouldn't understand the words. But he could read the numbers at least. He was smart. He'd figure out a lot of the stuff. He would love the book. I bought it.

His wife, Angela, was also a special friend of mine. I found an illustrated history book about Chernihiv. Again all in Russian. But the photos were many and beautiful and I bought it.

I prepared a parcel, including some strange and delicious Ukrainian candies, and wrapped everything with the greatest care, making the From and the To information crystal clear. No small task. I was proud when I finally finished.

I took a trolley downtown and carried my parcel to the main post office. Busy as usual. I took my place in a queue and gradually inched toward a clerk. When I got to her, she told me I was in the wrong place! I had to go outside this big building, walk around the corner, and go to a door at the end of the building. There were two doors. Of course, I picked the wrong door. Finally I got inside.

Another line. In fact, three lines. For different things. I stood in the line where everybody was holding a parcel. Smart choice. Finally it was my turn at the counter.

Guess what? The clerk asked me what I was mailing. I tried to explain. Whatever I said was not good enough. She ripped open my beautiful parcel and tore everything apart. I gasped.

Then she carried everything to a worktable. Selected an official Ukrainian Postal Service cardboard box from a selection of them. Plunked all my gifts in it. Ripped a big rectangle of heavy manila wrapping paper off a thick role. Wrapped the box securely. Glued it tight with a big brush from a paste pot. Set it in front of me. Filled in a form for me, and pointed where I should sign it. I signed it.

Then she went to a computer and spent minutes looking up something. It was the postage due. She scribbled it on a slip and showed it to me. I gasped again. It was four times more than I expected. More than $20. That was a huge price in Ukraine. What to do? I paid. Not a good experience.

The next time I had a parcel to mail, I simply carried the items to the post office in a plastic supermarket bag. That greatly simplified what would take place next. And that's the way I did it every time.

Sometimes I would stop in to mail a letter. This was in the main post office which I had entered the first time. I would always have to wait in a queue. All I wanted was a stamp. Finally my turn. The clerk would always weigh my letter though I never had more than a single sheet of paper in the envelope. It seemed to me she could tell just by hefting the envelope.

Then she would always go to a computer and study something on the screen. Then she would select the stamps. This was an operation in itself. It involved picking out the right ones from a folder. Then apply them. Then write "AVION" in red letters on the envelope ("By Air"). Then tell me how much. Then point to the big box in the corner where I should deposit it.

Finally I figured it out. Enormous inflation in Ukraine—more than 20 percent per year. Prices of the stamps changed quickly. She was checking the current price! Apparently it was too difficult to memorize the new prices. I bought extra stamps for future use, but when I brought in a letter to mail, a clerk would have to double check that I had paid the correct current amount.

Because of all this incredible bother, I stopped sending packages as gifts. I found easier alternatives. One was to send bank checks. Even that was more difficult than you might think. There was the problem of mailing them. There were a few mailboxes here and there in the city. But it seemed to me the mail in them might not be collected often.

I felt safest depositing my envelopes in the big blue box at the main post office. I hoped that the mail would be scooped out every day instead of twice a week, as I suspected might be the case at other boxes.

If I thought a check would be inappropriate, I used another strategy. I was so proud of myself when I thought of it. I would send an Internet gift card from a huge digital store. A store known to anyone who uses the Internet, one that I prefer not to name.

That turned out not to be not so easy. The first time I tried it, a clerk told me on the phone, "Gift cards can be purchased only within the

U.S.A." What! I asked to speak to her supervisor. I told her I was a terrific customer and a Peace Corps Volunteer in far-off Ukraine and she broke down. "Well, I guess I can do this for you," she said. Wonderful.

I thought it a brilliant idea. It was a true gift—more appealing than just cold cash. And the card had a huge and wonderful selection of tempting things that it could be turned in for, or in part for.

Well, I sent one to a friend. When he did not send me a note after I had waited and waited to hear from him, I inquired.

He told me, "Oh, I thought it was just another unwanted offer of a free credit card. I trash all those offers!"

I sent one to another friend but he did not want it. A very nice man. He tried to send it back to me! But the store would not allow that. True story!

I did send other gift cards. I assume they got cashed easily.

I developed another money problem back home when my condo association selected a new management company. I had been paying my monthly fees for services rendered by direct withdrawal from my checking account. The same amount each month. I had paid this way for years. Completely satisfactory.

The new-company manager said, "No!"

"Why not?" I asked.

"We need a paper trail," she told me.

It didn't make sense to me but my protest had no effect.

What to do? I discovered my bank had a newfangled bill-paying service online. I tried to enroll. Could not do so and I complained to my bank. They told me that I should update my Internet server program. My computer was less than four years old. The suggestion sounded crazy, but I did as suggested. The new program raised havoc with other settings on my computer. What a mess.

My only alternative left was to mail a monthly check. I hated that idea, and by now you know why. I decided I would do exactly what I was doing to pay my Deep River town taxes. I figured I would be away from home for another 12 months. So what I did was to write and sign 12 checks, the same in every detail except one, which this time was the date on each check. I mailed the batch to her, with a note to cash one every month. It worked perfectly.

Receiving parcels was just as much fun. Just joking. Far from easy, though always so nice to be remembered this way. The parcels would always be mailed to me at *Coursi*, my language school. If a small one—the size of a paperback book, say—it would be mailed to the school. Anything larger and I would receive a notice to pick it up at the post office.

The first time, I went to the big post office downtown. Wrong post office. I was told to go to a branch near the school. I did not know that branches existed!

I had to take a marshrutka to get to it. Finally I got to the counter. The clerk asked to see my passport. I had not thought that I might need it. I didn't have it. She turned me away. I had to make a return trip and stand and wait in line. But I walked out with my parcel in hand. Progress!

Just before Christmas I received another notice of a parcel. It was a gift from my daughter Monique and her husband, David. She had alerted me it was coming (did not reveal the contents!) but said it was a big package. I brought along a big babushka bag to put it in. I'd have to carry it to a transit stop, wait for a marshrutka, carry it to the stop close to home, then the final two blocks. I'd be glad to have that bag. I also had my passport!

My turn finally came. Always long lines. One reason, I found out, is that people pay their gas and electric bills at the post office and maybe other bills I was not aware of. The clerk took a long time searching in a back room. She came back lugging an enormous carton. It was hard for me to see her behind it. I always noted the postage. Always shocking. This time, $46!

No way could I carry this home. Too big. Too heavy. What to do? I opened it. I found it stuffed with plastic "peanuts" to protect the valuables.

I scooped all the peanuts into a plastic bag. I dug out all the gift-wrapped presents and got them into my babushka bag. I left the big carton behind and a bag full of peanuts, making sure to get the clerk's permission.

I trudged off to the transit stop, leaning sharply to port because of the weight of all my presents. It was a cold, windy day. I shivered as I waited for Marshrutka 31. Finally it pulled up.

How the heck would I get through the narrow aisle to a seat! I was so lucky. A seat right by the door was empty! It was the only free seat. I grabbed it and sat there, the huge bag on my lap. I finally made it home.

One time I went to the branch to retrieve an unidentified package from an unidentified sender. It turned out to be a small carton...but heavy...from my friends Peter and Angela in Connecticut. I noticed their name on it, of course, and the postage. It was a shocking $18.45.

What could this be? Two big jars of Skippy peanut butter! Not available in Chernihiv. Wow! What a thoughtful gift. Later I figured the postage cost 3 or 4 times more than the peanut butter. But how I enjoyed it!

For years I have taken pride in voting regularly. The right to vote is rare in this world of ours. I consider it a privilege to cast my ballot.

One day at *Coursi* I was handed some mail. One letter included an absentee ballot for Deep River's regular biannual election. It had skipped my mind. I received it two days before the election. But I noticed that the efficient Town Clerk had mailed it six weeks earlier. *Coursi* had received it during vacation, put it aside to give me when classes resumed, then forgot. I was disappointed but I understood. A simple human error. Shucks!

And know what? In that election, some 1,400 votes were cast for the two candidates for Town Clerk. My Town Clerk was retiring and we had two candidates. The winner won by 2 votes after a 3-hour recount. Imagine that! She would have won by three votes if I had received my ballot in time to vote. The winner was Amy Winchell, the wife of my good friend, Dale.

Now I believe you understand why I felt I should devote a full chapter to these assorted mail problems. Irritating in the extreme. I wish that Peace Corps had given us more detailed information about some of these potential problems. For anyone living abroad for a prolonged time, especially in a less developed country, mail is hugely important, even in this Internet age.

~ ~ ~

*Did you know* ... that's it's not only difficult to get into Peace Corps? It's also a process to get out, but only in a good sense.

Peace Corps calls preparing to get out and go home Close of Service—COS. It's a carefully thought-out procedure. It keeps in mind all kinds of eventualities that Volunteers may meet.

For us, COS stretched over three months. It started with alerts and notices from Headquarters and then it intensified. And it ended with a three-day retreat in a ski resort in the mountains.

We received much information as it proceeded. Went through a final physical exam. Had to write a report about our successes or lack thereof. And then sat through talks at our retreat. And filled out paperwork.

But we had a good time, too. In fact, it was wonderful, as you will read in an upcoming chapter.

# 24 / My expat friends

*I meet all four of them by accident.
How they have made my life better!*

While working at the library I had the good fortune to meet five expatriates who became my good friends. All men. I met them one by one over the months. Four were Americans and one was Italian. Four got to know one another through me. They were all strikingly different, each colorful in his own way. So interesting. I was so lucky to claim them as friends.

As I look back, they were essential in helping me weather my Peace Corps service. From what I observed, Volunteers usually worked alone in their community. In isolation! No other Volunteers around! I found this extremely difficult. My expat friends were my escape valve.

I met Rich first, just two months after I arrived. At the Post Office's Internet shop. I was doing my e-mails at one of its rent-by-the-minute computers. Six people waited in line. I finished and a man came forward to claim my computer.

His first words were, "What state are you from?" Somehow he recognized me as an American!

I told him Connecticut. He told me he was from Florida. Then he said, "I'm the next Hugh Hefner!" His chest seemed to puff up.

"What?"

"Yes!" he said. "How about chai?"

"Chai? What's chai?"

"Tea. We'll drink tea and talk."

I met him an hour later in a café across the street. He seemed in his late 40's. He was of Italian descent. He was with a knock-out young Ukrainian woman, about 20.

"She's my manager," he said and smiled. He gave her a pat on the shoulder and she squeezed closer to him. He told me her name. I'm changing it to Nastia for good reason.

I got to know him well. Never thought I would take up with a man so different in so many ways.

He had been a building contractor for 20 years in Florida mostly. He started by building decks for houses, moved up to houses. Had a good business, he told me. He married young. Divorce. He married again—"an emergency room nurse," he said proudly. Divorce again.

He heard about Ukraine and its dazzling marriage agencies. That was a big, big moment for him. "Such gorgeous women!" In just days he signed up with an agency in Kyiv. The package included round-trip air, hotel, and best of all, multi introductions to ravishingly beautiful women. The whole thing cost him several thousand dollars. "I dreamed of meeting the gal of my life!"

He settled in Kyiv. Remained there nearly three years. Met many women. Wined and dined many but never met the gal of his life.

Had to make money. Started a marriage agency of his own in Kyiv—thousands of American men want to meet a beautiful, sexy, devoted, low-pressure Ukrainian doll dreaming of living in Paradise, called U.S.A. But very competitive business. His agency did not do well. I admit I was fascinated as he told me the details. No time here to tell you all that. Sorry.

He was a man of ideas and energy. A born entrepreneur. Now for a year he had been working hard to produce and market a girlie calendar. He read my mind. "Definitely not pornographic!" he said. "No, no. Nice girls. Good girls."

He happened to have a copy. Showed it to me with prideful gusto. Lavish, glossy, beautiful. The kind you'll see in a bar or an auto repair shop. Luscious girls, in the tiniest of bikinis, often in poses that seemed anatomically difficult but intensely provocative, well, he hoped, I'm sure. One pin-up for each month, sometimes two for each month, cavorting in the surf or lolling on a golden beach.

"Aren't they gorgeous?" he said. "Isn't this a terrific calendar?"

"It sure is. Just like the 'Sports Illustrated Swim-Girl Calendar."

"Ah, come on! Mine is super better!" He flipped through its pages again. "This is the most beautiful bikini calendar ever! Here, look again!"

I had to agree. It was beautiful. Super sexy. No, not pornographic. But as close as you could get.

I turned to Nastia. A little beauty. I asked, "Are you on one of these beautiful pages?"

She frowned. "No, no. I help Rich find the girls." She stuck her nose up. "That's not for me!"

I got to know her, too. She was his shadow. One day Rich told me, "We live together." I suspected that, of course. I liked her. Petite. Charmingly cute. Definitely intelligent. Spoke the best English I ever heard by a native Ukrainian—could easily have passed as a born American. Had majored in English at a university in Kyiv.

I asked Rich whether he had ever considered posing her in a bikini. No, he said. "Wonderful, wonderful gal. Very pretty. So smart. But no breasts. No breasts!"

He was on the edge of success, he said. This calendar was his first. He was trying hard to promote it in the U.S.A. He had made a couple of trips back, flying on his air miles accumulated during his building years. Said he was talking to Wal-Mart and other big retailers. "I've been calling every one of them!"

He told me one thing after another about himself. One was very weird. His ex, the emergency room nurse, was financing all this!

And he lived just one floor beneath Tamila, my Russian teacher. I had walked by his door every time I went up to her apartment for class. He knew her. What a coincidence! Remember, thousands of such buildings in the city!

He had settled here because Nastia lived with her folks in the city. It was cheaper than Kyiv but close to it. And it had everything he needed.

**R**ich and I became good friends. I'd visit him every week or two. He'd talk to me about business, and I'd talk to him about my work. Each of us was an important outlet for the other.

He'd explain how he located girls for his photo shoot. Selected a great photographer, but reasonably priced. Found the perfect location at a certain beach in the Crimea, Ukraine's Florida. How he planned the whole week of the shoot...took all the gals there by train (20 hours each way), put them up at a hotel, fed them, made sure they had fun all while working hard.

How he hired a hairdresser for the shoot. How each bikini had to be tailored perfectly to the girl. All the photo retouching involved...a girl might be beautiful but had a tattoo that was unacceptable.

How he prayed for good weather for the shoot because he had invested so much money and the shoot was all-important. How Nastia would work all through the shoot as his Gal Friday, handling countless details, and, so important, keeping the girls happy.

They would have their expenses paid but got no cash for their modeling. The printed calendar advertised them as models, and a note explained the girls could be hired for modeling jobs through Rich. If they got a job, he would take a commission.

How then he had to sort through the hundreds of photos and pick the very best, considering many factors. Selected a graphic artist to design the calendar. Found a top-notch printing company at a rock-bottom price. And constantly promoted, promoted, promoted in the U.S.A.

Rich started coming to my English Club. Nastia would come with him. He dropped out but she enjoyed it and came often. He'd come only for something special. I took a liking to her. Talented. I hoped she would think higher. She impressed all the members by her English. She actually inspired some.

Whenever I visited Rich he'd bring out some food for us. Even cook something. He loved spaghetti with tomato sauce. It was a great treat for me every time.

He loved making French fries and often made a big pan full for us. Just a snack! He also loved to make ice cream sundaes. Ukraine made good ice cream. Always topped with genuine Hershey's chocolate syrup picked up on one of his flights to the U.S.A. Sometimes he would add caramel sauce.

When I bought a cell phone because Peace Corps told me it was essential, he taught me the basics. He'd give me all kinds of helpful tips about many things. The best place to change money. Where to find an honest money-changer on a Sunday. The best pizza shop in town. Where to have a watch fixed. Different restaurants and different neighborhoods. He gave me many insights about Ukraine—medical care, government regulations, the police, and all the corruption.

I found out that as an expat, he had to leave the country every three months. Sometimes he would go just to neighboring Moldova, stay overnight, and then come back in. He would time his trips to the U.S.A. to satisfy this obligation.

One day I noticed he had a Scrabble set. I was amazed. He had dropped out of high school. "But later I went back and got my GED!" He was proud of his GED. He loved the game. I did, too. We'd play just about every time I visited. His Scrabble skills were amazing. He had a talent for forming word combinations. He would beat me consistently. Now and then he'd say, "John, I think you're letting me win!" Not so.

He won because of pure talent. Yet in one way it was true he couldn't win without me. He was terrible at spelling. He'd say, "John, how do I spell neice?" I'd say, "It's not n-e-i-c-e. It's n-i-e-c-e." And he'd say. "Excellent! That's what I hoped." And score more points.

I invited him to come to the English Club with his Scrabble set and explain the game to the members. He did. He put a lot of excitement and fun into it. They crowded around him. They loved his demonstration.

One day he told me, " I'm going to the U.S.A. in three weeks. What do you need?"

"Are you serious?"

"Absolutely. Just give me your list."

I mentioned peanut butter—crunchy! Scotch tape. Elmer's white glue. And a few other things. I opened my wallet and took out money for him.

"No, no. Pay me when I get back."

One day while he was in the U.S., Nastia called me. "Rich just phoned me from Atlanta," she said. "He just got an order for 1,500 calendars! He was so excited!"

It was his first order. I understood.

He called me when he returned. I congratulated him heartily.

He beamed. "Yes, it's fantastic. But it's just the beginning. And oh, I didn't forget. I have all your stuff. Come on over."

I went. He told me he had gone to the U.S. with two big suitcases, one inside the other. He needed both coming back. "I bought so much!"

I looked. And howled! He had returned with both jammed with purchases. His favorite hot sauce. His favorite T-shirts. Favorite tooth paste. Favorite dungarees. All kinds of things not available in Chernihiv. He did that every time he flew home.

And for me he had not one, but two, jars of peanut butter. Plus the other things on my list.

We talked about his business every time. He was always upbeat. No, he had not sold Wal-Mart, dammit, but did have that order for 1,500. And promises of more.

He would invite me over for dinner on our big American holidays—which were just regular workdays in Ukraine. "I'll do the cooking," he would say. I remember our first Christmas.

*Rich was a character. I never thought I'd have a friend like him. Soon I knew I was lucky to have him. And he me.*

"But we'll do it on Dec. 19," he said. "Yes, that's early. But that's what works best for me."

I showed up with champagne and ice cream. He took them from me with pleasure.

He had a large, beautiful apartment and it was well-furnished. He kept it as neat as a pin. And he was meticulous in the kitchen. He had two stray cats that he loved and fed them only the best. I was the first to arrive. He and Nastia were busy making dinner.

"I brought this bird back from the U.S.A." he told me. "It was frozen. I triple-wrapped it. The airline lost my suitcases in Moscow!

Incredible! It took 18 hours for me to get all of them back! But this bird was still in good shape."

He was making mashed potatoes. I noticed something different. It was the first time I saw mashed potatoes made with the skins on.
"Look!" he said, pointing inside the bird. "Real stuffing just like my Mama made! And look!" He showed me two envelopes of mix-it-yourself turkey gravy. "I bought all this at Wal-Mart!"
"What kind of cranberry sauce do you have?"
"Cranberry sauce? I don't have any. I never thought of it. We never had cranberry sauce when I was a kid!"
Oh, well.
"One problem," he said. "I don't have a platter to serve the turkey on."
"Just serve it in the roasting pan," I said. "Everybody will understand."
That worked out fine.
It turned out to be a quiet but pleasant dinner. Rich and Nastia. Myself. And two friends who arrived just in time, Jackson and his girlfriend, Larisa. I didn't know them. Jackson was another American expat. I'll tell you about him and Larisa in a few minutes.
Rich was a fine host, generous and good-humored, and Nastia helped in every way. We offered toasts. The turkey was beautiful, but I skipped it, vegetarian me. The potatoes were delicious, skins and all. Everything was excellent. The sundaes were the biggest and best yet. I went home grateful. But I did miss the cranberry sauce.
Hugh Hefner was his supreme idol, his hero. Rich was continually inspired by Playboy. But one day he showed me a copy of Maxim magazine. It was my first look at it. He seemed to like it even better than Playboy. "I am going to publish a magazine like this," he told me.
Was he joking? I looked at him. Was he drunk? He could not be. I had never seen him drink. "It's part of my long-range plan," he said. "I'm gonna do it. Definitely."
I couldn't help myself. I launched into the numerous difficulties. The investment required. The expertise needed, and the many varieties of it...creative, editorial, financial, business, advertising, circulation, legal. He listened. But I don't think I changed his mind one bit. It's as if he had not heard a thing I had said. He had a vision. With a capital V.

Our friendship continued strong all through my service. Sometimes two or three weeks would go by, and then we'd meet again, play Scrabble again, eat a pan of French fries. He would tell me about his problems.

One day he told me he dropped Nastia. "Wasn't doing the job," he said. I was very surprised. He found another pretty gal. "She's terrific," he said. In three months he dropped her. I saw this scenario several times.

He always had a big order for calendars coming up. He hired himself a salesman in the U.S.A. on straight condition. But no big order ever developed that I was aware of. But he persisted. His ex always came through with the money. He would speak of her in the highest terms. Would visit her when he went to the U.S.A. "But no sex," he would say. "No, no. We're just great friends."

He created a second calendar and was planning a third when I finally left for home, my service completed.

I would give him advice. I thought it was sound, of course. I had started a business and ran it for many years, then a second business on the side. Most of all I hammered at one idea.

"Why do a photo shoot every year? Not necessary! Do one every three· years. You always take dozens of shots· of each girl. Take many more. Have the girls slip on different bikinis. Change their hair-do. Use the same girls in your next calendar. Nobody will notice. You'll save a ton of money. And so much aggravation."

He agreed. Well, in theory. It was clear he loved doing the shoots.

At the end he branched into other businesses. One was selling bikinis retail. He was buying the bikinis cheap in China through a catalog. He worked a deal with the manufacturer, set up a website, took photos of girls modeling the bikinis, and sought to sell them in the U.S.A., or so I thought.

"Sounds good," I said to him, "but why would a gal want to buy a bikini without seeing it for real, feeling it, and checking it for right size?"

"The price! I can sell them so much cheaper than they can buy them in a shop!"

"How long would it take you to ship a bikini to a customer in the U.S.A.? How much would the postage cost you? It would be so expensive." I knew how expensive from my own experience.

"No, no, John. Here! I'm going to have outlets here! And I'm going to publish a catalog. I'll have a website." He was working on this when I finished service and left for home.

He was also going back into the matrimonial-agency business. He had made a connection with the operator of a huge Internet agency. The details were fuzzy. But he was going to advertise girls on still another new website of his own, recruit men from the U.S. as customers, and then collect a commission for each customer from the agency. It was the very same idea that had attracted him to come to Ukraine.

He did get this started and did recruit men. But he was worried one day when I stopped by. His first commission check from the big operator was past due. He called him and complained loud. No check came. He called five days later. Finally the check did come. "It was for a big amount," he told me. "I think it's going to work out."

He plugged this matrimonial business, along with his calendar. "Matrimonial" was the wrong word. Few marriages seemed to result.

Rich was my good friend through my last minute in Ukraine. He was a good guy. Cheerful. Considerate. Amusing. Always ready to lend a hand.

I had a big problem leaving for the U.S.A., and Rich helped again. So much luggage!

Milady Annabelle had come to Ukraine for my last days. She had arrived with two suitcases, one filled with her stuff and the other as an extra for me. So thoughtful. I had so much stuff.

I had two large suitcases of my own. We would be taking all four home, each filled to the max! Three for me and one for her. So bulky. So heavy.

We'd be leaving by train for Budapest and would fly from there. How would we get all these on board the train? I worried about it.

Rich came to my rescue. He arrived in a taxi, carried down all four suitcases, loaded them on board, and drove us to the train. He put the suitcases onto the train himself, lugged them to our compartment, stowed two under the bunks—a very tight fit.

He hefted the other two high into the overhead bins. He was strong, and it took everything he had. He was breathing hard. "There you are, John!" he said. "You're all set."

Several other friends had arrived at the station to see us off. They saw Rich do all this. They were impressed.

I threw my arms around him. "Thank you, Rich! Thank you!"

Annabelle gave him a hug, too.

"Hey, I've got to hop off!" he said. "I'm not ready to go home with you! Not yet! Make sure to keep in touch!"

My next expat friend was Jackson—I had met him at Rich's Christmas dinner. He was about 55—just a guess. He had been the longest away from the U.S.A.—seven or eight years, I believe. He had started by moving to Moscow. He saw it as a hot opportunity. Had gotten work.

Now he had been living in Ukraine about two years. Jackson was his family name. I considered it unusual that he preferred that as his handle to his given name, which was Craig.

He was a tall and good-looking man. In the last months he had developed a neat goatee. "Just for a change," he chuckled, but he kept it. Well-educated and well-spoken. He generated a feeling of competence and trust.

Every now and then he would drop something about his past San Francisco was his home town and he still had his father there, elderly now. He worried about him. He mentioned Costa Rica a couple of times. Another time Cambodia. I got the impression he had traveled a lot.

Not a playboy. I felt he was a hard worker—had come to Eastern Europe because of a career opportunity. Basically he was a consultant. He would make contact with a big business of some kind and sign a contract to perform a service. When I met him, he was running an English-language school at Borispil Airport outside Kyiv. The school was for pilots and air controllers. English is the international language in the commercial aviation world. They had to learn it to get ahead. Especially the professional lingo.

I would see him now and then, usually by running in to him at a restaurant or a supermarket. Sometimes at Philharmonia. He was cordial and quick to make a helpful suggestion or give a useful tip.

Always had Larisa on his arm. She was a beautiful woman in her 40's. Very sweet. Impressed me a lot. They seemed an excellent match, and a tight and lasting one. She had a teen-age daughter and she lived with them. He liked the girl, and she liked him, he told me.

He worked in Kyiv and they lived there, coming to Chernihiv for weekends. It was Larisa's home town. When the big financial crunch hit the country, Chernihiv became their base. The living was cheaper and it was more comfortable than the big city. He still found work three or four days a week in Kyiv and he would go there for those days and put up at a rental apartment as needed. That was cheaper than a hotel.

When the recession got worse, he started an English-language school in Chernihiv as a sideline. He held the classes in his living room. He would come to my English Club now and then.

He perceived an opportunity there. Everybody in the club was interested in learning English, of course. He offered what he called a "Master Class" course. That term had terrific sizzle and he signed up students. But not for long, from what I could see. He was too expensive, I think. His students were also pinched by the recession.

He also made a try at another hot business idea. He heard about a great shortage of registered nurses in the U.S. Nurses abroad were being recruited to come and work in the U.S.

His new idea was to master all the entry requirements for nurses emigrating to the U.S.A.—everything that was needed to get into the country and then become accepted as an R.N. in the U.S. He set out to beat the bushes and find as many prospects as possible.

It sounded good to me. He would train and motivate them, help them with the paperwork, and help to find them jobs in the Great Land of Opportunity. He would charge them for the training, and then collect a commission when he found them a job. I may have some details wrong but that was his idea in general and he promoted it vigorously. But it didn't take off, I'm sorry to report. Or so it seemed to me.

At the same time he managed to convince Larisa that she should train to become a nurse. In fact, maybe she was one. Then the two of them, with her daughter, of course, could go to the U.S. together. That would be a momentous decision for her, certainly. He would find himself a good opportunity there, she would go to work in a high-paying job as a nurse, and life would be great. After a while he didn't talk about it any more.

Certainly he had a better deal as an expat than my other expat friends did. Somehow he had gotten himself a longer and more favorable visa. For one thing, he didn't have to exit Ukraine every three months. What a great headache that bureaucratic detail was. The others heard about that and prodded him for details. I never found out what was involved.

He had a lot of experience in Ukraine and I enjoyed hearing him talk about life here. He made me understand some things. I was always glad to see him. I enjoyed seeing him and Larisa—an ideal match, I thought.

Before me, he knew only Rich. He met the other expats through me. Whenever we planned anything as a group, we invited him.

As the end of my service approached, I intended to take Annabelle to Kyiv for a few days as a little vacation. He quickly gave me advice and even made arrangements with a realtor friend of his to find us a nice short-term apartment. As it turned out, that was not necessary. We chose a hotel. But he tried hard for me..A good guy.

Renato became another pal. Not American. Italian! Brimming with gusto. Smart. Fun. I met him at the Dba Gucia restaurant (Two Geese) near the library. That was his first name, Renato. He was in his 50's also.

He was proudly, incessantly, enthusiastically "Italiano." He arrived at any party with a brilliant ascot tie around his collar. Debonair! Women fainted for him. In fact, I used to describe him as 110% Italian—by his flair, his good humor, his bearing, and his rich Neapolitan accent.

He spoke English remarkably well. That impressed me also. American English, I mean. Italians feel the same about American English as Ukrainians do—it's important to learn it if you want to get ahead. A big reason that our friendship took off was his ease in it. He'd make small mistakes but they were part of his charm.

I loved the way he would roll his R's when he spoke. And how he said "Ciao" and "Mama mia" all the time. He'd kiss me on both cheeks whenever we met and parted. I got to hear "Mama mia!" often.

Like countless other foreign men, he had come to Ukraine to meet a woman. So his was a familiar story to me by now. He was divorced and had a daughter back in Italy. He would show me photos. Bellisima! Gorgeous.

He had been a Ph.D. mechanical engineer. Went to work for Fiat Automotive and made Fiat his career, becoming a high-level executive. Fiat decided to cut back and offered him a terrific retirement deal. Renato made it even better by his astute negotiating, as he told me a couple of times. He retired early on a fine pension.

He began exploring romance opportunities in Ukraine online and that's how he met Svetlana. The photos of her were beautiful and he could see she was smart. Their e-mails began shot back and forth. Things got hot.

He flew to Ukraine to meet her. He was excited by what he saw. She was as beautiful as her photos (which is not always true). She was an engineer, too, and worked in a factory. Had an engaging and nicely low-key personality. And was smitten with him.

She was divorced, too. She had a teen-age daughter. They lived in an old cottage next to Svetlana's father and mother on the edge of the city. Her English was fragmentary. His Russian was nil. But love conquers all.

He moved in with her. Life was wonderful. He loved Svetlana. Showered her with love. Bought a big TV set for the three of them. Bought other nice things. He loved her daughter. Bought her books and clothes and provided money for her. "She is learning English so quickly!" he would tell me. I could see his pride.

He found life in Ukraine very appealing. He was enjoying his new life and new family. And, what was so wonderful, most things were so much cheaper than in Euro-expensive Italy. He was accustomed to the good life and now could enjoy it with money to spare.

He began making his own salamis, which is quite a process. He wanted to teach me more than I cared to know about that. And about fine wines—he insisted that Italian red wines are the finest in the universe. Yes, he was totally Italian. Macho in a suave way.

He was attracted by the low real estate prices. After much looking, he bought a fine condo in a new-high rise going up. It was right across from the most beautiful park. Would be finished in six months. Exciting.

But in Ukraine, all you get for your money is an apartment with bare walls. No wallpaper, not even a paint job. No kitchen cabinets, no plumbing fixtures, no trim of any kind. He got estimates. It would cost him another $35,000 to finish. But that was okay. Then came the crisis. Real estate prices plummeted. And Ukraine tightened up on its visa requirements.

Now an expat could live here only six months in a year. Previously that had been a joke. The expats would go to nearby Belarus, say, enter that country, make a u-turn, and come back the next day for another six months.

Renato would do it by flying home to Naples—it took less than three hours. He'd visit his relatives, stock up on the best pasta and Italian delicacies he could not find in Ukraine, and fly back.

He contacted a notary (a lawyer specializing in real estate), signed the many documents, and plunked down his money. He was told it would take six months to finish the condo work. He planned every detail, made precise working sketches and plans, went out shopping for everything needed, interviewed workmen, and got started. Six months became eight, became ten, and the end still was not in sight.

Meanwhile, he had begun studying Russian feverishly. Absolutely essential—he was in Ukraine to stay. Walked around with a Russian dictionary in his hand. Spent hours with Svetlana tutoring him. Memorized lists of words. It all sounded familiar to my efforts with Russian.

"Big, big problem, John," he would say, knocking on his head with his knuckles. "I cannot remember! I am so, so discouraged. Mama mia!"

When I told him about my English Club, he became a regular. He wanted to make his English even better. This was a great opportunity to practice. He was always a hit at our meetings. Always had interesting comments to make. He'd keep things rolling with his questions. We all loved him. The young women swooned over him. He was used to this.

He enjoyed the concerts at Philharmonia as much as I did. We always sat in the same spots, far forward on the left. I sat on one side of the aisle and he and Svetlana sat on the other side. We'd chat at intermission.

A well-matched pair, I thought, although his Russian remained minimal and her English rudimentary.

He introduced me to Mikael Sukaj, the conductor. Renato would call him "Maestro," and Mikael would beam. Renato would go congratulate him and schmooze with him at intermission. I'd tag along. We had a great time.

It's through me that he became interested in the Korolonko Library—the Foreign Language Department, of course. He would stop by every day, made friends with the three librarians. I would see him often there. He'd practice his Russian on Victoria, Tanya, and Iryna. He became a part of our cozy coterie. He and I would have coffee together. Always good chats.

When I started the French Club, he attended regularly. French and Italian are close cousins and his French was quite good. We always looked forward to him in those sessions also.

Then surprise—he started an Italian Club! Recruited several students. He taught them for free! I sat in a couple of times. Very fine teacher. They loved him. Three of them were also members of my French Club and my English Club. How about that?

Suddenly bad news. His father died and he rushed home to Naples for the funeral, and then returned to Chernihiv in a pall of grief. A week later, his mother died! He flew back to Naples. "She could not live without Papa," he told me. He was desolate for many days.

Then troubles of a different kind. He began complaining that he and Svetlana didn't have that much in common. "She has a very, very good character." He told me that often. Was very pretty. But the spark was gone.

Renato would unload on me. "But she knows nothing about very simple things. I asked her about interest rates in saving accounts. She was no help at all! So many things she does not know. Mama mia!"

I got to know her quite well and thought her admirable. She did not know those things that he complained about only because she had never been exposed to them. They were not a part of her life.

Svetlana already was going through a terrible time. Came the recession and she lost her job overnight! Not a penny of separation pay!

**R**enato supported her, of course. He was good about that. She became even more dependent on him.

Like her father, she loved to garden, and now she became earnest in growing everything she could in the big garden right next to her door. She talked Renato into helping. He looked fit, but he had worked at a desk for 30 years.

He would have been happy to skip it all. She was proud one day when they harvested a 50-kilo bag of potatoes. That's a lot of potatoes.

But Renato snickered. "I could buy 50 kilos in the bazaar for just 2 or 3 Euros. Not worth the effort!"

The incompatibility grew worse. He told me more tales of woe. Then he met another woman in her 30's, a lawyer. Beautiful, of course. She was married but unhappy. "John, she has a very, very good character."

He found an apartment, left Svetlana. She spilled tears and so did her daughter. The new gal moved in. In two months he began telling me this relationship was not working well. Oops!

"I pay for everything. She does not press my shirts. Does not even cook a meal for me. Mama mia!"

Surprise again. He would call Svetlana whenever he needed special help. She always said yes. "We are friends. I give her money," he told me. "I promised her I would help her. And she helps me."

Then came the dire financial crisis. Real estate prices plummeted. His condo had been completed to the bare walls but he had not started the many finishing projects which were essential. He decided to lock the door and suspend work and wait and see. "I do not want to risk more than I have risked already." That made sense to me.

*Seeing my expat friends was a big outlet. I'd leave feeling buoyed for another day. Renato is in the center and Craig at the right.*

He dropped his girlfriend, the lawyer. And went out and found and rented a small house. Easy walking to downtown. "The rent is very little. And the owner is a good man. I am very happy."

That was the situation as I left Ukraine.

He said to me, "No more Ukrainian women! No more! Mama mia!"

I must say he added a lot of gusto to my life in Chernihiv. It was a pleasure to see him. I became very fond of him. He had traveled to many countries, but never to the U.S.A. I invited him.

"Come see me, Renato. I will have a bed for you! And breakfast!" I said it that way as a little joke, but I meant it. I hope he comes.

**N**ow about my friend Alain. Another dear and colorful fellow!

Just a few minutes' walk from the library was the biggest indoor shopping center in the city. It was called the Mega Center. Big by standards there. It was American style—a modern new building with a food supermarket in the basement and a variety of small shops on its two floors. It even had escalators—the only ones in the city!

I enjoyed it. It was full of life and activity. I'd shop for food. Browse in the bookstore. Walk through the big electronics and home appliance store. A great place to walk and exercise in bad weather.

Dead ahead as you walked in on the main floor—wide open in the very center of all this activity—was an attractive small café. You couldn't avoid it. On one side was a kiosk with a red awning. It served coffees and teas in surprising variety. It offered 20 flavors of ice cream, good ice cream. Plain in a dish, as a sundae, or in a cone—to my knowledge the only genuine ice cream cones in the city.

It had seven or eight nice round glass tables with chairs. The ornate steel chairs were unusual—they had flaming red seat cushions and backs and the backs were shaped like valentine hearts. Quite charming.

The owner was interesting. About 45. Tall, slim, energetic. With a very closely cropped beard. Dressed in a sweater and dungarees. Affable, chatting with this customer or that one as he went about his work. He was assisted by two women. Sometimes he'd sit at one of his tables and work on his laptop.

He was creative. He'd introduce a new product—a variety of buns, or little toys to catch the eyes of little children and their moms, or a new line of candies. He kept trying new products. He impressed me as an exemplar of the new breed of small Ukrainian entrepreneurs.

I'd stop by for an ice cream cone or a cup of tea. One day as he served me, he said, "What is your name?" He asked the question in English. Strangely accented English, but good.

I told him, then said, "And yours?" He paused, then said, "Alain."

"Alain?" It sounded French and he pronounced it a strongly French way. "That's a French name!"

"Yes, it is." We spoke a few words of French. Then surprise: he told me he was American. That's when I discovered that he was an expat here. From New York City! Born there. Yes, operating this little business in Chernihiv, Ukraine. Gosh! And he had lived in France. How interesting.

I began stopping in more often, always hoping he would be in. He was often gone. If in, he would sometimes sit with me for a bit, until needed. We became friends and we shared our stories, of course.

He was a true expat, had been in Ukraine for a couple of years, was living with a Ukrainian woman and they had a baby daughter. He showed me pictures. A darling little girl.

Sometimes she would come in with her mom. She was a beautiful young woman perhaps half Alain's age. The little girl was his princess. He would beam when he'd see her and dangle her on his knee. He had become a father quite late. I felt it was a splendid transforming experience for him.

We had many things, many interests, in common. I would stop by for a coffee or a dish of ice cream whenever I could. Whenever business slowed, he'd leave it to his two gals and come and sit and chat.

One thing he bemoaned was the pervasive under-handedness in the country. "It exists at every level. And for everything." He told me how inspectors would come in to inspect his little café. "Too often they find something wrong. But not really wrong, you understand? They are terrible."

He did not mention payola, but I knew that was a common practice.

He had other interests. He pointed to a big signboard at one side of the café. Not really part of the café. It was covered with 15 or 20 cards offering real estate for sale or rent. It was his billboard. They were properties that he was promoting for sale.

Quite often he would be absent for a few days. "Business!" he would say. Very few details. Kyiv, he would say. Or Prague. He would go to Prague every few weeks. To fulfill his visa requirement, I suspected. He had friends there. Said he had lived there. Jerusalem also. Same story.

Once he made a quick trip to London. He told me he was interested in buying a Mercedes van called the Sprinter, and on the Internet he had discovered a good used one there. He made the trip to look it over but came back disappointed.

One day I mentioned my solo trip around the world. I told him that I returned home with my passport crammed with visas. He was fascinated. He excused himself and came back in a minute with his passport.

It was full of official stamps and visas also. Amazing. He had traveled to so many places, and so often, that he had had to have extra pages added to it. I smiled and said to him, "I had to do the same thing with my passport!" But he had been to even more countries!

On another day I mentioned my digitalization program at the library. He leaped up, left for a minute, and came back with a box. In it was a digital scanner, brand-new. A portable model. You held it in your hand like a pistol and could snap barcodes—a barcode on this item, on that item, on so many things.

"I just purchased it," he said. "I will use it to take inventory."

Instantly I wondered whether it could scan books at the Korolenko Library! It didn't have one. Wouldn't that be marvelous....

"Yes. Certainly!" he said. "There are five basic kinds of barcodes. This one can read them all. I can purchase one for you. I can get a discount. I will give you the discount."

I was excited. I asked him if I could borrow it and show it to my librarian friends at the Korolenko. "Yes, of course," he said. He still had it in its original box. He put it in its box, made sure the instructions were inside, handed it to me. "Exciting!. Let me know what they say. Good luck!"

Well, you know now how badly this effort turned out. I returned the beautiful little scanner to Alain with great disappointment.

One snowy day early in the winter he noticed the Stabilicers on my shoes—my ice cleats. The name is spelled that way. He had never seen anything like them. "They are my life-savers!" I said. They were unknown in Ukraine, a country where snow is usual come winter.

He contacted the manufacturer in Canada, got samples mailed to him, and created a website to market them. Talk about initiative! I helped him to write the advertising copy for his website.

As it turned out, all this got done too late for that winter. "But for next year!" he said. One thing discouraged him—the price he would have to charge for them, including the shipping from Canada, would be expensive for Ukrainians. "But I will try."

I told him that two groups of Volunteers came to Chernihiv every year for their three months of Training. They would love this café. "Advertise to them," I said to him. "Offer them a free coffee on their first visit. Or a free ice cream. Tell them you can offer them free Wi-Fi for their laptop computers. They'll all come here! And oh, tell them about the Stabilicers!"

He created a big poster, "Volunteers! Welcome to my Café! I am an American here!" Plus more words. But he did not mention any freebies!

Whenever I ran into Trainees, I would always mention Alain and his café. I felt I was doing them a genuine favor. I did see one or two there but not many. I have no explanation except that they were busy.

When I began planning my vacation trip to nearby countries, he was quick to help me. I knew that buying my train tickets would be a hassle—the language difficulty, the impatient ticket clerks. He offered to go to the train station for me and buy them. And he did that.

On another day he confided to me, "I am going to be a father again. Yes, my girlfriend is pregnant."

That is the way he always spoke of her—"my girlfriend." I never got to know her well although she would come in and supervise things when he went off for a few days. The language problem, again.

I knew how happy his little daughter made him but as he spoke now, I was not sure whether he was happy or disappointed. I knew that abortion was common in Ukraine. I stuck out my neck and said, "You are going to have the baby?"

"Yes. But I have left it entirely to my girlfriend. To me, it is a mother's decision. Yes, she wants the baby." Suddenly he grinned. "I will have to work harder now. John, I need good ideas! Help me!"

I tried. Truth is, he was savvy. He had plenty of ideas of his own.

Several times he told me that if I went to Prague, he would arrange for me to stay at a friend's there I knew he was sincere.

I ran into bad luck. Alain announced that he would be away when milady Annabelle arrived from California for my final days in the city. He told me, "I am so sorry that I will not meet her!"

I was sorry, too. So was Annabelle. She was eager to meet him. And he was away during my last meeting of my two clubs. I had hoped he could attend them. It would have been a pleasure to introduce him.

He did send me an e-mail. He was not much of a writer but he got right to the point. "Good luck when you go home, John! We are friends. We will keep in touch! Alain."

I was not at all sure whether he would ever return to America. From what I could see and had read, after a long time away, it could be difficult for an expat to return home—home was no longer home. And how to come up with the cushion of money to fly back, rent an apartment, and stay afloat until landing a job, and so on? But I knew he was enterprising.

It is through me that he got to meet Wayne, and then eventually, Renato. I was sure they would become friends. I told him, and them, "It is important for all you expats here to stick together!" They agreed.

Yes, these non-Ukrainian friends became enormously important to me. They helped me. They were a key part of my social life. They boosted my morale when it sagged and took pleasure in my small successes. They added a layer of joy to my life that I did not expect. I was so lucky. Again I thought of Volunteers working in lonely isolation. With no friends like this around. Hard!

Strange to say, but at times I felt a bit like them, meaning like an expat. Like them I was struggling alone, or so it seemed, in a strange and challenging country, and doing my best to get by and be successful.

Yet I was always aware that I was a Volunteer and had taken an oath and was engaged in serious work. But looking forward to going home the minute my hitch was up and re-starting my comfortable routine. With none of the big problems they faced.

I was cheering for each of them, and they knew it.

Oh, you may be wondering why I didn't include my friend Wayne here (he's in Chapter 18). To me, he was not a true expatriate. He vacationed in Ukraine. Or to put it another way, he was just a half-expat.

~ ~ ~

# 25 / 'Expect the unexpected!'

*It's good advice. Mishaps befall me.*
*Quirky things come up. I get hurt.*

**O**h, my trials and tribulations in my first months! As a Volunteer I knew that it would be unrealistic and in fact crazy to think that I could get through 27 months in this strange country with everything perfectly smooth and easy. A lot smarter to think something would go wrong. The sensible questions were, "What will go wrong? How bad? And then what?"

And besides, maybe something wonderful and dramatic would come up! Who knows?

Let me tell you about a few.

**First, something quirky.** In my first week of Training after a long day I was riding the bus home to Natasha's little house half way to the outskirts. I was sitting half way back. Not only was it dark out but there were so many people on the bus, including standees in the aisle, that I had a hard time seeing out. I missed my stop. It was a couple of stops before I noticed.

What to do? I stayed on all the way to the end of the run. I figured that I'd ride the bus back and get off at the right stop.

Finally the bus got to the end and it pulled over. I was the only passenger still on board. I remained in my seat, expecting the bus would roll on in a minute. But it did not. It stayed put.

The driver and the fare conductor, a woman, noticed me and I tried to explain. She was sitting across the aisle from him. My Russian just wasn't up to it. They looked at one another and said nothing. The driver hunched his shoulders and shrugged.

I thought, *What are they thinking? Well, I don't think I look like a bum. They can see I'm not drunk. They must have noticed my heavy briefcase.*

The two set up a picnic lunch on the dashboard, turned on some music, and ate and sipped their tea and chatted for 15 minutes. They glanced at me now and then. I wondered how long we'd be stopped this way. At one point she got up and came and offered me a cookie, which I took. "*Spaciba!*" I said. "Thank you!" Finally, they started the bus again.

I was still the only passenger. At the next stop a man and a woman got on. On the next stop, a man. I kept peering out. It was so hard to see outside. I moved far forward and stood in the lurching aisle so I could see through the windshield. In the dark I could see my stop coming up. I recognized the kiosk next to it. That's where I waited to get on every morning.

I scampered the last two steps up the aisle. The conductora noticed me, told the driver to stop. He did. I put the fare in her hand. I felt that it was only fair for me to pay again. But she refused it.

"*Spaciba*," I said again as I got off. "*Ochen spaciba*." She smiled at me and gave me a little wave and the bus rolled on. That's when I figured that they had figured it all out. Very nice people, these Ukrainians.

Across the street, the single light in Natasha's kitchen looked very welcoming.

### A desperate voice in the snow.

On another night returning home around 8, I was the only one to get off at my stop. Very dark out. Cold. Four or five inches of snow on the ground. The bus drove on.

I had to walk about 300 feet and I started. I heard a voice off to the right. Somebody mumbling. About 15 feet away, I noticed a man lying in the snow. He was trying to get up but could not.

I went to help. Dropped my briefcase—so many books!— in the snow. Finally I got him up. He was tall and muscular. About 60. So drunk he could not stand by himself. Again, what to do? Somehow I held him up with one arm. Picked up my briefcase with the other. He leaned heavily on me. I wasn't sure I could keep him up. We trudged on, slipping and stumbling. He nearly collapsed a couple of times.

Natasha's house had a high fence along the front. Every house had such a fence for security and privacy. I got to the heavy steel gate. No way could I get him through the gate. I had to let him fall in the snow. I got through and hurried the fifty feet to the door. I knocked hard and fast.

Kyrill, Natasha's older son, opened it. I told him about the man in the snow. All he said was "Oh!" He stepped aside so I could enter. The heat of the house was escaping. He wanted to close the door.

"No, no, Kyrill! The man needs help! Come help me!" He looked annoyed. Finally I got him to come out.

The man was curled up on the snow. Kyrill ran in and got his mother. She came out with him. Again the man was struggling to rise. Couldn't. They saw they had to do something. They ran inside for their hats and coats and rushed back. I was trying to get him up. They managed to do it. Recognized him. A neighbor. Walked him home a block away. I went inside. Vodka is a terrific curse in Ukraine.

They returned. They were taking off their heavy clothes. Natasha turned to me and said. "John, you did good, good thing!" Then she led the way into the kitchen and we sat and had supper.
 I do admit I felt good about it.

**A drunk knocks me over.**
 He really hurt me although no broken bones. What follows is the account that I e-mailed to my family:
 "Hi, everyone. I am getting better but I ran into something bad last night. I finished teaching and walked to the bus stop to catch my ride home. It was about 9:30.
 There were three people there, two men and a woman, all about 35, all drinking beer. They knew one another. Each had a bottle. One man was drunk, the other man was tipsy, and she was happy.
 The drunk finished his bottle and noticed the woman still had some beer. He grabbed her bottle in a fooling-around way and put it to his lips and she, in a fooling-around way, tried to get it back. It escalated.
 I stepped away from them and moved to the edge of the sidewalk. I was looking out anxiously, hoping for the marshrutka when the drunk came reeling and bowled me over and knocked me onto the street. I landed on my right side. I was stunned. I was hurting but nothing seemed broken. Good thing I didn't hit my head. I tried to get up but couldn't.
 The guy who was just tipsy—not the drunk—ran over, reached down and grabbed my coat and tried to lift me up. I yelled "Stop!" I was afraid of him. And I was afraid he would rip my beautiful LL. Bean coat. It was a farewell gift from my friend Ton Coppejans back home.
 He let go and I slumped back down. A few minutes passed, I guess. A flashlight startled me. Three cops were standing over me. They had been passing in a cruiser. They helped me up. Saw that I was hurting. Asked questions. My Russian couldn't handle it. They thought I was drunk! Then they saw I was sober. They looked me over. Brushed some dirt off me.
 I tried to explain; pointed to the three drinkers. They had walked off a few yards and were talking but not looking at me. That was deliberate, I was sure.
 I pointed to them again. I thought the cops would go question them. They did not. That irritated me. They should have gone over and asked some questions. They eased me into their tiny cruiser. I had a card with my address on it. They gave me a ride home, thank God. They had little to say. They had given up questioning me.
 I was now living with my second family. One officer went up to the fifth floor with me. Ira and Slava were shocked to see me. In pain! With the cop! The cop tried to explain. But he had seen so little. It still rankled

that the three of them had done nothing about the drinkers. The cops hadn't even made a single note.

Ira and Slava were very concerned. Kept asking if I was okay. Looked me over. I explained everything to Slava and he explained to the cop. Now the cop made notes. Finally he said goodnight. I said to him. *"Spaciba bolshoi!"* Said it three times. "Thank you very much!" Slava and his mom thanked him also.

I was so grateful to the policeman and his two buddies. How would I have made it home without them?

Ira and Slava helped me to my room. My right shoulder and hip hurt. So did my wrist. I was lucky I hadn't broken something.

Ira made me a cup of tea and hovered over me. I usually ate at this hour. She said she would cook me something. I told her not to bother. I thanked them and said good night.

I undressed and dropped into bed. Did not bother with my pajamas. I ached. Had to lie on my other side. Could not sleep.

In the morning, right after it opened, I called Peace Corps Medical at Headquarters. Dr. Oleksander came on. I knew him. A good guy.

He asked me questions, told me to move my limbs this way and that. "I think you will be all right. You were very lucky." He recommended Ibuprofen pills and ice packs all day long. Lots of rest. Told me to call him the next morning.

Peace Corps had given us a medical kit loaded with stuff. I had the pills but not the ice pack.

Ira made me a nice breakfast and then went out and bought an extra-large bag of frozen peas. She placed it on my shoulder. She left for her office two hours later. I used the bag through the day. Kept putting it in the freezer in between. I could have used three such bags.

By evening I was still sore but better. Those peas now were only fit to be thrown away. Ira came home with fresh fruit and ice cream. I had been living there a while. Fresh fruit was rare. It was the first time I saw her bring home ice cream.

This made me realize that my living with a family was a smart idea. Suppose I had been living alone!

In the morning at 8:05 I called Dr. Oleksander again, as he had asked. He questioned me. He told me he wanted to check me and to come to the office. It was Friday. The office would be closed on Saturday and Sunday. He wanted me to come immediately. It would take three hours each way. I said okay. I was glad he was so attentive.

I rushed and made it to Kyiv by 1 p.m.. It was my first trip there alone. I was anxious about it. I had to take a bus, then a marshrutka, then the jammed Metro, then a walk. I was hurting but I felt the exercise was doing me good. I made it all right.

Dr. Oleksander saw me immediately. "Strip down," he told me. He noticed something. "Your undershirt is inside out!"

"Oh? I was in a rush, I guess."

"Very bad!" he said

"Oh?" I wondered what could be so bad.

"Yes. We Ukrainians believe that will bring very bad luck."

I was amused. But he was totally serious. Ah, cultural differences! He checked me. "I see the bruises on your back. I see how you fell." He called over a colleague, Dr. Yuri Radchuk. About the same age. I had read about him in a Peace Corps write-up about the doctors. He had a lot of orthopedic experience. He had me move my right arm in many ways, checked my hip. I took a liking to him also.

"Nothing is broken. You should be all right."

That was good news.

Dr. Oleksander gave me a brace for my wrist. "You'll have to use this for a while." Told me to continue with the Ibuprofen. Gave me a professional hot/cold pad to apply. Gave me detailed instructions. "Do not worry. You will be okay!"

As I write this weeks later, I can say he was 95% right. My wrist still hurts at times. I think I may have the pain the rest of my days. I'm grateful for his fine care. And to Ira and Slava for their attention and concern.

Finally the two doctors finished with me. I was happy. Felt optimistic. I got an idea. "I'd like to take a picture of the two of you. To show my family. In fact, all of you."

I roped everybody into the picture, including Dr. Valery; Natasha Nikolayeva, the indispensable medical assistant; Dr. Lesya Pasichnic, the female doctor; and Tarek Bushareb, the pharmacist. Arranged them in a nice pose. Snapped the picture. No picture! My battery was dead! They laughed. How I blushed! They forgave me.

Dr. Lesya was a newcomer to the department. I considered it great news when I read about her coming. After all, more than half the Volunteers were women. Like the other doctors, she treated everybody, but the women gravitated to her, of course. I never got to see her professionally but I did have the pleasure of a few words with her in the corridor.

Tarek Bushareb was the youngest, I judged. He was the pharmacist and worked in a cubicle lined with shelves stocked with little bottles and boxes. But he had graduated from medical school in Algiers, was a licensed doctor, and was studying to become a certified radiologist—in fact, he had the long program nearly completed by the time I returned to the U.S.A.

He spoke French fluently (Algeria) and I'd have a little chat with him in French. He enjoyed it also. In fact, he spoke five languages. His wife, Olena, was the travel specialist at Headquarters. I got to speak to her also. A delight.

As I got better, I wondered whether that drunk ever felt sorry for what he did to me. I'll bet he's forgotten it. He did that in just seconds. And I'm still feeling it.

**I get off at the wrong university.**

When I started working at *Coursi*, to return home I had to take a trolleybus about half way and then get off and take an autobus the rest of the way to my street. Then walk about 10 minutes to my home. Not easy, and not pleasant in the winter.

Marina, a fellow teacher, told me about Marshrutka 32. I could get it at the stop right across from *Coursi*. It would take me right to my street. A great improvement. It became my standard way home.

Then I wondered where I could pick up No. 32 to get to the school. I asked a couple of drivers on my rides home but they didn't understand me. Then I wrote the question in Russian for them but couldn't understand what they told me.

At home I asked Ira and her son, Slava. They didn't know but would find out. The next morning I had to go not to *Coursi* but downtown. So I walked to the stop where I could pick up No. 8 trolleybus to do that. A *Marshrutka* 32 stopped by! So this was the stop! I made a note for the next time I went to *Coursi*.

That moment came the next day. I got aboard No. 32. A mile farther, I expected it to take a left. But it took a right. Surprise. We traveled through foreign country for me. We crossed a lake, drove by an army camp, and went on and on to the edge of the city. I saw some of the tiniest houses I have ever seen. This was all new to me.

Now only two of us were still aboard. Now we came to the end of the line. The woman got off but I stayed in my seat. I knew that eventually No. 32 would go back and eventually I would get to my school. I was willing to pay another fare.

Noticing me, the driver told me to get off. I tried to explain. Futile. He pointed firmly to the door. I did not want to get off. I stayed put. How in the world would I get to the school if I were left here? He muttered and pointed again. He was angry. I picked up my bag and got off. There was another No. 32 parked there! Its driver was at the wheel, waiting to start the route. I had not realized there was another.

I got on, paid my fare. We started out. We retraced a good part of the route, then proceeded right across the city. This was better. I recognized this area. I kept looking out. My school was right next to the Technological University. I knew that.

The Technological University was a major landmark. I spotted it and got off at the next stop. But it was not the Technological University! It was another university, unfamiliar to me. It had a similar big blue sign above its door. That's what had confused me.

What to do? I wrote the name of the Technological University in Russian on a paper and showed it to this person and that one coming by. The first ignored me. Another looked but did not know. I showed it to an old lady. *She's as old as I am*, I thought. She was carrying a big bag of groceries. Heavy. She read my note, said "*Da*," and motioned to follow her. How nice.

We walked and walked and walked. There was snow and ice. Difficult. I seemed always three paces behind her. Her body tilted right because of her heavy bag. I stopped a couple of times, hoping for a taxi. She waved for me to keep up. No taxi. We trudged on. cutting through a big housing development.

Where was she taking me? I was limping now. We walked another block and went around a corner. Straight ahead was the Technological University! Hurray! What a relief! She pointed to it and I gave her a thumbs up. Then I worried. Maybe she wouldn't understand what that meant…or maybe it meant something different here…maybe naughty.

No, she understood. She smiled and gave me a thumbs up! Then she turned and began walking away in the direction we had come from. She was still tilting to starboard, poor lady.

It's then that I realized that she had gone out of her way…maybe way, way out of her way…to get me here. Gosh!

That ride and walk had taken me more than two hours. What had happened is that I had started out by taking No. 32 on the wrong side of the street! I should have taken it on the other side.

I tried that the next time. I got to my school in just 10 minutes. Very slowly I was getting to know more about the city. A difficult process.

## I am so late to meet a waiting journalist!

For a long time marshrutkas were a big problem for me. They seemed to have no schedule. One came along when it came along.

One afternoon, a terrible experience. I was due at school at 3 p.m. for an interview by a woman print journalist—a news agency journalist, meaning that her story might appear in not one, but perhaps many papers. Desirable publicity for the school!

I was at my regular stop waiting for Marshrutka 32. Often there were several persons waiting. I was alone again. One marshrutka passed me by. With some empty seats! How to explain it? Ten minutes later, so did another. Then another. Then another! Yes, four of them! Over a period of nearly an hour. All passed me! What was going on? What was I doing wrong? I couldn't understand it.

After the second one went by, my cell phone rang. It was Olena, my dean. She demanded, "John, where are you? She's here! You're late!" I explained. "The marshrutkas keep passing me by! Won't stop!"

Ten minutes later, another call. Olena again. Same scenario. She was upset and angry. I tried to explain. I said, "I know! I know! But it's not my fault, Olena. I don't understand why they don't stop for me. I would take a taxi but no taxi has come by!"

I felt like yelling, "Why don't you send a helicopter for me?" It was as if this were my fault! I hung up. Kept staring up the street, hoping for a marshrutka.

Finally, finally one picked me up. Getting off, I walked double-time. I got to school terribly late. I was out of breath. So anxious.

Olena and the journalist were sipping tea and chatting in her office. The young woman was quite relaxed. Natasha, I believe her name was. They were very cozy.

"Finally!" Olena said to me, glaring. "John! You are so, so late!"

She infuriated me. No word of understanding! No word of sympathy! She made me feel that I had done something wrong. I wasn't a culprit. I was an innocent victim! I was awfully upset, not only by the inexplicable marshrutkas, but her crazy reaction. I was angry. I spoke some sharp words.

Natasha was a witness to all this. Never blinked. What a lady she was. She brushed the incident aside. I calmed down. Olena calmed down. We went ahead with the interview. Olena did the translating back and forth. No idea how accurately she translated me...or whether she embellished. Anyway, at the end Natasha took a picture of me...smiling!

One day Olena showed me Natasha's newspaper. Her picture of me was pretty good. I didn't understand her Russian text but later Lina translated it for me. I liked Natasha's story. Natasha hadn't even hinted about her long wait for me. Or the terrible scene between Olena and me. Later I got good comments about the article.

Olena never brought it up. Neither did I. But I don't think either of us ever forgot it.

**I get to meet Vice President Joe Biden.**

What follows is the e-mail about this big event that I sent home the next morning:

I shook hands with Joe Biden today. Yes, the Vice President of the U.S.A., and in a heartbeat maybe our next President.

I was one of a frenzy of 300 people buzzing around him. One of about 30 who got to shake hnds with him. Lucky me. It was a big moment for me—I can't wait to tell my grandchildren about it.

It happened at the Hyatt Hotel in Kyiv. The Vice President flew in to talk with President Yuvchenko. I was a Volunteer in a group invited to come and meet him.

I am sure I had a much harder time getting to see him than he did me. It took me 35 hours. I got up yesterday at 5. Took a trolley downtown. I was loaded. Had a suitcase on a two-wheel cart and carried a heavy handbag. That little cart was a wonderful plus.

Then took a marshrutka for the miserable two-hour ride to Kyiv. Then the jammed Metro across the city. Not easy getting through the turnstiles and up the long escalators. Then plodded down the long hill to Peace Corps headquarters.

Arrived about noon. Already I was tired and the day was only half done. I was here because Peace Corps wanted to brief us about the Vice President's reception...how to get to it, what was involved, how to behave.

I had gotten a call that 30 Volunteers would be invited. We were nearly 10 that many in Ukraine. Names would be drawn from a hat. I wanted badly to attend. My chance was slim.

What an incredible scene in our Volunteers Lounge at Headquarters as we waited to go see the Vice President. What excitement!

Then came another call. Headquarters had been deluged with requests and had given in. We were all invited. I was so happy. Plus, Peace Corps announced it would spring for our expenses. But some Volunteers were posted too far out. No way they could make it.

Now I learned 130 of us were going! The whole headquarters staff seemed to be involved in getting us ready. What a hubbub. Volunteers were pouring in. Our Volunteers' lounge was wall to wall with backpacks and suitcases. It was an obstacle course.

All six computers in the lounge were in use and Volunteers were signing up to be next. All the plastic cups at the water cooler were long gone and no water left.

Six Volunteers were crowded on one couch. Every chair was occupied, sometimes by two people. Others were sitting on their suitcases, some on the floor. All chatting. All catching up after months apart. All excited. I had brought a brown-bag lunch. Was the envy of many. Some went out looking for a nearby eatery.

Staffers came in and explained things and answered our questions. They didn't have some of the answers. They told us to make sure we looked good. And to be sure we had our ID with us.

I was busy the rest of the day catching up with my colleagues. Soaking up all the gossip I could. Doing this and that. A long day. At 8 p.m. I took the Metro back to the other side of the city to the old Bratislava Hotel. It's high up on a hill. Peace Corps has a deal with it for us Volunteers.

There's a McDonald's at the bottom, a hundred yards from the Metro station. I was famished. I, the vegetarian and perennial dieter, ordered a cheeseburger, fries, and an ice cream cone! The first time I was eating a burger and fries in six months. It was delicious. But I felt guilty. Back on the wagon tomorrow. Then I trudged up to the big Bratislava with all my stuff and got a bed.

It cost 171 hryvnia for a twin-bedded room in the older half of the place. I'd have a roommate. About $15 apiece. Peace Corps was paying for all this. Our round-trip. The hotel. And allowing us a few dollars for street money. These sound like small sums. But these are substantial sums in Ukraine. This was going to be a big expense for Headquarters. But it was a command performance.

My roommate arrived. Geoff. About 40. New to me. Had served as a Volunteer previously. Enjoyed talking, and talked a lot. I enjoyed listening. It was 11 p.m. by the time we turned off the light.

My alarm on my cell phone went off at 5:30 this morning. We had been told to be at the Hyatt by 8:30. I had a problem. I told Geoff I had to go back to Headquarters to do a couple of things. He could sleep longer, and did. I put on my Sunday clothes.

Made sure to have my Peace Corps pin on the lapel of my jacket. Polished my shoes. I had planned to eat at McDonald's. No time. Got to headquarters at 7:15. The security guard who let me in (security was a serious issue…two big steel doors to get through) said I was the first to arrive. I had no time to spare.

Just then Keeley walked in. In her early 20's. I did not know her. She had arrived at midnight after a 14-hour train ride from eastern Ukraine. She was here to see Joe, too, of course. We decided to go to the Hyatt together. First, I had to get to a computer and write out something for one of my bosses. No computer available yesterday. I got it done. Keeley was impatient. She was happy when I said I was ready.

*A grand entrance! For the moment we were not Democrats, Republicans, Independents. We were all Americans! This photo says it all.*

From Headquarters we had to walk up a long, long hill. I'm not the walker I used to be. I was slow. I was careful. I was beginning to breathe hard. I felt that maybe I was doing an unwise thing. Keeley was sympathetic but kept glancing at her watch. Finally we got to the top. I am surprised that I survived to write this.

Then we took a Metro for five stops. Transferred to another line for three stops. Walked half a mile. Again mostly uphill. Arrived at the Hyatt—gleaming modernistic building with a lot of black glass. We saw a long line waiting—waiting but not moving—at the front door. I recognized some Volunteers. It looked just like the opening of a blockbuster movie. I was breathing a bit hard.

It was now 8:42. We were 12 minutes late but no matter. Slowly we moved inside. The Vice President was going to speak at 10:30. This turned out to be just like Super Airport Security! I showed my ID to a guard. Then we had to empty our pockets. Get frisked. It was a big deal.

We were led into a large hall with crystal chandeliers. There seemed to be 300 of us in here. Far too few chairs. Who were all these people? Well, besides us Volunteers, they were all staffers from our American Embassy and USAID. It's one of our big programs here. And important people in the city.

We milled around. I saw people I knew...had not seen them in months...said hello to this one and that one.

I had been hoping there would be food. I had had just four apricots and some crackers at the Bratislava...left-overs from yesterday. Nothing to eat here. Just water.

In gabbing around, I heard good stories and bad stories. Volunteers who were doing all right, enjoying their service, feeling they were doing something worthwhile. One or two who were disappointed, didn't have much to do. Were undergoing hardship. One was thinking of quitting.

I thought this hall was the staging area...we would soon move into an auditorium. No. At exactly 10:30 Joe Biden walked in right here, escorted by a hawk-eyed retinue. He was smiling and waving. All of us cheered and cheered. He was beaming and waving. His escorts were scrutinizing us.

He looked just the way he does on TV. Handsome. Very fit. Slicked white hair. Sun-tanned. Great big smile. He was getting his day's exercise just waving at us!

But it was hard to see him. Such a crowd here. I was way at the rear. Somebody mentioned Joe had flown in on Air Force 2. He had a party of 70 people with him. That's how many it takes. He was staying in a suite priced at $650 a night. It had a gold bathtub. That was the gossip.

He gave a fine talk. So candid. So upbeat. So funny at times. So grave at others. But he was a pro. Knew how to work us.

He said a few words about his mission here. But right now, how happy he was to be with us, all of us here in Ukraine in the service of Uncle Sam. He spoke with sincerity. He made me feel good.

I looked around. Every eye was focused on him. I was sure we weren't all Democrats. No difference. He was our Vice President!

Suddenly he spotted a tiny boy. Barely 2. Scooped him up from his Mom, cooed with him, tried to get him to smile. Looked at us and kidded about it. How come such a little tot was in the room? Unthinkable this might be a staged photo-op....

We had been warned, No candid photos! Apparently nobody heard that. Dozens of cameras were going off. He seemed to love it all.

Now he said he'd allow three questions. I had one. But somebody else was chosen, and then somebody else. He gave good answers. I tried again. He chose somebody else. Then said, "Sorry. Running out of time!"

The question that I wanted to ask? What did the Obama-Biden administration have in mind for Peace Corps: same size, smaller, bigger? The gossip was that we would get a lot bigger. Oh, well. I knew it's always smart to limit the questions. Some might be difficult.

But now he descended and walked in among us! Incredible to see how we all engulfed him. He was gracious. Kept smiling. Shook hands. Kept smiling and waving.

I was standing way back. Dozens of people ahead of me. I surveyed the situation, felt I could edge in from a far side. It worked. I got right up to him and extended my hand. He took it!

"What's your name?" he asked with a smile. "What do you do?"

"John LaPlante. I'm a Volunteer." And added a few more words. I'm sure he was surprised by my obvious age.

"Congratulations! Keep up the good work!" he said. And a few more words. Then reached out to take another hand.

People kept pushing in for pictures with him. Some didn't have a word to say to him. All they wanted was to squeeze in, face a friend holding a camera in hand, and hope for a sensational photo.

Finally it was over. He walked out, his guards squeezing around him. People began streaming away. I was one of the last out. It had lasted about 40 minutes.

It had been a big challenge for me to get here. An even harder one for some of my fellow Volunteers. I would be sleeping in my own bed tonight. Some would still be rocking and bouncing along on a night train.

I was glad I had said yes to the invitation. I had never shaken hands with a Vice President before. Someday I'll be able to tell my grandkids about it. I'll tell them that I got a good impression of Joe.

As I think back now on those many months, so many things turned out to be unexpected! That I would remain in the same city—Chernihiv—all that time.

That, contrary to my assignment, I would never be a teacher at a university. That I would teach not only English, but French. That I would get to live with three different families.

I know we look like old friends catching up. But it's not so.

That in mid-service I would get to go to China! That I would get to write for "Peace Corps Journals" (about this in a chapter coming up). And that while serving in Ukraine, I would get to meet and chat with our Peace Corps national director from Washington, D.C., and with the Vice-President of the United States And this remarkable list stretches on…

Over the following months, I went through many things that surprised me and at times made me a bit smarter and wiser. And one day, I thought, *When I really begin to really feel at home here, I'll bet it will be time for me to get on that plane and go home!* That's the way it turned out.

~ ~ ~

# 26 / Getting thru the holidays

*They're happy...but sad, too. It's true for Volunteers everywhere. It's hard for me, too.*

Thanksgiving! Christmas! New Year's Day! Easter! The Fourth of July! Labor Day! All the holidays that are a big part of our calendar!

I looked forward to each and every one even more than in the U.S., I think. It was easy to get homesick at these times. I loved holidays and holy days back home. Who doesn't?

But here, except for Christmas, each was just another working day. And Christmas here wasn't on December 25. It was 12 days later. So December 25 was just another working day, too. But New Year's was New Year's!

Of course, back home these big days had long become ingrained in my consciousness. For one or more reasons. As an American...family man. Working man...fun-loving man. Here in Ukraine, so far from home in miles and culture, they loomed even larger for me.

But I didn't look forward to them with the excitement and superficiality of youth. I did so with deeper meaning. Each one approached as a milestone not only in my American calendar but my Peace Corps experience. They became magnified in my mind.

As each came up, I harked back to old times. I focused more on my loved ones, current and departed. I missed the festivity of home and family. If anything, being so far away emphasized my family ties, my community roots, my Americanism. My memories of yesteryears became more poignant. And all the more so because I was facing these holidays alone.

I remember how some people back home looked at these days with boredom or irritation. For instance, someone would remark about Christmas, "Oh, I could skip the whole thing!" Or, "I am so glad the holiday is behind me!" about Thanksgiving. I admit I had felt that way at times.

Only during my around-the-world tour for my 75th birthday had I been abroad during several of our holidays. But that was different. I was traveling every few days from city to city and country to country. I

It was exciting to discover what it was like to be away on our big days. So exciting to look forward to every city coming up. New sights, new people, new cultures, new happenings. This is why I had gone off. Besides, I was going to miss them only once.

Now in Peace Corps, it was just the opposite. Day by day I was becoming more used to my new environment, my new work, and my new associates. Every day was less exciting and more humdrum. And the length of my absence from home more significant.

On the other hand, I had the Ukrainian holy days and holidays to look forward to. This was exciting. I wanted to experience them and learn all about them.

**My first Thanksgiving in Ukraine.**

This one was fairly easy. My fellow Trainees and I had been in Ukraine only seven weeks. We were up to our chin in the pressure of Training. The only time we had a few hours to relax was on Sundays. It was study, study, study.

We worried about how to do this or that, how to get here or there in the city on time and safely. How to work out pleasant relationships with our training staff, host family, even one another. How to make the most of our time. And how to remain in touch with those back in the U.S.A.

Besides, because being in Peace Corps was so challenging for me and so exciting for my family and friends back home, there were frequent e-mails back and forth, often daily ones. "How are you doing?" someone would ask me. "What's happening?" "Tell me all your news!" It was a pleasure to oblige.

So we Volunteers were far from home but still in the loop. That was true for me, anyway. We were so much better off than Volunteers of a decade or two earlier who were truly isolated—no Internet! Only slow stamped mail! I wondered how they had managed. And also fellow Volunteers right now in really backward countries in Africa, say. Ukraine was certainly not backward in that sense.

Thanksgiving would be an official Peace Corps holiday for us, of course. No classes! No studying! But just an ordinary work day for Ukrainians.

It was amazing how many of us Trainees got the same idea. A simple idea. To celebrate Thanksgiving with our host families and teach them something about this grandest of all American holidays.

I call it the grandest because it seems to become part of all of us, regardless of our color or religion or ethnic origin or birth culture and language. To my mind, it is also our most universal holiday and most distinctively American. Don't you agree?

The following are some of the things I heard Trainees saying as Thanksgiving grew closer.

"Where do you think I can find cranberry sauce?"

Or, "I'm going to roast a turkey for the family I'm living with. And make my Mom's favorite stuffing!"

Or, "I'm going to steam and butter some cabbage! These folks eat it always grated, always raw!"

Like my fellow Trainees, I was living with a family busy in the workaday world. Thanksgiving Thursday would be just another work day for them. Natasha would be painting in somebody's house and Kyrill would be attending classes at his university. Sick little Nakita would be staring at the TV set. No way could there be a genuine, relaxed Thanksgiving for us.

So for our Thanksgiving we would eat in the evening as usual. Despite my good intentions I wasn't up to cooking a whole Thanksgiving dinner for them, and I didn't have the skills.

The best I could do would be to provide special treats. Maybe cranberry relish. Maybe a pumpkin pie. If I could find them. And tell them about our American traditions…recount how the Pilgrims and Massasoit Indians sat down together to a true "thanksgiving dinner" after a harsh winter of death and suffering.

This in my own Massachusetts where I lived and worked for 40 years! Only a two-hour drive from where the Pilgrims first landed, on the now-enshrined Plymouth Rock.

Thanksgiving arrived. I was alone at home with little Nikita. No studying Russian today! I slept late. Tidied my room. Had a peanut butter sandwich and banana for lunch. I grinned when I thought about that. Then I took a bus to the Dba Gucia, our hang-out. I hoped to run into some of my young colleagues. Not one. I had my tea and pastry and sat forlornly in a corner. I didn't linger.

Then, watching the clock, I walked to the Post Office, strode into the big room with the two cashiers and the 20 phone booths. It was 5:30 p.m. It would be 10:30 a.m. on the Atlantic coast and early morning in California—my best time to reach everybody.

I went to a cashier. My Russian was not up to a conversation. I gave her three 100-*hryvnia* bills—approximately $60—and said, "*Cay Shay Ahh*"—"U.S.A." In fact, I had scribbled the three Cyrillic letters for her. She wrote "6" on the slip, gave it back, and pointed to Booth 6. I went in, closed the door, and began calling.

I called milady Annabelle and my family all over the country. I was lucky. In all those calls I had only one miss. I got only the answering machine at my son Arthur's in Florida. That was a disappointment—I missed them, him, my daughter-in-law Marita, and my three grandchildren there. I left an upbeat message.

I reached everyone else. I had only good news for them, and they had only good news for me. We got all caught up. How wonderful it all was. I felt terrific. Aglow. It put me in the Thanksgiving spirit!

The cashier gave me about half my deposit back. About $25. If I had known that, I would have talked longer.

One thing had amused me. They all told me the same thing: "Dad, your voice is coming in so clear! It's like you're just next door!"

When young I used to think my voice traveled over the phone lines. Why wouldn't I think that? Seemed logical. It was years later that I learned our voices get converted into electronic pulses, and then re-created into our voices at the other end. Another miracle of technology!

When I got back to Natasha's, the three of them were sitting shoulder to shoulder on the couch and watching their programs. Just another evening. I sat with them and told them about my calls home to everybody and some items of my good news. They were happy for me.

I went to bed early. No Russian vocabulary tonight! I hugged my pillow and wallowed on nice memories from family Thanksgivings of years ago. And a sad one or two, I admit. Such is life. I was thankful to be a Volunteer. But I'd be more thankful when Training finished.

Christmas far from home.

December 25, our Christmas, was just another working day for us Trainees. Ukrainians celebrate Christmas on January 6. It is a big day for them—a holiday and holy day, in fact.

They are far more homogeneous than we. They derive from the same Slavic stock, the same centuries-old culture. They are all caught up in the same problems and aspirations of their homeland.

All bound up in their common memories of oppression and hardship for so many centuries. All involved right up to their nostrils in surviving in their suddenly free and independent but hugely burdened new republic.

We Americans by the nature of our country are wildly more heterogeneous. We practice an incredible assortment of religions. We are hot and cold about Christmas. For some of us Christmas is Christ's birthday. For many, a big gift-giving day with good and bad aspects. For others, a day just to be ignored and suffered through.

The Ukrainians have a widespread and fervent interest in their January 6 Christmas. This intrigued me. Ukrainians as citizens of the Soviet Union practiced atheism, which was the official line. Or pretended to. No God!

Religion went underground. Yet people told me that in remote villages some people managed to keep their ancient churches open and to worship in them. Their religion never got quashed. People in the cities also tried to preserve the religious aspect, but had to veil it in whatever they did.

For most people, it was dangerous to admit being a believer. The best way to success...to a decent life...was through membership in the Communist party, which was open only to a few.

Communists had to believe and support the Communist Manifesto...had to be followers of Marx and Lenin...had to toe the line...had to reject religious faith and profess atheism. Some did so sincerely. Others put on a show. I met one or two who said matter of factly, "We had to go along. It was the only way."

I got to meet atheists but they seemed few. One was one of my favorite teachers at *Coursi*. She told me, "John, I don't believe in God. Or a god. My family does not believe. It is that simple."

As their Christmas approached, I saw a great excitement in the people. Even my friend the atheist was caught up in the excitement. She smiled. "It is our culture!"

A bigger day for them is January 1, New Year's Day. This is when everybody makes merry. When millions see the New Year come in. This is when Grandfather Frost fluffs up his long white hair, puts on his red suit and hat, and comes visiting the children with his big bag of gifts.

On December 25 and January 1, my thoughts kept drifting back to the U.S.A. I thought of my loved ones' Christmas celebrations and then New Year's celebrations. I missed them all. Truth is, my loved ones were so dispersed across the country from the Atlantic to the Pacific that even if I were back there, I would not be able to be with most of them.

It had been many years since we had been together as a family. But again, being so far away in such a different country made those two big days all the more significant to me.

First, about Christmas—our Christmas, meaning December 25.

I had it much in mind and I kept getting reminders from across the Atlantic. I received e-mails and cards from family and friends. The Internet emphasized to me how old-fashioned slow-mail is. An e-mail arrived in seconds.

But it took 10 to 15 days for a letter to get here, and that was by air. Some folks back home didn't realize this. My Christmas mail arrived much later. And the only envelopes that reached me were the ones mailed directly to Chernihiv—not forwarded through Deep River.

Some parcels took much longer than that. Sometimes four to six weeks! A good thing nobody was sending me a home-made cake. Always a delight however late something arrived, of course.

Yes, December 25 was just an ordinary day in Ukraine, with shops open and everybody working. But it was the winter school-vacation time, so as a teacher I had days off. I went to the Korolenko Library every morning to work on my projects, including my writing.

So on Christmas, off to the library I went. Closed! How come? Then I remembered: this was the last Tuesday of the month. The library always closed on the last Tuesday. To clean, straighten out the books on the shelves and get caught up on odds and ends. Disappointing! What to do?

Well, I took a walk to the bazaar. Always a lot of fun. Hundreds of stalls, selling anything and everything. All of them one-man shops, Correction: one-woman shops mostly. It was a cold but pleasant day. I had little to buy. I strolled and looked and enjoyed the crowds.

But to me this was Christmas! I was thinking of home! Of milady Annabelle and my family. Of friends. Of good old days. Of people now gone. It all weighed on me. So I began rationalizing—if I were at home, I would be with only one or two anyway. Or: I knew this was part of the deal when I signed up for Peace Corps!

Still I felt depressed. Then I got a good idea— to call *Coursi*. Dean Olena answered. I mentioned that this was Christmas back home and the Korolenko was closed!

"John, come here with us," she said instantly, with zero hesitation.

Again I appreciated her thoughtfulness and generosity. I hurried and spent the afternoon there. Very happily. I had a lot to do and the spare computer was all mine.

At 4 p.m. Olena and Lina invited me to have dinner with them in the restaurant downstairs. I jumped at it. Again, so thoughtful.

They did not have Christmas on their mind. This was just another day for them. We did talk a bit about Christmas in the United States. I told them about the Christmas morning my father had given each of his three grandchildren—my Arthur, Monique, and Mark—an envelope with a $100 bill in it. A big sum back them.

He had started a beautiful fire in the fireplace. We were in a sea of torn wrapping paper. How somehow the envelopes with the checks in them had gotten tossed into the fireplace and had gone up in flames. Olena and Lina gasped with horror. Then howled. I did also. Now. Not funny back then!

After dinner, I kissed both of them on the cheek. "You have been so wonderful! Thank you!"

Then I rushed to the big Post Office telephone office. I was lucky. Few were in line. I called everybody in the U.S., just as I had on Thanksgiving. Again I had only good news for them. Ditto they. This time I reached my son Arthur and his family. Perfect.

This hour on the phone turned out to be the best part of my Christmas. Just as I had hoped. I went home to Natasha's content. I felt only a pinch of homesickness. I thought about that. I was becoming accustomed to Peace Corps and to my life in Ukraine.

My first New Year's Day. In Ukraine, New Year's Eve is a big deal. Just the way it is for us. The whole country stays up to watch the New Year come in. Ira and her son, Slava, planned a big dinner at midnight. I am not a night owl, so prudently I went to bed at 8:30 p.m. "Please knock on my door at 11," I told Slava.

He did and I slicked up. They were in the living room, on the couch, staring at the TV, which was on loud. Right in front was the coffee table crowded with dishes of food and bottles of wine and spirits. They were watching a New Year's Eve count-down, à la New York Times Square.

It was not Times Square. It was Independence Square in Kyiv. I had been there…huge open plaza, the tall, glorious monument in the center, grand buildings all around.

It was packed with thousands. Jumping with joy. Mostly young people, as in New York. A huge band was playing on a great stage. Some of Ukraine's most ravishing young women in knock-out outfits were exulting in lavish dance numbers.

The emcee was keeping everyone properly excited as the clock ticked its way out of 2007 and into 2008. Then midnight! Cheering! Fireworks! In fact, local fireworks were also going off right outside our windows! Shhh! Boom! Boom! On and on!

Then right away the President of Ukraine came on. Handsome man. Brilliant red necktie. He spoke for 15 minutes or so, seriously, optimistically. I could not understand, of course, but I had a good idea. "What's he saying exactly?" I asked Slava.

"Oh, that everything is going to be okay. That the government has good plans for us. It's the same baloney every year!" He didn't use that word. He used a cruder one.

Now it was time for New Year's dinner. But we had to wait for daughter Olya and Viktor, her fiancé. She lived with him. They were detained. It was 1 a.m. when they arrived. They walked in with two friends from Moscow—boisterous Yvan, and his girlfriend, Natasha, a nice quiet person. Pretty. About 30.

We had a merry dinner. Lots of talk and laughter. Lots of eating. Lots of drinking, which meant lots of toasting. Viktor and his friend Yvan went to town on the bottles. First, a bottle of whisky. Then, a bottle of vodka. Amazing how many times they filled their glasses and proposed a toast. To Family! To Good Health! To Prosperity. To Success. To America! The last was for me, of course.

I worried how the four would make it home with Viktor driving. They did not look drunk, to my surprise. "That's because we eat a lot between glasses," Slava told me.

Olya sensed my concern. "It's okay," she said. Yes, she said "Okay." Then, "We will call a taxi to take us home!"

Viktor usually drove them over. They had come by taxi. Good thinking. It also made me aware they planned to get high.

I made an excuse and went to bed at 3 a.m. The dinner went on. I glanced at Ira as I said *"Dobrie noche!"* "Good night!" She looked drained with fatigue. She had worked all day getting all this ready. But she was gallantly sticking it out.

**The next morning** was New Year's, of course. All three of us slept late, naturally. Ira served a big holiday breakfast. The centerpiece was the wonderful pudding that she discovered I liked so much. Thoughtful, as usual.

Then she and Slava went and relaxed in the living room (her bedroom) and I went to my room. I stretched out on my narrow bed. My thoughts quickly drifted to America and family and friends. Yes, I was homesick.

I fixated on one memory. On New Year's afternoon we met at my Aunt Bernadette's and Uncle Jack's. They had no children. We were their children. After dinner we'd sit in their living room, the younger ones on the floor.

Uncle Jack would begin playing his old 33's from the Forties and Fifties. We knew all the songs. It was a wonderful tradition. It wouldn't have been New Year's Day without it. Aunt Bernadette had passed on. He was now 97 in the Rhode Island Veterans Home. I got up from my bed. Had to change my ideas.

I took a marshrutka downtown and spent a couple of hours at Ukretelecom. I sent e-mails, got e-mails, replied to e-mails. Always a pleasure coming here. I was tempted to call my family but I had called just a week earlier. Anyway, the time difference was a problem.

Then I took a walk around the city center. Very cold and very gray. Some ice, but the sidewalks were quite clear. I squeezed my fingers in my mittens to warm them. My mood was totally somber. I gravitated to our McDonald's. The only one in the city.

It was crowded as usual. I knew I was the only American. This thought emphasized my isolation. It was at moments like this that I'd love to have two or three other Volunteers around. Even if they were Americans from Nebraska or Mississippi or Alaska. At least they would be fellow countrymen, and that would be a comfort, despite our different accents and even cultures.

I rarely went to McDonald's. I liked the place...I liked a cup of coffee and an ice cream cone...and it was so tangibly American. But I didn't go often because I couldn't stand the music, which was always on, always loud, and always impossible. Well, to my ears. Now the customers were four thick at the counter. A long wait. I made a U-turn and walked out.

I spotted one of the roving coffee ladies with the big insulated hot-water bottles. And settled for a throw-away plastic cup of coffee from her. Then I strolled and nosed around in a few shops, just to see something different and kill time. I had my family back home on my mind. Wonderful old memories kept flashing up. And so the afternoon passed.

At 7 p.m. I took Marshrutka No. 8 home. I had to stand most of the way again, of course. I walked the final quarter mile home. I was alone on the street. The cold was crisp, but no wind, so quite pleasant.

Ira was finishing her cooking for dinner. She gave me a smile and told me dinner would be in 20 minutes. I joined her and Slava at the table. Her dinner was very good, though as usual I ate some dishes and skipped others. I worried this would offend them, but if it did, they never showed it. We talked. Only because Slava was at the table. Without him it was impossible.

I went to my room around 9. I did what I do every New Year's Day. I wrote down my successes during the past year, and then my disappointments. Quite short, my list of disappointments, fortunately. And as usual, I wrote out my goals for the New Year. I call them goals, not resolutions. I feel this emphasizes them more.

Then I went to bed and picked up Ned Follett's "The Man from St. Petersburg." I had found it at the Korolenko. I was two-thirds through the novel. A compelling tale with lots of Russian history thrown in. Excellent. I became engrossed. Which is exactly what I needed.

Our Easter, and theirs....

I grew up in a Catholic home and went to Catholic schools for 16 years before university. So I was familiar with Easter ...Lent ...Good Friday ...Easter!

I remember how for Easter, Maman would outfit all of us in beautiful brand-new clothes for this holy day. Then we'd walk so proudly to Easter Mass at Our Lady of Consolation Church. Communion! The choir giving their all! My mother went only because of my father...he was very devout.

Afterward, the Easter Parade! We'd walk around and meet all our neighbors and compare our Easter outfits, of course. Many snapshots of all of us in our beautiful duds. Our big Easter dinner, as elaborate as for Thanksgiving. Oh, in the morning we had all gotten up early—no prodding necessary—to check our Easter baskets with the chocolate bunnies and candy eggs. What fun.

Now in Ukraine, I was eager about the approaching Orthodox Easter. It's observed on a different Sunday than ours—they have a different liturgical year. I saw how excited people were about Pascha, as they called it.

I got very lucky. My landlady Ira and her son Slava invited me to go to church with them. Later I found out it was just about the only service they attended during the year. Here is what I wrote about it in an e-mail home that evening:

Today is Easter. Orthodox Easter! It is the most holy day of the year. More important than Christmas. People are really worked up. *"Kristos vospres! Kristos vospres!"* They are saying it to one another. "Christ is risen! Christ is risen!" What fervor!

Ira, Slava, and I got up at 4:30 and took a taxi to Holy Trinity Church for 6 a.m. Very rare to take a taxi. A very special day. What a huge and beautiful church. Many Orthodox churches in the city. This is the oldest and most revered, 16$^{th}$ century, with big golden domes!

Hundreds of people coming and going, every woman carrying a big wicker basket. It is to hold their special Easter bread, blessed by a priest. Many baskets also have Easter eggs, beautifully hand-painted, mind you. And a big fat sausage or two. And a nice bottle of vodka, of course.

Enormous church, jammed with people, young and old. Large paintings all around of saints and holy fathers of centuries ago, all with white beards and opulent robes.

Everybody is holding a lighted candle. What a sight. Hundreds of candles flickering in the dark church. Everybody is walking from one saint to another all around the church, pausing to say prayers and ask for blessings.

Some people had been there all night. Priests, old and young but all with a beard, walked around in their gorgeous vestments. They kept spraying holy water on us and crying, *"Kristos vospres! Kristos vospres!"* And the faithful kept responding, "So he is! So he is!" Very emotional. The priests seemed to enjoy spraying people.

Atheism was the official line in the Soviet world. Well, the religious spirit certainly survived nicely. Very vibrant today.

We walked out of the church and found it was a beautiful morning. Sunny. Blue sky. Dandelions. Couldn't be nicer. We were surrounded by faithful. Hundreds of them. All with their Easter basket. Ira made a suggestion and we said yes—to visit the nearby Patriotic Memorial Park.

We walked to it. It covers a beautiful green hill with great steps leading to the top. Hundreds of steps. As we approached, we fell in with many others going there. We walked up. A hard climb but we made it. Numerous others like us up there. In fact, a crowd.

In front of us was the sacred tomb of an Unknown Soldier (known only to God, as they say) of the Great Patriotic War (World War II to us).

The Eternal Flame burned on in his honor and that of countless others who were killed. More prayers. So appropriate on this Easter morning. A thought came to me: *We and the Soviets were allies in that war. Then the terrible Cold War followed and suddenly we were enemies. How ironic. War! How horrible.*

**P**riests here also. Again in their flamboyant vestments. Prayers. Chanting. The faithful sidled up to them, a few daring to touch their vestments.

Ukraine was no longer part of the U.S.S.R., of course. In fact, the two were increasingly bickering and standing back at arm's length. But I sensed an expansive cloud of fervor over the hill...patriotic, religious, and cultural.

A fantastic view of the city from up here. Very pretty right now with all the trees in leaf and the flowers. Then home we went for the big Easter dinner. So many people that we had to walk a long way before we managed to catch a marshrutka back.

I rested for an hour in my room. Then Slava knocked on my door, "John, dinner!"

Just the three of us in the kitchen. First, the holy bread. Ira cut a slice for each of us. She did it with solemnity. And we ate it with solemnity. Joyful solemnity. This was all new to me. I was going along with them. The table was covered with beautiful foods. The mood lightened.

There was enough food to last the week. All cooked by Ira, of course. This is what was expected of her. All week long she was a hard-charging little entrepreneur, but right now she was in her true role, her exalted role. Mother! We finished with chocolates. Those and the wine had been my contributions.

Then, dinner was over. "Thank you!" I said to her. I felt so privileged to have been invited. I returned to my room for a nice long nap. So good to put aside the cares of the workaday world for a bit. I got up in a while and noticed Ira and Slava were napping also. A perfect ending.

So, apart from the military observance, it was much like our Easter back home. Ignore the details, and so many things are the same all over the world. That's because we are all so much alike. That's what I've found.

I was struck by the gravity and solemnity. So many died...families torn apart.

**O**h, one more thing. Every such holiday made me pause and count how many months and days I had already served in Ukraine, and how many more until I finally flew home.

In fact, all my daily journal entries started with the day and the date and an extra notation.

For instance, I just opened my 2009 Journal at random and this is the entry that I found: Sunday, May 3 (Day 123 / 573). This meant that it was day 123 of 2009 and Day 573 of my service in Ukraine.

But I had another number fixed in my mind—622! Yes, 622 was the total days that I would be spending as a Volunteer in Ukraine.

I didn't like the idea of wishing my life away, but I was delighted to see this number 573 get bigger and bigger...and closer and closer to 622!

It's not that I regretted signing up. No, not at all. It was just a growing, yearning desire for home, sweet home. I was an American, more than ever.

**M**y English Club members enjoy an unusual Fourth.

In my second year, the Fourth fell on Saturday, so we celebrated it at my English Club on Sunday. Some of the members did not know a thing about our Independence Day.

I made sure our discussion was all about the founding of our country and its growth and its major role in the world today.

I told them, "In the United States, we are all immigrants, or the children of immigrants, or the descendants of immigrants. My father and mother were immigrants from Québec in Canada. People of all races and colors and religions and talents. There are just a few other countries like the U.S.A. in the world. Canada is one. Australia is another. Both fine countries. But no other country has done it on such a huge scale."

I paused. "Do you know that we have millions of Americans of Ukrainian descent?"

A few realized it. But my saying "millions" startled them all.

I continued. "I know you think the United States is Heaven!" Some laughter. "It is not Heaven. Your country has many problems. My country has many problems. Problems are part of life.

"Somehow we have become a very fine country. We have wonderful freedoms. Most of our people live well. It is possible for people to move up in life, which is hard to do in many other countries. Sometimes impossible. But we also have poor people. And people without homes. Yes, we do.

"But one thing is true. The United States is the country that most people in other countries who want a better life desire to move to! How many of you would like to live in the U.S.A.?"

More than half put up a hand. I was not surprised. Then I asked them, "Why?" This led to a discussion. This pleased me. Discussions were the essence of our club. Discussions in English! At the end I emphasized one thing one more time. "We are not Heaven! Stop thinking that it is. There is no Heaven on earth."

After that, we all took off for a party at Wayne's house. They had never experienced anything like that. An American cook-out! But I told you about this back in Chapter 16.

My final holiday in Ukraine was Thanksgiving. My second Thanksgiving here! It turned out to be very different. As I mentioned, every year two groups of Trainees came to Chernihiv for their training.

Yes, Thanksgiving was just another workday, so the Trainees attended classes. Previous groups had held a communal Thanksgiving dinner late on Thursday afternoon at a local school. Each would bring something from home for the dinner. It was very relaxed. Toasts. Jokes. Singing. Gossip.

Now a new group of Trainees had arrived. I told them about the past Thanksgiving dinners together. They liked the idea. But they were so pressed for time that the best they could do was a party at Marconi's, a local pizzeria. I was invited and I was grateful. And so was milady Annabelle, who was visiting me. I was struck by how young most of these Trainees were—in their early 20's. There was only one other couple over age 60.

There were about 25 of us. We sat face to face at a long table. Limited opportunity to socialize. Those around us were all youngsters. We found little to talk about. Yes, it was pleasant being together on this holiday. After all, we were all Volunteers. But that was all that we had in common.

We had a beer. Pizza, of course. The two of had just one piece because we'd be sitting down to dinner at home with my host mother Tanya in just two hours.

The young woman at my left was working on her laptop! After just 20 minutes we noticed the older couple saying goodbye. We were just marking time here. We soon left. As well-intentioned as it was, this get-together missed being Thanksgiving dinner by a mile.

Our real Thanksgiving dinner was scheduled for the following Sunday. We were invited to my expat friend Rich's for the traditional dinner. He had gone to the U.S.A. He had told me, "I'll bring back a nice big turkey again. Better than any turkey in Ukraine!" He had done this last year, too.

But he had so many purchases to lug back that he had skipped buying the turkey. Three days before our dinner, he called and said, "John, no problem! I'll have a beautiful roast chicken. With the stuffing, the mashed potatoes, everything! It will be wonderful!"

Of course. The turkey wasn't so important. It was being together in the Thanksgiving Day spirit.

But then a scheduling conflict arose. So Sunday became Monday. It was going to be just for the three for us. But when Annabelle and I arrived, he introduced us to three friends. All strangers to me. Sasha was a young man who was a professional soccer player. The two women were in their 30's. Pretty.

Rich said, "They are my masseuses. They come and do me just about every week." He noticed my bewilderment and added, "Yes, together. "

It sounded interesting. He had never mentioned that.

I think Sasha also was meeting the gals for the first time. It turned out that Sasha knew a few words of English. The two gals did not. It did have a crippling effect on our dinner.

Rich was meeting Annabelle for the first time. She had been very good to him. When he heard she was coming to Ukraine, he asked if she could bring him a bottle of his favorite hot sauce. "Sure!" Then he changed his order to three bottles. "No problem!"

Then he asked for some Drake's Cakes. "I love them!"

So Annabelle went shopping but couldn't find any Drake's Cakes. She reported to him, "They're available only east of the Mississippi."

Okay. Then he asked me, "Well, can she bring two boxes of orange-flavored Alka Seltzer tablets for colds?"

This had become so complicated that soon he was dealing directly with Annabelle through e-mails.

She brought them all. I mention this only to show you what an interesting guy Rich is and a nice lady Annabelle is.

He did serve a good dinner, and he made it all. A golden, juicy chicken. Thick mashed potatoes—mashed with the peels on, as usual. Buttered corn. Delicious stuffing.

I provided a can of whole-berry cranberry sauce! I had been saving it a long time for the occasion—sent to me by one of my children. And a box of fancy chocolates and a bottle of Georgian wine.

I, the vegetarian, got along without the chicken. But Annabelle dug right in and enjoyed everything. She told him, "You're a fine cook, Rich!" He beamed, of course. And rightly so.

For dessert, he came up with his usual wonderful extravaganza. Huge portions of chocolate ice cream drenched with Hershey's chocolate syrup.

He had plenty of stories to amuse us, thank God. He was a marvelous story-teller. We chuckled and laughed and I supplied a few of my own. I don't think our new Ukrainian friends got to enjoy them much, limited in English as they were. But they nodded and approved and smiled a lot. And obviously they loved the dinner.

It was all very nice. Rich deserved every compliment we gave him. But again it was not Thanksgiving Dinner. Yet when I looked at my watch, I was surprised how long we had been at the table. It was dark outside!

We took a taxi home. On the way, I said to Annabelle. "Next year we'll have a real Thanksgiving!"

For sure. My Peace Corps service would be done and I'd be home!

Throughout my service I was lucky in that I got to observe every one of our American holidays and was the recipient of genuine hospitality. What could be nicer than that?

Yet every one of them was a reminder that I was an American at heart and would go home proud and pleased about my service. But so glad to be re-entering American life on our own shores.

And in America, I would tell stories about the Ukrainian holidays and holy days I got to experience and enjoy.

~ ~ ~

***Did you know*** ... that during your service you will most likely have more than one job? Concurrently. At least that's how it was in Ukraine.

You will have your officially assigned job, and you will be urged to undertake another job, or even more than one, that you dig up for yourself. Something significant, of course.

As you'll see in these pages, I found several. It made my life very interesting.

# 27 / I meet the PC doctors

*I get to see them for this thing and that.*
*And then, two emergencies come up!*

**O**ver my 27 months, I got to see our M.D.'s in Kyiv for a variety of reasons—often enough to get on a first-name basis with all of them. Far more often than I thought I would. I have already told you about the care I received after being knocked over by the drunk.

The doctors were all Ukrainian nationals, as I've explained. Graduates of Ukrainian medical schools. At first I admit I had a reservation or two. I wondered, *How good are they?* Hey, wouldn't you ask the same thing? Well, that got quickly resolved. After a few months I decided they were very good. More than that, I became impressed by their cheerful attitude and their obvious determination to do a good job. I got to like every one of them.

They had a dual approach. First, they were ready to handle any problem that came up. Second, they emphasized preventive care—what to do to maintain our good health and avoid problems. They drummed this into us all the time with pep talks and how-to demonstrations.

Please don't get the wrong impression. I never became a big problem for the doctors. I never became sick during my Peace Corps time. I never lost more than a two of work time. But I did have to go to Medical for a variety of things.

And like all the other Volunteers, I had to go through the various physicals that were scheduled for us at intervals, get shots for this and that, receive reminders to take certain procedures and behave in certain ways. We all heard from the doctors in person. And there were often medical notices to all of us included in our weekly e-letter from Headquarters. I found it impressive.

As you know, it took me months to get into Peace Corps. Over and over during that time, I heard that Volunteers get top care. I got this from the Peace Corps recruiters and the Peace Corps advertising materials. Of course I felt that this might be inflated marketing buzz. I got to see that Peace Corps kept its word.

If you remember, Peace Corps put me through all kinds of medical tests before clearing me for service. That's when I got to see for real that Peace Corps Medical was exacting and thorough.

Then in my more than two years of service I got to have sufficient experience with our doctors for one thing or another that I became sure that our care was indeed excellent.

And it was all free, mind you. Even the medications. Even the outside consultations that were arranged for me were free.

I had excellent coverage before I entered Peace Corps. As a retiree, I had been covered by the Medicare umbrella, of course. Additionally I got fine coverage through Blue Cross / Blue Shield Medex. I was one lucky senior citizen!

Peace Corps assured me that I could suspend the Medex coverage while in service, and could resume it without penalty after leaving Peace Corps. You can be sure that I ascertained that that was totally true! It was.

*I got to know these doctors well, found them good: from left, Dr. Valery, Dr. Yuri, and Dr. Oleksander. Dr. Lesya was excellent also. She wasn't available when I took this photo.*

And when I returned to private life, I did get my precious Medex coverage back. All it took was a routine letter from Peace Corps.

In every country where Peace Corps serves, it guarantees medical care for its Volunteers. In a tiny country, it may be one doctor or a physician's assistant or a nurse practitioner. With 300 Volunteers, Ukraine was Peace Corps' biggest deployment and had the largest medical department.

You know now about its four doctors (one a woman) and its pharmacist and office manager. All spoke English, but as a second language. Impressively good English, I must say.

In time I learned that this intensive coverage was the main reason I was assigned to Ukraine. As you know, I expected to go to a country where French was important.

**W**ell, when Peace Corps began its Fifty Plus Program for older men and women, it reasoned they would need a wider range of medical services to back them up. It would be smart to send them to countries where such were available. They developed a list of ten. It included Ukraine.

In an earlier chapter, I described the extensive medical and dental tests Peace Corps put me through to enlist. Later, from other older Volunteers I heard similar stories. All the tests that were ordered for them. All the money they had to spend for these tests.

Peace Corps wanted to be as sure as possible that those chosen would survive the 27 months without creating big medical problems, losing work time, and running up huge bills for Uncle Sam.

One woman, 55, told me she had paid $1,600 for dental work before Peace Corps let her in. Another woman, a Ph.D. who had been a professor, said to me, "It took me two years! The testing went on and on. I kept telling Peace Corps, 'I am 70! Of course everything about me won't be perfect!'" Another woman told me she had to spend thousands of dollars for two super-tech hearing aids.

It seems over the years Peace Corps had learned it had to be prudent in selecting Volunteers.

My first experience with Medical in Ukraine came during our initial orientation at the Post-Graduate Institute right after arriving. I told you about that.

That is when I met Dr. Valery Gontarenko, the senior doctor, and Dr. Oleksander Gonta, about 35, I thought. My medical record was reviewed and I was told about the medical department in Kyiv and given a couple of inoculations. It was a promising introduction.

**I** saw Dr. Oleksander for the second time during Training. He came for a day to brief us. How to stay healthy. He had a great variety of tips and suggestions.

He focused heavily on HIV/AIDS. The rate of infection in Ukraine was very high. He said, "An essential way is to engage in safe sex! Really safe sex! Take no chances!"

There were 15 of us in the room, and most were gals, of course.

At one point he opened a box, took out something, and plunked it on the table. Gasps! Astonishment! It was a model of a phallus, stiffly erect, plus its testicles, in plastic but vividly realistic in every detail!

He opened a box of condoms and placed it next to the phallus. Then he said, "I want each of you to take one of these condoms and come here and learn how to put it on properly!"

He pointed to a gal. She got up with great embarrassment. He handed her a foil envelope. She unwrapped it, took out the condom, and set to work. She was blushing. She started with the condom wrong side out, which drew some laughs. Finally she finished the job.

"This is not a joking matter," Dr. Oleksander said. "You're doing this right could be a matter of life or death."

Then he called upon another Volunteer, and another, and another. Some did the job easily, which drew some titters. Some were awkward. But was this feigned?

My turn was coming up. I was going to be a good sport certainly. Then Dr. Oleksander looked at his watch. "That's enough," he said. "You're doing all right. I have other things to talk about."

Thus was I spared. But I had noticed something. "Dr. Oleksander!" I said. "But people have to be very careful after intercourse! If they are not careful in removing the condom, a bad accident can result!"

"Yes, of course." And he talked about that. Everybody in the room had listened with total attention, which was good.

Twice at other times when I met him, he thanked me for mentioning that. "I talk about that every time now!"

He came back several weeks later. This time it was to explain to us how to preserve our emotional health. He stressed that ours were challenging assignments and the risk of emotional illness was serious. He gave practical, down-to-earth advice. I paid a lot of attention. I think everybody in the room did. Already we were all under stress. We needed all the advice we could get.

I mention all this again to show you how thorough Peace Corps was and how it tried hard to cover all the bases.

Oh, one more thing I must mention. On the very day Dr. Oleksander had told me to come to Kyiv to be examined, I felt something tiny—something strange—in my mouth. A tiny screw! I had had dental implants. Loved them. This screw belonged to one. Gosh! I tucked it away safely.

**W**hat to do? I called Dr. Oleksander again. Immediately. "Incredible coincidence," I said, and explained it all.

He said, "We'll get you into a dental clinic tomorrow. After we finish with you. Your timing is perfect!"

And right after treating me for my injuries, he gave me directions to the clinic. He had made an appointment for me.

I thought I'd have to find my way to the dental clinic by Metro and then on a trolley. I worried about that. To my surprise, a Peace Corps driver took me right to the door. The clinic was very high-tech. Its dozen dentists served the business and international community in the capital. It was my impression Peace Corps sent all Volunteers to it.

I was assigned to Dr. Viktor. About 35, I'd say. I was delighted that he spoke good English. I got a good opinion of him the first time

"Not a big problem," he said, examining my mouth. Quickly he screwed it back in.

"What would have happened if I had lost it?"

"We would have ordered one. No problem."

"This one I got in California. Would the replacement have had to come from there? What would I have done during all that time?"

My questions went unanswered. So I said to him, "Can you cement it in so this won't happen again?"

"No. If we had to take it out, we would not be able to.'"

"Can you make it very tight?"

"Yes." And he applied so much torque I thought something might snap. Nothing did.

"Can you take a look at my other teeth while I'm here?"

He did, and found a cavity behind a molar. It required a couple of shots of anesthetic. I was amazed by how painlessly he gave me the injections. Remarkable. Then he repaired that tooth. Another good experience!

Out at the front desk with him, I signed the paperwork for Peace Corps. I asked him, "How much is this costing?"

"Why? Nothing for you. Peace Corps will pay for it."

"Just curious."

He did some figuring. "One hundred dollars is the total charge."

"Thank you." I did not mention how much replacing the screw and repairing my molar might have cost back home. Quite a bit more, I was sure.

Amazing to me also was that all this could go on in such easy English. Supposing he had known only his Ukrainian!

Outside, I found my Peace Corps car parked nearby. My driver was reading a newspaper. What service!

We chatted on the way back. We were driving along a fine avenue. A dozen people clustered in front of an impressive building. "What is that about?" I asked.

"The Polish Embassy. All those people are hoping to get visas to go to Poland. More jobs there. Better jobs there."

This street and the neighborhood reminded me of the charm of Paris. I'd been there numerous times. I mentioned the similarity and he was surprised. Yes, Kyiv was impressive.

I am pleased to tell you that over the weeks the therapy for my bruised shoulder and arm worked quite well.

The second emergency arose on a Sunday morning in my room at home in Chernihiv. Suddenly I felt very hot. Began to itch horribly on my arms, chest, and legs. Developed red blotches. Wanted to scratch, scratch, scratch. Terrible! And my breathing was getting difficult! Had never experienced this!

What to do? I knew the medical office was closed, but I called Peace Corps and spoke to the guard on duty. He said he would contact Dr. Yuri. He was at home but on call.

While waiting, I got out my digital camera and took pictures of my blotchy arms and legs. Awful! The pictures might be useful.

Dr. Yuri called within minutes. I told him everything. He asked questions.

"Sounds like an allergic reaction," he said. "Take two of the Benadryl pills in your medical kit right away."

Every Volunteer received a kit the size of a shoe box. It was stuffed with pills, capsules, ointments, lotions, bandages, surgical tape, a thermometer, scissors, tweezers, even an emergency whistle (!), plus a booklet of instructions.

I didn't have those Benadryl pills. Olena, my dean at *Coursi*, had come down with runny eyes and nose plus a fever. So bad that she couldn't work. I had given my pills to her. I was sure I would never need them.

"You should not have done that!" Dr. Yuri said sternly. "Go to your nearest drugstore and phone me. I'll give them a prescription. Take the medicine immediately."

But instead, I called Olena. She had most of the pills left and got them to me immediately. Within an hour my symptoms disappeared!

A day later I saw a big spider by my bed. I called Dr. Yuri. He said, "No, I don't think it was a spider." He explained that the reaction on my body had not been localized.

I have wondered, of course, what caused the attack. No idea. Might it happen again? Yes. That was a problem. Without knowing the cause, I had no idea whether I should change anything I did. I kept the pills handy for a long time. In fact, I tucked one in my wallet in case of an attack at school or somewhere else. Never needed it.

I had to go to Headquarters soon later. I stopped in to see Dr. Yuri. He gave me a special one-shot hypodermic needle packed in a special tube. "If you begin to breathe hard and you get frightened, stick this into your leg!" He showed me how. It would inject an exact dose.

I carried it around with me for a long time. It was scary how dangerous such an allergic reaction could be.

The Medical Office in Kyiv was efficient! One day I got a message that I was due for my mid-service physical. I had no idea such was required. I was told I would get a third physical at the end of my service, just before I returned home.

The exam took two days. My doctor this time was Dr. Valery, the senior doctor. I liked him very much, also.

He had come to Peace Corps some nine years ago after many years as a heart surgeon. He told me that after his first thousand heart operations he stopped counting. He told me that on weekends he sometimes worked as a surgeon in the trauma unit at a hospital. "I do not want to lose my skills!"

At every session I learned something new about him. This time that he was a speed ice skater—skated 5 or 6 times a week all winter—worked out under a coach. He did look remarkably fit—would run up the stairs!

What I liked is that every session with the doctors was relaxed and pleasant. Nobody was counting the seconds and minutes.

He checked everything from my ears down to my toes (literally) and lots of things unseen, including my prostate. He questioned me about many things. He gave me another two shots as inoculations.

He listened to my heart. Surprise. He told me he would send me to his old cardiology hospital for a check-up. "It is just routine," he said.

He asked about my eyes. I told him that they were both 20/20 with my bifocal eyeglasses on.

"Good," he said. "But please stand over there and read that eye chart on the wall, anyway."

I did it with supreme confidence. But it turned out my left eye was only 20/40 with my glasses on! My records showed it had been 20/20 just 18 months earlier. That difference bothered him. And me!

"We must check that out," he said. He set up an appointment with an ophthalmologist to coincide with my next visit to headquarters.

When he got done, a PC driver named Andrei drove me to the cardiology hospital. That was all it did, heart work. Natasha, the medical assistant, came along to shepherd me through the process.

I sat in the rear. Andrei noticed I wasn't wearing my seat belt and told me to buckle up. It had been so long since I had ridden in a car that I had forgotten I was supposed to do that.

Big hospital. Dozens of patients sitting and waiting in the main corridor. I was embarrassed when Natasha took me right to the head of the line. In just 10 minutes I was introduced to the cardiologist, a lovely woman in a white lab coat. Wore a beautiful necklace and earrings.

She spoke English. "I have been to Boston, Washington, and Baltimore!" she said proudly. "To study how American doctors do things." She glowed as she said it.

She ordered me to strip down to my belt and told me how to position myself on the table. Natasha was looking on and I was embarrassed. Neither paid attention.

The doctor gave me an electro-sound. She was tiny but flipped me easily from side to side. She was pushing the probe so hard that I winced. She kept looking at her monitor and reading off readings to an assistant, who jotted them down.

Then she wrote a detailed résumé and read it aloud to Natasha with special instructions for Dr. Valery. I looked at it later. It was in Russian, or maybe Ukrainian, so I understood nothing.

Surprise. I still had to see another cardiologist. I followed Natasha to another office. For an EKG, she told me. I was the only patient this time. And this time I had to strip just to my T-shirt and the examination was easier. It was far more pleasant.

The doctor came in, also a woman in a white lab coat but older. No jewelry. She gave me a once-over. Then a woman technician started the test. Easy. She gave the cardiologist her readings and she reviewed them and hand-wrote a report and gave it to Natasha.

Then in Russian she said to me, "Have a good day!"

I followed Natasha out into the freezing cold and across the snow to the big Toyota, which Andrei was keeping running to stay warm. We had driven a long way from the center, and again I was impressed with how lovely many sections of Kyiv were.

Back at Peace Corps, Dr. Valery studied the reports from the two doctors and gave me news that alarmed me. "Your mitral valve shows calcification. Not good."

Calcification meant that the valve was hardening and he explained that to me. He flipped through my records and looked up my tests of 18 months earlier. There was calcification then—mild calcification.

Did I feel any symptoms? No. I had no pain. No hard breathing. Nothing abnormal.

He picked up the phone and talked to the cardiologist about my electro-cardiogram. "A very excellent cardiologist," he said of her. He asked questions in Russian.

"I have good news," he told me. "The inner leaflets are not affected. They are the parts that move. It's the shell that's affected. This is less significant. You have little to be concerned about."

He said it's all a normal part of aging, and there is little that can be done. After all, I was going to turn 80 very soon. How lucky I have been! Of course, I was prepared for bad news at any time. We have to be realistic.

I had to stay overnight. More tests the next day as part of my mid-service physical! I had expected to be sent to a hotel. Then Dr. Valery gave me good news.

"You can stay here in our sick bay," he said. "But you will have a roommate. He has been with us for five days." The sick bay was a bedroom with twin beds on the first floor.

This Volunteer was Martin, about 23. He was a dark young man with a black beard. A Latino from Los Angeles, I judged. His face was swollen and his left eye had an ugly blue bump under it.

He told he had been walking home alone late one night in his nearby town and was attacked by two youths. They whacked him, pummeled him, and knocked him down. Then ran off. But hadn't stolen anything.

He staggered and got up. In pain. Ran his hand over his face and his hand was wet. Blood. He managed to call Peace Corps on his cell phone (we were all ordered to have one). The night guard took his call, then asked if he could make it in by himself.

He said yes. He hurried, of course. I didn't get those details. Anyway, a doctor had been called in and was waiting and went right to work on him. And here he was in sick bay, with another appointment with his doctor in the morning.

I didn't ask Martin and he didn't say but I suspected it was a hate crime. Minority members in Peace Corps are cautioned to be extra careful and are given special instructions.

I felt awful for Martin. I asked him if he was thinking of quitting and going home.

"No," he told me. "I did think of that when I was still down on the sidewalk. It was the first thing I thought of. But right away I decided I wouldn't go home. I would stick it out."

He said he had trained to be a high school teacher, was a high school teacher, liked the work and his students. Well, most of them.

I marveled at his English. He was a very educated young man. He impressed me in every way.

It turned out there were three other young Volunteers at Headquarters, two men and a woman, all for medical care. They were planning to walk to a Mister Snack nearby for supper (yes, that was its name) and invited me along. That pleased me. Remember, I was a grandfather and at times I felt separated from my young colleagues by my age. But certainly nobody's fault.

"I'm going, too," Martin said. "I need a break from this room."

We walked out together. It was icy and Martin held me by an arm. But it was to help me, not himself, though he was in pain.

A nice, clean little place, Mister Snack's. A franchise, I believe. My young friends all raved about the special barbecued chicken sandwich with cheese, so I too ordered that. It was a thick sandwich— my first flesh in four months. I needed a break from my vegetarian diet. I devoured it all. Delicious.

Incidentally, the meal with drinks cost us $6 each. About the same as in the U.S., I thought. All Volunteers complained how expensive Kyiv was. Remember, we were receiving an allowance of less than $300 a month.

We stayed and talked a long time. Another young Volunteer, Brian, told me that on a previous visit to Kyiv, he had been attacked one night by a big guy who had stolen his wallet. It included not only every dollar, but his passport, credit cards, other important documents, his girl friend's picture, everything.

Peace Corps had advanced him money to get back to his post. "It took me two months to get my passport and credit cards replaced!"

I asked them all about their experience in Peace Corps. They were generally happy but concerned about some things. Their being alone in their community bothered them but more than that they were struggling about their role in Ukraine. Not sure how much they were achieving.

I was impressed by all of them. *What fine young people*, I thought. I was sure they would do well in life.

Afterward, back at Peace Corps, I spent two hours on a computer in the Volunteer Lounge checking my e-mails and reading American newspapers online. My young friends were doing the same thing.

We Volunteers had two rooms set aside for us on the top floor, across the hall from the medical offices. One room was a sitting room, and the other a computer room.

The sitting room had a big couch and a couple of stuffed chairs, a coffee table, and lamp tables. High bookcases lined two walls. Loaded with used books. Hundreds of them. "Leave one, take one." That was the general idea. I always found a couple to take home, then would return and exchange them on my next visit.

Peace Corps had placed a big empty cardboard box next to the couch. A sign said, "Help Yourself!" Volunteers could drop in clothes or boots or anything else that they no longer needed. Many dropped in things when they prepared to go home.

I had never looked into the box. One day I went to sit on the couch and glanced into it. Just a couple of pieces of clothing. Then I noticed a camera case. It had a camera in it. A Canon... digital...

*Must be broken*, I thought. Then I thought, *But nobody would want to donate a worthless broken camera.*

I took it home. Replaced the batteries. It worked! Quite a coincidence. I had just lost (but maybe it had been stolen) my own fine digital camera. This was quite a find!

Oh, in a corner of the lounge was a table with cold water and hot water, tea bags, a box of Ibuprofen capsules, and a box of condoms. Help yourself to what you want!

The computer room had half a dozen Internet-connected computers along two walls, comfortable chairs, and a printer in a corner. Everything free for us to use. What a much-appreciated and thoroughly-used amenity!

Next to it the printer had a cardboard box with thrown-out printer paper. "Recycle!" a sign said, meaning "Use the Other Side." I considered it a joke, considering the huge sum it was costing to keep this Peace Corps operation in Ukraine going. But maybe its symbolism worked.

I had a good night's sleep in the sick bay. A good shower. A meager breakfast (a cake of Ramen noodles in boiling water and a leftover apple that I had brought). Then my second day in the medical office.

All went well there. Finally I was done and it was time to go for my mid-service dental appointment. All I needed was a cleaning. Natasha had had a hard time getting me one because it was the holiday season. I was hoping for the same young dentist again, Viktor.

On the way out, I reported to Tarek, the pharmacist. As always, we spoke in French, both of us just for the practice. He filled a bag with the vitamins and other minor things Dr. Valery had ordered for me.

A driver named Varil drove me to the clinic. He had to go that way. But this was a different branch. Also beautiful. Also very high tech. A lovely young woman in white sat me in the fancy chair. I thought she was the dentist. No. She was the dentist's assistant.

Another young woman in white appeared. Wore huge protective goggles—I never got to see her face. Was she the dentist? She gave me a meticulous exam with a pick (ouch!) and then a cleaning. Not sure whether she was a dentist.

For the cleaning she used a super-fast electric drill with a hand piece. My first experience with such. I never got to see the fitting she used on it. A lot of whirring, whistling noise. Painful at times. Her assistant kept shooting water into my mouth to cool the drill and wash stuff away. Twice I was afraid I might drown. They got the job done in 12 minutes.

She wrote a report for Dr. Valery and jotted down the fee. I glanced at the form before turning it in. Wouldn't you? It was $55 for everything. Uncle Sam would pay.

Then I walked out and Varil was waiting in the big Toyota. He was listening to a Mozart CD. I had my overnight bag in the car in preparation for going home. I wanted to take the Metro out to the end of the line and catch a *marshrutka* for the two-hour ride back to Chernihiv.

Nicely, Varil went out of his way just a bit to let me off at my most convenient Metro station—meaning the one where I could take a single train to the end instead of two. It was cold and snowy and dark. It would have been unpleasant doing all this on my own.

On the way, we had a nice talk. He spoke good English. Had been a Peace Corps driver for 18 years. Knew every highway and hotel and café in Ukraine, he said. Had driven officials to Poland, Moldova, and Romania, but never nearby Russia. "It is sealed off!" he said.

I mentioned that I planned to travel around Ukraine during my upcoming vacation. He gave me some good tips. "Go to Uman," he said. " It's just a small city. But it has the most beautiful park in Ukraine. It's our Versailles!"

Hey, he was an expert. I made a mental note. {And on my vacation weeks later, I did get to Uman. And enjoyed it.)

He told me he had one child, a son who had just gotten his doctorate in comparative philology—Latin, ancient Greek, old Russian, and Ukrainian—and was headed for an academic career. Varil was so proud. How many people become experts in comparative philology?

Lots of traffic. Varil made sure he left me off in a safe spot and wished me good luck. Another good guy. I hoped I'd see him again.

Later I learned that that dental office had not been a branch. It had been a different office. Peace Corps was using the other much less because its charges were too high, I heard.

On my ride home in the dark on the snowy road in the crowded *marshrutka*, I thought of many things I had experienced in the last 48 hours. And I felt very good about Peace Corps. Again.

I returned to Medical a couple of weeks later for my eye examination. Dr. Valery had made an appointment with an ophthalmologist. A Peace Corps driver took us to a special hospital for policemen. A big, old building, impressively clean. "I know this doctor," he told me. "Excellent!"

Again the doctor was a woman, about 60. She spoke some English. Told me she had worked in Tunisia. A lot of French spoken there, I knew, so I said a few words in French. It turned out she loved to speak French. We carried on in French while she did her checking. Dr. Valery was impressed. She and I became instantaneous friends.

I had a complex vision problem, she said. I understood. I had had cataract surgery and I had implant lenses in both eyes, each of a different focal length. Plus I wore glasses—bifocal glasses, for near and far vision.

After her refraction test, she told me it would be difficult for me to be fitted with a single pair of glasses like the pair I was wearing at the moment. She told me I should have two pairs of glasses made, one for normal street wear and the other for close-up work.

That was not good news. But what could I say? She gave Dr. Valery the two prescriptions.

From there the two of us went directly to an optician's. Dr. Valery explained my prescriptions. No problem. I selected two frames—I made sure they were different styles so I could tell which pair was which. "They will be ready tomorrow," the optician said—a woman also.

Again I stayed in the sick bay. Martin had left. I missed him.

The next day Dr. Valery accompanied me back to the shop. I was given both pairs. Made in the U.S.A., I noticed. I pointed that out to him. He noticed my American pride, of course.

I also had business with him now of a different kind. I was the president of SNAC, our Peace Corps club for Volunteers 50 and over. He was the club's advisor and Headquarters liaison. I wanted to discuss our forthcoming big meeting. I had some specific ideas.

He was reluctant but I talked him into walking to a Chinese restaurant for lunch and we worked everything out. The restaurant was so pleasant and the food so good that I decided that it would be our restaurant of choice for one of our group dinners during our SNAC get-together.

I returned to Chernihiv happy about my new glasses. But it turned out that I did not like them. Each pair was fine individually. But what a nuisance to walk around with two pairs of glasses and switch for near and far situations. I set them aside and returned to my original bifocal glasses.

I knew that when our two eyes have different strengths, whether for near or far, the brain always accepts the input from the better eye. That's why I had not noticed I had one eye 20/20 but the other eye 20/40. How about that?

I continued to wear my old glasses until I returned to the U.S.A. and had a new pair made. Just one pair. Bifocals again. God bless America!

Twenty-seven months is a long time. I had to visit Peace Corps Medical for this and that over the stretch. Little things. I got to know all the doctors. They were always willing to do anything they could.

One day Natasha, the staff assistant, assigned me to see Dr. Yuri. We discussed my little problem. Then when I stood he noticed I was limping. I said I had a bad callus on the sole of my right foot. He took a look, then said, "Maybe I can do something about that."

He got a scalpel and carefully shaved off as much of the callus as he could. What a great relief! I walked out smiling, not limping. His parting words were, "When it bothers you again, stop by."

As time passed, my usual doctor became Dr. Valery. It just turned out that way. I would have been pleased with any one of them. Always a pleasure to go see him. He was a fine physician and a warm–hearted man

Natasha was invaluable. I would get a call from her. "John, don't forger about your flu shot." Or "John, it is time for your dental cleaning." And she would book me, even at the dental clinic. I am sure she did the same for all Volunteers.

One day, her e-mail said, "Let's please make an appointment for your Close of Service Physical." Getting into Peace Corps is a process. So is getting out. A physical examination is a requirement at the end.

It took place two weeks later, and that's when she booked my dental cleaning. Thoughtful of her to schedule the two for the same day. Getting to Headquarters in Kyiv and then back could take up the whole day. She saved me a trip.

The C.O.S. physical was an Event, with a capital "e." Very thorough. Let me remind you: I went through many medical hoops to get into Peace Corps. Then like all Volunteers, I went through another medical evaluation upon arriving. Then my mid-service physical. And now this final one. Dr. Valery was going to be the doctor.

He did not miss a thing. My medical file was open on his desk and he reviewed it. This was not a 20-minute quickie. He had a long checklist. He drew blood, took measurements, palpated me. As he examined me from head to toe, he checked off one item after another.

I had noted that I had a hearing deficit. At age 80, that is expected. It was not serious probably but he would check.

"Maybe you have wax in your ears," he said.

He selected a long probe. It was a stiff wire. At its end was a tiny cup, smaller than a pea. He pushed it way into my ear, rotated it carefully, and scraped out bits of wax. Both ears.

"See if that makes a difference," he said. It did. I had never seen such an instrument.

He mentioned that if a significant medical problem of any kind turned up, one that had developed on Peace Corps time, I would receive a voucher that would cover treatment for it when I got home after exiting Peace Corps. Very nice, I thought.

After his examination, he sent me off to a private cardiologist again for an electro-cardiogram. The results were normal for my age. "You are remarkably healthy," he said after explaining them to me. I did feel remarkably healthy. But it was nice to hear it.

One bit of good news did not surprise me. I had lost 25 pounds in my 27 months. I knew by my belt that I was losing but I was surprised the total was so significant.

"Are you happy about this?" he asked.

"Of course!"

"How did you do it?"

"I am getting a lot of exercise walking. I walk, walk, walk. And you Ukrainians use smaller dinner plates than we Americans do. Yours are six inches wide. Ours are eight inches, sometimes bigger. And I never take second helpings. I am careful about I what I eat. Nearly total vegetarian now. No alcohol. Few sweets. Just one little ice cream cone per week!"

One other factor—plain good luck

His congratulations delighted me.

"Well, we have just two more things left to do," he said. "Your TB shot. Dr. Oleksander will give it to you that when you go to your C.O.S. retreat next month. And then your HIV/AIDS test at the very end of your service."

"An HIV/AIDS test? I definitely won't need that!"

"It's mandatory. Every Volunteer has to take it."

When I got to the retreat, Dr. Oleksander gave me my TB shot. I did not have to remind him. The Medical Department was impressively pro-active all the time.

A few words about my dental appointment after my C.O.S. physical. I had cracked a molar and needed a replacement crown. In fact, I needed a root canal procedure. Three appointments in all. I had a new dentist, Dr. Sasha, and I was impressed by him also. And he spoke good English. What a plus! I was going for my final appointment. I was due at 2 p.m.

I took a Metro train, in fact, had to change to a second train. Bad luck. I overshot the station where I was supposed to get off and had to backtrack. I was afraid I'd be late and took a taxi. Still I got there five minutes late. "No problem at all, John," he assured me.

He had the crown all ready. He showed it to me. Beautiful. It fit perfectly. In 20 minutes he had it glued in and polished. Once more he checked all my teeth. He paused after examining one.

"This one is unstable. It moves a bit. And it has a crown. We should investigate this. It might even require a new crown. I can't tell yet. First I must get Peace Corps' permission. I will contact the medical office there."

Then one of his assistants cleaned my teeth. Unpleasant, as you know. But I appreciated its importance.

Afterward he filled out a report for me to hand in to Medical. I glanced at it, of course. I noticed his charges. At the current exchange rate, it was $44 for the crown, and $8 for the cleaning. I was astounded by how much less this was than what I was accustomed to paying in the U.S.A.

I mentioned this to him. He nodded. "I have Ukrainians who now live in the United States. And they come back when they need extensive care. For them, the money that they save is like getting a free vacation trip back to Ukraine."

Dr. Yuri happened to be my doctor at Headquarters on this day. When I got back there, I mentioned my unstable tooth.

"Yes, Dr. Sasha called me about it. But I'll have to send a message to Peace Corps in Washington about this. They will decide."

He explained to me that the doctors were required to clear with Peace Corps in Washington whenever something unusual came up. This was unusual because I had only three weeks of service left.

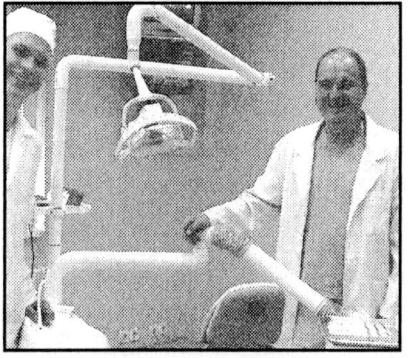

*I had fine dental care from Dr. Sasha (right). He tackled complex work.*

I thought to myself, *They'll probably nix it. They might decide,* "It's not that urgent. Let this Volunteer attend to it on his own when he gets home.'

In four days Dr. Yuri called me. "Good news, John. We'll go ahead with this tooth and the crown."

Getting the tooth fixed took two more appointments with Dr. Sasha. On the first one, he removed my crown and X-rayed, prepared, and medicated the tooth. At my second appointment, he said, "We are lucky. I can re-use your crown!" And he completed the job.

I was greatly impressed. It would have been so easy for him to say, "Sorry, this crown will not fit now."

His total charges amounted to a bit less than $200. Another bargain.

As part of my exit physical, I had to have a more sophisticated stool test. Again mandatory. Two samples taken days apart were shipped to a specialty lab in Washington. I was shocked—the tests came back positive.

I had cyclosporiasis! I had tiny parasites in my colon! Usually the result of fecal matter on food. Incredible! How could this have happened?

It's common in undeveloped countries. I told Tanya at home. After all, we ate the same food. She just discounted the whole thing!

I was put on Bactrim for a week. It's a pill. Then I provided two more stool samples for the lab. Negative! No cyclosporiasis!

Just one more test to go—the HIV/AIDS test. This was done on as close to the final day of service as possible. It took place after my three-day Close of Service retreat with other Volunteers in my Group 33.

It happened Dr. Valery was away on vacation so Dr. Yuri did the test. I told him that I had absolutely no reason to be nervous.

"I have to do the test anyway. It takes only a minute."

I asked him, "How many positives have you found here?"

"Just one case. Two or three years ago."

"I'll bet some people are uptight when they take this test."

What I had in mind was the obvious sexual activity among Volunteers. I've mentioned how Peace Corps routinely handed out free condoms. I had seen Volunteers take a handful of them. I had seen Peace Corps send condoms to our recent Close of Service conference.

"Yes," he said. "There can be a lot of suspense involved."

The test took just a minute. Amazing. Just one drop of blood. You get an immediate Positive or Negative.

"Negative!" Dr. Yuri said. And he smiled.

I told him a story Dr. Valery had told me. "Ah, human nature!" Dr. Valery said. "Usually a patient will tell me, 'Oh, I used a condom. But it broke!' But one time a Volunteer told me, 'I was in a hurry! Didn't use one.' I was impressed! He was honest." And he chuckled.

In my final session at Medical, Dr. Valery gave me documents to take home with me to the U.S.A. They included a résumé of key findings to give to my primary care physician. And one was a Corps Care card.

Corps Care is a medical insurance plan for Returned Volunteers. It is not free but Peace Corps said it was a good buy. The card would provide free care for my first month back home in the U.S.A. Nice.

Volunteers were free to purchase additional months. Peace Corps emphasized the importance of coverage. We were free to choose a different insurance carrier if we wanted to.

As explained earlier, I went right back to my Medex policy. I was impressed and so grateful that a law guaranteed my doing that.

I have only good words to tell you about Peace Corps Medical. If socialized medicine were like Peace Corps medical care, I'd vote for it in a minute.

~ ~ ~

# 28 / A troubling op-ed

*A former Volunteer criticizes Peace Corps.
I respond. Our top director has his say.*

One day not long after I began my service, milady Annabelle e-mailed me a New York Times op-ed about the Peace Corps. Its title was "Too Many Innocents Abroad." Written by a Robert L.Strauss.

Its writer had been a Volunteer and then a Peace Corps recruiter and then even a Peace Corps country director. And here he was excoriating Peace Corps in our most important newspaper! Wow!

I read every word. It was a revelation. After all, all I knew about Peace Corps was just the surface stuff—the good stuff that I had heard over and over again and had assimilated without question.

I had no idea someone could have genuine, serious criticism of the famed organization that I had committed 27 months of my life to serving. Remember, public opinion polls had always ranked Peace Corps one of our top federal agencies.

Robert L. Strauss? I had never heard of him. His details were interesting. He had been a Volunteer in Liberia (1978-80) and then a Peace Corps recruiter in Denver, then in time the country director of Peace Corps in Cameroon for five years (2002-07), and now was an international development consultant and a free-lance writer.

I Googled him and found he had impressive credentials. In fact, he had criticized Peace Corps before in magazine articles. I read his op-ed again. Then one more time.

Yes, he was loudly and harshly and publicly criticizing Peace Corps. This was all new to me. He shook me up. It seemed impossible that he could be right. How come I had never heard any of this before?

He attacked a basic policy of Peace Corps. From the start Peace Corps had been a young people's game. Now he was charging that the young people who have been the traditional Volunteers all these decades were too immature for the work!

He said that too often they were not up to the job even in the early days of Peace Corps and this was even more true now! He said these are more sophisticated times, even in developing countries. He said the young Volunteers are not savvy enough. They lack know-how. They just flounder.

343

What are needed now, he said, are older Volunteers, 50 and up, and many more of them. They bring essential job and life experience to their assignments, and have a much bigger and better impact. He acknowledged that yes, Peace Corps has been seeking more older recruits as part of its new Fifty Plus program, but he insisted that it needed far more.

Furthermore, he went on to argue that in its recruitment efforts, Peace Corps should set its entrance requirements much higher. It should select only the most able.

Quantity has always trumped quality, he said. Peace Corps does not select higher, he said, because it's afraid it could not meet its recruitment goals. It would be an embarrassment.

*Strauss spoke from experience. Photo taken in 2004 when he was Peace Corps director in Cameroon.*

He complained that Peace Corps has been "mythologized into an agency that cannot be questioned or improved." The result was that in these changing times it no longer serves its host countries as well as it should, and this when we need a lot more friends around the world.

I was so happy that Annabelle had sent his op-ed to me. But disturbed and angry. I thought hard about Strauss' complaints. I believed differently.

**I** was no expert about Peace Corps. But I knew why I had joined and in large part that had been based on the store of favorable impressions about Peace Corps that I had absorbed over the years.

And now I had four months of first-hand experience in it as a basis to judge it by. It was very limited experience, true, but it was re-assuring to me. I had positive vibes about Peace Corps.

I felt somebody should reply to Strauss. I had this on my mind when I went to bed. I decided that I would reply. I got up and wrote a reply and e-mailed it to the Times.

Certainly I agreed with him about one thing: the more older Volunteers, the better! And Peace Corps recognized this also. Consider its current Fifty Plus program, which Strauss had acknowledged as meritorious. It's in reading about Fifty Plus that I became motivated to join.

Fifty Plus was the initiative of our then national director, Ronald Tschetter. Traditionally Volunteers aged 50 and over had comprised about 5 percent. This was being raised to 15 percent over two years. Certainly this was a big step in the direction Strauss was urging.

It's this new emphasis on maturity and experience that made me feel I would be welcomed into Peace Corps. I would not have joined any outfit where gray hair was considered odd.

Of course I agreed with Strauss that the career and life experience of older folks was particularly valuable and desirable. Who could disagree?

But one of his charges—that young people were not up to the challenge—made me indignant. I had just finished training with a group in which the great majority were young, some barely in their 20s.

I, too, wondered whether they could be up to their assignments, even with the serious training we had been put through.

We were all going to be English teachers in secondary schools and universities. If they didn't have much experience, they certainly had plenty of enthusiasm and energy.

They certainly had done far better at learning the language than I had! I gave these young people the benefit of the doubt. After all, Peace Corps had been recruiting youngsters for decades: it must feel they are entirely satisfactory.

In some cases, I even thought the younger Volunteers might do a better job. Especially those teaching in high schools, with younger students in their classrooms. It was my impression that everywhere the teachers of younger children by and large were younger teachers. They seemed more natural for the job.

In fact, in Ukraine, Peace Corps had a program called Youth Development that was right up the young Volunteers' alley.

They worked with children and teen-agers, not only in the classroom, but after hours in recreational activities and in the gym and the playing field.

During vacations, they ran a surprising variety of camps and workshops. By the very nature of their work in this program I felt younger Volunteers must do a better job.

Strauss spoke of their immaturity. Well, he served as a young Volunteer; he must have suffered from this same "immaturity!" Did he feel his service was wasted or unappreciated? I'll bet he did not.

During Training, I was impressed by my young colleagues in general. And I thought to myself, They *are as mature as any people of that age could be!* I was sure they would be excellent role models for their students and would be impressive young ambassadors for our country.

Oh, subsequently I had a doubt now and then. One day in the Volunteer Lounge, I ran into a young Volunteer who had a ring in his upper lip! I was startled. What kind of impression must he give here? I had never seen a Ukrainian with such. If I were Country Director, I would order him to remove it!

I also noticed some young Volunteers who dressed sloppily for work. How could they get away with this when Peace Corps kept emphasizing that we must be "professionally dressed."

In fact, I thought of this admonition whenever I saw Volunteers sloppily dressed, younger and older ones also. Which was too often. In my school, *Coursi*, and others I visited, I saw the professional personnel dressed admirably well. This although they were all receiving scanty salaries.

Maybe Strauss did have a point about the immaturity of some.

I sent my response not only to the Times. I copied it to every Volunteer in Ukraine whose e-mail address I had. Some 100 people, most of them young people, of course.

The Times did not print it. Shame on them. But maybe that was because I could not give them a phone number to reach me (a number was required so the newspaper could confirm that the writer was authentic).

And I did not get a single comment from my colleagues who got it. That disappointed me. I had been sure I would get dozens of replies.

I felt they would jump right in to affirm that they do a good job and are worthy and that Peace Corps' long experience with younger Volunteers testified to that. I was defending them! Why weren't they defending themselves!

After reflection, I thought we needed Volunteers of all ages for different assignments. Furthermore, I thought it was good for the people we served to see Volunteers not only of all races and backgrounds but all ages. Yes, I do.

Maybe Strauss was right in saying that Peace Corps recruiters did not set the bar high enough. I didn't know enough about that to comment although I had read that only one in four applicants, or maybe it was one in three, got invited to join.

I did feel his thoughts deserved careful weighing in Washington.

Let me quote some of his words in the Times. They deserve your consideration:

"The Peace Corps recently began a laudable initiative to increase the number of Volunteers who are 50 and older. As the Peace Corps' country director in Cameroon from 2002 until last February, I observed how many older Volunteers brought something to their service that most young Volunteers could not: extensive professional and life experience and the ability to mentor younger Volunteers.

"However, even if the Peace Corps reaches its goal of having 15 percent of its Volunteers over 50, the overwhelming majority will remain recently minted college graduates. And too often these young Volunteers lack the maturity and professional experience to be effective development workers in the $21^{st}$ century.

"The Peace Corps has long shipped out well-meaning young people possessing little more than good intentions and a college diploma. What the agency should begin doing is recruiting only the best of recent graduates— as the top professional schools do—and only those older people whose skills and personal characteristics are a solid fit for the needs of the host country.

"…while Volunteers generate good will for the United States, they do little or nothing to actually aid development in poor countries. The agency has no comprehensive system for self-evaluation, but rather relies heavily on personal anecdote to demonstrate its worth.

"The Peace Corps was born during the glory days of the early Kennedy administration. Since then, its leaders and many of the more than 190,000 Volunteers who have served have mythologized the agency into something that can never be questioned or improved. The result is an organization that finds itself less and less able to provide what the people of developing countries need — at a time when the United States has never had a greater need for their good will."

Now here are excerpts from my reply to the Times:
"My group arrived on Oct. 1. There were 86 of us. Eight of us were age 55 or older. This is considerably less than the 15 per cent that is the Corps' goal. I am the oldest by far. I will be 79 in April.

"The rest of us, of course, were what he says Peace Corps has been shipping out since its start: 'well-meaning young people possessing little more than good intentions and a college diploma.'"

"Well, if Peace Corps has an excellent reputation at home (polls say it does), surely it's because of the efforts of such immature young people. Which makes me ask, Is it possible for any young people to be more mature than these high-minded, brave young people?

"Yes, there are excellent native English-language teachers. But I have seen how students take a shine to our Volunteers. Our Volunteers provide something extra. They are notable examples of real Americans, enthusiastic and high-minded, not the less-than-noble types depicted so often in the media at home and abroad.

"It's embarrassing to tell you how many claims have been made on this ordinary American to appear in various classrooms. I am sure there are better English teachers than I, many of them Ukrainians. But the students want to see me, a flesh-and-blood American, something quite rare here in Ukraine.

"In fact, being a nice, good American is my most important job here. Well, that's my opinion. I am a small ambassador for my country. We could use plenty more.

"One last thing. Peace Corps sends Volunteers only to those countries which invite them in. Look at the roster of current countries. Not bad, eh? Would the invitations keep coming if our work were so mediocre?"

Robert L. Strauss interested me a lot. I looked up everything I could about him. I found he had two master's degrees from Stanford University, including an M.B.A. He had worked on projects of international development in more than 50 countries.

I believe his article in the April 2008 issue of Foreign Policy magazine is must reading for anyone interested in Peace Corps. It is entitled "Think Again: The Peace Corps." It is a harsh and scathing review. It forces us to confront many of our favorite notions about the Peace Corps.

It drew quick responses from both sides. Nine responses were published by the magazine in late May. You will find it useful to read the comments.

One who took vehement exception was Ronald Tschetter, our national director. He denied each and every one of Strauss' assertions. That was expected, of course.

He wrote, "I was greatly disappointed with both the tone and misrepresentations of Robert Strauss's article. It is ironic that Strauss is a former Peace Corps country director. Your readers should be aware that the responsibility to monitor the performance and effectiveness of Volunteers fell directly into his hands.

"As the current worldwide head of the Peace Corps, I can tell you that each of his arguments is false and with all certainty, our agency is thriving. In April, President Bush met with Volunteers leaving for Guatemala and said the Peace Corps 'really is the best foreign policy America could possibly have.'"

Then I contacted Strauss. I wanted a discussion with him. It was easy. In fact, I sent e-mails to him several times. His replies were immediate. I never felt I was getting the brush-off. He responded with care and sincerity.

I admired him for his continuing interest in Peace Corps. And I felt his contrary point of view was healthful and valuable. Even if exaggerated or wrong, it must force Peace Corps to re-think itself. Maybe he was correct!

I wondered why he was living, permanently it seemed, in such a strange place: Madagascar. I asked him. He said that after service in a Francophone country in Africa, he and his family enjoyed living in Francophone Madagascar. He added that it was a convenient base for him as a consultant in international assistance.

I mentioned his name to some people knowledgeable about Peace Corps. "Oh, him again!" That was a typical response. I got the feeling some considered him a curmudgeon.

At one point I wondered: *Maybe he's setting himself up to become the next national director of Peace Corps!* I put the question to him. His answer was an emphatic "No!"

My bottom line: I am glad he spoke up. I welcomed his thoughts. At one point I thought, "If we Volunteers could vote for our national director, I would vote for him!"

**O**h, if you are not aware, I must tell you that the national director of Peace Corps is a political appointee and has always been. I feel that ability should be the first criterion. But the prevailing thinking is that key policy jobs throughout the federal government should always be held by appointees of the President.

Strauss also had written about another topic he was familiar with, international development as a mission of our State Department. If you're interested in this topic, I believe you would also find Strauss' strong and inflammatory article about it illuminating. Google his article, "Looking for the Right Road in the Third World" in the Stanford University Alumni Magazine, May / June 2007.

Now guess what? With this background about Strauss' complaints, imagine my surprise when I heard that Ronald Tschetter was coming to Ukraine on an official visit. The very Ron Tschetter who had made it a priority to sign up more older Volunteers. Truth is, I had not even known his name.

Better still, our Kyiv Headquarters sent all of us older people an invitation to come meet him. I decided yes on the spot. I was sure younger people would have enjoyed going also, but I understood the problems of inviting all Volunteers in a country as big as this one.

Not long after came another e-mail: Peace Corps would cover our expenses. These were days of budget austerity for us in Ukraine. They were cutting this and that...even our free subscriptions to Newsweek Magazine. They really wanted us present! Well, I'd attend!

I researched him online within minutes after deciding.

**R**on Tschetter and his wife Nancy had been Volunteers in India in the '60s. He was born in South Dakota in 1941. After college, with friends he hitchhiked through Europe, Lebanon, Syria, Israel, and Egypt. That impressed me. He had started as an investments salesman and had risen to great success. To the top.

He was only the third of 17 national directors who were former Volunteers. He was the first appointed by a Republican President, George W. Bush. To me, having served as a Volunteer seems essential for the job. I liked the idea of having a former Volunteer as our top boss.

For 20 years he had been active on the side in the National Peace Corps Association, the national private group of former Volunteers, achieving board chairman. It carries weight in influencing policy.

All in all, an impressive background for the post, in my opinion.

**A**bout 20 of us made it to Headquarters to meet him. So not all older Volunteers attended. I must mention some of them would have faced up to a 24-hour train ride each way. I had it easy. I was only three hours away.

We met in the staff conference room. As it was, every seat was taken. It was a pizza luncheon. Enough pizza was ordered in for three luncheons. Afterward, he spoke.

Ron Tschetter was a big, affable, silver-haired man who commands attention. In his late 60s, he was vigorous in body and voice. He was accompanied by his wife, Nancy—she had served with him in India, as I've said. And by his chief of staff and a couple of assistants. He had a staff photographer who kept shooting pictures.

Tschetter took off his jacket, loosened his tie, munched pizza with us, then got down to business. He spoke in easy and colloquial words. He was enthusiastic. He took credit for the Fifty Plus program, gave statistics about its success, both in terms of numbers of recruits and the effectiveness of older recruits.

But even as I wrote this for you, Fifty Plus was still far short of its goal of 15 percent. There were fewer than 500 of us in a total enrollment of about 8,000. It was closer to 7 percent.

**O**h, I found out the answer to a big personal question.

I have mentioned that I expected to be assigned to a "French" country and was so surprised when I found out I was going to Ukraine. It did not seem reasonable. But recruiting older Volunteers on an organized scale was a new idea.

Tschetter said this was an experimental period. Peace Corps wanted to make sure we older folks had a good supporting infrastructure wherever we were going, such as "a decent hospital nearby." So we older ones were limited to just 10 or so countries of the approximately 75 on the list.

He talked about how Peace Corps is doing (generally quite well), talked about our important work around the world, and gave some specific examples of great projects that he had seen for himself.

One was a Volunteers' project to show people how to make very useful methane gas from cow dung, in India I think it was. And another in South Asia where rice farmers often suffer badly in good harvest years because rice prices plummet as a result of enormous quantity. Volunteers had organized a cooperative that could release supplies of rice gradually, as needed, assuring higher prices in general. He did not tell us about any project failures.

Then he opened the meeting to questions. It became a lively discussion. One topic was inflation. Inflation was serious in Ukraine; some 20 percent last year. Higher and higher prices make it harder for Volunteers to get by on their allowances. Also more difficult for Peace Corps to operate. He said he was aware of all this and it was being discussed. There were other topics.

I was surprised that Robert Strauss and his stinging article had not come up. So I brought that up. I voiced Strauss' complaint about Volunteers being too young and immature and his call for Peace Corps to recruit many more Volunteers 50 and over.

I said to him, "We know that you are the one who made recruiting older Volunteers a priority—a priority for the first time in the history of Peace Corps. You want to jump from 5 to 15 percent in two years! Excellent. But if Mr. Strauss is right, maybe your figure should be 25 percent and eventually maybe even 55 percent!"

He shot back, "Did you see my reply?"

I had not. That in itself was strange because I had searched and had found some replies but nothing from him. I never got to see what his reply had been. (Later I was told his reply was not in the Times. That seemed strange. I was told it had appeared in some specialty publication.)

He did not explain his reply but continued, "What is important is that we're on the right track. It's difficult to set a specific target. We'll get there. Absolutely!"

I thought he gave a good answer. It was the right track. I thought he did a good job all around. But this was his $42^{nd}$ or $43^{rd}$ visit to Peace Corps countries around the world, so he had plenty of experience in fielding questions and making a good show.

Later I had a chance to say a word with him. He was genuinely cordial. He shook hands and said, "Keep up the good work!" I felt he must say that a hundred times a day.

His photographer took a picture of us. It turned out to be a lucky shot. He caught both of us smiling like old friends. (I prized that photo. Planned to print it here. It has disappeared. Sob!)

It was a whirlwind visit. Earlier, he had met with our local Kyiv staff, which was about 90 percent Ukrainian. I had also heard that he had been trying to meet with Ukrainian leaders. Somebody mentioned that he was miffed when President Yuvchenko turned him down, and that he had declined to meet with a lesser leader.

I also heard complaints about his huge number of visits around the world. Somebody said they seemed even more numerous than Condoleezza Rice's, our then Secretary of State. Were they primarily pleasurable sight-seeing jaunts or essential inspections? I don't know. Maybe both. But I applaud him for Fifty Plus. A genuinely sound idea.

It definitely bolstered my morale to see our top boss in Washington come and meet us, eat pizza, and answer our questions. Our morale was something that I wondered and worried about. I speak about it later.

Then I found out that Sen. Christopher Dodd (D-Connecticut, which is my state, of course), himself a former Volunteer, had written a bill to double the size of Peace Corps. That will make Robert Strauss happy, I thought immediately.

It made sense to me. Consider: Ukraine had a population of some 44 million, and we were only 300 strong here. What kind of dent could we possibly make? And we were the largest Peace Corps group in the world!

I write about Senator Dodd in Chapter 42. Very interesting what he was up to. Unfortunately, our economic downturn derailed his plans.

~ ~ ~

***Did you know*** ... that when you enlist, you will be agreeing "to go wherever and do whatever." And to do so even with the possibility of hardship.

Of course, Peace Corps uses common sense in its assignments. They will try to seek a country and a job that are a good match for you. But it's understandable at times that a match may be less than perfect. Simply because a better one is not available. So "flexibility" is expected.

I heard Volunteers complain that they were badly mismatched. I met one who found her assignment so wrong that she refused it – and "resigned" in lieu of being sent home because of her refusal.

# 29 / Off I go to Shanghai

*My friend Wu is getting married there.*
*Annabelle flies from L.A. and joins me.*

Yes, I had to go to China. My friend Wu in Shanghai had invited me to his wedding. "John, please come! Finally you will meet Elaine! We will be married on March 23!" He also invited Annabelle and my sister Lucie. He knew both well.

Annabelle said yes in a minute. Lucie had to decline.

It would be an opportunity to see my dear young friend Wu again. It would be a visit—no, more than that, a little adventure—with Annabelle. She and I had been apart too long. I needed a break. And it would refresh my batteries for my final stretch in Ukraine.

I checked with Headquarters, of course. An unusual request. But no problem. They said okay.

Going to Shanghai turned out to be an important but wonderful interlude. The timing was perfect. It came at the end of my first year of fast-paced service. And after a hard winter of snow and ice and gloom.

Annabelle and I did some serious planning for it. She was in California, some 7,000 miles from me. Our e-mails zipped back and forth.

The idea was that I would fly east across Asia on Aerosvit Airlines, the national Ukrainian carrier. And Annabelle would fly west from Los Angeles across the Pacific. We'd fly in opposite directions around the world! And we'd meet at Pu Dang Airport in Shanghai at about the same time. This would maximize our time together and make it easier for Wu to pick us up.

Easier said than done. Aerosvit flew only once a week to Shanghai. I could have used another airline; however, no other flew non-stop there. But savvy Annabelle managed to book a flight for herself that coordinated nicely.

I ran into a difficulty immediately—the hassle of getting my visa to enter China!

My friend Wu had also been perturbed. He sent me three e-mails about it. The last: "John, let me know the minute you receive your visa!"

Now let me explain why I wanted so much to go. I consider Wu my Chinese "nephew".

I had met him in Nairobi, Kenya some four years earlier. I was on my solo trip around the world. He was a businessman from Shanghai vacationing there. We were strangers sharing a dorm room at a hostel but we had dinner together. He was alone also. Then the next day we went sightseeing together. I had to stop at an e-mail shop to write an article for my newspaper again. He got curious.

"How can I read these articles?" he asked.

"Easy. When I e-mail it to the newspaper, I send it to friends also. I'll put you on my list."

That started our long e-mail friendship after we each returned home.

Wu is in his early 30's. An electronics engineer. A high-achiever. He has really moved up. He is the director of marketing for Europe for his Shanghai electronics company. He travels to Germany, France, and Belgium. Right now he was negotiating a $1.5 million contract with a European buyer. That's a lot of money in China. A busy fellow.

During our first early months I mentioned that I would write a book about my trip around the world. He e-mailed right back: "It should be published in China!"

My book published in China? What a crazy idea!

"No!" he said. "Chinese people will like your book. We have had a closed society for many years. Now it is opening up. We are making more money. We can go to other countries just like you. People will be fascinated to read how you did it.

"One other reason. You made the trip at age 75. Nobody here will believe that a man can go around the world alone at 75!"

Well, Wu was insistent. And optimistic. He bought the rights to publish my book in China! A less-principled man could have bought a single book and had it translated and published and I never would have been the wiser.

I make a joke about it. I say, "Wu did not pay me a million dollars, believe me. But he paid me enough for all the chop suey I want for the rest of my life!"

Translating the book and designing it was a big job for him. He worked at it with two other translators. A year later he got it published. He invited Annabelle and me to the PR kick-off in Shanghai. Of course I went!

Annabelle wanted to but could not. Sob! My sister Lucie went with me. Wu was a super host. We were scheduled to stay one week. We stayed three. "The Chinese New Year is coming up!" he said. "You must stay and enjoy it."

We did indeed. Then Lucie and I went on to other countries in Asia. After a month she had to return home for a big event. I traveled on to more countries. It became another adventure for me. I came home and wrote and published a new book, "Around Asia in 80 Days. Oops, 83!"

Wu and I continued to be in touch. (And we still are.) Meanwhile, he met Elaine. A beautiful university graduate, an accountant in a government office. He was smitten. He did not tell me her name for a while. He called her Miss Right!

Young Chinese are fascinated by America. Many take American names. It's a popular thing in their English-language classes. She became "Elaine". I have never gotten to know her Chinese name. She is Elaine to me.

In fact, he told me about her before he told his father and mother. And he asked me for advice. He was serious about it. I started making up advice, some funny but some serious.

*Downtown Shanghai is stunningly modern. Easy to see the American influence. This was my second trip there and my third to China.*

I would say to him, "Remember what Confucius said: that a young man should make sure he gets to see his sweetheart when something goes bad? It's a good way to get to see the real person!"

Or, "Remember. You are choosing more than a bride. You are choosing her family. How do you feel about that?"

Wu would always write back, "Brilliant!" I smiled every time.

Then he announced they were engaged.

**B**ut you need a visa to enter China! China has different categories of visas. All I wanted was a plain and simple tourist visa. What hurdles!

I had to make three separate trips to Kyiv to get it. The first time, the Chinese consulate was closed. So I had to go back again, of course. I waited in a long line. Awful. But I got the application filled out. Then I had to go again to pick it up. Each trip took me away from work a full day! And I got charged $130 for just a 14-day visit. You would think the Chinese would make it easy for visitors to go to their country and spend dollars there!

I happened to mention my China trip to Dr. Valery. He was excited.

"One minute, John," he said. He looked in a book and scribbled something on a paper for me. "Put this in your wallet."

It was the name of the official Peace Corps doctor in China. Yes, we had Volunteers there. "Dr. Gao Jinat at Sichuan University in the city of Chengdu." His contact information was included.

"If you need medical help, contact him!"

How thoughtful. As it turned out, not necessary.

Life is so strange. What a surprise to be back in China—back in Shanghai! Annabelle also had been here—25 years ago for a vacation. When we first met, she showed me her album of snapshots taken here. Particularly charming were the cute little children in their tiny Mao outfits. "I never thought I'd ever come back," she told me.

Shanghai is a stunning city. It's "wow!" this and "wow!" that. Remarkable because this ultra-modern and progressive metropolis is where we got the verb "to shanghai." Not a nice word. It made the city notorious.

Today all that is history. Shanghai has emerged as the biggest and the richest and glitziest city in China, surpassing even impressive Beijing. Beijing is the Washington, D.C. of China, and Shanghai is the New York City, and some say—in fact, I do—that it is more awesome than even Manhattan.

It's a city with a metro population estimated at 16 million and a city population of 8 million, with more millions shouldering their way in. The city has jumped over the river to an old wasteland and slum area called Pudong, and that has become a glittering co-city of big high buildings

Shanghai has high buildings beyond number and the downtown is studded with some extra-high ones. Big-name architects from America and Europe and, yes, Asia have come to town to cash in on the possibilities. They strive to embellish their reputations by designing buildings that somehow stand out from all the others around.

They struggle to outdo one another. One trick is to put something stunningly unusual up at the top. Maybe a giant sphere, or a pyramid, or some other novel shape. It is remarkable what they dream up. I saw one with a miniature castle way up at the top!

There's no end to the construction going on. We were staying in a 30-story building. A new one was going up across the street, but nicely set back. Forty floors!

Shanghai is a city of thousands of restaurants, some seating hundreds, some just a few. Plus thousands of stores, from great emporiums and smaller department stores to ordinary little shops, and exquisite boutiques. Thousands of mom and pop little businesses. McDonald's is there. KFC has many stores. Starbucks, Pizza Hut, Burger King. They are all there. Plus many that we have never heard of.

It's a city where streets and avenues are jammed with traffic. Thousands of buses and trackless trams—beauties, very high-tech. It has thousands of taxis. I believe Shanghai has more taxis than private autos..

I asked Wu why he didn't own a car. "Too big a problem. Too hard to find a place to put it. Too hard fighting the traffic. Better to use the Metro or a tram. Our Metro is one of the best in the world. On Saturday I rent a car. We go for a ride in the countryside!"

It's a city with millions of bicycles and motor scooters. Often they are the most practical private vehicle you can have. Shanghai is a flat city.

Pedaling is not difficult. It's easy to park a bike. Low operating cost. Even old people ride bicycles. No helmets.

All the principal streets have bicycle lanes, and during rush hours it's amazing to see the countless two-wheelers streaming by.

It's also a city of museums and libraries and theaters and nightclubs and churches and temples and hotels and office buildings and government buildings.

Downtown Shanghai is as beautiful as downtown New York City, I think. In fact, more beautiful. One surprise: everybody was in Western clothes.

And the parks! Many parks, big and small. So beautiful. So well-maintained.

Here parks aren't an afterthought. They are a necessity, so people can go outside and stretch their legs and sit in the sun and enjoy the cheapest pastime of all. People-watching! And there are people everywhere.

Shanghai is a roaring, rushing non-stop economic engine. A capitalist powerhouse. China's biggest! And what a paradox!

This is the city where the Chinese Communist Party got its start in 1931. Communism! No free markets. No free enterprise. Ironic!

But it didn't work, as we know. It's only when China junked that system in favor of a capitalist free-for-all again that its economy took off. It's amazing us by its vigor. It's setting records.

That's when China became today's booming country—the Factory to the World.

It's all so contradictory. How can a country at the same time have a Communist government grounded in Marxist precepts ("from all according to their talents, to all according to their needs")?

And a capitalist free-market system based on cutthroat competition? But that's the system it is today. Some say that's what explains its amazing success.

We all know that the 20$^{th}$ Century was America's century. That's when our country became big and wealthy and powerful and almighty.

Well, I am one of those who believe that this will be China's century. And that Shanghai will dominate the Chinese playing field.

Westernization is the driving force. They want to be like us in the West. I've mentioned that children take on English names for fun. Men and women and children dress like us. In our two weeks in China, I saw only two old men dressed in the long gowns and skullcaps of yesteryear.

It's eye-opening how much English you see on signs on the streets and in the stores. And much of Shanghai looks like a Western city, though with its own distinctive touches. Traditional Chinese architecture seems to be reserved for temples and Chinese-style tourist neighborhoods and restaurants. That's my impression.

Can't tell you how often Annabelle and I were approached by smiling university students as we walked around. They would say, "Hello! Where are you from? What is your name?" Such cute kids. We got caught up in it a lot, Annabelle especially. All they wanted was to meet real Americans and practice their English. So many study English in school.

Annabelle flew over on China Air. She told me most of the passengers by far were Chinese. The attendants served everybody meals with both chopsticks and knives and forks. Take your pick.

"I looked around," she said. "Most people were using forks and knives. Not chopsticks."

Yes, Westernization is the big thing, at least in the major cities. But I'll bet she was using chopsticks.

*Happy at his work on the sidewalk. So many new sights for us to enjoy.*

But it didn't take the two of us long to notice something else. We thought this rampant Western emphasis might have swept away all remnants of traditional Chinese life. Not so. We saw this on our first day in the city.

We decided to go for a walk. We would walk straight ahead, and then straight back. No darting down a side street, and then exploring another. We wanted to make certain we did not get lost! We couldn't say even "Hello "or ""Thank you" in Mandarin.

But we each had a precious paper in our pocket, which Wu had typed out for us. It had our address, and Wu's address, with his phone numbers, as well as the name of one of his friends, Lu Man, with her phone numbers, just in case we got lost.

Our neighborhood was all high-rises. But in just two blocks we entered Old China. That's what I called it. It was a pocket neighborhood of the old days. And the old ways.

For three blocks, old buildings lined both sides, only two stories high. Drying clothes hung from lines running from building to building.

For the whole stretch, the ground floor of buildings was a series of small shops. Very small, the size of a bedroom, say. Crammed with stock, and usually with just one attendant, the owner, often a woman, probably the owner's wife. China has millions of such tiny businesses, it seems.

But the sidewalks out front were also prime retail area. A barber would be cutting somebody's hair on the sidewalk Ladies would be sewing clothes for people. And mending.

All kinds of peddlers were set up there. They had plastic sheets put down on the sidewalk to show all their fruits and vegetables. Or tubs of fish. I saw tubs of live turtles. Turtles are considered a nice dinner. So many other strange delicacies.

Women had pushcarts crowded with their wares, all kinds of household stuff. One man was baking huge potatoes that people bought as a lunch. A lot of people were running what we would call yard sales, with all kinds of used stuff. A lot of jewelry and jade items, and samples of calligraphy. Calligraphy is a great art form, highly prized.

A lot of sidewalk restaurants were set up. A man out in the open air was cooking noodles on a tiny stove, and people were eating bowls of noodles at little tables as people walked by. A woman was washing the bowls in a pan of cold water.

Nearby a woman was serving bowls of fried rice. Another offered an amazing variety of Chinese pastries.

And all along this stretch, so many side alleys, maybe just 15 feet wide. Too narrow for a car, but with plenty of bikes and motor scooters parked in there. With two-story buildings stuck side by side all the way back, all crowded with people in tiny apartments. Many clotheslines strung up, with pants and shirts drying.

Little chance for the sun to reach down into here. People working at this or that outside. Two ladies having a neighborly chat. A kid repairing a motorbike. A dog chasing another dog. A young woman nursing a baby.

I was fascinated.

**W**u's wedding was the big event, of course. It was spectacular. It was a production, and in a real sense. We'll never forget it.

He went out and hired a professional wedding consultant to choreograph the whole thing and make sure every detail went right. Wu greeted us at the airport, making the long ride with a friend who had a car. The wedding was the next day! He still had so much to do.

He put us up in an apartment hotel in a quite new high-rise. It was what I would call a studio apartment with everything provided, from a washing machine and microwave right down to cups and teaspoons.

I must mention the building's elevators. It had four passenger elevators. So quiet and smooth and fast. We were on the 16$^{th}$ floor. One day I checked. It took us just 13 seconds to whiz up to our floor. Amazing.

Now, about the wedding. It was going to be on Sunday at 4 p.m. Wu told us that his friend Lu would pick us up. And he had his mother Lu with him. Wu and Lu. Yes, confusing, I know. Lu turned out to be their family name!

Warm embraces! I had met them both. I introduced Annabelle. They were shy but that would pass, I was sure.

I knew Lu from my previous trip. Good guy. About Wu's age. One of China's new young capitalists, dealing in stocks and bonds, making a name for himself in the Shanghai stock market crowd. I knew his mom also. A sweet little woman.

We took a taxi. The

*The bridal couple. Wu is handsome, Eileen lovely. We did not know what to expect. We found ourselves at a wedding part Chinese and part Western. We enjoyed it all.*

wedding would be in a hotel. A handsome, modern place. We entered and walked up the grand staircase to the ballroom.

Then what a surprise! Wu and Eileen were standing at the top, directly in front of us. She was gorgeous in a white gown. Wu was handsome in a dark suit, white shirt, and silk tie. We expected a Chinese wedding.

This looked American. We expected exquisite traditional Chinese garments. I was disappointed in a way. A violinist and a clarinetist played as we arrived. Those are not Chinese instruments. And those weren't Chinese melodies.

Wu and Eileen greeted us warmly. I embraced him. What a smile he had. I kissed Eileen on the cheek. She was startled—yes, that's the right word—but smiled. It was our first meeting. I took to her right away.

Two men had approached. Wore gym suits and baseball caps. Certainly not guests. Each had a huge TV camera on his shoulder, and they had them focused on us! They were filming a DVD of the wedding—another of the wedding producer's all-out ideas.

Then we were we led to a side table with a great big crimson book on display. It was open. Every page was crimson. It was the wedding guest register.

We were showed where to sign. I looked at the names on the page. I couldn't read any of them. All in Mandarin. I signed and Annabelle signed. It amused me that other guests probably wouldn't be able to read our names either.

There were 180 of us attending. We were at Table 9. As we entered the ballroom, no wonder so many eyes focused on us. They weren't used to seeing the likes of us. That was obvious.

I spotted a huge word on the wall up front: "Wedding!" Yes, in English! The room was lavishly decorated with colorful silks and tassels. An interior decorator had been at work. Truly gala.

There were large circular tables for eight. White linen tablecloths. Linen napkins. Chopsticks delicately poised on chopstick blocks. Each table had bottles of Chinese whisky, rice wine, red wine, beer, soft drinks. One brand of beer was Budweiser. Again, Budweiser in Shanghai!

I would be sitting next to Lu Man, a lovely lady about 40. She was a friend from my last visit. She could speak excellent English.

Right away I recognized Wu's thoughtfulness. She explained everything. There would be two speakers. She would be one. And surprise! I would be the other.

G̲uests entered. What struck me was the variety. All ages, some quite elderly, some children. Some persons were dressed quite formally, the way Annabelle and I were, though I did not wear a tux or Annabelle a gown.

Some came with an open-necked shirt, no tie. In slacks. I saw a couple in jeans. All that seemed acceptable.

Wu and Eileen entered. Great applause. They were beaming. They were led to their seats of honor way at the front.

I knew Wu's father and mother and I knew they were here but I could not make them out. We did not know Eileen's parents.

The waiters began bringing the food. Each table had a huge Lazy Susan. Astounding how much food. A total of some 40 dishes! There was beef and lamb and chicken and pork and shrimp. Plus other meats and seafood. No way could I tell what many things were.

I took Lu Man's word for everything. The most dramatic was a big fish. It looked asleep on the plate. Shanghai cooking is sophisticated. Then all the vegetables and fruits!

Now, the toast! Somebody up front said something. We couldn't understand, of course. Our glasses were filled and ready. For that, red wine had been chosen. I asked Lu Man about this. It turns out that red wine is new in China.

We raised our glasses. Wu and Eileen raised theirs. They were radiant. We weren't sure what exactly we were drinking to, but it was fine by us.

E̲verybody ate with chopsticks, of course. The Bud and the red wine seemed the only Western items. Oh, for the soups they used big, funny ceramic Chinese soupspoons. I like them a lot better than our metal spoons.

All of us would reach into this dish or that one with our sticks, pick up a morsel, and lift it into our mouths. So all the sticks dipped into all the dishes. We frown on that. Not a problem for them. And it's not impolite to make noise as you eat. It's good to slurp your soup. It shows you relish it.

Everybody laughed when Annabelle picked up her sticks. Chopsticks are tapered. The working end is whittled down. Annabelle was holding hers by the wrong end. A pure accident. She's been using chopsticks for years. She's good with them. I am learning. I have little accidents.

Our Lazy Susan was wonderful. What a great idea. The centerpiece was that big fish. People reached over and picked at it with their sticks. Soon there was just a long skeleton on the plate. Even the head and the eyes got eaten.

Finally came the rice and the noodles. They signal the end of the serious eating. Then the waiters brought us a good-looking fruit concoction. Oh, the wedding cake! Yes, it was a Western cake. We each got a piece. I noticed some folks were unsure about it. Some refused it. Shanghai Weight-Watchers?

Then the ceremony! Quite brief. First, Wu and Eileen stood and faced one another, held up their glasses, and pronounced some solemn words to one another. All in Mandarin, of course.

Then they extended their right arms and touched palms. Held them together all while taking turns speaking more solemn words. I don't know whether they were memorized words or personally composed words. Impressive, especially the touching of palms..

I could not make out a religious official or any other official. Maybe there was one. Maybe not. Then the solemn part was over. It had lasted just a few minutes. Maybe something had preceded it—Lu Man had mentioned that both families had met at Wu and Eileen's condo for something important in the morning.

Now applause all through the room. Happy music. A big TV screen came alive. Being shown was the DVD of messages sent in by friends from near and far. In fact, it was being shown on two screens, so everyone could see. Wu had incorporated my modest contribution. It was amusing to watch myself. I wished I had done a better job.

Then Lu Man rose and walked to the podium up front. She had a script in hand. She spoke in a clear and positive voice. Obviously she had given this much thought. Again, all in Mandarin. Applause. She returned to our table but did not sit. To my surprise, she took me by the arm and escorted me to the front.

I had thought about this and I had decided that I would smile a lot. Which I did. When you can't say much, smiles help a lot!

It was my turn now. I spoke. Lu Man translated. So the two of us went back and forth. I kept it simple but I put in a lot of emotion. I felt a lot of emotion. Wu meant a lot to me. My Chinese "nephew"!

I was looking directly at Wu and Eileen, of course. At one point I paused and bowed to him. Then I turned to Eileen and said nice words and bowed to her. I knew folks couldn't understand but they could see. And understand how I felt.

Lu Man was doing her best to translate, I was sure. I joked. I chuckled. Finally I finished. Applause. People were being too generous, I thought. Lu Man escorted me back to our table.

Now things got loose and informal. A magician came on and did tricks. Imagine, a musician at a wedding reception! He was good.

I heard a rich baritone singing up front. An Italian aria! From Verdi. Could it be there was an Italian opera singer in this room? I looked. It was a small Chinese man singing. He was about 50. What a strong and compelling voice! I nudged Lu Man.

"Eileen's father!" she said. "He loves to sing opera. It's his hobby. Very good, don't you think?"

"He's marvelous!" People can be so surprising.

Wu and Eileen, hand in hand, began visiting all the tables. They chatted and laughed and lavished attention on everybody. They made their way to our table and they were gracious and sweet. Wu gave us each a hug. That's definitely not a Chinese thing.

Oh, I must tell you! During a part of this Eileen had stepped out. Maybe to the ladies' room, I thought. But she came back in a completely different outfit. Again, stunning. At another point she left again...and returned in still another outfit. Three outfits during the dinner!

Everyone was merry now. All those bottles on each table had been opened. Many wedding presents, of course. We saw many envelopes being proffered. All red envelopes. Lu Man explained to us.

"People don't know what to give. They don't know what the bridal couple needs, or what they already have. They give money. But it must always be presented in a red envelope."

I told her we have the same problem back in our country. But why red, I asked Lu Man. "It's the wedding color." she said. I recalled that crimson guest book.

"How about white?" She hesitated. "For us white is the color of death." Instantly I recalled how at the top of the stairs Eileen had been beautiful in her pure white gown. Well, it was clear some traditions were being changed here. Just as some of ours are.

*All smiles as they begin their married life. Wu and Eileen are excellent examples of China's rapidly-rising modern middle class.*

Annabelle and I had been stumped about a wedding gift. My sister Lucie had a good suggestion. "Go to the Shanghai Museum. It has a fine gift shop, remember? They'll have an excellent selection. And everything would be exchangeable, I'm sure."

We did that. We found an antique classic painting in a fine frame. We wanted something with enduring value. Their eyes glowed when they opened our package.

Annabelle had asked Wu for suggestions. He mentioned a travel guidebook about California. When she pressed him, he also mentioned a certain music CD. She had bought them both.

She had also brought an exquisite set of silver chopsticks. She had bought them on her trip to China 25 years before but had never used them.

Now a surprise. Two older couples approached us. Wu's parents and Eileen's parents! Broad smiles. Happy faces. We shook hands. After all, it's our American custom.

They bowed. We bowed back. Warm words on both sides. We didn't understand their words and they didn't understand our words, yet we all understood everything. That's the best way to put it.

Now it was time for Wu and Eileen to leave. It's always an emotional thing. They were closing a big chapter and starting a bigger one. Leaving their families. Starting a family. Wu had mentioned that Eileen had become his best friend. I hoped that would never change.

They were going on a honeymoon, of course. But not now. In May. Off to Australia. Wu always said he would come to the U.S.A. and stop by to see us again. He had mentioned they would honeymoon in the U.S.A. The problem was that Eileen could not get a visa. The War on Terrorism!

All in all, a spectacular day. Once more we were reminded that many of us on our planet are of different color and culture but very much alike.

The rest of our two weeks was wonderful. We went off sightseeing and scouting. Visited museums and the big central library. Toured parts of the city. I went shooting pictures in Old China just two blocks away. We saw Wu several times. We attended dinners with him, met more of his friends. It was clear that he had an active life covering family, work, and community.

We had memorable experiences time and again. One day on the street a middle-aged man approached me. Searching hard for the right words, he asked, "How old are you?"

I told him 78. He scrutinized me, seemed satisfied, and walked away. It happened again. This time a woman. I told her 78. She nodded and stared.

It happened another time. I thought for a second and said, "I am 99." The fellow looked at me hard. But seemed satisfied. I decided then and there that 99 would be my age in China. Then another thought.

I turned to Annabelle. "Oh, my God! He believed me. I must look 99!"

She just laughed.

Annabelle and I found out one thing. We got to know what it's like to be pandas in a zoo. We were stared at wherever we went.

Our trip to Shanghai was wonderful in every way.

I asked Wu why Australia for their honeymoon.

"We want to see the kangaroos!"

"You can see kangaroos at your Shanghai zoo," I told him. He laughed. I did, too. But it was true.

Now a word to you, dear readers. Go to Shanghai if you can. Go before the yuan, the Chinese "dollar," skyrockets in value. It will. Go! Such a fantastic city.

Annabelle and I left China in the same way, flying in opposite directions. She flew east and I flew west. That was remarkable in itself. She got home to California without a problem. I landed in Kyiv determined to get right back to work and carry on full tilt. Just 15 months to go!

~ ~ ~

**Did you know** ... that being a small "ambassador" for our own country at your overseas post can be challenging? Even taxing?

In time many people will know that you are an American, if not a Peace Corps Volunteer. This is a concept unknown to most people. But those you associate with will learn about it, and they will measure you in keeping with what they think being a Volunteer means.

Many eyes will be on you, at work and in your private life. It can become a weight to live up to it at all times and under all circumstances.

Of course, every Volunteer wants to make a good impression. But you become conscious of little things that never occurred to you before. You are more careful about the way you dress. How you act in stores and restaurants. It carries over in surprising ways.

# 30 / Annabelle visits me

*It's time! She flies to Ukraine, meets my friends, and gets to see my life close up. Just as I hoped.*

Her coming to see me some months later was so exciting! Since I had arrived in Ukraine, the two of us had been shooting e-mails back and forth almost daily. We knew how we were doing. We were up to the minute despite having been separated for many months and by thousands of miles.

The e-mails were wonderful. But there are distances of the heart that e-mails still cannot bridge.

Yes, we had met in China for two weeks. But what I wanted was for her to see me at work in Ukraine and share a bit of my life. Her desire, too.

How to put her up for a month? I had mulled several options. They ranged from a hotel room to an apartment of our own. But the ideas fell apart when I went looking and thought things out. I had told my host mother, Tanya, that Annabelle was coming. She was happy for me, and genuinely so, I thought.

One morning I braced myself. "Tanya," I said. "Would it be possible for Annabelle to stay with me here?"

"No problem," she said. "We will manage, the three of us."

Within two days she made it easier. "I have been planning to go on vacation," she told me. "I'll be going to Bulgaria for 10 days."

And she departed the day before Annabelle arrived! Was that a coincidence? I didn't think so. We had her place all to ourselves!

How could the two of us best spend this golden time together? This had also required thought. I had my teaching to do at *Coursi*. And I had my two clubs on Sundays to run. And I had to continue slogging away on my library-digitalization project and my public-transit project. But I had vacation time coming and of course I was ripe for a vacation. I'd use the time to squire Annabelle around.

What we put together was a calendar of work and play. This would be good several ways. Annabelle would tag along for everything and get a close-up view of what I did and what Peace Corps was all about. She would meet just about all my associates and some of my students and get an idea of how I spent my days.

I thought she would find this fun for the sheer variety of it and she agreed. Plus, we would have true vacation time.

An excursion to Kyiv would be a must. And I planned a weekend to Ukraine's second most famous city, Lviv. It is in the west, at the foot of the Carpathian Mountains. It's renowned for its history and architecture.

Then we planned a long trip in the opposite direction, to far-off Sevastopol. This famous seaport is right on the Black Sea, in the fabled, sunny Crimea. SNAC, our seniors' group, would be holding its summer meeting there. I would be attending it anyway. There Annabelle would meet more Volunteers, and closer to our age.

As usual, SNAC would be planning a fine weekend. Annabelle would get to sit in on our business meeting, which she would enjoy and where she would learn a lot. And I knew she would be welcomed on all our fun activities.

Good weather would be an essential, but this would be late summer and Ukraine is marvelous then!

Annabelle arrived joyfully but exhausted—three flights, the first to Newark from Dallas, where she had been visiting her daughter Katie and family. The second to London. Then the last to Kyiv. So much airport scrambling within a squeezed schedule! Thousands of miles in the air over eight one-hour changes!

**I** was at Borispil Airport outside Kyiv to meet her. I was lucky. I had expected to have to take a *marshrutka* to Kyiv, then another to the airport. A half-day deal for sure. At the last minute I found I could take a *marshrutka* directly from Chernihiv to Borispil, a 2.5 hour ride. And this direct service was only a month old. What progress!

I waited on my tiptoes as the passengers filed in with their suitcases. Finally I spotted her. She was wearing one of her signature hats, as usual. It made me smile.

We took the same *marshrutka* back. Annabelle fell asleep against my shoulder. She was exhausted. Now the usual dull ride to Chernihiv. But she was all eyes when we drew close. The sight of the gleaming white church with its golden domes atop the hill stirred her. It stirred me every time I saw it. It stirs everybody, I believe.

"How beautiful!" she murmured.

Quickly we entered the city. She gave its centuries-old plaza an appreciative glance. "It's much more attractive than I thought."

Then a taxi to Tanya's. She stared at the big blocks. "These buildings were designed more for comfort than beauty, weren't they?"

"Yes, correct." She was being generous. There was zero beauty to them, in my opinion. "Practicality" was their key word.

The driver even lugged Annabelle's luggage up to Tanya's third-floor flat. I was hoping he'd do that.

Home! Tanya soon arrived. She smiled, Annabelle smiled, I smiled. Annabelle knew the language barrier would be difficult. But the smiles and Tanya's ease and grace made it all easy. As did Annabelle's.

The next morning she slept late, of course. She got up because she had to. Sasha, my tutor, was coming to give me my Russian lesson.

Sasha arrived, beaming as usual. And excited. She knew all about Annabelle's coming. "*Stradzvuite*," she said to Annabelle as if to a dear friend. "So happy to meet you!" And that set the tone.

"Hello, Sasha," Annabelle said. "I feel the same way!"

Annabelle tagged along everywhere and enjoyed it. Here dinner at school.

She knew all about Sasha, of course. Sasha was a senior at the Pedagogical University. I had met her at the Korolonko one day—was struck by her wonderful American English. She became my Russian tutor—visited me at Tanya's for private lessons twice a week for some 18 months.

I paid her 133 *hryvnia* a month (about $27), the amount provided by Peace Corps, which was a fair price. She tried hard to teach me, and never gave up.

We became friends. And now here she was. Friendly chatter ensued, but Sasha was here to teach me, and we had to sit and do the Russian. It wasn't easy. The two of us worked at my desk, as usual.

Annabelle went out to the living room with a book about Chernihiv to read. She sat on the divan there. I had a thought, *I have never sat on that divan in all the months I have lived with Tanya.*

Sasha and I worked away. I suspected Annabelle was listening to us as we did our best to carry on as usual. Finally the lesson ended.

Sasha left with a smile for me and a hug for Annabelle. The two of us went on to a relaxed day. Better to start slowly. We caught up fully. I kept talking about my life in the city and all the people who were part of it. I filled her in. I wanted her to understand. And she was greatly interested.

It was an unseasonably cold and windy day but we ventured out. There was so much for her to see. Important not to waste time. And the walking was good for the exercise. We walked to the Soiooz market nearby. Soiooz is a big food-store chain.

We came to it. It was on the first floor of a five-story apartment block. It was only one-tenth the size of one of our big American supermarkets.

"This is a supermarket?" Annabelle said unbelievingly.

"Yes. To them it is. Few people have cars. They can't carry much, so they go shopping nearly every day. So there are branch stores like this at every big bus and trolley stop. And at big apartment buildings like this. The stores carry all the basics. But just basics. But that's changing."

Inside, I walked to the wall of lockers. I put my shoulder bag in one, told Annabelle to include her pocketbook, then locked the small door and pocketed the key.

I told her, "This locking-up is the standard practice in every store. And see that man over by the door. He watches everybody. All stores have these sharp-eyed guys."

We sauntered through the store. I pointed out how big the cookie section was, and the candy section, and the alcohol section. True, they were the biggest departments in any store.

Sasha came for my Russian lesson as usual. You can see that I didn't have my heart in it. She was determined.

Annabelle picked out a bottle of Chardonnay—or what she hoped would be Chardonnay. It seemed to look like her favorite. No labels in English here. I assured her it was. I had learned a bit of the lingo.

She noticed how small the produce section was. Just a few apples and tomatoes and other common fruits and vegetables.

I told her, "That's because most people buy their fruits and vegetables at the big bazaar. In fact, we have four bazaars in the city. Their prices are cheaper. I'll take you to a big one later."

We inspected the meat department. She noticed most of the items were sausages—a huge variety of sausages. Few roasts and steaks. The sausages are budget stretchers.

Manny kinds of breads. Ukraine makes delicious breads. We went down the aisle of breakfast cereals. The variety was limited. Yes, she found corn flakes, but just small boxes. Same thing in the detergent sections—all small boxes. Small bottles of everything.

"That's because people must carry their purchases home. They walk. Or take a bus or trolley. No big car to pile the stuff in. This is why people buy just two or three apples at a time. Or a few onions."

She saw familiar brands. Colgate. Kleenex. Coca-Cola. There was a small department of house wares, both plastic and steel. She checked and saw most of this stuff was imported from China. She said, "China is huge here, too!" Yes.

Finally we stood in line at the small check-out. I took out my money. It was the first time she saw *hryvnia* and *kopecks,* the bills and coins of the land.

The young woman in the snappy red and white uniform scanned the purchases—yes, the stores are computerized here—and added them up on her register. Annabelle saw the amount tally on the electronic window: 32 *hryvnia,* and 47 *kopeck.* A bit less than $6.

I paid and the clerk gave me my change and receipt. "*Pakete?*" she asked. I shook my head. No. I had brought my own plastic bag. She would have charged another 6 *kopecks* for one.

Annabelle had gotten several surprises in that store. Outside, she looked at our small purchases. She said, "How much did the wine cost?" I told her about $2.50.

"Well, that's a bargain," she said. "But the other things we bought didn't seem to be."

"That's true. Ukrainians find food expensive. It's a big, big item in their budget. And the prices go up and up. Huge inflation here. More than 20 percent per year. And salaries drag far behind."

I thought of something else. "Maybe that's another reason why there are few fat people here. They eat less. And they walk a lot more."

Back home, Tanya was out. Annabelle made supper. She checked Tanya's cupboards and refrigerator and saw onions and carrots and noodles and rice and other things. Tanya had told us several times to make ourselves at home. I took her at her word.

Annabelle made a tasty supper and quite quickly. We were sitting and eating at a tiny table in a tiny kitchen in a huge apartment block in a city whose name she still could not pronounce. But we were eating a nice American meal! It felt good.

The next day Annabelle rose earlier. She was getting adjusted. It was Sunday. She would accompany me to my two clubs in the afternoon.

I wanted to show her some sights, so we left the flat at 10 and took Trolleybus No. 6 downtown.

It was an oldie. They were all oldies. Forty years old, I estimated. Few passengers because Sunday. We were able to take seats! On weekdays we'd have to stand. I gave Annabelle two coins and told her to give them to the *conductora* when she approached. I pointed to her, a big forty-ish woman with a yellow and blue frock, the Ukrainian colors.

I had told Annabelle that old people rode free. I had long ago stopped paying because everybody was startled when they saw me paying. One *conductora* had refused my money. But Annabelle was obviously a senior citizen, yes, but obviously a foreign tourist. Better to pay.

The *conductora* approached, Annabelle gave her the coins, and the *conductora* took them and gave her a tiny receipt and moved on. Annabelle now had one more key experience under her belt.

The trolleybus bumped and lurched along. Rubber tires. No tracks. "I like it," I said to Annabelle. "It reminds me of sailing on Narragansett Bay back in Little Rhody."

Rhode Island is where I was born and grew up. She smiled. She had done a lot of sailing also.

**W**e arrived at the *rinok*, the big central open-air bazaar. Perhaps 500 or 600 tiny stalls, one next to another in long rows. As I've explained, each a tiny one-person business, man or woman.

Each was a specialty shop of one kind—pots and pans, soaps and detergents, men's sweaters, stationery items, ladies' underwear, electric switches, curtains, bathroom stuff, pillows, men's shoes, women's shoes, children's shoes, hardware, auto parts.

Sharp competition, with many shops offering the same goods.

Few visible prices. You ask the price and you are told the price. Maybe some folks haggled, but I rarely did. They knew I was a foreigner, probably suspected I was an American. I didn't want to create a bad impression. On the other hand, I didn't want to act like a rich tourist by accepting whatever price they mentioned. Sometimes I declined, always with a smile.

Also a large area in the center of the market for food. Dozens of vendors, many selling the same items. Tomatoes. Onions. Squashes. Cabbages, Carrots. So many other vegetables. And so many fruits.

So many egg vendors. All eggs had prices—so many different prices. So many varieties and sizes of eggs. Two white eggs of the same size, or two brown eggs, might have different prices. No idea why. Ukrainians are connoisseurs!

We had little to buy. Besides, we had to go on to the library for my French Club and then my English Club.

We bought a juicy pomegranate and a couple of nice oranges. They were merely handed over to me. No bag was offered for big items—just for grapes or mushrooms. I put everything in my shoulder bag. "This is Ukraine!" I said to her.

At one corner there were six or seven women standing in a line. Middle-aged and hefty. Each, each wore a big apron and a cap. Each was standing in front of her own insulated box. Each was hawking something. Hard to make out what.

They were selling what I called "grease cakes." Hot, golden, deep-fried dumplings. Six or eight kinds. Stuffed with mashed potatoes, or with cabbage, or sausage.

I approached her and pointed to item No. 2 on her sign—with mashed potatoes—and said, "*Pashalusta, dba.*" "Please, two."

She had a plastic bag over her right hand as a mitten. She opened her chest, dug deep and moved things around, and picked out two. I paid her. I gave one to Annabelle. "Try this, dear." I bit into mine.

She was hesitating. It was hot in her hand and greasy. She took a tiny bite. "Not bad," she said. She smiled. "Hits the spot!"

Not a fib. She ate it all. We were lucky. Later in the day, that goodie might have been sold cold.

"Mashed potatoes inside," I said. "I like it. Especially on a bitter cold day in January!"

A bit farther, I stopped at another woman, younger this time. No apron. Standing in front of a big steel thermos bottle. She had various tinned coffees and teas on a small table.

I pointed to one tin. "*Dva,*" I said, motioning to Annabelle and myself. And "*Adyn y adyn.*" "One and one."

The woman picked up two four-ounce plastic cups from a stack. Small by our standards. She dropped a teaspoon of coffee in each cup, then a teaspoon of sugar —"one and one!"

She filled the cups half full of water from her steel bottle. I indicated "more" and she put in a little more, but stopped short of filling the cups. That's because we'd be walking. She didn't want us to spill and scald ourselves. I paid her. About 70 cents for our two cups.

The cups were thin plastic. Too hot to hold. I showed Annabelle how to hold them by their rim. No problem that way. We walked along, sipping our coffee. She wasn't quite certain about all this but was being a good sport.

We walked around the huge bazaar for another 30 minutes. Always a lot of fun. We got to the big library at 12:40. Right on time.

Annabelle had seen pictures of it. "It is very, very grand!" she said. She was familiar with it from my e-mails. How it began as a bank. How in World War 11 it had been taken over by the Germans as a headquarters. How then it had become a museum. How the library moved in when it needed more room. How it was named for the great writer, Korolonko.

We walked up the great marble steps inside and turned right and found our way to the Foreign Language Department, my department—the only one I ever went to.

A big, sunny room with big windows at the end. Big cacti on the sills. Attractive modern furniture. Half a dozen reading tables with two chairs at each. A long wall filled with books. Modern equipment—four computers, a big TV set. Big cacti and other plants on the sill for the big windows. There were two young women doing research at one table, "readers." We'd call them "patrons" in the U.S.A.

**T**wo of the three librarians were working today, Tanya and Iryna. Victoria, the head was off. All were my friends now. Both of them smiled and quickly came forward.

"Well, this is milady Annabelle!" I said. But they already knew. "Hello!" they said in Russian. "So happy to meet you finally!" Their enthusiasm was clear.

They had heard me use the word "milady" before. They understood: we were a long-time committed couple but not married. They accepted that.

Annabelle already knew about them.

I loved all three. But Iryna was my special friend, as you know. Besides being a librarian, she was a professional teacher of English. She took delight in both my clubs. She was always helping me—so much so that I began calling her "my partner."

*We were all excited on hearing Denys was getting married. A happy day!*

She showed Annabelle the impressive Window on America section of books, made possible by our American Embassy. She was so proud. And then the smaller European Union collection, made possible by that group. She went on and on about the department. Annabelle was all ears.

Then a young man and two young women came in. All smiling. "Hello, Denys," I said. "Hello, Lilitt. Hello, Ira." They were the most regular members of my French Club. And three more entered. It was time to get started. I said to them all, *"Bonjour, mes amis!"*—"Hello, my friends!"

I introduced Annabelle. "You all heard about her," I said to them. They nodded and smiled.

One more arrived—my friend, Renato, the Italian expat. He was a regular at both my English and French clubs.

Renato also knew about Annabelle. And she about him. I could see they were both pleased to finally meet. Two others arrived. All friendly. We arranged three tables into a big U and all of us sat down at our usual places, I front and center. Our club was in session. The meetings lasted 75 minutes.

They were very informal. We chatted about different topics. The idea was to speak French and perfect our French. Some spoke better than others. Only two were truly good, Denys and Ira, both 22. But we all tried our best. I led the conversation. I was so happy when I got them to talk back. It was the toughest part of my challenge.

Today the whole meeting centered on Annabelle. She had studied French in college, could read it a bit, but had lost whatever speaking ability she had. Everybody was sympathetic. They knew that to preserve their French—or their English—they had to practice, practice, and practice. I drummed that in constantly.

We talked about her flights, her home state of California, her children, her brand-new impressions of Ukraine.

Annabelle was interested in everybody. Seemed to enjoy it. Certainly I did. The clubs were the best part of my week. I believed that my students enjoyed it. Hoped they got something out of it!

Then followed our English Club, a bigger group. We moved to a large room upstairs where the chairs were arranged in a big oval. About 20 came in, the average size. Mostly university students, but a few high school students and some older people. Male and female, about half and half. I knew most of them. They were regulars. But we attracted two or three newcomers every Sunday. Today was typical.

I called the meeting to order. Many were studying Annabelle. They smiled at her, fixated on her. They knew! I introduced her, calling her Milady Annabelle, as I always did.

She stood, smiled, said "Hello. I am so happy to be here with you. John has told me about you. All good things!"

Present here also was Iryna, my partner. She welcomed the group, then made special mention of Annabelle. Annabelle beamed.

As usual, I asked each person in the circle to self-introduce. Some said just their name and university or job. Some were shy, some incapable of dredging up enough English to get it done. Others elaborated. I knew by now what most of them would say.

Then I introduced the topic: air travel. Most topical, given Annabelle's presence. I asked Annabelle about her long trip, all the many details...what airlines, the many stops, how she planned it, how she shopped for the best prices, and Annabelle explained. It made everything more interesting. I was observing their reactions. They were fascinated.

I asked how many of them had traveled by plane. Only four hands went up. I asked them for details. Not many were offered. But I kept asking and asking. I cajoled. I wheedled. I talked about my experiences of plane travel. The whole point was to educate while entertaining, give encouragement, be helpful in any way possible, and open their minds about the U.S.

Then I gave them my pep talk. "This week find someone to speak English with. Read something in English every day. Read aloud to yourself. Memorize new words. Watch American DVDs. Listen to English on the radio. It's all up to you. Yes, you. Have a good week." They had heard this from me before.

A few lingered to chat. Afterward, Iryna led us back down to her Foreign Book Department. Then into the off-limits book room next door. The three librarians had a cozy nook back there. Iryna made us a cup of tea, offered cookies, and we sat and chatted around the cozy table. Pleasant. I could see the two were taking to one another.

Later Annabelle and I talked over the experience. She felt the members got a lot out of both meetings. Even those who said little. "And I could see they all like you!"

I believed this was true. But it made me feel good to hear her say it. I gave her a hug.

The next day I took her to *Coursi*. Olena and Lina, the dean and the methodologist, had been alerted and were totally charming and welcoming. Then as teachers strolled in, I introduced Annabelle. Smiles and good wishes from all. They knew about her and her coming.

I gave Annabelle a tour of the classrooms, all quite modern and pleasant. "Much nicer that I thought," she said. "Very nice. The staff, too! I see why you are happy here."

I did not have a class of students to speak to that day, but I did have a private lesson scheduled with Anton, my 14-year-old friend. He, too, knew about Annabelle. He arrived eagerly, as always.

"Hello!" he said with his usual big smile. He was not bashful, and soon he was asking questions of her and making comments.

The three of us sat around a table and talked for the whole 90 minutes. Today our topic was, yes, air travel again. It was such a natural. Anton had never been in a plane.

We talked over many aspects. How she chose the airlines, made reservations through search engines. Airport security. The crowded plane, sitting for hours, the role of the attendants. Then landing, collecting luggage, going through Customs and Immigration.

There was a lot to talk about. Our time went by quickly. I could see Annabelle was impressed by his fluency. My dream was that he would take the FLEX exam. I was sure he would ace it.

**I** had told her this was why Anton signed up with me. "He is eager to talk, talk, talk in English. Wants to be fluent. And he's good at writing English. I'd like to have more students like him."

Additionally, I always assigned him a paper to write as a home task. I would read it, correct it, and then discuss it with him. It was heartening how proficient in speaking and writing he was becoming.

During her stay Annabelle returned to *Coursi*. She got to feel close to Olena and Lina. And Anton. And I think they did to her.

We had planned to go to Kyiv the next morning for the day. The forecast called for cold and gray and it was accurate. We put off the excursion. It was two days later that we went. Annabelle was incredulous when I set the alarm for 4:15 a.m.

I explained to her, "The trains are few. We have to catch the 6:12 morning *electrika*. Yes, it's an electric train, not a diesel. We'd waste too much time if we waited for the next one."

We could have gone by *marshrutka*. This would be a new experience. A good one, I hoped.

It would have taken two hours by *marshrutka* on the main highway, skirting everything. Always a terribly dull ride, as I've mentioned. This train took three hours, but we made 10 or 12 stops. We got to see bits and pieces of towns and villages. I found it interesting and so did Annabelle. Surprising how smooth our ride was in some stretches and how bumpy in others. This definitely was not Amtrak.

We were in one of nine cars. We sat side by side. Our car was mostly empty. As we went along, more people got on. Finally only one seat was left, right across from me.

**A** man came in and took the seat. He was short, energetic, about 50. I nodded to him and he nodded back. He spoke some English....was

Russian...now lived in Calgary, Alberta...was a pipeline engineer...was back here on assignment. His name was Alex. We had a lively chat..

Like us, he was going to Kyiv. There he walked with us into the huge station. I wanted to make reservations for our upcoming weekend in Lviv.

He offered to help us. How lucky we were. He led us through the maze of people to the right clerk, one of dozens, told her in Russian what we wanted, and completed all the arrangements for us. All I had to do was pay. All this had taken more than half an hour. It would have taken us forever. What a good guy.

He knew Annabelle was a first-time visitor. "I have a suggestion for you," he said. It was about a good sight-seeing tour of the city. "Its office is very close to here." We jumped at the opportunity. I was astonished: he walked us over to the office!

A nice big bus was parked out front. A tour was departing in 35 minutes. Alex again did the translating. He made sure we got on the bus all right, then said goodbye.

I tried to press money into his hand. "No, no!" he said. "My pleasure." He strode off, never to be seen again.

The bus filled and we started. Our guide was a Russian speaker. Surprise. This tour would be all in Russian, not English. Oh, well. I had been to Kyiv perhaps 10 times, always on Peace Corps business. I had seen very little. As Alex said, this was a fine tour.

Annabelle understood not a word. I, to my embarrassment, understood very little. But we appreciated the many marvelous sights. Independence Square. Government buildings. Parks. Churches. Monuments. The session went by quickly.

Our guide soon saw our language problem. He would lean toward us and say "St. Vladimir's Cathedral." Or "Chinese Embassy." He knew a few words of English! When we got back, he came over and said, "So sorry. My English very bad!" A good man!

I was so impressed by our tour that I felt all new Volunteers should get such a tour when just arrived. It would make them appreciate Kyiv so much more, and give them such a better introduction to the country.

Next I took Annabelle to Peace Corps. It occupied a small four-story building tucked in an enclave behind other buildings. No sign of any kind on the building. No American flag out front. Intentionally discreet, I believed.

There were always several big Toyotas out front, all part of Peace Corps' fleet.

We came to the front door, an enormously heavy steel door. Just plain steel; no window in it. We pushed a button and we heard a click!

The unseen guard inside had unlocked the door. I was aware there were several TV cameras scanning the environs. Inside, the guard could see us on his monitor, I was sure. Annabelle was impressed by the tight security. The door was heavy to open. Finally we got in.

Inside we were in a small ante-room. The guard sat at a desk. TV monitors showed him the whole approach to the building and who might be ringing to enter. He unlocked the door only when he considered it safe.

We showed him our IDs. I had told Annabelle there were several guards on the staff. Guards were on duty 24 hours a day. He knew me but not Annabelle. What I had was a special Peace Corps ID. She had to show her passport. The guard made notes in his log. He gave us passes to wear around our neck while in the building.

A luggage-inspection machine was nearby. We did not have to use it. In fact, I never got to see it used.

Now the guard tapped a button. It unlocked another heavy steel door just four feet away. Hard again to get it open. So heavy. We made it through. The door closed and locked. Finally we were inside Headquarters.

"Gosh! What security!" Annabelle said.

"I know. It was never explained why it was necessary."

To repeat: some 75 people worked here. The country director and a cadre of other executives and specialists of various kin—language education, Volunteer training, site selection and placement, medical care, security, finance, communication, on and on. Two Americans held the top jobs and all the others were Ukrainian nationals.

I marveled at how large an administrative staff was needed to run a corps of 300 Volunteers or so who were assigned to jobs in towns and cities across the country.

On this day I had business with Medical, way up on the fourth floor. Dr. Valery was waiting for me. A jovial and helpful man. Happily I introduced Annabelle.

He beamed and said, "I hope you will have a nice stay in our country, my dear." He said "my dear" to all of us, whether men or women. It was part of his charm.

I had a small problem and he was treating me. We got through it in a few minutes. He chatted with the two of us. Another doctor was walking by, Dr. Yuri. I knew him well also. Another nice chat. I wanted her also to meet the others in the department. Unfortunately, not available. I considered all of them good friends.

I walked her next door to the Volunteer Lounge. A pleasant sitting room with sofas, a big TV set, plenty of books and magazines to read—in fact, shelves of books, many from Volunteers going home to the U.S.A., all free for us to take.

There were backpacks and jackets here and there, parked by Volunteers visiting Headquarters. In a corner were a hot-water pot and cups and teabags. We went to serve ourselves.

"What's this?" Annabelle said. She pointed to an open box half full of foil-wrapped condoms.

"They're free," I said. I chuckled. "Very popular. They are supplied by the Medical Department.." Then I got serious. "AIDS is an enormous problem in Ukraine. We're asked to speak about AIDS whenever it's appropriate at our jobs."

I showed her the Computer Room next door, with half a dozen computers and a printer. All free for us to use. Two young Volunteers were at work. I recognized one, Peggy, a secondary school teacher, and I introduced Annabelle, and we had a good catch-up for 10 minutes. Then Annabelle and I sat at computers and checked our e-mails.

The lounge was for use of Volunteers here on business, or taking a break while visiting in the city. Ill Volunteers were sometimes kept overnight. The Medical Department had a sick bay with two beds. The Volunteers could relax and enjoy the lounge during their treatment.

I told Annabelle about Mandy, a young Volunteer in my Group 33. In fact, we had been in the same cluster in Training. She had been bitten by a dog and had reported it to Medical. She was ordered to come in immediately. She had to take the mandatory rabies treatment—several injections over several days. This is where she had spent her free time. "I'm careful around dogs. Believe me!" I said.

Just then Diana Schmidt strode in. Our country director. How propitious. "Hello, John," she said amiably.

I introduced Annabelle, and mentioned she was from southern California. Diana—we all called her Diana—mentioned she and her husband, Hugo, called that home also. He was a dentist. Hugo was retired now, and here in Kyiv with her.

Now a coincidence. Hugo was from Newport Beach! His dental office was right across the street from where Annabelle lived! I had been treated by the dentist who had taken over his practice!

Afterward, I checked in with my regional manager, a young woman named Iryna Shevchenko. She was busy at her computer. Among other things, she was the one who reviewed my articles for a feature called Peace Corps Journals on Peace Corps' national website in Washington. More about this in a subsequent chapter.

"Annabelle," I said. "Iryna here is my immediate boss. She's pretty good." I smiled as I said it. Iryna smiled also.
"I have heard about you," she said to Annabelle. "Welcome!" She couldn't have been nicer.
We left Headquarters with good feelings. Now we had three hours before our train back. We walked this interesting neighborhood of the city and returned to the railroad station. It was still early. I knew of a Trolleybus, No. 5, whose route gave a nice view of the city. We boarded it and made an interesting circuit.
"I love Kyiv!" Annabelle said. " I do! Surprising that we don't hear more about it."
"Yes, a shame. Ukraine should promote itself much more as a tourist hot spot. There's a lot to enjoy. And prices are much lower than in western Europe."

**B**ack at the station, we went to its special lounge for senior travelers. Very nice. An oasis of quiet. Comfortable stuffed chairs. Small tables for a picnic lunch. A pleasant supervisor to provide information and assistance. Clean toilets next door.
We were tired. This was a good place to rest, away from the frenzy of the rest of the station. The time came and we boarded our e*lectrika* for home. The seat across from me was empty. Facing Annabelle was a woman, about 45. Impossible for the three of us to converse because of our language inadequacy. It was so awkward just staring at one another.
She offered us grapes. Insisted we take some. Offered us cookies. Insisted we take some. We had nothing to offer her in turn. It was embarrassing but we appreciated her kindness.
Finally we arrived in Chernihiv. We went out to the bus stop to wait. She came to the same stop. She saw we were unsure. She asked me where we lived. I could understand at least that. I dug into my wallet and showed her my address. She nodded.
A *marshrutka* arrived and she motioned that we should board it. She got on also and sat close to us. She told us where to get off. Surprise. She got off also. It was late and very dark. She walked us to our street! Very fast pace. Took about 10 minutes.
Finally I recognized where we were. She said good night and turned around and headed back. She had done all this...gone way out of her way...to help us! I did not learn her name.
We got home to Chernihiv very tired. But pleased. We talked about Good Samaritan Alex, and Good Samaritan Lady X.
"The people are so nice," Annabelle said.
"Amen!" I replied.

Our time together in Chernihiv was so busy. We went out to meet friends and associates. We explored the city. Tanya, my host mother, returned from Bulgaria and our threesome worked out fine. I had been her tenant only two months, so we were still quite unknown one to another.

She let me use the computer in her living room, and Annabelle also. It was Internet-connected! Annabelle could keep in contact with her family. Evenings and weekends Tanya went out more than usual. She was giving us all the privacy she could. How nice of her.

There were memorable moments. My tutor Sasha invited us to watch her university team playing volleyball and we went. She was the captain. We found our way to the gym at her Pedagogical University.

We spotted her: No. 4. She looked even taller in her shirt and shorts. She was so happy to see us, rushed over to find us better seats in the bleachers closer to center. This was an international game—they were playing a team from nearby Belarus.

The teams took their positions, a whistle blew, and the action started. Wow! I had seen pick-up volleyball games at the beach and at a picnic on the Fourth of July, say. This was different. This was wild. This was exciting. This could have been professional volleyball. So fast. They slammed that ball back and forth. The power! The agility! The determination!

Sasha was outstanding. Truly. I had never seen this aspect of her. She ran and jumped and gave orders. I could see how her teammates respected her. The score went this way and that, always close.

One time the ball came zipping at me. Missed me, but so close that I took off my eyeglasses and put them in a safe pocket. This was furious. Another time the ball grazed Annabelle's hair. With just a few minutes left, Sasha's team was ahead, then Belarus rallied and won the game by just three points. Shucks.

They played another game. Same finale, sadly. But Sasha came running over, sweaty and smiling. "How did you like it?" she said.

"Fantastic!" I said. "What a player you are, Sasha!" Annabelle said. "You deserved to win!"

"Thank you," she said. "But they were terrific, weren't they?"

Again I marveled at her good attitude. Her team was terrific also. And how good her American English was.

Another pleasure was our evening at the Symphony. I had been hoping that the Chernihiv Philharmonia Orchestra would play while Annabelle was here. I had primed Annabelle well. She knew about the beautiful concert hall. How I considered the orchestra first-rate. How excellent was Mikael Sukaj, the conductor. I was excited and so was she.

Again the weather was rainy and cold. But our evening made up for it. Annabelle was astonished to see people from the audience running up at the end to give bouquets to the conductor and soloists. I wished I, too, had thought of bringing a bouquet for Mikael. That's what I called him to myself. Mikael! A fine evening.

We looked forward to our two big excursions to far corners of the country. Sevastopol came up first in the Crimea. Ukraine's "Florida."

I went to our station in Chernihiv three days early to buy the tickets. A problem. This was the busy tourist season. I wanted two lower bunks. I could get tickets, but we'd have to settle for an upper and a lower bunk. Not good. But I agreed. I would take the upper.

I had to take vacation days for this trip. It necessitated a full day of train travel each way. More than 24 hours!

On Thursday morning we rose at 4:30. We rushed. Still I was worried about missing our 6:18 a.m. *electrika*. It was dark out and cold. We waited and waited for a bus to take us to the station. I was anxious. Would we miss the train? A lone taxi approached and I stopped it. We got to the station in six minutes. We were in time. I felt much better.

On the train, guess what? Again we ran into Alex, our Good Samaritan! All the more remarkable when you consider that the train had nine cars, and the three of us were in the same one. How weird! He saw us first. Again, he lived up to my Good Samaritan title.

In Kyiv we would have to change to our through train to Sevastopol. To enter the station, we had to cross many tracks. It involved climbing an enormous outdoor stairway, crossing on a bridge, then going down a long stairway. We had five heavy pieces of luggage.

Alex insisted on accompanying us. Insisted on helping us. He grabbed our two heaviest pieces. We wouldn't have made it without him. Then he got us settled in the station. We had an hour to wait.

I said, "Alex, let's go get something to eat." I was pleased when he agreed. Annabelle said she preferred to stay put.

Alex and I found a restaurant nearby. We got into a good conversation. He explained that was a drilling engineer on searches around the world for oil and natural gas.

On a job site he worked at a computer and, studying geologists' maps, decided the direction the drill should take: it could go down vertically, or at an angle, or go down and then travel horizontally, even work its way around a rock or other obstruction. Directing it along the best route was Alex's responsibility.

"Yes, I like my work very much," he said.

He had emigrated to Canada for a better life. On a trip back to Russia, he had met a gal from his hometown there. "We went to secondary school together!" Now they had been married one year. He was very happy.

We talked for 40 minutes. I felt I had met a very good friend. I hoped our friendship would continue. Finally we returned to the station. Alex had to go to work. I got a stranger to take my camera for a picture of the three of us. What a nice souvenir. It was time to say goodbye to Alex, and "Thank you!" We shook hands. What a grip he had!

Alex was the Good Samaritan who helped us so much. And what an interesting man. I insisted on a photo (wish it were better!).

Annabelle and I whiled away the time until train time. We were on the last car of a 20-car train. What a hike with all our luggage! Finally we made it.

We had a cabin for four. In it, a young man on a lower bunk, noticing I had an upper bunk, offered to swap—I hadn't even suggested it. He was a stock broker—something very new in Ukraine. He spoke fair English and it's surprising how long we talked in different sessions.

He was pessimistic about the United States. I felt in him a strong animosity toward the U.S.A. I could see he was sincere. I didn't get excited. This was a chance to be a decent American and to show tolerance and friendliness. He noticed and I felt he appreciated that.

Sometimes the ride was rough. Too rough to read. Little of interest to see outside. Sprawling fields, patches of forests, poor country houses, a horse or a few cattle. A stream or river now and then.

We'd order tea and a waiter would bring it to us. We had snacks with us, a good idea. The toilet was at the end of the car. As the hours passed, it got very messy. We hoped not to have to use it.

My friend the stock broker got off about half way. I was sorry he was leaving. A couple came into our cabin. They were part of a group. A fresh conversation. So many Ukrainians study English in school. When they found we were Americans, this couple invited their friends from the next cabin. They crowded in. Finally there were eight of us! They asked many questions. I did my best to answer. Annabelle and I fascinated them.

At one point I suggested an arithmetic game: I would show 4 fingers to mean 4, 8 fingers to mean 8. If I nodded, it meant "add." If I shook my head, it meant "subtract." I'd run off a string of numbers this way, two additions, then one subtraction, and so on, trying hard to memorize the totals as I went along. At the end, they had to tell me the right answer in English.

They loved it. They did remarkably well. Suddenly we were all best friends. It was getting late. Finally we broke up. A memorable evening!

We got to Sevastopol at 6 Friday morning. What a long and hard ride. But a beautiful morning. We were going to share an apartment with two Volunteer friends, David and Rebecca. I handed the address to a taxi driver. He got us there in less than 10 minutes. I paid what he asked for although he was grossly overcharging us. I swallowed my protest.

We had a devil of a time finding our apartment, but it turned out to be attractive, clean, quite well furnished, and convenient. A good deal. David and Rebecca arrived in less than an hour. It was our first meeting in person. We liked them. This would work out well.

I had spoken to Rebecca on the phone in the past. She is the one who had brought Tanya's apartment to my attention—where I was now living. She and her David had lived in my room at Tanya's during their Training.

It was a perfect day for this famous Crimean city. In the afternoon we met the rest of our group and our co-presidents, Phil and Carol. Friendly familiar faces, friendly new ones! We were Volunteers: all for one, one for all! We met at the high school where Phil and Carol taught. It was a grand and ornate building with a must-see central staircase.

Then Phil and Carol led us to the hill with the unique Panorama atop it. It's a round building, and unique because its inside walls were a 360-degree painting. You walk in a big circle to see the whole thing. And what a story it depicts.

It's a hugely dramatic rendition of the monumental Battle for Sevastopol during the Crimean War. The bombardment of the city by British, French, and Turkish started on June 6, 1845, and lasted 349 days. The armies were among the largest ever seen. The Russians lost. Some 250,000 were killed on each side. Think about it—half a million dead.

This unique masterpiece shows the scope of the battle in impressive detail. It was the work of a French painter named Rimbaud. His artistic extravaganza is much better known than he is, sad to say.

Afterward we visited Greek ruins on another side of the city. Broken pillars, blocks of marble on a hillside. It is said that Prince Vladimir was baptized a Christian here in A.D. 988. The date marks the beginning of the Ukrainian Orthodox Church. The weather continued perfect. How good.

In the evening we went to a restaurant for dinner on an edge of the city. Charming, good food, good company.

We had our business meeting the next morning. We discussed our tried and true topics—how to help young Volunteers, how to boost Volunteer morale, in what ways training might be improved.

It was a significant meeting for me: I was elected president of SNAC for the coming year. SNAC became a significant commitment for me. I tell you all about it in the next chapter.

After that, we went on to more interesting things: the main one being a fine auto tour along the mountainous coastline with expansive views of the sea. Our guide was a young teacher named Vladimir, a colleague of theirs. Excellent.

We were to get as far as beautiful Yalta, queen port of the Black Sea. We stopped to tour two famous castles.

The first was the charming and marvelously photogenic Livadia Palace. It was a summer get-away for Czar Nicholas II of Russia in 1911.

And then the Vorontsov Palace, forever famous as the site of the Big Three meeting in 1945 during the ending days of World War II. Our President Franklin Roosevelt and Britain's Winston Churchill and the U.S.S.R.'s Josef Stalin met there to make post-war plans.

A lot of squeezing and horse-trading went on. Their decisions changed the geography of Eastern Europe. We stood by the three great chairs in which they had sat. Sitting around the circular table with them were a score of assistants. Truly it was the biggest table I have ever seen. I believe it was made for that occasion.

In one point, at one point we all felt excited to look down from high up on our highway upon the Swallow's Test way down below. It's the small but picturesque castle so famous on calendars and postcards. Chances are you've seen it. You might call it the iconic "Eiffel Tower" of the Crimea. It's perched dangerously (or so it seems) on the tip of a rocky peninsula overlooking the sea.

Then, a big disappointment for Annabelle and me. We never made it to Yalta. Merely got to its outskirts. We could see it across the bay, gleaming white buildings at the foot of great mountains. Unreachable. We had to turn back. What bad luck.

For the next morning, a hike was planned on some craggy hills with views of the sea. Annabelle and I didn't feel up to that. Through Phil, I hired Vladimir, who had guided us toward Yalta. "Show us Sevastopol!" I told him. It was his city. His English was smooth and easy. It turned out to be a smart move.

He led us downtown for a relaxed morning. Sevastopol sets beautifully on an exquisite harbor. It was very busy. Ferries were darting from side to side. A fleet of gaff-rigged sailboats were racing, their taut sails a beautiful sight against the blue sea and sky.

We walked through a beautiful park, standing aside to let a squad of 18-year-old Russian sailors march by, their haircuts precise, sailor suits pressed, buckles shining. Russia holds a lease on a great naval base nearby.

And we had the benefit of our guide's commentary at every statue and sight. It worked out beautifully.

Late in the afternoon we started the long train journey back to Chernihiv. It took us exactly 24 hours. We both felt it remarkable that we could survive a challenging round trip like this. In fact, we enjoyed it.

Two days later it was my first anniversary in Ukraine! I let it pass quietly. I was glad to be a Volunteer. Happy to be in Ukraine. Pleased that I was coping. Hoping that I was making a contribution. Most of all, determined to complete my 27 months. My eyes were on December, 2009. That's when I would go home. Mission accomplished, I hoped.

Our next vacation destination was Lviv in far western Ukraine. I had read wonderful things about it, and Olena and Lina at *Coursi* recommended it enthusiastically.

We planned a long weekend, Friday through Monday. We'd sleep on the train going and returning. As usual, I notified my regional director Iryna that I would be away overnight. Peace Corps insisted on notification—they wanted to know where we were!

Annabelle and I went to the station a week ahead of time to buy our tickets for two lower berths in a four-berth car. This time we succeeded.

As the date approached, the weather got worse and worse. Blue skies would be important. No blue skies in the forecast. We decided to cancel and re-book for the following weekend. This required another trip to the station. We were charged a penalty for canceling—a whopping 30 percent! Awful.

Bad news. Originally we would have taken the train directly to Lviv. With these new tickets, now a big detour—we'd have to go to Kyiv first, then transfer to the Lviv train.

Well, we decided on doing the first part differently. We would take a bus to Kyiv, not a train. Then we'd take the night train to Lviv.

Yes, a big bus, not a small, crowded *marshrutka*, which would always take the boring highway. The bus would take longer on a secondary road, but it would stop in villages and towns. We'd see more. We planned to leave at 8 in the morning. This would give us time to do enjoyable things in the capital. It worked out just as planned.

In Kyiv it was gray and cold, but no rain at least. We walked to the railroad station to check our luggage in the big basement storage room till our evening departure time. Good idea, but we had to stand in a long queue for 25 minutes to get it done. But worth it. This freed us for our sight-seeing.

We had a good time. When we got tired, we'd get on a trolleybus just to ride and rest, all while getting a look at different neighborhoods. We took such breaks three times.

Trolleybus No. 24 was especially good. It gave us a long ride up through one of the nicest neighborhoods...right by the Rada, which is the Parliament, and other impressive buildings. It re-enforced my belief that Kyiv is a very attractive city. Americans should target it more.

We were tired when we returned in late afternoon to the station. It was throbbing with travelers coming and going. Another wait in a long queue to pick up our luggage. Such a pleasure finally to enter the quiet of the lounge for senior travelers. The same lady was on duty. She nodded at us. I went out and came back with supper for us. Annabelle had found a table for us.

Soon it was time to board our train. Again, an enormously long train. It could be a hike to get to the right car. It was.

I couldn't help muttering to Annabelle, "This is another reason I prefer a long-distance bus. It's easy on and easy off."

The train was modern and clean. Better than our train to Sevastopol. Many passengers. We found our cabin. Two double-bunks. We had the lowers, thanks to buying our tickets early. With us were a young couple.

The train started so smoothly—no jerk this time. The conductor came and checked our tickets, and immediately Annabelle and I changed to our night clothes and took to our bunks. The young couple walked out when they noticed. Nice of them. They tip-toed in when they returned and made hardly a sound climbing up to their own bunks.

Again the track was smooth in stretches and rough in others, but I felt comfortable and content after our busy day. I fell asleep within minutes. I awoke when the conductor stopped in at 6 a.m. to tell us we'd arrive in half an hour. We hurried. So did our companions. It was raw and raining when we got off at 6:48 a.m.

We strode into the station, ate breakfast, and went to its business service center. I knew that as in Odessa, there would be sleeping accommodations there. The attendant shook her head, "No!" That surprised me. Certainly there were empties at this early hour, or would be. "No!" she said again. So disappointing. What to do?

We were a mile from the center. We'd find a hotel there. We took a taxi downtown. It was daylight now. A gloomy day with rain on and off.

On the way I browsed in my guidebook: all the major attractions were clustered in a big square in the very center.

Annabelle and I huddled and talked and made a decision. I said to the driver, "Please take us back to the railroad station." I saw he was confused and I repeated. He turned around but was obviously puzzled.

We changed our train tickets to return home that very evening. We were cutting our visit short. This time we got a small refund, which was incomprehensible. The previous time we did this, we got fined! We checked our luggage for the day. Then took a tram downtown. One quick look at the ancient and ornate buildings and Annabelle said, "This will be interesting."

But it was still drizzling so we took another tram that seemed headed in an interesting direction—just to keep dry while getting a better look. It was after 11 a.m. when we got back to the center. The rain was letting up.

It remained cold and gray all day. The rain took long pauses and now and then and I was able to take some interesting pictures. The center of Lviv was indeed postcard-pretty.

The Opera House was stunning. There were many statues on the square, grand statues, one or two strikingly different. Striking buildings all around. I found them as interesting as any museum. I took one picture after another. I was having great fun composing the shots.

Annabelle also was having a good time. Dozens of intriguing shops. The window-shopping was marvelous. Like Kyiv, this was a city that deserved far more attention by tourists.

Lviv was also a capital, so to speak—the main city of western Ukraine, which is a stronghold of Ukrainian language and culture, in contrast to the Russian sections of the county, primarily in the east.

We found an interesting restaurant right on the square. Very few customers. Three ladies sat at a table nearby.

"A nice place," Annabelle said as we ate. I had to agree. So nice that I walked over and asked one of the ladies to take a photo of the two of us at our table. She did. And that started a good chat with her and her companions. Thank goodness they spoke a bit of English.

The day continued pleasant. When we finally returned to catch our train, we felt one day in Lviv had been enough. We had seen the highlights, all wonderful.

But Annabelle had caught a cold. She didn't let it slow her down. The ride back through the night seemed bumpier. We reached Kyiv early in the morning.

Good, the weather was clearing. This was now Sunday. Another quick decision: we'd go visit the Pyrohovo Outdoor Historic Village (sort of like our Olde Sturbridge Village in Massachusetts) on the outskirts of Kyiv. We had to take two buses to get there, but worth it.

Many buildings of olden times formed the village. Many had been moved to it. Town houses, farmhouses, barns, sheds, all rustic. Many charming. Many with hand-carved wooden decorations around windows and doors.

There were ingenious fences. Ancient farm implements, so crude. Some buildings were small museums of sundry arts and crafts.

There were hills all around, and positioned on some were big, old-fashioned windmills. They were bold silhouettes against the brightening sky. The wind provided the power for the mills to process grains.

The village offered a million photo opportunities. I was glad we had made this long side trip.

We got home to Chernihiv late that night. Very tired but pleased. The weatherman had not cooperated. But we had made the best of it.

The next four days went fast. Olena and Lina at the language school invited Annabelle for a farewell treat. They hosted us at a fine lunch in a private dining room…borsch, canapés, salmon, potato pancakes, Chardonnay, a luscious cream cake, espresso. They gave Annabelle a beautiful necklace of green beads. She was greatly touched.

"Thank you, Olena." I said. "Thank you, Lina. How kind of you!" She had gifts for them also. They loved them.

Annabelle's cold worsened. She was coughing and coughing. Late one evening Tanya walked into our bedroom. If she knocked, we didn't hear her. Annabelle was in bed. Tanya insisted on applying a big, hot plaster to Annabelle's chest, and another to her back. I recall how my grandmother had used plasters on me once.

Tanya's plasters worked surprisingly well. Something moist was inside them but no idea what. Annabelle got a decent night's sleep.

*Time for Annabelle to leave. We're on our way to the airport.*
*It was all too short. But very good.*

In the morning I investigated. In the plaster were hot mashed potatoes! I don't know what my Grandma used. Not mashed potatoes for sure.

Tanya offered more plasters the next evening, but Annabelle was better and declined. She was grateful and Tanya could see that plainly. I was grateful, too.

In two more days, time for Annabelle to depart. We took the express marshrutka back to Borispil Airport. We had much to say to one another, and in between, our silences were cozy ones. At the airport, we rushed to get Annabelle and her things inside.

She faced a two-hour wait but it was an urgent rush for me: my marshrutka was heading back to Chernihiv in 20 minutes. No other until 11 a.m. the next morning! But I made sure Annabelle was all set.

Hugs and kisses, of course. Sweet words. Then, au revoir! I was pensive with a hundred thoughts all the way home. But happy.

She sent me an e-mail the minute she got home. Good flights back. Everything fine at home. And nice words of thanks and love that I prefer to keep to myself.

~ ~ ~

***Did you know*** ... that every country will have its own Peace Corps headquarters and staff. And that this staff will be predominantly local—will consist of native people. The top executives will be Americans, and these will be fewer than you may expect. I believe this is true of our embassies also.

My country, Ukraine, had the largest Peace Corps group in the world—close to 300 Volunteers during my service. Our headquarters had a staff of 75. And 72 of them were Ukrainians. Most of these were working career jobs, it seemed to me, meaning for long stretches. They would stay on and on.

But the few Americans at the top were limited to just a few years because of the "Five and Out" rule. I did see an exception made for our country director, who was kept on longer, undoubtedly for a valid reason.

I have heard it said that having such a large number of key administrators who are natives with consideble tenure inevitably gives the headquarters a local, native uniqueness. After all, they do exert influence. "They know their country best, and they feel they can best adapt Peace Court to their country."

If this is true, it might be argued that each country has a different Peace Corps. Which is quite a thought.

# 31 / I get involved in SNAC

*SNAC is our Seniors Club. It's not long before I get involved deeper and deeper.*

As a Trainee in Peace Corps, I would hear about SNAC now and then. There would be an item in our Friday e-newsletter from Headquarters about SNAC planning a weekend in a distant city. Or I would hear an older Volunteer mention how much fun SNAC was.

I became instantly interested because it was our Seniors Club in Peace Corps. It was a social and travel club and I liked that. I was a senior in Peace Corps. In fact, as you know, the most senior Volunteer in Ukraine. And before many more months, in the world. Certainly a title that I never aspired to.

I was so senior that at times I felt isolated by my age. Oh, nobody ever did anything to make me feel on the outs. No. No. But it's natural for folks to feel closest to those of the same age. Youngsters hang out with youngsters, the forty-ish with the forty-ish, seniors with seniors. Natural and understandable.

My guess-timate was that the average age of us Volunteers in Ukraine was about 27. In SNAC I would still hold the title of oldest, but at least I'd be associating with a group whose average age might be 65, say. All of us in it would have more in common. I liked that idea.

SNAC held three meetings a year, usually in interesting cities here and there in Ukraine. Places that were interesting historically and culturally and geographically. That appealed to me a lot. And I loved the idea of hanging out with fellow Volunteers, at least on weekends away.

Remember, most of us Volunteers worked alone in our communities. The new friends we made were Ukrainians—our fellow workers, our students, the folks we lived with, the people we saw often.

I've mentioned that when I joined, I expected I'd work with at least a few colleagues. It never happened. A huge disappointment. I worked in isolation in Chernihiv. What a pleasure it would be to get together with other Volunteers, of any age but especially of my approximate age. To compare experiences, learn, gossip, let off steam!

I am sure you realize SNAC is an acronym. But what does it stand for? The answer is Senior Networking Action Committee. When asked what the full name stands for, most members hesitated, thought hard, and stammered. They were not sure. Everybody called it just SNAC. I think they liked it because the name was short and snappy. Who cares what it means? That seemed to be the attitude. Well, at one point I cared very much and I made an issue of it. More about this later.

I went to my first meeting only five weeks after arriving in Ukraine, even before I took the Volunteer oath. I remained very active all through my 27 months of service. I was elected president at the end of my first year as a Volunteer and kept the job until shortly before returning home. But my term ended abruptly—you'll find out why!

My first meeting was in Kyiv in early November, in the offices of American Council (I'll tell you about AC in a minute). I was still a Trainee—had been here just a month. Invitations had been sent to the eight of us age 50 and up in our Group 33, but only three of us attended.

In all, we were about 15 at the meeting. That was about half of all the Volunteers in Ukraine who were age-eligible.

That was the typical ratio at all the meetings that I attended. So, a tiny club. The modest turn-outs always bothered me.

Now about American Council. Its full name is American Councils for International Education. It is a private organization with a broad range of services. One is a contract to manage FLEX, which is a program funded by the U.S. State Department. FLEX sends gifted teen-agers to the U.S for 10 months. A very interesting program, as you'll see shortly.

Before the SNAC meeting, I had stopped at Headquarters in Kyiv. I got lucky. A Peace Corps driver had an errand to do near American Council and would give me a lift there. I jumped at it. I was a rank stranger in the city and I expected to have to get to American Council by Metro and foot! That was scary. I got a good look at the city—very attractive—and an easy ride right to the door of American Council.

FLEX had a suite of offices on the first floor of a big building. They were primarily business offices. Lots of desks. This was a Saturday, so the place was empty except for us.

It was easy to tell American Council focused on education. On the walls were many posters of American colleges and universities. And many shelves of books about our colleges and universities and about higher education in the U.S.A.

It also had a room with many computers. It was called the Internet Center. I have no idea who used it regularly. But I was alone in there. I couldn't resist. I managed to get online and I spent an hour in there checking my e-mails, leaving just in time to get to our meeting.

It was held in a pleasant conference room. People were sitting around a big U-shaped table. They were chatting and enjoying snacks and cold drinks placed here and there. All seniors, of course. But some were less senior than others. Most were very young seniors.

A man was sitting at the head of the table. Was studying us. I took a seat next to a woman. Her name tag said Jane. I introduced myself. "Who is he?" I asked, pointing to the man.

"Rich Brownell. Our president. And that woman next to him is his wife. Cathy. She's a Volunteer, too."

Just as she said that, he started our meeting. He ran it briskly but easily. He asked us to introduce ourselves. "When you do," he said, "please give us a tip or two about anything that might be helpful to us as Volunteers."

What a good idea. I liked that. This is what I was hoping for. I listened carefully as each person spoke. I had my turn.

I had a simple tip to offer. "I'm just a Trainee—a stranger in using the Metro. I was so glad I had a map of the Metro in my pocket when I got on this morning. I got a seat but there were so many standees that I could not see the monitor that announces the stops My little map saved me!"

Afterward, I felt foolish. Maybe they were all aware of that! Well, I had tried. I did pick up useful tips. Yes, SNAC might be a great club.

Then Rich Brownell moved on through business—minutes…reports…election of officers…new plans…discussion of the next meeting site. Obviously a serious club!

FLEX was the big topic. I told you about it earlier—the fine American program that chooses outstanding boys and girls and sends them to live with a family in America for a year. I became involved in FLEX later. I valued this introduction to it.

**E**verybody here was new to me. Except one—Dr. Valery, our senior Peace Corps doctor. He was here to give flu shots and as a liaison from Headquarters. He was friendly and mixed easily and told us about a Puccini opera getting good reviews at the Opera House that evening, if interested.

I found out that he was a regular at SNAC meetings and was warmly welcome. Not only for his injections and medical advisories but his insights about Peace Corps and so many things Ukrainian.

Other interesting things to do in the city were suggested. Rich and his wife, Cathy, were returning to their hotel, the Bratislava. It was one of countless hotels in Kyiv but the one that Headquarters recommended and where it had leveraged discounted rates for us. It had a renovated section and a non-renovated one. We Volunteers got put up in the cheaper one. I had a reservation there. I went off with them.

They were good company. To my delight, they invited me to dinner at 7:30 p.m. Attractive restaurant off the lobby and good food. Best of all, I spent more than two hours with them at the table. They were the very first Volunteers I was getting to huddle with. In fact, the first husband-and-wife Volunteers I was meeting. They were friendly and outgoing. They gave me numerous tips.

Soon I asked, "What's it like to be a married couple in Peace Corps?"

Rich said, "It's been terrific." And Cathy said, "More couples should sign up together. But they have to be married! If they are just engaged, they will not serve together."

Rich and Cathy saw that I was a raw Trainee. Two or three times they told me, "There is life after Training!" They remembered how tough Training was. I appreciated their words. They saved me later. I never saw them again. They were heading home, their service completed.

I finally went up to my room encouraged by everything. I was happy to have accepted the invitation to attend the meeting.

Interestingly, SNAC's format and line-up of activities became the pattern for all the other meetings to come. A happy combination of club business, friend-making, information-swapping, and, especially at later meetings, local sight-seeing.

### My next meeting: Odessa in April.

This famous city is at the northern tip of the Black Sea in the Crimea—considered Ukraine's "Florida." Odessa was famous enough even then for Mark Twain to visit it. Ukraine's three biggest rivers converge there.

It is said the sun shines all year and its winter temperatures are balmy. It was a famous watering hole for good workers during Soviet days. They went there as a reward. It still attracts many tourists from Russia. It's Ukrainians' favorite vacation spot.

It was a 14-hour overnight train ride from Chernihiv. I decided immediately to go. It had all the right ingredients: besides SNAC, it offered a historic and important destination, an authentic old city (it wasn't bombed as much as Chernihiv, say, in World War II), and dramatic improvement in weather and scenery. And it was an adventure to get to it!

My quandary was, what hotel to make a reservation at? Location, amenities, price...so many factors. I might just as well throw a dart at a list of hotels. Then inspiration. The railroad station's Service Center!

I had read in my Ukraine guidebook that major stations have Service Centers with overnight accommodations. Much cheaper than good hotels, and high quality. But you couldn't make a reservation.

Odessa was one of the country's biggest cities. So I took the train without knowing where I'd be sleeping.

Getting off, I walked into the Service Center—it was part of the big, station station. Passenger trains aree all-important in Ukraine. I was lucky. I got a room.

Actually, it was a bed in a three-bed room. I had to walk several flights up. I was pleased: an attractive, modern room with new-looking furniture and a comfortable bed. A clean and bright bathroom down the hall. I would describe the Senior Center as an upscale hostel. The price was $15 per night. Reasonable.

On the first night, I was the only occupant. On the second, one roommate—a professional musician. He was quiet. Minded his own business. He remained only two hours, leaving at 8:30 p.m. to catch a train. I slept alone all night long in that three-bed room. I had a "single.".

In the morning I had a terrible time finding our meeting place elsewhere in the city. I had the address and took a trolley there. Walked up and down the street, looking. The building numbers seemed senseless. I arrived 35 minutes late, tired and irritated.

Seeing familiar faces perked me up. Our meeting was good. I missed the introductions and the sharing of tips and information, all good stuff. But I was in time for other good topics as well as a discussion of Robert Strauss' damning op-ed in the New York Times about the Peace Corps (Chapter 28).

I had e-mailed his op-ed to the club as a suggested topic for discussion. Had included my reply to his op-ed that I had sent to the Times.

The discussion was much less intense than I had hoped. It lasted all of five minutes. Members agreed that older Volunteers are desirable. No surprise in that. But showed appreciation for our younger, much more numerous Volunteers. My sentiment also.

Interesting to me was a discussion about how to improve Volunteers' morale. I had been a full Volunteer just a few months but already I had seen that Headquarters did little to boost our pride and lift our spirits.

In fact, I had written to our director Diana about this. I had suggested some simple strategies. One was not only simple but cheap. Remember my disappointment at the Swearing In about not receiving a Peace Corps pin?

I told her every Trainee should get a pin at a "pinning" ceremony, done with solemnity and ritual. And Volunteers should be encouraged to wear the pin throughout their service. This certainly would build pride. I had also made other suggestions to her.

Now at this meeting of ours everyone agreed that our morale could use a boost and Headquarters should give this more priority. And they said they liked the idea of the pinning ceremony.

**D**r. Valery was right there listening. I was sure he would report this back to Diana. Besides, she certainly would get a copy of this meeting's minutes. I hoped something good would result.

Our new officers for the coming year were Phil and Carol Arnold. They were teachers right there in Odessa. You read about them in the previous chapter.

"We are going to be co-presidents," Phil said to us. Then he joked, "You will have the two of us to blame if you are not satisfied!"

I had gotten to know them both. Felt they deserved our votes. And was sure they would do a good job. They were off to a good start as our leaders—had lined up many sight-seeing opportunities and the usual evening at the opera or symphony.

But I wanted to explore on my own, and went off solo, my camera in hand. I had a great time riding Odessa's old trams, exploring here and there, getting a few glimpses at the Black Sea (such a terrible misnomer, I thought), and taking photos.

The city square in front of the cathedral was crowded with artists selling their paintings. It was so festive. So colorful. I spent two hours there, enjoying all of it and clicking often.

The city offered so many possibilities...fascinating architecture, busy markets, stores of all kinds, and history aplenty. I returned to my room at dusk and got a good night's sleep. Sleeping on the train had been tough.

We had a nice get-together in the morning. I had only another three hours to look around and I made the most of that. Odessa was a picturesque and historic city. Fascinating. Like Kyiv and some other Ukrainian cities, with proper promotion and advertising it would boom with tourists.

Then back to the station for my long train ride back to Kyiv, and then my final three hours back to Chernihiv. I got home happy. Odessa had been time well spent.

**N**ext meeting: **Kyiv again in June.**

This meeting was a surprise one. It had not been booked. The circumstances were extraordinary. This is why it was in Kyiv.

It was announced that Ronald Tschetter, our national director in Washington, was coming for a visit (Chapter 28 also). He was the initiator of the Fifty Plus program that I have told you about—the program for older Volunteers that had attracted me.

His visit was of interest to all Volunteers in the country. But no way could all Volunteers in Ukraine, about 300 now, be invited to come meet him at Headquarters. Too expensive. And too disruptive to their normal activities. I think that was the reasoning. But invitations went out to all us older Volunteers.

Phil and Carol, our SNAC co-presidents, had a great idea: why not have a special SNAC meeting there at the same time? Just before Tschetter's arrival. To consider issues to present to him. It made sense.

It gained irresistible impetus when Peace Corps sent us another e-mail—it would spring for our travel expenses.

Our meeting preceded the meeting with Tschetter. We did have a worthwhile discussion. Suddenly, an extraordinary development. It had nothing to do with our official business.

We were at Headquarters, sitting around the big table in the staff conference room. A woman of older age—a newcomer not known to me—came in and took an empty seat. It happened to be right next to me.

Our meeting was in session, someone had the floor, and there was no way that she and I could exchange hellos.

Some minutes went by when perchance I noticed that she was dabbing her eyes with a kerchief. She was crying!

"What's the matter?" I whispered.

She merely shook her head in a kind of "Nothing! Never mind!" way. And continued with her kerchief.

"Can I help you?" I said. "What's wrong?"

A long pause, then a tearful whisper. "Peace Corps is sending me home!"

What! I was astonished. But I had to wait for a break in the program to inquire more. Then came the moment.

I asked and she told me her name. I'll call her Veronica here. She was not a Volunteer. She was a Trainee. She had been summoned to Headquarters to meet Diana. And Diana had just given her this bad news.

"Why are you being sent home? Why?"

Veronica let it out in bits and pieces. She was finishing Training and had been assigned to a distant village far in the east and she felt this assignment was totally unacceptable. She asked for a different assignment. But Peace Corps was adamant. They asked her to try it at least. She said no.

By her refusing the assignment, Peace Corps had found her intransigent. Told her she would be dismissed from the corps if she did not resign. Peace Corps considered resignation a smart grace-saving alternative in such a case. She had not agreed yet. Now here she was, tearful about it.

She had an additional problem. She had a deal with a university back in the U.S.A. whereby her experience in Peace Corps would count toward a master's degree—a degree costing her a lot of money. Now this good deal would be lost.

How to help her? True, every applicant agreed to go wherever assigned. But Peace Corps' action seemed so arbitrary. And heavy-handed. I thought of all the time and effort Veronica must have put in just to enter Peace Corps—and the time and effort getting through Training.

And I wondered, *What is she doing sitting here in this SNAC meeting, right next to me?* I mentioned this to her.

She told me she had seen the meeting in progress and stepped in thinking it would be a place to sit, absorb the shock, and calm herself. She continued to sit right there.

A break came in our meeting. I got everyone's attention, introduced Veronica, and spoke about the awful experience she was going through.

"It seems unfair," I said to everybody. "Couldn't they find a better assignment?

"Do you think that we could ask Diana to review Veronica's situation...let Veronica state her reasons one more time? Who knows, Diana might now find reason to re-consider her tough decision."

Then and there I picked up paper and pen and drafted a paragraph. It went like this:

"Diana: Veronica has told us that she is being sent home and why. She is broken-hearted about it. It is such terrible news. Is it possible to speak to her one more time... to give her one more chance to make her case?"

I read it to our members around the table and asked if they would sign the request along with me. There was a brief discussion.

Veronica was asked to explain the situation to everyone and she did. A vote was taken. Yes, we'd sign the note and pass it on to Diana.

Dr. Valery had been sitting with us. Hearing all this, he had excused himself. What he had done was to go and speak to Diana. Her office was just down the hall. We never got the chance to send our note.

Dr. Valery returned with her. She stood in front of us. "Yes, I'll tell you as much as I can. But I am limited. I cannot breach the confidentiality of some aspects."

Veronica had left the room when she saw Diana arrive.

Some of the details were familiar. Peace Corps had asked Veronica to at least go see the place, and at least try it for a few days. No! Absolutely unacceptable!

Diana reminded us that when anyone joins Peace Corps, it is to go wherever and do whatever. Flexibility is essential. Diana said she had discussed the case with others at Headquarters. They had made the painful decision to ask Veronica to change her mind or to resign—painful for Veronica and themselves.

I wondered, of course, about the confidential aspects that might have been part of Veronica's evaluation. Maybe they had been a deciding factor.

Diana told us, "I am sure you understand we take no pleasure in this. It is just the opposite of what we try to do." That decision would stand, she told us emphatically.

Hearing all this, I for one sided with Peace Corps. And so did the other members. But we felt good to have made an effort to help a colleague in distress—well, in this case a prospective colleague.

I knew that SNAC in the past had often discussed ways to help fellow Volunteers, and here was a good example of something that had come up spontaneously and had put that spirit to the test.

And our club had risen to the challenge. I felt this was an appropriate role for SNAC. I felt good about it.

### Our next meeting: Sevastopol in September.

In the preceding chapter I told you about our visit to this beautiful city. We went to attend a SNAC meeting. Now I will tell you about that interesting meeting in detail.

There were only 15 of us again—about half of those eligible. I wondered how more could be encouraged to come. I wondered why more did not attend. A prime reason probably was the long train ride necessary for some, and just for a Friday through Sunday weekend. It would make sense to tack on vacation days, especially for such a famous locale as this.

Our business meeting covered the usual issues, but I found them enjoyable and helpful. I liked new tips and new information to make my Peace Corps experience better.

Secondly, this was the major opportunity to think and talk about the big subject involving us all: Peace Corps—what it was doing, how it was heading, what we liked and disliked. To pick up gossip and share some.

Besides, most of our core group were SNAC regulars. It was nice to look forward to seeing them again and chat. For me SNAC had become truly a nice little club.

Oh, Phil and Carol had received an e-mail from disappointed, tearful Veronica. It was an update, and all good news.

She said that within hours after quitting Peace Corps she had found a job teaching English right there in Kyiv. She enjoyed it, mentioned the high demand for private English-language teachers in corporations ("they pay as much as $50 per hour!"), had worked things out with her university, was making friends, and was glad she had resigned.

She even said that Peace Corps had been helpful in working out many details for her! Wonderful. It pleased me to hear it all, especially about Peace Corps being helpful.

Phil and Carol had sent out a notice asking who would be interested in running for president. I had replied that I would.

**W**ell, it turned out I had a competitor, Don, a lawyer. His wife, Karen, was also a Volunteer. Somebody nominated him from the floor. I felt that if he got elected, she would act as his co-president—like Phil and Carol. They would do a great job, I was sure, especially as a team. But Don declined. So I was elected by acclamation. And so, as I wrote to my family and friends, "It was easy. Nobody else wanted the job."

Afterward Annabelle asked me, "John, why did you want this? It's a lot of work, isn't it? And there doesn't seem to be much help."

She made this last comment when she saw how difficult it was to get someone to Volunteer for the only other elected job, secretary. I was lucky and got my new friend David Rodgers to put up his hand. So, he too got in by acclamation.

Yes, I was sure it would be work. As it turned out, David got busy with something else. But I felt SNAC was important, I had an idea or two for it, and I liked to keep busy. I went ahead as a one-man band.

On the way home afterward, I felt excited but apprehensive. I thought Phil and Carol had done a swell job while in charge. I hoped to do as well.

### Our next meeting: Kyiv in April.

Back in Chernihiv and alone again—Annabelle had flown home to California—I began planning our spring meeting —my first as president.

One thing had bothered me since arriving in Ukraine. I had been to Kyiv perhaps 10 times, always on business to Headquarters. I had never gotten a good look at our capital city. I felt this was true for most Volunteers. I decided our first SNAC meeting should be in Kyiv and was determined to include a thorough sight-seeing excursion for our members.

I broached my idea to Dr. Valery, who was an important part of all our club meetings.

"Yes," he said. "Excellent idea!"

I got him to plan the excursion. I got him to arrange for a suitable vehicle and driver. In fact, in a lucky stroke, I got him to be our excursion leader and commentator. He agreed to everything. How lucky I was.

Annabelle had been right. This was a challenging add-on to my other activities. But I got it all done, doing the publicity, handling the many e-mails from members and the reservations, answering questions, and planning the many other details of our get-together.

Our meeting would be at Headquarters. I had several key items on our agenda.

One was to re-name our club, abandoning "SNAC" in favor of "The Fifty-Plus Club." It would have instant meaning for everybody in Peace Corps.

Others were:

~ Should language-training be modified for older trainees?
~ In what way can we be of service to our younger colleagues?
~ Why not a Peace Corps anthem?
~ Why not a group tour to Moscow this summer?
~ Open Forum: "You bring it up…we'll discuss it."
~ Why not beautiful and historic Ivano-Frankivsk for our summer meeting?

And I had booked our director, Diana, as our headliner. She accepted quickly. She told me, "You can all ask me any question. Don't be bashful. I'll answer." That impressed me.

Dr. Valery and I had come up with an assortment of entertainment suggestions: the great Kyiv Circus…a ballet…a symphony concert…a visit to the Pyrohovo Museum of Folk Architecture on the outskirts…a visit to the big French retailer Auchan's huge new store, just opened.

But the major attraction would be our "Grand Tour of Grand Kyiv." A first! Our Saturday morning club meeting would conclude with a pizza lunch in the conference room. Then we'd do our Grand Tour. I expected it would take three hours. Maybe longer.

Oh, to thank Dr. Valery, I had designed an attractive certificate proclaiming him the Ukraine Fifty-Plus Club's first Honorary Distinguished Member. It included a heartfelt commendation in a nice frame. I had also bought a bottle of Moldovan cognac as a gift. It would be a Kodak moment for him. I was sure my members would go along.

Our meeting started promptly. With our secretary far afield again, I had talked a colleague in my Group 33, Berta

Dr. Valery was a regular at our meetings. It was a pleasure to make him our first Distinguished Honorary Member.

Schweinberger, a lawyer from San Francisco, to serve as secretary "for this one and only meeting."
Graciously she said yes. As it turned out, I had to make the same request at still another meeting, and again she said yes. Nice, eh?

*A few of our small group. Friendships blossomed quickly. But we did have very different ideas.*

Here's how our various agenda items were decided.

~ Should language-training (Russian and Ukrainian) be modified for us older trainees? This led to a long and passionate discussion. The decision was: Perhaps. A committee was named to explore the question and report back.

~ A group tour to Moscow this summer, perhaps with a side trip to St. Petersburg. Some interest. A committee would consider the matter.

~ Our summer meeting in Ivano-Frankivsk. Yes.

~ A better name for SNAC. I felt this would be a sure thing. Surprise. No! I was astonished. They liked SNAC! So be it.

~ The certificate for Dr. Valery. He was delighted. But a big goof. I had made it out as coming from The Fifty-Plus Club. But the name change had just been voted down! Much laughter.

I announced that I would take it back and make the change. I got it done and sent the certificate to Dr. Valery. How I had mis-judged the sentiment of our members!

We broke for lunch, then re-assembled to hear our headliner, Diana. She kept her word. Questions popped up and she answered, fully and candidly. So many that time ran out.

One I enjoyed was how Diana became a Volunteer. Here is what she told us:

"The reason I have BA, MA, MBA and PH.D. degrees is that I loved going to school and couldn't imagine life outside of the university environment. But, once I became a university professor of psychology and then business I began to realize that I needed to find another way to both entertain and support myself.

"I loved my career in teaching and business but always wanted to join the Peace Corps. I kept putting it off until the day I was hit by a car when I was riding my bike in Southern France with my husband, Hugo.

*What a good time we had touring Kyiv. A success. Fine weather. Dr. Valery is in the center. Our director Diana is at his left. I'm at t he left, with the cap. We were all friends, for sure. But our thinking conflicted at times.*

"While I was lying on the road, waiting for the ambulance, I asked Hugo, 'Can we join Peace Corps if I live through this?' Of course, he said 'Yes!'

"It took me a year to recover and then we joined Peace Corps as Volunteers in January 2000. And here we are. So, Peace Corps has been a wonderful life-changing thing for me. And Hugo."

Oh, we never got to discuss the Anthem! That was an item of my own, and I put great stock in it. Well, I would bring it up at our summer meeting in Ivano-Frankivsk.

Then, our Grand Tour! With Diana coming along as our guest, we filled every seat in our comfortable *marshrutka*. The tour was thorough and delightful, and Dr. Valery outdid himself.

At the end, we assembled on the great steps in front of the Kyiv Circus (which occupies its own impressive building; it's not a tent!). We smiled for a group photo and gave Dr. Valery three cheers, American style. He beamed.

*With Diana, our director. Several dealings with her. One or two frustrations. But I admired her.*

The weather was perfect, and we went our different ways for the entertainment options that appealed to us most. I had gone to the circus on the previous evening (wonderful!) and went to the symphony on this evening (wonderful!).

The Grand Tour had been such a success that I sent an e-mail to Diana. I said, "There should be a group tour like this for all Volunteers, but in their first few days in the country. They will have a much better understanding of Kyiv and the country!"

I did not get a reply.

I did find out later that SNAC again held the Grand Tour the next year, for the advantage of new members. I'd love to hear that Headquarters made it a routine event for every incoming group of Trainees.

### Our next meeting: Ivano-Frankisvk in August.

Ivano-Frankivsk was well worth the trouble of getting to it. It was a fine success if measured as a social together or a tourist weekend. John Jensen, who was my on-site partner making many of the arrangements, did an excellent job. He deserved a commendation.

He put me up in his apartment and was a fine host. I enjoyed him enormously. He was so interesting. He had expertise in many fields. Had been an Army officer—the National Guard, I believe. He was an Iowan—had an exhaustive knowledge of growing corn and raising hogs. Was interested in starting a museum focusing on cream separators. Yes, cream separators! He convinced me it was a good idea.

Most recently had been a croupier on a river boat casino in Mississippi, I believe. He loved to ski—it was fortuitous that his assignment in Ivano-Frankisvk was to help promote tourism. The nearby Carpathian Mountains offered wonderful skiing, and he made it a point to do first-hand tourism research on their slopes. I was most fortunate to have him as my sidekick at this meeting.

But measured by what I hoped to achieve, our meeting was a failure. I take consolation in that I was probably the only one who thought so.

Again I got a member to serve as one-time secretary, Jim. He and his wife Robyn were serving together. They were the only Alaskans among us in Ukraine, I believe.

I wanted SNAC to vote to have Peace Corps modify its language teaching program for older Volunteers. The ad hoc committee appointed at the previous meeting had done little. Indeed the chair—I'll call her Alice—had e-mailed me that not many suggestions had surfaced. In other words, that language teaching was pretty good as it stood.

I was dismayed. I felt it could be improved half a dozen ways. I sent her a long e-mail explaining these ways. She replied that my suggestions sounded interesting. But nothing happened. In fact, she eventually e-mailed me that she was ill and would be absent at this meeting.

I wanted the club to change its name from SNAC (the Senior Network Action Committee). For the second time I proposed calling it the Ukraine Fifty-Plus Club, perfectly understandable because of Peace Corps' program by that name to recruit Volunteers 50 and older. I felt that SNAC, the acronym, was inaccurate and incomprehensible. I got the same bad vote. "No!" What a disappointment.

I had a brand-new item for discussion. I wanted the club to recommend to Peace Corps that it start a Volunteers' Club—somewhat like an officers' club in the military—close to Headquarters in Kyiv. Now and then Volunteers have to go to Headquarters on business.

The club would be a convenience for Volunteers and would offer numerous amenities, which I described. It would be a morale improver and save Peace Corps money—it was putting us up in a hotel, the Bratislava, that involved a long Metro ride. Discussion postponed for one year. SNAC would have a new president. Who would remember to bring it up next year?

I wanted the club to vote to recommend that Headquarters urge our ambassador in Kyiv and appropriate officials in Washington to do something exciting. What was that? Peace Corps would observe its 50$^{th}$ anniversary in two years, 2011. There would be great celebration and great festivity. My suggestion was that Peace Corps should lobby Ukraine to invite all Volunteers who had ever served in the country to return in 2011 for a two-week celebration on the occasion of the Corps' 50$^{th.}$

I did this because I had heard South Korea was doing it. South Korea wanted to show its appreciation although Volunteers were no longer serving there. How wonderful if Ukraine did it also!

The motion carried, but only because there was nothing to lose. Besides, I offered to do all the work of writing to everybody to promote the idea. There was no enthusiasm.

The meeting was a turn-down and disappointment on one thing after another. Even my friends did not go along with me. For a minute I was tempted to resign.

But we did have a grand time socially. Some went on a rafting ride down the local river. We all went on a cook-out in a nearby park. We ate a lot, drank some beers, and lolled on blankets on the lawn. Ivano-Frankivsk was a most interesting city. In our free time we walked around and enjoyed the city's fine architecture. We kept our cameras working!

But afterwards, I asked around. Why had so very little been accomplished at our meeting.? How come? Weren't those great ideas? I couldn't get any direct answers. So, I developed my own conclusions.

First, the big appeal for everyone in SNAC was a good time, period. Members felt that recommending such things to Peace Corps was useless. The recommendations would fall on deaf ears.

Picnic time! John Jensen is preparing the fire. SNAC was a fine social outfit. For sure.

And remember, everybody was in Peace Corps for a relatively short time—not many years; just 27 months. Some were leaving in just a few months. So why bother?

I had a different belief. We had an opportunity to make Peace Corps better. I was serious about striving to give SNAC a serious side. I was one of those getting out before long. In fact, in just four months. But I cared. To me this meeting made a mockery of the high role I hoped to give SNAC

And I had a pragmatic belief. If you don't ask, usually you don't get. If enough people in an organization ask and argue hard, usually they will be listened to. Surprising what dramatic results even a 51% vote can achieve.

### Our next meeting: in Poltava in November.

This was going to be our final meeting of the year and my last as president. New officers would be elected at this meeting.

We chose Poltava for two reasons. It was an interesting mid-size city with much to see. Historic. And more convenient to get to for most of our members—much easier than Ivano-Frankivsk had been.

Again I managed to get an excellent local Volunteer to agree to handle many details in Poltava. It was Berta Schweinberger, who had served ably as acting secretary for our Kyiv meeting.

Meanwhile I worked at my end to promote a 2011 reunion in Ukraine for all Volunteers who had served here. Immediately I wrote a letter to our ambassador in Ukraine, William Taylor.

He was the one who had inspired me in his talk to us when we arrived in Ukraine, and later at our Swearing In. I knew he had recently retired. His replacement had not arrived. I felt that the chief of staff at the embassy would place my letter in the pile being prepared for the new ambassador!

Of course, I made my letter as forceful as I could. After all, Ukraine had the largest group of Volunteers in the world! Peace Corps had been serving here steadily year after year since 1992, the year after Independence! Some 2,000 of us had come and labored to improve things!

I stressed that Volunteers serve in any country by invitation of the hosting government. If so many of us came here to Ukraine, surely it was because Ukraine appreciated us! This was a grand opportunity for Ukraine to show its appreciation!

To the argument that Ukraine is a poor country, I replied, "What country that Peace Corps serves in is not poor?" I added that this need not break the country's back. Volunteers would buy their own tickets, but surely Ukraine could get us discounts from Aerosvit, the country's big international airline. Then hold an appropriate ceremony of recognition and thanks. And could make other arrangements to give us a good time.

I asked him to use his influence at the highest levels of government to make this a reality.

I followed this by sending copies to our country director and to the director of the Ukraine Desk at national headquarters in Washington. I asked them to use their influence wherever possible.

I am sorry to report that I did not get an acknowledgment from anybody at the Embassy. Or any of the others. How about that?

Then bad luck. The swine flu hit Ukraine. It had also upset the United States and some other countries. The media were ripe with reports of an epidemic in western Ukraine. It was centered in Lviv.

Just a week before our meeting, Ukraine shut down all schools and universities for three weeks and appealed to people to stay home.

From what I had read, I believed this reaction was greatly exaggerated. Why would anyone close schools for three weeks? That's a long time. Think of all the kids, teachers, families affected. Why not one week, with an alert that it might be prolonged if deemed necessary?

Peace Corps e-mailed us a notice that all meetings were canceled! It should not have said "canceled"! "Postponed" would have been a better word. What to do? That meeting would be my finale as president.

Well, guess what? A few days later, all this was relaxed by Peace Corps. We could hold meetings! We tried to re-vive our reunion in Poltava. But the university there that would have hosted us was unrelenting. It would remain closed for the whole three weeks.

We had put in a lot of work preparing and planning. This would have been an important meeting because we'd be electing officers for the next year. Over the winter they would have planned for the spring meeting. Again, what to do?

I received a suggestion from one of our members, Peter Maguire, a native Rhode Islander like me. He was a retired university professor and dean. He suggested that we appoint an ad hoc election committee that would request nominations for the various offices, set a time-table, and hold an election. All this could be done by Internet.

Within hours I appointed him chair. He started immediately.

The next day I e-mailed a notice about all this to everyone.

I attached a copy of my letter to Ambassador Taylor and another of my long e-mail with my many suggestions how Peace Corps should modify the way it was teaching us Ukrainian and Russian.

I urged them to follow up on these matters in whatever way they chose best. I wished SNAC the best of luck and expressed thanks for whatever help and support the members had given me.

I signed it and added, "Your retiring president." But this did not mean that I quit before my term ended. No! Circumstances had abbreviated my term of office. So ended my tenure. It happened less than a month short of my last day in Peace Corps.

SNAC greatly enriched my Peace Corps experience in several ways. I am grateful to the unknown Volunteers who were inspired to start the club years ago. How wonderful! I hope that every contingent of Volunteers in every country that we serve in has a SNAC, or the equivalent. Oops, sorry. I just remembered that we Fifty-Plus Volunteers are assigned to only 10 countries or so. But the list will get longer.

I worked earnestly for SNAC. We succeeded nicely as a social and travel club but we fell far short of what I hoped SNAC could become. I went home with my tail between my legs about this.

~ ~ ~

***Did you know*** ... that you will have excellent medical coverage wherever you are assigned? All covered by Uncle Sam. Everything from medical care to special examinations and tests and prescriptions.

I can vouch for it personally, as you see in these pages.

In a country with a large group of Volunteers, there will be one or more medical doctors. Probably more. In a smaller country, maybe a physician's assistant or a nurse practitioner.

In every country, the medical staff will have easy contact with Peace Corps Medical in Washington. It provides impressive back-up service. I heard of and got to know Volunteers who were flown out for specialized care, then returned. What more could be asked for? Peace Corps Medical is excellent.

# 32 / My life with Tanya

*She gives me a good home away from home.
A wonderful gal. But oh, what frustrations!*

I lived with Tanya for my final 17 months. So, it turned out to be nearly two thirds of all my time in Ukraine. I'd say she was 95 percent perfect. But my previous two landladies were also 95 percent perfect. How lucky I was all those months!

Let me tell you about Tanya. As you know now, every woman in Ukraine has two names, one formal. In Tanya's case, that was her informal name. Her formal name was Tatiana, which I consider even prettier. But for me, she was Tanya from first to last. Never Tatiana.

She was in her early 50's, I believe. Truly beautiful—a knock-out. Was a university graduate from Russia and had a responsible job. And was a single mother, with two fine adult sons, one married.

She had 100 virtues and good qualities. Make that 150. And only one bad one. But that bad one irritated me so much that one day I nearly blew my top. Thank God I was able to restrain myself. I'll explain in a few minutes. I am proud to tell you we had a fine relationship right to our last day.

After Training, many Volunteers preferred to live on their own in their own apartment. One day Ed Novick, a fellow Volunteer and close friend, asked me why I preferred living-in rather than renting my own flat, as he was doing. And why I was living with my third family all while remaining in Chernihiv. I thought for a minute.

"For one thing, Ed, I like coming home to somebody at the end of the day. I like the security of that. And I like somebody else doing the cooking. And I like not having to go out to buy the groceries and wash the sheets and scrub the bathtub and vacuum.

"And why three 'host mothers'? Good question. Well, Peace Corps chose the first one for me for Training—you went through that, too. I had hoped to stay with that family. But that didn't work out. I didn't want to live alone, so I found another. Then I moved to another to improve my circumstances.

"And know what? Those changes were a good thing. Each one was an education for me. In fact, it was like looking out on Ukrainian life and culture through three different windows instead of just one."

I must say there was one big difference. Living with Natasha, my first host mother, and her two sons was living with a family. And living with my second one—Ira, and her son Slava—also was living with a family. But living with Tanya was not. I was really living with a single person.

True. She and I in our time at home were all alone in her flat. But she went off to her job in the morning five days a week. She got home at 5:15 p.m. And I went off to my work at *Coursi* around 2:30 p.m. But I was teaching in the evening, Sometimes it was 10 p.m. before I got home. So our time together was limited.

She was concerned for me. If I didn't get home on time, she would phone me, "John, where are you?" I would explain. Soon she realized I was a big boy and gave that up. But her calls made me feel good.

I saw little of her sons but I liked and admired them. Arkady, the older one, about 30, was living with his wife and child some blocks away. He was a self-employed carpenter, and a good one, as I got to see. His English was limited but quite good. I wished my Russian could be that good!

Andrei was 20 and mature for his age. He graduated from the prestigious national university in Kyiv while I was there and then started his own career in a city far away. Until then he had been coming home one weekend a month. I was always delighted to see him show up. He spoke impressive English. We always had great talks.

I have mentioned their good English. On the other hand, their Mom knew practically none. But we worked that out. English had been far less important in her younger days.

**O**ur relationship started off as strictly business and it remained that. Yes, we became friends. We got to appreciate one another. But it was strictly an arm's-length relationship from beginning to end. I kept the door to my room always closed, whether I was in or out.

We ate some meals together but I never sat down with her for a cup of tea, or joined her in the living room to watch TV. Nothing like that. I never let it become more than that.

I got to know her well and she me. I knew that she would go to the "*vanna,*" the steam house, every Sunday morning. And go dancing with her woman friends every Thursday evening. She saw that the light in my room would be on until nearly midnight (she could see it under my door). She knew that I loved apples and they had to be a staple in the kitchen.

And she knew that I would not emerge from my room in the morning until after she left to walk to work at 7:45. She never had to worry that I would catch her with her hair curlers on. Or that I would compete with her to use the bathroom in the morning. Or that I would come in and crowd our tiny kitchen while she was rushing through her own breakfast. It worked out fine for both of us.

I paid the rent every month on the 12tth without being asked. One month on the 12th she went off on a vacation before I had a chance to pay her. And I had the 1,150 *hryvnia* all ready!

*My Volunteer friend Ed Novick and I had different opinions. I preferred living with somebody. He preferred his own place. Peace Corps approved both.*

On the day she returned, we had lunch together. And very quickly she asked, "John, did you forget the money?" I had by then. I went to my room for the envelope I had prepared and paid her instantly. It made me aware once again that our arrangement was all business.

Within one week after my moving in, our pattern was clear. I would be a tenant in one room that I rented from her—my bedroom. But really it was my mini-apartment within her apartment.

At first she would barge in even if I happened to be in. She kept some things in a corner of my closet and might need an item. Or she might want to ask me something. I put a stop to that. "Tanya, please knock," I told her. Well, she knocked every time.

The room had everything I needed. A comfortable double bed—what a heavenly contrast to my cot at Ira's! Two large windows on the end wall, so lots of sunshine. A long bookcase that I quickly

*Home for a quick lunch. I'd sit across from her at our tiny table. But the language barrier was difficult.*

filled. A small divan that I relaxed on and so did any friend who visited. A desk which became the operations center for my various activities.

And then, best of all, a computer table—the kit table that I had bought back at Ira's and had moved here. On it I set up my Mac Mini, my speakers, my CDs and DVDs, and all my extra computer stuff, including a multi-hub and a portable hard drive. And in time, my Skype equipment.

No printer. I would go elsewhere when I needed one, which was not that often. Or use the printer at *Coursi*. I had it made!

I had one straight-backed chair that I could move from one desk to the other as needed. A clothes closet that was much too small but which I made do. And that was it. Oh, I had to keep a few sweaters and shirts on a shelf in her closet in the living room. That was where she slept, on the divan. It was a usual Ukrainian practice, as you know now.

My work at *Coursi* and the Korolonko Library took me out afternoons and evenings. Mornings were my leisure time—for the first time in my life! But they were always busy. This is when I did my private writing, which I did a lot of just about every day. And of course I had to prepared my classes.

I would eat breakfast alone. I fixed it myself and it hardly varied. A bowl of muesli and corn flakes, half and half, with cold milk. One toast with a slice of cheese. Half an orange in season. An apple when oranges were rare. And half a banana, which I sliced into my muesli. And a cup of black tea. That's all.

One Saturday morning early on, she noticed the cold milk. She offered to heat it for me. She was startled when I said no. She had never seen cereal eaten with cold milk. She liked her muesli with hot water.

I would eat my supper late in the evening, at 8, 9, or 10, depending on when I got finished at school. I knew she

*Tanya invited me and I went with her to a friend's for a nice dinner. A good time. Our problems were very few.*

always ate at 6. For a few weeks she cooked my supper for me. After that I was usually on my own.

I'd go in to prepare it. She would be watching TV in the living room. Sometimes she would pop into the kitchen to point to a dish she had left warm on the stove for me, or a pot of something in the refrigerator. For sure there would be a pot of borsch—the national soup.

She might heat it for me, but most often I did. Then she would return to her TV. By 10:15 she would turn off the light and go to bed on her convertible divan. She kept the blankets and pillows underneath. It would take her just two minutes to prepare it for sleep.

We had lunch together on some workdays. At 12:10 I would hear the door to the flat being unlocked. She was returning from the macaroni factory. Through my closed door I would yell, *"Privet,* Tanya!' – "Hello!"

She would always respond in English. "Hello, John!" Then she would add, "You want to eat?"

I would answer *"Da!"* most of the time—"Yes!" But often that would be too early for me—I had had breakfast only three hours earlier. For her, the noon meal was the big meal of the day. I preferred to eat at 2 p.m. or so. But at times I would eat with her.

Unfortunately, I always felt uncomfortable at the table with her and I sensed she was uncomfortable also. More so as time went by. For one reason alone: our language problem. I knew too little Russian and she too little English. There were long, awkward silences.

Yes, she worked in the macaroni factory just two blocks away. That's what everybody called it in Russian. Finally, I understood. What they made was pasta. All kinds. Their brand name was a national one.

She was the purchasing agent—she bought everything that the factory needed except the raw materials for the pasta. I mention this here as a refresher. Forgive me, please.

When I moved in, I felt that her lack of English would encourage me to pick up Russian faster. Wrong.

She was more interested in learning English than I was Russian, and she improved much faster than I did.

After a while, she always spoke to me in English. Even if I said a few words in Russian, she would continue in English. It was remarkable the progress she made. And how I limped behind.

I think that my seclusion in my room bothered her in the beginning. I am sure she wondered, *"What is John doing in there all these hours all alone?"* I hope she didn't think it was because I didn't like her. I liked her a lot. Sometimes I thought she might consider me strange.

But I always had much to do. In fact, I was happy that I had much to do. It was better for my mental health. And I took pleasure in my work, which was often writing something. And I liked my own company. That is a great blessing. I have found that too many people do not like their own company. How sad.

Once in a while we had to have a serious talk. How to do that? She provided the solution. She would ask me to sit next to her at her computer in the living room. She'd sit in her big stuffed armchair. I'd pull up a stool. She'd turn on the computer, then turn on a two-way Russian-English translation program she had. It turned out to be remarkably good. A godsend!

She would type a sentence or two in Russian. Then would click "English" on the program menu. And her words would appear on the screen in English. It was magic!

Then she would push the keyboard to me. I would type whatever I had to say. Then she would click "Russian," and my words would appear in Russian. I was amazed the first time. The translations were not perfect but quite adequate. That program of hers saved the day for us many times.

I wondered why Peace Corps didn't tell us about such programs. I think I knew. They didn't want to give us an easy way out.

Her sons Arkady and Andrei would arrive now and then. Always separately. Arkady, the carpenter, would come when she needed something fixed. He could also do plumbing and electricity. He was always in good humor and we always exchanged pleasant words.

Andrei would come home from his university in Kyiv one weekend every four weeks or so. She would cook for him and fuss over him. "I love my son," she told me. I could see that for myself. Actions speak louder than words, as we know. He would sleep on the divan with her.

*She worked hard at the office and hard at home. Took it all in stride. Here she's preparing pears for winter.*

He could play the guitar and I enjoyed that. He'd come and sit with me in my room and we'd have long chats. His English made it easy. A smart guy. He got up on the sunny side every day. More than once he solved an annoying computer problem for me. He did it cheerfully. He would return to Kyiv at daybreak Monday. His Mom would hand him his clean laundry, a big lunch for the *marshrutka* ride, and extra food to heat up at his university hostel. I was sorry to see him go, too.

He would soon graduate. He was on full scholarship because of ability. His major was physics. He surprised me. One day he said, "But I do not want to be a physicist. I like to work with people!"

He surprised me also when he said he had been to the U.S.A. "I was a waiter in Wisconsin for a summer." He had paid an agency to find him the job and it had been a wonderful experience. "I learned how to make pancakes. And my English improved!" Fantastic, I thought.

He had also been to Poland. And to South Korea, I believe. He had a knack for finding such opportunities. And he was just 20. I foresaw a brilliant future for him.

One day I saw him studying Chinese. Wow! "China will be very important!" he told me, and of course I agreed. He had enrolled on the side in a course on Chinese. Actually it was Mandarin, which is what most Chinese speak. He already knew several hundred of the symbols called ideograms. He was doing this challenging work mostly on his own.

One weekend he brought home a young Chinese friend from the university. A big, smiling fellow. Andrei was excited when he introduced us. "Kwan is a musician!" he told me.

So he was. Kwan was from near Beijing, if I remember correctly. He was studying music in Kyiv because the program was excellent and more affordable than in the U.S.A. or Western Europe. I found out he was tutoring Andrei in Mandarin. And in turn Andrei was teaching him Russian. A smart arrangement. A win-win situation, as we say.

Just before I ended my service and left for home, Andrei came home again. Long train ride. He wanted to say goodbye to me! How nice.

He had graduated and was working in distant Dnipropetrosk, one of the largest cities. He had gotten a job with a Christian church group. It was American-based.

"No, I am not in physics," he said, smiling. "I work with university students." He had told me he hoped to work with people. He made it happen. I was happy for him.

Now back to Tanya. She was very honest. If she found a coin on the floor that she thought was mine, she'd leave in on the stand by my bedroom.

One month I paid my rent and board as usual. My rent and board were 1,000 *hryvnia* at that time. I peeled off eleven 100-*hryvnia* bills for her.

She was startled. She counted them again, looked me straight in the eye, questioning me...then handed me 100 *hryvnia* back. I never would have noticed my mistake.

That total amount was about $200. I know this sounds low to you, but it was a substantial sum in Ukraine. It consumed the biggest chunk of my allowance from Peace Corps.

When I discovered that she went online with her computer at home, I asked if I could use it. I did not have Internet in my room. She said yes, and charged me 25 *hryvnia* per month, which was fair.

Finally I got lucky. I got my Mac Mini connected to the Internet in my room. She charged me 50 *hryvnia* per month, which was also fair—she was paying out 100 for the two of us. One month she handed me 20 *hryvnia* back. "It has turned out to be only 30 for one month," she told me. How nice of her.

What a hard worker she was. Up at 6:45 a.m. every morning, not easy on dark January mornings. Out the door to work at 7:45. Back for lunch at 12:10. Out the door to work at 12:50. Back at 5:15 to make supper. Week in and week out.

She always cooked everything except breads, which she bought. She made four or five kinds of jams, putting up two dozen big jars per year. Many big jars of pickles. Worked at this and that all the time.

At 8:30 in the evening she would sit at her desk and study English or turn on her computer for a while. Then often get on Skype and connect with Andrei in Kyiv or a distant friend and chat and laugh away. Then to bed right after 10, as I've said.

On weekends she would do the heavy housework, such as vacuuming, changing the sheets on my bed or doing the laundry or washing the kitchen floor. Cooking or tending her houseplants or changing the water for her tiny fish. Quite a story this. I'll explain soon..

*Andrei brought his friend Kwan home for a weekend. We had a good time.*

I knew very little about her background. I did know she was born in St. Petersburg in Russia, a fabulous city, and graduated from famed Moscow University. I suspect she came to Chernihiv after she married. I never heard a detail about her marriage or husband. He was never mentioned. I knew he lived in the city—her son Andrei mentioned one day he was going to visit his father.

There was no man in her life. She was not interested. I was sure she could have had her pick.

Like me, she was not a churchgoer. She was a spiritual person and a cultured one. She had an amazing collection of books. Unfortunately, she had little time to read them at this stage in her life. She led a busy social life, in person and on the phone. I found her admirable in many ways.

It soon became clear to me that her major motto was, "Save, save, save in every way!" All without depriving herself too severely.

She saved three ways. One was to do everything herself that she possibly could. One day I saw her put on a rubber glove to fish deep down into the mucky toilet to find what was blocking it.

Another was to buy in bulk. She'd lug home a bushel of potatoes to store on the balcony. She bought big bags of carrots, beets, cabbage, onions, and squashes for the balcony. Or oats and apples and sugar and rice and pasta in bulk— I'm sure she got the pasta at a bargain price at work.

Another way was to buy the lowest quality acceptable. Her tenet seemed to be, "Not the best. Just what's good enough!"

On the weekend she would go to the big central bazaar and scout the many fruit and vegetable stands for the best buys. When she bought apples, they were usually drops. And when tomatoes, always the worst-looking.

She would make her own croutons by slicing a big bread into tiny pieces, then toasting them in the oven. We boiled water on the stove for our tea. If I let it boil a minute too long, she brought it to my attention.

One day I went off without shutting the hot water faucet completely. When I returned, I saw a big sign above the sink, "John, please turn off!" I felt 10 years old. I made no comment. I let the sign stand. She took it down the next day. I suspected she regretted putting it up. Neither of us brought it up.

At first she bought small standard packages of muesli for me. Then she began making a big batch of her own version. She would mix oats with raisins and peanuts and some nuts. She would mix a two-gallon pan of it at one time. Just like Ira did in my previous place. A smart move.

Many families had cable TV connections, but she used a vintage rabbit-ears antenna for her set, and it had only a 12-inch screen. And that set was her major source of entertainment. One day I bought her a remote control as a gift. You should have seen her smile!

She insisted on washing the dishes without detergent, just hot water. We used the same small bottle of detergent all through my many months with her.

Oh, I would wash all my breakfast things and would wash the lunch dishes also, plus any pot or pan—she had to rush back to work. But often she insisted on washing them. I would only put things away and wash our table. In time, I began doing the dishes...she protested...I insisted...it became our routine. She would cook; I would *wash the dishes*.

Most of our food was the simplest. More than once the entrée for my dinner would be a boiled potato with a bit of butter and salt. With a side dish of coleslaw, prepared by her. Or a dish of plain spaghetti with a slice of cheese placed on it to melt, or just a dab of butter. Plus coleslaw.

She knew how to make a delicious apple cake. I loved it. Now and then she would make another apple cake. I knew she was doing it for me.

On Sunday she would make a big pot of borsch. We'd eat it till it was gone. It might last several days. One day I said, "It's delicious, Tanya. But not every day!"

The only time she did real cooking was when she invited a girl friend over. Or when Andrei came home. She would cook meat for him, or fish. She and I didn't eat either. She didn't eat even sausages, and Ukraine offered a thousand varieties. But maybe she ate those things when with him.

What a loving mother Tanya was. When he'd come, on Sunday she would wash his clothes and hang them up to dry and iron some of the pieces. Oh, she had a marvelous little Italian washing machine. But no dryer. Dryers were rare. She'd hang the clothes to dry on the balcony or on clotheslines running back and forth above the bathtub. She went all out to help him and make his life easier.

Within a month I noticed that she could feed me for a week on what she spent on food for him on a weekend home.

Not once did she ever cook a Sunday dinner or a holiday dinner for just the two of us. It would be the same old thing.

I think I had it figured out. A very intelligent and hard-working lady. And a single mother who was on her own. Money was scarce. She had to raise her two boys and run the home...do it all by herself while holding down a demanding job...and her primary strategy was to manage it by saving every *kopeck* in any honest way possible.

Frugality was her way of life, and I understood the necessity of that, and she was a master at it. I never saw her drink milk. Milk was for me.

Yet she took intense pride in her appearance and found money to buy fashionable clothes and boots. She must have had 20 lipsticks in our tiny bathroom. She looked terrific every time she walked out the door.

I did do a slow burn when I picked up an apple and had to cut the worms out. Or picked up a banana that was mushy because she had bought it too ripe. She never ate bananas, by the way. Those were reserved for me.

Later I heard the story about bananas in Ukraine. They were unknown in Soviet days. She grew up back then. When they appeared, people would buy just one. So expensive. I think she never got over that.

Gradually I saw her life improving. A new nozzle on the shower in the bathroom. A new metal cabinet for her cosmetics in the bathroom. Then a new toaster. She gave the old one to Andrei to use at the university.

Then one day—she was so excited—she bought an aquarium. A small one, the size of a shoebox, and a single tiny guppy, brought home in a plastic bag of water.

And the following week, four more tiny fish, all different. She gave them the greatest care. She set them up right next to her computer in her tiny aquarium, with a rose-colored light above it. It was beautiful. She would sit and study the fish. I think she had a name for each one.

One morning she was aglow. She pointed inside the aquarium. There were new tiny fish in there—tinier than a grain of rice. Just born! How was it possible? Who was the mother? The father? Mystery!

I was afraid the bigger fish might eat the babies. I mentioned this and she became concerned. She scooped the babies out one by one and plopped them into a big jam jar. They'd be safe by themselves.

But she dropped one baby on the floor. She dropped on her knees, searched for the tiny thing, found it, and carefully scooped it up. It was lifeless. She had tears in her eyes.

I worried about one thing. Her aquarium had a tiny pump that blew bubbles in the water. Oxygen! The babies in the jar also would need oxygen. What to do? The next time I was at our only McDonald's, I brought home one of their nice sipping straws.

Every morning before breakfast I'd blow bubbles in their water. They must have felt it was a hurricane. I did it every time I entered the kitchen. She did, too. The babies thrived.

Finally came the big day. She put the growing guppies in with the big fish. She kept count. Soon she found some were missing. Those big guys were cannibals!

When she'd go off for a few days, it was my job to feed them and turn off their light and the air pump at night, per her instructions. I did the job conscientiously. I didn't want to see her in tears again if she found one or two floating when she returned.

**S**he continued to make improvements. One day, white toilet paper instead of the common, coarse gray. Another week, a new hand vegetable grater—she grated and shredded cabbage and carrots and onions just about every day.

How long she had had the rusty old one? She thought and thought and laughed. "*Mnoga!*" A long time! Since she was a bride, I was sure.

She took vacations. Ten days in Bulgaria. A week in Moscow. Ten days in the sunny Crimea. Now and then a weekend in Kyiv. But again she knew how to stretch her money. On long journeys she would sleep on the train coming and going. She would pack a large picnic basket for herself. She never considered it deprivation. She was enjoying life.

And one day I realized something: all these improvements were possible primarily for one reason—the cash that I paid her for my room and board. She had taken in a Volunteer couple before me, and now me, and she got to like that steady stream of cash. I was glad she was better off because of my presence. She was a savvy lady. I was sure she was figuring how to find another Volunteer when I left.

Then another thought. All of us Volunteers in Ukraine were doing the same thing—spreading cash around—and I imagined how it rippled through the economy.

Not only to host mothers and companies of all kinds and also the many public services. As well as to the Ukrainian government through the retail taxes on everything. Plus all the money that Peace Corps spent through its Headquarters in Kyiv. I appreciated the terrific multiplier effect of it all!

We Volunteers—in fact, Peace Corps itself—were doing a lot more good than we thought, and in more ways.

In January, a big scare. Russia threatened to turn off the heat. It was the big supplier of gas to Ukraine. It was claiming Ukraine was not paying enough for the gas. Ukraine was counter-claiming Russia was not paying enough rent for the pipelines it used through Ukraine.

One day Tanya came home distraught. Apartments and businesses were going to have their gas shut off! Everybody at the macaroni factory was being laid off for two months...no paychecks...it was shutting down!

We sat at the kitchen table and made a plan. How would we cook without gas? I gave her money and told her to go out and buy an electric two-burner hot plate right away. She ran off. And returned several hours later, empty-handed. There had been a run on hot plates.

We worried for the next few days. The gas was continuing to run. Then big news. The politicians in Russia and Ukraine had worked out a deal. The factory did not close. She did not lose a single hour's work. We didn't lose an hour of heat.

We were both interested in improving our language skills. Her English. My Russian. We decided to study together every evening for an hour. We would do exercises. She would read English words aloud—strive to pronounce them properly with my help and memorize them. I would do the same with Russian words with her help.

Not good. Her voice was too soft. She was not patient enough with me despite her good intentions. I gave up after a week. She continued diligently on her own. She went out and bought herself a paperback, "How to Learn English Fast!" but in Russian. I knew she studied it every evening. And her progress was truly fast. I admired her and told her so.

As for my studying Russian, I threw in the towel completely in a couple of months. I discussed all this in another chapter.

She followed through on everything I had asked for in my first meeting with her. She respected the fact that I was vegetarian. But not hard for her as she was a vegetarian herself, it seemed.

She changed my bed sheets every week or so and gave me fresh towels. She was surprised that I took a shower every day but never made a comment. She did my laundry the first week but I put a stop to that and did my own. A few times she insisted on taking my jacket and trousers and ironing them, which was thoughtful.

One evening I came home. It was only 6 p.m. and she was in bed—excuse me, on the divan. So early. Extraordinary. She was curled up with the blankets nearly covering her head. Very sick. Stomach complaints. Without saying a word I called her son, Arkady.

She heard me and protested, "No, no, no, John!"

Arkady was worried, asked to speak to her. I handed her my cell phone. She mumbled something...a re-assurance, I was sure. The next morning she was better and went to work.

In January she sat me down at her computer and started her translation program. She had something important on her mind. She typed, "I must raise the rent. The terrible inflation! It must go up from 1,000 to 1,300 *hryvnia* every month."

That was a huge increase. It would gobble up a great percentage of my monthly allowance from Peace Corps.

I put my fingers on the keyboard and began typing, "That is an increase much higher than inflation! I must get in touch with Peace Corps!"

I did check with my regional manager, Iryna. We reasoned that Tanya would have all the same basic monthly expenses if she lived alone in her flat. The extra expenses that she paid for me were for my food and the extra electricity that I used. That was all. I felt she deserved more money, but less than she demanded.

But Iryna told me she and Peace Corps could have no role in this— it was entirely between Tanya and me. I realized that.

I waited a week before bringing up the subject. I told her, "I will pay 1,100 *hryvnia* per month," I said. "Just 100 more than now." And I explained. I did not threaten to move out but of course I'm sure she realized that I might.

A long pause. "All right," she said. And that was it. It remained 1,100 all the rest of my time with her, some 11 months. Oh, plus the extra *hryvnia* for Internet service.

I was delighted when Tanya said okay about milady Annabelle coming and living with me for a month. She was most pleasant about it. I offered to pay more, of course, and Tanya mentioned 350 *hryvnia*, and I paid it, no problem. She was impressively nice to Annabelle and Annabelle took an immediate liking to her.

When I moved in, Tanya had wanted to buy new furniture for me— she insisted on taking me and my librarian friend Ira to a furniture store. She knew Annabelle would come and visit sooner or later. We looked at beds and dressers and bureaus. She had a special interest in a new bed for me. Finally I said, "No, no, Tanya. The furniture you have now is fine. Buy new furniture for yourself after I go home to America."

I didn't want the worry of scratching new furniture or leaving a circular mark on the dresser with my hot teacup.

But exasperated, she said to me, "The bed creaks!" I didn't get it at first…and then I did. I laughed. "No problem," I said. "Don't worry."

Tanya and Annabelle were together just a few days. Tanya went off on vacation. I believe she timed it to give us more privacy and to make it easier on herself. It worked out fine. Again I admired her thinking.

As the weeks went by, she simplified her life by preparing big batches of simple foods. A whole pot of borsch, or of soup. And she would serve them once a day, sometimes twice, until the pot was empty.

She would cook a pot of macaroni, or rice, or buckwheat (*kasha*), or a two-inch stack of thin pancakes (*blinis*), or a pan of beans. And we'd eat these meal after meal until gone.

She would take a leftover out of the fridge—one that had been a leftover two or three times— and check it by sniffing it, and nearly always serve it again.

They were all good foods, mind you. Nutritious and healthful. I never got sick from anything she made. In fact, I lost pounds, which made me happy.

What I minded was the monotony of it, and the priority that she assigned to feeding me as cheaply as she could.

On the other hand, she was eating what I was eating. But now and then she'd announce that she would not be home for lunch or dinner. It occurred to me she might be splurging at a restaurant. I never found out.

**I** would have accepted it heartily if she served the big batches not so consistently. If she served rice one day, then beans the next, then borsch, then the rice again, and so on. She could put up the food in smaller batches to make this possible.

*A big moment. This is her first bread coming out of her brand-new oven. I felt what I paid her made it possible.*

I started asking at school and the library. "Do you eat borsch every day? Do you eat rice three days in a row?" The answer seemed to be no!

But it's surprising how often she did serve borsch. I did enjoy it. But no meal could be cheaper to prepare: water, small bits of beets and potatoes and cabbage and carrots and onions, and some seasonings. Most of these seasonings were right out of the garden and the yards nearby, not store-bought, mind you. Borsch twice a week would have been perfect.

I am the one who brought beans to her attention. "They are high in protein," I said. "Because I am a vegetarian, I need more protein."

She began soaking beans every week for me. But again, it was always the same kind: huge, beautiful, white beans. Delicious. But there were so many kinds available. They came in so many colors. And they were all cheap. It was so easy to achieve variety.

Sometimes I'd come home and find only two things in the refrigerator: eggs and borsch. Usually I chose the borsch.

One night my irritation got the best of me. I was hungry. There was so little in the fridge. I sat at my computer and typed a long letter to her. I mentioned all her good qualities. "You are a fine person. I like you."

Then I got around to the food. I asked for more variety. Made simple suggestions.

Then I re-read it. Decided to tone it down a bit. Finally I was satisfied. I copied it on my flash drive and carried it into the living room.

I wanted to put it on her computer for her to translate and read. But she had gone to bed early. I didn't want to wake her. I returned to my room and went to bed.

The next morning I re-read my letter. Thought about it. Then pushed it aside. And I never showed it to her. Everything considered, I liked living at Tanya's. Maybe I could make my complaint known to her in a more delicate way

Valentine's Day! "John, I love you!" Tanya scrawled at our English Club. A joke!

About one month later I came home from teaching late and looked in the refrigerator. What could I warm up? Only a pan of soup in there. I looked for the cheese. No cheese. I looked at the fruit bowl for a banana. No banana. My blood pressure shot up.

Just then she walked in from the living room. She was checking on me. I pointed to the pan of soup and I scowled. She got my point.

"John, we eat soup every day in Ukraine!" she said.

"Maybe you do. But I don't want to!"

She could see my anger. Could feel it.

I pointed to how empty the refrigerator was.

"What do you need?" she asked.

I rattled off a short list—cheese, bananas, oranges, more milk.

"I go to market!" she said. It was past 10 p.m. In three minutes she had her jacket on and was rushing out. I thought she had meant in the morning. To what market at this hour?

She returned in 30 minutes and took the items out of her bag. She let me see them. She had them all. She had also bought a chocolate bar for us—a sure sign of contrition.

I had eaten my supper by now. Yes, the soup. And I had calmed down. But still had things to say.

"Let's go to your computer!" I said. We sat down at it and had one of our digital chats. I was concerned. She was concerned. We both had a lot at stake. I did not want to move out. I was sure she did not want to lose my monthly check.

I typed, she typed, back and forth, and we read one another's words. It became more relaxed. I told her what I expected. She nodded. Again I pointed to how empty the refrigerator was. She nodded again.

Finally I offered her my hand and she took it. We shook! I knew she considered this gesture a crazy American thing. But she understood and was glad to shake. And she smiled.

Things definitely improved.

I tried to be thoughtful. I would leave a big chocolate bar—dark chocolate was what she liked—on the kitchen table. I gave her a bouquet of flowers on Women's Day—the equivalent of our Mothers' Day, but broader. I slipped money in her hand whenever she left on vacation.

But gosh, she could be so picky. Wouldn't overlook anything. One day I left the light on in my room when I went to work. She brought that to my attention. Another night I forgot to close the apartment door. Yes, left it ajar. "John," she said, "how could you do that?"

I wanted to say, "Because I was distracted!" But she wouldn't understand those words. What I said was, "I am an old, old man!" She laughed. I was sure she was in total agreement.

We did some nice things together. One day she suggested we go to the circus. I love a circus and said yes. I paid for the tickets. We had a good time.

Another day she said we were invited to her friend's house for dinner—a friend who had taken in a Peace Corps Trainee—and I said yes. We had a good time.

On the way home, she reached out and took me by the arm. I liked the idea of being gallant but did not want to give a wrong message. At one point, she had to let go and I did not offer my arm back. We continued home side by side, without touching. She understood.

She loved to dance. Mid-east belly dancing. Sometimes I'd come home and she'd be dancing in the living room, to music from a CD. She was fleet and graceful. She loved it. Sometimes one of her girl friends would come over, and they would dance and practice and practice. They were terrific together.

One day she invited me to an annual belly dance show downtown. She and her friend were going to be one of the acts again. Would I like to go? Yes! Then she told me my ticket would be 45 *hryvnia*! Oh, well. I bought a ticket and went.

All the gals were wearing filmy, see-through outfits that would excite any sheik, believe me. They put on a fantastic show. My son had just sent me a tiny *FLIP* video camera. A beautiful gift. It was my first time using it. I shot her whole sequence. At home afterward in the kitchen I played back the sequence. Nothing there! She was so disappointed. So was I. I had goofed somehow.

On a nice spring day, I discovered a gleaming red mountain bike on our balcony. With a 10-speed derailleur! I looked it over. I had been an enthusiastic bike rider for decades. This was a good bike and had everything. A beauty. Tanya had bought it for herself.

Three weeks went by and she did not use it once. I figured it was because it was such a huge job to get it in and out of the flat and down and up the many stairs. I suggested she should store it in the basement. That might be more convenient. She said, "No room!"

"Maybe we can make room. Please let me see." Finally she took me down there.

Each apartment had a closet, maybe six by eight feet. Hers was at the end of a narrow corridor, then left onto another. She unlocked the door to the closet. The ceiling was very low. The floor was dirt. The room was stuffed to the ceiling with boards and old furniture.

I said, "Let's go look outside." I found a perfect spot for the bike under a balcony on the first floor. The bike would be protected from the rain and snow. I showed her how her son Arkady could screw a big ring into the wall there, and she could chain her bike to it. "It will be convenient for you!"

But she insisted on keeping it upstairs and lugging it up and down. So be it. I would encourage her to ride it. And she did, usually on Saturdays.

I would see some men riding bicycles, even old men. A bike was so practical and saved so much money. But never a woman. She rode her bike happily and proudly. How I admired her.

But I never got her to buy herself a helmet. She really had a mind of her own. In fact, never did I see any Ukrainian bike rider with a helmet on. I must mention that Headquarters insisted that Volunteers wear a helmet when on a bike. Later I was told that most never did—did not want to stand out.

One day in my final summer I announced that I would go off and travel for my month of vacation. "Very good!" she said in Russian. Immediately she began planning improvements to her kitchen to be done in my absence. When I got back after a month, I saw a complete new kitchen in the making. Very impressive.

"But big problems," she said. "Did not have time to finish!" But Arkady would come with his tools in the evening. He finished in a week.

What a big improvement. A beautiful brand-new window. New laminate flooring. New wallpaper. New cabinets. New sink. New countertop gas range. A new kitchen table. A big shelf above her washing machine. She was ecstatic.

But no new oven yet. "No money!" she said with a little laugh. "*Patom!*" Later!

Before long she had the oven. Immediately she baked an apple cake. It was beautiful. "Very good oven!" she said. She cut me a slice then and there.

But I felt badly when she began putting her mis-matched dishes and bowls and her old and worn pots and pans into her beautiful new cabinets.

She read my mind. "*Patom!*" She'd buy some later. She'd save up for them. But she didn't manage to do it before I left.

I asked her, "What will be your next project?"

"The bathroom. Big, big job!"

"Great idea!" I was sure it would happen. Especially if she got another Volunteer. And I was confident she would.

Little daunted her. Here she's repairing a pedal. I never saw another woman of her age and status riding a bicycle.

In my last few months, a dozen people in my English Club began playing volleyball at the high school after our Sunday meetings. It was a great idea. I mentioned this to Tanya.

She showed up the following Sunday and went with the group to the gym afterward. She'd participate every Sunday. I think it's why she came. I was told she was terrific—the second best. She could have been the mother of nearly everybody else playing!

As the days passed, I looked forward increasingly to my going-home date. Now it was coming fast. I think she dreaded it. She could see her income taking a tremendous drop. I liked to think that she would miss me. I believe that she would.

I had a lot of things to give away. Surprising how much I had accumulated in my more than two years. Impossible for me to take a lot of it home. Much good stuff.

I made a list of people to give things to. I put her name on it but reluctantly. Such a fine and good person. But she had been so stingy with me. I hoped she would read a message in that. I struck her name out. Then I relented. I put it back on my list. And I felt better about that.

I must say she was wonderful when I mentioned that Annabelle would be flying in to spend the final 14 days with me. "Is it all right if Annabelle stays here with me again?"

"Yes," she said. "Very good!"

She was totally amiable about it. But I wanted to be clear about the details. We had another computer "chat."

I wanted to settle one thing. "How much will I pay for Annabelle's stay with me here?"

She knew that I had been paying for a full month every month, even for days and weeks when I was away. In fact, I had been gone for nearly four weeks on my recent summer vacation. Besides, we'd be leaving for the U.S.A. two weeks before my final rent and board ran out.

She thought for a minute. "Everything will be all right," she typed. "No problem, John!"

That was very nice. She could tell by my smile I was happy.

One night I got up to go to the bathroom. It was midnight. I was startled to see her painting the trim on the kitchen door.

She didn't say so but I knew she was getting ready for Annabelle's arrival. In fact, she spent many hours making little improvements.

Annabelle's stay worked out nicely. Annabelle arrived and the two greeted one another with smiles and embraces and genuine warmth.

Annabelle had a beautiful gift for her—a very mod fashion belt from her favorite store. It was glittery and obviously high quality. Tanya loved it, tried it on right away. She wore it to the English Club the following Sunday.

And guess what? Our food improved! She came home with walnuts and a pomegranate and even a grapefruit. These were firsts for me. The apples were nicer and so were the bananas. I was very happy.

I had asked her to teach Annabelle some of her vegetarian recipes. She translated and typed them out. I saw the two of them side by side at the counter in the kitchen. She was teaching. Annabelle was absorbing.

Very soon Tanya began skipping lunch. She announced she would not be home till 9 p.m. She announced she was going to Kyiv for a long weekend. What she was doing was making it easier for us. Giving us more time alone. On the other hand, maybe she herself was also enjoying the break from us.

One night I could not connect to the Internet. I tried and tried. No luck. How come? I asked Tanya. She had had my service disconnected.

"It was the start of a new month for paying!" she said. She realized I would be here just a few days more. But why didn't she alert me?

Then she asked for another computer chat with me. Sure. We sat side by side. She hit me up for another 200 *hryvnia*! Shocking!. We had settled all this.

In fact, she had signed the Peace Corps end-of-service form that I owed her absolutely no money—it was a mandatory form that all Volunteers going home had to get filled out.

It was a minor sum for me, about $30. But the idea of it! I had no taste for argument. I gave her the money and insisted on a receipt.

What was remarkable was that in all our months together we never exchanged a bad word. I told you that she was 95 percent perfect. Well, that was true. All in all, I was fortunate in staying with her. I would stay with her again. I admired her. Liked her.

How about me? Well, I believe I was 95 percent perfect, too.

I hope Tanya finds herself another good Volunteer. Better still, I hope she finds a good man all her own—though I'm not sure she was ever out looking. She deserves one. The guy would be lucky, too.

~ ~ ~

***Did you know*** .... that during Training over there and perhaps a bit longer, you will be asked to live with a family chosen for you—your "host family." Peace Corps will pay them for your care.

This is done for the best of reasons. To help you learn the language, the culture, and the way of life, and also to give you an easier start during the intense weeks of Training—a safe environment, home-cooked meals, guidance, language practice, and so on.

You will be very busy in Training, and this will free you from many worries and time-taking things.

Afterward, you may select any arrangement you choose. You may continue to live with a family or you may opt for- an apartment or even a house. You will now pay for this out of your monthly allowance.

There are good arguments for both ways. I chose to live with a family. It was not perfect but I believed it was the better way. As you will read.

# 33 / My life with the bosses

*I get to deal with the brass. I develop a big problem and some irritations*

Life with bosses is rarely perfect. Of course, there were bosses in Peace Corps, and at various levels, meaning in Washington, around the world, and at the local level—in my case, Ukraine—and then at the very bottom level, mine in Chernihiv. I did not expect perfection.

In fact, I was astonished to find our Headquarters staff in Ukraine had 75 full-time people. I mentioned this earlier. Yes, 75 to manage a group of fewer than 300 Volunteers at that time. Plus a cadre of part-timers. Huge, it seemed to me.

*Why so many?* I wondered. *What is this all about?*

Well, I found out. The answer was that it took not only administrators, but also specialists of various kinds—in education, in language instruction, in relations with the Ukrainian government, in personal security for Volunteers, in travel arrangements, and still others who had deep and broad knowledge about Ukraine itself.

Plus a medical staff of four doctors and a pharmacist and a medical assistant. Plus secretaries and clerks. Plus a surprising number of drivers and a surprising number of guards. Yes, guards.

I was also surprised when I learned that 73 of the 75 were Ukrainian nationals. Why so many?

I could only surmise. Certainly they were cheaper than Americans. You didn't have to fly them in from the U.S., and then fly them back home. Surely you didn't have to give them the same big package of salary and perks.

Certainly they provided essential expertise about the country and its culture and its way. Good contacts with key Ukrainian departments and agencies and their staff people. Think of the drivers and the guards, for example—important for them to have local knowledge!

I suspected that some of these, at all levels, had worked in Ukrainian government before being hired by Peace Corps.

And one more reason. Peace Corps has a strange rule. It's called "Five and Out!" All key administrators may serve a limit of five years, and then they must leave. It may be a rule unique in the federal government for appointed employees. In fact, it seems a controversial policy.

Sargent Shriver, founding director, believed that "Five and Out!" would keep the organization fresh and dynamic. The agency would get a steady and continuing infusion of new blood. This rule covered our two top administrators in Ukraine.

The Ukrainian nationals, however, had the possibility of making Peace Corps their career. They were not limited to five years. This assured an increasing depth of expertise.

It also assured continuity in its support structure as the highest administrators came and went because of that rule. I got to meet several Ukrainian staffers who had been there 8 or 10 years. I met a driver or two, for instance, who had been there nearly since the arrival of Peace Corps in the country in 1992.

I did see there could be exceptions to the rule. Our country director, Diana, finished her five years

*Iryna, my regional boss. Pleasant. Capable. Impressive My gripe: how she "reviewed" my articles.*

and then got an extension of two years. In fact, her extension got another extension during the very close of my service, for a total going on eight years, as I understand it.

She was still working when I left and said she was delighted to have been appointed as a roving country director, ready to serve a temporary hitch in this country or that one as the need came up.

Remember, too, that this Ukrainian staff was supported by a huge hierarchy in Washington and across various States. Well, huge at least to my eye.

It's in full honesty and with pleasure that I tell you that I had pleasant relations with everybody I got to deal with. In fact, I never had an ugly moment with anyone in Peace Corps. But I did have a few incidents that gave me a sour taste and made me wonder.

**M**y immediate boss throughout my two years of service was my regional manager, Iryna Shevchenko. She ran Region 1. There were eight regions. What is remarkable is how little I got to deal with her. Days and weeks would go by without hearing from her.

She was a calm and considerate person. When I think of her, I think of the old carpenter's adage, "Measure twice and saw once." Iryna always thought twice before she spoke once. There was always a pauseful deliberateness to her. I would wonder, *What is she thinking now?* But I got used to it.

She was in her 30's, I believe, always polite, always attentive, always all-business, and always careful to have the Peace Corps rules and regulations at her elbow, I thought.

She may have been unique among the more than 70 Ukrainian nationals at Headquarters—to my knowledge, she was the only one to have lived and worked in the U.S.A. For some five years she had studied—earned an M.B.A., I think—and then worked in Texas as a business consultant.

So she had a big plus—the actual cultural experience of living and working in the U.S.A. It's impossible to pick this up even if you are an eager learner of everything American unless you have lived on our shores.

All the Ukrainians at Headquarters spoke English, those at the higher levels very well. Iryna spoke it with easy fluency and wrote it the same way.

She co-shared a small office at Headquarters. It was as tidy as a *babushka's* kitchen. She had her mobile phone on one side and her laptop on the other. Her pens and pencils and records and pads were at the ready.

Usually I would see her by appointment. But sometimes I would drop by. She was always welcoming.

Nobody ever explained to me what a regional manager did. But I got to see that it was a demanding job. I am sure that what I got to see of her responsibilities was true for all the regional managers.

She spent a lot of time in the office, keeping records, attending staff meetings, supervising us, and checking up on us. She would e-mail and call us. (I know this sounds contradictory to what I said some paragraphs back, but it's my impression.)

Also she had to deal with the organizations that we were working in, and with our official Counterparts at those places. I believe she had something to do in choosing these organizations for us, and what host families we'd live with. There was a lot of paper work, and I think a hard part of her job was getting us Volunteers and Counterparts to turn in required papers and reports on time.

I think another headache was making sure we observed the rules. A key rule was that we alert her to any overnight absence from our home base—before (!!!), not while or afterward. This was a serious offense with tough disciplining, but I got the feeling some Volunteers did it. I heard of Volunteers sneaking off early for a weekend or a vacation out of town, and returning late—or did both.

The rule made sense. Peace Corps had to know where everyone was because of a possible emergency. Iryna shot off many e-mails to us, "Please make sure to notify me before you leave! And when you are returning!"

We accumulated 24 vacation days a year, but even Saturdays and Sundays while on vacation counted as vacation days. This struck most of us as unfair. So 24 was not as many as it sounds.

Also, I am sure she had a tough role whenever anyone got into serious trouble. After all, we were her responsibility. The penalties for the violators could be getting kicked out, or even facing criminal charges. But there didn't seem to be much of the latter.

Early in our Training I did hear of one young fellow who had been sent home for public drunkenness. The rumor was that he had been caught drunk, had signed a contract with Headquarters not to do it again, but got drunk again. All in a few weeks. He was quickly driven to the airport with a ticket home. We heard about it. And we took it seriously as a warning.

And what a shock—one of our colleagues had the police waiting for him when he got off his plane in the U.S. while on a trip home. They found child pornography on his computer. A trial! Imprisonment! He was quickly terminated, of course.

The details of such serious happenings were not made public. Not even the names of those involved. They should have been.

We would hear gossip, and that's notoriously unreliable. It's so often exaggerated. Why shouldn't we be in the know? We didn't need every awful detail. But we should have been notified of the basics, including the person's name. That's the wise approach.

I knew the guy in the child pornography case. I considered him a friend. He had helped me when I had a problem with using the video feature on my digital camera. He impressed me as a Volunteer.

Well, a few vague words about it arrived from Kyiv. What Volunteer could this be? I went right online to Google and typed in "Peace Corps Volunteer. Child pornography."

Bingo! Immediately I found half a dozen news stories, all based on an Associated Press feed. I knew all the basics. Even his prison sentence eventually. Wouldn't it have been smarter for Peace Corps to give us the straight facts?

Back to Iryna. She was required to spend time on the road. She'd go off in one of the big Toyotas with a chauffeur. Sometimes for just one day to a city or town. Sometimes for two or three days with several stops plus overnights, of course. She had to visit us Volunteers, plus our Counterparts. Sometimes routine visits, sometimes special and urgent. She was a wife and mother, but this was her job.

Sometimes she had to stage a regional conference in one of our cities. She would have to plan not only the program but all the logistics, and then run the program—recruiting speakers, assigning roles and responsibilities, making all the arrangements, demanding feedback and written reports. So it took many talents. I never felt that Iryna fell short.

She irritated me seriously about one thing. This is when she edited the articles that I wrote for the editor of "Peace Corps Journals" in Washington. The reports were published on Peace Corps' global website…www.peacecorps.gov. That's when Iryna would swing into her "censor" role. That was my word for it, not hers. But I'll get into this in the next chapter, "My Writing Life."

I felt Iryna's motives were good. She was being thorough and responsible and conscientious. I am not sure but I think her problem was that she did not have an American concept of journalism. Hers was Ukrainian, perhaps still tinged with Sovietism, though I am sure she was unaware of this. Perhaps Peace Corps itself had this restrictive view.

**I** have a sharp memory of one instance of what may have been a hangover from Soviet days for her. She was visiting me at *Coursi*. As I've explained, the school occupied space in a big building. In fact, it was a hotel. A high-powered conference was in swing in the big auditorium. An imposing head table was lined with men and women in expensive clothes. News photographers, TV cameramen.

Iryna and I walked out of the building together. I was startled to see the parking area crowded with big, gleaming cars. Highly unusual. Policemen were standing at the alert around an even bigger car—what would be a Hummer if Hummers were available in Ukraine. "What's that all about?" I asked her as I pointed to it.

She told me in a very low voice, "Do not point like that, John!"

I was startled. "What do you mean?"

"Those police may come and question you!"

"What?"

"That is the car of a very important man. They may wonder why you were pointing like that."

She was serious. I think she was intimidated. This from a woman who had spent five years in the U.S. and, you'd think, soaking up our culture.

She told me the man in the double-breasted suit with others clustered and fawning around him was a big, big man in their Rada, which is the Ukrainian Congress in Kyiv.

When we got out of range, I said to her, "In America, things are different. Nobody will get upset if I pointed that way. If I were holding a gun, yes, or acting threateningly, yes. But we are a free country!"

What I was saying without saying it was, "Ukraine is a free country also, yes, but a very young one. Less than 20 years old. The culture of the old days still has not caught up to the new times.

"This is why we Volunteers are here. Among other things, to make you aware of how we think and live and behave. Of our principles of freedom in their every-day applications." (As I write this, I am not sure I was totally correct. Our War on Terrorism has changed some things.)

I remember two other specific visits Iryna made to me. One was after I had moved into Tanya's flat (my final landlady). Iryna wanted to see for herself what my accommodations were, how good or how rough, and if everything was up to Peace Corps' regulations. And of course she wanted to chat with Tanya.

I alerted Tanya that Iryna would come. "Oh!" she said. Immediately I felt that Tanya knew this Iryna Shevchenko from Kyiv.

And she did. This was Tanya's second time of renting to a Volunteer. I felt instantly that Tanya had dealt with Iryna before. The prospect made her nervous.

Iryna was a quiet person. She arrived, noticed the three locks on our two front doors, and nodded approvingly. She said hello to Tanya and looked around. She entered the kitchen, examined everything, noticed something missing. Where was the big red fire extinguisher provided by Peace Corps?

I pointed to it under the kitchen table. The kitchen was tiny. There was little room. She nodded. That was okay.

She looked around again. Where was the Peace Corps-supplied combination smoke and gas detector? I wasn't sure myself. I had forgotten. I thought a minute. I took her into the hall and pointed to a shelf high up in Tanya's big bookcase. "Up there!" I said. In fact, Tanya had put it there.

"No. Not good!" She reached way up and took down the battery-operated device. Returned to the kitchen, appraised the gas stove and other equipment. "Better here," she said, placing it atop the fridge right across from the stove. It made sense.

She entered my room. I always make my bed in the morning, always hang up my clothes, always dump my socks and underwear in the laundry basket, and firmly believe in a place for everything and everything in its place. But I'm a busy guy. My room often looked like me. A bit rumpled.

She saw all the books and papers and office odds and ends on my big desk. My computer and monitor and their many accessories on my secondary desk. The bookcase full of this and that. The big cardboard box I used as a file cabinet. The shelf where I kept my camera and cell phone and DVD player and their chargers.

"Gosh! You've got a lot of stuff, John!"

"True. But some of that stuff is Tanya's." I pointed to Tanya's items in the far end of the bookcase. "Don't you think my room looks nice and comfy?'

She had one of her thoughtful pauses. "Yes, I think so."

She sat and we had a catch-up. Was everything okay, she asked me?

"Yes" I assured her.

She covered several bases. She had her pad out, her pen in hand. The language school? The library? Other things? "Yes." "Yes.""Yes."

Then she went out and chatted with Tanya, returned in a few minutes. "No big problems, it seems."

I agreed. I felt better for Tanya's sake.

I was aware that Iryna's chauffeur was sitting and waiting in the big Toyota in the yard. She didn't seem hurried.

*How many hours do those drivers spend sitting and waiting every day,* I wondered.

Finally she said, "I'm glad you're doing all right."

"Yes. Not bad at all." And I meant it. I told her I was enjoying my work, liked being a Volunteer, thought highly of Peace Corps. She smiled.

**I** asked for a favor. Another item Peace Corps gave each of us was an oil-filled electric room heater. Some apartments were cold, it seemed. In the past, Volunteers left their heater behind on site when they returned home. A souvenir gift! Now, as an austerity necessity, Peace Corps wanted the heaters back. Mine was still in its box, "Can you take it back for me, Iryna?" I said.

"Sure. But you still might need it!"

"No." And I convinced her. It was winter, and Tanya's flat was nice and warm. Here in Chernihiv, it was the city that provided the heat. The city turned it on for everybody on one day in the fall, and off for everybody on another in the spring. Excellent service.

Her taking the heater would save me a huge nuisance in the fall. That's when I'd be returning home. It would be hard enough for me to get the fire extinguisher and the smoke and gas detector back to Kyiv. The heater was heavy. I offered to carry it down to her car.

"No, no. My driver will be glad to come up and get it."

He was good about it. The four of us (including Tanya) exchanged a few more words, and off the two of them went. She had been truly helpful and had done her job thoroughly.

By the way—if ever she tires of Peace Corps, she'd have a great future as a tour guide. There were few corners of this big region of Ukraine that she was in charge of that she was not familiar with.

Later I saw Tanya felt relieved. Who likes an inspection? Even when everything is hunky-dory.

**I**ryna came to see me in Chernihiv several times. Always pleasant. But one time I was apprehensive. It was about a painful matter and I worried about its outcome.

It was caused by my ugly debacle with Olena, my dean at *Coursi*. You may remember the details from my account in Chapter 13.

Here was the essence of it: Olena began accusing me of talking too much to my students in class. Well, that was the assignment she had given me—to talk! She told me, "You are not a teacher. You are an entertainer!' She made her complaints in front of other teachers. Awful.

This is where my manager, Iryna, came in. I brought up this problem with her. She thought for a minute. "I will go sit in one of your classes." And she did that, although my class was in the evening and she had to drive out from Kyiv.

She decided my teaching was fine. I assume she told Olena the same thing. Later she wrote me an e-mail summarizing her visit and her satisfaction. How happy I was. I had nothing but praise for her.

My sole problem with her came in her role as the reviewer of my articles. I leave that for the next chapter. More appropriate there.

If I'm writing of bosses, I must remind you that during Training our immediate bosses were our LCF's and TCF's—our language and cultural and technical teachers. All fine people. All excellent in their roles. I was irritated with my TCF at the start but that got straightened out. It turned out fine.

**O**ur top boss in Kyiv was our country director, Diana. You know her well by now from my numerous mentions.

I found her always pleasant and efficient and quick to respond. But cool and detached. Maybe she had found this was the way it had to be as the big boss. I would send her a query or a note, and she would answer with a quick "Thank you" or a few sentences. It was always adequate but I could see this was always nothing but business. No criticism about that.

My most important dealing with her came only a few months after Swearing In. I had something serious on my mind—Volunteers' morale.

The morale should have been better. I wrote her a long e-mail. The following is an abbreviated version:

"Our outfit is called the Peace Corps. ' Corps' is a key word. Right away, think 'Marine Corps.'

"As you know, the word suggests a group closely bonded by a common and usually high purpose, with impressive morale and spirit, and with the members committed to that purpose, dedicated to it, proud of it, and honored for it.

"Much of that fits our Peace Corps. But an important ingredient is missing. We are not made to feel as a Corps.

"Here in Chernihiv, where I take my role as a Volunteer very seriously, I sometimes feel more like an expat than a Volunteer. I know a couple of expats here—that's why I can say that.

"Like many other Volunteers, I work alone. I never realized this is the way it would be. I find this isolation hard. I'd like to feel part of a tight-knit group. It's remarkable how little contact I have with Headquarters, and how little contact Headquarters has with me.

"The only regular communication I receive is the Friday e-mail report. It brings us valuable information but it is cold and impersonal.

"For a dozen years in my younger days I worked on the editorial side of a big newspaper with hundreds of employees. We had a very smart editor-in-chief.

"He knew the importance of high morale. He did that part of his job brilliantly, and without spending a lot of money."

Then I wrote many details of how he did all this. And I suggested simple ways that Peace Corps could be doing the same thing.

Finally I said, "I offer this suggestion with the best of motives. If you like it, you might appoint a committee to think it over, refine it, define its policies, and make sure it gets a smooth start."

Well, a nice surprise—she sent me a pleasant note that gave me real hope. She said she would soon attend a meeting of country directors from around the world. In Thailand or Cambodia, I believe. She would bring up my suggestion and get back to me. That's what she assured me.

Given her impressive background in Peace Corps (remember, our group was the biggest in the world) and her impressive previous career, I was sure she would wield heavy leverage in that assembly of country directors. I was optimistic.

Guess what? I never got a word back from her about it. A big disappointment.

I brought it up again some months later. She responded, but without enthusiasm. She made a 180-degree turn. She said, "Why should it be our job to keep Volunteers pumped up?"

I was disappointed. Stunned. The human-resources profession keeps drumming the importance of high morale among employees. I was taken aback hearing these new words from a Ph.D. in industrial psychology—assuming that means what I think it means.

I was also disappointed when I suggested early on that Peace Corps pins should be given free to Trainees for their Swearing In. And that the "pinning" should be a small but dramatic part of the ceremony. It would have built up our pride. Would have been a golden opportunity for good PR in news releases about us back home.

It got brushed off. "No money!" But such a trivial amount. For the record: I am happy to tell you that now the pinning is now part of Swearing In.

Some months later, I had more reason to contact her when I became president of SNAC. This time it was a new matter. For my first meeting as president, I invited her to be our main speaker. She accepted graciously, attended, and did a fine job.

"Ask me any question and I'll answer," she told us. That's what happened. It was all about business, of course. I should have brought up my question about morale but I got distracted and did not.

Her talk finished, she stayed through our full meeting and remained for pizza with us. Afterward, she came along as our guest on a guided bus tour through Kyiv. A good day it was, and she was a big part of it.

I had occasional dealings with her. One was when I suggested that a free online language-instruction program was available with a few mouse clicks. Russian instruction, in my case. The outfit was byki.com. Its program should at least be made known to Volunteers as a supplement...might even save Peace Corps money. My idea got nowhere.

Another instance was my proposal that Peace Corps should develop an anthem. We still did not have one after 50 years. Why is an anthem considered so nice...so important...by so many other groups? The anthem could be developed in time for Peace Corps' massive 50th anniversary celebration coming up.

Another when I proposed the idea for a Volunteers' Club in Kyiv —comparable to an Officers' Club. I discuss this in detail in a further chapter.

Another when I heard that some countries (South Korea!) were inviting Volunteers back for a financially-supported visit as part of Peace Corps' 50th anniversary celebration—and wrote her that we should encourage Ukraine to do the same.

I never got the feeling that she approved of any of these—her right, of course. I saw no encouragement. In the case of the Officers' Club, she gave me a flat turn-down.

All this after I got such a promising start with her. That was when I was looking for money from USAID for my big digitalization project at the Korolonko Library. The new director at the agency had not been replying to my e-mails. Promptly Diana put in a call to the lady (maybe it was an e-mail), who quickly contacted me. How auspicious.

I had more dealings with her and they were pleasant. During my Close of Service interview with her just before leaving Peace Corps. And during our Close of Service retreat in the Carpathian Mountains later. I saw a warm side of her there. I talk about all this in Chapter 38— "Preparing to go home."

My bottom-line impression of her: a good administrator who liked her job, enjoyed her own hitch in Peace Corps, loved Peace Corps, and understood what it was like to be a Volunteer. With no interest in shaking things up in any way for the better.

To my surprise I even got to deal with executives at the highest levels of Peace Corps. I never entered Peace Corps with any thought of becoming an activist. It's just that opportunities arose and I felt I had to respond.

The first time was with National Director Ronald Tschetter, which you know about now (Chapter 28). That was my only meeting with him, but I liked him. One thing I liked is that he had been a Volunteer himself. Furthermore, he had remained active as a returned Volunteer during his long civilian years in the investment business.

He was the founder of the Fifty Plus Program. That's when I asked him whether that program should be greatly expanded. As you know now, I liked what he said and appreciated the way he explained it.

My second encounter was with Acting National Director Jody R. Olsen, Ph. D. She had been a Volunteer and had had a long association— many years—with Peace Corps. Ron Tschetter, a political appointee as I have explained, phased out after President Obama's election and she took over until the President appointed Tschetter's successor.

I contacted her as I had Diana Schmidt about that hot theme of mine, how to bolster Volunteer morale. I had a specific new suggestion to improve morale. A Peace Corps anthem! It was time we had one! The following, boiled down, is what I wrote to her.

"Think about it. The Army has an anthem. The Navy has one. All our services have one. Why is it we don't have one?

"Anthems are so important. They are essential in any spirited organization of noble purpose. They symbolize what we stand for and strive to do. They bond us together. They make us feel proud.

"Don't you agree we should have one?

"After nearly five decades of accomplishment, Peace Corps has a rich and proud history! We have a golden opportunity coming up—Peace Corps' $50^{th}$ anniversary! The planning is already under way. The timing is perfect. We have so many wonderful things to sing about.

"The anthem could be sung for the first time as a highlight of our $50^{th}$ Anniversary Celebration on the mall in Washington in 2011. It will be a huge celebration—thousands of Volunteers and ex-Volunteers and their families, I'm sure. It will have enormous publicity everywhere.

"Think of what a dramatic addition to the ceremony the premiere of the Anthem would be. Think of how President Kennedy would beam. And how proud we Volunteers and former Volunteers would be."

I gave specific suggestions of how to do all this:

"Why don't we launch a contest for the best anthem?

"It would be wonderful if the composer were a Volunteer or a Returned Volunteer.

"I understand we have a total of close to 200,000 PCVs and RPCVs. It's an enormous pool of talent. We should offer a big cash prize, and publicize the contest far and wide, and honor the best composer and lyricist (hopefully one and the same person) by being introduced and applauded by President Obama right there at the premiere!

"The winning anthem should be selected by a distinguished jury. Maybe the musical directors of our great armed services bands."

I went on to suggest ways to select a jury to choose the winning anthem. I added, "The key to the whole thing is enthusiasm at our highest level and a huge public relations roll-out."

I fretted for several weeks. Finally I received a note from Dr. Olsen. She said my letter was being passed on to the $50^{th}$ Anniversary Planning Committee. I was pleased to hear there was one. She did not answer my question of what she thought of my idea. I did not sense any enthusiasm. She did scribble a note: "Keep up the good work!" Very nice. She probably scribbled that often on a reply to any Volunteer.

I never heard a word from the planning committee. I couldn't help getting the feeling that suggestions or questions from mere Volunteers on the lowly front lines were not appreciated, sad to say.

Then President Obama announced Aaron Williams as our new top man. He got confirmed and took over. I write about him in a later chapter.

Upon taking office he had sent an e-mail to all of us soliciting good ideas! So I sent my anthem suggestion to him. Never heard from him about it. Imagine my frustration.

Then came our big national recession. Millions of Americans were being pummeled...losing their jobs, their houses, and their morale.

One night in bed I got an idea. Peace Corps was doing its best to attract older Volunteers. Here in this recession was an enormous fresh pool of potential candidates. Peace Corps could be terrific for them!

What a perfect way for someone reeling from all that to take a break by joining Peace Corps. They could catch their breath, do something new, learn new skills, make new contacts, re-group, maybe find a new direction, all while helping our country and some needy folks overseas.

I promptly wrote an op-ed and e-mailed it to the august New York Times. But this whole matter is better for the next chapter, "My Writing Life."

Oh, an interesting experience with another official from Washington. One day Dr. Valery told me the head Peace Corps psychologist, Dr. Richard Pyle, was coming for an official visit, and he wanted to speak to Volunteers about their Peace Corps experience.

"John, are you willing to be interviewed?"

Immediately I replied, "Of course!"

I made a special trip to Kyiv and had a long and pleasant session with Dr. Pyle. He wanted "the real scoop" and I was quick to oblige..

I spoke about several things, particularly the isolation and aloneness of being a Volunteer and the importance of developing a program to build up morale. He made many notes, said he appreciated my forthrightness, also said he would discuss some of my points with colleagues back in Washington. In fact, he wanted a photo of me and took one. I felt I would hear from him in time. But I did not.

I must say good words about past national director Ronald Tschetter. I got excellent vibes when he visited us in Ukraine. Also, later my daughter Monique had sent him a suggestion about something else, not germane to this. He replied personally to her! That impressed her and me.

This chapter has focused on my dealings with Peace Corps bosses, all the way from the front trenches up to the summit. Everything was largely pleasant and satisfactory at the lower levels.

I can't say the same about the higher-ups that I dealt with in Washington. No response. Or lukewarm at best. This was so contrary to the impression I got from reading the national website,peacecorps.gov, which projected an aura of fellowship, togetherness, and sunshine.

# 34 / I came here to write

*I start early. Compose articles...feel I'm being censored! Begin my book.*

Yes, absolutely true. Writing about Peace Corps and my good and bad experiences in it was one of my major goals if I got accepted as a Volunteer. I am a journalist at heart. Reporting is my thing.

Most Volunteers, I believe, sign up for several reasons. So did I. A key reason was to report on my life from my first day as a Volunteer to my last. And to do so in detail. The challenges. The difficulties. The satisfactions and pleasures. The whole deal. To report on all of this accurately, fairly, interestingly.

The minute I got the idea of Peace Corps, I thought, *"What a spectacular opportunity to report. And write!"*

Millions of words have been written about Peace Corps. But darn little about the experience of one Volunteer, and in particular, an elderly one in the Fifty Plus program.

This at a time when Peace Corps was planning to add many Volunteers, with a focus on older ones. I was sure a book like the one I had in mind would be helpful to many considering the idea. Younger ones and older, too.

What made sense to me was a very personal book, reporting my experiences and my emotions and my insights and reflections about it all.

I decided I would write not only this new book. I would also write newspaper articles—regular reports as I went from Trainee to Volunteer. About every aspect of the experience.

Training. Learning a new language. Starting work. Becoming part of the Peace Corps system. Living with strange people, in a strange land. Adjusting to countless differences. On and on. Right to my last day. There would be plenty, for sure. And then summing it all up.

Would I rise to all these challenges? Or would I be humbled by them? After all, that is the gist of any adventure—to be confronted by a challenge that will be difficult and very uncertain. One in fact that carries the risk of failure—but which, with pluck and luck, you will complete and prize.

I suspected it would be a life-changing experience for me, but in which ways I was not at all sure.

Peace Corps is popular. Surprising how many consider joining it. They have many questions. They hesitate. My book could help them to make the big decision.

There was no way that anyone who knows me could think that I would not write about all this. I had been writing for more than 50 years, often for pay, but at times just for the pleasure of telling about something interesting and perhaps important.

I went into journalism not by accident but by choice, enrolling in graduate school to study it. I aspired to a career in journalism. A life in journalism. I spent a dozen years at it and moved up through the ranks...and finally left it because I felt squeezed out and in fact betrayed. This I must explain.

I had risen from a cub reporter to an editor and an executive on a fair-sized paper. Even at this upper level I was dismayed by the poor money and felt constricted by it, of course—I was married and had children.

At the paper I was the editor of my own section—our very own Sunday magazine, not one that we bought ready-made and with our name printed on it. I had been making nearly all the decisions with the blessing of our editor-in-chief.

We got a new editor-in-chief with a different style. I bridled at the emphasis that he placed on editing by consensus rather than experience and instinct. Particularly mine.

The fun was out of it. Whereas before I put up with the poor pay because my work was so satisfying, now I had to put up with the meager salary just to continue doing something that had lost its sizzle. A good offer came up in PR.

As I have recounted elsewhere, I made much of that, in time launching my own office and running it till close to retirement, when I sold it.

In retirement, all while doing something else very interesting—getting into Elderhostel and eventually managing a big Elderhostel program—I returned to journalism as a free-lancer. And happily. I continued scribbling and publishing for a dozen years, including two books, right up to entering Peace Corps.

I've told you how I brought my computer to Ukraine in anticipation of this. How it was out of commission for several months. How I made do. How finally I got it up and working and connected to the Internet while living at Tanya's. And how all that made my life not only easier and better. Now I could begin my writing in earnest.

Peace Corps told us we could <u>not</u> make money in any way from our service. Which meant, for one thing, that I could not write for pay. I accepted that. I also accepted that anything I wrote for publication would have to be reviewed and okayed by my Peace Corps boss. I would play by the rules. Then came an absolute fluke, potentially embarrassing. I'll explain that.

The basis of anything I wrote would be reportage—careful accounts of every aspect of this Peace Corps life—illuminated with my own point of view and my own interpretation and judgment. I went about it in earnest, even in private e-mails to my family and friends. The same when through that fluke my first one home popped up in a digital paper. In fact, two!

I put in as much detail as I could…the essential facts, big and small…and telling anecdotes. As I went along, I took care to save all these e-mails that I wrote. They would be a treasure-trove for my book.

Still I felt that I would need more data. While living with my first landlady, Natasha, I began writing a daily journal—what was called a diary in my youth. I had brought three sturdy notebooks, 8.5 by 11 inches, blue ruled, good paper, stiff covers.

I opened to Page 1 and wrote, "May all the entries scribbled in these pages be good entries. And may the negative ones be not too bad." After all, not everything goes perfectly, right?

What I intended were just raw notes and quick comments. Nothing fancy. Just the essential facts of happenings every day. Plus unusual emotions, good or bad. This was important—my feelings. Plus details about the weather and any local or national news with a bearing on me.

Again I was doing this to prepare for my book. Two years in Peace Corps would be a long span. We cannot trust our memory. It is selective and plays tricks for good and bad. While writing my book, I would dip into this personal record of my service often. It became priceless

Here is the very first paragraph. "4:30 p.m. To *Coursi* by *marshrutka* to meet teachers for the first time. Dean Olena and Lina welcome me warmly, give me a bottle of cognac. I meet the director of the whole shebang, a lady named Iryna. About 65. Pleasant but aloof. No wonder—she knows not a word of English! Leaves early "for an appointment."

"Meet 10 teachers, all women, all part-timers (teaching at *Coursi* after a full day in public school). Have small gifts for me! They're very quiet. I ask if I may speak. Yes. Speak for 10 minutes. Successful. We mix for a bit…a glass of wine and crackers and cheese. Nice people. Restrained. Am I the first American they ever talk to?

"Manage to leave early for the Philharmonia Concert at Red Square. No idea how to get to it. Teacher Ira—I just met her!—insists on taking me, puts us on the right trolleybus, gets off with me and leads me practically to the door!"

And the entry went on....

It became my nightly ritual to record my day this way. It was my last thing before brushing my teeth. That first notebook had 200 pages. I filled every line and every page. Then I scribbled through two more notebooks. Milady Annabelle sent me two more. By the time I went home, I was deep into the fifth—nearly 1,000 pages.

As I progressed, I got fancier. For instance, Saturday, March 21, 2009, says, "Day 79 / 530 (this meant the $79^{th}$ day of the year and my $530^{th}$ in Ukraine). First day of spring. 21 degrees Centigrade and windy, but fair."

In all that time, I failed only once to write my entry. One evening I went to bed tired at 7:30 for just one hour—and woke up at 4:30 a.m.! I was appalled. I hurried to my journal, scribbled a quick entry, then went back to bed, my guilt appeased.

I kept up my journal even on trips and vacations. Not always easy. But important. I wanted a detailed record.

And of course some of my entries were disappointing ...angry ...bitter. That's life also, isn't it?

My batch e-mails flew off regularly. I sent out big ones at important points—thousands of words ...after my Swearing-In ...my first six months ...my $500^{th}$ day ...my $80^{th}$ birthday. And so it went.

The response to them was interesting. So was the lack of response. All the recipients were my family and friends. A few would reply nearly every time, always with words of appreciation, and, what I was eager for, news about themselves. Some replied now and then. Some never—and this would disappoint me.

What I had hoped for was an exchange: I would send them my news and they would send me theirs—didn't have to be elaborate. This is what I expected, though I had never discussed it or made it a condition.

After a while, a pattern established itself. I knew who would reply and who would not. I even knew whether they would be brief or expansive. After a while, I became philosophical: we just have to accept people as they are. But of course, my affections did grow for those who did respond. Relationships are like tender plants. They have to be nourished.

One thing that I hoped to do was to write regularly for my hometown media. Notice that I said "media." This requires explanation. After retiring, I had returned to my first love—started writing features and then a column also for our local weekly newspaper.

Meanwhile a digital newspaper—www.lymeline.com—had started up. It was "a newspaper without trees." It was being run by Olwen Logan. In fact, she launched another.

She had been a free-lance colleague of mine on the weekly. However, we had never had an opportunity to become close. I began writing for her. I liked it. She liked it. In time, she used my pieces in a second digital paper she was launching. I hated the idea of giving up that writing when I entered Peace Corps.

She was paying me. Now my pieces would be freebies. We had a small agreement. When I came home, she'd host a dinner for Annabelle and me!

In Ukraine, immediately I began thinking about possible articles. As I've told you, Peace Corps was stern about Volunteers writing for the public. We Volunteers were guests in a host country, and we were told we must be sensitive and understanding, and we must not do anything to offend or embarrass.

We could write anything we chose to—we were not military; we were free Americans. But the message was implicit...we might well be riding that morning flight back to the U.S.A. if we did publish something that gave Peace Corps, or Ukraine, umbrage.

**M**y first report for lymeline covered many things and I passed it by Diana Schmidt as the expected courtesy. She wrote back that it was fine except for one statement.

I had written that our flight to Ukraine was supposed to be on United Airlines to Frankfurt, Germany, and then on Lufthansa to Kyiv, but it turned out to be Lufthansa all the way. I wondered in my article how American taxpayers would feel about our tax-paid flights being provided by a German airline and not an American one.

Diana explained that Ukraine and Lufthansa "code share," which to me suggested a partnership, and which she understood to be perfectly okay. I wondered whether readers would agree it was okay.

I sent the report to lymeline with the code share explanation and Olwen used it. No problem of any kind. Wonderful.

To save myself time and trouble, I also e-mailed this piece to a list of family and friends. It was my easy way of keeping them informed. This personal list of mine had many names. It included Olwen. But I did not notice that.

The next thing Olwen received from me was a report e-mailed not specifically to her at lymeline, like the first one, but to her as one of my friends. She was one. But she thought she was receiving if for publication and she published it. I regretted that but understood.

She received more e-mails like this...and published them. All because it was some time later that I discovered she was using them. I was flustered. Concerned. Olwen did not do anything wrong, mind you. It was innocent on her part. Also innocent on my part. Truly.

In these pieces I wrote about the hardships and difficulties of being a Trainee, but nothing "insensitive or embarrassing." Still I worried; after all, I had bypassed Peace Corps. But I never heard a peep about it.

With this precedent set, I continued to e-mail my reports straight from my computer to my friends and to Olwen, meaning lymeline, with no advance copy to Peace Corps in Kyiv. I had good intentions but felt torn.

As a journalist I wanted to tell the whole story, good and bad. But I didn't want to offend Peace Corps. In the first months, all my early feelings about Peace Corps were jolly. Later I did develop misgivings and criticisms although overall I approved heartily of Peace Corps.

**B**ut never a grumble from Peace Corps. I'm assuming that Peace Corps never got to read any of those e-reports. Maybe it did but decided to leave well enough alone. Bottom line: I was fortunate.

I do feel that my scribblings were generous and helpful to Peace Corps. I would get messages from my readers with appreciative comments. They enjoyed what I wrote and they learned a lot about Peace Corps and what it does and how we Volunteers carried out our roles and the kind of complex life we were leading in doing our jobs. I was positive Peace Corps could view it only as very favorable stuff.

Also, I wrote articles for other outlets. The Volunteers in Ukraine published a newsletter every other month, *"Nu Shcho."* I know, it's unpronounceable. It's Ukrainian slang. It means "What's up?" I began writing for it and wrote half a dozen pieces.

One was about FLEX, the program that sends gifted students to live with a family in America for a school year. Another was about two taxi drivers I met during my travels—one remarkably good and the other remarkably awful.

Still another was about CCP/USA. It was a Boston-based program that triaged kids affected by Chernobyl radiation and flew some to Boston for treatment. Doctors, nurses, therapists, lab technicians there did their best to help them in any way possible. This care was free. Just as my articles were.

**S**o were the articles we Volunteers contributed to *"Nu Shcho"*— unpaid. It was just one more way to be of service. I enjoyed doing it.

Our editor was Jessica Benes, in her 20's, who had worked as a journalist for a bit after college. Was doing a good job. I encouraged her...hoped she would return to our profession after Peace Corps. Journalism is important and challenging, but it's tough in working conditions and pay. Not sure she would.

One day I got an e-mail from a Peace Corps official not in Kyiv, but in Washington. Amber Smigiel described herself as a marketing specialist. She had the assignment of editing and publishing "Volunteers' Journals" on Peace Corps' national website, peacecorps.gov. I took a look at it. Volunteers around the world wrote in about their experiences. I learned from it and enjoyed it.

Well, someone had sent in something that I had written. I don't know who or what. But Ms. Smigiel liked it. And she invited me to become a contributor, one of a handful around the world.

In an e-mail she said, "I know that you like to write long, and we prefer shorter items, but I'm sure we can work that out."

She mentioned it was a serious commitment, with contributors feeding in pieces on a fairly regular basis. There would be no payment— it was just one more way a chosen Volunteer could help. I accepted and went to work.

I wrote five articles and as usual, they were long. But no problem. All these had to be shown to Peace Corps in Kyiv and I went about it dutifully. The articles would be shunted down, landing finally on the desk of Iryna Shevchenko, my manager. As usual, she was caring, serious, sharp-eyed, and extremely cautious.

On the first piece she found a few nits. They didn't bother me. I made the small changes and sent the article on to Washington. It was published.

*Memory is unreliable. Every night I would jot down the happenings of the day. I filled five journals.*

I did the same with my next piece. Here Iryna discovered some things more grievous. She sent it back with numerous suggestions. I was taken aback. To me, nothing in it seemed offensive. The hair went up on my neck. What to do?

I decided not to comply. I sent her a note that I simply would not send the piece to Volunteers' Journals. I would withhold it. That's what I did. She accepted that.

What I had found was that Peace Corps Ukraine, meaning Iryna, was censoring my work without ever calling it censorship. She was merely being "sensitive and careful." Maybe she did not consider it censorship. Anyway, now I was very careful.

My next pieces all made the trip to her in Kyiv and back without ruffling anybody's feathers. I sent them on to Ms. Smigiel.

But now she reported a problem. Not with me but with Volunteers' Journals. It was being shut down for re-design and would be up and running again quite soon. Not to worry. The weeks went by. I queried her.

"It won't be long," she assured me. "Your pieces will be published."

My patience ran out. I stopped writing for her.

After many weeks, I received a group e-mail from her. All of us correspondents were told that Volunteers' Journals was in business again, better than ever, and to resume writing.

I e-mailed her again, and my intention was to be helpful. Some of my pieces in her backlog would need editing or updating because of this lag, but if she would let me know which ones, then I would do the work. I received no reply.

Volunteers' Journals was a disappointing experience for me. I had put in a lot of thought, time, and effort. How could I not feel that I was dealing with a big and insensitive bureaucracy?

In Chapter 27, I told you about the op-ed that I submitted (unsuccessfully) to the New York Times. This was in response to Robert L. Strauss' op-ed about Peace Corps' direction as it approached its 50th anniversary.

Some months later I sat down and composed a second op-ed about a topic totally different. It was provoked by our severe recession. I had a great middle-of-the-night idea.

Many people back in the U.S.A. were losing their jobs, including older folks with much experience. I got up and wrote an op-ed urging them to consider Peace Corps. It would be a win-win for them and Peace Corps. I felt the fact that I was a senior-citizen Volunteer strengthened my case.

Big newspapers pay for op-eds. But this would be a freebie, per Peace Corps' regulations.

I sent it to the New York Times. No response. I sent it to the Christian Science Monitor, where I had been published. No response. I sent it to the Hartford Courant, the dominant paper in Connecticut, where I had been published. No response.

How come? This was such a topical piece. It would be of genuine help to many people. And it would help Peace Corps recruit able people...more experienced and more mature people.

Oh, I had also sent my op-ed to friends. What a favorable response I got. One, Bill Clark, Ph.D.—my old educator friend now retired in Florida—took it upon himself to send it to his big daily down there. He thought it was that good! He also got a rejection.

What else could I do to advance my op-ed? A new idea.

I sent it to the New London Day in Connecticut, the daily serving my quadrant of the state. I had been in its pages. It used it, but only after considerable prodding. I was pleased.

The Day is a fine paper. But it has a readership measured in the thousands. I felt that millions should hear my message. But one newspaper after another had turned it down.

So, I contacted Peace Corps in Washington. It has a public relations department. Their job is to publicize Peace Corps and make its opportunities known. All in an effort to build public (taxpayer) support and recruit more and better people. I e-mailed my op-ed, in fact, to a specific specialist, David Briery.

I was sure Peace Corps had a lot of influence in the newspaper world. I made a straightforward suggestion: "You have media contacts all over the country. This op-ed can interest many people and can gain new recruits for Peace Corps. Please send it out."

I never got even an acknowledgment from him. I thought, *Well, maybe he never received it from me.* So I sent it to him again. Total silence.

What should I make of this? At the very least, shouldn't a well-intentioned Volunteer with a novel and topical idea at least get a reply? I consider that common courtesy.

That brought my brainstorm to a dead end. I was disappointed and frustrated. Wouldn't you be? What kind of apathetic bureaucracy was I dealing with? Somebody explain to me, please.

**M**eanwhile, I went ahead with my book. I worked on it nearly every day in bits and pieces. I organized the work with care. I felt I had a terrific vantage point.

I was open about this work of my own. Not devious. Many were aware—my associates, students, and people I got to know on a daily business. Not rare that someone would ask, "How is it going?"

My teaching assignments gave me the opportunity to get close to some students and learn a lot about their life and their society. So did my work with my English Club and French Club, which attracted older people as well.

So did my projects of digitalizing the big library and developing the public-transit handbook. So did my dealings with the library staff, the staff at the language school, and my relationships with my three host families and the expats I got to meet in Chernihiv. Plus my work with Peace Corps officials in Kyiv, and assorted people in the city.

I have mentioned my daily journaling. But in addition to my personal reactions to everything that came along, what I needed was a solid basis of factual information. So from the very start, I began to save every e-mail I wrote or received that contained useful information relating to Peace Corps.

I had had two e-mail accounts for years, Hotmail and Yahoo. Why two? Just in case one developed a problem—you never know. In time, my Yahoo account had more than 2,500 saved messages in it, and my Hotmail another 1,000. To me they were enormous and important files, and the "Search" function made it easy to find things and pop them onto the screen.

For instance, if I wanted to locate info about Robert Strauss, I would just type in "Strauss" in the Search Panel of Yahoo, say, and in a few minutes could examine every mention of him that I possessed. Fabulous! Or any other Strauss, of course, including the great composer.

Steadily my book took shape. I settled on a working title. I planned the layout...some 40 chapters...all in a natural and common-sense order. Slowly I began the writing. A humongous project. What a satisfaction when I finished Chapter 1!

One chapter followed another, some more difficult than others. I finished 25,000 words. 50,000. 100,000. I was getting there. It wound up as what you are reading now—more than 225,000 words.

Writing a serious book is a big job. The book itself is just the tip of the iceberg. What is invisible to you, dear reader, is the huge mass of ice under water—all the facts and comments and information and statistics and news items and gossip and odd remarks that have any relevance to the subject, and which have to be saved, organized, and reflected upon as the writing gets started. And the editing and double-checking that complete the job.

**I** have said it before. Writing a serious book is as much labor as building a house. I know. When newly married, I built a house. I was 30. My wife Pauline and I bought a pretty one-acre lot out in the country, with Golden Guernsey cows browsing in the fields on three sides of us.

We selected a house plan, hired a builder, and situated the land on our lot so that we'd see the sun setting through our picture window. I did whatever unskilled work I could do after my day's work at the newspaper... tarring the foundation, nailing up sheet rock, painting, lugging rocks for a stonewall. A huge job.

And so is writing a book. But different in that it is totally sedentary and solitary. It's just you and the blank monitor screen. The only things that move are your brain and your fingers. Well, so it seems.

I put in countless hours on this new book. I wrote between my various responsibilities in Chernihiv, plus early in the morning and late at night. It went on till the end of my service. There were not many days when I did not work at it. My vacations were my only big pauses. I gave the book a high priority. My goal was to have it 95 percent finished when I went home.

As the book developed, there were chapters that I could complete…could wrap up! This because they were all past tense: How I got the idea of joining, what Training was like. Other chapters had to remain open-ended until I completed my 27 months. I started these chapters early and added to them bit by bit as the months passed.

Like my other books, I knew this one would need photos. I kept this in mind. I took photos for two reasons. One was to preserve important information about an event. The other was for possible use in the book.

The book became more than a job. It became an outlet. A great relief from the stresses and demands of my work as a Volunteer. It was one more important purpose in my life. I was delighted to shoulder it. I never considered it a burden. But a challenge, yes.

As I got closer to my Close of Service, I was able to complete more chapters. When I did leave, it was indeed 95 percent finished. That percentage is a metaphorical goal, you understand. Just a thoughtful estimate. But this was all raw reportage. It had to be refined. What I faced was a great big edit. But I was up to it. I'd be returning home in mid-December. I'd relax for the Christmas season. Then right after New Year's, I'd get to it!

And that is the way it has been. It took me more than a year back in the U.S. to complete it. That sounds like a long time. Yes. But I had to resume my normal life. Squeeze in visits with my family (in four states!) and friends. And I had an accident.

I fell down stairs head first, my head slamming against a closed door. No broken bones, which was astounding, but big problems requiring months of visits to doctors, tests, and physical therapy. And I am just now getting back to normal.

But here is the book. I hope you're enjoying it. Finding it helpful. Maybe even thinking of becoming a Volunteer!

~ ~ ~

# 35 / I get to travel a lot

*Peace Corps offers tempting opportunities.*
*I pack up and go. Even to other countries.*

It is a rare Volunteer who completes his service without giving in to a huge urge to go off and gallivant and broaden his horizons geographically and intellectually. I am sure that hoping to travel is a major motivator for everybody attracted to Peace Corps.

Of course, I planned to make the most of this golden opportunity, although my age was beginning to catch up with me. I was losing some of my steam. Not that I intended to quit taking to the road. What was required now was greater care in selecting and planning my trips. I had to see as much as I could with less physical effort. In plain English, with less hoofing and lugging.

What excited me right away is that Volunteers got two days of vacation per month of service. The three months of Training did not count. So, 24 months left meant 48 days of vacation meant 24 per year. How appealing! You couldn't take it in advance, of course. I must tell you that for too many years I got just two weeks of vacation per year.

There were regulations. Any overnight stay away from home base required a notice to our regional manager. You had to give the notice before departing, not while at your destination, and definitely not afterward. Beforehand!

Peace Corps wanted to know where you were and how to contact you. Emergencies do come up. And any trip outside the country required the permission of our top boss in Kyiv. Plus it required an itinerary with contact info. It sounded reasonable. No problem.

But then a wrinkle. Those 24 days per year included the intermediate weekends. One of my Volunteer friends brought it to my attention. "That isn't fair," she said, and explained why. I had to agree.

It really wasn't 24 days a year. 'All Volunteers received two days off per week...because they worked the normal work week in Ukraine...which was five days per week. So why should their normal days off during vacation suddenly be counted as vacation days? It did not hold water. Unfair! But there was no fighting it. That's the way it was.

An extraordinary opportunity popped up quickly. My friend Wu in Shanghai invited me to his wedding. Yes, China! It is he who translated and published my "Around the World" book there. I felt I must go. I wanted to go!

And I got an inspiration. Why not have milady Annabelle meet me in Shanghai and enjoy it all with me? After all, Wu was her friend also; he had been her house guest in California. Annabelle jumped at the chance. I applied to Headquarters and got its blessing. How nice.

Annabelle and I flew to Shanghai separately. I described all this in a previous chapter. You know what a fine time we had. After a fabulous two weeks, I flew back to Ukraine and Annabelle to California, zooming in opposite directions around the globe. Seems incredible as I write about it now.

I came back very grateful. But the down side is that this cut sharply into my vacation days to travel locally.

SNAC—our Peace Corps Seniors Club in Ukraine—was my big travel opportunity within Ukraine. Yes, I wrote about this earlier. I mention it here as a travel opportunity. It held three meetings a year, usually in different cities. They were chosen to be as convenient and interesting as possible. Of course I went to every one.

My biggest opportunity came in the summer of my second year. I had 30 days of vacation in all—24 plus 6 left over. It made sense to take it in one block if possible. And before September, when the school year would begin again.

**W**here to go! What to do? These became urgent questions as spring ended.

I finally decided on two loops ending in late August. Back to back. First, a small loop in Ukraine. Then a big loop outside Ukraine. I would travel these loops alone. Truth is, I had nobody to travel with. Not a problem. In fact, I enjoy my own company, lucky me. And I would make it a point to travel the way I like best.

What do I mean? Most people in Ukraine travel long distances by train...usually night train. This way they can avoid some hotel stays. I planned a different way if possible.

I have traveled by train quite a lot. In the U.S.A. In Europe. In India. Even in Asia—three days on the tracks from Singapore all the way up the Malay Peninsula to Bangkok. All my trips to SNAC meetings were overnight by train—all the way to Odessa, then to Sevastopol.

Trains are fine in general. There are excellent ones—the TGVs (the super fast and super-modern and comfortable European trains) that I have ridden. But too many trains are old and bumpy and tedious.

My chief complaint is simple: in every train, you ride a route that is chosen to be as level as possible. Not for its appeal. Many trains, especially in Europe, let you see outside well only on one side. And when you enter a city, what you see is the back of everything: the back of the factories, the back of the warehouses, the back of the houses, the back often of the worst neighborhoods, and then finally the vast, dismal, always similar train yards—acres and acres of parked freight and passenger trains at major stations.

What I prefer are long-distance buses. Yes, buses. There are plenty of bad and mediocre buses, mind you. Most buses in Ukraine are terrible by Western standards. I've told you about the awful *marshrutkas*, always jammed full, notoriously dangerous. I got to make some 20 round trips from Chernihiv to Kyiv by *marshrutka*. Never enjoyed it.

Back in the U.S.A. I have traveled Greyhound many times, and on journeys of thousands of miles. Not perfect. I admit that. But it does have some fine equipment and excellent drivers. By and large, I am an admirer of Greyhound.

Europe has some fine bus companies. In some ways better than Greyhound. Especially the buses on long international runs. Some are truly state of the art. Panorama windows. Air conditioning. Generous seats which recline (well, a tiny bit). A clean toilet aboard with a wash basin—always a last resort for me, however.

Usually a coffee machine that will offer everything from Americano to espresso to cappuccino plus others. Plus teas. Movies with personal earphones. Sometimes a stewardess.

And when you enter a city, often you ride right down the main streets, seeing the fronts of everything! You get on right at the curb and get off at the curb, not a huge hike away as for the trains, and your luggage goes into the big bins underneath, and often the driver will do it for you. Same in the U.S.A., by the way.

Just take a small bag aboard with snacks, your camera, sunglasses, and all such items. Everything is so much easier. And know what? Invariably cheaper than the trains. Considerably cheaper. Yes, no wonder I prefer these fine buses.

The big minus is overnight travel. Trains offer bunks, though the bumpy tracks can spoil your dreams. Sleeping on a surging and braking bus is hard. I admit it. But I've accepted that because of the advantages.

I have another preference I'm sure you'll consider strange. I prefer hostels to hotels. True, there are bad hostels just as there are bad hotels. I have been lucky. I have stayed at many hostels. I have never stayed at one that was a dump. And I have stayed in some notably fine hostels.

Why this preference? When I first started traveling on vacations and enjoying hostels, I hesitated to say I stayed at them. I worried people might think I was smoking pot, or was just a cheapskate. I don't give that a thought any more. I preach hostels all the time now. Well, for adventurous souls.

Most hostels (like most hotels) are reputable and meet reasonable standards. And they are a better deal in just about every way. Not for a honeymoon, I admit, or a luxury vacation.

But if you want to go on a tour (be a tourist) and especially if you are traveling alone, you should choose hostels. It is the smarter choice.

You will have less privacy, but not a big deal. You will have more fun, meet more fellow travelers, learn a lot more, and save much money. I learned this quickly.

It is worth re-telling my first hostelling experience as a retiree. I was in my early 60's, the director of marketing at a hospital in Massachusetts.

**J**ust before retiring, I had to attend a trade conference in Philadelphia. My hospital booked me into a four-star hotel. Quite plush.

At the end of my day's business when I returned to my fine hotel and fine room, it was just me and the TV set. Got to tell you the TV set is not my favorite companion.

When I ate in the dining room, I sat at a table alone. I never got a chance to talk with anybody at the other tables. Only the waiters when they took my order and handed me my check.

The magnificent Chernihiv train station was the starting point for many of my trips within Ukraine and beyond. Never a terrible trip.

Fast forward some years. I was now retired—a man of leisure. I decided to take a solo trip across the United States, yes, alone, and I bought a Volkswagen Microbus (the famous, clever little self-contained RV) for the trip. I stopped in Philadelphia because it is such an interesting and impressive city.

Wanting a break from the Microbus, I checked into a hostel converted from a fine old mansion (in its heyday!) right by the Schuylkill River. I liked it right away.

Like most hostels, it offered dorm beds (4, 6, or 8 to a room), lockers, toilets and showers of course, a kitchen where you could bring your food and cook your meals and eat if that's what you wanted to do, but often at a table with other hostellers and try to start a conversation.

The hostel most often would also offer a washer and dryer, a computer or two with Internet, book shelves with a variety of books ("Leave one and take one"), and a lounge with TV, comfy if sometimes worn furniture, a table for cards and other games, sometimes a pool table, other good things. And plenty of pamphlets about local attractions and a friendly person at the main desk for questions and advice.

Best of all, the chance to meet other travelers, most often quite young and most often interesting, including foreign ones. Occasionally a retiree or two.

As in all good hostels I had to show a passport or other picture ID. It keeps the riffraff out.

One evening after a day of sightseeing, I went into the lounge. There was a ping pong table. I love ping pong. A young couple was sitting on the couch. In fact, cuddling. I looked at him and said, "How about playing a game?"

He looked at his lovely girlfriend, searched her face, and then looked at me. "I'm sorry, sir. We're on our honeymoon."

They were from England. In Philadelphia. How nice. But for a honeymoon in a hostel? Oh, well. Then I got an idea.

"Why don't the three of us play one game?" I said. I made it a point to include her. "The two of you at that end of the table, and me at this end. Could be fun."

He looked at his bride and she looked at him. To my surprise she was the one who spoke. "Yes," she said, smiling. "Let's try that."

We played for an hour. Had a wonderful time. Then I sat with them and chatted. And I couldn't help thinking of the lonely evenings I had had in that plush hotel just down the river. And the fun I was having here. And that's how my enthusiasm for hostels blossomed.

I know that in a hostel I'll have a decent bed. Make that a decent bunk. Double bunks usually, but I have seen some triples. Invariably the clerk makes sure I get a lower bunk, and I appreciate that. Often I ask for a quiet corner and most times I get one. Most often the rooms are not full. At times I have slept all alone in a multi-bed room. Got to tell you: for four years starting at age 10 in boarding school, I slept in a dorm for 50 kids. That was good preparation for hostelling.

I must mention that nowadays hostels sometimes have mixed dorms....men and women in them. That's something new. I like the old-fashioned dorms better. But I haven't found this a problem.

I like to prepare my own simple vegetarian meals. I like to walk into another room just a few steps away and use a sometimes free computer and go online. I like to have reading materials around and sometimes the variety is fascinating. Sometimes I, too, have left a book behind and taken one with me when I checked out.

I like being in a setting where I can chat with this one and that one. I learn so much and have such a good time. I have made long-time friends in hostels. My friend Wu in Shanghai is an outstanding example. We met at a hostel in Nairobi, Africa!

I don't mind a toilet down the hall. I don't mind waiting my turn to take a shower. In fact, I have simple strategies. One is to get up very early in the morning. Typically I'll have these things to myself.

Here's another of my strategies. It is possible to have a thief present. Hey, when you're sleeping, it's tempting for somebody with mean fingers. I have worried about that. I tuck my wallet and my watch and pocketknife and flashlight deep down in my pillowcase. Then I sleep on my pillow. This has never failed me.

I like having somebody at the front desk who is friendly and helpful, and that is often the case. Hostels are a bargain, comparatively. Often hostels are centrally located close to train and bus stations. Some (in the U.S.A.) even have a free pick-up service. And I like to use money wisely.

As it turned out on this Peace Corps travel, I did have to stay at a couple of hotels. The hotels were decent, but overall the experience proved I was correct about hostels being better for me.

Let me put this whole thing another way. I no longer think of renting a room for the night. I think of renting a bed for the night.

I shared a room with a young woman at a hostel in Prague on this trip. Dora, about 26. We were just the two of us in a dorm for eight. It would have been less awkward with other people in the room.

We sized one another up, of course. I assume she felt she had nothing to fear from this grandfather. We took our turns changing in the bathroom in morning and evening.

Gosh, she impressed me! She was Australian, traveling around Europe alone for three months. She was a "beauty therapist" (a new expression for me) in Melbourne, did hairdos and nails and pedicures and gave massages, gave skin treatments, things like that.

I noticed Dora took a lot of time making up in the morning. She would emerge from the bathroom very beautiful. I complimented her. She smiled and said, "I have to set a good example!"

I have met many Australians here and there. They live so far Down Under, so far away from the white world and so encroached by Asians, that they yearn to get to the U.S.A. and ENGLAND (notice my capitals; that's where their ancestors migrated from), and then Europe.

It is a big cultural thing for them. They graduate from university, work feverishly for a year or two, save every pence, buy a multi-destination plane ticket, and take off. Sometimes around the world.

"When I return home," Dora said to me, "I want to open me own shop. My girlfriend and meself. And then get serious, don't you know, and settle down and think of getting meself a hubby."

We talked about some of that. For one thing, we discussed partnerships...their strengths and weaknesses. I told her, "In my experience, partnerships work during the honeymoon stage. But most go sour and collapse." And I explained in detail. "You should go into it planning to buy your girlfriend out as soon as you can." She listened attentively.

*Dora! What a nice gal. We had a serious talk. She thanked me later.*

The next morning as I packed to leave, she insisted on taking my photo. "I'll remember your advice, sir," she said. "Thank you." I took her photo also. I liked Dora a lot.

I told you I split my vacation time into two loops. The first loop was terrific—to as many towns and cities in Ukraine as I could crowd in. All by bus and *marshrutka*. One week. Many fine experiences. Not a bad one.

**M**y second loop was ambitious. A dozen cities in seven countries in three weeks. Alone. Poland. Lithuania. Latvia. Estonia. Back down to Poland again. Then Germany. The Czech Republic. Austria. Hungary. Then home to Ukraine. I wondered whether I had enough time to cover them all and whether I still had what it takes. I decided to try. After all, if too difficult, I could quit at any point and return to Ukraine.

I chose these countries because no visas were required for an American. I wanted to keep it simple. Visas are such a pain. This is why I eliminated Russia and Belarus. They require visas. Also, I had been to both.

This is one of the great pluses of the European Union, by the way. A citizen of the EU can travel freely from one member country to another. No red tape. True for Americans also who visit there. This is so different and so much easier than when I traveled in Europe years ago.

I knew that the trip would not be easy. There would be all the language problems. But how lucky I was to be an American—to be able to speak English. Many Europeans speak at least a bit of English. It would have been infinitely more difficult if my language had been Portuguese or Greek or Arabic, say. Wow!

Plus other problems. A big one was the challenge of working out a mix of travel by train, and bus, and *marshrutkas*. Which to use when?

Plus those of using different currencies in some of the countries. Croons in Estonia, Forint in Hungary, something else in Poland, still something else in the Czech Republic. What a pain! These countries are all part of the European Union but their economies are not yet strong enough to permit them to use the wonderful Euro.

And the challenge of finding decent lodgings every night. This is something I thought about every day on the road: *where will I sleep tonight?* It made no sense to make reservations. But I was game.

In Budapest very late one evening I was sure I would be spending the night on a bench in the bus station. But I got lucky at the last minute and found myself a bed. More about this in a couple of minutes.

I learned long ago that solo travel is very hard work. It is hard physically and sometimes emotionally.

I also learned that the safest assumption on any trip is that something will go wrong. Just pray that it will not be serious. And I was right on both counts on these loops.

*A quickie village stop. She in the apron just sold me this delicious ear of corn. I never knew what would happen next. Fun!*

**A**s it turned out, I traveled by bus mostly. Such fine buses in western Europe! Some were luxurious. Good companies. The biggest is Eurolines, which covers just about all of that vast area. It is a consortium of bus companies, all using the same brand name—Eurolines—and the same website. Highly recommended.

Another is Ecolines, smaller, I believe, and totally new to me. It covers several countries, at least. Excellent also. I found its prices cheaper.

There are numerous regional companies. Two lines that I used were Orangeways (orange buses) and the Student Agency Bus. Strange name, I know, and I never figured it out.

I thought it was for students only. It was for anybody and everybody. I would be pleased to use any of these again. If you plan to travel, check their websites.

A problem came up on the very eve of my taking off. I cracked a molar and lost a crown. Right away I called Peace Corps Medical in Kyiv. Right away they booked me into their favorite Dental Clinic, a top-notch outfit where I had gotten good service before.

It turned out that I needed root canal therapy. Not the first time, by the way. This one was one of my easiest. In three days I was given clearance to travel, and I had an appointment to have the work finished upon returning at the end of the month. It all went well.

I decided I would skip museums. I did not have the inclination or the time to visit museums the way I used to. I have seen many museums. There are good museums and there are countless mediocre and lousy museums. Sometimes, of course, you may have a very special interest, such as seeing postage stamps or getting to see the house where Karl Marx lived and wrote. Then it makes sense.

What I did everywhere was to emphasize the cities themselves. The cities that I visited would become my museums! In them I would get to see how people live and work and relax...would get an idea of how well they are doing and what their culture is like and what their values are. And get to look at many of the famous sites that we see on postcards.

I have learned that cities have an inner core that truly expresses the city's personality. Think of Paris and its Eiffel Tower. Or London and its Parliament. Or Madrid and its Prado.

The outskirts are just, well, just the outskirts. Humdrum and generic. It is true in Kyiv and Shanghai and Tokyo and Rio di Janeiro and Cairo and Panama City. In major cities all over the world. Little need to go beyond the city center unless you have someone to visit. So my plan was to skip everything outside the core.

In the cities, I would use buses and trams and trolleys a lot. If I got tired, I'd hop on a tram or a trolley and sit and ride for 15 or 20 minutes, then cross the street and take another one back. If it happened to be a double-decker bus, even better. I'd climb to the upper deck and sit in the very front if possible. What a wonderful way to sightsee. And to rest.

Metros (subways) are wonderful when you have to get somewhere fast—for everyday commuting, say. But what do you get to see underground? So I would use subways only when essential.

You may be interested in other ways that I prepared for this travel.

One day in Chernihiv I spotted a two-wheel cart. Lightweight. It folded in half vertically when not in use. That's for me, I decided.

I packed things that I needed at night into a sturdy cardboard box and placed that on the cart. On top of the box I placed my handbag with the things I needed during the day. I lashed both of these on. That was the rig I used every day. Much easier than a suitcase, even one with wheels.

One of my friends laughed. "John, that cart is for *babushka*s," she said. A *babushka* is a grandma, as you know now. Yes, this was a *babushka* cart. Well, I was an old grandpa! Five times a grandpa! My *babushka* cart really lightened my day.

Oh, I also had a shoulder bag with my camera and maps and travel guides and snacks and a bottle of water—unwise to drink water from a tap in most of these countries. I have never traveled so lightly!

Got to tell you about my money. I had my Visa card. But I also had cash, of course. Some Ukrainian cash and American cash. I have been pick-pocketed a couple of times. It is unwise to carry all your money in one pocket or in your wallet or purse. Some people use money belts, but all you can stuff into them are a few bills.

So I divided my money. Some in one pocket (I make sure to buy pants with really deep pockets). Some in my chest wallet under my shirt. Some wrapped and stuffed next to my leg in a sock and some more wrapped and tucked in my other sock. My thinking is simple. They can't steal it all! What a problem it would be to be stranded without a dime.

A great surprise. Often my Visa credit card would not be accepted for a purchase. And a few times my dollars were not accepted! In all my travels, I had never seen a dollar being refused.

And many countries would not accept my nice fresh, crisp Ukrainian bills, either. Even in next-door Poland! I'd be insulted if I were a Ukrainian. In many of these places, it's the Euro that is king. So I had to have some Euros.

In Berlin, I desperately needed some Euros, and there was no money-exchange shop nearby. I couldn't even use a toilet; in most public places you have to pay. I saw a McDonald's. In many countries I knew a McDonald's would accept an American bill from an American customer. Their computers are programmed to figure the exchange rate.

I walked in and asked for the manager. I explained and showed him a $50 bill. He told me, "You have to buy something and we give you your change in local money. But a $20 bill is the biggest we'll accept."

The $50 was the smallest bill I had. "I'm in a bad fix," I told him. "Can you make an exception?" He took my $50, went into a back room and then came and gave me the change I needed in Euros. I overwhelmed him with my thanks. When I walked out, I realized I hadn't bought anything and felt bad about that. I counted the change he had given me. Yes, a nice guy, but I think he cut himself a hefty commission.

I entered Poland just the way I had hoped, on a great big gleaming Eurolines bus.

Night was falling. I couldn't see much. This was going to be an all-night ride, but no choice. Sleeping on a bus is awful. Finally I nodded off. Then a big stop. The frontier. We had to get off and go through that tedious business. We started again. I nodded off. Very soon another stop. But why?

*Kyiv—so interesting! This lady was selling kvas, the big summer drink. I got to like it.*

Our big, beautiful bus had broken down. No idea what had happened. We were stuck there for four hours. Finally a replacement bus pulled up.

It was an oldie, held in reserve for just such incidents, I think. A bit of sleep again. Then the sun rose. 'Twas a short, short night.

I sat by a window on the shady side of the bus. The shady side was a big plus. I kept that in mind whenever I got on—choose the shady side! I made full use of the panoramic window. The Polish countryside was beautiful, but so was Ukraine's. I kept in mind, of course, that the frontier had shifted back and forth more than once over the years.

But the road here was better. Much better. And the houses seemed better, and better maintained. The towns seemed more prosperous. This impression lasted throughout my stay in the country—things were better here. Poland turned out to be a wonderful surprise. These people were with it. I was impressed. No more bad Polish jokes!

Oh, on one ride I was sitting in the wrong seat. The seats were assigned. My seat was indicated on my ticket. I didn't know that. Now a woman was claiming it. I found that assigning seats on buses was the practice in every country. On Greyhound, it's first aboard, first choice.

I had to move to my rightful seat, which was on the sunny side. But people would get off at various stops, and I'd jump to a better seat whenever possible. Always on the shady side and as far forward as possible. This jumping to other seats seemed fine. Nobody got mad.

All the cities I was going to were big cities. Most were capital cities. Famous. That's why they appealed to me. And you don't have to spend a month in a city to catch its spirit, or lack of spirit. A day or two will do it.

After that, the marginal return gets very slight (that's a concept that I still remember from Economics 101}.Yes, I'd cover the center in a day or two. Then move on to the next city.

**W**hat I found is that all these cities have an old town—and usually that is what it is called, Old Town. And it's usually right on a river. That's where you'll find the great plazas and squares, the cathedral.

In fact, also government buildings, palaces and other great buildings always of wonderful architectural interest, with fascinating windows and roofs and doorways and amazing ornate ironwork. Cobblestone roads, narrow and twisty lanes.

*Each day I wondered where I would sleep. Here I'm in Poland. I got a bed in the hostel above the pizza shop.*

And for sure, all the tourists, with their cameras and guidebooks. I was delighted to be a normal tourist just like them.

And every city would have the New City. That's what I called it. The Old Town would be tucked in close to the New City, which was the modern, active, humming workaday center, often very large and spreading out into suburbs.

Most often the New City would be largely a new creation, partly or nearly totally rebuilt in the recuperation from the horrendous damage of World War II. Amazing how these cities could rebuild themselves so splendidly in just a few decades.

I found this New City everywhere nearly equally exciting to its Old Town. I would find dramatic new buildings, grand boulevards, parks, downtown shopping neighborhoods, often with exquisite shops, on and on. Impressive.

To my eye all these New Cities had exciting vitality. I could sense their energy. I could feel their importance and understand their claim to fame. That's why these ancient cities in modern dress attract so many tourists. Why they attracted me.

**L**et me tell you a word or two about each of them, in the order that I visited them.

**Lviv.** The last big city I visited on my loop in Ukraine. In the far west, near the Polish border, in fact part of Poland at one time. Rich in history and culture. Many architectural treasures. It is the stronghold of those who are Ukrainian in language and sentiment, as opposed to those in the big far eastern cities, who have a Russian predilection. (I took milady Annabelle here on our way home to the U.S.A.

**Krakow.** Considered the cultural and historic and intellectual heart of Poland and a must-see. A strong medieval look in its older quarters. Comparable in this sense to our Boston or Philadelphia, but much older and much richer in visible remnants and souvenirs of this legacy…buildings, monuments, narrow streets. A must!

**Warsaw.** Close to 2,000,000 people. The dynamic political and financial capital of Poland. Rich in architecture, old and new. It's more than you would expect, in my opinion. Famous as the home of Copernicus, the first great astronomer who reversed our thinking that the sun circles the earth. I loved his statue—probably there's more than one.

**Vilnius.** The proud capital of Lithuania, a country which in past times had a huge role and impact on a much greater area, including my Ukraine. Exploring its Old Town gives you an instant appreciation of its might and splendor in centuries gone by. Elegant buildings. Fine statues.

**Riga.** The attractive capital of Latvia. The country is squeezed between its neighbors in the small Baltic trio and you would think that it would succumb to one or the other, but it seems to be holding its own. You quickly sense its own culture and pride. The three countries always seem to be mentioned in a single breath, and when you visit, you understand why.

**Tallinn.** The capital of the northernmost of the three Baltic countries, Estonia. Like the other two, proud of its past and clear-eyed about its future. Positioned right on the sea, it enjoys a great strategic advantage. No wonder it shows influences of the Scandinavian countries just across the cold waters.

**Gdansk.** If anywhere in Europe there is a city that can be described as "picture-postcard pretty," this Polish gem would be a strong nominee. Amazing to see the fine, grand buildings running up and down its broad avenues and ringing its plazas. Most amazing of all is to see how a single style of medieval architecture is uniform throughout its Old Town, and how so many of the buildings were similar not only in style but size. Talk about a master plan! What mighty person mandated all this?

**Poznam.** A big, important city in Poland, "with it" in the modern sense but so rich in architecture of a previous time that it is a close runner-up in this category to famous Krakow. A fine city in which to live and work, I would think.

**Berlin**. One of the great cities of the world. Strikingly modern. The German capital of the Nazi empire in World War II. Notorious the way it was split up for years by the Berlin Wall. Little signs of the wall today. Has fashioned a dynamic future for itself. Wished I could stay longer.

**Vienna**. Austria's great pride, with reason. One of the most famous cities of Europe for its musical and cultural and intellectual attainments. No tourist can go wrong in visiting it. An enriching experience.

**Prague**. Most lustrous of the Czech Republic's cities. One of the most popular tourist destinations in Europe. A living museum at least in the architectural sense. Hundreds of impressive buildings, all worthy of having a camera focused at them. One reason is that contrary to cities like Berlin and Budapest, it suffered little damage during the war, and thus retains its old charm.

**Budapest**, Hungary. Really two cities, Buda and Pest facing one another across the great Danube River. It is a close contender to the previous two as an attractive vacation destination. I've been twice and would be pleased to go again.

A bit more about Lithuania, Latvia, and Estonia. All are ancient countries and thus, proud. They are some of the tiniest countries in Europe. Nevertheless, each has its own history, its own culture, its own language, its own government, and of course its own money.

How much longer can this go on in this age of mass media, super mobility, and vanishing frontiers? The European Union will put an end to some of those, and quite soon—their distinctive money, for instance.

They made me think of the three states in lower New England where I have spent my years—Rhode Island, Massachusetts, and Connecticut. All very small, as you know, much smaller in total than some of our enormous western states, such as Montana or Texas. In the geographical sense they are much like these three countries.

Now imagine what it would be like to go from Little Rhody to Massachusetts and then Connecticut and have to stop and confront all these differences! A different this and a different that!

To me it's inevitable that the melting pot will melt many of these differences down. And in so doing, of course, all three will lose so much of what they value so highly now. It's the sad and even tragic aspect inevitable with progress.

I had bad moments. In my first loop, through Ukraine, one day my bus ended its run in a small city at 10 p.m. All the passengers scattered in the dark. I looked around for a hotel. Could see none. I needed a bed!

I went to the bus driver, who was about to pull away. "Hotel," I said in my primitive Russian. "I need a hotel. An inexpensive hotel."

He scratched his head. (Of necessity I must abbreviate these tales). "Hop in," he said. Remember, I was the only one on the bus. He drove here and there through town, after 10 minutes finally found a hotel. He stopped.

Motioned for me to stay and wait. Ran into the lobby. Ran back in a few minutes. "They will have a bed for you!" he said. And they did. What a Good Samaritan. Refused my tip. I shoved it into his shirt pocket.

*Late at night! No hotel! He's the driver who went way out of his way to find me a room.*

In the next small city, my bus pulled into the bus station late in the afternoon. The end of the line. Same story; I needed a bed.

The driver hailed a nearby taxi driver who was lounging by his car and told him I needed a hotel, an inexpensive one.

The taxi driver approached. I told him what I needed. He was puzzled. I repeated.

He pointed to the big bus station, saw that I did not understand, took me by an arm and led me inside. Took me right into the office of the manager, a woman. Spoke to her. She led me down a corridor and opened a door.

A bedroom! Very plain and simple, but adequate, with toilet and shower down the hall. I grabbed it. I knew big railroad stations had rooms but not bus stations. I'd spread the word about this.

The taxi driver had been waiting. He was happy for me. He patted my shoulder and strode off.

In the morning I got on my next bus, which would leave at 7:30. Suddenly I saw last night's taxi driver approaching. He boarded the bus. He was looking for me.

He found me and said, "Did you have a good evening?" I gushed, "Yes, yes. Thank you so much!' Before I had a chance to do anything else, he gave me a wave and. I was amazed. I wanted to tip him.

He could have taken me on a long ride the previous evening, built up the mileage, found me a hotel, and soaked me. What a kind man.

In Vilnius our bus was due at 9 a.m. It was 8 a.m. It stopped in a city in front of a big railroad station. Rest stop. We all got off. I went to the toilet and was late in coming back. My bus was pulling away! All my luggage was on board!

I was frantic. I ran across the street to a taxi. "Please catch that bus!" I told the driver. Well, tried to. Finally he understood. The bus stopped two blocks away and we pulled up behind it. I hopped out, knocked on the bus door. The bus had no passengers. Strange. "My luggage!" I told the driver. "My luggage!"

He pointed backward. I did not understand. He pointed backward again. I did not understand. He closed the door and drove away! I was stunned.

"Can I help you?" a young woman on the sidewalk said. In English! I explained. She told me the bus driver said all my luggage was left at the station. She led me back to it and took me inside. We went to several departments. She did all the talking. She found me all my stuff!

She told me this city was Vilnius! How could it be? Vilnius was still an hour away. Well, we were supposed to change our watches at the border. Well, nobody had told me that.

**O**h, this taxi driver. He was searching for me. He had been waiting to be paid. I had changed my money and in my wallet I had Lithuanian bills. I hadn't had a chance to study them. I opened my wallet and proffered it. I wanted him to pull out whatever money I owed him. But he kept pulling out one bill after another. I was afraid he would take them all! I had to put my hand on his hand to stop him. The rascal!

Later I wondered. *How can one taxi driver be so good and honest? And another so greedy?*

I took a big gleaming bus in late afternoon from Prague to Budapest. Of course, it would end its run at a station. But it ended at a street corner. No station in sight. Again everybody rushed off. The bus drove off. I stood on the corner with my cart and shoulder bag. All alone. It was night time. What now?

I got directions and walked to the huge bus station about a kilometer away. *Why hadn't the bus taken us there?* No idea. It was late. All the ticket offices were closed. A few people rested and lounged in a huge waiting room. *Where would I sleep tonight*? I worried.

I went from one person to another. I kept saying, "English? "*Français*?" If only I could find somebody I could speak with! Finally a young man said, "Yes, I speak English." Hallelujah! His name was David. I explained my plight.

Again I must simplify the tale. He called a taxi driver. "He will be an honest man," he said. "I know of a good hostel." The taxi arrived.

David gave the man instructions. The man turned on the meter and drove into the city. About 15 minutes.

He stopped at a huge building on a street corner downtown. He found the hostel inside and walked in to inquire for me. They had a bed! The driver charged me exactly what the meter said. How remarkable. I paid him. He thanked me and left.

In Vienna I found my way to the Metro. To use it, I had to buy a ticket in a machine. A friendly man—a banker—explained that I should buy a two-day pass. Five Euros, I think it was. A great bargain. He said I could pay with a credit card. VISA was one of the logos on the machine. I have a VISA card. But it would not work.

I compared my card with his card. His had a round silver implant that mine did not have. What to do? I had some Euros. But only four. I was one Euro short. I had not had a chance to buy more. I expected to buy some here. He saw my problem. He dug into his pocket and gave me the extra Euro I needed. My smallest American bill was $5. I offered it to him.

"No, no!" he said. "Good luck!" Yes, in English, and went on his way. How remarkable again. Thanks to him I managed to buy the two-day pass. Wonderful.

I must say it's astonishing how many people in these countries speak at least a bit of English. I believe English is mandatory study in many schools and universities.

I met countless good people along the way. So many helped me. Not enough pages to tell you about others.

I must tell you about Iryna in Poznam. About 24. Talented. Beautiful. She had been a member of both my French and English Clubs in Chernihiv!

She had moved to Poznam in search of a better teaching job and found one. We had been in touch. "When you come to Poznam, please contact me, John," she had said. In fact, had insisted.

I did. She came and met me at my hostel—very nice, by the way—at 10 a.m. and then took me out to see her city. We walked and roamed all day. She showed me all the big sights, and some minor ones.

She even took me to her favorite place, the city's famous tropical garden, enclosed in a huge glass bubble of a structure. She took me back to my hostel at 6 p.m. A perfect day. How wonderful.

Oh, she told me that she was earning four times as much as she would back in Chernihiv. And she was engaged to Andrei back in Chernihiv, her high school boy friend, an IT specialist. And he was moving to Poznam.

She was living in a convent of Catholic nuns...they took in several young women...were kind. They were trying to find a job for Andrei. She glowed when she told me.

Now, about some more special people I happened to meet..

On one train I met Francois and his fiancée from Canada. He was a captain in the Canadian infantry, but retiring after 13 years—12 years short of a pension. He had just finished a year of service in Afghanistan. The Canadian Army had 80,000 troops—3,000 were in Afghanistan. He said it was hard and dangerous there. He was glad to be back.

"The Army is too much of a bureaucracy," he told me. "I was frustrated. Angry." Now he wanted to get into "green construction"—building houses that are environmentally friendly.

He was a native French speaker but spoke English well. We spoke in French.

He had graduated from Canada's Military Academy and then been commissioned. "I wanted to be a soldier ever since I was a little boy." He had served all over Canada. Had gone to our West Point for special training...also to our Rangers School at Ft. Benning, Georgia, for special training. "I enjoyed it very much," he told me.

The two were heading to Ukraine because she was of Ukrainian descent. "She wants to get a feeling for her roots. We'll be married back home in October."

Iryna moved to Poznam for a better life. What a fine welcome she gave me there.

Sitting next to me on one bus was a big man who was coal black. About 40. He was reading a newspaper. It was in English. I sparked a conversation.

"My name is Raymond," he said. "I am Nigerian but I work in Prague. For an American company. It is called Monster Online."

He told me that it was an online people-placement company. It helped people to find jobs, and helped companies to recruit personnel. "It is very big—the biggest in its field."

He spoke fine English. The problem was his accent. I had to strain to understand him.

He was married and had two children. He told me how terrible things were in Nigeria—he called it an "artificial country" that forced incompatible tribes to live and work together. So difficult, he said.

He said he belonged to the Ibu tribe and gave me some background. I knew nothing about all that but I got the feeling he knew what he was talking about. I was sorry when he had to leave the bus.

On another day my seat companion was a man about 50. I sized him up as Chinese. I was wrong. He was South Korean. He, too, spoke excellent English but his accent was more manageable.

He was working in Qatar, the little up-and-coming Emirate country on the Arabian Peninsula. He gave me his business card. His name was K.J. Na (Kyung-Joon). He was Regional Director, Middle East, for Hyundai Engineering & Construction Co. in Qatar. An impressive title.

*A joy of solo travel is making new friends. With Kyung-Soon my ride ended too soon. He was so interesting.*

Hyundai, of course, is the South Korean company that builds increasingly fine automobiles and trucks. What I didn't realize is what a variety of fields this huge company is engaged in. In Qatar the company was doing big construction jobs.

He said the work in Qatar was hard and the company gave all the Koreans there 45 days of vacation a year. He returned to Korea three times a year to be with his wife and three sons. He said he was surprised to be assigned to Qatar.

He told me that military service in South Korea is compulsory. He had served and become a naval officer. He laughed. "Our three sons had to serve. One in the Army, one in the Navy, and one in the Air Force!'

I asked if he had relatives in North Korea. "No!" he said. The freeze between South and North Korea was a tragedy for families with members on both sides of the border. They never see one another. Inconceivable to me.

He was very pleasant. Asked me questions about Peace Corps. I mentioned that Peace Corps had sent Volunteers to South Korea for 20 years, stopping some years ago.

I told him that in 2011 Peace Corps will observe its 50th anniversary. There will be big celebrations in Washington and many host countries. Korea was inviting all Volunteers back for a reunion (more than 2,000 of them!). It wanted to show its appreciation. (I wish Ukraine would do that!)

"Very, very good," K.J. said. He knew nothing about Peace Corps' 20 years of effort there. Was impressed.

At breakfast in the hostel in Poznan I sat at a table with an Asian man. About 32. He was making free Skype calls on his laptop. Happy calls. In his language.

He turned to me. "I am sorry," he said. "I am speaking to my Mom and Dad." I was astonished—he was speaking English and his parents were in Baltimore!

Then he explained. He was Chinese, was born in China, but had moved to the U.S.A. with his parents when he was a boy. He had graduated from Johns Hopkins in Baltimore. Computer science. Then he had traveled around the world alone. Nearly 50 countries.

"How did you finance that?" I said. He laughed. "Credit cards!"

Now he was living in Sweden. His wife was a beautiful Swedish gal. There he was a small building contractor—remodeling kitchens and bathrooms and so on. Business was good.

Was he still an American? "Yes, sure." He knew he should explain more. "I think Sweden is a perfect country. Everything runs like clockwork. Education. Health care. Public services. Everything is high quality. Taxes are very high. But people accept that. I like Sweden a lot."

I asked about the long, frigid winters. "It's true. But they're really not bad. We get together with friends. Go to movies and concerts. Enjoy life at home. A lot of people like the snow and the cold. And the long summer days are so, so wonderful!"

Any children? "No, not yet. First things first. But the time will come! Meanwhile, life is good."

On another day, across from me was a man about 45 with a boy. In front of him were a woman and her husband. Behind me was a woman with a girl.

I said to him, "What is the time, please?" He did not understand. I pointed to his watch. Then he understood.

They were Iranians. He was a dentist. Next to him was his son. In front of him were his sister and her husband, who was a teacher. Behind me were his wife and their daughter. They lived in Germany and they were on their way to Prague for a vacation.

His wife had a big picnic basket. Thick sandwiches, fruits, potato chips, drinks. Happily they munched and drank. She passed something to me. I said, "No, thank you." She offered me something else. Again I said "No, thank you."

We were becoming friendly. I stood up in the aisle with my camera and asked them to crowd together. They did. The bus was lurching and bouncing. It wasn't easy. I urged them to smile. They did. I clicked the shutter. My picture was beautiful. I passed my camera around for them to see the picture. They were delighted.

*These Iranians—the wonderful family across from me. My new friends.*

When they spotted something interesting out the window, they would alert me. I would do the same for them. All this time I remained aware they were Iranians, citizens of a country we're not getting along with. And they knew I was an American, from a country their homeland did not like.

The feuding at our top levels wasn't even hinted at. We were just fellow human beings on a bus, handicapped by a lack of a common language but drawn together in friendship.

Shortly, the dentist's wife passed a plate to me. It held a banana, a peach, a cucumber, and a kiwi. I repeated my "No, thank you" line. Her husband insisted that I eat. He smiled but was emphatic. He pointed to the banana. I ate it. Then the cucumber. I ate it. It was the first time in my life that I ate a cucumber by biting into it as I would an apple.

He insisted I eat the peach. Impossible, and I patted my tummy and he understood. He accepted the plate back. But he was happy that I had finally accepted their hospitality. They were beaming.

We stopped for a five-minute break. Right there was a fancy bakery. I spotted beautiful rolls. I asked for an assortment. Back on the bus, it was my turn now. I insisted they each choose one. They did. Then I insisted they all choose another. They did. We were in a merry mood. Few words between us because so difficult, but warm vibes. Our countries were feuding but we were not.

In Prague we went our separate ways with big waves. I left with a nice feeling about Iranians and I suspect they had a good feeling about Americans. In our small way we had done a little something for peace. And we felt good about it.

Now about Pete and Donney. I met them in the hostel in Warsaw. They were about 45. They had the lower bunks in a room with two double bunks. Using an upper bunk is a problem for me. I mentioned that. Pete quickly said, "You take my bunk, mate. I'll take the upper." A generous offer.

Pete was English and Donney was American. They were on a trip of many months. They had met in some city three months earlier and had teamed up.

I looked at them and said, "Traveling together like this is tough. Are the two of you still talking to one another?"

They both laughed. "Barely," Donney said. "Yeah, barely," Pete also said. But they were joking, or so I hoped. They seemed a good team.

I never got to find out about Pete's background or Donney's but Donney quickly told me he wanted to be a writer. He seemed serious. He was keeping a journal.

I told him that I did some writing and he asked many questions and I did my best to answer them and give him honest advice. He asked for my e-mail address and I gave it to him.

They had to get up at 4 a.m. to catch a train. Donney had a cell phone and he set its alarm for 4. "I am worried that it may not go off," he said. So I set my phone for 4 also. Our phones went off seconds apart. I said a groggy "Au revoir and good luck!" to them and went back to sleep. They were extra quiet in packing up and moving out.

Since then I have received messages from Donney from different cities, and I believe he's got what it takes to become a writer. They are still together.

In these travels outside Ukraine, I did take a train—a fast, smooth, modern train into Germany to Berlin. But with its small compartments, many empty, it did not provide the opportunity for personal contact that the buses did.

And in my Ukraine loop earlier, I made it a point to visit three libraries, all to compare them with mine in Chernihiv and assess their progress toward digitalization. I discussed this in Chapter 17.

Well, finally I got home to Chernihiv. I plopped into bed. Weary but happy. One thought was firm in my mind: I had had a lot of fun but I had learned so much, too. Yes, learned so much. And here I was an old man. How even more wonderful and valuable it would have been if I had done this traveling as a young man.

Every young person right out of college who shows some gumption should go off for six months with a backpack and travel around cheaply in country after country. What a way to cap off the school years and get ready for life in the real world.

So many students finance their education. They should finance this last part of it as well. Of course it would be possible to find work here and there along the way.

This would be education in the finest sense. It would pay off later in greater confidence and awareness. And they would learn so much about themselves in the process. And like Dora from Australia, then they could settle down and start a good career for themselves and a good life as adults. And of course, advance the cause of peace between nations.

All this I believe. Don't you think so?

My two vacation tours were challenging trips but I had much pleasure. To my surprise I made it. I found it all so worthwhile. It was a highlight of all my time in Peace Corps. I had only three months to go.

I was ready, in fact, eager, to wind up with a strong push.

~ ~ ~

***Did you know*** .... that a big surprise for me was that I wound up working all alone in my city. No other Volunteers around! I was disappointed.

I had hoped that I would be posted with at least a few others. I found it hard to be alone. I would have enjoyed having a friend or two or two, sharing a meal with them, and venting! Many days...many weeks...would go by without my seeing another Volunteer.

I found out other Volunteers felt the same way. I believe Peace Corps did it this way because it's afraid that Volunteers would spend too much time together and would not immerse themselves in their new community as deeply.

# 36 / And back home, what?

*27 months of separation can generate stresses. And some things can go sour.*

When I joined, I wondered how my living overseas so long might affect things back home. Relationships! Maybe for the worse. I worried about it, and rightfully. Some painful changes did occur. Inevitable, I believe, though I worked hard to keep everything smooth.

But one thing made separation easier and minimized the difficulties. Modern technology! It was so much easier to keep in touch. What made the big difference were my computer, and in time, my own Internet connection, and in more time, amazing Skype. I told you about this in Chapter 22, "My Computer Life."

In the second half of my service, I finally had a comfortable set-up with all this technology at my fingertips in Tanya's flat. This new technology was such a blessing that sometimes I wondered, *How did Volunteers manage to make it 40 years ago, even 10 years ago? In the wilds of Africa, or the isolated villages up in the Andes, or aboriginal Fiji?*

Here I was, getting by all right in a country difficult to describe as backward or primitive. Things were quite developed in Ukraine. Oh, some Volunteers had it hard in remote villages. I felt badly for them.

But I enjoyed indoor plumbing, running cold and hot water, indoor heat, steady electricity and gas. Food aplenty. No serious crime. Fantastic public transit. In a city with schools and universities and hospitals and banks. Stores and shops of all kinds. Reliable mail, Internet, and telephone. Restaurants, theaters, night clubs, even a symphony orchestra. Plus the many pleasures and resources and perks of Peace Corps.

Still I found it difficult and frustrating at times. Consider! Back home I owned my own home with all comforts and conveniences. No mortgage. No consumer debt. I wasn't a millionaire, but I was financially secure. I owned income property, and I had a variety of investments, and I had the time to run these things.

I was happily retired with no need to work. But I did continue to work because I got such a kick out of it. And I had a car! I had never imagined a life without a car.

I was settled in an important relationship of 15 years with Annabelle. I was lucky to have her. We were living a bi-coastal life, part of the year in Connecticut, part in California. We traveled a lot, to visit our children and have a good time.

I was a father with three children well married and well settled. And a grandfather four times. And I was delighted in my second year in Peace Corps with another grandchild.

I was writing a newspaper column and features because writing was important to me and I liked the challenge. I had published two books and was having fun giving talks at churches, clubs, and schools.

And the town that I was living in—Deep River—was my home not because I had been born and grew up there, or earned my living there, but by pure choice. How many folks can say that?

I was lucky to belong to Deep River's Rotary Club, a perfect place to make friends and work on interesting community projects. I enjoy being with nice people and I had a circle of friends in a variety of fields—a circle that stretched far and wide.

My point is that I had a lot going on. I considered myself fortunate. No wonder some folks were surprised when I mentioned I was applying to join Peace Corps. One or two thought I was crazy.

I had one major concern in committing to Peace Corps. *How could I keep all this going smoothly while far off in a strange land for many months?* For one thing, my various relationships. Somebody long ago said that absence makes the heart grow fonder. Yes and no. Some relationships thrive. Some die.

True, everyone entering Peace Corps runs into difficulties. Young people have difficulties of their own. So do older Volunteers. But I believe I had more, and they were more complicated. How come? Because of the breadth of things I was engaged in.

Peace Corps recognized that service in it could have great appeal, but often practicalities of daily life could intrude and deter. You just can't go overseas for many months and let things run themselves.

Peace Corps suggested that entering Volunteers appoint an attorney to run things for the duration of their service. Perhaps a legal attorney but not necessarily. Some Volunteers gave a person close to them power of attorney to act for them—someone experienced and trustworthy. Some solved the problem by selling their house, their possessions, their car.

Hiring a manager sounded good but could be a less than perfect solution. It could involve considerable expense. Sure, you might be lucky and find someone who would do a fine job. But you might appoint someone and be terribly disappointed with the results during your service or when you came home. You might be relieving yourself of some responsibilities only to find that you had wound up with big problems.

What I kept in mind is that a Peace Corps hitch was a limited thing—27 months. And if things got tremendously complicated, I could quit and go home. Of course, I hoped this would not be necessary.

My decision finally was not to divest, and not to appoint somebody, but to organize things as well as I could before leaving. I resolved to supervise and administer everything myself from afar. There were things that I could automate, such as the payment of routine bills. Through the Internet I could keep an eye on many things. And through the Internet I could keep in touch with people and maintain a tight liaison.

I have discussed some of these things already. And I told you how some of them worked out. I mentioned the problems with my mail and my taxes, both my federal and state taxes and town property taxes.

As the months progressed, I found some solutions to the problems, or at least easier ways to handle them. How fortunate I was. And I shared them with you.

Of course, you are wondering about my relationships back home. Did they flourish or founder?

Well, to repeat myself, relationships are like plants. They must be watered and fertilized. It took me a while to learn this. After college, like so many graduates I moved away and got immersed in career. I lost some good friends because I didn't understand this need for continual nurturing. Friendships withered. So easy to happen. It happens to many.

I entered Peace Corps a lot smarter. I did my best to water my relationships through numerous e-mail contacts. I suppose that at first my friends found my e-mails exciting because of the novelty of what I was going through, but less so as the newness died and my days became more humdrum. All very natural.

The truth is that I wrote e-mails to many dozens of people, but I would hear back from only a small percentage. In my heart, these few became my dear inner circle. How good it was to spot their names in my Inbox. I would gladly name them but this would be unwise.

In time I learned how long it would be before any particular person would reply. A few would send me a message in mere hours! I also got to know which ones would remain silent.

I was disappointed that many would never acknowledge receiving my e-mails. Before I shipped out, I had informed a long list of people that Peace Corps had accepted me. I had asked if they wanted to receive e-mail reports of my adventure. Quite a few said yes.

I understood that nobody was under the gun to reply to my e-mails, though a reply could be just a dozen words. Even less. "Am fine. Work is good. Happy you are not quitting!" It did not have to be the 2,000 or even 4,000 words that I sent them. I never grumbled about this.

But I admit I took offense when some never replied. I never struck a name off my list for this reason, although doing so would have eased things a bit for me. But friendship is friendship. It has to be watered by both parties. I felt I was watering but they weren't.

One other thing. I had a firm policy. Whenever I received a reply from anyone who wasn't an obvious screwball, I would always reply. A personal reply, mind you. Not a form reply. Even to a stranger who had read my e-mail through somebody else—it's surprising how many e-mails get forwarded and forwarded!

And I did not take days to do it. Often I would reply immediately. Some people noticed this and would commend me for my promptness. I wanted to be considerate, and replying quickly was one way. But doing it quickly also made my busy life easier.

I have never forgotten a definition that I read many years ago: "A stranger is a friend you have not made yet." Maybe it was from Confucius. I took it to heart. I make it a point to try to turn promising strangers into friends. Of course, all the friends we possess were once strangers to us.

Another saying that I have gotten to appreciate is: "He is blessed who has many friends." Imagine the bleakness of having no friends. I like the thought of being rich in friends.

As we know, the most important events in anybody's social life are birthdays and holidays. I was extra attentive when these approached. On these occasions I sent truly personal messages. And gifts when appropriate. I was always in touch when I heard of a retirement or a graduation or a death. I took pride in keeping in touch.

**O**ne pleasant surprise was that the reports that I e-mailed won me several brand-new friends in the U.S.A. I would receive e-mails from complete strangers—they had received one of my reports from somebody else and had decided to contact me. I would send that person a reply. And presto, this would lead to more e-mails. And friendship.

High up in my relationships was Annabelle. She and I exchanged e-mails usually on a daily basis. That kept us linked tight.

More than once, I marveled about one thing. If all these contacts had been by stamped mail, imagine how difficult it would have been for both sides. The hassle. And what the postage would have added up to. E-mail was magical.

And then came Skype! Other Volunteers had it. They brought it to my attention. And I had friends in far places that used it. It was all new to me. "A miracle!" they said. They sang its wonders. So did I.

I encouraged my family members to get Skype, but the only one who did was my son Mark.

Remember, I also had to keep current with my business dealings. What an enormous help Skype was in this. Especially in my second year.

A big reason was my income real estate back home. I mentioned that I owned a rental condo. I had also rented out my own for the duration. So I had tenants in both. I had automated the routine part of this—how they paid their rent and how I kept track of it.

Well, problems came up. A tenant would get behind in the rent. Or a tenant would leave. I would need to find another. I had a fine real estate broker to help me, but still easy communication between us was important. E-mail could do the trick.

Or a thermostat did not work. Or a garbage disposer was broken. Imagine how a Skype phone call could simplify things!

Before I got Skype I had to handle what turned into a nasty problem. A tenant who was a good friend decided to leave. It started with e-mails back and forth. There was miscommunication and he misunderstood. Both of us became unhappy. In fact, angry. Finally it got settled. But that friendship went down the drain, sad to say. The outcome might have been happier with Skype.

One day came a bigger problem. The tube supplying the ice maker in a refrigerator had leaked and ruined a section of the plaster ceiling below. In fact, in the condominium lobby down there. The problem involved back and forth calls—unthinkable without Skype. Finally the ceiling got repaired and I paid the bill.

On another day, a tragedy. I had a tenant I'll call Rita. She had moved in after I had left for Ukraine, so I never got to meet her. She lived alone. We did have a nice e-mail correspondence at the beginning. She turned out to be excellent in every way, as a person and a tenant.

One morning I was shocked by an e-mail. She had been killed in an auto accident! She had been driving home alone late at night. Drove off the highway at a curve and hit a tree. Was killed instantly. She was wearing her seatbelt. No brake marks. Only 24 years old. A tragedy with a capital T.

That led to a number of challenges for her family and me. They had to move out all her possessions, of course. And I had to make sure the condo was ready and find a new tenant. That was in my pre-Skype days. It all went smoothly. We got it done with e-mail. Suppose this had happened to me as a Volunteer in Liberia 30 years earlier, say.

I am afraid you are concluding that I was kept busy with all this. Not so. These were sporadic happenings, months apart.

One important relationship was a big worry—my Uncle Jack. I mentioned him earlier. He was my uncle by marriage. He was the husband of my dear Aunt Bernadette, who had died eight years before. She was living with my mother and father when I was born. So I got to know her as well as my mother.

My aunt and uncle married when I was one year old and moved in right next to us. If I did not like what *Maman* was serving for supper, I would go next door, enter without knocking, and sit down at the table and eat with them. They never had children. I became more than a nephew.

They lived into old age and he outlived her. In time he became my responsibility and I accepted it gladly. Then he became ill and had to enter a nursing home. I had to sell his possessions and his home for him.

Remarkably he recovered. He was a World War II veteran (life-scarring memories of action in France and Belgium and Germany) and through good luck I found him a place at age 92 in the Rhode Island Veterans Home in Bristol, R.I. A fine place.

He was 96 when I got the idea of Peace Corps. He was my greatest reason for not entering Peace Corps. What to do? I felt guilt. But how much could I do for him when I was living so far away—100 miles away when I was in Connecticut, and 3,200 miles away when in California? I decided that I had to be true to myself and say yes to Peace Corps.

It was difficult for me to break the news to him. He was 97. But there was something that I hoped he would understand. He had served our flag. I never had, but now I had the opportunity in a small way through Peace Corps. I told him I had other reasons also. He took it badly. Became angry.

My daughter, Monique, took over for me and did an excellent job. I kept in touch with him. I would send e-mails for him to his social worker and she would read them to him, and then give him the printout. He remained bitter but I never quit.

I would not have been surprised if he had died while I was in Ukraine. Well, he did not die while I was gone. I made it home in time to visit him. In fact, I got to see him twice before he passed on. My whole family assembled from the far corners of the country for his funeral and I was among them. And I gave the eulogy at his memorial Mass at the Veterans Home.

When I entered Peace Corps, several of my closest kin excitedly assured me they would come and visit me. I know they were sincere. Life is strange. Difficulties arose. Not one of them made it to Ukraine. I was disappointed. I believe they were also. I understood. Well, sort of.

Milady Annabelle was terrific. As you know, we saw one another three times during my service. We met in China for two weeks. She came for a month at the end of my first year. And she came to be with me for my final days. I wanted her to be part of everything. Then we flew home together.

Conclusion: I came home with my relationships quite intact. I had preserved and strengthened the most important ones, apart from my uncle. I had lost two or three friends, without really understanding why. Sad. But I could not blame myself. And I had enriched my life with numerous new friendships.

As always, it was a reminder that life is imperfect. We cannot always have our way. My losses could have been far worse. My new gains helped salve them.

~ ~ ~

*Did you know* .... that Peace Corps' mission has remained unchanged since the start?

It has three goals for you as a Volunteer. The first is to assist the people in the country that you work in.

The second is to be a good representative of our country and get those you work with over there to understand more about us.

And the third is to take on a new role when you return home, which is to spread the word about Peace Corps and your efforts in its behalf, and what it's like in your host country.

Some people think that Volunteers are on a mission to advance our strategic political interests in their host countries, and even to do uncover work for the CIA. Not so! Peace Corps prohibits this and will not tolerate it.

# 37 / My successes & failures

*I put my best into all this. I work hard.*
*Some things go well. Some could go better.*

I am positive of one thing. All 86 of us recruits arrived in Kyiv on Oct. 1, 2007, committed to digging in and achieving 100 percent of everything Peace Corps asked us to do and expected of us.

We had signed up "to go wherever and do whatever." We expected a challenge—make that a challenge and a half—but we were bright-eyed and determined and very proud to be Volunteers. No way did we come way over here to fail.

Amy and Adam and Jennifer and the other younger ones among us were just starting out in the real world of work. They had good personal and academic records but little career experience to build on. Every challenge here would be new. That could be scary.

Those of us a decade or two older like Brian and Sara and James were more seasoned, with some impressive accomplishments for sure. But perhaps some of these had signed on because they needed a break from what they were doing. Maybe they were bored, dissatisfied, frustrated, who knows? But surely they had a good track record. Peace Corps would not have accepted them if it had found otherwise during its checks.

We who were the younger ones in 50-Plus like Evonne and Joann had a lot more strengths and successes on our résumés.

And we who were well into retirement like Nancy and Tom and Berta and myself were coming over most probably for much different reasons. Certainly not for job experience or career opportunity. And certainly not to learn a new language that we could use for advancement once we returned home.

Maybe the main factors for us were to escape boredom. Or bury a grief or a disappointment. Or prove we still had good stuff. Maybe to make new friends in the Corps and in whatever new country we got sent to. And I'll bet to travel and enjoy an adventure or two.

And, probably not least on our list, young or old, was an ambition to do some good for our Stars and Stripes as well as for the Ukrainians we would get to serve.

Of course, all of us wanted a perfect score card when we got through. We wanted success. But life is not like that. Some things will go better than others. We might rack up some brilliant successes. We might do well in other areas. And, woe on us, we might rack up a flop or two.

If a terrible flop, whether in performance or behavior and we saw it coming, we might opt out before completing our 27 months and head home. This if we suspected Peace Corps might be thinking of giving us the choice of resigning or being fired. More than two dozen in my Group 33 went home early. No idea if any went because of this fear.

Certainly some left because of a disappointment—they hated the weather, say. Or a change in plans—they spotted a big opportunity for a scholarship, maybe. Or mom or dad was very sick. As you know, Volunteers may leave at any time without protest or prejudice.

As each of us finally approached Going Home Day after 27 months, for sure we looked deep to see how we had done. In fact, during our Close of Service interview, we would be asked for an estimate of our service. Yes, a written assessment of what we had accomplished.

Maybe some of us wanted to write something stronger and tried to exaggerate but knew our regional manager—our immediate boss—would be scanning what we wrote with a critical eye. Not easy to admit a failure. Writing that COS assessment was a challenge for all of us. I'm sure. Peace Corps may read these reports with a jaundiced eye.

What did we succeed in? How often are we ever asked such a probing question. Well, I've told you so much in these pages about my experiences, good and bad, that I can't duck now. So here goes.

### How did I do? Any successes? Did I fail, or come close?

Let me tell you the bad stuff first. Without a doubt, my big failure was in learning Russian. I put up a heck of a good try nearly to the end. I was interested in learning. I put in countless hours. Trying to memorize words and phrases. Understand the grammar. Pronounce correctly. Practice in speaking and writing. My teacher, Tamila, and my two personal tutors, Luda and Sasha, would attest to that, I'm sure.

I've been a good student all my life. Here my age was my enemy. I'm not saying this as an excuse to cover up lack of effort.

During Training, I felt I might be sent home for my obvious deficiency. Diana Schmidt, our country director, who had the final say, told me when she visited one day that I was being kept on because I was trying so hard. I tried hard for another 18 months. Honest!

The problem was not the grammar. Not easy, but I could grasp it. The problem was retaining the many new words I was stuffing into my noggin. I finally gave up, after much anxiety, when I had to accept that the study was ruining my day and depressing my spirits. It reached the point that I hated to pick up any of my Russian books.

I was sure my long-time tutor Sasha must hate our sessions. Must be frustrated. "Haven't you had enough of this?" I asked her more than once. She kept saying no, no. Sweet gal.

Besides, my failure was not hurting my work. I didn't find it difficult to get along without the Russian. Most people I dealt with spoke some English. I always had my two-way Russian-English dictionary with me—it could always get me out of a jam. And what purpose would knowing Russian serve once I got home? I didn't aspire to join the Foreign Service or become a journalist posted to Moscow. My career was behind me.

When finally I told Sasha, "I'm quitting!" she wasn't startled. She said, "I understand, John. I really do." Immediately I felt a huge weight lifted. I slept much better.

I feel terrible about it. I envied the younger Volunteers who had broken through to a high conversational level. If I had been their age, I would have, too.

How effective was I as an English-language teacher at *Coursi*?
Quite good, I believe.

As you know, I became a classroom speaker more than a teacher. I would go in and speak to this class of students or that class. The idea was to let them hear an American speaker and to encourage them to speak back. I'd emphasize that: "Speak back, please!"

Of course, I sought to speak about interesting subjects and to speak slowly and effectively. It would have been stupid to do anything but. But it was extraordinary for anyone to speak back, even to ask a question. Imagine my frustration.

The regular teacher, whoever it was, always assured me, "They understand, John. They are just shy." I stopped believing that. My senses told me differently.

I did have some very satisfactory teaching experiences. These came with the few opportunities I got to have a class of my own. Only a few students signed up, but they must have been the best and most far-seeing of all our students.

I emphasized to them that much of what they learned in English would apply to their native Russian or Ukrainian. So they were getting a double helping of good stuff. Some got to appreciate this.

Another was my English Conversation Class. Only four students, and they were all Computer Science majors. One young woman and three young men. I got to like them very much. We covered many topics. Slowly they answered my pleas to speak, speak! I began to feel closer to them in more than a "teacher" way. If I can help them in the future from home here, I will be pleased to do so. I believe they will all be successful.

I believe that my students liked me. Would go out of their way to say "Hi." Would stop to say a few words on the street or in a store. It was obvious they enjoyed having me come to their class. I believe that I inspired them.

How? I went beyond just teaching. I encouraged them. Exhorted them. I would say, "You are the leaders of tomorrow. Be good leaders." I would say, "Somebody has to be a leader. Why not you? Yes, why not?"

I would say, "You must not limit your study of English just to these few hours in class. You must find ways to read and speak every day."

I would say, "It is easy to lose a second language. You must keep it up. Must practice, practice. Or all these hours, all this effort will turn out to be a complete waste."

"Your country is just a teen-ager. Of course, it's going through growing pains. Things will get better."

What teacher ever knows what his impact is on his students? I remember my own experience as a student. Did I ever tell my good teachers how much I appreciated them? No. It never occurred to me. But maybe my enthusiasm in class said that for me.

In time, to my frustration, I became under-employed at *Coursi*. Or so I felt. (Over my 27 months I came to see other Volunteers felt the same )

Many teachers wanted to have me work with their students in the beginning. But it declined. They needed the classroom hours to teach the nuts and bolts. As the semester went on, they were desperate to cover everything before the final exams. I got fewer requests.

I tried to stimulate "gigs" for myself. I sent out suggested topics that I was able and ready to talk about. I would ask individual teachers, "Would you like me to come to your class later this week? Or how about next week?" Few takers. The most enthusiastic were Marina, English teacher, and Louba, French teacher.

I would suggest to Olena ideas of things I could do. In writing. Usually she would find some reason to trash my suggestions. This amused and irritated me. After all, for many years I had earned my living in part by being a consultant, offering ideas and implementing them.

I know exactly when things began to sour. It was when our application for a grant for a "white board" failed. Peace Corps did not provide grants for equipment. It was that simple. But Olena pinned the defeat on me.

My two years at *Coursi* concluded on a happy note. Hallelujah! Both Olena and I extended ourselves to patch things up. She was generous about this and so was I. How good that was. We parted with genuine hugs and best wishes. What I like to remember is how so often she was so kind to me. She was a loving queen at those times.

How well did I succeed in my two clubs?
Here the results were clearer. The list of those attending would change over the weeks. But in both clubs some came week after week, or nearly every week. Their interest spoke for itself. And so did their warmth toward me. They became more than my students. They became my friends.

I taught them English and French. I recognized their talents. I encouraged them not only as students but as persons. I gave them all kinds of tips and advice about doing well in life. I gave them more self-confidence. I widened their horizons. I made them feel better about my country and my fellow Americans. I was a good small ambassador.

I knew that I was effective with them. It became even more obvious in my final weeks. I would say, "I am preparing to go home. Just six more weeks!"

I would hear sighs. Someone would say, "Oh, no, John!" I believed them. I knew I was hearing the truth.

I also heard this from the three staff librarians in the Foreign Book Department, Victoria, Tatiana, and Ira. I felt a great closeness with them. Ira in particular.

I think that this work of mine in my clubs at the library was my best. In truth, I got more pleasure and satisfaction in my clubs than I did at *Coursi*. At *Coursi* I sometimes felt like a puppet with little say. In my two clubs it was totally different.

I'll never forget my final Sunday with them—my farewell party. They were all so nice. Their comments and good wishes were heartfelt and their gifts so thoughtful. And Annabelle was at my side!

How about my Library Digitalization Project?
You read all about the great Korolonko Library, which I visited nearly every day. Some one million volumes, a staff of close to 100, the central library for the whole oblast (province), proud of its history and role. And generously supported by our U.S.A. with gifts of books, computers, and such hi-tech goodies as TV sets and digital cameras.

I told you how I love libraries—I consider the library a city's premier institution after the food stores! How I size up a city by its library. A good library suggests a good community.

I told you how old-fashioned the Korolonko was, like one of our libraries two decades ago. A whole-room—the Catalog Room—filled with many dozens of card cases and hundreds of catalog drawers.

I explained the tedious problem of using the library...finding the books you wanted, getting possession of them, and checking them out. You saw how, if you wanted books in different fields, you had to go from one mini library to another and endure the difficult process.

I explained how usage was declining. Fewer people were using books, particularly university students. More and more had access to computers and knew about Google and Wikipedia services offered in their own languages. It was less important to use the library.

How librarians were fearful for their jobs. For them, career jobs! Computers save work! Computerization would slash the payroll!

In time I got to suspect that the annual statistics were being fudged. I surmised this was to assure a good operating budget from higher authorities every year.

The situation became plain to me. And gloomy. Keep this up and the library would die!

I began preaching digitalization. Nobody wanted to hear about it. But I persisted. I explained and explained. Sure, computers save work. But the staff could be trimmed not by lay-offs but by natural attrition. By retirements mostly. All workers would be guaranteed their jobs. And new services would require employees of their own. Think of all the services our American libraries provide in addition to books!

I made slow progress. Some people saw the sense of what I believed. Finally the library found the money for a library software program—Russian, but adequate. A consultant came in for a week to educate the staff and give basic instruction.

My department—the Foreign Book Department—became the focus. Finally the first book was digitalized. The tiny numbers on its barcode had to be typed in by hand. How laborious. The project would take forever. But, yes, it was a start.

Finally today the need to digitalize is generally accepted though still dreaded. I have received e-mails that the work goes on. The library is committed to joining the modern age.

Would this have happened without me? Probably. Some day. All I could take credit for was giving the library the big kick in the pants.

Now what about my Public Transit Information project?

This was another monumental challenge. Again you know the situation. A big city of 300,000 people. Most people too poor to own an automobile. Owning one just a dream, but one nourished by the new capitalism.

A vast system of public transportation. Three levels. One level provided by a limited number of very old trolleys operated by the city. A bigger level of buses operated by a growing number of profit-driven entrepreneurs. And a third level—a much newer level, born just a few years ago, of *marshrutkas*—16-passenger vans; many fleets of them of varying sizes, again the creation of hopeful capitalists.

All traveled numbered routes. The trolleys the fewest routes, the buses more routes, and the *marshrutkas* the most routes. And different fares—the trolleys the cheapest (with seniors riding fee and students getting discounts), the buses charging more, and the *marshrutkas* even more.

There was no publicized, systematic way of getting basic information. Not sure how to get to an unaccustomed section of the city? You'd have to ask a neighbor or at a tobacco kiosk and hope for the best. You had to be born in the city to get a basic understanding and still there would be great voids.

My idea, as you read in Chapter 18, was to provide a centralized information source. At first I dreamed of an annual handbook à la Yellow Pages. Supported by advertising in the same way. The handbook would be sponsored by the Korolonko Library.

It would be a profit-maker, and the profits would be put to good use by it—for digitalization, let's say!

The recession hit. That killed the idea of paid advertising. I adjusted my thinking: let's make it a website instead of a printed handbook! Paper and ink cost money, but pixels are free.

I worked at this project with the same fervor as the library digitalization project. This time I explained and preached to city bureaucrats. Of course, as the economy recovered, slowly paid digital advertising would be a big possibility.

My indispensable ally was Ira, my librarian friend at the Korolonko. She found the right contacts at City Hall and set up interviews for me and accompanied me. She would sit at my right and translate back and forth. Cumbersome, but it worked.

For the most part it was friendly but there were sparks of frustration, irritation, and brusqueness. I dealt with two officials in succession. Nice guys, quick to smile and make jokes. But tough and short-sighted. I coaxed and wheedled promises from them, but these got broken. I think they had good will. They ran up against stone walls within City Hall.

As my days in Chernihiv got fewer, I told them I would spring for a graphic artist to create the map and website. Yes, from my own pocket. This sparked interest.

I did this. And by my final days, I got to see a pretty good composite map. But it needed more tinkering. I got a promise that it would get done. Unfortunately, that did not happen.

In my time back in the U.S.A. I have received e-mails from Ira. "It is happening, John," she tells me. This makes me feel good. I am feeling even better now. Ira has sent me a link to a website and I can check for myself.

Our map is up and running on the city's official website! Not perfect. But quite good. It will appear on four other websites. And it will get better. It will help many people. All our effort—mine and hers—paid off.

How did my writing and publishing succeed?

Peace Corps Journals, which had been such a frustration for me for months, became a happy experience again. Amber Smigiel, its editor, e-mailed me one-day that finally its website was running again. Some of my original articles that she had put on ice got edited to become timely again and were published.

And I continued to write others and they got posted for readers. I hope, of course, that my scribblings were helpful and interesting to readers, which was the whole point of Peace Corps Journals.

And I wrote scores of reports—many thousands of words in all—to the folks back home. Through e-mails to them and via two digital newspapers serving my home area.

As I've said, there was no money in this for me. Not a penny. I knew before starting my service the Peace Corps edict: No Volunteer can profit monetarily from his service while in service. So, this writing was just another way for me to be of service.

How about my year as president of SNAC, our seniors' club?

Was I successful? How do I measure this?

First, I must explain one thing. I was really a one-man band. A secretary had been elected with me, but things happened and he never served. So I was the only officer.

But I planned, developed, and produced all three meetings in my one-year term of office. In three different and attractive cities, Kyiv, Ivano-Frankivsk, and Poltava. I was lucky to find a Volunteer in each city to arrange the local logistics.

Our meetings attracted only half of those eligible, I'd say. Each meeting had appealing features in addition to our Saturday morning business meeting to spark interest. Attendees could tack on additional vacation days, which made much sense for Volunteers attending from far points. If what I heard was true, the attendees were delighted—most of them attended all three get-togethers.

Did something practical and helpful result? If you mean, did people have a good time? Yes, definitely.

But I hoped to give SNAC a serious dimension it did not have. For instance, to consider ways to make language instruction better. That was just one of my proposals. It became plain there was no interest. What members wanted was just a nice, inexpensive vacation in an interesting locale along with the opportunity to hang out with fellow Volunteers.

Very desirable things, I agree. But I felt we could have done more. In that we missed the boat.

**Is** there any other way to look back on my successes and failures?

Yes. I felt I was successful in other ways, some immeasurable, unfortunately.

In the city I achieved a reach, an influence beyond my classes at *Coursi* and my clubs at the library.

A lot of people got to know me. The families that I lived with. Neighbors. All the teachers at *Coursi*. So many staffers and regular readers at the library. The clerks in my regular stores and restaurants and cafés. All the regulars at the Philharmonia concerts—and some of the musicians—knew that I was a regular, too.

So many people at the huge central bazaar. The regulars I would encounter at my usual trolley and bus stops. The friends that I developed along the way…friends who had no connection with Peace Corps…the expatriates, for instance. City officials, too.

I was on TV and I was written up in local papers several times. There were pictures of me. So many people got to know I was a Volunteer. And remember, I was the only Volunteer around.

I was conscious of that. I tried every day to live up to that. I think they got a good impression of me, and through me, of Peace Corps, and of the U.S.A.

In Peace Corps itself, everyone—Volunteers and staffers—knew I was the oldest. That gave me a certain repute. I was aware of it, took it seriously, and behaved to be worthy of it. I wanted to show that older folks could be effective Volunteers.

I think that getting through the 27 months successfully and happily was an achievement. As I've mentioned, about a quarter of my group quit and went home. My goal was to finish the whole hitch and I made it.

I came hoping to learn as much as I could about the country and the culture. I took a great interest in this from start to finish. I went out of my way to get broadening experiences, develop contacts, ask questions and learn things and absorb everything I could.

**F**rom the beginning I developed a good relationship with everyone that I came in contact with and for any reason. They included Peace Corps headquarters staff and my various teachers, the Korolonko personnel, my students, my club members, the families I lived with, the expats that I became close to, and the acquaintances that I made in various shops and businesses.

I know one reason. Long ago I read "How to Make Friends and Influence People" by Dale Carnegie. It's the classic it deserves to be.

I don't remember even attracting a bad stare. My single bad experience was the cold night when a drunk bowled me over into the street.

Again, my only relationship problem in all my undertakings was my hard time with my dean at *Coursi*. But that ended happily, as you know.

Another success was maintaining my back-home relationships with family and friends. Not 100 percent true, however. I came knowing that relationships must be nurtured, and I worked at nurturing them. There were some who drifted away. It is hard to avoid, I believe.

All of us progress in life up through various circles of family and friends. The childhood years, the teen-age years, the college and university years, the early adult years, the early married years, the career years, the retirement years, with new circles forming every few years. On and on. There is a normal and understandable attrition. You have to expect it and accept it.

I regret some losses. They were unfortunate. But that's life. I consider my record very satisfactory.

I was successful in something else. And Peace Corps deserves much of the credit. I returned home healthier than when I went over.

When I entered Peace Corps, I was a border-line diabetic. My doctor kept warning me. I was not on insulin, but I was assured I would be. By the end of the first year, this fear was gone. Problem over!

How come? I was more active—walking a lot more, out of plain necessity for one thing. I was eating less. For one thing, using a smaller dinner plate, but only because everybody used smaller plates. And out of long, long habit, I never took seconds.

I have a notorious sweet tooth, but I had this under control for years also. I ate a small piece of candy now and then. I had an ice cream cone only on special days, and Ukraine must have the smallest cones in the world. My first two families always had desserts on the table. Which was bad. Tanya, my third, rarely did. Which was good.

And my long process toward vegetarianism accelerated. In my final six months, I believe I ate meat only twice, and only because I was famished. I felt healthy, and I liked the idea of not killing anything in order to eat it.

A success was keeping in good shape, emotionally and physically. I did not come down with depression or failure pangs. I did my physical exercises every morning and every evening.

I passed my final physical shortly before going home with everything fine and normal. What wonderful news. The belt that held my trousers up told me I was losing weight, but no idea how much. Twenty-five pounds when Dr. Valery led me to a scale. In 27 months. Oh, joy!

I walked even on cold and icy days, not for the pleasure of it but the importance of it, even when physical limitations slowed me. I walked up onto my home-bound plane without breathing hard and carried my luggage out to the curb at the end of the flight. Not bad.

I came to Ukraine to experience, understand, appreciate, and evaluate the Peace Corps experience. I went out of my way to learn from others about their experience. I managed all that. I also came to write a book about it. This project has been a success.

I drove myself to have that draft 95 percent finished by the time I left. That is, finished to the extent possible. Mission accomplished. It was all on a CD in my hand bag. Now, a year later, it exists.

I arrived in Ukraine proud to be a Volunteer and returned home with my pride undiminished. Even magnified. I landed eager to plunge in. I wanted to spread good words about Peace Corps. I was resolved to promote it in any way I could. It is a fine organization, though not perfect. What organization is? Already I have given some talks. I plan more. Contact me if there's a group you'd like me to speak to.

I returned home with something precious. Something impossible to pack in my suitcase. The number of friends I had made in my various centers of effort. The glow of these friendships will last a long time.

Did I do some good? I believe so. I will never know how much or in which way. Deep in my heart I feel I did a good job and touched numerous lives in a positive and encouraging way. I hope I will continue to do so through the pages of this book and my humble efforts here and there to support Peace Corps.

Bottom line: I am glad I did it all. I wish I had done Peace Corps right after college. I'll be proud to wear my Peace Corps pin on the Fourth of July. I hope my obituary will mention my service.

I wish there were a Peace Corps anthem. I would sing it with pride. At the concerts at the Coast Guard Academy, I'd love to stand finally with the others who served our Stars and Stripes.

One more thing. I joined for numerous reasons. They included sentiments of patriotism and altruism. The feelings President Kennedy sparked in me when I was young. They were decisive in my joining.

At times during my service I'd be doing something I would rather be skipping. I would say to myself, *This is why you joined—to help our country, and to do some good.* I knew that I was the only American many Ukrainians got to meet. I kept this in mind—was careful how I behaved.

I returned home feeling good that I had been serious about all this all the way.

~ ~ ~

# 38 / Preparing to go home

*It's a process to join Peace Corps, another to get out. But at the finale, there's fun, too.*

One of the first Peace Corps expressions we learned was "Close of Service." We called it just C.O.S. It's the formal check-out process that Peace Corps would put us through as we reached the end of our 27 months. That expression, C.O.S., came up often in our thoughts and our talk. It is a process!

All Volunteers who completed the full hitch went through it. We heard about it from those who preceded us in Groups 32 and 31. It escalated through several weeks. Serious. Important. But there was fun and fellowship to it also.

C.O.S. débuted several months before our service ended. We began getting e-mails from Headquarters, some long and detailed—all the steps that awaited us and what each would involve.

We were told our official separation date—our last day in Peace Corps. The dates seemed to vary by individual. Mine would be Dec. 19, which was about 12 days ahead of the full 27 months. That was a surprise. A pleasant one. Then we were told that we could leave as much as one month early, without penalty. How wonderful. I double-checked. It was correct. Later I thought, *Maybe it's a budget-stretcher.*

After conferring with my regional manager, I settled on Dec. 1. That would be my final day. That meant that I would serve 26 months instead of the full 27 months. Nobody explained, and I didn't object. I was ready!

Then another e-mail told us that if we wanted to, we could receive cash in lieu of the plane ticket home that was guaranteed to us. This was interesting. I'll explain in a minute.

Another asked us to confirm our address of record. The address that Headquarters had for me was in Deep River, CT. Oops, a problem! I sent in a correction. I said it should be Newport Beach, CA.

This is why. When milady Annabelle and I became a pair (16 years ago), we became bi-coastal for common-sense reasons. She was a Californian. I was a New Englander; Connecticut was my home state now. We had our individual families, of course, and our own sets of friends.

What developed is that come fall, I would move in with her in California. And come spring, she would move in with me in Connecticut. It gave both of us wonderful opportunities to enjoy the best seasons in both places. And to get to know and enjoy one another's friends and home towns and lifestyles. And to continue to live our normal lives in our hometown communities. For instance, I'd continue to vote in my state, and she in hers.

If one of us had packed up everything and moved permanently to the other's home, it would have been hugely disruptive. It would have meant giving up many important things, hometown friends not being the least. Our way worked out ideally.

When I became serious about Peace Corps, I was in California. I interviewed there, went through the whole process right through Nomination and Invitation there. Then it was time for me to return to Deep River. It was from there that I entered Peace Corps. Peace Corps sent me a train ticket to Philadelphia, and after our Staging there, put me and all my fellows on the plane to Ukraine.

Now Peace Corps wanted to send me back to Deep River. But this was the normal time for me to be in California! What did this mean in practical terms? Well, I would be given a ticket to Hartford, CT. There I would have to fly on to Annabelle's on my own.

I wrote all this to Peace Corps and they understood the logic and honesty of it. They said they would send me by plane all the way home to California. Excellent. But then I opted for cash instead. Here's why.

As I have mentioned, Annabelle had been a good sport about my disrupting things and entering Peace Corps. I was grateful. In my first year in Ukraine, I had invited her to come and visit and she had, for a very nice month. Now I had another thought.

I invited her to fly and spend the last days of my service with me. There would be pleasant goings-on at *Coursi*, at my two clubs, at the library, and with my expat friends. I wanted her to enjoy it all with me. I wanted her to have a better understanding of my life as a Volunteer. She thought it wonderful and accepted in a minute.

We made it happen. A problem of timing came up. As mentioned, I decided to "separate" some three weeks early, on Dec. 1. Why? I wanted to take Annabelle to Kyiv for a few days. I had gone often but had never gotten to enjoy it much. It's a beautiful city with many offerings. Foolish not to grasp this opportunity. And we wanted to enjoy time together after a long separation.

The problem: I hated to fly home immediately afterward and arrive smack in the frenzy of the pre-Christmas season. Better to arrive just in time for a calm and enjoyable Christmas with our families. So, after

Kyiv, we took the train to Lviv in western Ukraine and then Budapest in Hungary. A few days in each. Wonderful. Then finally we flew home.

It worked out beautifully. One headache was my luggage at the airport. I still had too much though I had sent much stuff home early. I had to pay hefty overweight charges. *C'est la vie.*

Good news from Peace Corps was a reminder that we had a Readjustment Allowance coming to us. I am sure none of us had forgotten. Peace Corps had been setting aside $225 for us every month. It amounted to close to $6,000.

We could use this any way we chose—to rent an apartment, buy a car, start graduate school, provide support while job-hunting, just to live it up, and so on. We could receive this in several ways. I chose direct deposit to my bank. I received one third on my official date of separation, and the rest a few weeks later.

All through this I became impressed by Peace Corps' thoughtfulness and efficiency. Organizing all this was an enormous undertaking for Headquarters, I am sure, but I found it all smooth and easy. This was probably why the staggered departures.

As the weeks went by, the C.O.S. process continued. In Chapter 4, I told you about the medical exams to enter Peace Corps. At the end of C.O.S., the big exit physical exam. That's when I was shocked to learn of the "worms" found in my gut. A prescription cleared that up. After that, imagine my elation—I was in great shape! (If a bigger problem had come up, I would have been given a voucher for care back home).

Gradually I alerted everyone about my departure plans—many people, at work, in the city, and back home in the U.S.A. In many cases, I received replies of surprise. "John, it's already that time!?" Yes!

I felt this way myself! The big day had come! I remember as every new month had dawned, I would re-set my count…16 months to go, 15, 14, and so on. In fact, I even kept a record in my daily journal of the days, as you know.

Here is one example: Tuesday, Feb. 10, 2009 (Day 41 / 492). This meant that it was the $41^{st}$ day of the year and day 492 of my service. Officially my service had been for 823 days. Now, suddenly the days were flying by. I was racing to get everything done. Amazing!

**I** began scrambling to finish my big projects. First, my library digitalization project. Then my public transit handbook. I began thinking of someone to succeed me as the leader of my two clubs. Highly unlikely that I would find someone to take over my French Club.

But I found an excellent candidate for my English Club: Wayne Purves, my expat friend from Sacramento, CA, and a former Volunteer himself. You have read a lot about him. He got excited about taking the reins! Lucky me. I couldn't think of anyone for my French Club. Sad.

And I tried to squeeze in more travel. I wanted to see as much of Ukraine as I could. I had vacation days left. As you know, I rushed off to tour some key sites in the country. Hectic but wonderful.

I began trying to remember those that I had arrived in Kyiv with—my fellows in Group 33. We had gotten to meet at Staging in Philadelphia and most of us had parted just a few days later to begin Training. We got together again only for Swearing In, which was frantic.

Here's where we gathered from around the country for our going-home retreat, Peace Corps wanted to brief us well. And.we had fun.

Now I had gone nearly two years without seeing most of them. I had gotten to see their names on batch e-mails from Headquarters. That's all. Nevertheless, it was amazing how I felt bonded to them.

Our C.O.S. retreat took place at a resort hotel in Slavske. Slavske is a well-known village tucked in the mountains in the western corner of Ukraine. Headquarters liked it. It was small, attractive, and beautifully sited for skiing. And it had many amenities. We took advantage of them. Except the skiing. Too early for heavy snow. Which made it cheaper for Peace Corps, I suppose. That was smart. Besides, no time.

We all arrived for dinner at 6:30 p.m. on Tuesday. Check-out would be after breakfast Friday. We were put up in twin-bed rooms with private bathroom.

A big picture window looked out on the mountain slopes across the valley. I could see several ski slopes. Bleak and forlorn right now, unfortunately

The village spread out in the hollow between our lodge and the slopes. We all went to the village for a few minutes when possible. Picturesque. Touristy.

I was rooming with Brian Woods, early 30's. He was organizing his things. We shook hands. I remembered him only by sight. I stretched out on the bed as he puttered.

"Hey, Brian, look!" I said, and pointed to the ceiling. A great big mirror up there. "What is that for?" He grinned, "Ah, come on, John!" Enough said.

Brian was a fine roommate. He had graduated from the University of Southern Mississippi with a degree in radio and TV production and had worked as a TV news cameraman in several cities. In fact, he had worked his way across the country twice.

He had also tried the entertainment business in Los Angeles. Not many details; we were so busy. He was friendly and considerate with a sunny disposition.

Dinner turned out generous. A lavish buffet. We few vegetarians received a separate entrée. I liked all the meals. No shortage of anything.

I managed to get a count of us. On Oct. 1, 2007, 86 of us arrived in Ukraine. There were 8 of us in the Fifty-Plus category. Now we were only 56. So 30 had gone home, for a variety of reasons.

I asked around. It seemed only one had been sent home, Tedford, (not his real name), in his early 20's, for public drunkenness, it was said. There were only three of us still around from our original group of eight in our Fifty Plus category. The five who had left had done so early. At times I wondered if they had regrets.

Our Peace Corps bosses told us our Group 33 was a fine group. But maybe they said that about every group. Well, I know we were a fine group. Of course!

Quite an attrition, in my opinion. Not unusual, I was told. But consider all the expense involved in these early departures. Any private enterprise would be devastated with a grim statistic like that over just 27 months. It must be a concern in Washington.

*I'm with Ruth Alexander. We held the records in our Group 33. She was the youngest and I the oldest.*

I gathered other interesting facts. I knew we had more women than men. But we were so lop-sided: 40 women and 16 men! How to explain it? Are women more idealistic? More adventurous? Tell me.

And our group was so young! Take a look: 31 were under age 25 (the youngest had just turned 23); 17 were 26 to 30; 5 were 31 to 39; there was nobody 40 to 49; then we three oldies were the only survivors in Fifty Plus.

My two colleagues in Fifty Plus were years younger than I. Berta was a lawyer from San Francisco, and Nancy had been a teacher of

French for a while, then had operated a restaurant in Vermont for many years. Excellent Volunteers. A pleasure to know them.

Of course, I felt isolated by my age in this crowd of youngsters. Who wouldn't be? I joked that I was Group 33's "*dedushka!*" "Grandpa!"

Everybody at C.O.S. was exceedingly nice to me. They would leap to help me with my luggage or open a door. They insisted that I sit in the front row for our group photograph. They cheered me wildly when my name came up during the awards night on the final evening (everybody got an award). Time and again I said to them, "I wish I were the youngest rather than the oldest." True. It was fun to speculate how that might have changed my life.

I did get to meet the youngest in our group, Ruth Alexander of California. A pleasant, attractive, self-assured young woman. She sailed through Peace Corps with flying colors. I made it a point to learn as much as I could about her.

She told me, "I was 20 when I arrived in Ukraine and 23 when we came home. Everybody in our group was a college grad, remember? It happened because I got through college in three years. I went to UC Berkeley and majored in psychology.

"I became a teacher in a high school in Kharkiv. It's a small town. It was great."

I asked her, "What did folks in Ukraine think when they saw how young you were?"

"I don't think my age was a big deal, but some of my older colleagues thought that I was inexperienced and incapable of dealing with hard tasks or big responsibility. I was babied, kind of needed to be."

"Do you feel that your youth a problem in any way?"

"Not as much as I thought it would. I thought my students wouldn't respect me once they found out that I wasn't much older than they were. But not a big problem. Most of the other teachers of English—all Ukrainians, of course—were young too, although I was the youngest.

"The only issue I sometimes faced was gaining respect among the other teachers. I didn't want to speak back, or assert my position strongly against someone with 10-plus years more experience."

"Did you have a problem making friends?"

"Luckily I had an amazing site mate also from Group 33. I can't imagine what my service would have been like without a close friend at my site. I also made friends with the other English teachers and my neighbors.

"They were a huge support to me. I think becoming a friend is one of the most important things a Volunteer can do."

"Did you live with a family, or by yourself?"

"I lived with a host family my first month at site and then moved into an apartment, which I stayed at from then on."

"As a Californian, how did you get through the cold and the ice and the snow?"

"Not well. I had no idea how to walk in snow, and did not bring proper boots with me so I had to wear Yak Traks everywhere (boot slip-overs with steel grips in the soles). That first winter was long and hard. I remember being colder than I thought was possible and not seeing a ray of sun for days.

"If I hadn't kept myself very busy I would have been really depressed. Spring finally returned and on sunny days I would skip and sing down the street. People probably thought I was crazy, but I was very happy after being vitamin D-deprived for so long.

"The next winter was much better. I didn't fall once, had great boots, and knew what to expect."

"**W**hat's the best thing that happened to you over there?"

"I don't know if I can say that there was one best thing, I had many wonderful experiences and became friends with some truly inspirational people. I learned a lot, which is probably the best thing that happened. I learned mostly about myself and my confidence and independence and acceptance. Testing how far I was really willing to go.

"Also pulling off successful events like camps, seminars, and theater performances were highlights. Creating a new home for myself!"

"Very impressive, Ruth. What's the worst that happened?"

"Winter. And drunk men."

"Were there any Peace Corps regulations that you didn't like? Anything at all that you didn't like about Peace Corps?"

"Not that I can remember. As I look back, everything seems beautiful and shiny."

"So, what was the best thing about Peace Corps for you?"

"The life experience. And the cross-cultural experience. So valuable. I had thought of volunteering overseas for some time. You know, before being tied down with a career and a family of my own.

"I checked out a number of opportunities and settled on Peace Corps. Very happy about that."

"So, what's next?"

"Well, right now I'm back in California. Living with my parents for now. I volunteer as a reading specialist for foster kids, and am taking classes. I am planning on going to graduate school next year. I want to be a psychiatric nurse practitioner."

"Is this your career path?"

"Yes, definitely."

"Is this what you were thinking before Peace Corps?"
"Pretty much. I knew I was going to be some sort of therapist."
"Would you do Peace Corps again?"
"Maybe after I retire, but not anytime soon. I would recommend it to others who are very patient and motivated. Who are looking for adventure and would like to make a real impact on a small town far away."
"What's your special advice for young people thinking of joining?"
"Although nothing will prepare you, try to get experience in the field that you are interested in. Talk to Returned Volunteers before joining, and learn as much about the country and language as you can.
"Think about how long 27 months really is and see if you actually want to commit that amount of time to people and a place you have never been to.
"Oops, scratch that. I'm just going to say, 'Do it!' Peace Corps is an amazing life-changing experience. Guaranteed!"

Yes, C.O.S. was a combination of business and fun. It was very serious business. Well organized. There must have been eight staff people there from Headquarters, led by our country director, Diana.

The remarkable thing was that this was the first time many of us were together since Swearing In! We had dispersed all over the country. I was startled by how young they were. The great majority of them could have been my grandchildren. In fact, there were only three of us who were Fifty Plus Volunteers. Two years back, we had been eight!

We had eight long group sessions together, two each morning and two each afternoon. One or several staff persons conducted each meeting.

We reviewed our Peace Corps experience and provided feedback. We were given instructions on our final steps, including closing our various projects, bank accounts, and the mandatory Description of Service that each of us had to write. This was our own assessment of what we had done and how well it had turned out.

We had to return our Peace Corps passports we had been on. We had to do this and that. Much detail. Deadlines.

Dr. Oleksander Gupta was on hand to explain the final C.O.S. physical each of us would go through and the medical benefits that we would go home with. One important item was the option we had of purchasing a recommended interim medical and hospital insurance policy called Corps Care, with the first month free.

Not important for me. I had Medicare. I also had a Blue Cross-Blue Shield Medex policy. I had canceled it on the eve of entering Peace Corps, but I had a guarantee that I could renew it without question or surcharge. I intended to do this.

Dr. Oleksander gave me a TB shot and asked for two stool samples for a parasite check—the "worms" I told you about. All of us had to take this test. He came with a suitcase full of medications. I had a bad cold. He immediately handed me a couple of medications.

He was there throughout our retreat. He paid attention to everybody. Oh, upon arriving, he left a box of condoms in our assembly room. For one thing, AIDS was a concern. And he never wanted to hear of an "accident."

We sat through a long session on the challenges of re-entering our life back home. We were warned about the perils of readjustments and reverse culture shock. And given specific tips.

We were told the federal benefits we were entitled to. We were assured that Peace Corps had a department that could help us with a variety of challenges, including starting graduate studies or finding a career job.

If some wanted to work in the federal government at some levels, they would have bonus points added to the score of the competitive exam they would be required to pass get in. All very encouraging. There was even more—good information about scholarships and fellowships. Not much of this pertained to me, of course. For the younger people, it was all terrific.

**We** were also told about the National Peace Corps Association, based in Washington, D.C. It is a private group made up of Returned Volunteers and Peace Corps workers and former workers. It publishes a magazine, advocates for Peace Corps, and has some 130 sub-groups, by state or country of service or interest. Our first year of membership would be free. I planned to join.

The fun came in the breaks between meetings and in the evenings.

I made it a point to sit with various groups at meals. My young colleagues were a joyful and fun lot. From beginning to end I was struck by their serious motives, high spirits, and obvious talents.

*We were kept busy...discussions, forms, meetings. And we had a good time. But we were aware that soon we'd be going our own ways.*

During one session I felt moved to speak up and did so.

"I wish that our fellow Americans back home could sit in with us and see you young people for themselves. How talented and high-intentioned you are. What fine Volunteers you have been. I am so proud to be in this room with you." I got applause.

The second day was sunny. A nice change. There were all kinds of small groups catching up on the two years that had passed.

*Eunice was my friend from start to finish—still is. What a gal. She's out of Peace Corps now, but off on another adventure.*

Threesomes and foursomes went out for walks. Some to the village. One group strolled to the back yard. I was with them. There were four sheep in a pen. We had bread from the dinner table in our hands. They spotted it and came running and ate it from our fingertips. Fun.

**O**ur final evening was fantastic. Our farewell dinner. Then we gathered upstairs in a handsome vaulted room. We were excited. Laughing. Joking. Some Volunteers had planned a farewell party for our whole group, and they got it going quickly.

Our emcee was one of our young Volunteers, Michael Seifert. Extroverted. Jovial. He was wonderful in the job...spontaneous and funny and at times pointedly serious.

I remembered him from Staging. Now I got to see a new Michael.

He was the buddy of Matthew Mozingo. Matt was the tall, quiet, serious

*Many friends to catch up with. Good to see Michael (left) and Matt again. They were planning to stay in Ukraine!*

young fellow who had looked out so carefully for me on our trip from Philadelphia to Kyiv, and was doing the same again here. He and Michael had gone through service as close buddies.

I mentioned a new Michael. It turned out that he had discovered God. Yes, and he spoke about that with great conviction. I found it impressive. And so had Matthew, it turned out, although he didn't talk about it as much.

And both were staying on in Ukraine. They had been engaged in youth work. They had gotten the idea of building an orphanage. I was dumbfounded when I heard that.

"It's going to be tough," Matt told me. "But we're going to tackle it." My! How ambitious. I felt it would happen. I wished them luck. We all did. As I thought about this, I looked around. I felt that all these young people were winners.

I was interested in everybody. But I must mention two more. One was Eunice Bonaparte. In her 30's, I think. A sweet gal, so talented. Had lived in California and New York City and other places. Had taught school back home. We became friends way back in Staging when we sat at the same discussion table.

She visited my Chernihiv quite often and looked me up whenever possible. Always upbeat. She did so well in learning Russian and seemed so successful in her service. She had numerous friends, including Ukrainians.

She loved adventure. Will do well in life. I'll be hearing more about her. I knew Peace Corps minorities had a tough time in Ukraine. But she never gave me any inkling of that. I did worry about her.

Here we are, the final trio in our "Oldies" group. And having a good time at our last get-together. Nancy (left) and Berta.

Another was Richard Lechtenberg, from southern California. Early 20's. Good-natured. Self-confident. He entered directly after university. Had both American and Brazilian citizenship, which interested me—I had been to Brazil.

He served as a high school teacher in Peace Corps. I got to meet him late in the game. I admired that he had gotten a bicycle to get around his little town. It was so practical, though it was something Peace Corps frowned on because of safety concerns.

I got to spend quality time with him during my travels late in our service. Shared some train rides with him—he, too, was always on the look-out to help me. I enjoyed his company. He has a promising future.

I took a liking to all my fellow Volunteers. A fine bunch, for sure.

And it was a pleasure to get together with the staffers from Headquarters. An impressive group. I knew several well. I considered them good friends. They were smiling and friendly and convivial. They were celebrating our success with us.

At the end, awards! Everybody got one even if it sometimes did not make much sense, well, to me. All funny. Many insightful. Pointed. Loud applause. Laughter. I'd like to tell you what mine was for. I've misplaced it. Don't remember. Sorry.

I was not knowledgeable but I knew some genuinely deserved a special award and I was glad to see them receive one. I noticed one who was omitted somehow. Nothing deliberate, I'm sure. Jessica Benes. A young gal. She had been the unpaid editor of *Nu Shcho*, the journal produced by Volunteers. It was a lot of work and a real responsibility.

Richard. was another who kept an eagle eye out for me. A fine lad.

Jessica had done a fine job. I was one of its contributors, so I knew. I got everybody's attention and nominated her for an impromptu award. Many hands clapped. Unanimous approval.

She came and said to me, "That was nice of you, John. Thank you!"

I was pleased to do it.

**O**ur Peace Corps officials were not overlooked. Some in our group had passed around sheets. Each one bore the name of a Peace Corps official who had worked for us. We were urged to write words of thanks and encouragement and sign our names. Some comments were emotional, some funny. We all scrambled to scribble, of course. These were awarded to each person in public. High moments! Wonderful.

Our top boss, Diana, had received a sheet with words of thanks and praise from many of us. She was highly admired and respected. She got up and began to speak.

Surprise! She broke down and began to weep. I was astonished. I think we all were.

She said, "I feel very emotional like this every time a new group arrives. And every time one goes home. Like right now." She dabbed at her eyes. "The truth is that it has been so good to have you here to work with us. The spirit of Peace Corps shines in you. You are the best of America."

She got terrific applause. As you know, she herself had been a Volunteer, along with her husband Hugo

"Peace Corps has been my life for quite a while now," she told me later. "It's been wonderful. Before, it was mostly about sales and marketing."

Thus did our C.O.S. retreat end. This was the last time that I saw my fellow Volunteers in Group 33 with one or two exceptions. It was a difficult leave-taking.

But our service was not over. We had several weeks of service to go, in my case five. And the final three days would be in Kyiv at Headquarters. For the last-minute obligatory steps, including an HIV/AIDS test at the very end.

Well, I got through it all—but this is not news to you at this point in the book. I'll never forget those terrible fearful days of mine during Training. In the same breath, let me say that I have wonderful memories beyond number that will always shine in my memory.

December 1, 2009, was my last day as a Volunteer. The next morning I was on my way to Kyiv for a few days of R & R, Annabelle at my side.

What fine days they turned out to be. For one thing, the weatherman cooperated. The days were short in daylight and terribly gray (as expected), but no rain, no snow, no ice, no cutting wind.

We put up at the two-star St. Petersburg Hotel. It's an oldie, rooms big enough to dance in. Comfortable beds, immaculate linens, a big sink in a corner, and the toilet and shower room down the hall. Immaculate. I didn't mind this a bit and Annabelle again was a good sport.

The St. Pete was increasingly favored by Volunteers. Its rooms were easy on our budgets. It was superbly located for what interested us!

We arrived mid-morning on Thursday and left late to return to Chernihiv late on Sunday afternoon. We visited Headquarters for a final goodbye. Took in the famous Kyiv circus (its own majestic building; no canvas big top!).

We enjoyed a marvelous concert of the National Philharmonic Orchestra in its splendidly ornate hall. Spent an afternoon strolling Khreshchatik, the city's own Champs Elysées, so to speak.

Attended Bizet's "Carmen" at the Opera—I'm not an opera buff but I found it interesting and the opera house was gorgeous. At the National Art Museum we saw countless paintings, major and minor. Some amazing. Enjoyed cozy restaurants. Walked and gawked! Had the good time we had hoped for.

*Happy faces! Our Group 33 in our Farewell Photo. I'm at the left in the second row. You can see how we Oldies were outnumbered!*

On Sunday we enjoyed a leisurely breakfast at the hotel with fellow Volunteer Ed Novick from Phoenix, Arizona. He was a senior also, and a widower. A good friend. He was a C.P.A. and also had an M.B.A.. He had been an executive with American Express.

We had met when he attended my English Club while in Training. Came often. In fact, was our speaker one Sunday. We hit it off, met often until he got assigned to a distant small town as a community developer. In fact, at his invitation I spent a weekend with him at his site. It was clear he was doing a fine job.

When he heard we would be in Kyiv, he made it a point to rendezvous with us. Annabelle took a liking to him, too. He still had many months to go. He wished us good luck, and I returned the wish with pleasure.

*Preparing to go home, mission done. I was so glad Annabelle had come to Ukraine again and was with me.*

I had been impressed by Kyiv since my first visit. Beautiful, with many parks, many trees, and most remarkable of all, an amazing abundance and variety of architecture. How frustrating it must be to visit there without a camera.

I call Kyiv an open-air architectural museum. There seemed always a building in sight to stare at and study—one 150 years old replete with rococo, or another just built with minimalist modernity.

I can sum up my feelings about Kyiv easily. A first-class city in a less than first-class country. But Ukraine is catching up. Truth is, the country has innumerable pleasures, charms, and delights for tourists. They need more publicity. As for Kyiv, it should be on anyone's should-see list.

And so, it was time to depart Ukraine. I had arrived as a stranger. But now I felt comfortable. At ease, so to speak. But I was excited. Eager to get back to my native land.

But I felt a sadness. I would miss many things and many people. Was sure of it. Already had a notion that I would like to return for a visit. And knew that I would try to keep in touch with my new friends in the meanwhile.

I am in Deep River, Connecticut, as I write these words. This is home. Things are so different here, and so much better in so many ways. Home is where the heart is. It's true. But my heart is in Chernihiv, too.

*We rested in Kyiv. Such a fascinating city. Look at that ancient church behind Annabelle!. It was chilly. No problem.*

Quite often I find myself looking back and marveling at the whole Peace Corps experience. I've had a rich life. Fascinating variety. Adventures big and small beyond my imagining. But I must tell you one thing. My Peace Corps service in Ukraine were a brilliant highlight.

Ukraine was a country that I would never have thought to visit. Now I tell people to go there for a vacation! How about that?

~ ~ ~

***Did you know*** ... that Peace Corps enlists more women than men. This was a surprise for me. Also, I knew that most Volunteers were in their 20's, but their high number also surprised me.

I knew that the recruits of retirement age would be few, but they turned out to be even fewer than I expected. Older Volunteers were sent to just some 10 countries—those with medical services capable of serving their needs.

# 39 / Life after Peace Corps

*Peace Corps can be such a life-enlarging experience—how good to have tried it.*

Your life post-Peace Corps will be largely up to you, of course. Hopefully your future will turn out to be as successful and satisfying as you're dreaming and hoping.

But as we know, luck plays a big role in anyone's future. Success is not only a matter of talent and skills and experience. It's also a matter of luck. Essential it is to keep in mind—you may have discovered this by now—that often we make our own luck, good and bad.

There can be genuine good luck, of course. Good luck smacking us right out of the blue. Such as getting a letter that we have received a bequest of $1 million from Uncle Harry, who disappeared long ago. But that's accidental good luck—also known as sheer good luck.

But here I am speaking of good luck of our own making! We assure our own good luck of this kind by preparing well and making smart moves and decisions—and Peace Corps can certainly be a very smart move. We assure this good luck by working hard and pleasing our boss and using our talents and initiative and developing good habits and values and taking sensible risks. On and on.

And bad luck also can be accidental. We're all familiar with this. Being hit by lightning! Or losing our house to a tornado! But again we can create our bad luck. By coasting through our education. Turning down opportunities to learn new skills and meet helpful people. Taking up with the wrong crowd. Doing something dishonest. Taking up drugs. Blowing our credit rating. Being lazy—so common. On and on. In one sentence, we invite bad luck my doing bad things and making stupid decisions.

With all this said, I believe that we open ourselves to good luck for years to come by joining Peace Corps. The younger the better, but it's never too late. This is an important message that you get when you research the advantages of a Peace Corps hitch.

I was having coffee with my friend Raymond. About 33. An assistant professor at a state university. A former Volunteer.

I said to him, "Ray, do you really believe that Peace Corps service means as much for future career opportunities as Peace Corps says it does in its promotional materials?"

"Yes, I do. For one thing, on a résumé I believe Peace Corps experience is worth as much as a master's degree. Maybe more."

"That's impressive, Ray. But hard to measure, isn't it? Why do you say that?"

"Hard to measure—that's true. But it's my gut feeling from what I've experienced. From what I've gotten to see. From talking to other Volunteers.

"Think about it. Most people who review applicants for whatever reason know what Peace Corps is all about. Learned about it from TV. They've seen movies. Read books and newspaper stories. Peace Corps service has become enshrined in our culture.

"They are familiar with the Peace Corps scenario. Being sent off to a strange country for more than two years. Having to live with a native family for a while. Committing yourself to whatever you're assigned to do.

"Then the personal difficulties. The ones every Volunteer bumps up against. Arriving in an unknown, unchosen country. The intense training. The language and cultural immersion. Carrying on, often all alone, with no other Volunteers around. The break-even income.

"Being expected to find other outlets for service on your own. Hardship in some cases. Loneliness. Homesickness. Frustration. All too some degree or other. It's an awesome challenge.

"That's one side. The hard side. But then there's the bright side. Your Peace Corps service says so much about you. The practical, worldly experience you've acquired, and the self-confidence. The many new contacts and connections you've made. The spirit of adventure that is needed to make it. Plus the initiative. The adaptiveness. The determination. The perseverance. Your sense of responsibility. Hey, it reflects courage. Idealism. Patriotism. Altruism.

"Over the years Americans have picked that up. They have a high opinion of Volunteers. They attach prestige to having been a Volunteer. I'm not imagining all this. Look at how Volunteers are depicted in news stories and novels and movies. Numerous opinion polls have shown that Americans are impressed by Peace Corps. They have respect for it. I have felt all this myself.

"Who has ever heard of a Peace Corps scandal?

"So, if somebody comes into your office looking for a job after Peace Corps service, wouldn't you give that person extra consideration? I'm sure you would."

It's impressive how he went on and on, don't you think? Well, he didn't say all that. He said some of it. Some of the comments were made to me by other Peace Corps alumni. Some were things that I found out myself. Some I've picked up in my reading.

What I've done is assemble them. For a simple reason: it is a good way to make the case that Peace Corps service is time well spent. A fine investment. It can have an enormous pay-back, immediately and long-term throughout a person's career.

Peace Corps service can be a powerful head start for anybody in taking the next step after service. In getting a job. Or starting a graduate program. Going into business. Changing career. This is true for a young person who enters Peace Corps right after school. True also for somebody part way through the working years.

It can provide an important change of view and change of pace. Can lead to wider opportunities, better jobs, higher pay, and greater prestige.

But how about for a retiree? Well, the pay-back is more abstract. Now it's not so much about opportunities and dollars and cents. It's more about how your family and friends and neighbors look at you. They have a higher respect. Greater admiration. Plus something else that is part of the pay-back: your own heightened self-esteem. Your satisfaction with yourself. Your pride.

After Peace Corps, you have a choice. What to make of your Peace Corps experience? You may store it away in your memory and leave it there, locked in a trunk and increasingly forgotten. Or you may use it as a firm stepping stone to your fresh start in life.

By deciding on the first or the second of these, you are choosing different roads to the future. In my opinion, deciding to use your Peace Corps service as a stepping stone is the way to go. To put it another way, it can be a terrific front door to what you envisage as your career, you hope. How smart.

This choice is up to you. You decide how to spend your money, don't you? Well, it's up to you how you will use this valuable new capital.

Why is Peace Corps service such a good asset? Gosh! Because you are now stronger, more experienced, more mature, and more deserving. Probably possess a firm idea of what you want to be and do. How good this would be! So many people float through life rudder-less.

Certainly Volunteers have an enlightened social consciousness and a broader national and even international outlook. And a better understanding of people of other nationalities and cultures. And sympathy for them.

We Americans live in such a big and mighty country that often we look down on and even unthinkingly disparage people in other countries, especially undeveloped ones. It's just another example of unfair discrimination.

My experience is that intelligence and talents and personal qualities have been uniformly distributed to people around the world. My time in Ukraine only re-enforced this opinion.

To my mind, Peace Corps experience is beneficial in many ways. Often un-anticipated ways! And the younger you are, the better it is.

It is hard for me to believe that Peace Corps experience might do you harm, unless it exposed you to bad situations that you succumbed to. Such as my young Volunteer colleague who got drunk in public in his first couple of weeks in Ukraine, got warned by Peace Corps not to do it again, and repeated the same stupidity. As I mentioned, he had to "resign."

He was a dramatic example of someone who was making his own bad luck. Let's hope he has learned from that.

It's common for Volunteers to go on to success in various fields, often in public service in a government department or elective public office. Or in teaching at all levels. Or in commerce and industry. Or journalism. And other fields. It is expected that a returned Volunteer will succeed. The surprise comes when he or she does not.

More than once over there, I thought, *I wish I could buy stock in Albert! And Maria. And Dorothy! And Jack!* And other Volunteers that I got to know. That's how confident I was about these people to whom I've given these fictitious names, and about many others.

It is pleasing to see how people in the news—people making good news, not bad—often have Peace Corps service listed as part of their background.

A good question is: did they reach their impressive level at least in part because of their Peace Corps service? Or would they have reached it anyway because of their talents and drive? It's common sense to believe that Peace Corps helped tilt the scale the right way for them.

Peace Corps is valuable even for older Volunteers. That's been my own personal experience—I who turned 80 while in service. It became a broadening experience. Made me feel better about myself.

And talk about opening opportunities? I am giving public talks about Peace Corps. And you are reading this book that I wrote as a direct result. Sometimes I think, *"How sad if I had turned down this opportunity!"*

One thing is sure. Smart people will recognize you for having done a brave and noble thing, although perhaps you did it for a combination of altruistic and mundane reasons. I suspect all of us do.

Your enhanced reputation will bless you for the rest of your career, whatever it becomes, and the rest of your life. Your service will be a highlight in your obituary, I'll bet. That's something to think about.

As a returned Volunteer, you will be part of an elite fraternity for sure. Be proud that you responded because you heard of President Kennedy's call. Or pleased that you read a Peace Corps brochure or heard about the opportunity by chance. Make the most of what you did in serving abroad. Enjoy the perks. Wear your Peace Corps pin on special occasions, at least. Good luck!

And inspire others to follow in your tracks.

~ ~ ~

*Did you know* ,,,, that it's just about guaranteed that you will have to undertake to learn a new language. I say "just about" because there may be a country or two where English is the language of the land. Your new language may be important or unimportant in your later career.

Studying Mandarin or Russian can be enormously valuable later. Studying a minor language in an African country may turn out to be valuable also, but it may turn out to be worth not a dime. It all depends.

There's luck in what language becomes your challenge.

# 40 / So, what do I think now?

*It's natural that I've formed strong opinions.*
*I like Peace Corps. But it needs changes.*

I won't waste any time or mince my words. I think Peace Corps is a fine outfit. I am going to say it all again. I am glad I became a Volunteer. Glad that I served in Ukraine. Glad that I got the assignment that I did although I would have preferred one tied in with my profession of journalism or proficiency in French.

As I said on the previous page, I am proud to have been a Volunteer. I will wear my Peace Corps pin without fail on the Fourth of July and whenever I speak publicly about it, which I expect to be doing. I'll be happy to recommend Peace Corps to anyone who seems a prospect.

I say all these positive things before I go on with my next comments. Because I do have criticisms and recommendations. I would be delighted to see some improvements.

First, let me talk about Peace Corps in general. I was chatting with a Peace Corps official one day. He said something that stuck with me.

"At your level—for you as a Volunteer—Peace Corps is exciting. It's fun. But at my level as an administrator, it's just another government bureaucracy."

I got to understand what he meant when he called it a bureaucracy. The word invokes thoughts of bosses and workers, friction, timetables, assignments, committees, deadlines, reviews, paperwork, boredom, competition, frustration, struggle.

What he was saying was, "It is not fun. It is not exciting. It is a good job. We're working in an agency with high-minded goals. But a job."

I understood that. It's unfortunate, but most jobs are like that. I believe that most people in the world would call in sick tomorrow if they could get away with it.

For me Peace Corps was fun, yes, but not all the time. It was work most of the time, and most often it was pleasant work. It was exciting once in a while. But I had problems and worries. I was working in a poor and struggling country and some things were hard. And people are people, meaning they are imperfect. But definitely it was an adventure.

Yes, it was. To me an adventure is a stimulating, challenging undertaking that shows promise of success, but can fail. The possibility of risk is essential for something to be an adventure. As you know, I nearly failed in Training. I struggled to get digitalization started at the Korolonko, and the public transit website up and going, and both became a fact, though I wondered and worried about that, So, yes, an adventure!

I've never been in Peace Corps' headquarters in Washington or even seen a picture of it. But I know it has its own impressive building with its own staff of more than 1,000 administrators and employees (the Paul D. Coverdell Peace Corps Headquarters, 1111 20$^{th}$ St., Washington, DC 20526). It takes that many people to direct 8,000 Volunteers working around the world. No doubt it's a bureaucracy.

I've mentioned more than once that just in Ukraine, it took a headquarters staff of 75 full-timers in Kyiv, plus numerous part-timers spotted here and there in the country, to manage our group of about 300.

Yet, Peace Corps is still a small outfit in any list of federal departments and programs—even with a corps of some 8,000 and an annual budget of some $400 million.

In my few dealings with the Washington office from afar, I did find beyond doubt it is definitely an impersonal machine—one which after nearly 50 years of existence has developed its own set way of doing things and its own culture.

I have given you instances in which I approached it with suggestions, and the total lack of response that I got.

I discovered bitterly that it can be aloof and indifferent to Volunteers in the field. In fact, I feel that's how Headquarters in Washington treated me. And more than once. More about this shortly.

**W**hat's interesting is that I found out Peace Corps has a policy said to be unique in our federal government. I was surprised to hear about it. All appointed persons are supposed to serve for just five years at the most.

I am speaking of those hired for leadership positions for a specific length of time, as opposed to those hired for ordinary jobs that can go on and on as long as they do the work competently. It's the "Five and out!" policy which I have previously mentioned.

This applies to the top levels of the hierarchy in Washington and to the country directors and assistant directors who head the more than 70 national staffs around the word. Yet there could be exceptions, I found out. As my Group 33 was leaving, our country director Diana Schmidt got an extension of a couple of years.

This rare policy was instituted at the very beginning. The idea was to have continuing fresh blood and not to be burdened with leaders who would continue in their well-entrenched ways long after they might have exhausted their ideas and energy.

But if this is such a good idea, why don't other federal departments and programs adopt it!? What makes Peace Corps so special? Or, does this policy hurt Peace Corps more than it helps it?

Doesn't it seem wrong to automatically furlough somebody just when he or she is really building up steam and accomplishing things? Don't you think that such a person during his or her final months would be preoccupied with finding another job? Isn't that awfully costly and sad for Peace Corps?

One other thing. Most federal departments—there are exceptions—are led by political appointees. The incoming President appoints them when he takes office. In reality the process can take place over several months. Many require congressional approval. Not a big problem in many cases.

Those already in those jobs—appointed by a previous president—know their days are numbered. They will be quickly replaced by the new President. Some of our national directors served only two or three years. True also of numerous other political appointees in Peace Corps.

The President of course chooses people he feels can do the job. It's inconceivable that he would choose a jerk. He makes such an appointment often as a thank you to someone who has served him well, either during one or another of his election campaigns on his way up or during some phase of his life as a governor or senator or whatever.

Or as a thank you to a heavy financial supporter. Or as a favor to someone with enough clout to request such an appointment for some friend or relative. It is called favoritism. It is also called a pay-back.

There is justification for this way of doing things. The President is our Number 1 executive. He wants to make sure that he will have someone running the many departments that he is responsible for who will do it his way and in accordance with his line of thought. If we happen to have voted for that President, of course we approve of that. We want him to follow through on his campaign ideas and promises.

But there is criticism of the number of political appointees Peace Corps has—a far higher percentage than most other federal departments and agencies have, including much larger ones.

I've heard that it has the most political appointees of all—more than 30. Some have not been Volunteers. There are questions about how much these appointees know about Peace Corps when they first show up for work.

How can outsiders walk into the headquarters cold and take over? They need a lot of background knowledge. So how do they manage?

They have a chief of staff or counterpart who presumably knows the ropes and is familiar with the problems and the possible solutions. And they have the benefit of an ongoing core of administrators. But remember, only for the balance of the five years these people still have.

Who knows? Maybe these top subordinates are the ones who set the agenda and the pace, who explain the problems and the priorities, and who may provide the convincing opinions about how the Corps should forge ahead. Of course, newly appointed directors must have a full head of steam of their own. Presumably they do.

Setting this pattern was Sargent Shriver, the first director. Truly he was the creator of Peace Corps—and of other significant federal programs (the Office of Economic Opportunity…"the war on poverty," Vista, Head Start, the Job Corps, and others). In 1994 President Clinton awarded him the Presidential Medal of Freedom, our highest honor for a civilian.

The national director when I was sworn in was Ronald T. Tschetter, the 17th in the position. He was a former Volunteer who had become a prominent leader in the investments business.

During that career he remained deeply interested in Peace Corps and rose to eminence in the National Peace Corps Association, becoming board chairman. He was a pronounced Republican and was appointed by President George W. Bush, a Republican, of course.

The director who was appointed just as I had my Close of Service in sight was Aaron Williams, also a former Volunteer (the Dominican Republic, 1967-1970).

He was the fourth Volunteer to be named to the top post. He was appointed by freshly elected President Obama. Williams is a Democrat, of course. He is also a black man.

He said in an interview with TV host Tavis Smiley that while growing up on the south side of Chicago, he wanted to see life beyond the borders of his city and thus joined Peace Corps. In his assignment to the Dominion Republic, he worked in a rural program to improve local teaching. He met his wife there.

He served for many years in USAID. He had been cleared for an ambassadorship when this nomination came up. The President does not have the total say in these appointments. As mentioned, they must be approved by the Senate. It's uncommon that one is voted down.

I like the idea of having a former Volunteer chosen for the top job. It makes sense. It's good to realize that our top leader has gone through the experience and has learned about Peace Corps from the ground up.

It's also good to see someone chosen who has risen through the ranks of government service with success and distinction. He received high honors, so this seems to have been the case for Williams.

I say this because we know that the President appoints numerous people to high positions—ambassadors, for instance—who know so little about the country they are being recommended for that they have to look it up in an atlas! Some Peace Corps directors have been appointed with just an ounce or two of knowledge about it. Not true for Williams.

In his first speech Williams said that one of his priorities would be to bring "Peace Corps back to America." He also mentioned change. There was a strong likelihood of change.

President Obama had spoken of change in Peace Corps more than once on the presidential campaign trail. And as I wrote this, the Senate had been considering a bill to greatly enlarge Peace Corps and bring it in tune with the times, but the prospects suddenly dimmed when the Republicans turned stronger in the mid-term elections and took control of the House.

With all this said, what do I think of Peace Corps global? I had a high opinion when I looked at it from afar, before joining. Before I got to experience it. As my experience developed, my opinion became a wee bit clouded, sorry to say.

I did get an excellent feeling when I got to meet and listen to Director Tschetter when he came to Kyiv to visit in the middle of my first year. He was the driving force behind the Fifty Plus program that lured me into service.

Tschetter was well-known for his visits to Peace Corps posts abroad—had racked up a legendary number. I heard some criticism. It is understandable that he wanted to get to see for himself what was going on, but 40 international trips in two years?

After our question-and-answer session with him, I did walk out upbeat about Peace Corps and our Washington leadership.

But after that, my experience with Peace Corps at the national level was all downhill.

My next experience with Washington came when our big economic recession began to impact millions of Americans. As mentioned earlier, I wrote an op-ed intended for back-home newspapers. I wanted to spread the word that this was a great time for Americans to consider Peace Corps.

So many were losing their jobs. Their homes. Standing in line for unemployment checks and seeing the weeks that they would collect these checks running out fast. Finding it difficult to land new jobs. Sitting at home twisting their thumbs in futile waiting and becoming demoralized.

My message was simple: consider Peace Corps. It can be a good deal for 27 months. Can open new doors for you. Can re-instill in you a feeling of worth. Let you discover new skills. And so on.

Three big newspapers turned it down. I had also sent it to a number of friends. Smart people! I got numerous comments back: what a great message! Finally the New London Day, the daily that covers my corner of Connecticut, published it. That pleased me.

The Day is a fine paper. But it has a readership measured in the thousands. I felt that millions should hear my message. So, I contacted Peace Corps in Washington. Specifically one of its press people. They have media contacts all over the country. I included my op-ed. Surely he could see how timely it was...how it could help some desperate people...and how it could gain Peace Corps able new Volunteers, including certainly some older ones.

But total silence! However, sometimes e-mails never reach their destination. I re-sent it, and to that specific individual, mind you. Not even an acknowledgment! That brought my brainstorm to a dead end. How would you feel about that?

My next initiative got slightly better treatment, but still not satisfactory. The 50th anniversary of Peace Corps would be coming up in September, 2011. It would be a big deal, and rightly so. I got an idea for it—my Peace Corps Anthem idea. I brought it to your attention in a previous chapter.

Ronald Tschetter had retired. We now had an acting director, Jody Olsen, Ph.D. She had served as a Volunteer, then had joined the Peace Corps national staff and had worked her way up. I sent it to her. Not just the mere idea. I added suggestions on how to promote it with a national song-writing contest and even a plan how to stimulate submission of anthems and select the winner.

I thought an anthem would be a great morale booster. Would help to popularize the Peace Corps. These are the very reasons so many organizations have an official anthem. I also thought that premiering the anthem at the 50th anniversary extravaganza Peace Corps was developing would have national impact.

She bounced it up to the 50th Anniversary Planning Committee. I never heard a word back about it.

Then Aaron Williams was appointed national director. In a mass introductory e-mail to all of us, he mentioned that he welcomed suggestions. I dusted off my anthem idea and sent it to him. Why not? It was just as good then as it was earlier. Weeks went by. No acknowledgment. Again, sometimes e-mails seem to wind up in limbo. So I sent it to him again. No reply. What is a sensible conclusion?

Now what do I think of Peace Corps Ukraine?

First, let me tell you what I read in a Peace Corps document published during my stay about the Ukraine program:

"Following the independence of Ukraine in 1991, Peace Corps entered post-Soviet Ukraine in 1992. During this time, programming has primarily focused on English education, HIV/AIDS prevention, community and economic development, and youth development. Volunteers serve in 210 villages and small towns across the country, and over 1,800 Volunteers have served in Ukraine. Currently, Peace Corps/Ukraine has 277 Volunteers, the largest Peace Corps program in the world."

A questionnaire was developed and tested on the Headquarters Ukrainian staff. Improvements were made in it. Then it was used in 127 interviews in 78 villages and towns, as well as with some host families. Certainly a minuscule sample in a country of some 44 million. I wonder what a professional pollster would think of it. But it was the best they could do, I assume.

The results (I am rounding the percentages):

~ Broadened perspective: 75%
~ Better understanding of us and the U.S.A.: 73%
~ Improved English: 43%
~ Increased skills and professional development: 34%
~ Motivation for further achievement: 21%
~ Cross-cultural exchange: 20%
~ Increased self-confidence, self-esteem, independence: 18%
~ Increased tolerance: 13%
~ Impact on family or community: 11%

This final statistic was astonishing to me. I would have thought it would have showed a much greater impact. It's where I for one felt I made the biggest impact.

But one more thought. How much of a difference can 300 Volunteers working in isolation from one another make in a country with 44 million people?

To put it another way, how can a single Volunteer like me in a city of 300,000 possibly make a difference?

I am not sure of the answers. I know that I impacted some lives in a positive way. But they were relatively few. And I felt I got some big improvements started—the digitalization of the Korolonko Library and the creation of the city public transit website. But there was so much more that could be done.

What was a constant surprise throughout my service was how very few people around me knew anything about Peace Corps! Time and again I had to explain. When somebody did know something about it, it was usually wrong. Headquarters in Kyiv could have hired one more staffer—a PR person to churn out news releases for local media about Peace Corps and our efforts.

Maybe what Peace Corps should do is bring many more Volunteers into a country, even if it has to serve far fewer countries. Maybe the investment our country makes through Peace Corps would be more effective, for that country and for our own. It's an idea that deserves study.

My experience during my months there was that in general Peace Corps was well intentioned and motivated and eager to do a good job. I think it had a dedicated and talented staff, and please keep in mind that this staff had some 75 people and all but the two at the top were Ukrainian nationals. I felt good about them.

I am pleased to tell you that I was always well treated and in fact the people that I dealt with at times went out of their way to be helpful. I got to know some on a first-name basis and considered them my friends. When I left, told some that I would have a bed for them if they made it to Connecticut—in fact, bed and breakfast! That made them chuckle.

My most serious problem was my difficulty in the Russian language program. I feel that everyone concerned at that point was sympathetic. As I've said, I think that I came close to being sent home but was given a break because, as Director Diana Schmidt said to me, "You are trying so hard."

Over the months I contacted her a number of times by e-mail. Sometimes I sent her a copy of an e-mail directed to someone else, sent just to keep her in the loop. But now and then I sent her a suggestion or an idea, directly and only to her.

I am pleased to say that until nearly the end, I always received a reply, though at times she was skeptical or critical, and that was her right, of course. At the end, there were a couple of times that I did not receive a reply. Maybe she was busy, or away, or tired of my e-mails, or so contemptuous that she did not feel my e-mail was worthy of a reply. Whatever her reason, I was disappointed. I felt that any polite and well-intentioned e-mail from a Volunteer should get a reply.

I respected her for her credentials for the job and her obvious efficiency. It pleased me that she was a former Volunteer, and had not served as such as a pup right out of college but as a mature person high in her career as a professor and marketing specialist, if I am correct. That impressed me.

There was one time when she immediately went to bat for me. That is when I sent an important e-mail to the new director of the USAID office in Kyiv and then re-sent it because I received no acknowledgment.

I brought this to her attention and immediately she contacted that person, who promptly contacted me.

I must tell you that I liked her. She was always nice when she saw me, though I felt at times that she did not like me. That, too, was her right.

The first serious suggestion that I made to her was sparked when she sent all of us an e-mail that our Ukraine budget was being scrunched and it was important to economize.

I had seen this emphasized at Headquarters. The Volunteers' Lounge on the top floor had a photo-copying machine. Free for all of us to use. A wonderful amenity. A sign next to it urged us to double-side our copies. A box by it had waste copies with one side blank and we were urged to use them up. I liked that. I am all for economizing and recycling. Practicing these easy economies is an everyday habit for me.

Headquarters had a fleet of half a dozen big Toyotas. My suggestion in a detailed e-mail was to see if the office could get along with at least one less, maybe two. I itemized some possibilities.

Her reply—I am slimming it down—was that all this had been studied and that the fleet was as economical as it could be, given the demands placed upon it. Furthermore, the vehicles—the big Toyotas in our case—had been supplied by Washington. That was the end of that.

I laughed—I was thinking of the mere pennies being saved by getting us to re-use that once-through photocopy paper. And I was aware of the many dollars that could be saved by dispensing with just one Toyota. It wouldn't have been difficult to achieve an economy like that. In my opinion.

There may have been economies put into effect, but the only one that I got to feel was our subscriptions to the international edition of Newsweek Magazine were cut. In my case, it was the only publication of world news that I got to see. True of other Volunteers, too, I believe. I complained about it to her. I am pleased to say that about this she was sympathetic.

At one point, I also e-mailed her that I considered Peace Corps' language-teaching wrong. I explained this to you earlier. She told me that language education was set in Washington by experts and its methodology was the same for all Volunteers in all countries. And again, that was that.

She expressed no appreciation for my taking interest, or sympathy for my point of view. As a Volunteer, she had gone through the same language curriculum. Maybe she thought it was excellent. I felt that her response fell short. At the least, she could have offered to forward my comments to Washington.

One day I e-mailed her that I had discovered a wonderful online foreign-language instruction program. It was www.byki.com. It's an acronym for "before you know it." Byki offered instruction in some 75 languages, including Russian and Ukrainian, the two of most interest to us.

Byki had two programs, one free and one you purchased. I had downloaded the free one and found it good. My suggestion was that we study it for use by all during Training. It would be part of the program.

She e-mailed me back that she was sending it on to our country director of language instruction, Iryna Krupska. I admired her.

Iryna sent me a detailed reply, quite pleasant. In essence she said, "Thanks, but no thanks." That ended that. I realized, of course, that extensive use of byki might reduce the number of language teachers on the staff.

Another time, I e-mailed Diana that I felt strongly about a lack of any organized effort to build up our morale and keep it nourished.

I made a number of practical suggestions that would cost very little. I was happy to get a reply. She was interested!

She said that she was going off to a national country directors' meeting in southeast Asia—Thailand, I believe. She would bring up my suggestions. She flew off and flew back. I waited and waited. I got no further word about it.

I brought it up again with another e-mail some months later. This time she wrote back promptly. The essence of her message was that it was not Peace Corps' business to build up our morale.

I got another quick and emphatic turn-down when I made another suggestion. The Kyiv office knew from experience that all of us Volunteers had to go there on business a number of times a year. For many this would require an overnight stay, or even longer.

We were given a monthly allowance to stay six times a year at the Bratislava Hotel, a hotel that it favors. It was a mediocre property, shabby in its older section which was where we put up. And it was a long Metro ride and walk to and from Headquarters.

You know by now how I enjoy hostels and how I have stayed at many interesting and pleasant ones.

I suggested that Headquarters operate what I called The Volunteers' Club. Essentially a hostel, but quite upscale, with many amenities.

It would be close to Headquarters and a Metro station. Close to restaurants, a McDonald's if possible. I had noticed how Volunteers enjoyed the McDonald's in downtown Kyiv. They thronged there.

I suggested that not only would such a club be a better deal for us, but it might even save Peace Corps money. She turned down my idea cold. Here's the e-mail she sent me:

"Hello John, As far as a PCV club goes, it is absolutely impossible for us to run such a type of club. We are forbidden by the PC regulations and although it might be fun for the PCVs, it would be a nightmare for us.

Headquarters was tucked in a yard, out of sight. Peace Corps liked that, I think. Here are some of its Toyotas (beyond the vehicle in foreground)—huge vehicles in Ukraine.

"We are not in the business of hospitality but in the 'business' of training and providing support for Volunteers as they fulfill the goals of Peace Corps. – Diana."

Well, I didn't know what the PC regulations said, but I felt my proposition did fit nicely within the definition of "providing support for Volunteers." If our Armed Services feel such clubs are important, why shouldn't Peace Corps?

Earlier I told you about the nit-picking of my regional manager in the reports that I wrote for Volunteers' Journals on the Peace Corps website. I considered it really censorship. I won't belabor it here.

As my months passed, I got to resent some things. One was that I never heard it mentioned, or saw it printed, that most Volunteers serve alone in their community. It was a surprise for me, and a disappointment. I believe it would work better to assign several Volunteers together, for better morale at least.

Another complaint was that before arriving in country we were not informed of basic and important things. One was that computers and cell phones would be essential. I arrived with a computer and bought a cell phone when I was told to. I had never owned one. I brought this up with my regional manager.

She told me a computer was not essential. Wrong. Ninety-five percent of my contact with Headquarters was by e-mail, for one thing. Maybe it was not called essential. But it would be extremely difficult to live and work without one. True about the phone, too.

Maybe they were not called essential because if Peace Corps did call them essential, it would have to supply them. It certainly called them essential for all their desk personnel at Headquarters.

One more complaint. Why didn't Peace Corps issue us ice crampons to keep us reasonably safe walking the icy sidewalks? At one time. Peace Corps had issued them. As you know, I had my own—what a blessing.

Peace Corps Medical was outstanding in its preventive care—TB shots and flu shots and other shots. Free vitamins. Free condoms. Free resistance bands for muscle exercise. Good advice and good care for all kinds of perils. They lent us fire extinguishers, electric room heaters, and combination gas and fire alarms.

A bad fall on the ice could mean a broken limb or a concussion or worse. Winter was long. Imagine how much a bad fall would cost Peace Corps in dollars and time lost.

I had specific recommendations about how to improve our Training, but got nowhere. Some three months after Swearing In, a new group of Trainees arrived in my city for Training. I got to meet some and have good talks. I learned from them and they learned from me. A win-win!

I had reflected about the Training and had come up with a list of things that could be made better. I sent a long e-mail to Iryna Krupska, our training manager, about this also.

She replied with her usual charm and punctuality. She complimented me for my interest, said she had shared my points with her staff. But turned everything down. Why? Trainees should learn many things on their own!

Her words: "It's actually one of our goals to facilitate trainees' ability to successfully apply such important tools as observation, community mapping, needs assessment, information collection through interactions with community members, participator analysis, etc. Besides, it's part of your PCV experience (including Training) to explore your communities and get integrated!"

My opinion was different: This is what Training should be all about! Trainees should be given the best start possible! If Iryna had been one of us, I feel she would have felt the same way.

One thing I became aware of was how many Volunteers felt under-used, under-employed. I got this impression time and again. There was a lot of hanging around, a lot of waiting and hoping for something to come up. I have no statistics to back me up on this. But I believe it was a problem.

Yes, Peace Corps emphasized that we had to use our initiative and be enterprising. But maybe young Volunteers new to working for a living needed more than that simple urging. More direction and better assignments. Maybe this was one reason so many in our Group 33 went home early.

Early I mentioned that I came to Ukraine with the intention of writing a book about my experience. You now have it in hand.

Maybe some of you have thought, "Certainly John had to find some critical things to write about. How could he write a book reporting one superlative after another? How dull! How unbelievable! Maybe the rascal initiated some of these ideas and recommendations of his in order to generate good 'copy'—juicy stuff to tell us about!"

Valid questions. But I did not do that. My conscience would not permit it. It's not my style. I raised these matters because I thought not only that they were legitimate but might make Peace Corps Ukraine even more efficient and effective and Volunteer life more pleasant.

I began this chapter by calling Peace Corps a fine outfit, including Peace Corps Ukraine. I mentioned that I had found everybody pleasant and competent and helpful on the whole. I said that I liked and appreciated everybody on the staff that I had gotten to meet. I affirm all that again as I close this chapter. I am glad I served in Ukraine.

I have found perfection very rare. I have never seen it in myself although I have strived for it. I believe that when we do find imperfection, especially imperfection that affects us, it behooves us to bring it to light and do something about it. This is my way of doing that.

~ ~ ~

***Did you know*** .... that most Volunteers get posted to smaller cities and towns and even villages? At least this was the case in Ukraine.

I worked in a city of 300,000. Residents there considered it a small city. I considered it large. I knew of a few Volunteers who worked in larger cities. The rumor was that Peace Corps considered large cities too expensive.

The great majority worked in places much smaller than mine. Some in towns of 5,000 or less.

# 41 / Tips & Advice for you

*I learned so much during my service.
I want to be helpful, so I'm passing it on.*

If you are tempted at all to serve in Peace Corps, this is something you're interested in—tips and advice!

Well, here are some straight from me to you. All of them are the fruit of my hard-won experience day by day. I wish I had known some of these before I signed up. I hope they'll help you.

But a caveat. You may be male, or female. You may be 21, or 71. We all have traits in common with other people. We also have traits which make us different. Some of what I write may fit you. Or may not. Choose or chuck as you deem best.

Remember that I am far from being the typical Volunteer, if such exists. I am an octogenarian. I have worked at many things and gone to many places and have had a wealth of experiences. Younger folks have not had such opportunities yet. This may explain some of the things I have chosen to speak about, and the emphasis that I give them.

Also keep in mind that my Peace Corps service was in a pleasant and quite developed country. Plus, I was a Volunteer in the largest contingent in the world. Close to 300! I might write differently if I had served in a primitive and harsh land, or in a small contingent of 75, say.

So, the advice that you are seeking might be better coming from a younger person, or one who served in a contrary setting, or one of different personal background. With all this said, still I believe some of my tidbits will help you.

My first piece of advice?

Very basic. If you have a background in medicine or nursing and think you would probably be assigned to work in public health, it would be wise also to seek advice from a Volunteer who did that. More than one if possible.

If you are black, you would be smart to get in touch with a black returned Volunteer. And so on. Later I'll point out how you might locate such Volunteers.

One more thing. What do I mean by "advice"? And what by "tips"? When I say advice, I mean big, broad principles to guide you. When I say tips, I mean little, practical suggestions. Okay?

## ADVICE

— Be philosophical. Remember that most experiences in life are imperfect and contain good and bad elements. This is how your Peace Corps experience will be. Think that it will be overwhelmingly good. And there will be some bad.

— Be honest with yourself. Probe yourself to find out why you want to serve. If you are like me, or most of us, you probably want to do it for reasons, plural. All of them may be valid. But maybe not.

— Probe yourself in another way also. Try to assess your strengths and weaknesses.

We all get to know some things about ourselves early in life. Whether we can carry a tune, or learn to count easily. Or memorize a list of things fast. Or like hanging out with others or prefer being by ourself. Or like to work with our hands or sitting and thinking.

Some things we discover about ourselves pop out only after exposure to varied experiences. Do you have a sense of initiative or prefer to carry out someone else's program? Do you like to make decisions, or prefer deferring that to someone else? Do you like to take risks—moderate and calculated risks, but sometimes dangerous risks? Do you usually complete what you start to do, or are you an easy quitter? Do you like to paddle your own canoe?

Why ask yourself such questions? Because by its very nature Peace Corps service is an adventure. I'm repeating myself, I know. But this is an important point.

—Face reality. You will most likely wind up working alone in a small to medium-size community. You will be assigned your primary job, and you will be expected to find and work at and hopefully complete secondary undertakings. These will require initiative and determination and stamina and perhaps some discomfort. It would be fortunate if you feel up to this. And if you are not sure, wonderful if you are determined to give it a good try. Think all this over.

More than once I saw Volunteers twiddling their thumbs, unable to get started, and feeling anxious and frustrated, and, I suspect, going home at the end disappointed and perhaps guilty.

— You may not do the whole hitch. Be mindful that we all serve for 27 months. Three months of Training in the country that we are assigned to, and 24 months of Service. But that is not really true.

We are expected to serve 27 months. Some of us serve much less time than that. Our service is open-ended. We can leave whenever we choose. Peace Corps tells us they will not hold it against us if we go home early—but I am not sure this is totally true, either. Some—a few—are asked to resign because of this or that.

Numerous resignations must be upsetting for key officials. After all, think of all the money that has been invested in us. Think of all the training and the ongoing support services.

An attrition of 35% has to be worrisome. That is what it was in my group. We arrived 86 strong. Only 56 of us made it to the finish. Any private enterprise with a heavy drop-out like that would do something about it. Maybe Peace Corps would not be able to meet its recruitment needs with a more stringent policy. And maybe my group's rate was abnormally high. I am only speculating.

But I repeat. You are free to quit whenever you want to. Bottom line: your risk is minimal. You can come home at the end of 10 days! After all the expense involved, I suspect Uncle Sam would weep.

Remember the advice Diana, our country director, gave us. "Give a thought of quitting the 10-day test!" Don't quit impulsively. That advice is good anytime, anywhere, for any big decision.

— Take into consideration at what stage you are in life. If you are fresh out of college and not sure what you want to do in life, serving in Peace Corps may be an easy and awfully smart decision. You'll get experience, learn important new things, make connections, pick up a new language, and return home with stronger self-confidence and a beefed-up résumé, plus nearly $6,000 in transition money.

If you are 45 and a lawyer and are thinking of closing—or far better, selling—a practice that you have been building for 18 years, you should think long and hard about that.

Or of quitting a reasonably good job because of frustration, ditto. It may be smarter to find a way to improve your job. Be cautious about burning important bridges behind you.

If you are 66 and retired and bored after a year of getting up late and spending the morning watching TV, Peace Corps may be meaningful and exciting indeed. But do you have enough of a sense of adventure to cope with the challenges? Do you have the strength of mind and body? Does anything in your past suggest you are up to this?

— Remember that one of the assurances of Peace Corps is that you will nearly certainly learn a new language. That sounds great. A new language may offer great promise for your future. But it is not necessarily true.

What Peace Corps will strive mightily to do is to *teach* you a new language. In my experience, it is a rare Volunteer who becomes truly adept at the new language. Any new language is difficult, and becomes more difficult the older you are. The key question: are you motivated to learn a new language?

Your Peace Corps work may place you in a situation where the new language is essential. Which means that you will pick it up faster in your daily life. But you may be an environment where your native associates speak English to some extent. Perhaps well. This was my case. They were *eager* to learn English. This greatly de-emphasized the importance of Russian to me. I was embarrassed by how little Russian I knew when I returned home.

And some languages are more valuable than others. Potentially Mandarin (the main language of China's one billion people) may be far more valuable than Tagalog (Philippines), especially if you are 22 and hoping for an international career of some kind.

As a consequence, the market value of your new language when you go shopping for a new job back home may have more or less significance.

— Remember, too, that when you join, you are expected to agree "to go wherever and do whatever." This is true in theory. But Peace Corps is practical about it.

Consider, say, the possibility of being assigned to go "wherever." Surely Peace Corps will want to send you to a place that makes sense. It's only after I arrived in Ukraine that I learned that although Volunteers work in some 75 countries, older ones are sent to only 10. These are countries where there are pretty good medical facilities.

So if you are a retiree, it is good for you to understand that "wherever" is quite limited. You can rule out more than 60 countries.

If you are younger, you face something different. Perhaps Peace Corps in deciding where to send Volunteers reaches the bottom of the list of both countries and applicants, so to speak.

It may have 25 assignments still to fill here and there. And it may have only 25 Volunteers left to send off. And lacks enough information about anybody to decide which person might be best in this position or that one. So it just makes matches as best it can. The fit for some Volunteers might turn out to be inappropriate. Call it just bad luck.

The same is true of being assigned to do "whatever." If you have zero agriculture experience and come from a non-agriculture place, such as the Rocky Mountains of western Montana, it is doubtful that you will be assigned to teach agriculture.

But again, bad luck can come into play for you despite Peace Corps' best efforts.

— Be aware of the special advantages that Peace Corps may give you. Some Volunteers go on to careers in public service (elected or appointed office) or private enterprise with international aspects. Peace

Corps can help you with education in certain fields, or with extra points in competitive exams for federal service. Check this out with your recruiter.

You may find your new networking opportunities very valuable. Membership in the National Peace Corps Association may open new doors for you. It is worth considering.

— Remember that it is possible to negotiate with Peace Corps. I did not realize this.

Consider my case. Peace Corps told me, "John, we are sending you to Eastern Europe." I gulped but said, "Okay." I expected to go to a country with a relationship with France—where French would be helpful.

Maybe I should have objected. Maybe I would not have won. But I should have tried

— Remember that the reality of your service may be far from romantic. Peace Corps says Volunteers may serve in conditions of hardship.

Let me give you an instance. While in service, I met a Volunteer in his 60's. He had had a hip replacement—or maybe it was a knee replacement. It had been wonderful but not perfect. I saw that when I watched him walk.

He had found himself housed in an apartment on the fourth floor of a five-floor walk-up. Those stairs were a great challenge.

Then he discovered his place had no running hot water. He was long beyond the Boy Scout age. He had to heat a kettle of water on his gas stove and limit himself to sponge baths.

His assignment was "community development." He had done a lot of consulting; this sounded right up his alley. Consider his reaction when he learned that he would be working to help impaired children—physically and mentally impaired! A stunning surprise. But he accepted that. How admirable.

Another Volunteer in his situation might have decided to return home. And people would have understood. How would you feel if that happened to you?

I heard of an older woman who had been assigned to work in far-eastern Ukraine. It was a 14-hour overnight train ride from Kyiv—how often would she get to visit this fine city? Not often.

All her life she had enjoyed indoor plumbing. Now she had to use an outhouse. What a pleasure that would be—especially in frigid and snowy January and February. She grumbled. Who wouldn't? But she, too, accepted it. How would you take that?

— Remember that getting in may take longer than you expect and may cost you money. It will undoubtedly take at least six months. It may take a full year. A woman friend told me that she had to spend $1,700 for dentistry in order to satisfy Peace Corps. In my case, Peace Corps asked for a second opinion about an old medical problem, then for new X-rays of dental implants. At my expense.

— Do not burn your bridges behind you. Maybe you hate your present job. But tell your boss your plans and ask if your job would be waiting for you when you leave Peace Corps. You might be delighted to get it back. Use this strategy wherever you think it might apply.

Your 27 months of service will seem long, but to your surprise, they will end. It's important to return home to a warm welcome.

Leave home with the best of relationships, if possible, and then be mindful to nurture them from afar, and come home to resume life with one and all easily and comfortably.

## TIPS

— Investigate, investigate, investigate. Ask hard questions of your recruiter. Try to talk with returned Volunteers. Explore the Peace Corps website. Read everything you can about Peace Corps.

— You will need three letters of recommendation. In my opinion, those letters are all-important—may be decisive. Be as choosy as possible in selecting those whom you ask to write in about you.

First, make sure they are not only good recommenders, but good writers! Second, choose as high as you can. The more significant they are, the more significant you become. Third, if you have separate important talents, it might make sense to choose writers who have experienced these different talents of yours.

Oh, another thought. Do not hesitate to add additional testimonials. You are marketing yourself! Do the best job you can.

— Try to take money of your own when you go abroad. Your monthly allowance from Peace Corps will be adequate. I found it so. But I did spend extra. I believe numerous Volunteers do. You may appreciate a cash cushion for splurges, travel, and just the plain good sense of greater comfort and extra security. But do not act like a wealthy American! That would go counter to what Peace Corps is all about.

— Abroad, Peace Corps will provide all the necessities. But it's not quite true. In Ukraine all of us found it necessary to have a cell phone. And a computer. After all, 99 percent of Peace Corps communications are online. The phone and computer were at our expense. Equip your computer for Wi-Fi (wireless Internet); very useful in some places. It bothered me that Peace Corps never mentioned the importance of a computer and a cell phone.

An absolute necessity for me were my Stabilicers—the crampons which I attached to my boots on bad days of winter not to slip and fall on ice. I brought them from the U.S.A. (They were a gift from a friend; I did not know such things existed.) Peace Corps said that its budget did not permit these (the cost was about $30 retail; less wholesale, I'm sure). How much would it cost Peace Corps to take care of a Volunteer with a broken leg, or a brain concussion? Be sure to buy a pair if you are bound for a frigid land.

— Homesickness is a common ailment. But in most cases, it passes and seldom re-occurs, much like seasickness. But remember, you can fly home for a quick fix, then return to work! But again, this will be at your expense, and on your vacation time.

— A must is a camera. You understand why, I am sure. Some cell phones can take photos. But a good digital camera is surprisingly useful.

On one occasion I had to have a wall divider built in a condo I own in Connecticut. I drew a sketch of it and a floor plan showing where it should be placed. I photographed my sketch and my plan, uploaded them to my computer, and e-mailed them to the U.S.A. It took a matter of minutes. They were a great help to my carpenter.

Another time I had to sign and return a contract. Maybe I could have faxed it. I wasn't even sure that the technology existed in my city. I didn't waste time. I signed it, photographed it, and e-mailed it home. It was just another jpg. The recipient merely had to print it. And of course, I retained that jpg on my computer. It was my own copy of that legal document, speak. I photographed legal documents this way several times during my service.

Taking photos is a sure way to lock memories into our brain. We all know a photo is worth a thousand words. Sometimes ten thousand!

— I wish I knew more about cell phones when I had to buy one in Ukraine. I had never owned one. I certainly would have bought one with photo capability—one always ready for a quick snapshot.

By the way, your cell phone back home may not work in the country you get posted to. Be sure to check that out.

In fact, my Nokia phone purchased in Ukraine was useless in the U.S.A. What a shame.

— Be kind to yourself. Take along everything that you consider very important, whether it is a certain book, certain photographs, a certain good luck charm, certain mementoes, or a portable DVD player or Scrabble set or special accessory for your computer. All while respecting Peace Corps' luggage limit.

On the other hand, be aware that many items are available overseas. No need to take along an extra tube of Colgate toothpaste, or more changes of clothing. You will find them available.

— As soon as you know where you are going, e-mail your Country Director there. Ask if he or she can connect you with a Volunteer there similar to you. Establish an e-mail friendship and ask questions.

My final point: Joining Peace Corps is a big decision. One that may turn out to be momentously significant. But to repeat, it involves little risk. You can quit and return home at will. Peace Corps will buy you your ticket and give you your separation allowance for your months served after Training. Plus a ride to the airport. There's comfort in knowing that.

~ ~ ~

***Did you know*** .... that some Peace Corps rules and regulations apply to Volunteers everywhere? I suspect that most of the rules are global.

Some, however, are strictly local, based on the local situation.

In Ukraine, I believe that our prohibition of driving a motor vehicle was a local one. Or perhaps it applied to some other countries with a similar background. I have heard of Volunteers driving Jeeps in some countries of Africa, for instance.

In Ukraine it meant any vehicle with a motor. A car. A truck. A motorcycle. Even a bicycle with a tiny motor. Why? Because driving one was considered, dangerous given the condition of many of the roads, the alcohol culture, and maybe the level of general driving skills.

Ukraine has special highway police. I often saw them at work. In my city. And on highways. They worked in pairs, sometimes in three-somes. On any day they could be seen at any location. Unpredictable where they would be tomorrow. It could be during the day and during the night.

They wore distinctive uniforms with reflective patches on their jackets and trousers. And they carried a white swagger stick. They would stand at an intersection or stand by the side of the road and survey traffic. They might spot a car or truck and point the swagger stick at it. That meant stop! And stop it did. Maybe for a legitimate violation. Maybe not.

I got to hear complaints about these police. They were considered arrogant. Considered bullies. And they were notorious for being on the take. A "fine"' paid on the spot could quickly resolve a problem.

Maybe this was a factor in the Peace Corps' prohibition.

# 42 / Thinking in the night

*What would JFK think now? How will Obama carry on? What's coming up?*

President Kennedy was at his idealistic best when he made his historic speech on the steps of the University of Michigan late that night in 1960.

But let's not forget that he was a seasoned politician. Which means that he was realistic in his assessments of anything. I am sure he hoped for great things, but he was accustomed to negotiating and compromising and settling for the best he could get.

At one point he hoped that 100,000 Volunteers would be serving. He was way off. At one time early in Peace Corps' history, the total in the field approached 15% of that—a record high! Then it slumped. Lately it has been rising. But today the total is still less than 10% of his dream.

How would JFK feel about that? Your guess is as good as mine. Mine is that he would say, "Dammit! We've got to recruit harder. Get to it!" Of course, he would say it in finer language. Certainly he would be grateful Peace Corps was still alive and kicking...and growing.

Surely he found it gratifying when his idea took off. Exciting when he saw the thousands of young people applying to sign on.

He believed that Peace Corps would attract huge numbers—and Congress would provide the funds. He visualized 1,000,000 returned Volunteers. Well, after nearly half a century, the total is nudging the 200,000 level. Not a huge number, everything considered. The Corps currently attracts about half of what it did 30 years ago, though the number is rising.

This despite heavy and ongoing advertising and marketing and the build-up of a lode of romantic lore about Peace Corps.

It's sad but true. Why is that? Many opinions, too many for us here. Certainly we have alternate opportunities to volunteer for idealistic and altruistic motives. AmeriCorps, for instance (sometimes called informally "the Domestic Peace Corps"; it presently has 4,000 Volunteers). Plus a plethora of private ones, large and small, including religious ones, some offering attractive short-term enlistments.

Of course he would have been delighted that Americans love Peace Corps. And that both Democrats and Republicans give it good support, though there are loud dissenters.

Peace Corps has been around a long time. It is older than other historic legislative acts, including the Civil Rights Act (1964) and Medicare (1965). We have had nine presidents since then. Five major wars. Have entered a new age—the Age of Terrorism. Think about that juxtaposition: Terrorism! And Peace Corps!

What is most interesting is that its passage into law was the first time that "public service abroad" became an integral part of our foreign policy. It was a new concept. And it endures. It seems beyond dispute. It seems to be a permanent value in our Americanism.

Tragically JFK died not long after Peace Corps was established. It seems to be stretching it to believe that he would have had a grandiose dream that his new baby would become one of our most popular programs decade after decade.—one apparently destined for an even more lustrous future as it begins its second half century.

Isn't it remarkable that the spark that he ignited that night at the University of Michigan continues to excite people year after year? There are some alive today, I am sure, who are surprised that his idea survived. Astonished that it's celebrating its 50th anniversary. With no end in sight. That his idea took off. And who believed that it would peter out after the first rush of enthusiasm.

Some people thought, "Idealistic! Impossible! Crazy!" Who would dispute them? Wasn't it far-fetched? Didn't it sound too good to happen?

Remember the dire predictions for his idea by some of his contemporaries. How Eisenhower scoffed at it as "Kennedy's juvenile experiment"? And Nixon as "a haven for draft-dodgers." But maybe this was true to some extent.

During my service, I met Volunteers who had signed up years ago as youths, and who had signed up again and were now part way through a second hitch. I met one man who was doing his third hitch!

I met one who did his first hitch in Brazil. Another in the South Seas. Another in Africa. I met a couple who had served in Colombia. Another couple in Korea. Imagine what JFK would have thought of that!

Please remember: the Peace Corps is not like the Army or the Navy, say. You can't just roll on from one hitch to another and build up retirement time and a nice pension. The rule is that hitches must be interrupted by "civilian" time. But again, there are exceptions. And there is no "retirement time." Not a dime of retirement money.

JFK's memorable call—"Ask not what your country can do for you. Ask what you can do for your country!"—is known even to the young people now entering Peace Corps. It's a motivating factor.

It's right up there with Patrick Henry's "I am sorry I have only one life to give for my country." Or Abraham Lincoln's glowing description of our democracy as "a government of the people, by the people, for the people." Or Franklin Delano Roosevelt's "We have nothing to fear but fear itself." Or Martin Luther King's "I have a dream!"

But let's skip forward to now. Barack Obama several times during his presidential campaign came out in favor of a sharply enlarged Peace Corps. No doubt he had studied the polls and understood and appreciated the Peace Corps' ongoing popularity with our people.

Why do our people feel this way? The answers are difficult to pin down. Is it the appeal of giving back and doing good for the good of it? Seizing opportunities for travel and adventure? Getting marvelous experience that will pave the way to future opportunities? Building up an address book of helpful contacts? All with Uncle Sam picking up the tab?

My belief—I expressed it earlier—is that most people get excited for multiple reasons. True of me, as you know. It would be interesting to parse it out for every person. That would take skilled psychologists.

But I like to think President Obama supported Peace Corps because he believed in its nobleness and effectiveness. Not just out of political opportunism.

Our newly elected President Obama stepped into office intent on building up Peace Corps. It was a time when our people were becoming increasingly divided about our wars in Iraq and Afghanistan. He had campaigned to end them and was trying hard.

Soon he was burdened with the enormous challenge of rescuing our tumbling economy. And delivering on other huge promises—universal medical care and financial reform. People were losing their jobs by the millions, their incomes were plummeting, the national budget and debt were setting staggering highs, and tax revenue was shrinking.

Let's remember that Peace Corps' annual budget is in the millions, not billions, which is what it is for many of our other undertakings. It's a drop in the bucket. Well, a few drops in the bucket.

He continued to endorse a build-up of Peace Corps, even when, of course, that would mean increased expenditures for it.

On June 27, 2009, Senator Christopher Dodd, Democrat of Connecticut and chairman of the Senate's Foreign Relations Committee for Peace Corps, stood and introduced Senate Bill No. 1382, "The Peace Corps Improvement and Expansion Act of 2009."

A plea for expansion and reform! Bad news to some who are opposed. Good news to others, who feel that Peace Corps should get much bigger, all while believing that some things about it should be reformed and its priorities re-shaped to fit today's realities.

If somebody had to submit that bill, it was appropriate that it be Dodd. He himself had served as a Volunteer. At the tender age of 22 he signed up and got shipped to the Dominican Republic and served in a rural village from 1966 to 1968. Apparently that service helped to motivate him to a career in public service—a distinguished one though his reputation got tarnished in the very same year as this important bill.

His bill sought an expansion, yes, just as President Obama had promised. Furthermore, it urged a reassessment—it urged modifications! In fact, a make-over!

Important questions must be asked, he insisted. Here is the way he expressed it in his speech:

"How can Volunteers be better managed? How can they be better trained? Can we improve recruiting? Are we sending our Volunteers to the right countries?

"Why do we have Volunteers in Mali and Tanzania, but not in Haiti, Egypt, Brazil, or Vietnam? The answers are unclear. Are we still achieving the broader goals of the Peace Corps and helping our country meet $21^{st}$-Century challenges?"

These words echoed thoughts expressed earlier by others. One especially, former Volunteer and Peace Corps country director and vocal critic Robert Strauss, if you remember (Chapter 28).

Senator Dodd's bill proposed increases in the Corps' budget. Up from $350 million to $450 million for fiscal year 2010. To $575 million for 2011. $700 million for 2012. The final sum approved for 2010 was $400 million—which nevertheless turned out to be the biggest increase ever.

These sound like enormous sums, and they certainly are to us modest taxpayers, but they pale in comparison to what other federal departments get. Some call Peace Corps' appropriations a drop in the bucket. Well, a few drops in the bucket.

Yet we have been going through a harsh recession when our resources are greatly strained. I for one have supported growth and change for Peace Corps. Will this really happen?

I listened to President Obama's State of the Union address on January 23 of this year. I appreciated his call to Democrats and Republicans for conciliation and cooperation. But terribly disappointed that in this momentous $50^{th}$ anniversary year he made no mention of Peace Corps! What a bummer!

Let's hope it was just an oversight, or lack of air time. Peace Corps deserves better. Indications are that he is becoming more centrist, all in a bid to strengthen his bid for re-election. It's wait and see.....

Remember, I was around when JFK kicked it all off way back in 1960. I didn't do anything about it because I was too busy getting my career going. But I never forgot.

If a palm reader had told me that nearly five decades later I would serve as a Volunteer in a far-off country called Ukraine that did not exist back then as a nation unto itself, and that I would write a book about it, I would have said, "You are out of your mind! What are you smoking?" How I'd love to know 50 years from now what turns out to be the sequel to JFk's grand idea.

How wonderful it would be to hear that peace now exists in all nations, and that the quality of life has risen so markedly in undeveloped countries that Peace Corps has phased out. No longer a need for it!

I doubt that. I believe Peace Corps will still be around, working hard to do good, with even more Volunteers in service. Some putting in not one hitch or two, but 20 years. 30 years. Making it a career! And getting paid appropriately. What's wrong with that idea?

And that more than ever, Peace Corps will be acclaimed as one of JFK's biggest achievements. And one of our country's more noble undertakings. And that you will be one of the growing number with a proud Peace Corps pin.

~ ~ ~

***Did you know*** .... that some Volunteers maintain close ties with Peace Corps after completing their service?

Some "re-up." This means they serve a second enlistment to a different country. The policy is that they cannot go directly from one enlistment to another. There must be "civilian" time in between.

I met several Volunteers who were serving their second, third, even their fourth hitch. I met a couple who served right after college, then were serving again as Fifty Plus Volunteers.

Some sign up for Peace Corps Response. It sends Returned Volunteers abroad for short terms for emergency types of work.

Some Returned Volunteers in standard careers join the private National Peace Corps Association, based in Washington, D.C. It carries on suitable programs activities and lobbies for Peace Corps, advocating a much larger corps, for one thing.

Some join state Peace Corps associations. Nearly every state has one. Check NPCA's website. It's www.peacecorpsconnect.org.

# 43 / Now what about YOU?

*Are you interested in becoming a Volunteer? Yes? No? Maybe?*

I've done my best to let you know what Peace Corps does and what it's like and what you can expect. If you have gotten this far, you certainly have more than a trifling interest.

Did you pick up my book just because Peace Corps is an important and interesting program and you wanted to know more about it?

Or you know someone who has been a Volunteer or is one?

Or have entertained the question, whether fleeting or pressing, "Does Peace Corps make sense for me?"

If your answer to any of these is yes, my effort will have been worthwhile. This is my hope.

If you've read the book because Peace Corps has an appeal for you personally, I hope you have decided it makes sense. Maybe your answer is that it does not. Fine. Move on to whatever you see next as good for you.

If your answer has been "yes," then take the next logical step. That is to go to the national Peace Corps website, www.peacecorps.gov.

You will find it interesting, in fact fascinating. You will find tons of information. You can spend a long time exploring it.

Do go to its "Volunteers Journals." You'll be able to read the accounts of Volunteers around the world about the jobs they are doing, what they are confronting, the lives they are living, and theisatisfactions they are reaping. I was one of those sending in reports, as you know.

Also go to www.youtube/peacecorps.gov. You'll get to read many more Volunteers and a wider range of experiences, good and not good, serious and funny.

Also look up the website of the National Peace Corps Association, www.peacecorpsconnect.org (I am repeating it for emphasis). It is based in Washington, just across the street from Peace Corps Headquarters. Its membership is made up of former Volunteers and Peace Corps employees and some people who are fans.

NPCA carries on helpful programs for RPCVs, as they are called (Returned Peace Corps Volunteers). It keeps an eye on Peace Corps, critiques it, supports it in some ways and fights for change and improvement. It publishes a magazine, "World View," which provides interesting reading. You will learn a lot.

If then you still feel excited about the possibilities, call or e-mail your local recruiter. There are recruiters in our major cities. You will receive a cordial welcome. Very little pressure. You will get information about local meetings that you can attend. You will get the names of RPCVs you may contact.

You will be able to decide whether you want to meet a recruiter and discuss the specifics of your situation. Easy to arrange. Its toll-free number is 800 424-8580. You can reach your local recruiter through that call.

You can begin the process even online at www.peacecorps.gov. May cancel the process at any point. Or extend it to the max. Truth is, it can take several months, even a year or so, to get accepted, as you know now. It depends. All this will be explained to you. One in about three makes the cut. Remember, life in large part is what you make it!

Let me put it as succinctly as I can. I believe Peace Corps can be a life-changing experience, and in more ways than one, and for the better. It can change not only your immediate future, but can open a whole new future for you. It can give you surprising satisfactions and benefits. It's worth investigating.

All the best to you! Good luck!

E-mail me at johnguylaplante@yahoo.com. I'll try to be helpful.

~ ~ ~

***Please remember*** .... that life should be an adventure. You may disagree. Fine. But if you agree, be aware that Peace Corps can be a wonderful adventure. At any stage of your life. Whether you are a man or woman. Regardless of your race, ethnic lineage, or religion, or any other demographic. Any American may apply.

If you serve, you will be doing good for your country, for people in another country, and for yourself. Isn't that quite persuasive?

And if you are unhappy overseas, you can resign at any time. And Peace Corps will pay for your trip home. And give you the transition money you've earned.

# Interested

## in leaning more about the Pleasures and Pains and Opportunities (!) of serving in Peace Corps?

I'll be glad to speak at your Library - Church - Club - School Bookstore - Society - Synagogue - Picnic - Association - Fraternity or Sorority - Company - Party - Union - Resort - Cruise ship - Gated community – Newspaper, Magazine, TV - Radio Station - Rotary, Lions, Elks, American Legion ... or any other upstanding and friendly gathering.

In fact, any group where good people gather to think about new things, discuss lively topics, and hope to pick up a new idea or two to improve their life.

I am well-practiced. I know how to keep people awake and interested. I'm energetic. I talk straight and don't exaggerate. I love to sow seeds of inspiration. I take pleasure in answering any and all questions. I can offer you plenty of testimonials and assurances. I won't break your budget. And I sign books.

All it takes to get things started is a quick e-mail to me:

**johnguylaplante@yahoo.com.**

I'll waste no time in giving you all the info you need. Just tell me the name of your group, where, tentative date, size of audience, and budget. Don't be bashful.

Remember: Peace Corps could be a life-expanding thing for you. At your age. Now. Think about it. Why not? Yes, why not?

*John Guy LaPlante*
Volunteer / Ukraine